18.99

Social Policy

Social Policy

Edited by

**John Baldock, Nick Manning,
Stewart Miller, and Sarah Vickerstaff**

OXFORD
UNIVERSITY PRESS

OXFORD
UNIVERSITY PRESS

Great Clarendon Street, Oxford OX2 6DP

Oxford University Press is a department of the University of Oxford.
It furthers the University's objective of excellence in research, scholarship,
and education by publishing worldwide in

Oxford New York

Athens Auckland Bangkok Bogotá Buenos Aires Calcutta
Cape Town Chennai Dar es Salaam Delhi Florence Hong Kong Istanbul
Karachi Kuala Lumpur Madrid Melbourne Mexico City Mumbai
Nairobi Paris São Paulo Singapore Taipei Tokyo Toronto Warsaw

and associated companies in Berlin Ibadan

Oxford is a registered trade mark of Oxford University Press
in the UK and in certain other countries

Published in the United States
by Oxford University Press Inc., New York

British Library Cataloguing in Publication Data

Data available

Library of Congress Cataloging-in-Publication Data

Social policy / edited by John Baldock . . . [et al.].
Includes bibliographical references and index.
1. Social policy.   2. Great Britain—Social policy—1979–
I. Baldock, John, 1948–
HN17.5.S5986   1999   361.6'1'0941—dc21   99-12998
ISBN 0-19-878173-3

10 9 8 7 6 5 4 3

Typeset by BookMan Services
Printed in Great Britain
on acid-free paper by
The Bath Press,
Bath

Contents

Part Five
Consequences and Outcomes of Social Policy   513

Detailed Contents

4 Welfare, Ideology, and Social Theory

11 Cash Transfers   253

14 Social Care 344

19 Arts and Cultural Policy   488

20 The Impact of Social Policy   515

Guide to the Book

Welcome to Social Policy

That you are reading these words suggests something about you, your interests, and even your values. You may have done no more than pick up this volume in a bookshop or library. Alternatively, perhaps you are already a student on a social policy course, have bought or borrowed this book, and are expecting it to provide some quite specific information. Whatever the reason, there is a good chance that the term 'social policy' resonates with definite positive or negative views you have. This is because 'Social Policy', the academic subject, is not one that is easily neutral in its content or implications. Rather, it tends to involve aspects of life where values and commitments are important.

This is because a social policy is always a proactive attempt to change a given social order—to make things different from how they would otherwise have been. In the post-communist era of the new millennium, this inevitably means intervening to modify market forces and to redistribute resources amongst a population. Social policies *are* redistribution; and the subject 'social policy' is about why, how, and with what outcomes these redistributions take place. There is a strong probability that you are broadly in favour of social policy interventions. There is a lesser probability that you are rather sceptical about the benefits of social policies, but the odds that you do not give a damn either way are rather low.

What is Social Policy?

The term 'social policy' is used to refer both to the academic discipline 'Social Policy' and to what it studies, social policies themselves. There is no agreed and established definition of what a social policy is. Part One of this book explores this uncertainty and shows how it is part of the nature, evolution, and politics of welfare systems. However, this book is organized round two fairly conventional definitions:

A 'social policy' is defined as a deliberate intervention by the state to redistribute resources amongst its citizens so as to achieve a welfare objective.

A 'welfare system' is defined as the range of institutions that together determine the welfare of citizens. Amongst these are the family and the community networks in which it exists, the market, the charitable and voluntary sectors, and the social services and benefits provided by the state.

Clearly these two definitions raise further questions, in particular what is meant by 'welfare'. Seeking answers to that question is very much what studying the academic discipline of social policy is about.

The classic justification for a social policy is that it will lead to greater social justice, though that is by no means the classic outcome. And the classic statement of that justi-fication is the Beveridge Report's call for an 'attack upon five giant evils': want, disease, ignorance, squalor, and idleness (Beveridge 1942: 170; the full quotation appears in Chapter 1). This conception of what social justice required formed the basis for the post-war British welfare state. But it does not apply so readily in other times or places. Different societies and different groups within those societies have varied and even conflicting views about what is socially just. This means that social policy has become the central task of modern politics: deciding which redistributions should be enforced with the authority of the state.

Beveridge's Report was produced in wartime, and he saw social policy largely in terms of redistribution between whole categories of people: from the employed to the unemployed, from those of working age to those in retirement, and from the healthy to the sick. However, today welfare is often seen in more individualistic terms. State social policies help provide the context in which individuals choose and organize their own lives. This perspective sees individual lives as subject to a whole range of risks, particu-larly risks of dependency and exclusion. Richard Titmuss, who in 1950 was appointed to what was effectively the first professorship of social policy in Britain, distinguished between 'natural dependencies, as in childhood, extreme old age and child-bearing', and 'man-made dependencies' such as the risks of industrial injuries and of unemployment and under-employment (Titmuss 1976: 42–4). Titmuss suggested that as economies and societies became more complex and industrialized, so the numbers of these man-made risks increased, turning life into something of a lottery unless social insurance and welfare services were developed to meet the new dependencies.

Today many of us are able to live our lives taking for granted the guarantees provided by the welfare state and social policy. It is this context which allows what a more recent commentator, Ulrich Beck, has called 'institutionalized individualism', a self-centred consumerism which none the less depends on a welfare system constructed when people subscribed to more communal values (Beck 1998). Social policies are fundamental to the organization of our societies and implicit in the choices we make every day of our lives.

So it is unlikely that you will be neutral, disinterested, or uninterested in the issues of social justice and redistribution described in this book. They are part of what makes social policy an exciting subject: it is relevant to both our values and our lives.

The Scale and Volume of Social Policy

The moral and political importance of social policy is also reflected in the sheer scale and number of activities it represents. To study the operation of welfare systems is not to study some marginal aspect of the economy. During the 1990s the fifteen nations of the European Union were spending very close to an average of 30 per cent of their gross national products on 'social protection' (Eurostat 1997: 243). This amounted in 1994 to between £5,462 per person in Luxembourg and £1,177 in Greece, with the figure for the UK being close to the average at £3,435 (ibid.: 138). (Throughout this book technical or specialist terms like **gross national product** and **social protection** are printed in bold when they are first used, and a definition is supplied in a glossary at the end of the chapter.) These levels of expenditure effectively make welfare provision what might be called the largest industry in developed economies. Certainly, organizations such as the National Health Service or the state education system in the UK are substantially larger in terms of amounts of money they spend each year and the numbers of people they employ than most major corporations in the private sector. For example, in 1997 the National Health Service spent just over £35,000 million pounds and employed just under one million people (Treasury 1998). In contrast, the private company with the largest turnover in 1997 was Shell Transport and Trading, which reported a turnover of £31,290 million and employed 42,000 people (UK Equities Direct 1999). If the number of employees is preferred as the key measure of size, then Unilever, with 287,000 employees in 1997, came closest to the NHS (ibid.). The production of social welfare is arguably the largest industrial sector found in the richest economies of the world.

What does Studying Social Policy Involve?

While the making of social policy may be driven by values and politics, the study of social policy should be informed by evidence. Social research, collecting data about how people live, is central to the traditions of 'social policy' as an academic subject, and it has a long history, rooted in the work of the early social scientists such as Edwin Chadwick (1800–1890), Friedrich Engels (1820–1895), Charles Booth (1840–1916), and Seebohm Rowntree (1871–1954).

Consequently you will find a great deal of empirical data in this book, particularly evidence about how resources are allocated. Studying social policy is an excellent way of getting to know about the material world and how people live in it. In this book much of the material is about the United Kingdom. Social policies are still largely the product of the nation state, and therefore even a more international approach has to take the form of comparing the detail within one nation with that in another. But, as market forces are increasingly global in their operation, so social policies will have to follow if they are to have any redistributive impact. We have tried to recognize the developing internationalism of social policies in this book by giving at least some account of what is happening in other countries.

The Objectives of the Book

- To provide a comprehensive introduction to the subject matter of 'Social Policy' as it is currently studied in schools, colleges, and universities. It does this by reviewing the key debates and issues and by setting out some of the basic evidence that is relevant.

- To provide students with a substantial proportion of the information they will need to prepare for seminars, classes, and presentations, and to write essays.

- To provide gateways to the further study of social policy issues. This is done by defining and structuring the core topics, by explaining the meaning of key terms (particularly in the glossaries at the end of each chapter), and by listing a large and accessible literature (in the references and guides to further reading at the end of each chapter).

The Structure and Organization of the Book

The chapters are the basic building blocks of the book. It will often be necessary to read a whole chapter to understand an area of welfare needs and the social policy interventions designed to deal with them. Each chapter is an essay within its area. This is because Social Policy, the academic subject, takes the form of sets of interconnected arguments and evidence. There are limits to which particular topics can be taken out of their contexts.

The core chapters are those in Part Four, 'Delivering Welfare'. Here the main ways in which governments intervene to redistribute resources and to provide services are described. All the main organized service areas are found here: social security, education, healthcare, social care, housing, and criminal justice. To these we have added two areas which are increasingly seen as part of the core social policy responsibilities of government: the natural environment, and people's access to cultural and leisure activities. We have not included chapters on two other important sources of welfare provision, the voluntary and charitable sector, and the private for-profit sector. This is not because we underrate these two sources: they are of growing importance in all welfare systems. Partly it is because their activities crosscut the more traditional areas of provision. For example, the voluntary sector is of increasing importance in the provision of social care and private companies have a growing role, in the UK at least, in the criminal justice system and in healthcare. Secondly, the charitable and private sectors receive less attention because we have adopted a conservative and established definition of social policy, that is, deliberate interventions by government and state institutions designed to redistribute resources. Therefore, while we have discussed voluntary and for-profit sources of welfare in the core chapters where they have an important role, we think readers should be alert to the fact they are not thoroughly dealt with in this book.

The chapters found in the other four sections of the book are designed to set the core activities of welfare systems in a broader context. These sections are designed to add background and depth to the accounts in Part Four. Thus readers of the core chapters will often find they are referred to chapters in the other sections for further explanation of the context or related issues.

Part One, 'The Origins, Character, and Politics of Modern Social Welfare Systems', is designed to show how, since the industrial revolution, the state's responsibility for managing the welfare of its citizens has grown and become more and more the central subject of politics. The social policies of the present are rooted in their historical origins and in the political conflicts and ideological differences that determine what the state does.

Part Two, 'The Social and Economic Context', is designed to give substance to a fundamental truth that is often ignored by students of social policy: that the vast bulk of human needs are not met by the public welfare system, but by the market economy and by the family. It is these last two institutions that define the context and the starting-point of social policies. Again, readers of Part Four will often be referred back to these chapters. In Chapters 6, 7, and 8 we have sought to provide much of the fundamental evidence about how the family and the market both meet many needs and produce others. It is also in these chapters, particularly Chapter 6 and Chapter 8, that important data about population and demographic change are presented. Social Policy is rightly called a multi-disciplinary subject, and Chapters 4 and 5 seek to provide students with some of the social theory that they need to weigh arguments, particularly those found in political science and economics. Although inevitably technical, these chapters are designed for the non-specialist reader. They should be read by any student planning to do a substantial or extended piece of work on a social policy issue.

Part Three, 'Planning, Financing, and Implementing Welfare Policies', is intended to explain and document how social policies are managed and how they are paid for. The state largely intervenes by using public servants to inspect and provide welfare services and by making decisions about taxation and expenditure which allow it to pay for what is provided. These two chapters contain the subject-matter of what are often called Public Policy Studies and, again, they form a fundamental foundation to any discussion of social policies and social services.

Part Five, 'Consequences and Outcomes of Social Policy', consists of two essays: one on the achievements of social policy in the United Kingdom, the second on trends and debates about the future role of social policy and the welfare state. Broadly, they seek to outline how far social policy has come and where it might be going. Both the chapters are inevitably speculative and involve judgements about what the evidence means. Some readers might wish to start their investigation of social policy with these two chapters. Earlier, we described state welfare systems as the largest 'industries' to be found in developed economies. The academic subject of Social Policy might well be expected to offer an account of whether the resources these industries consume are well spent, of whether they have produced welfare gains, and of how they may develop in the future.

How to Use the Book

The book is designed to be used by a student seeking to prepare for a class or seminar discussion, for a presentation, or an essay on a social policy topic. The following route is suggested:

- Chapter headings. If there is a chapter title which broadly covers the topic you are researching, then read all or most of that chapter.
- Subheadings. At the beginning of each chapter is a list of the subheadings used and these may refer to the particular topic or area you are interested in. If not:
- The index. This is at the back of the book and lists the pages on which a topic is discussed. Where a page reference is **emboldened** in the index then a glossary definition of the term appears on this page. This will be at the end of one or a number of chapters. The references to the term within the chapter (the first use is also emboldened) and the context in which it appears will also be worth exploring.
- The glossaries. A particular term may occasionally appear in more than one glossary and be slightly differently defined in each. This is because social policy is a multi-disciplinary subject, and one where argument and differences in emphasis are normal. These differences are usually worth exploring.

Glossary

gross national product Gross national product is all of a country's output of goods and services (usually in a calendar year) plus income from assets abroad, but with no deduction (i.e. gross, not net) for depreciation in the value of the country's assets. Gross domestic product is this, but not including income from assets abroad.

social protection benefits These are direct transfers in cash or kind to households and individuals which are organized by the state to meet risks and needs associated with old age, sickness, childbearing, family expenses, disability, and unemployment. Within the European Union the constituents of social protection statistics have been harmonized according to ESSPROS, The European System of Integrated Social Protection Statistics. These include the bulk of public health and social services and social assistance benefits, but do not include state education expenditure.

References

Beck, U. (1998), 'The Cosmopolitan Manifesto', in *The New Statesman* (20 March).

Beveridge, W. (1942), *Social Insurance and Allied Services: A Report by Sir William Beveridge* (Cmd. 6404, London: HMSO).

Eurostat (1997), *Eurostat Yearbook 1997: A Statistical Eye on Europe 1986–1996* (Office of Official Publications of the European Communities, Luxembourg).

Titmuss, R. M. (1976), *Essays on the Welfare State* (3rd edn., London: George Allen and Unwin).

Treasury (1998), *Pre-Budget Report, November 1998* (H. M. Treasury, London: The Stationery Office).

UK Equities Direct (1999), *Companies A–Z at http://194.200.168.251/equities/index.htm* (London: Hemington Scott Publications).

About the Contributors

John Baldock is Reader in Social Policy at the University of Kent at Canterbury. His main research and teaching interests concern the ageing of populations in industrial societies and the provision of care services for older people. He has also published widely on the personal social services. A book on all of these issues, written with Clare Ungerson, *Consumption, Markets and Community Care*, will be published by Cambridge University Press in 2000.

John Butler is Professor of Health Services Studies at the University of Kent at Canterbury. He has taught, researched, and written extensively about many aspects of health and healthcare in the UK, and has carried out research on these issues for the World Health Organization, the Department of Health, and the National Health Service. Amongst his most recent publications are *Patients, Policies and Politics* (Open University Press: Buckingham, 1992) and *The Ethics of Health Care Rationing* (Cassell: London, 1999). He is an Honorary Fellow of the Faculty of Public Health Medicine and a Foundation Fellow of the Academy of Medical Sciences.

Michael Cahill is Principal Lecturer in Social Policy and Deputy Head of the School of Applied Social Science at the University of Brighton. He is the author of *The New Social Policy* (Blackwell Publishers: Oxford, 1994) and of a forthcoming book on social policy and the environment. Currently he teaches on the history of social policy, policy analysis, transport policy, and social policy and the environment. His research centres on the social dimensions of transport and environmental policy.

Michael Calnan is Professor in the Sociology of Health Studies at the University of Kent at Canterbury and Director of the Centre for Health Services Studies. A medical sociologist with a specific interest in health policy and the health services, his recent books include *Going Private, Why People Pay for their Health Care* with Sarah Cant and Jonathan Gabe (Open University Press: Buckingham, 1993) and *Modern Medicine: Lay Perspectives and Experiences*, edited with Simon Williams (UCL Press: London, 1996). He convenes the MA in Health Studies at Kent and is currently conducting research on health promotion consumerism in healthcare and the health of health professionals.

Tina Eadie is Lecturer in Social Work at the University of Nottingham. Earlier she worked as a Probation Officer and Senior Probation Officer. Her teaching and research interests have followed the changes taking place in the Probation Service, specifically in relation to the professional role of probation officers. Recently with Meryl Aldridge she published 'Manufacturing an Issue: The Case of Probation Officer Training', in *Critical Social Policy*, 17/1 (1997).

Tony Fitzpatrick is Senior Lecturer in Social Policy at the University of Luton. His research interests include social security reform, post-modernism and cyber-theory, environmentalism, political ideologies, informal activities, criminology, and globalization.

He has published articles in journals such as *Critical Social Policy*, *The Journal of Social Policy*, and *Body & Society*. His first book, *Freedom and Security*, was published by Macmillan (London) in 1999.

Andrew Gray is Professor of Public Sector Management at the University of Durham. He is Director of the Centre for Public Sector Management Research, which aims to enhance understanding of the challenges facing public management and ways of meeting them. Recent research projects have included 'Professionalism and the Management of Local Authorities' (for the Local Government Management Board) and others on various aspects of health service management. Recent publications include *Business-Like but Not Like a Business: The Challenge for Public Management* (Public Finance Foundation, CIPFA: London, 1998) and chapters in *Politics UK* (Prentice-Hall: London, 1997).

Bill Jenkins is Reader in Public Policy and Management at the University of Kent at Canterbury. His main research interests are in public-sector management, public administration, modern British politics, and public-policy evaluation. Together with Andrew Gray he has published a range of books and articles in these areas, including *Administrative Politics in British Government* (Wheatsheaf Books: Brighton, 1985) and, with Robert Segsworth, has edited *Budgeting, Auditing and Evaluation: Functions and Integration in Seven Governments* (Transaction Books: New Brunswick, 1993).

Derek Kirton is Lecturer in Social Policy at the University of Kent. He has been a social worker in the field of childcare and has taught at several universities, primarily on topics related to social policy and social work. His main research interests lie in the area of fostering and adoption, on which he has written various articles, and is the author of the forthcoming *Race, Ethnicity and Adoption* (Open University Press: Buckingham, 1999).

Mark Liddiard is Lecturer in Social Policy at the University of Kent at Canterbury. He has worked on a variety of research projects and has a particular interest in qualitative methods. He is co-author, with Susan Hutson, of *Youth Homelessness: The Construction of a Social Issue* (Macmillan: London, 1994). More recently he has focused specifically upon cultural policy issues, and has published on museums, art subsidies, and the impact of the mass media on public attitudes and on policy-makers. He is currently working on a book about historical exclusion in museums, entitled *Making Histories of Sexuality and Gender* (Cassell: London, 2001).

Nick Manning is Professor of Social Policy and Sociology and Head of the School of Sociology and Social Policy at the University of Nottingham. His recent research has focused on Russia, with EU-funded projects on employment and labour-market change, and on poverty, ethnicity, and political stability. He has published widely on these issues and also on aspects of mental health. His recent publications include reports for UNICEF on women and social policy in Eastern Europe, for the High Security Psychiatric Services Commissioning Board on security and personality disorder, and special issues of the journals *Policy and Politics* (on mental health) and *Social Policy and Administration* (on the millennium). Forthcoming books will deal with research methods, citizen action, and unemployment in Russia.

Stewart Miller is Honorary Lecturer in Social Policy at the University of Kent at Canterbury. He has taught and written on social politics, citizenship, and social problems. Together with Vic George, he edited *Social Policy Towards 2000: Squaring the Welfare Circle* (Routledge: London, 1994).

Rebecca Morley is Lecturer in the School of Sociology and Social Policy at the University of Nottingham. She teaches women's studies, social policy, and cultural studies. She has also taught and researched for many years in the area of men's violence to women. Her publications include *Preventing Domestic Violence to Women*, with Audrey Mullender (Home Office: London, 1994), and *Children Living with Domestic Violence: Putting Men's Abuse of Women on the Child Care Agenda*, edited with Audrey Mullender (Whiting and Birch: London, 1994). She is currently principal investigator on a three-year study of the impact of changing housing policy on women's vulnerability to domestic violence. This study forms part of the Economic and Social Research Council's Violence Research Programme.

Jan Pahl is Professor of Social Policy at the University of Kent at Canterbury, where she teaches a course on 'Work, Employment and Family Life'. Her research interests include the control and allocation of money within the family, domestic violence, employment in the social services, and community care for elderly people and for those with learning disabilities. Her publications include *Private Violence and Public Policy* (Routledge: London, 1985) and *Money and Marriage* (Macmillan: London, 1989). Her current research is concerned with couples and their money in the electronic economy.

Chris Pickvance is Professor of Urban Studies at the University of Kent at Canterbury. A sociologist by background, his research interests include housing, local government, and urban protest. He is co-editor of *Place, Policy and Politics: Do Localities Matter?* (Unwin Hyman: London, 1990); *State Restructuring and Local Power: A Comparative Perspective* (Pinter: London, 1991); and *Environmental and Housing Movements: Grassroots Experience in Hungary, Russia and Estonia* (Avebury: Aldershot, 1997). His articles have appeared in the journals *Sociology*, *The Sociological Review*, and *The International Journal of Urban and Regional Research*.

Peter Taylor-Gooby is Professor of Social Policy at the University of Kent at Canterbury. His research interests include the future of welfare and European social policy. Some recent publications are *Risk, Trust and Welfare*, edited (Macmillan: London, 1999), *European Welfare Futures*, with V. George and G. Bonoli (Polity Press: Cambridge, 1999), *The End of the Welfare State?* edited with S. Svallfors (Routledge: London, 1999), *Choice and Public Policy: The Limits to Welfare Markets*, edited (Macmillan: London, 1998), and *European Welfare Policy: Squaring the Welfare Circle*, edited with V. George (Macmillan: London, 1996).

Julia Twigg is Reader in Social Policy at the University of Kent at Canterbury. She has written extensively on issues concerning informal carers, in particular the role of services in their support. More recently she has been concerned with the management of the body in community care, exploring, through a study of bathing services, the experiences of both recipients of care and of frontline staff who provide it, in *Bathing, the Body and Community Care* (Routledge: London, 2000). At present she teaches courses on gender and social policy and on the social politics of food.

Sarah Vickerstaff is Senior Lecturer in Social and Public Policy at the University of Kent at Canterbury. She has a long-standing research interest in training and vocational education policy and practice. Recently she has been involved in international projects investigating the impact of privatization and marketization on industrial relations in central and eastern Europe. Recently, together with John Thirkell and Krastyu Petkov, she published *The Transformation of Labour Relations: Restructuring and Privatisation in Eastern Europe and Russia* (Oxford University Press: Oxford, 1998).

Part One

The Origins, Character, and Politics of Modern Social Welfare Systems

1 Social Policy and Social Welfare Systems

Stewart Miller

Contents

Introduction: A Social Policy Textbook

This is a book about something called **social policy.** You may be reading it as a student specializing in an academic subject of that name or studying it as part of a professional course in, say, social work or nursing; or as one looking at the practical area of social policy from the point of view of sociology, economics, politics, or history, or indeed any one of several disciplines which are likely to look at the welfare, or social policy, systems of Britain and other countries; or you may just be interested in this area. In what is an extensive and wide-ranging volume, we try to cater for all of these interests.

Something of the range of what we regard as included in or related to social policy may be gathered from the titles of the chapters which follow: these include 'Cash Transfers', 'Health and Health Policy', and 'Social Care'—all areas of policy and practice conventionally associated with social welfare; but also 'Work (and) Employment', 'Crime and Justice', 'The Environment', and 'Cultural Policy'. So what ideas and issues hold together this varying selection of topics? Perhaps it will help if we begin by considering some ideas central to any analysis of issues in the social policy field. Let us look at two crucial concepts, social policy itself and the welfare state.

Social Policy

We hear reference to social policy in a variety of contexts. Political decisions about a wide range of matters—from economic planning and taxation to crime and housing—are described in the press, in political debate, and in academic commentary as having social policy implications or impacts. Governments are expected to have social policies, and to bear them in mind when making many decisions. The phrase crops up in the context of public services like social security and health which have a clear **social welfare** function, but it also seems to be related to action about employment, tax, and other economic matters, and also to issues of law and order.

Students are faced with books, articles, and whole degree courses including the phrase 'social policy' in their titles; sometimes it refers to the kind of practical business we have just referred to, and sometimes to an academic discipline which has social policy as its subject matter. The latter sense of the phrase is one with which many of the authors of this book are familiar; they teach in departments and on courses of 'social policy'. Writers have spent much time, effort, and ink on the questions of whether it is a coherent academic subject, and what its boundaries are. But the former sense is what comes first: what is the real-world phenomenon of that name? So for the time being, we shall not be using the term 'social policy' to describe an academic subject, or assuming that we are all working within that academic tradition. Rather, we are concerned with the practical phenomenon of social policy, in which not only social policy students are interested, but also those in sociology, politics, public administration, economics, and other subjects.

The question arises—is 'social policy' a useful label? Or does it smack of the post-war monolithic pattern of state-dominated welfare services, and is it redundant in a world of mixed economies of market and **collective welfare**? We would argue that it is indeed still useful, and that it can be used to define a reasonably cohesive area of human endeavour. Of course, the phrase 'social policy' means something more than the sum of its parts, the adjective 'social' and the noun 'policy'. It is a shorthand term for a field of activity which we cannot define by a process of defining the two words and putting them together. Writing in 1975, as part of an attempt to define an approach to social policy for the Irish government, David Donnison argued that **distribution** was the key to social policy:

What distinguishes a policy as 'social' is . . . the fact that it deals with the distribution of resources, opportunities and life chances between different groups and categories of people. . . . It follows that *every* Government department, programme and policy may have social aspects. Meanwhile social policies always have other aspects which for many people will be more important. Health and education services, for example, are primarily designed to raise general standards of health and learning usually without much regard to their distribution or distributional consequences. Policies for these services become social, in the sense defined here, when they deal with the allocation of resources and opportunities between potentially competing groups, and—as a consequence which may be more distant but equally important—with relations between groups in society, their status and self-respect, their power and their access to broader social opportunities. (Donnison 1975: 26)

This passage raises, directly and indirectly, at least five issues. First, although the term 'policy' is usually taken to mean something like 'the principles of government action' on a particular matter, the phrase 'social policy', defining an area of activity and interest, appears to include consideration of the means used in pursuit of policy, the organizations involved, the people affected, and indeed the problems which give rise to policy. Second, the elements of distribution and redistribution remain crucial to the concept of social policy, and we shall turn to these below.

Third, what is implicit in Donnison's description, with its references to 'opportunities and life chances', is that social policy is largely about what is often called people's *welfare*. He argues that welfare policies such as those on health and education policies only become social 'when they deal with the allocation of resources and opportunities between potentially competing groups and . . . with relations between groups in society'. But it is fair to say that, at least as context, such issues are seldom absent from at least the context of policy and practice in these areas, except where they deal with purely technical matters. Fourth, policies and institutions are not exclusively 'social' or 'non-social'. Social policy aspects crop up in economic, transport, and other policies, and considerations other than those of social policy inform, at least in part, many public actions quite properly thought of as social policy. And fifth, all the above, especially in respect of distribution, applies even where the ultimate (re)distribution is carried out by non-state agents. Continental Europeans are well used to the idea of 'social' or 'welfare' provision in which the state has a stake and some influence, but which is on a pattern far removed from the post-war British model of public agencies, some of which combined everything from policy formation at a legislative level to actual service to clients. This will lead us to the issue of whether or not the term 'welfare state' remains a useful one.

Distribution and Redistribution

When people earn wages, or make gains (or indeed losses) on the stock market, or leave assets to their heirs, they are engaged in processes of distribution, and social scientists and governments alike have long been interested in the patterns of distribution—particularly of income and of wealth—in society. It may be thought, for instance, that a highly unequal distributive pattern encourages some people to work harder and improve their position—but equally that it so disadvantages others that it deprives them of the opportunity of experiencing a decent standard of living.

But in modern societies there is also a great deal of redistribution. This takes place when important social actors adjust the distribution of income, wealth, or other resources by 'robbing Peter to pay Paul'. Frequently the actor involved is the state, and this is particularly the case in complex industrial societies of the kind characteristic of the late twentieth century—or, indeed, the early twenty-first. Partly because some patterns of distribution are judged inherently undesirable, and partly because governments are committed to providing common services—defence, police, and roads, for instance—

some redistribution of income and wealth is inevitable, through tax and public spending. But the redistribution that takes place in a modern society is enormously extensive, and takes many forms.

All the social services have redistribution at the core of their being, and much of the political controversy over them revolves around this. How are we to finance old age pensions when the proportion of pensioners in the population is rising inexorably? By merely compelling people to insure themselves, or by using redistributive mechanisms like tax and income-related contributions systems to take enough from the well-off to guarantee pensions for the poor? What are the incentive effects of redistributing pension opportunities? Nor, as we shall see below, does all redistributive social policy take place within the policy areas conventionally identified with it.

Social Welfare

The other major element in defining the 'social policy' field is the idea of social welfare. The particular kind of redistribution which social policy seeks to bring about is that of enhancing the welfare—or, if you prefer, the well-being—of individuals and families. In particular, social policy is used to guarantee levels of income and access to resources at or above what are judged to be the minimum acceptable. To the extent that social policy is working adequately, people are not allowed to fall into destitution, homelessness, or avoidable illness as a result of accident, social forces, or indeed their own inadequacy. Sir William Beveridge, author of the famous 1942 report on social security, on which much of the post-war welfare system was based, spoke in ringing terms of the evils against which social policy ought to be directed:

The Plan for Social Security is put forward as part of a general programme of *social policy*. It is one part only of an attack upon five giant evils: upon the physical *Want* with which it is directly concerned, upon *Disease* which often causes that Want and brings many other troubles in its train, upon *Ignorance* which no democracy can afford among its citizens, upon the *Squalor* which arises mainly through haphazard distribution of industry and population, and upon the *Idleness* which destroys wealth and corrupts men, whether they are well fed or not, when they are idle. (Beveridge 1942: 170. Emphasis added)

Social security, health services, education, housing policy, and employment policy, which Beveridge saw as combating the five respective 'giant evils', are clearly the very stuff of social welfare and social policy. It is worthwhile pointing out, however, that Beveridge did not rely entirely on the gains for **individual welfare** to justify his extensive social policy system. Ignorance is presented as a collective evil in a democracy; idleness is to be combated for its 'corrupting' effects. Elsewhere he made it clear that the 'many other troubles' he refers to in relation to disease included deficient economic performance, and that the ability of the country to defend itself militarily was an important consideration in social policy. Whatever view we may take of Beveridge's attitudes, this concern with collective as well as individual welfare is characteristic of social policy debate, and it presents policy-makers with some of their most acute dilemmas. Since the 1997 election the Labour government has struggled to convince its supporters and its critics that it has struck a defensible balance here, between, for instance, the two perceived needs, first to secure social security claimants a civilized standard of living, and second to encourage as many as possible of them—including many single parents and disabled people—out of total dependence on benefit and into paid employment.

And Beveridge also hinted at some of the range of policies involving redistributive social elements. 'Squalor' was said to arise 'mainly through haphazard distribution of industry and population'—so the social policy to combat it would need to involve not just housing but physical planning allied to regional economic policy for employment.

It is because of the centrality of distribution and redistribution, and of social welfare, to social policy that there is also a chapter in this book relating 'patterns of inequality and difference' to 'social need'. Social policy is largely concerned with meeting social need, and that need is largely defined in terms of social inequalities and differences. It would be intolerably complacent to suggest that, in Britain in the 1990s, we can assume that everyone has their basic human needs met and social policy can concentrate on something of a different order which we might call 'relative need'. The presence of the homeless, of children who are receiving no effective schooling or who may be subject to even fatal cruelty, and of elderly people who find themselves denied healthcare, as well as of families on unconscionably low incomes which lead to disease and squalor (to use two of Beveridge's terms) should guard us against that complacency. But the fact is that there are elements of inequality and difference in these problems as well as in a wider range of issues of need which social policy deals with.

Incomes which are low in relative terms lead not just to an inability to 'keep up with the Joneses', but to exclusion from the markets that the Joneses participate in. We know that the poor pay more for their food because they cannot buy in bulk, and often do not have access to the private transport facilities involved in getting to the cheapest outlets, like out-of-town shopping centres. When local school systems have effective patterns of academic or social selection, the provision and the opportunities for those who fail to be positively selected is likely to suffer in terms of resources and quality.

It is not only differences of class or income that arise. Social policy in the late twentieth century has been involved increasingly with differences of ethnicity, and perhaps particularly with differences of sex. There has been a struggle—by no means entirely successful—for policies to cope with the disadvantages of women in a traditionally male-dominated society in a permanent state of flux. The almost automatic poverty of female single parents has constituted a policy problem on a range of fronts, from child poverty to childcare and employment opportunities.

So social need, the individual and collective need that social policy is concerned with meeting, is largely defined in terms of inequality, and even in the thrusting 1990s and beyond that inequality must remain central to its discussion and teaching, and therefore to any book such as ours. And this is true even if other concepts used by those concerned with social policy are changing significantly. Some of the issues mentioned above have come to be discussed in terms not so much of 'poverty' as of 'exclusion'. A 'Social Exclusion Unit' has been set up in the Cabinet Office to monitor policy effects and feed informed input into the development of programmes across a wide range, from social security to juvenile crime. It is entirely appropriate that such a term should be used to bring attention to the plight of people unable to participate fully in society at large or, say, the labour market. But essentially exclusion remains one part of a spectrum of inequality of access and opportunity.

Social Policy Beyond 'Social Welfare'— And Other Policies Within It

We have already observed that social policy exists and works not only in readily recognizable 'social' areas of public policy. Michael Cahill, whose book *The New Social Policy* includes chapters on communicating, viewing, travelling, shopping, working, and playing, reminds us that, as Donnison observed, social policy can permeate well beyond the 'famous five' areas of British institutional welfare—usually enumerated as social security, health, social care, education, and housing—and beyond the tax and employment areas that we have come to place alongside them. This is particularly obvious if we note Donnison's use of the word 'opportunities'. There are many policies through which governments can redistribute opportunities for citizens to secure their own welfare; education and employment are the most obvious, but the subsidization and regulation of transport spring to mind too.

It is also the case that economic policy in various forms has direct and indirect effects on distribution and individual welfare. Sometimes these are the incidental effects of the success or otherwise of the economy, and in particular the rate of economic growth. But the importance of such effects, and the fact that sometimes they are direct and predictable, mean that governments of welfare states have to bear them in mind. While adjusting interest rates may be primarily a policy to control the money supply and economic activity, its direct effects on the cost of personal borrowing, especially the cost of house-purchase mortgages, means that governments have to consider such social factors when contemplating this kind of decision. (In Britain government has recently sought to distance itself from interest-rate decisions and leave them to the Bank of England, but government retains influence and can affect the decisions by its actions elsewhere.)

Public expenditure and taxation policy constitute another area—perhaps the most obvious—where economic and social policy overlap. To the extent that social provision is publicly funded out of taxation, the connection between them is clear. But the relationship is more complex than merely one of raising the money to meet agreed needs. We shall see below and in other chapters that need itself is a contested idea. But, even if it were not, the effects of raising or lowering the level of public expenditure as a proportion of the Gross Domestic Product (the national income, measured annually), and of raising or reducing taxes, would be bound to make decision-making in this area economically vital, highly politicized, and often bitterly contested.

It is worth emphasizing not only that almost any area of policy may have social effects and implications, but that some things that happen even in the 'core welfare areas', particularly involving the technicalities of, say, medicine or educational methods, may have a relatively low social content.

The corollary of all this—essentially, the point that social policy considerations per-

---

Box 1.1 The scope of social policy

Core welfare areas	Social security Healthcare Social care Housing Education
Essential areas of redistributive policy	Taxation Public expenditure Employment
Further policy areas potentially affecting redistribution	Monetary policy Transport Legal aid Physical planning . . . and most other areas of policy, acting through employment, etc.

---

meate other areas of policy—is that social policies are also subject to non-welfare influences. In an industrial society, systems of support for people in and out of work are likely to be structured so as to provide or maintain incentives to work productively, and these may clash with the goal of guaranteeing decent standards of living for the un-employed. Programmes for the welfare of offenders are unlikely to be able to ignore the perceived need for a degree of punishment. It is in this contested and uncertain context that the 'welfare state' has its being.

Welfare State

The term **welfare state** is one which is often presented these days as outmoded. The phrases 'after the welfare state' and 'beyond the welfare state' are highly current. But writing off the phrase 'welfare state' would not be constructive, for it stubbornly re-mains a current one both in academic analysis and in 'live' politics. As we write, the British government presents 'the reform of the welfare state' as one of its primary aims. The question is, what does the term mean and what it can be useful for?

Bryson deals with the term as follows:

The term *welfare state* is used when a nation has at least a minimum level of institutionalized provisions for meeting the basic economic and social requirements of its citizens. When a nation is defined as a welfare state the major emphasis is on the classic forms of social welfare. However, regulation of the labour force and working conditions, general public health meas-ures and some active intervention to at least partially redress inequality is usually implied as well. As Mishra notes, the concept refers both to intention (that is, 'the idea of state respons-ibility for welfare') and the services and provisions (1984, p. xi). (Bryson 1992: 36)

The term is a useful one for something which is rather narrower than the **welfare system.** The latter phrase usually used to refer to all institutions which are primarily aimed at, or used to deliver, welfare objectives. To enlarge on this: the welfare system of a country includes a wide range of welfare-oriented organizations. This takes in not only those in the state sector, but all those driven by broadly welfarist goals: voluntary organizations, independent 'trusts' of various sorts dedicated to social provision, and private sector (for-profit) companies contracted to deliver social services.

It is possible to imagine a society in which high levels of welfare were achieved which might not fit all Bryson's criteria for a 'welfare state'. But it would be a mistake to think that even quite striking developments—such as the increasing use of markets and contracting-out in a welfare system, as has been happening in Britain lately—necessarily mean moving towards a qualitatively different, 'other than welfare' state. A decline in the proportion of the national product spent by the established bureaucracies of the 'welfare state', if it were to occur, might well indicate no more than a change in the methods by which social policies are delivered—it does not necessarily mean a shift to something so qualitatively different as to render the 'welfare state' redundant.

Moreover, the mere fact that fewer and fewer welfare personnel are directly employed by the state would seem to many Continental observers to amount to a coming into line of the UK from its unusually monolithic pattern of post-war welfare to something much more normal, where the state uses and/or regulates the welfare activities of a plurality of private and voluntary organizations: a welfare system. It is important to appreciate that there are and will continue to be a huge range of patterns and degrees of welfare provision, and we shall enlarge on this point below.

Furthermore, not only Britain but all other welfare states are changing, under the strain of economic, demographic, social, and political changes within and beyond them. But Pierson, whose title *Beyond the Welfare State?* includes an important question mark, concludes that it will long remain appropriate to use the term as a description and a basis of comparison. The strains on the welfare state are those on society as a whole, and while the degree and pattern of dependence on state welfare is changing and will continue to do so, its disappearance is scarcely more likely than the disappearance of organized society itself.

Methods of Intervention

When the state creates social policy and intervenes in the pursuit of welfare, it employs a variety of methods of intervention. Direct *provision of services* to client citizens is one, and social security benefits are perhaps the most obvious example in the British context, where these are distributed by an agency of central government. The Benefits Agency acts on behalf of the Department of Social Security to pay Retirement Pensions and other insurance benefits, as well as to assess claimants for income-tested benefits like Income Support and to make the appropriate payments. Local government also provides services directly, notably schooling—although it no longer provides *all* public-sector schooling. These examples remind us that direct provision can take the form either of benefits in *cash* or of services in *kind*.

The distinction hinted at above, between those benefits and services which require the testing of income for eligibility, is an important one. In Britain, a payment called Child Benefit is made to all mothers of children under 16 (or 18 if in full-time education) without any test of financial need. Such benefits are often described as 'universal'. But there are also benefits which are only available to those whose income is low enough to qualify; Income Support is the 'ultimate' means-tested benefit, making the claimant's income up to a specified level, and withdrawn pound for pound as net income increases. The corresponding description is of **selective benefits**. It will be obvious that this terminology is a conventional shorthand—the terms could be used in quite other senses.

Even **universal benefits**, however, may have qualifications beyond the simple contingency they are designed for. Full retirement pensions are only paid to those who have paid the necessary contributions, a condition not attached to Child Benefit, or indeed hospital care—two examples of universal services funded from general public funds rather than through a contributory social insurance system.

Subsidies constitute another mode of social intervention, for instance in transport. Where a bus or train route is fulfilling a social function, such as enabling a needy population to avoid isolation, the cost of maintaining it may be underwritten by the local authority, which will probably also subsidize the travel costs of pensioners and/or other groups in need. And tax credits of various kinds also subsidize expenditure and behaviour thought socially desirable, such as borrowing for owner-occupation of housing or investment in retirement pensions.

Regulation of others' provision is a further way in which governments seek to pursue their social objectives. The management of residential homes and other facilities of social care—particularly those whose clients are publicly funded—is subject to the regulation and inspection of local authorities. This often goes along with subsidization: there is a common Continental pattern of health services, schooling, and, indeed, social insurance, where voluntary organizations are empowered to provide services on a subsidized basis within a strict code of government regulation. But regulation can also be a matter of law in employment and other matters, seeking, for instance, to prevent discrimination on grounds of sex or race.

In these two methods of intervention—subsidization and regulation—the actual service provision is made by non-state organizations. This is also true where government retains responsibility for a service, but meets that responsibility through **contracting-out**: buying the services of others, or commissioning them to act on government's behalf. This is what happens when a local authority pays a catering firm to provide dinners on school premises, for instance; or, indeed, if it houses some or all of its applicants for housing through housing associations rather than in its own stock. Inasmuch as local authorities provide social care these days, they do it largely through voluntary or commercial agents.

This last point leads to a further one: that public authorities in some instances may do no more than advise citizens on how to acquire services—as do Housing Aid centres—or act as gatekeepers and arrange for provision to be made, as can happen with community care where the client is charged the full cost.

In what has come to be called 'the mixed economy of welfare', these and other modes of delivering welfare involving various combinations of government, publicly funded,

Box 1.2 Modes and methods of social policy intervention

Basic modes of intervention	Variant methods	Examples
Cash benefits	Universal (Non-contributory)	Child Benefit
	Universal (Contributory)	Retirement Pensions
	Selective	Income Support
Services in kind	Universal	Hospital services, schooling
	Selective	Free prescription medicines, higher education grants
Subsidies	Vouchers	Nursery vouchers, bus passes
	General subsidies	'Social' public transport routes
Regulation		Equal opportunities laws
Contracting-out		Catering services in schools
Advice		Housing Aid Centres
Gatekeeping		Some community care

voluntary, and commercial organizations and providers, and collective and individual recipients, have all become common.

We have tended to think of the British welfare system in terms of direct state provision, whether in cash or in kind, universal or selective. But it is possible to envisage a system consisting almost entirely of the third, fourth, and fifth mechanisms enumerated above, using regulation, subsidy, and other methods which keep government at a distance from the direct provision of service. Indeed, it is increasingly the case that as the 'mixed economy of welfare' develops, regulation is returning as a significant mode of state welfare. One might argue that we have been there before: much of nineteenth-century protective intervention—such as the Factory Acts—was of a regulatory nature.

There is a further vital point, especially important as governments seek new ways of meeting welfare responsibilities. Policies and programmes often straddle more than one category of intervention, or sit uneasily within a category. In Britain plans are afoot to replace a social security benefit, Family Credit, which is paid to families with a low-paid wage-earner, with a tax benefit, the Working Families' Tax Credit, which has a not dissimilar form but which will be administered within the tax administration, the Inland Revenue. In advance of this the Inland Revenue is assuming some responsibility in the social security field. It will be interesting to see both how the new credit figures in the financial accounts of government, and how writers on public policy classify it!

One final dimension of variance should be mentioned. Citizens are not left at liberty in all cases to decide whether to avail themselves of social policy provision. Schooling between the ages of 5 and 16 is mandatory, as is membership of the National Insurance scheme for social security, contributions to which are deducted in a similar fashion to income tax. Compulsion is justified on grounds of collective welfare, the benefits of large-scale operation, and avoidance of later dependency.

Models of Welfare

Given what has been said so far, it is not surprising that variant notions of the nature and limits of the welfare state exist alongside each other, providing contrasts between countries and conflicts between groups and ideologies within them. As Bryson, in her discussion of the welfare state concept, goes on to observe:

(There) is a great deal of cultural variation in the extent to which liberal democratic capitalist societies measure up in terms of welfare state criteria. Some, such as the USA and Japan, have a weak form which is often referred to as residual. In contrast, the well-developed welfare states of the Scandinavian countries are referred to as taking an institutional form. As well as there being variation between countries in state provisions, within countries different groups have their welfare catered for to varying degrees. In particular those of the non-dominant races and women are likely to receive fewer general societal benefits, even though they may be well over-represented as recipients of state support. (Bryson 1992: 36)

Among the dimensions along which welfare-state models can vary are: the level of public expenditure; the level of direct state provision of services; the use of agencies, franchising, and market-based techniques; and the level of private provision. Broadly speaking, states and political actors of the right favour minimizing state activity in favour of market-based private provision; the USA's pattern of healthcare fits this idea, even though it still involves substantial investment in a residual public healthcare sector. As Bryson observes, the Scandinavian countries have provided examples of an opposite, leftist model, involving high public expenditure, high taxation, and direct government provision, on a non-income-tested ('universal') basis, of a wide range of welfare services.

The famous British analyst of social policy, Richard Titmuss, wrote of the first of these as 'the residual welfare model', and the second as 'the institutional redistributive model'. The common European welfare state, seeking to balance the perceived needs of individual social and collective economic welfare, he described as 'the industrial achievement-performance model' (Titmuss 1974: 30–2). His sympathies lay with the second, but his 'right–left–centre' formula has also been followed by writers seeking to appeal to a sense of moderation and promote a 'third way'.

It is worth observing here that the major variable on which Titmuss focused was the relative balance between state provision of services and reliance on the market. The assumed antithesis between the state and the market has long been a central idea in British social policy. The 'Third Way', as discussed by Anthony Giddens among others, is an attempt to break this antagonism and to develop social welfare (and other) institutions in which state provision and the market are used in complementary ways (Giddens 1998).

The Social Justice Commission, a body set up in the early 1990s by the British Labour Party leader John Smith, to stand back and consider the future of the welfare state and related policies and institutions, took this approach. They rejected the prospects both of a 'Deregulators' Britain', where the rule was 'every person for themself', and of a 'Levellers' Britain', where a stifling egalitarianism would undermine incentive and productivity. Their preference was for an 'Investors' Britain', where social justice (taking full account of welfare needs) and economic growth would be reconciled. The so-called 'New Labour' government elected in 1997, while not accepting all of the Social Justice Commission's thinking, has echoed its orientation; references to a 'third way' permeate their public declarations and position statements. Interestingly, while this 'third way' view predictably rejects the right-wing of the previous, Conservative governments, it also distances New Labour from the social-democratic, statist approach of earlier Labour administrations.

The complexities of these ideological variations and conflicts form part of the subject matter of the next chapter. What has been established here, we hope, is that they are a further dimension of what is the complex and fascinating world of social policy. Later chapters explore specific areas of policy and particular themes and approaches; here we have sought to lay some groundwork for that exploration.

Glossary

collective welfare The good of the whole society.

contracting-out Arrangements by which services are provided by private companies, individuals, or voluntary organizations under contract to, say, a local authority or a hospital trust, rather than directly by that body itself.

distribution The processes by which resources and opportunities are shared out in society, through birth, employment, policy, and other means. Includes 'redistribution', by which distribution is altered or amended. 'Distribution' is also used to describe the results of these processes.

individual welfare The good of the individual citizen.

selective benefits Commonly used to describe 'means-tested' benefits; those only provided to those whose incomes and resources fall below a prescribed level.

social policy The principles and practice of state activity—including state policy for private or voluntary action—relating to redistribution in pursuit of welfare.

social welfare The enhancement of welfare through formal social arrangements.

universal benefits Conventionally, welfare benefits provided to all who fall into certain contingencies (such as having children, in the case of Child Benefit; being of school age; being over the age of retirement; having become unemployed) regardless of their income or wealth.

welfare state The main instruments by which the state seeks to ensure minimum levels of welfare, or through which it redistributes resources other than how the market decides. This concept is usually used to refer to the main institutions of the post-war welfare settlement, the National Health Service, the social security system, the state-funded education system, the state role in the provision and funding of housing, and state personal and social work services.

welfare system The organizations and mechanisms primarily concerned with providing or guaranteeing the social welfare of citizens. These may include non-state organizations such as those in the voluntary sector and those in the private (for-profit) sector. This is a wider definition than the more traditional one of the 'welfare state'.

Guide to Further Reading

Alcock, P., *Social Policy in Britain* (London: Macmillan, 1992). An introductory text which pursues important themes and issues through the British welfare state.

Bryson, L., *Welfare and the State* (London: Macmillan, 1992). A useful discussion, by an Australian analyst, of the role of the 'welfare state' and 'social policy' in modern society, critically considering conventional definitions of these and other terms, and going on to look at the distribution of state welfare, with a particular emphasis on gender differences.

Cahill, M., *The New Social Policy* (Oxford: Blackwell, 1994). Explores social policy beyond the welfare system, in communications, arts, transport, and other areas often neglected.

Esping-Andersen, G., *The Three Worlds of Welfare Capitalism* (Cambridge: Polity Press, 1990). A scheme of classification for welfare states, embracing a range of industrial countries.

Macarov, D., *Social Welfare: Structure and Practice* (Thousand Oaks, California: Sage, 1995). An account of social welfare from outside the British tradition, by an eminent Israeli academic.

References

Beveridge, W. (1942), *Social Insurance and Allied Services: A Report by Sir William Beveridge* (Cmd. 6404, London: HMSO).

Bryson, L. (1992), *Welfare and the State* (London: Macmillan).

Cahill, M. (1994), *The New Social Policy* (Oxford: Blackwell).

Commission on Social Justice (1994), *Social Justice: Strategies for National Renewal* (London: Vintage).

Donnison, D. V. (1975), *An Approach to Social Policy* (Dublin: National Economic and Social Council and Republic of Ireland Stationery Office).

Giddens, A. (1998), *The Third Way: The Renewal of Social Democracy* (Cambridge: Polity Press).

Mishra, R. (1984), *The Welfare State in Crisis* (Brighton: Wheatsheaf).

Pierson, C. (1991), *Beyond the Welfare State? The New Political Economy of Welfare* (Cambridge: Polity Press).

Titmuss, R. (1974), *Social Policy: An Introduction* (London: Allen & Unwin).

2 The Development of Social Policy

Stewart Miller

Contents

Introduction: Welfare and History

In modern societies, the 'welfare state' is well named, despite the changes which have overtaken it in recent years. Since the middle of the twentieth century, the public social services such as healthcare, schooling, and social insurance have furnished many of the key points of contact between the state and the citizen. Moreover, most of the money raised by the state in taxes is spent on the kinds of social policy programmes and institutions discussed in Chapter 1. It was not always so, and this chapter seeks to describe and explain the development of the redistributive, welfare-oriented sphere of social policy (described in the previous chapter), leading to its prominent role in the modern state.

We begin with some discussion of the relationship between welfare and industrialization, then look at the development of social policy in Britain, the first industrial nation and also one which is sometimes thought of as a pioneer of welfare. After a brief look at earlier periods, we turn to the recent history of the British welfare state.

Much of this chapter will therefore be about Britain, but the experiences described have been, in some respects, and with important differences, those of many other countries which industrialized in the nineteenth century and came to constitute the so-called 'developed world' of the twentieth. There have been times when Britain has been a leader in social policy thought and development—the Beveridge Report of 1942 quickly became a point of reference for the policy-makers of other countries, even if they did not all seek to follow its advice—but Britain has equally looked for examples from elsewhere, and in particular has been influenced by practice in Germany. There is no such thing as a welfare state entirely 'typical' in its development, and Britain's has been idiosyncratic in some ways and at some times, not least in its relation to **industrialization** in the nineteenth century.

Industrialization and the Emergence of State Welfare

Many writers have sought to theorize the phenomenon of welfare state development, particularly in industrial countries. Rimlinger (1971) sees welfare development as varying with national patterns of industrialization. Wilensky and Lebeaux (1965) describe the development of welfare in terms of a reluctant response by the state to the problems of an industrial society. Some Marxists have seen it in terms of the gains forced from such states by workers' struggle. Marshall (1950) emphasizes the construction of civil, political, and social rights in a complex process of conflict and gradual enlightenment. Pierson (1991) describes the later twentieth-century welfare state as bound up with the ideology of social democracy.

What is not at issue is that the welfare state is a phenomenon of the modern, industrial nation. Not before the twentieth century in most cases, and in no case before the nineteenth century, did the machinery exist, at national or local level, to sustain the taxation and service provision characteristic of the welfare state. It hardly makes sense to speak of 'social policy' in these earlier times—and therefore it hardly makes sense to speak of the 'social problems' to which that policy is often a response.

That is not to say that institutions did not exist whose history is part of the history of social policy, because they came to be transformed into or replaced by more recognizable institutions of welfare. The English **Poor Law,** which was codified by legislation of 1601, had a welfare function alongside its role in disciplining the landless workers who fell through the bottom of the social system as feudalism broke up and wage labour became increasingly important in the local and national economy (Lis and Soly 1979). Similar laws emerged in most European countries as they formed themselves into something like the nation states we know today. Here England was a leader, since its evolution into a nation state was an early example, like that of France. But even in England the limits of a national state whose officers could not swiftly move around the country or, indeed, communicate with outlying areas, whose authority still depended substantially on the co-operation of local magnates and whose leadership remained highly personal and particular in the monarch, could not even aspire to run complex

Thousands	1801	1851	1901
England and Wales	8,893	17,928	32,528
Scotland	1,608	2,889	4,472
Glasgow	77	363	904
Birmingham	71	265	761
York	17	36	78
Brighton	7	66	123

Table 2.1 Nineteenth-century growth in population and urbanization: population of England and Wales, Scotland, and selected towns
Mitchell and Deane (1962): 'Population and Vital Statistics', 2, 8.

services or systems of regulation. The question did not arise. And something similar remained true at county level, in a rural, agriculturally dominated society.

So it was only with the creation of an industrial society, with its concentrations of urban population, its development of improved transport and communications, its need for an educated workforce, and its nationalized political and administrative system—as well as its problems of rapid growth and the undermining of the more traditional family and community systems of social support and control—that the state, which by that time was British, showed either the capacity or the inclination to develop the modern range of social policies and institutions. See Table 2.1 for the growth of population in the nineteenth century: during that period, the urban proportion of the population of England and Wales grew from approximately 20 per cent to 77 per cent (Burnett 1978; Wohl 1984).

In Britain, the first country to experience the transformation now labelled 'the Industrial Revolution', it is perhaps not surprising that the state's response lagged so far behind economic events. In contemplating the nineteenth century, we find ourselves faced with a picture of what appear to us as urgent and massive social problems arising from the phenomenally rapid and unplanned **urbanization**, met by the reform efforts of a state slowly transforming its identity from one vested in the old, preindustrial order into one capable of keeping pace with the hectic rush of modern industry and commerce.

Again, we can consider the Poor Law. The story of its development in the nineteenth century vividly illustrates the painful nature of this transformation and the essential fact, never to be forgotten, that social reform is not purely—and is sometimes hardly at all—a matter of altruistic generosity, but is often one of 'necessity of state', helping to remove obstacles to economic progress and social order as these are perceived by those with influence on policy. Nor are such necessity, progress, and order uncontested concepts; they are often the objects of fundamental conflict. When Edwin Chadwick (1800–90) and his fellow reformers sought to establish institutions of (to us) modest and severe assistance to, and control of, the poor, he was met with bitter opposition from those likely to have to pay for them through property taxes. Yet, as with the **public health** measures which were promoted against equal opposition, the Poor Law reforms were no more than an attempt to act in the best interests, perhaps the enlightened interests, of the owners of property and capital as investors and employers.

By the early nineteenth century local initiatives over many generations had made the Poor Law a thing of great variety across the country. In particular, some local authorities were much more prepared than others to give financial aid to 'paupers' (as applicants were known) without requiring them to enter the poorhouse. Moreover, some differed from others in that they provided allowances in aid of wages when times were bad, and not even all those in employment could afford bread. To Chadwick this practice undermined the best operation of the labour market, and the variety of practice sent confused messages to workers. Better that the Poor Law be administered, under central guidance, in such a way that it provided for the truly destitute but did so in such a way that no able-bodied worker would *elect* to depend on it rather than work— that is to say, the lot of the pauper should be less *eligible* (or *preferable*) than that of the labourer in employment (see Box 2.1). This 'less eligibility' principle underpinned the reformed or 'New' Poor Law from 1834. The investment involved in setting up the local provision—including 'modern' poorhouses of several different kinds, or with several departments for different classes of pauper—and the new administration at local and

---

Box 2.1 Less eligibility: from the Report of the Poor Law Commissioners, 1834

[PRINCIPLE OF ADMINISTERING RELIEF TO THE INDIGENT]

'The first and most essential of all conditions, a principle which we find universally admitted, even by those whose practice is at variance with it, is, that his situation (that is, the situation of the "pauper", the recipient of Poor Law relief) on the whole shall not be made really or apparently so eligible as the situation of the independent labourer of the lowest class. Throughout the evidence it is shown, that in proportion as the condition of any pauper class is elevated above the condition of independent labourers, the condition of the independent class is depressed; their industry is impaired, their employment becomes unsteady, and its remuneration in wages is diminished. Such persons, therefore, are under the strongest inducements to quit the less eligible class of labourers and enter the more eligible class of paupers. The converse is the effect when the pauper class is placed in its proper position, below the condition of the independent labourer. Every penny bestowed, that tends to render the condition of the pauper more eligible than that of the independent labourer, is a bounty on indolence and vice . . .

A well-regulated workhouse meets all cases, and appears to be the only means by which the intention of the statute of Elizabeth (of 1601), that all the able-bodied shall be set to work, can be carried into execution.'

Source: Report of the Poor Law Commissioners, 1834: 261–2. Material in brackets added.

central levels—Boards of Guardians for new 'unions' of parishes, and a national Poor Law Commission to supervise them—was substantial. It was intended to lead to a hard, minimal but efficient system of last-resort relief which would also help to smooth the working of the labour market.

It was largely the information gained through the operation of the New Poor Law, from 1834, that led to the attempt at a public health reform that would create a similar pattern of central control and local provision to improve sanitary conditions. But not even epidemics of cholera in the 1840s could persuade the politically enfranchised and influential to opt for a truly effective national step in that direction until a further generation had passed. Nevertheless, many local authorities took important initiatives, and gradually there was emerging a state capable of tackling some of the problems of an urban industrial nation, even if there was reluctance to realize its potential.

Other countries industrialized later, and their governments took more of an active role, from an earlier stage, in promoting that industrialization and building into it the beginnings of modern welfare; so that when Britain introduced substantial but limited schemes of social insurance for healthcare and unemployment benefit in 1911 it was after such influential political and administrative figures respectively as David Lloyd George and William Beveridge had visited Germany and been impressed by the arrangements initiated a generation earlier under Chancellor Bismarck.

At the same time, Britain had been cautiously extending its originally patchy public education system in the face of the demands of both industry and democracy. It is no accident that the legislation intended to ensure elementary education throughout the country was passed in 1870, only three years after the vote was given to men from a wider range of social and economic classes. This field of public endeavour, too, was developed and expanded in the years before the First World War, when Germany was demonstrating the advantages of an educated workforce.

By the time of the First World War, then, Britain had an extensive central and local state, whose activities ranged beyond the traditional activities of defence and public order into welfare (including housing), education, and a large number of regulatory measures in industry and commerce. Its taxation system, too, was beginning to assume a modern scale and comprehensiveness. The expansion of the state was to continue for most of the twentieth century (see Box 2.2).

The war of 1914–18 enhanced the tendency to examine social problems and propose solutions in further state action—and indeed, an ambitious 'reconstruction' programme was formulated and partly enacted—but that action was cut back in the light of post-war economic problems. Indeed, social policy between the two world wars was dominated by these problems. On the one hand, there was a succession of *ad hoc* attempts to respond to the massive unemployment of the period; on the other, a cautious government allowed many other issues to be squeezed out, and by 1939, at the outbreak of the Second World War, a backlog of unanswered social questions had built up. It was in that context, as well as that of a new form of total war involving the civilian population to an unprecedented degree, that in 1942 a blueprint was produced for something like a welfare state—although the phrase was one which the author of that blueprint abhorred. The Beveridge Report marks a distinct change of gear in the progress of British social policy.

Box 2.2 The state's expansion in the twentieth century: general government expenditure as a percentage of Gross Domestic Product

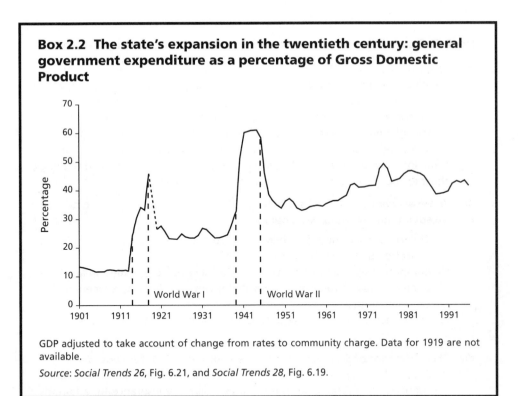

GDP adjusted to take account of change from rates to community charge. Data for 1919 are not available.

Source: Social Trends 26, Fig. 6.21, and *Social Trends 28*, Fig. 6.19.

The Beveridge Report and After

Probably the most famous document in social policy history anywhere, the Beveridge Report was commissioned as a technical examination of the social insurance system that had grown and developed piecemeal in Britain since 1911. The idea was to determine what adjustments might make the existing system work better and more comprehensively. William Beveridge, one of the luminaries of the twentieth-century social reform 'establishment', had been around for a long time, as we have seen, and had always been active in social and educational administration. He seized the opportunity to produce in part what the government had asked for, but which went far beyond the brief. The Beveridge Report, *Social Insurance and Allied Services* (Beveridge 1942), included not only a proposal for a comprehensive system of income maintenance through social insurance (National Insurance) with a means-tested backup (National Assistance), but also a broadly sketched design for much of the post-war welfare policy system (see Box 2.3).

It was immediately attractive to the Labour Party, whose leaders had joined Churchill's National Government in 1940. Labour's adoption of Beveridge's main principles and recommendations probably gave them a critical edge in the 1945 election over their erstwhile partners, the Conservatives, whose leader Churchill had been much more reluctant

> **Box 2.3 Beveridge on social security: from the Beveridge Report**
>
> '300. *Scope of Social Security*: The term 'social security' is used here to denote the securing of an income to take the place of earnings when they are interrupted by unemployment, sickness or accident, to provide for retirement through age, to provide loss of support by the death of another person, and to meet exceptional expenditures, such as those connected with birth, death and marriage. Primarily social security means security of income up to a minimum, but the provision of an income should be associated with treatment designed to bring the interruption of earnings to an end as soon as possible.
>
> 301. *Three assumptions*: No satisfactory scheme of social security can be devised except on the following assumptions:
>
> (A) Children's allowances for children up to the age of 15 or if in full-time education up to the age of 16;
>
> (B) Comprehensive health and rehabilitation services for prevention and cure of disease and restoration of capacity for work, available to all members of the community;
>
> (C) Maintenance of employment, that is to say avoidance of mass unemployment . . .
>
> 302. *Three Methods of Security*: On these assumptions, a Plan for Social Security is outlined below, combining three distinct methods: social insurance for basic needs; national assistance for special cases; voluntary insurance for additions to the basic provision.'
>
> *Source*: Beveridge, W. (1942), *Social Insurance and Allied Services* (Cmd. 6404, London: HMSO), 120.

to publicly accept a set of 'promises' he was uncertain could be kept, and which in any case he had regarded as an undesirable distraction from the conduct of the war in 1942.

The contemporary importance of Labour's welfare programme is indicated to some degree by Kenneth Morgan's remark in *Labour in Power*:

By the time of the general election of February 1950, the main defence of the Labour government by its supporters lay less in the achievements of nationalization or industrial reform, than in the creation of the welfare state, including full employment. (Morgan 1984: 142)

A full employment policy, and the creation of a 'national health and rehabilitation service', had been assumptions which Beveridge built into his design for a comprehensive social security system. Although he did not go into these in great detail—and, indeed, would have had no business doing so—his endorsement of them greatly added to the weight of the economic and healthcare progressives who were campaigning for them, and the planners who were sympathetic to these ideas. So Beveridge's importance goes well beyond the social security system, itself a massive construct.

But despite its attractions for Labour, it would be wrong to describe the Beveridge blueprint as 'socialist'. It was not particularly egalitarian, except in as much as any plan for a National Minimum would inevitably involve enough redistribution to narrow differentials at the bottom end of the income scale. It accepted, and indeed consolidated, the subordinate role of women in the family. (Married women were to depend on their husbands' entitlements in social security.) It was a plan for state intervention, not only to guarantee the welfare of the elderly, the sick, the unemployed, and others, but also to enhance the collective welfare of Britain as a capitalist economy and society. Moreover, he emphasized the limits to state responsibility and the need for voluntary action. This is typical of what George and Wilding (1994) have called a 'middle way' or 'reluctant collectivist' approach. But, like the creation of a national health service which accompanied it in the forties, the social security reforms were also radical in their way and characteristic of what becomes possible in the exceptional context of war and its aftermath. At that particular time, what emerged as political orthodoxy was something like a social democratic ideology: a preparedness to tolerate, indeed an enthusiasm for, statist strategies such as public ownership, universal welfare provision, and regulation, all in the service of what was to remain essentially a capitalist society. Maynard Keynes came into his own as adviser both to the wartime and the post-war governments, and indeed he negotiated with Beveridge during the preparation of the latter's report, so that Beveridge knew he was not just crying in the wilderness but making proposals which had support within government.

The Reforms

The succession of social reform measures began even before the war ended, with the Education Act of 1944 and the Family Allowances Act of 1945. But it really got into its stride after the election of the Labour Government under Clement Attlee (Churchill's deputy during the war). There were three great Acts, which we shall note briefly here, as well as a string of other, less memorable but not unimportant ones to do with housing, planning, childcare, and so on.

The National Health Service Act (1946) created a national healthcare system, almost entirely free at the point of use, and funded principally from general taxation (with a small contribution from National Insurance to emphasize continuity with the previous National Health Insurance system and make contributors feel properly entitled to use the system). The service was, in practice, an amalgamation of the local authority and voluntary hospital systems and a development of the general practice service available on a limited basis under the old National Health Insurance system. It sought to make healthcare available and accessible to all, and was in principle a model universal social service. Its sponsor was the left-wing Minister of Health, Aneurin Bevan; this measure was not part of the Beveridge social security package, although we may note Beveridge's assumption that something like it would happen. Had that not been a safe assumption, Beveridge would have had to design a social insurance system that covered the cost of healthcare itself, and not just (through sickness benefit) loss of earnings.

The National Insurance Act (1946) stemmed from the core recommendations of the Beveridge Report of 1942. It provided for a universal, contributory **National Insurance** system to provide income in retirement, sickness, and unemployment, as well as in other contingencies. Like the NHS Act, to some extent it generalized and systematized provisions from which some people had been able to benefit since the developments earlier in the century.

The National Assistance Act (1948), which began by formally winding up the centuries-old Poor Law, complemented National Insurance with **National Assistance,** which was intended as a safety net for those few who were expected to slip through the contributory benefit system and require means-tested assistance. (We shall see that National Assistance and its successor systems played a far larger part than was envisaged for them.)

The 'big three' Acts did not constitute the sum total of the post-war settlement, even in the welfare field. There were further legislative measures, and the whole framework of welfare rested on a particular brand of economic policy. It was at least partly on welfare grounds that the Labour Government committed itself to the maintenance of **full employment** (see also Chapter 5). As a strategy of government policy, this was an innovative move, although not a unique one to Britain. The general commitment of western governments to such a strategy was a vital part of the international economic and political settlement of which the founding of the United Nations Organization, the Bretton Woods agreement on international finance, and the Marshall Plan for American aid to Europe were other elements.

A Period of Consensus? The Fifties and Sixties

The decades immediately after the Second World War and the 'post-war settlement' are frequently described as a period when the big issues of the time had been settled and when the major British political parties, although they competed fiercely with each other, displayed a high degree of overlap in their approach to policy. This phenomenon has been characterized in the term 'consensus'.

'Consensus' is basically another word for 'agreement'. In this context, it tends to be used to describe a substantial degree of agreement between the parties competing to form governments in Britain; or at least, enough of an overlap between the crucial leadership elements of these parties to ensure that the Opposition at any given time was not proposing or promoting radical or revolutionary change; and that, when the government changed hands, there was considerable continuity of policy. As we shall see, not all commentators agree that such a consensus was more strikingly present in the fifties and sixties than at other times.

Interestingly, it is quite often argued that the present time is one in which a new consensus has emerged about the degree of state intervention in social and economic life, the need for reform of the welfare state, and a range of related matters; and the lack of 'clear blue water' between the Conservatives and Labour before the 1997 election, and the limited degree of change afterwards, are cited as evidence of this. To the extent that this is a plausible analysis, it certainly points up one element of consensus: that it does not require parties to be particularly friendly towards each other. They tend to be just as mutually hostile and critical at times when one can sensibly speak of there being 'consensus' as when not. Indeed, if almost all that divides parties is personality and assessments of competence, friendliness is not usually conspicuous.

Sullivan (1992) remarks on the frequent assumption that at least part of the post-war period has been characterized by consensus about the role of the state:

The orthodox interpretation, in relation to the United Kingdom at least, is that for close on thirty post-war years significant continuity characterised the domestic policies of the Labour and Conservative parties. That continuity reflected, or so it was believed, substantial agreement at the level of principle about the need for government intervention to ensure economic growth, full employment and the provision of more or less comprehensive welfare services. (Sullivan 1992: 1)

As Sullivan observes, the emergence of this consensus is often thought to have been aided, or at least marked, by 'Butler, Chancellor of the Exchequer in the 1951 Conservative administration, aping the economic policies and principles of the previous Labour Chancellor, Gaitskell' (Sullivan 1992: 3). Indeed, the allegedly consensual approach of the fifties at least is often referred to as 'Butskellism', a term coined by the *Economist* magazine from the names of R. A. ('Rab') Butler and Hugh Gaitskell. The 'consensus', or agreement, is said to have consisted of the general acceptance of a capitalist state with a substantial public element; a mixed economy, economically dominated by private industry but with an extensive industrial public sector, including coal, steel, the railways, and the utilities, and a range of public services, including a largely universalist welfare state. All this was to be managed in such a way as to ensure continually rising living standards and to avoid mass unemployment on the 1930s scale.

Certainly all of the governments of the 1950s and 1960s seem to have felt constrained to operate within a framework which can be defined largely in these terms. The Conservatives did not denationalize more than a couple of the industries that Labour had taken into public ownership in the forties; Labour did not attempt to take industrial nationalization any further. The welfare system legislated for by Labour was consolidated by the Conservatives.

Nevertheless, the two parties argued and competed vigorously, each trying essentially to convince the electorate that it could run the state defined by the post-war settlement better than the other. As Taylor-Gooby (1985) points out, there were areas of policy where disagreement between the parties still went well beyond rivalry into ideological conflict. Glennerster (1995) takes this point so far as to argue that 'consensus' is not an accurate description of the period at all.

One particularly bitterly contested area was housing. The Conservatives' achievement in building numbers of houses in the 1950s was considerable, and difficult for Labour to challenge them on, especially as more and more prospective Labour voters became owner-occupiers. But their commitment to a shift from public to private provision led the Conservatives to introduce one of the most controversial housing measures of the century: the 1957 Rent Act. This attempt to revive the ailing private rented sector by undermining rent control was a political disaster, as well as a calamity for many tenants—although one of its chief characteristics was its sheer ineffectiveness: private renting stubbornly refused to be revived.

In social security some of the government's critics were shocked that, throughout the fifties, about a million pensioners were dependent on National Assistance, notwithstanding the fact that the value of the National Insurance retirement pension rose in real terms. This was the result of problems of the practical relationship between National Insurance (NI) and National Assistance (NA) in the post-war social security system. Although NI contributory benefits were intended to prevent poverty, they often failed to provide, unaided, an income higher than the minimum guaranteed by NA once rent and other allowances had been taken into account. Many people receiving full NI pensions or other benefits but no other income were forced to subject themselves to NA means tests to obtain their full entitlement. However, in a way, this 'creeping selectivism' rather suited the Conservatives, many of whom were far from convinced of the desirability of extensive universalism in welfare. The post-war scheme had built in a degree of means-testing which they could approve of. A pamphlet of 1952, Macleod and Powell's *The Social Services: Needs and Means*, put the thinking Conservative's position as follows:

The question . . . which poses itself is not, 'should a means test be applied to a social service?' but 'why should any social service be provided without test of need?'

In broad terms, then, Conservative policy towards the social services at this time trod the fine line between the two (to them) unacceptable options of a return to anything that smacked of the family means tests of the 1930s on the one hand, and 'signing the blank cheque' of unmodified universalism on the other.

The main engine of welfare expansion in the fifties and early sixties was undoubtedly economic growth—even if, in comparative terms, Britain's performance in this field was modest (Chapter 5 contains a discussion of the links between efficiency, economic growth, and welfare). The issues of redistribution which arose after the early sixties were almost absent during this 'never-had-it-so-good' era. And the absence of large-scale national (as against regional) unemployment also served to suspend some of the questions and dilemmas that would eventually have to be faced. When Labour came to power in 1964, promising both better economic performance and welfare state improvement, the crunch began to come.

1964–70

Taylor-Gooby (1985) refers to 'the political dilemmas of a Labour Government committed to meritocracy as well as egalitarianism, incentives as well as redistribution, the support of sections of the middle as well as the working class'. These dilemmas might be easily resolvable in an economic vacuum; but the years from 1964 to 1970 presented in aggravated form the 'fine-tuning' problems of Keynesian economics in a series of sterling and balance-of-payments crises. As a response to these, the government felt obliged repeatedly to revise its economic and social strategies of planning and reform. The Labour Prime Minister, Harold Wilson, and most of his colleagues in government saw growth in the welfare system as a product of growth in the economy, without which it was impracticable. The economic circumstances of the mid- to late sixties were perceived to compel severe cutbacks in their expansion plans on these grounds.

It would be a mistake, however, to conclude from the experience of the Wilson government that susceptibility to economic vagaries is a distinguishing characteristic of social policies, since the attempt to engage in serious economic planning was also a casualty at this time. Moreover, positive aspects of economic and social policy sometimes ran together. Statutory redundancy payments and earnings-related unemployment benefit were introduced, with the aim of encouraging the mobility of labour between jobs as technological and economic change demanded, as well as that of providing for individual welfare.

There is a consistent strand through the attempt to manage the economy, the substantial reorganization of government and administration, and the meritocratic approach to education which gives something of the flavour of the Wilson government, and which can be summed up as **managerialism.** Great faith was placed in new structures and techniques, and in the essentially consensual idea that what was required to solve Britain's ills was a kind of post-ideological modernization. This is also the period of a rapid growth in the number and influence of pressure groups and of a kind of corporatism in their mutually dependent relations with government. This form of politics, particularly the links between the government and the trade unions, came under strain in the seventies and in the eighties was declared anathema, undermined, and all but destroyed by Margaret Thatcher and her colleagues.

One of the great themes of social policy debate in the sixties was the conflict between the **universalists** and the **selectivists**, with the Labour government pressed by its friends to pursue universalism, while it actually strove to keep its options open and took hardly any decisive steps in either direction. A nice example is the case of family allowances, which the government raised in 1967 and 1968, nevertheless counterbalancing these increases with a 'clawback' scheme to recover the extra value from taxpayers with children, thus translating an apparently universal policy into a selective one. This kind of compromise sufficiently disappointed some of those who had had great hopes of Labour for them to turn towards the Conservatives in the hope of generating a welfare bidding match, and by 1970 part of the poverty lobby was campaigning under the slogan, 'The poor get poorer under Labour'.

It would be a mistake, however, to dismiss the Wilson administration of 1964–70, which, even if it ended up improvising frantically, began as a reforming government and maintained some of its momentum right up to its rather surprising defeat in 1970. It tidied up social assistance by translating National Assistance into Supplementary Benefit, a system which, for all its limitations, secured many more people their entitlement than had NA. It brought about the building of large numbers of houses, both in the public and in the private sector. It promoted the 'comprehensive' reform of secondary education. It modernized local authority social services.

The whole period we are looking at here is one of adjustment to a new kind of competitive international economics, and a new kind of affluent but highly imperfect kind of social life and organization. The modest but continuing growth and the low unemployment seem both to have permitted something like consensual politics to operate and to have disguised the seriousness of Britain's economic and political decline. In the 1970s any delusions under which Britons were labouring were stripped away, and a set of ideological positions was developed, or rather recognized, which provided theoretical backing for a rather different style of politics.

Post-Consensus? After the Sixties

This section will examine the post-Butskellism decade of the 1970s. One of the important features of that decade is the 'U-turn' phenomenon. Both the Conservative government of 1970–4 and the Labour administration of 1974–9 began with high degrees of commitment to programmes that are recognizably ideological: they set out to do roughly what one might expect of governments of their respective colouring. But both were knocked off course by economic forces: the Conservatives abandoned their anti-collectivist programme for a highly interventionist brand of social democratic centrism, and the Labour government felt itself obliged to adopt a 'tight money' approach which was not far from that of its Thatcherite successor.

It is perhaps ironic, then, that this was the period in which the death of consensus is often seen as having occurred. Many commentators, and some political actors, identify consensus politics strongly with the growth of the welfare state. Sullivan (1992) is explicit about this, suggesting that consensus was a prerequisite of welfare growth, and Johnson (1987) asserts that what he critically refers to as 'the providential state' was a product of a kind of consensual politics. The strong political consensus of the 1950s and 1960s went beyond the main political party leaderships, and embraced other political actors. One feature of the 1970s was the high degree of conflict between governments and others, such as the trade unions. Indeed, it was largely conflicts between the two governments of the 1970s and the trade unions that unseated both of the former.

As pointed out earlier, political agreement and support for the expansion of public welfare was easier in the context of steady economic growth. Although the 1970s as a whole were to experience economic performance which the 1980s Thatcher government must occasionally have envied, the decade also saw the end of automatic annual growth, as well as acute crises brought about by developments in the Middle East and in the developing world. These tensions made the commodities required by the developed countries, particularly oil, hugely more expensive, and produced a new combination of rapid inflation and growing unemployment. Perhaps it was small wonder, then, that the 1970s should prove to be a decade of political conflict unprecedented in the post-war era, and a time when the welfare state came under an altogether new degree of criticism and attack. Indeed, this is the time of what was often called 'the crisis of the welfare state', when its very future seemed to be called into doubt as it was severely criticized simultaneously by the left and the right. (In fact, that crisis was to continue well beyond the close of the decade, and indeed up to the present day.)

On the left there was a great deal of disillusionment with a set of policies and institutions which had failed to abolish poverty or a number of other problems of late industrial society, despite decades of economic growth and social organization. On the right, the cost of those very policies and provisions was held to be an intolerable burden on the economy; both sides, in slightly different ways, deprecated the degree of bureaucratic control welfare state organizations exercised over their clients. While some of these criticisms had surfaced from time to time since the war, during the 1970s they ceased to be cries in the wilderness and became part of an increasingly conflict-ridden norm of political debate.

In this period these criticisms of the welfare state found a material context in which particularly those of the right flourished. Affluence had led people to have higher expectations of services, expectations which were frequently not met by the welfare system. Britain's economic performance was poor, simultaneous unemployment and inflation both undermining the tax base on which services were financed and—combined with the effects of an ageing population—raising the level of demand for social provision. And the class structure had become more complex in ways which loosened what had become almost traditional loyalties to the welfare state among working people (George and Miller 1994: 9–10).

It is no surprise either, then, that policy in the 1970s saw the introduction of a range of means-tested benefits, like Family Income Supplement, intended to plug gaps in the system while keeping costs down or, like the national schemes of Rent Rebates and Allowances (the forerunners of Housing Benefit), designed to replace less selective provision—in this case, general subsidies to council housing. These were Conservative measures. Where universal benefits were improved, measures were taken to cover their costs. Although Labour expanded the contributory pension, creating the State Earnings Related Pension Scheme, part of the programme was a reform of contributions towards social insurance schemes designed to bring in more revenue to pay for it. And while Labour also improved on family allowances with the Child Benefit scheme, this was also paid for by increased revenue through a withdrawal of tax allowances.

Another measure which, like pension reform, had long been sought was a reorganization of the National Health Service in the hope of making it more efficient. This was enacted by the Conservatives and implemented by Labour, and was part of a general move towards bigger units of public administration, including ministries; the new NHS structure was one of several which did not last long (see Chapter 13). Longer lived was Labour's Homeless Persons Act of 1977, which placed responsibility for the homeless on local authority housing departments but failed to guarantee the resources that would make for civilized treatment in areas of housing stress.

The Triumph of Ideology

The **New Right** ideology which came to the forefront at this time owed much to nineteenth-century liberalism, and cherished economic freedom, which was cited as the chief ground for minimizing the state, particularly the welfare-oriented parts of it which now dominated public expenditure. Public welfare benefits were seen to undermine work incentives and the flexibility of the labour market. Indeed, free markets were presented as the ideal economic arrangements wherever possible, and state interference with them was seen as ill-informed (however well-intentioned) and damaging.

So pervasive did some of these ideas become, and so irrelevant were previously fashionable Keynesian ideas thought to be in this new environment, that when the Labour government ran into a financial crisis in 1975 it was constrained to adopt a monetarist policy of retrenchment in public expenditure, as the price for loans from the International Monetary Fund to support the pound. Even before this a Labour cabinet minister, Anthony Crosland, had declared, 'The party's over.' It was assumed that welfare state growth was impossible without an expanding economy.

The Conservative Party, in office between 1970 and 1974 under Edward Heath, turned on its defeated leader in 1975 and elected Britain's first woman party leader, Margaret Thatcher. Although a member of Heath's cabinet, she had succeeded in distancing herself from it, at least in retrospect. (Certainly personal relations between Heath and Thatcher thereafter bespoke a sense of betrayal on both sides.) But the evidence suggests that both the Conservatives in 1975 and the electorate in 1979, when Thatcher overturned Labour and became Prime Minister, were seeking a change from personnel perceived to have failed in leadership roles. Thatcher's subsequent pursuit of a New Right ideological agenda surprised many people.

The Labour Party under Wilson and then Callaghan had tried to pursue a standard post-war strategy of the balancing act between keeping the economy growing and developing the welfare state, and had failed to carry it through. Moreover, its relations with the trade unions who largely funded it had reached a new low point as unemployment was allowed to grow. When Labour in turn was defeated in 1979, their moderate leadership also felt the pain of rejection; and the party swung for much of the 1980s towards a leftist ideology in direct contrast to that of the Conservatives, and also, as it turned out, towards an electoral exile that was to last even longer. As far as the two main parties were concerned, consensus was indeed a thing of the past.

Thatcherism and Conservative Dominance

The story of social policy since 1979 forms an important part of contemporary policy realities and is dealt with in detail in subsequent chapters of this book. Here we attempt no more than to pick out the main themes, with particular examples of their realization. What is clear is that this period was one in which the welfare state was subject to a new degree of hostile governance; a period which it survived, but from which it emerged substantially changed.

From 1979 to 1997 British government was in the hands of a party which was inspired by the ideas and ideals of the New Right—economic liberalism combined with a tendency towards social conservatism which was a reaction to the progressivism of the previous generation. Famously, the Thatcher government declared almost immediately that 'public expenditure is at the heart of Britain's present economic difficulties' (HM Treasury 1979: 1). An early commitment to reducing the absolute amount of public expenditure became one to reduce it as a proportion of Gross Domestic Product; and while the government did not succeed in this so far as they wished, they certainly reversed the pattern of incremental growth which had been a feature of most of the post-war period till then, under Conservative governments as well as Labour (Chapter 10 gives a detailed account of this).

This policy goal manifested itself in the introduction and extension of techniques of financial management designed to control growth and throw responsibility on to service providers—seen by the Thatcher and Major governments as principal authors of welfare state expansion. **Cash planning,** making as little allowance as possible for inflation, combined with limited budgets, close control (or 'capping') of local authority revenue-raising and spending, and devolved financial management all ensured that no service decision could be made without its costs forcing themselves into consideration at every stage. In healthcare, personal social services, and education this slowed down expenditure growth and brought a new managerial style to bear on administration. In housing it resulted in unprecedented cuts in building, maintenance, and subsidization.

In social security, for the most part, such techniques could not be employed. It is generally held to be impossible to budget a service in which claimants have specific rights to money benefit; they cannot be turned away with the information that the money has run out for the year. The social security budget is said to be 'demand led'. The entitlements themselves must be reduced if money is to be saved. The government began by altering the basis on which pensions and other benefits were increased from year to year (pegging rises to prices rather than wages) and continued by imposing successively tighter conditions on benefits for the unemployed, and rewriting the formula by which contributory pension entitlements were arrived at. And indeed, they did achieve the impossible by reducing the system of special payments to social assistance claimants to a small, residual scheme, the Social Fund, with a cash-limited budget (Chapter 11 describes this in more detail).

Both the economic liberalism and the social conservatism of the Thatcherite programme were evident in the Child Support Act. Benefit costs were to be cut by pursuing absent parents, mainly fathers, for contributions to the support of children of lone parents on social security benefits. The Act was intended to apply more widely where there were absent parents, but in its implementation families with benefit recipients were quickly prioritized, to the almost total exclusion of other cases. Thus, at a stroke, money was to be saved and a blow struck for social responsibility and the biological family.

It is worth saying that a concern for the family has been a persistent theme of social policy since the nineteenth century, albeit with varying emphases. In the Major period, after Thatcher, family policy went under the slogan 'Back to Basics'; and the Labour Home Secretary Jack Straw's 1998 White Paper, *Supporting Families*, suggests that this preoccupation is still in the mind of government.

Towards the end of the Thatcher period an attempt was made to change the whole basis on which decisions about local authority spending would be taken in the future. The Community Charge or 'Poll Tax', which replaced Domestic Rates (the local government property tax), was formulated so as to bear obviously on individual local taxpayers and to deter them as voters from supporting parties likely to increase expenditure. It proved not only hugely unpopular and impossible to administer but also, during its short life, ineffective for the government's purposes: voters blamed central government as much as their local councils for the level of the tax. Moreover, its admitted inadequacies as a revenue raiser resulted in more local revenue than ever having to be provided centrally: Valued Added Tax was increased by $2\frac{1}{2}$ per cent to cope with this. Finally, it proved the last straw for Margaret Thatcher's premiership.

The abandonment of the Poll Tax by the succeeding Major government marked a small recognition of the limits to which an anti-welfare strategy could be taken. But by the end of the Conservative period in 1997 the welfare state, while still very much extant, had been radically altered by the massive introduction of market-based devices for injecting business methods and objectives into its management and undermining the post-war public service ethos among its practitioners.

In the National Health Service, health authorities had been broken up and an 'internal market' introduced where some parts of the service held budgets and bought treatments on behalf of patients from other parts (NHS Trusts) who were in competition with each other. In education, many schools and almost all colleges had been removed from local government control and similarly set to compete for business. In all services, provision was to be made as far as possible by contracted entrepreneurs rather than by employed public servants.

However, the degree to which the welfare system was financed by the state had not been greatly reduced, and in some ways the British welfare state in 1997 resembled, more than previously, those of several Continental countries whose systems had always operated on a contractual, 'mixed economy' basis, with higher welfare investment in some cases than Britain over a long period.

Conclusion: The Survival of Welfare

We can deduce from the foregoing story that social policy has been an intrinsic part of British society since the Industrial Revolution; and during the twentieth century, particularly since the Second World War, the British welfare state has grown to form the major part of the relationship between the citizen and the state. This growth has occurred not regardless of the party in government, but within a range of variation which itself has widened and narrowed according to the circumstances of the time. There have been periods of apparently drastic change, such as those of the post-war Labour and the Thatcher and Major Conservative governments. But, although the opposition has often been fiercely critical, on assuming office neither party has reversed much of the policy which it inherited.

Social welfare, with a substantial state involvement in it, continues to be as stubbornly essential to industrial society as it was seen to be by William Beveridge when he designed a social security system to allow British citizens to play what he saw as their parts in the economic and social life of the country, even if his blueprint has had to be revised from time to time. The National Health Service is criticized and reorganized, but it is also still with us.

This British story has had echoes in most of the developed world. Britain has emerged as neither a leader nor a laggard in welfare state development. Welfare systems—and, crucially, welfare *states*—in industrial countries have come to live with the continuing expansion of demand, combined with the reluctance of governments to raise taxes to meet this; they survive, but constantly change to meet the demands of their political masters and the wishes of the electorate as the political élites see fit to interpret them. As Pierson observes, this permits major decisions and variations, but not the disappearance of the welfare state itself:

the 'real' issue is not going to be whether we have a welfare state (nor even how much it will cost), but what sort of a welfare state *regime* it will be. The state's allocation of welfare may be changing (perhaps to become more fiscally regressive), but nowhere is it disappearing or yielding to a minimal state uninterested in the welfare status of its population. (Pierson 1991: 216–17)

Meanwhile, the demographic growth of what has come to be seen as 'need' continues: the elderly grow in numbers and proportions; lone parent families refuse to go away in the face of conservative discouragement. Much of the rest of this book constitutes a discussion of how governments, other providers, and welfare clients are coping with the demands of a changing but perpetual set of tensions which, like the welfare state itself, seem unlikely to pass from society.

Glossary

cash planning The practice of determining budgets from year to year in terms of firm cash amounts rather than 'in volume terms', that is, in amounts which are subsequently adjusted to take account of inflation and maintain their real value.

full employment A state of the national economy when all those currently defined as available for work are in employment. Effectively this has been defined at varying low levels of unemployment at different times.

industrialization The process by which economies change from an agricultural to an industrial base, and the ongoing development of that process.

managerialism In the 1960s and early 1970s, this tended to refer to a belief that many problems of policy could be solved by finding more efficient structures of organization and management for the public service. It led to reorganizations (not all of which were to last) of local and central government and health and other services. In the 1980s and 1990s the term came to mean the introduction of business-oriented principles and personnel into the running of the public service. (The term 'management' tended to replace 'administration'.) In the National Health Service, both the introduction of general managers and the creation of an internal market provide examples.

National Assistance/Social Assistance (in Britain, successively National Insurance, Supplementary Benefit and Income Support; and some other programmes) Social security arrangements by which citizens are entitled to financial help on the basis of need, for instance when they do not qualify for enough social insurance benefits for subsistence. Invariably subject to a test of means.

National Insurance/Social Insurance Social security arrangements by which citizens are members of a scheme entitling them to benefits in certain circumstances, such as retirement, usually in exchange for financial contributions.

New Right A school of thought combining economic neo-liberalism and social conservatism. The former gives a high value to liberty, defined as absence of state restraint without reference to the resources to exercise such liberty—'we are all free to dine at the Ritz'. The latter emphasizes the value of traditional social forms such as the nation and the married-parent family.

Poor Law Not only the law under which provision was made for the destitute from the seventeenth to the early twentieth century in Britain, but the whole associated system of administration and provision, including aspects of education and healthcare as well as welfare and regulation.

public health The general health of the population and measures taken to enhance it. Often taken to be central to social policy in the nineteenth century.

selectivists Those favouring selective, or 'means-tested', benefits and services on principle.

universalists Those favouring universal benefits and services—provided to all who fall into certain contingencies—on principle.

urbanization The process by which populations become concentrated in towns.

Guide to Further Reading

H. Glennerster, *British Social Policy Since 1945* (Oxford: Blackwell, 1995). A lively and combative account of the British welfare state's development since the Second World War, criticizing conventional accounts (such as the one in this chapter) of post-war 'consensus'.

C. Pierson, *Beyond the Welfare State? The New Political Economy of Welfare* (2nd edn., Oxford: Polity Press/Blackwell, 1998). Discusses the relationship between welfare state development and factors such as social democratic ideology on a comparative basis, and assesses the impact of 'the new political economy' on the welfare state and its future.

N. Timmins, *The Five Giants: A Biography of the Welfare State* (London: Fontana, 1995). An economic journalist's account, detailed yet highly readable.

References

Beveridge, W. (1942), *Social Insurance and Allied Services: A Report by Sir William Beveridge* (Cmd. 6404, London: HMSO).

Burnett, J. (1978), *A Social History of Housing 1815–1970* (London: David & Charles).

Central Statistical Office (1996), *Social Trends 26* (London: HMSO).

——(1998), *Social Trends 28* (London: HMSO).

George, V., and Miller, S. (eds.) (1994), *Social Policy Towards 2000: Squaring the Welfare Circle* (London: Routledge).

George, V., and Wilding, P. (1994), *Welfare and Ideology* (London: Harvester Wheatsheaf).

Glennerster, H. (1995), *British Social Policy Since 1945* (Oxford: Blackwell).

HM Treasury (1979), *The Government's Expenditure Plans 1980–81* (Cm 7746, London: HMSO).

Johnson, N. (1987), *The Welfare State in Transition: The Theory and Practice of Welfare Pluralism* (Brighton: Wheatsheaf Books).

Lis, C., and Soly, H. (1982), *Poverty and Capitalism in Pre-Industrial Europe* (rev. edn., Brighton: Harvester Press).

Macleod, I., and Powell, E. (1952), *The Social Services: Needs and Means* (London: Conservative Political Centre).

Marshall, T. H. (1950), *Citizenship and Social Class* (Cambridge: Cambridge University Press).

Mitchell, B., and Deane, P. (1962), *Abstract of British Historical Statistics* (Cambridge: Cambridge University Press).

Morgan, K. O. (1984), *Labour in Power, 1945–1951* (Oxford: Clarendon Press).

Pierson, C. (1991), *Beyond the Welfare State? The New Political Economy of Welfare* (Oxford: Polity Press/Blackwell).

Rimlinger, G. (1971), *Welfare Policy and Industrialization in Europe, America, and Russia* (New York: Wiley).

Sullivan, M. (1992), *The Politics of Social Policy* (Hemel Hempstead: Harvester Wheatsheaf).

Taylor-Gooby, P. (1985), *Public Opinion, Ideology and State Welfare* (London: Routledge & Kegan Paul).

Wilensky, H. L., and Lebeaux, C. N. (1965), *Industrial Society and Social Welfare* (New York: Free Press).

Wohl, A. S. (1984), *Endangered Lives: Public Health in Victorian Britain* (London: Methuen).

3 The Politics of Welfare

Nick Manning

Contents

Introduction: Politics and Welfare

Social policy is inextricably bound up with governments and politics. Political party manifestos routinely include substantial proposals for changes in social policies. Social policy itself involves attempts to change current social arrangements in one way or another, and hence involves the exercise of power. There are strongly held views about what these changes should amount to. Individuals, pressure groups, professionals, community groups, industrial and trade union groups, and others try to influence the direction of social policy.

In this chapter we will present some of the institutions, structures, and people who are involved in the politics of social policy, and who try to alter its course.

Box 3.1 Healthcare reform in the UK and the USA

A major commitment made by Bill Clinton when he was elected President in 1992 was to reform the delivery of healthcare to US citizens. The USA is unique amongst industrial nations for its inability to deliver healthcare insurance to 35 million people—about 15 per cent of the population, many of them black. There has been a long history of attempts to reform healthcare services in the USA. The vested interests of the American Medical Association and the private insurance industry combined forces to exclude health insurance from the 1935 Social Security Act. Only with the successful Democrat years of the 1960s was it possible to get limited support for the healthcare costs of poor and older people in the 'medicaid' and 'medicare' amendments to the 1935 legislation. Clinton faced the same coalition of interests, now bigger and stronger with the growth of the healthcare industry since the 1960s, but with a weaker command of political resources. It is not surprising that he failed.

A major reform of the NHS was similarly initiated by Margaret Thatcher in 1994. In contrast to the US, British healthcare has been delivered since 1948 to all citizens free at the point of consumption, and independent of their employment status. Healthcare indicators are relatively good, and the cost is about half of the US system, at 6 per cent of GNP. However, market mechanisms were introduced into the system, so that both private and public providers could compete, and a large number of new bureaucrats were employed to undertake the detailed paperwork caused by the complex commissioning and contracting system set up to ensure that the marketplace worked.

The outcomes of Clinton's and Thatcher's attempts at healthcare reform were determined by politics rather than rational planning. 'Politics' in this case means both the rules under which each leader has to operate, and the resources they can bring to the debates and the decision-making arena. These are shaped by the context in which each leader has to work.

One of the reasons for the British state's relative success in 1948 was that under British political rules, the ruling party has greater freedom of action than the US equivalent. The US constitution is designed to restrain any particular part of the state, including the President, from any great freedom of action. Since the foundation of the NHS, the British state has managed to exercise much greater control over healthcare than its US counterpart, keeping costs very much lower, but with a comprehensive service. In a series of reforms in the 1970s and 1980s, state direction of the NHS steadily increased, and the independent power of the medical profession has slowly weakened.

Concepts

Politics: Institutions and Structures

Modern **welfare states** are so-called because they are part of the modern nation state. States as such are a relatively recent invention. Although we think of England as having a very long history, some nation states such as Germany and Italy only emerged in the nineteenth century. States in general have a familiar set of structures and institutions for administering those concerns of their citizens that are considered as legitimately within the public domain. In the welfare area, for example, these might typically include a **government department** or **ministry** for dealing with different aspects of healthcare. In the UK this is called the Department of Health, in France and in Russia it is called the Ministry of Health.

The staff of these government departments would typically be full-time career **civil servants**—an essential component of the modern welfare state. It is the role of these bureaucrats to carry out and implement whatever **policies** are laid down by the government of the day. For example, where a new government, such as New Labour in the UK, plans a new scheme, such as the movement of more young people from unemployment into employment (from 'welfare to work'), then civil servants are duty bound to implement this policy. More details on the complexities of this process are discussed in Chapter 8.

The right of governments to develop and implement such policies within the state is conferred mainly, although not exclusively, through the process of **liberal democracy**. This is a mechanism now very widely diffused throughout the world for registering the **consent** of citizens to government action of various sorts, and for making the legal, financial, and military **resources** available to the government to act. In the field of social policy, financial resources or the lack of them are a pre-eminent constraint on government action, but legal arrangements are also of great significance. For example, modern medicine seems to cost more and more each year, partly as the result of the progress of medical science in developing new technology, but also partly as a result of the ageing of the population and the survival of people with significant healthcare needs. Both the medical profession and the public often turn to governments to find the money for this steady expansion of healthcare.

In addition to these resource problems, the **rules** under which such services operate, many of them inscribed in law, are both a mechanism for government control—through new legislation, for example—and a site for argument and dispute. For example, where a child has become very disruptive in her classroom there might be a clash between the child's right to education, the parent's obligation to secure that education, the teacher's right to particular conditions of employment, and so on.

One source of such rules in modern states is the existence of a **constitution** which lays down the structure of government, and the various rules through which it should be set up and should operate. This can be very important indeed for social policy changes and provision. A good example is provided by the USA. After the Declaration of Independence in 1776, at which Jefferson famously declared that 'all men are created equal', the constitution and the first ten amendments (such as freedom of religious expression) were adopted. There have been more than twenty subsequent amendments to the constitution, many of which have had profound consequences for social policy. For example, the abolition of slavery, and the right of black Americans to equal access to services such as education, was guaranteed in a series of three amendments (the 13th, 14th and 15th) passed soon after the northern States won the American civil war in 1865.

Box 3.2 US Constitutional amendments

13th   'Neither slavery nor involuntary servitude . . . shall exist within the US'

14th   'All persons born or naturalised in the US . . . are citizens of the US'

15th   'The right of citizens of the US to vote shall not be denied . . . on account of race, colour, or previous condition of servitude'

Britain never rejected or completely neutralized the monarchy, as did the French, the Russians, and the Americans in their revolutions. Without this break it has been difficult to establish a case for a written constitution in the UK, which makes it difficult to lodge a fundamental appeal to the basic rules which govern British society in a case where some feel that there is a fundamental injustice to be corrected. Charter 88, for example, have argued that a written constitution would provide safeguards for citizens against welfare injustices perpetrated by mistake or intent.

However, in the case of the US, the varied interpretation of constitutional amendments by the Supreme Court has often undermined their original intentions. This was most explicitly the case for the access of black Americans to education from the late nineteenth century through to the civil rights movement of the 1960s. There were two Supreme Court interpretations of the constitution that clearly show how a written constitution can be undermined. In the first, the court ruled that discrimination on the grounds of race did not take place where service provision was 'separate but equal' (in the case of Plessy *vs.* Ferguson, Louisiana, 1896). This justified the rapid development in the late nineteenth century of effective apartheid in the southern US states. In most areas of welfare and public service provision, including education, and in private provision such as bus transport and restaurants, blacks were excluded, by force if necessary, from white services up until the 1960s.

In the second example the supreme court reversed the 'separate but equal' ruling in 1954 in relation to the access of black children to white schools (Brown *vs.* the Board of Education Topeka, Kansas). However it ordered that the new ruling should be implemented 'with all deliberate speed', which was taken to mean as slowly as possible. Almost no school desegregation took place over the next 10 years, which was a major stimulus to the development of the 1960s civil rights movement. The rules of government enshrined in constitutions are not therefore independent of interpretation, and cannot in themselves guarantee particular outcomes.

The rules and resources which shape political institutions and structures typically give rise to a pattern of government action in the arena of social policy which has been classified by Julian Le Grand (1993) into three mechanisms: direct provision, financial support, and regulation.

Direct provision is where the state provides both the resources and the rules by which they are to be used. For example, in the UK health 'insurance' was provided from 1948 to 1994 through the National Health Service, directly supplied by the government to citizens who needed healthcare. This approach was felt by British labour governments for most of the twentieth century to be the most efficient and fairest mechanism for social welfare provision. It entailed either nationalizing existing services, such as the hospitals in 1948, or providing services from scratch, such as local authority housing from the early 1920s, or local authority social work since 1968. Taking these services into public ownership was part of a wider strategy of enlarging direct state provision where capitalism was seen to be inefficient or unfair, and included rail and air transport, steel production, and, for a time, car manufacture.

This policy was tolerated reluctantly by British conservative governments as an unpleasant but practical necessity. It had been necessary for the development and co-ordination of the many activities essential to the prosecution of the Second World War, including the Emergency Medical Services. This had amounted to the effective nationalization of many aspects of the country's production and service provision, and demonstrated that widespread direct state provision could work. Much of the British welfare state set up in the immediate post-war years was typified by this means of direct service provision.

For other services, however, **financial support,** but not direct provision, typifies state action. Here the state provides the financial resources, but not always the rules for their disbursement. This form of state intervention has often developed in areas where existing private provision is defended through well-organized interests. For example, British governments give people financial help to get privately provided legal services, because lawyers do not wish their service to be nationalized. Housing is also mostly provided by the private sector, but the British and US governments spend large sums in helping purchasers to acquire cheaper finance for their houses, for example by defraying income tax where income is spent on repaying mortgages. Indeed, this idea of government relief from paying income tax on money spent on services amounts in effect to extensive government spending in terms of 'tax expenditure', discussed in more detail in Chapter 12.

In many countries, healthcare provision operates in the same way, through the government subsidizing private provision, since doctors have been powerful enough to resist nationalization. The American Medical Association has been notoriously successful in this respect, but private insurance companies have also lobbied hard to defend their interests. However, they have also lobbied hard to attract government financial support, and on occasions they have been tempted to corruption, such as when they have submitted claims for the funding of fictitious treatments.

For this reason government financial support often requires the monitoring of service providers to check that the money is being used in a proper manner. This leads us to consider the third area of state action, **regulation.** Here the state is concerned more with the rules than the resources necessary for any particular action. In France, for example, the government merely legislates that all citizens should be insured through non-profit independent 'insurance societies' who pay for healthcare, and in the USA most citizens have private health insurance paid for by their employers, or, for about 15 per cent of the population, no cover at all. Regulation is a non-market method of state intervention to ensure the delivery of services to, or requisite behaviour from, defined groups or individuals in a manner defined in law or subject to bureaucratic surveillance. Parents are required to ensure that children's education takes place, normally, of course, at a recognized school. Those children are known to the state, since all births must be registered with the state. The provision of medicines is closely regulated as they may be dangerous; people of working age seeking income support are required to seek work; all car drivers must take out insurance against the costs of accidents; and so on. What the law requires, and the efficiency or fairness of bureaucratic surveillance, is the subject of sharp dispute from time to time, often organized by **pressure groups** concerned to secure the well-being of particular groups such as poor, older, or disabled people. We will look at the political practices of such groups below.

State action also takes place in most countries through lower levels of government. These also have considerable consequences for social policy. In very large countries, such as Russia or the USA, the next layer of government structures below the national level are what amount to 'mini-states' within the state. These have considerable powers of their own, including the ability to raise finance independently from the central state, upon which they will nevertheless usually be partly dependent. In smaller countries—in Europe for example—these lower tiers of government are likely to have rather less autonomy, and may range from rather loose regional groups to specific counties, as in the UK.

Social provision such as education is often undertaken at these lower levels of government. However, this raises a problem of the relative affluence of different areas, and hence the possibility of social provision varying between citizens of the same country as a result of geographical location. This variation may well be cumulative, so that relative differences are compounded for education, housing, healthcare, employment, and so on. Such regional disadvantages have been termed **territorial injustice** by Bleddyn Davies (1978).

Local governments also have rules, resources, and different modes of intervention, as we have seen for central government. For example, in the UK local governments can significantly vary the types of schools provided, typically between comprehensives and grammar schools. They can also vary the level of funding they choose to give to schools, and hence the size of classes, as well as provision of books and equipment and kind of food. As for central government, these variations in rules and resources lead to different types of intervention. Some local authorities provide most schooling directly themselves, as in Nottinghamshire, whereas in others almost all schools are independently organized, as in Kent.

Power and Authority

It is important to remember at this point that governments are not the only providers of welfare services, although they remain extremely important, especially when we are considering political matters, as in this chapter. Elsewhere in this book we suggest also that the private market, the voluntary sector, and informal, neighbourly, and family networks are significant shapers of and providers of welfare. Politics, and especially power, suffuse these areas too.

The rules and resources deployed by governments and other groups involved in the field of welfare are an exercise in power—the ability to implement plans of action and persuade or coerce others to follow suit. **Power**, in Stephen Lukes's view (1974), is not merely about the ability to pursue those options that are 'on the table', but also, crucially, the ability to control what the options are in the first place—either including the unthinkable, as Margaret Thatcher so often did, or more often excluding what some might think should be considered, but which governments or other powerful groups do not favour. Politics in the field of welfare can often be a struggle over the agenda for policy debate as much as over the policies themselves, as we shall see when we look more closely below at the key political players and the processes of change.

Power, in a government which is legitimate, is normally defined as **authority**. The classic work on authority was by Max Weber (1947), who suggested that modern governments exercised authority on a rational-legal basis. This meant that there were clear and explicit rules understood by all citizens as to the basis for a government's claim to have power. For example, where a new need comes to be widely recognized, such as the needs of those at risk of HIV/AIDS infection, or those unable to find work, government is the accepted source of authority for action: 'someone should do something about it', we say.

The frequent response is to either provide a new service or to finance some new activity such as healthcare, or to produce new regulations to guide behaviour—even intimate sexual behaviour. These are accepted as legitimate because we understand these state actions as rational and legal.

Legitimate authority can also be seen in the operations of the market, where the price mechanism regulates the legitimate exchange of money for goods and services. Similarly, charities such as those concerned with the welfare of children have a powerful and legitimate voice, raised from time to time in the interests of children's needs. Even in family life much—but by no means all—parental authority stems from the rational basis for action in the superior knowledge of parents about the best interests of the child.

However, from time to time the rational basis for authority in all these areas, including that of the state, is contested. A major independent source of authority which is frequently brought to bear on questions of welfare, whether within the state or the family, is based on the **professions**, such as medicine, teaching, or social work. Here, although authority is ultimately state-sanctioned, for example by the state registration of practitioners, specialized knowledge is deployed to criticize and develop welfare policies in many ways. Another claim to legitimate authority is made by pressure groups

---

Box 3.3 Max Weber on the basis of authority: charisma, rational-legal, traditional

charismatic authority
  the ability to command support for policies through personal magnetism

rational-legal authority
  the ability to command support for policies because they are in accord with widely accepted rules

traditional authority
  the ability to command support for policies because they appear natural or sensible as a result of long use

operating in the particular interests of sections of the community, whose needs may be felt to have been overlooked, or for whom the very definition of appropriate needs has been challenged. A very significant example of this challenge to existing legitimate authority, and the posing of alternatives, has been the achievements of the women's movement over the last 30 years. For example, this movement has successfully challenged the rational-legal basis of the notion of the dependence of mothers on the 'family wage' of their husbands, enshrined in state employment policy and social security for much of the post-war era. Similar challenges have been made to medical treatments, such as those for women's mental illness, or to the expression of husbands' authority over sexual or physical matters in the home.

However, there are a number of widely accepted activities by government and other welfare groups that have been around for such a long time that the original reasons for them may have become obscured over time. An example is the close association between the aristocracy or senior church figures and voluntary charities, which gives charities their good status and provides an important asset for raising money for some. Here Weber talks of authority as having a traditional basis, sanctioned more by its longevity than its intrinsic merits. The American and French revolutions were a general replacement of traditional by rational-legal authority. But in England this did not occur, and there is consequently a long tradition of historical analysis of social policy which stresses the tradition of *noblesse oblige* on the part of the aristocracy to help those less fortunate than others.

Tradition is not a monopoly of the aristocracy. Traditional authority can also be found in the deference of many of us to 'the doctor' or 'the teacher', or to senior members of our families. Here we can see power exercised in terms of obligations, such as to take the medicine, to undertake the duties of caring, or to be grateful for charitable help. However, traditional authority at the level of our daily lives is not as easy to overthrow as the *ancien régimes* of old, and may perpetuate the following of rules or the use of resources that, on reflection, we would not consider rational. For example, where medical treatments have grown out of accepted practice rather than scientific assessment, patients have been asked to accept them on the basis of traditional medical authority. There is now a growing movement in favour of 'evidence-based medicine', which raises by its very nature doubts about accepted practice such as hospital treatment for heart attacks or giving birth. These are discussed in Chapter 15.

Turning to change rather than stability, it is clear that some new ideas in government or other areas of welfare can develop through the exercise of exceptional personal qualities that can persuade citizens that the merits of the person themselves are a satisfactory form of authority, and on that basis the ideas can be accepted. This personal form of authority was described by Weber as 'charismatic'. It can open up room for changes normally regarded as 'unthinkable': for example, for many people Margaret Thatcher possessed this personal quality, through which she was able to exercise power for a considerable period of time and to make a number of radical changes to the British welfare state.

Charismatic authority can be a force for good or ill. It may be the vehicle for challenging and overcoming policies that have become ossified by tradition, even if they were rational at one time. Margaret Thatcher felt that this was true of many areas of public life, including central and local government and some of the professions. Echoing Joseph Schumpeter's characterization of capitalism as causing waves of 'creative destruction', she felt that many traditional ways of delivering welfare services, in the National Health Service, in housing, or in education, should be subject to market forces to weed out cosy but irrational practices that had accumulated unjustifiably over time. The eventual acceptance of some of her ideas by many of her critics, both in other countries and by 'New Labour', indicates how new they were, from the use of contracting in health and social services to greater independence for schools or increased owner-occupation. Other ideas were dropped, the Poll Tax being the best-known of these.

But charismatic authority is also common elsewhere in the welfare field, particularly in the voluntary sector. Many well-known voluntary agencies were built up by a charismatic innovator who managed to carry the authority to develop new ideas and services by sheer personal drive. Leonard Cheshire, Cecily Saunders, Elly Jansen, Maxwell Jones, and Paolo Freire are contemporary innovators of this type, just as Florence Nightingale, Octavia Hill, the Webbs, Lord Shaftesbury, and Elizabeth Fry were for an earlier generation. Once again, while much of the work of these welfare innovators was good, charisma does not always coexist with critical reflection, and can lead to such leaders overreaching themselves while rejecting criticism.

Thus, while rational-legal and traditional bases for authority are relatively stable, charismatic authority is doomed to decay because it is dependent on a particular per-

---

Box 3.4 Charisma and welfare innovators

Leonard Cheshire	founder of the Cheshire homes for permanently disabled people
Cecily Saunders	founder of the hospice movement for people who are dying
Elly Jansen	founder of Richmond Fellowship houses for people with mental illness
Maxwell Jones	founder of therapeutic community movement for radical democracy in mental health care
Paolo Freire	founder of a radical movement for education for the 'real world'
Florence Nightingale	originator of the nursing profession
Octavia Hill	founder of the Charity Organization Society for the improvement of the lives of poor people
Sidney and Beatrice Webb	social reform campaigners in a variety of areas, and founders of the Fabian Society and the London School of Economics
Lord Shaftesbury	social reform campaigner, for example to protect working children
Elizabeth Fry	prison reformer

son's powers, and by definition these cannot be exceptional forever—they will become normal, routinized, or mundane after a while, and disenchantment with the person's ideas may develop. Generally, as in the Catholic Church, a division of labour develops between the exercise of charisma and the maintenance of normal government. In the case of Thatcherism this can be seen in the way in which new leaders, such as William Hague, seek the official blessing of Thatcher. In general, however, charismatic decay leads to changes in government or voluntary organization in time, and a new round of normal authority ensues.

Citizens may or may not comply with the exercise of government or other authority. Where this is seen as a problem for the community at large, it might typically be classified as illegal. However, the problem may be of little concern to the community, but of some consequence to the individual or her family. In social policy, for example, the non-take-up of benefit entitlement may increase poverty in a family, or for children, in a way which can undermine the assumptions that a government might make about the extent of its support for family needs. In other cases the individual's and the community's interests might both be threatened where, for example, a potentially violent schizophrenic fails to take the medication which makes continued community living possible.

Etzioni (1975) has classified examples of compliance into a number of different types, depending on the nature of the individual's compliance and the means at an organization's disposal to enforce compliance, which we can usefully adapt here. The government can achieve compliance because it can coerce people, reward them, or persuade them. These latter mechanisms show a close resemblance to Weber's types of authority —and perhaps students could take the time to compare and contrast the ideas of these two authors.

The individual can comply with government rules for different reasons. Those such as Max Weber, who have defined government as the legitimate monopoly of the means of violence in a society, may observe that ultimately citizens comply because they have to. This begins with the obligation to have one's birth registered. Thereafter, as Michel Foucault (1973) has observed, a citizen is subject to continued, if mostly discrete, surveillance by the state in one form or another. A periodic mandatory population census supplements this, as do childhood vaccination requests, and school attendance checks. There are technical limits to this surveillance, although, as was the case in Eastern Europe, with enough effort it can become almost all-encompassing in its reach—and highly resented.

Box 3.5 Etzioni's types of compliance

coercive compliance
  where a person has little power to resist a policy

calculative compliance
  where a person perceives it to be in her interest to comply with a policy

moral compliance
  where a person strongly believes in the basis for a policy

Some have argued that the use of surveillance to compel compliance is particularly marked in the social security services, where concerns that citizens should seek and accept legitimate, even if low-wage, work, have overridden the original spirit of this most expensive part of the welfare state—to provide income for the destitute. New Labour's 'welfare to work' programme, discussed elsewhere in Chapter 8, continues this element of compulsion.

However there are two more common reasons for compliance. Most people comply because they can see some advantage to themselves in doing so. This is akin to Weber's rational-legal basis for authority. For example, in Talcott Parsons's famous model of the 'sick role' (1951) he characterized the role of the patient as being excused the normal obligations of work and family life, but only in return for a commitment to follow the doctor's orders. Similarly, students may work hard in the expectation that exam passes will bring future rewards. Etzioni suggests that such instrumental calculations are widespread in modern societies. However, there are limits to the calculations that individuals are capable of making. For example, left to their own devices people heavily discount contemporary or future risks that we know statistically they face, such as health misfortunes or the problems of old age, and fail to undertake sufficient insurance.

But others are not as calculating as this, and are actively committed to comply because, Etzioni observes, they see this as a moral commitment to a belief in what the government or another group is aiming to achieve. This third type of compliance includes the acceptance of duties. Duties can be borne positively and happily: for example, traditional analyses of the welfare state stressed the positive altruism exercised by British citizens for the unknown stranger, typified by the 'war-time spirit' of the 1940s in Britain. The generalization of this type of compliance to an explanation of social policy in general has been a naive and idealized view held by parts of the political centre in Britain which has mourned the supposed loss of such spirit. Richard Titmuss's 1970 analysis of the British blood donor service (the only one in the world to be entirely voluntary), was a classic statement of this concern. But duties can also be owed to the community which may in themselves feel burdensome, such as the obligation to help one's family, pay taxes, or do voluntary work. The fostering of commitment to obligations has been a prominent feature of right-wing welfare analysis in recent years, such as Mead's *Beyond Entitlement* (1987), and has found its way into New Labour policy through Frank Field's 1998 Green Paper on Welfare Reform (see Chapter 13). The argument is that, in reality, the acquisition of full citizenship rights depends on being able to discharge one's obligations as a citizen.

Welfare Politics: The Players

Who raises the issues that are to be dealt with through the political processes which permeate the welfare field? The main players include welfare clients, social movements, professionals, bureaucrats and policy networks, and politicians and political parties.

A simple model of the dynamic interplay of these social actors might be to consider the way in which social problems arise in society. When there appears to be a problem, such as the appearance of a new disease like AIDS, or a sharp rise in unemployment, this would normally be brought to the attention of government agencies by professionals such as doctors, or social movements, or pressure groups. The latter two groups overlap considerably, and can be thought of as organized associations with the primary aim of changing the direction of state intervention in a particular area, generally through raising an issue on the agenda of public debate. Politicians and government bureaucrats might then be expected to respond to these collectively expressed requests.

Welfare clients such as patients, unemployed workers, and students may also be active in these attempts to change social policies. In this way they are making their voices heard rather than passively accepting existing arrangements. Hirschman (1970) has described the alternatives here in terms of 'exit, voice or loyalty' (Box 3.6). Attempts to change policies are an example of 'voice', when collective or individual disquiet or innovation is expressed in the political arena. Loyalty is the option to support existing policies and welfare arrangements—perhaps the most typical. The final option is to try to escape the situation through individual solutions: for example by setting up a new business rather than expecting government to solve unemployment; or choosing private medicine instead of trying to persuade the government that health policy is wrong.

Box 3.6 Hirschman's 'exit, voice, or loyalty'

Where a person disagrees strongly with a policy, there are only three options:

exit	leave the situation
voice	express dissent and try to change the situation
loyalty	change position and learn to accept the situation

However this model of attempts to solve social problems through professional concern, collective action, or individual solutions is too simple to adequately explain political actions in the welfare field. This is for three reasons. First, much social policy is not to deal with new social problems, but ongoing issues of long standing. Second, much debate about policy arises from within government agencies rather than outside them. Third, much state intervention has unanticipated consequences—indeed, not infrequently having little effect or even making matters worse.

Routine Issues: Party Political Debates

New social problems are only infrequently the reason for changes in social policy. For example, expenditure on social security is dominated by the costs of pensions and unemployment. These problems have existed ever since the origins of income insecurity arose as a consequence of the rise in wage labour in the eighteenth century. For these areas of relatively routine party politics it has been suggested that a consensus of 'normal' policies can develop, where political disagreement between political parties can recede in favour of a consensus. A striking example of this was the general social policy agreement that existed between the post-war Labour Party and subsequent Conservative administrations for the first thirty years of the British welfare state. This was known as the 'Butskell' consensus, after the two ministers Butler and Gaitskell, from the two parties who were in broad agreement over public expenditure.

However, of course, on many matters there is serious disagreement between the parties over social policy—as was especially clear during the years when Margaret Thatcher was Prime Minister. As described at the beginning of this chapter, the British governmental system does enable a determined political party to pursue its policies relatively unchecked. During the 1980s this resulted in the introduction of market principles into many areas of social policy, the weakening of local government control, and the development of more independent **QUANGOS** (quasi non-governmental organizations) and agencies to undertake government work. Many of these agencies were staffed by Conservative sympathizers, such as school governing bodies or health-service trusts, who became in effect an extension of the party into government work that bypassed the traditional civil service (see Chapter 11 for more details on this).

The ideas that sustain political parties are frequently developed through pressure groups and **think tanks,** who take on the task of thinking the unthinkable as far as future policy options are concerned. For the last Conservative government, the Institute of Economic Affairs (IEA) and the Adam Smith Institute were important influences. The current Labour government will be drawing on ideas from the Fabian Society, the Child Poverty Action Group (CPAG), Demos, and others. In addition, **professional associations** such as the British Medical Association (BMA), the medical Royal Colleges, and **trade unions** and **business groups** will be offering advice or warnings to the government, and may be actively consulted from time to time.

Debates Internal to Professional and Government Bureaucracies

Debates about policy changes, however, often arise within those groups of professionals and bureaucrats with responsibility for the area in question, rather than from political parties or pressure groups. The key players here are seen to be a constant set of state functionaries, regardless of which party is in power. Rhodes (1988, 1992) has proposed that government within the UK can be usefully conceptualized in terms of five types of **policy networks,** ranged between two polar types of network: the policy community, and the issue network (see Box 3.7). The continuum between them concerns their relative integration, stability, and exclusiveness. Policy communities are characterized by relatively tight-knit and stable relationships, continuity of a restricted membership, vertical interdependence based on service delivery, and insulation from other networks, the public, and Parliament. Issue networks, on the other hand, typically have a large number of participants, limited interdependence, less stability and continuity, and a more atomistic structure. In between these polar types, varying both in terms of stability and interests, are professional and producer networks serving professional and economic concerns respectively, and intergovernmental networks oriented horizontally towards common positions within the structures of government.

A network is defined primarily in terms of 'resource dependencies', with network

---

Box 3.7 Policy networks

There is a range of networks, depending on how tightly they are integrated:

policy community
   tight-knit and stable relationships, continuity of a restricted membership, vertical interdependence based on service delivery, and insulation from other networks, the public, and Parliament

professional/producer/intergovernmental network
   These networks are intermediate in terms of how tightly they are organized, and in addition they are focused on different substantive areas, respectively a profession (such as medicine), or producers who deliver goods or services (such as the pharmaceutical industry), or government units (such as regional or local government)

issue network
   large number of participants, limited interdependence, less stability and continuity, and a more atomistic structure

---

interactions chiefly oriented towards resource maximization. However, Rhodes has also included a wider range of factors when considering the way in which policy networks change. Not only are economic considerations relevant, but ideological, knowledge-based, and institutional issues are also identified by him as significant. Thus, although Rhodes stresses the effects of changes in party ideology (such as the rise and fall of Thatcherism), clearly this could be extended to include a more general consideration of the world views of those individuals who make up the network—their social values, normative assumptions, and so on.

As far as knowledge-based change is concerned, he cites examples from professional networks such as the health service. While this may seem a straightforward case of a particular variety of resource dependency, work in the sociology of science alerts us to the possibility that scientific and technical knowledge is socially constructed and constrained by pre-existing structures of power (Manning, 1985, chapter 7). Medical knowledge, for example, in so far as it underpins new moves towards community care in terms of mental and physical health, may in fact be a contestable justification for policies favoured more for their economic than their health implications.

When Policies Go Wrong: Public Inquiries and Citizens' Movements

Key political players in the field of social policy may, however, only be revealed at times of change. For example, when policies go badly wrong there may be an **official enquiry** to ascertain the exact role that different groups and individuals played. An illustration of this process is given by the long series of public enquiries into cases in which vulnerable children have died in family circumstances where social workers and other professional groups have been unable to help, such as those of Maria Colwell and Tara Henley.

A similar series of enquiries have examined failures of institutional care in mental hospitals, children's homes, and schools.

In other circumstances we can see policies being undermined by the resistance of ordinary citizens who either cannot or will not accept them. The single largest example has been the sudden collapse of the East European welfare states in 1989–91, when citizens gained the confidence to engage in mass defiance of government policies. But specific cases can also be found. For example, when the US federal government decided in the 1960s to force local governments to develop racially integrated schools in the southern states and many northern cities, this led to the active physical resistance by parents of children being 'bussed' between school districts, and to the effective undermining of the policies through 'white flight', where white parents moved house, or moved their children to private schools, in order to avoid the effects of the policies.

Models of Welfare Politics

So far we have described some of the main institutions of government and the key players involved. But there are major questions we have not yet asked, such as how much room for manœuvre there is in the system, and whose voice is the strongest in this complex process. What is the range of options, and do all the players have an equal voice? There are a number of well-known approaches to answering these questions.

Pluralist

The classic liberal view from within American political science is that the political system is pluralist. This means that it is open to external influence in a myriad of ways, and that concerned citizens, individually or in organized groups, have many opportunities to influence the shaping and implementation of social policy. For example, the fact that politicians have to be elected means that they will be keenly aware of their constituents' interests. They will invite representations from citizens through regular clinics, and attempt to take up cases of concern. In addition, many interests are represented through the many pressure groups, voluntary associations, churches, trade unions, and business organizations that lobby politicians about matters of concern. Within this general process, social policy interests are well represented.

Elites

Criticisms of this model have been raised on the grounds that in reality it is very difficult for ordinary citizens to have an impact on social policies in this way. The idea of policy networks introduced earlier illustrates the relatively closed world of policy-making that actually characterizes particular social policy areas. This is a world of élites, where influential individuals and groups from particular backgrounds, and with common worldviews, actually dominate the agenda. For example, top French civil servants are almost exclusively recruited from graduates of the Ecole Nationale d'Administration. In the UK, pupils from public-school and Oxbridge backgrounds are commonly to be found amongst higher civil servants and politicians of all parties. These key players tend to have common ideas about appropriate and sensible social policies, and to share assumptions or, at worst, prejudices about what policy options there might be for particular issues. For example, many of the groups cited in the pluralist model of open government are in reality run by élite members. These people have careers that may have encompassed the professional administration of different, and possibly opposing, organizations. The argument here is that their élite status in effect narrows the policy options, and can exclude the views of ordinary citizens from serious consideration.

Corporatist

In another view the groups that shape social policy derive less from a culturally integrated élite than from several élites generated by the corporatist structure of power in modern industrial societies. The three key corporate groups are proposed as the trade unions, representing the power and interests of working people, the business community, and the state itself. These three are held to be in effect the key organized blocks of power that between them determine the shape and structure of social policy. They bargain between themselves in a corporate round of regular discussions to determine general wage rates, public expenditure on social and other services, rates of tax which are needed to pay for these, and the type of state intervention (provision, regulation, and so on). This is typical of many European countries, especially Sweden, Germany, and France. One consequence of this bargaining process is that the needs of weak or vulnerable groups such as disabled people can be ignored.

Marxist

A final model of the politics of welfare argues that the group with most power in the system to shape the way in which social policy develops is the business community. This combines elements of the previous two models to suggest that indeed there really is only one main élite, but that its essential nature derives less from a common cultural world view than from its possession of economic power. This is a Marxist analysis, which proposes that the whole level, shape, and structure of social policy is bent to accommodate the interests of economically powerful groups. Where there might be conflicts arising between the economically powerful and other groups, such as the trade unions, the professions, or local and central government departments, that have vested interests in particular policies, then this model argues that economic interests will tend to prevail. For example, Bowles and Gintis (1976) have demonstrated how educational policy has evolved to match students to the needs of industry for particular types of labour.

Models of Welfare Policy Change and Development

In the previous section four different models were presented of the way in which the politics of welfare operate in the contemporary world. However, the historical development of political conflicts over welfare are important for two reasons. The first is that many current issues are shaped by structures and processes that are rooted in the past—particularly the nineteenth century, when the current system of wage labour and its associated insecurities matured—some of them even as far back as the Elizabethan Poor Law of 1601. The second reason is that many of the ideas used in welfare debates originated in the past. In this section we shall explore three influential ideas about the way in which welfare policies have developed.

Wage Labour and Labour Markets

The first approach is to locate the origins of the welfare state in the emergence of wage labour and labour markets in the late eighteenth century in Britain. The insecurities of wage labour underlay the origins of much demand for and rationalization of the growth of welfare policy, both in the voluntary and state arenas. Since that time, labour market changes have repeatedly been critical to social policy development.

The defining moments of twentieth-century welfare innovation, such as the 1930s US New Deal, the 1940s UK Welfare State, and more recently the 1990s renovation of those systems in Clinton's 1996 US welfare reforms, as well as the British Labour Party's 1997 'welfare to work/minimum wage' package, have gone hand in hand with assumptions about the labour market.

This was most explicit in the American case through the simultaneous enactment in 1935 of the Wagner Act alongside the Social Security Act. These Acts were the culmination of actions by the Federal government to deal with the consequences of the 1929 Wall Street crash, and the subsequent depression that spread round the world. The Wagner Act attempted to regulate American industrial relations by granting greater trade union rights and placing obligations on employers. This, it was hoped, would stabilize the economy and hence provide the means for funding pensions and unemployment benefits which were introduced by the Social Security Act. In turn these arrangements, it was hoped, would reduce the need for poverty relief.

At the founding of the British Welfare State a decade later, the 1942 report on social security prepared by Beveridge also made it clear that the design adopted depended on a crucial assumption: that full employment would ensure the funds to pay for pensions, and minimize expenditure on unemployment benefit and poverty relief.

However, full employment in the West has proved unattainable. Unemployment has been a plague for European governments for the last twenty years, both because it drives up the costs of social security, and also because it generates political instability and a host of related social and health problems. Governments in Eastern Europe are now faced with the same problems. The creation of social needs and the social policies designed to meet them are crucially related to the operation of the labour market. Work not only provides the means to exist through meeting income needs (in Beveridge's time at the level of the 'family wage'), but on the whole it is good for our psychological and physical health.

In general, work has become an essential passport to other benefits, either through entitlement to social security benefits (typically pensions or unemployment benefit), or through work-related provision such as occupational pensions, subsidized housing, and healthcare. In both the US and Russia, for example, this so-called 'occupational welfare' has been very extensive. In the European Union the very definition of social policy is closely related to employment issues. Thus, in the EU, the right to the free movement of labour and other employment rights, such as equal opportunities, the relatively high levels of expenditure on education and on employment initiatives, and the relatively low levels of expenditure on health, housing, or social security, highlight the close relationship of social and employment concerns. This was symbolized in the replacement in the final draft of the 1989 Social Protocol of the term 'citizens' by the term 'workers'.

Citizenship

A second approach to understanding the development of state intervention in welfare has used the concept of citizenship.

Novel, important and true ideas are rare. Such ideas which are then developed into a coherent theory are even scarcer. T. H. Marshall is one of the very few to have had at least one such idea, and to develop it. That is why it is important to understand and to improve upon his theory of citizenship. (Mann 1987: 339)

The classic formulation of citizenship rights in industrial society by Marshall contained three elements (see Box 3.8). First was the legal constitution of citizens as of equal standing in relation to the law; second was the access of all citizens to democratic apparatus for the exercise of political power over the state; and third was the provision of sufficient means for all people to engage in full social participation. The coexistence of these civil, political, and social rights, which he argued amounted to the conditions necessary for full citizenship, seemed to Marshall to be both a historical description of the development of industrial societies, and the necessary precondition for their continued existence.

However, Marshall was at pains to point out that these rights did not exist without tension. Ironically, the development of citizenship rights had occurred alongside capitalism and its associated inequalities. In particular the limitation of political rights to the formal exercise of voting rights resulted in the juxtaposition of multiple inequalities in the economy and in family life, with political interventions that attempted to mitigate these inequalities through social and other policies. Moreover, he argued that the best condition for the successful development of industrial societies was to maintain a balance between the economy and social rights. Too much economic freedom would undermine the long-term stability of the economy through the loss of political legitimacy and the breakdown of social reproduction. Too much political and

---

Box 3.8 Marshall's model of citizenship

eighteenth century	civil rights
nineteenth century	political rights
twentieth century	social rights

In combination these have resulted in the 'hyphenated society' of democratic-welfare-capitalism.

social intervention, on the other hand, would stifle the dynamic growth of the economy, upon which everything else depended. In sum, Marshall argued that a balance between economic growth via capitalism, political empowerment through democracy, and social integration/participation sustained through social policy was both historically and theoretically necessary for the sustained achievement of any one of these goals.

In recent years the globalization of economic and political relations, and the political challenges which have been mounted to the traditional provision of social rights via the welfare state, have thrown some doubt on aspects of this model, and have stimulated new debates about citizenship. There are several problems. First, Marshall only ever referred to England in his discussion of citizenship, but other regimes have also achieved citizenship integration, such as fascist and state socialist ones.

A second problem relates to the decline in the strength of organized labour and the growth of single-issue politics. Citizens are also concerned about the environment, about gender, about race, about religion, and so on. Marshall's model is thus in need of extension, not only geographically, but in terms of the history of the substantive issues that are in contention. Turner (1990), for example, argues that Marshall neglects the realm of the 'private', including the experience of religious tradition and beliefs, and ethnic and racial identity, and suggesting that more emphasis could be given to citizenship struggles from below (such as social movements), in contrast with a view of citizenship as a privilege handed down by ruling groups.

A final problem with Marshall's model is its normative emphasis. He describes the sequential unfolding of rights of different kinds to the point at which full citizenship has been achieved. But this ignores the great variation with which such rights are actually exercised in civil society. This is particularly the case for Eastern Europe, where the lived experience of citizens over the last twenty or thirty years was increasingly separated from the official state view of a citizen's rights.

Welfare 'Regimes'

A third model for understanding the way in which the state has intervened in the field of welfare contrasts sharply with Marshall in that it is explicitly comparative across different countries, eschews normative commitments to any 'best' welfare arrangement, and explicitly incorporates political forces in its analysis. It draws on a tradition of analysing different types of welfare state, often contrasting less generous with more generous welfare provision. This work culminated in Esping-Andersen's (1990) highly influential book, in which he described three types, or 'regimes' as he called them, of 'welfare capitalism'. These were generated by considering the welfare situation of male wage workers only, and while there has been substantial criticism of them for ignoring gender issues, they have nevertheless dominated social policy debates in the 1990s. His argument was that in different countries social policies were organized around certain internally integrated features, so that social policies of different types shared certain consistent assumptions and effects: in terms, for example, of the nature of state intervention, the stratification of social groups, and—most crucially—the extent to which markets were replaced by bureaucratic distribution in a process of 'de-commodification' (see Box 3.9), in favour of the distribution of goods and services according to needs.

Box 3.9   Esping-Andersen's three worlds of welfare capitalism

neo-liberal (American)

de-commodification	low
stratification	high
state intervention	regulation of markets

social democratic (Scandinavian)

de-commodification	high
stratification	low
state intervention	direct provision or finance

corporatist (Franco-German)

de-commodification	high
stratification	high
state intervention	regulation of markets or finance

He suggested that there were three such types: neo-liberal (American), social democratic (Scandinavian), and corporatist (Franco-German). The neo-liberal type had a relatively low (and falling) level of de-commodification, a relatively high level of stratification in terms of income inequality, and state intervention typified by regulation of markets rather than the provision or finance of social welfare. By contrast, the social democratic type had a high level of de-commodification, low level of stratification, and direct state provision or finance, as well as regulation. Corporatist types had a mixture of these features: heavily stratified by both income (especially in France) and social status, yet with considerable de-commodification, if only through the heavy regulation of non-profit providers, rather than direct state provision.

The origins of these different regimes are linked to the political strength of labour movements in different countries against a context of relatively similar levels of economic growth. Esping-Andersen here follows a well-worn path of attempts to explain the origins of different levels of 'welfare effort' in different countries. The crucial question is why welfare-state effort—for example, the percentage of GNP spent on social security—has grown to a relatively higher level in some societies than others. Explanations typically include either the direct effect of economic growth, or the indirect effect of economic growth through the development of left-wing political power, centred on trade union strength and its political representation in government.

From this perspective the origins, size, and generosity of welfare states are contingent on political forces, and especially the alliances that can form between different social classes. Where the middle classes are persuaded that it is in their interests to side with working-class demands for an expanded welfare state, as in Scandinavia, then private-sector service provision is crowded out, and middle-class concerns for quality permeate the state sector. Where, however, working-class interests are poorly organized (as in the USA, for example), or where middle-class interests have turned away from state provision towards the private market (as in the UK), then welfare effort and quality will suffer.

Beyond the Nation State

Much of our discussion has been about the politics of welfare at or below the level of the nation state. As we observed earlier, however, the nation state has only existed for about 500 years, and much less in many instances. Some observers have wondered whether the nation state is in decline, and have suggested that we should also look at higher levels of organization in order to capture the full range of contemporary and future politics. For example, the European Union has grown in importance for social policy over the last twenty-five years, particularly in relation to issues of social security and employment. A growing volume of legislation and legal precedence is accumulating at the European level. Many local authorities now have direct administrative and financial connections to Brussels, and some now maintain permanent offices in Brussels to keep abreast of new developments. A parallel development has occurred in voluntary-sector organizations which are particularly relevant to social policy. With the commitment of the UK government to the social chapter, and the development of the European Monetary Union, this growing integration is set to continue. Moreover, with the number of countries in the European Union also set to grow, perhaps the nation state is in decline?

A further erosion of nation states can be traced through the development of global institutions which are increasingly moving into the area of social policy. While the World Health Organization may have always been concerned with social policy, the World Bank and the International Monetary Fund have only recently developed clear views on it, particularly in the field of social security in countries which are deemed to require 'structural adjustments' in their public expenditure profile, for example in Eastern Europe, South America, and Africa. Very often an individual country that needs credit from the IMF will have to commit itself to a detailed social security policy which in the past was traditionally under the control of the nation state and its political élite.

For some commentators this represents the 'end of history' as it has traditionally developed, such that in future a global society will develop with an increasing convergence towards one type of (limited) welfare policy. Others disagree, suggesting that with economic growth comes choice over social expenditure, and that there is a parallel regionalization of social politics through which a variety of social policies will continue to evolve. For example, the development of Irish, Welsh, and Scottish assemblies in the UK may lead to greater social policy divergence. The evidence from 200 years of US Federal efforts to integrate American social policies suggests that local autonomy can indeed survive and flourish for long periods of time, and it may therefore be premature to anticipate a decline in the politics of welfare.

Glossary

authority Legitimate power.

business groups Representative organizations for employers whose major allegiance is to further the interests of their members' economic interests.

civil servants Permanent salaried administrators available to a government whose duty it is to undertake to develop and implement policies determined by government ministers, and who take a neutral stance to the ideological position of the government.

consent Uncoerced agreement to a course of action.

constitution Basic rules formulating the structure of and procedures for government, either written or customary.

direct provision Where a social service is organized, financed, and provided by permanent government employees.

financial support Where a social service is financed by government, but organized and provided by non-government organizations.

government department A major branch of central government responsible for a significant section of state activity, such as healthcare or social security.

liberal democracy The system of government based on the universal right to vote for candidates chosen from a range of alternatives to represent the interests of sections of the community, combined with the freedom to organize and propose policies on issues of the day.

ministry *see* government department.

official enquiry Government-sponsored review of the operations of a particular area of policy.

policies Plans of action formulated in general terms by political parties, and their representatives in government, especially ministers, and often developed in detail by civil servants.

policy networks Informal affiliations of actors with a conscious interest in shaping policies and their outcomes.

power The ability to bring about preferred policy outcomes, or to prevent unwanted outcomes, or to shape the way in which policy options are considered.

pressure groups Organized groups aiming to develop or influence government policies.

professional associations Representative organizations for different professions, sometimes with a legal monopoly over the interests of a particular profession.

professions Occupational groups based on a presumed monopoly of specialist knowledge attained through a lengthy training.

QUANGOS QUAsi Non-Governmental OrganizationS; that is, only partly independent of government influence, often appointed by government, but supposedly free to pursue policies independently.

regulation Where social service provision, whether by government or another organization, is monitored carefully in accordance with legally enforceable rules and standards.

resources Capacities for action, often financial, but also personal, cultural, scientific, or political.

rules Agreed course of action, established in law or by custom and practice.

social movements Collective non-parliamentary attempts to change substantial areas of social life, major social institutions, prevailing ideologies and identities, or government policies. Often split between 'old' social movements, such as the labour movement, and 'new' social movements, such as environmentalism, feminism, or anti-racism.

territorial injustice Where social service provision in relation to need is unequal between different geographical areas.

think tanks Groups relatively autonomous from government which specialize in policy innovation and advice.

trade unions Representative organizations for working people whose major allegiance is to further the interests of their members' working conditions and wages.

welfare states Those that have a self-conscious commitment to the provision of adequate minimal access to income, healthcare, education, and housing for all citizens.

Guide to Further Reading

N. Deakin, *The Politics of Welfare: Continuities and Change* (London: Harvester Wheatsheaf, 1994). Covers a range of social policies, and the political issues that affect them.

R. Klein, *The New Politics of the National Health Service* (3rd edn., London: Longman, 1995). Does the same, but in depth for the National Health Service, which turns out to be a highly political arena.

V. George and S. Miller (eds.), *Social Policy Towards 2000* (London: Routledge, 1994). Explores alternative political party positions for all the major social policy areas, through a detailed review of election commitments.

References

Bowles, S. and Gintis, H. (1976), *Schooling in Capitalist America* (London: Routledge & Kegan Paul).

Davies, B. P. (1978), *Universality, Selectivity and Effectiveness in Social Services* (London: Heinemann).

Esping-Andersen, G. (1990), *The Three Worlds of Welfare Capitalism* (Oxford: Polity Press).

Etzioni, A. (1975), *A Comparative Analysis of Complex Organisations* (2nd edn., London: Macmillan).

Foucault, M. (1973), *The Birth of the Clinic* (London: Tavistock Publications).

Hirschman, A. O. (1970), *Exit, Voice, and Loyalty: Responses to Decline in Firms, Organisations, and States* (Cambridge, Mass.: Harvard University Press).

Le Grand, J. (1993), 'Paying for or Providing Welfare', in N. Deakin & R. Page (eds.), *The Costs of Welfare* (London: Avebury).

Lukes, S. (1974), *Power: A Radical View* (London: Macmillan).

Mann, M. (1987), 'Ruling-Class Strategies and Citizenship', *Sociology*, 21, 339–54.

Manning, Nick (1985), *Social Problems and Welfare Ideology* (Gower).

Mead, L. M. (1987), *Beyond Entitlement: The Social Obligations of Citizenship* (London: Free Press).

Parsons, T. (1951), *The Social System* (London: Free Press).

Rhodes, R. A. W. (1988), *Beyond Westminster and Whitehall* (London: Unwin Hyman).

——and Marsh, D. (1992), 'New Directions in the Study of Policy Networks', *European Journal of Political Research*, 21, 181–205.

Titmuss, R. M. (1970), *The Gift Relationship: From Human Blood to Social Policy* (London: Allen & Unwin).

Turner, B. S. (1990), 'Outline of a Theory of Citizenship', *Sociology*, 24, 189–217.

Weber, M. (1947), *The Theory of Social and Economic Organisation* (Oxford: Oxford University Press).

Part Two
The Social and Economic Context

4 Welfare, Ideology, and Social Theory

Nick Manning

Contents

Introduction

For the major part of this chapter we will examine the characterization of social policy along various ideological dimensions, and the ideals that have been at the heart of social policy debates in the twentieth century. Social policy has become more urgently discussed by politicians since conservative-oriented governments came to power in the 1980s in the USA and the UK. Yet the implementation of supposed right-wing policies of the 1980s and more left-wing policies of the 1990s has not been straightforward (Box 4.1). There is sharp ideological dispute over social issues, but also confusion about what traditional political ideologies dictate in specific policy terms.

What does this mean? We seem to have in both the UK and the USA a long period of relative cross-party agreement, followed by a sharp swing towards the right in public debate combined with a relatively weak implementation of the new political hopes. Yet with the exhaustion of these views in the 1990s and the election of ostensibly centre-left parties we find some of the most draconian welfare reforms being implemented. In the remainder of this chapter we will discuss the significance of ideologies for social policy.

Concepts: Theories of Ideology

The concept of ideology, while an essential part of debates about social policy, as we shall see later in this chapter, has been much debated within social theory. There are

---

Box 4.1 Swings in welfare ideology in the US and the UK

In the USA the main lines of modern social policy were laid down in Roosevelt's 'New Deal' in 1932. This was a pragmatic response to the economic depression which had engulfed America shortly after the famous Wall Street stock market crash in 1929. There was cross-party agreement on the New Deal until 1980, when President Ronald Reagan was elected on a distinctly right-wing programme that appeared to spell the end of the New Deal consensus. In the event, Congressmen lost their political nerve and failed to follow through the dramatic reversals to welfare programmes that were expected. In the UK we can trace a remarkably similar pattern. The British welfare state was laid down in the pragmatic 1942 Beveridge report, *Social Insurance and Allied Services*. This had long-standing cross-party support too until 1979, when Margaret Thatcher was also elected on a right-wing programme. During the 1980s, however, the welfare state was not dismantled in the manner expected, and public expenditure actually rose for some central areas such as healthcare and social security.

Ironically, during the 1990s in both countries more ideologically moderate leaders, Clinton and Blair, have undertaken strong welfare reform policies, attacking groups such as lone parents in an attempt to get them 'off welfare' and into work. This shows how welfare ideology and welfare policy can oscillate dramatically, but not always in the same direction.

two theorists who have dominated discussion about ideology: Karl Marx and Karl Mannheim. Marx's theory was embedded in a much wider project to analyse the nature of capitalism, while Mannheim was more interested in a theory of knowledge, of how we think and know about the world we live in.

Marx

Marx initially suggested that ideology, like religion, reflects the frustrations of the physical and secular world. Indeed, religion itself, he claimed, was an ideology. Marx suggested that ideological thought was misleading as to the real relations involved in any particular issue, including social policy: 'it is not consciousness that determines life, but life that determines consciousness' (Marx and Engels 1976). Writing in the nineteenth century, he felt that the market commodity lay at the heart of the new industrial society dominated by market mechanisms. He wondered why the real work involved in making a product was not actually reflected directly in its real nature for us, but in its market price. In the market it loses its real character, for example that of a painting, sculpture, football team, that of mass-produced clothing, and so on, and turns into something quite different—a commodity or an investment. This, he implies, distorts our relationship to and understanding of the real world, usually for the worst: either we don't appreciate the real circumstances under which products are made, or on occasion (as with bad art!) we value things for the 'wrong' reasons. Even people can become commodities in the market, and lose their character as people *per se*. For this reason he would have been alarmed at the development of an internal market in the NHS.

This distortion in the 'life process' under market society, Marx suggested, can be generalized to suggest that other relations can also be distorted: social security may not really provide security, healthcare may not make us well, education may not make us better informed, professionals may not really serve their clients' best interests, and so on. The official ideas about how these major institutions in our societies are supposed to work may be ideologies.

Mannheim

Mannheim (1968) developed Marx's ideas as a special case of a more general issue. To what extent is the common intellectual currency of a historical period ideological, which makes up the totality of perceptions and ideas shared by members of a society about their world, including social policy? These ideas cover such fundamental areas as human nature and the society on which we all depend in one form or another. Mannheim suggested two different types of ideology: the particular and the total.

By the **particular conception of ideology** he refers to doubts we might have about the validity of someone's ideas. We suspect that he or she might be more or less consciously disguising the real nature of a situation which, if it were revealed, might be disadvantageous to them. We often hear politicians extolling the virtues of a social policy such as 'welfare to work' or 'evidence-based medicine'. Such ideas might be discredited by showing that they spring from undisclosed personal, group, or class interests.

Mannheim's second type, the **total conception of ideology**, is more sophisticated than the first. He argues not just that a particular deception is in someone's interests, but that there is a correspondence between their social situation and the total perception of the world that they and their associates profess. For example, the government's definition of a social issue will be bound up with its job of maintaining an ordered equilibrium in society—of maintaining law and order, employment, and so on. The poor must be educated and motivated to 'join in'. This might suggest that while ideological differences are stressed by political parties in opposition, in power the constraints of government begin to change the ways in which governments and ministers think.

The End of Ideology?

In more recent years there have been two challenges to the arguments of Marx and Mannheim. They suggest that mature industrialism has resulted in the exhaustion of ideological differences—the 'end of ideology'. The first argument is associated with Daniel Bell's book, *The End of Ideology* (1960). Writing in the late 1950s, he argued that the big ideologies of communism and fascism had become exhausted. Fascism had been eliminated with the Second World War, and communism, once the excesses of Stalin's terror of the 1930s came to light, and with Khrushchev's criticism of him after his death in 1953, no longer held an alternative beacon to the world.

A more recent reworking of this theme emerged with the fall of the Iron Curtain and the collapse of the USSR. Here a similar idea is taken up by Francis Fukuyama (1992) and described as the 'end of history'. His starting-point is to observe that there is no longer any practical alternative to liberal democratic capitalism. This is to be explained through the effects of scientific and technological change which is irreversible and cumulative, and which gradually constrains all societies onto a common developmental path. In addition there is a deep-seated aspiration in all people for 'recognition'. This, he argues, is a basic aspect of individual identity, and results inevitably in a steady struggle towards democratic political systems, since they are the best, indeed only, way in which individuals can gain such recognition. Technology and democracy will also drive welfare states towards common solutions to common social problems.

The second type of criticism is that there has never really been a pre-eminent ideology. Mann (1970) and Abercrombie *et al.* (1980) argued that the **dominant ideology** in any society was merely the shared values of the ruling élite. Most people neither need nor want such an overarching set of values, but get by in daily life through a pragmatic adjustment to the constraints of work and family obligations. Survey evidence from the West suggests that a variety of values are held by ordinary people, and a range of accounts from Eastern Europe confirms that many, probably the majority of people did not really believe in the ideological prescriptions of state socialism.

This scepticism about the adherence of ordinary people to big ideologies has now widened into a new descriptive term for the current era: **post-modernism.** This term started in architecture as a means of denoting dissatisfaction with modern architecture, particularly the production of high-rise, prefabricated, mass housing which was disliked by those who lived in it. It represented the rejection of the expression of the big idea or **grand narrative** in architecture, associated more than anything with Le Corbusier's designs for high-rise housing. Social policy took about ten years to catch up with this change in architecture, and in the mid-1980s developed the idea that industrial society in general had entered a new era, the post-modern (Harvey, 1990). Drawing heavily on the work of Foucault, the argument was that different ideas or viewpoints, or 'knowledges' as he termed them, coexisted, and that none was to be seen in any essential sense as dominant or superior. This helps us to understand the ideological and policy confusions that seem to characterise UK and US social policy in the 1990s.

Ideas and Ideologies: What 'Ought' to Be and What Is

Ideas about how welfare states should be constructed have been hotly contested in recent years. Frequently these ideas have been expressed in terms of left- and right-wing ideologies. Following the discussion of Marx and Mannheim, we can define an ideology as having three components. First is a particular view which emphasizes or weights an argument, explanation, or judgement to the exclusion of other points of view. For example, in developing an approach to unemployment we might choose to emphasize the individual characteristics of a worker and her particular capacities or attitudes. These might be seen as causing unemployment, and hence remedies could be sought in terms of skill training or the development of better work habits for that individual. The argument might even extend to blaming the individual for their unemployment. This approach, however, tends to hide alternative explanations, such as industrial restructuring or global competition (see Chapter 7).

A particular, possibly one-sided emphasis in an argument could be a mistake or oversight. However, the term 'ideology' is also used to denote a second aspect—the interests of individuals or groups in the outcome of the argument or characterization. This means that they have something to gain from the argument being put in a particular way. For example, to continue the discussion of unemployment, whether an individual or a whole industry is the most appropriate level for explaining and dealing with unemployment is likely to vary with the interests of the individual or group concerned. Industrialists have tended to consider unemployment in terms of the inability of individuals to adapt to changing employment opportunities, or, in a famous phrase, to resist 'getting on their bikes' to search for work. This, it could be supposed, is because industrialists require a flexible workforce.

A third aspect of an ideology is the way it spills across more than one particular issue, referring to a wider set of relatively coherent ideas which might include not merely a specific item of social policy, but also ideas about family life, the nature of individuals, the rights and duties of citizenship, the authority of the state, and so on. Thus, to continue our example, industrialists might also consider it the responsibility of all adults to seek work in order to support their families, that people will find work if the alternatives are unpalatable enough, and that the state should ensure that such incentives are clearly structured and known to citizens.

To sum up, ideologies are particular, sometimes biased, sets of ideas that are held because they are in the interests of the groups of people articulating them, and which integrate views about a range of issues and social institutions.

Normative Ideals

While ideologies contain ideas about the way welfare states or specific social policies have developed and work, they particularly include also ideas about how things ought to be. These are statements about **normative ideals** which can be end states, but also the means of attaining those states.

End States

The desirability of health, happiness, or economic growth can be endlessly debated, and frequently they are. In the field of social policy one of the most commonly desired end states is the meeting of a 'social need' (discussed in Chapter 6). It has been argued by Doyal and Gough (1991), for example, that there are two basic human needs: for health, and for the capacity to survive and reproduce (which they interpret as the need for education in an industrial society). We might all be able to agree on such basic needs, but one of the problems is that some end states are incompatible with others. For example, economic growth can lead to pollution and ill-health; or more widespread education can lead to the devaluation of educational qualifications. This potential for end states to interact and even conflict means that arguments about the choice between them will revolve less around evidence than around ideological divisions between individuals, groups, and political parties over the right goals to pursue.

Means

Not only are end states disputed, but also the means of attaining them. In the early years of industrialization, when rapid urbanization had changed traditional family and community life, mutual aid and co-operative arrangements within working-class communities sprang up to deal with new risks: illness, for example, or lack of shelter. Voluntary charitable societies were founded by energetic reformers to help find, or to impose, solutions to the new social problems accompanying industrialization. New professional groups emerged to deal with issues of healthcare, planning, and social statistics. These in turn emphasized different means of working towards the desirable ends concerned, using the authority of knowledge and professionalism. And behind much of this change lay the growth of state intervention, sometimes as provider, sometimes as funder, and sometimes merely as regulator, but always raising issues about who should determine goals and the means of attaining them.

As with end states, there are incompatibilities between different means. Do professionals know best? Is the knowledge base on any particular issue partial or complete? Should local communities be consulted on new developments in their area? Can the state be trusted to represent the interests of minorities? Participation on the basis of ignorance might not be helpful to communities; democracy might lead to the comfortable majority ignoring or even oppressing minorities. Professions may misuse their power to protect themselves at the expense of their clients. Again, the room for disagreement and incompatibility between these means of social change opens up plenty of space for ideological debate.

Explanatory Ideals

Although ideologies are typically concerned with statements about what ought to be, they also express coherent views about why and how social policies have got into the position they are in. These are ideas about explaining social policies rather than trying to change them. Of course, explanation and prescription are often inextricably linked, but we can separate them for the purpose of exposition here. Just as we can separate ends and means when considering social ideals, we can separate social policy explanation into questions of why and how: why policies have developed in different times, places, and issues; and how they work in practice.

Why Did Welfare States Appear?

There is widespread agreement that this was in reaction to the dislocating effects of the dependence of individuals and families on waged work which had spread throughout the United States and Europe during the nineteenth century. However, there are two ways of looking at the origins of welfare states. The first is to consider them as the rational response to economic insecurity created by industrialization. From this point of view, technocratic élites realize that it is neither in their own interests nor the interests of those affected for severe poverty or inadequate access to health, education, and housing to develop. They organize a collective sharing of the risks of these misfortunes, often provided or regulated by the state, and justify this sometimes through the idea of social needs that ought to be met, and sometimes through the idea of investment in creating a healthy and happy (and therefore more productive) workforce.

From this point of view the growth of welfare states can be thought of as a functional or technical issue, and has often been written about as an inevitable by-product of industrialization. The traditional study of **social administration** as the progressive uncovering and meeting of social needs (discussed in Chapter 2) is typical of this **functionalist explanation**. Broader explanations, as in the study by Kerr, *Industrialism and Industrial Man* (1960), recognized that industrial élites could organize this process in more than one way, but argued that in the end all industrial societies are moving in the same direction, whether the UK, USA, Russia, Japan, or South East Asia.

A second way of understanding the origins of welfare states is to regard their development as a highly political process of social conflict. From this point of view there was a series of intense struggles between different groups, working people represented by labour parties, the liberal middle classes represented by democratic parties, and élites represented by conservative parties. All these groups saw that industrialization had created economic insecurity and exclusion, but they had very different ideas about what the appropriate mechanisms should be for dealing with this, and especially disagreed about the ideal social policies that they would like to see in place.

Celebrated examples of these more political analyses of welfare states include Marshall's (1963) account of welfare states as part of a wider political struggle for the establishment of **citizenship** rights (see Chapter 3). From this point of view social citizenship (that is, access to welfare) has only developed as a result of political struggle and political mobilization, rather than technical or élite intervention. For some writers,

> ### Box 4.2 Evidence for political explanations of welfare
>
> Evidence for political explanations of the development of welfare state expenditure was first explicitly presented by Castles and McKinlay (1979). This statistical study of western industrial democratic states measured public welfare in terms of social security transfer payments, educational expenditure, and infant mortality. It found that political factors such as left-wing mobilization and the absence of right-wing government have the strongest statistical association with public welfare.
>
> Several further studies in the 1980s confirmed this finding, even when the measures used for welfare changed and when the period of time covered was extended. For example, Hicks and Swank (1984) measured the impact of political 'capitalist and working-class-linked actors' on changes in direct cash transfer payments for income maintenance between 1960 and 1971 in eighteen 'advanced capitalist democracies'. Political actions by both right-of-centre parties and trade unions were the main determinants of transfer spending. In a supplementary study, Hicks, Swank, and Ambuhl (1989) confirmed this finding between 1957 and 1982. An extensive discussion of 'state activism' is presented in Hage *et al.* (1989).

such as Stephens (1979), this struggle has been characterized as the success of left-wing parties in taming capitalism; others have argued more cautiously that where there has been generous welfare state development this is almost always due to the relative strength of the Left in government. This approach now has an extensive body of empirical support for its approach (see Box 4.2).

Political analysts, moreover, argue that the technical or functionalist approaches to explaining welfare states only developed in the context of an unusually quiet period of political consensus about the means and ends of welfare states in the middle fifty years of the twentieth century. This, they argue, misled some writers to consider this as typical, whereas in fact struggle, debate, and dissent are more typical of public debates over social policies. There are two points being made here: first, that social policy is a politically disputed arena, and second, that left-wing political ideas are supportive of more extensive social policies. In short, social policy is about ideals rather than technique, and therefore requires an analysis that examines the ideological context of policy debate and development.

How Social Policies Work

In addition to this debate about the reasons why welfare states developed, there are passionate discussions about how ideals are turned into practice. In part these discussions overlap with normative issues about the ends and means of social policies, and many writers cover both simultaneously. Nevertheless, the way in which social policies work is not as simple as we might suppose. Social policy refers to some kind of intervention into social structures and processes (and, occasionally, a deliberate non-intervention). We have seen in Chapter 1 that there are basically four types of social provision: state, voluntary, market, and informal. Government intervention is particularly powerful since the state can both regulate (through laws) and provide resources (through taxation) for social policies. But the state is itself controlled through the ballot box, and therefore the commitments organized around political party ideologies are of central importance. The voluntary sector, typified by charity organizations, is also driven by social ideals, often associated with the beliefs of a key founding individual (such as the Rowntree Trust and the ideas of **Seebohm Rowntree**).

Beyond this, the market and the informal sector appear less overtly ideological. The market simply enables the production and distribution of those social services which people purchase directly, or indirectly through private insurance. Informal care, typically unwaged work by women, arises most often through family obligations. However, it can nevertheless be argued that the market and the informal sector contain fairly explicit, though hidden, ideologies. Markets inevitably imply that the possession of money, or more often credit, is the measure of a citizen's rights. Access to money, typically through wage labour, is from this point of view the morally preferable route to social welfare. This is why New Labour argues that paid employment is an ideal solution to a variety of social problems. Finally, feminists have argued that informal, unwaged work both sustains and is justified by an ideology of family privacy in which men as a class exercise unwarranted power over women.

Other key actors in social policy implementation include the professions and the bureaucracies that occur throughout the state, voluntary, and market welfare sectors. In many respects they reflect and reproduce ideologies appropriate to their sector. Professions also have a long tradition of independent values, of which the doctors' **Hippocratic oath** is perhaps an archetypal expression. Commitment to public service, discretion, honesty, and knowledge-based practice have been proffered by professional associations as a set of beliefs and practices which are detached from the interests and commitments of politics or markets. Their ideology is perhaps a claim to rise above ideology itself.

Ideologies of Welfare

Social policy, it has been argued so far, is not a neutral or technical matter. Typically, given the dominance of the state in social policy, social policy ideologies have been analysed through the familiar left-to-right framework used as a shorthand for identifying different political ideologies. There are a number of examples of this in the literature (see Box 4.3).

Clearly it is not easy to separate different ideologies cleanly: they tend to shade into each other. A major reason for this is that writers have tended to blur the normative ('ought') parts of an ideology with the explanatory ('why and how') parts. Thus two ideological positions might share the same ideals, or end states, but differ over their analysis of the 'why and how' of social policies, and hence the means advocated of attaining common ideals. For example, Marxists and socialists mainly differ over their analysis of how to attain a fairly similar ideal. Even Marx's description of life under communism is expressed in the kind of individualist imagery of personal choice that supporters of the new right would not disagree with: 'Communist society . . . makes it possible for me to do one thing today and another tomorrow, to hunt in the morning, fish in the

---

Box 4.3 Ideologies of welfare

Wedderburn (1965)

| Anti-collectivism | Citizenship | Integrationism | Functionalism |

Titmuss (1974)

| Residualism | Industrialism | Institutionalism |

Taylor-Gooby and Dale (1981)

| Individualism | Reformism | Structuralism | Marxism |

George and Wilding (1994)

| New Right | Middle Way | Democratic Socialism | Marxism | Feminism | Greenism |

Adapted from George and Wilding (1994), 9.

---

afternoon, rear cattle in the evening, criticize after dinner, just as I have a mind' (Marx and Engels, 1976). Perhaps this explains how, from time to time, social policy analysts have crossed over and changed their ideological position as a result not of changed ideals, but of their analysis of how to get to them.

Fine distinctions between ideologies are therefore difficult to work with, and here we will present a relatively simple three-dimensional view. On the one hand, the left and the right can be separated from a middle position. Second, there are a number of new social movements (NSMs) that cut across this traditional political spectrum, such as feminism and greenism. Finally, there is a group of beliefs ignored in the studies illustrated in Box 4.3, but possibly more significant than any other for social policy around the world—religious beliefs.

The Left

The Left draw their inspiration either from Marx or from the variety of democratic socialist ideas embedded in the European labour movements of the late nineteenth and early twentieth centuries. In many respects their ideals are quite similar. They are both concerned to harness industrialization (which they do not especially criticize) for the good of all members of society. An egalitarian distribution of goods and services is thus a central concern. The main disagreements between Marxists and other socialists is over means rather than ends. Marxists have been perfectly happy to advocate quite authoritarian means, including a powerful state, to achieve these ends: the USSR was a particularly clear example of this. Other socialists, on the whole, have been concerned to empower ordinary people through democratic parliamentary mechanisms in order to secure their active consent to social policies. Getting the majority of citizens to support policies is critical not merely to retain parliamentary power, but to crowd out alternative services, such as private, market-based ones. A particularly good example of this approach has been realized in Sweden for much of the post-war period.

The Middle

In the middle is a wide range of views united not so much by ends, as were the left, but by the means for developing social policy, with a much less clear idea of what the ends might be. The means they are concerned about are on the whole defined negatively in terms of avoiding the dangers of either too much unregulated capitalism or too much collectivism. This was classically defined by Marshall (1963) in his idea of **hyphenated society,** by which he meant democratic-welfare-capitalism. He argued that in the twentieth century the development of social policy was an essential element in the functioning of modern industrialism, just as the development of civil and political **rights** had been in previous centuries. This is a functionalist model in which the modern welfare state is seen as a pragmatic way of adjusting society to the inevitable market failures that are thrown up by capitalism from time to time. Much policy-making, from this perspective, is concerned with anxiously avoiding pitfalls that might arise from the unintended consequences of policy intervention, such as undermining work incentives, erecting poverty traps, condoning professional arrogance, missing unrecognized need, encouraging fraud, and so on.

This pragmatic response to social ills as they appear and are recognized has little time for passionate debate about the ideals of social policy. Notions of fairness and balance in social affairs, combined with the support of social institutions such as the family, are the goals of the middle way, anodyne enough for George and Wilding (1994: 73) to observe that 'few would quarrel with Middle Way goals'.

The Right

The right are exceptional in the energy with which they have stated both their ideals and their favoured policy mechanisms in the last two decades. They have made the running in terms of policy debate around the globe, both within nation states and within the numerous multinational agencies that advise and cajole those states over social policy, such as the World Bank, International Monetary Fund, and the Organization for Economic Cooperation and Development. While the right can trace their ideals at least as far back as Adam Smith in the eighteenth century, their basis can be located in the **Social Darwinism** proposed by Spencer and Sumner in the nineteenth century. Unlike the European roots of socialist ideas, the right has thus typically been an Anglo-American development; modern exponents such as Murray, Friedson, and Hayek have been based in the USA and the UK.

Social Darwinism drew on Darwin's ideas to suggest that, as in the animal world, social and economic success depended on the fitness of individuals and groups to survive in the brave new world of competitive industrial society. Indeed, it was seen as a useful mechanism for weeding out weakness naturally, and against which there was little point in intervening—intervention, it was thought, might well have highly adverse consequences. This view has reappeared in modified form in recent writings from the so-called new right. Their central argument is that society is not perfectible in any particular form. They claim that they do not, therefore, have an ideal society in mind, but argue instead that we should devote our attention to the appropriate means or mechanisms which will allow the maximum chance for any particular pattern of life favoured by an individual or group. Thus freedom from constraint, and the recognition of individuals as paramount judges of their own welfare, are central ideas to the new right. The key mechanism for ensuring these possibilities is the market; the state should have a substantially reduced role.

New Social Movements

The previous familiar political spectrum has been extremely important in debates about social policy over the last hundred years. However, since the 1960s a number of new ideologies have come to prominence in social policy discussions and analysis which cannot be located on that single left–right dimension. They are frequently referred to collectively as the **new social movements,** and share a criticism of the standard left–right model that the dimensions are either incomplete or wrong.

There are three sets of values highly pertinent to social policy issues which the traditional ideological division cannot accommodate: feminism, anti-racism, and environmentalism. The first two are discussed by Williams (1989). She argues that while the move away from traditional social administration in the 1970s was made possible by the critical appreciation of the impact on social policy of the social and economic organization of work and production, which informs much left-oriented analysis, such an analysis in relation to work leaves two further themes unexamined, of family and nation:

These themes, Work, Family, Nation, which shape welfare policies, reflect the divisions of class, gender, and 'race' respectively. In this picture the welfare state has to be understood as developing within the social relations of imperialism and the social relations of patriarchy, which themselves have changed over time. (Williams 1989: p. xiv)

For feminist social policy writers, such as Wilson (1977), Dale and Foster (1986), and Pascall (1997), the central questions include those about why women play such a major role in social reproduction, both in the family and as state welfare workers, and how the division of labour in both waged and unwaged work affects their interests. Since social policy is concerned with **social reproduction,** that is, the physical, emotional, ideological, and material processes involved in caring for and sustaining others (both children and adults), feminist writers argue that it is incomprehensible that feminist work should not be at the heart of social policy analysis. As feminist questions and analysis have expanded they have become entwined with some of the traditional left–right debates, such as those about commitment to equality, or the appropriateness of the state or the market for engineering change. Within feminist writing, therefore, we can locate relatively left-, middle-, or right-wing positions.

Anti-racism reflects the omission of issues of nation from social policy concerns. Within the welfare state welfare services are labour-intensive, and black and immigrant workers have played an important role as a reserve army of cheap labour: nurses, cleaners, caterers. Moreover, welfare services contribute to the reproduction of inequalities in British society. Black children do less well at school and in the youth-training and labour markets than their white counterparts. Access to appropriate healthcare and housing have been repeatedly documented as discriminatory against black people (Denny, 1985). Finally, it can be argued that the welfare state has historically been as much about the maintenance of political stability as the meeting of social needs, and the presence of black people has justified the frequent revamping of technologies of social control to contain and incorporate a perceived cultural threat. Mechanisms for this have ranged from the pathologizing of black diets, family life, and psychologies, to direct policing.

Environmentalism is not central to Williams's 1989 analysis, but is included (along with feminism, but not anti-racism) in the 1994 edition of George and Wilding's influential book on welfare ideologies. Green ideology is of two varieties—light green and deep green (Ferris 1991). The first is compatible with the current aspirations for most industrial societies, especially the attempt to solve social problems through economic growth. Concern here is that economic and social policies should be sensitive to their effects on animals and the environment. So, within housing, there is concern about energy conservation, or within healthcare there is concern about testing drugs on animals, or the development of genetic manipulation without proper ethical and legal controls. Whether these ends are best pursued via market pricing or state intervention is now discussed more extensively by light greens, as their agenda has seeped into the mainstream of left–right debate. Deep greens, on the other hand, see the welfare state as little more than an extension of the over-industrialization and over-population that is ruining the planet. There is little debate about social policies *per se* in deep-green ideology.

Other smaller social movements, ranging from more traditional political interest groups to protest groups, have developed, or in some cases have renewed and reinvented themselves, within the welfare arena in recent years. For example, action to highlight the needs and rights of disabled people, older people, children, and sufferers of various medical conditions appear from time to time. Some of these groups have developed more extensive ideologies than others, such as Disability Alliance (Oliver, 1990).

Religions

What is almost universally missing from these debates over ideologies around welfare issues are the ideas embedded in the major religions of the world. These are important for several reasons: in terms of ideals, religious beliefs affect the functioning of family life, community organization, and the vigour and focus of the voluntary sector. Understanding South East Asian welfare states, for example, is impossible without appreciating the values embedded in Confucian beliefs, especially about family life. With migration, religious beliefs of all kinds have been transplanted across industrial societies, and understanding and respect for religious belief are important components of discussions about anti-racism and social policy. Second, with the apparent end of ideology discussed earlier, religious ideas have become increasingly central to issues of national and regional identity both in the UK and in other countries. The biggest example would be the resurgence in the Orthodox church in Russia, and Islam in the Central Asian republics; but also within Western Europe, in the Netherlands, for example, we find that religion can be the main organizing principle and structural division in the national society. Without its religious component a clear understanding of the Dutch welfare state is impossible.

In addition to ideals, religion affects the structure and functioning of welfare states. There is comparative evidence from the statistical analysis of western industrial societies that central-government welfare-state development is affected by the extent to which Catholicism is predominant in a society (Wilensky 1981). Moreover, in so far as the charitable and voluntary sector is an important component of welfare activity both within a given society and in the international aid and relief business, religious inspiration has been an important element in the motivation for and justification of welfare work.

Normative Concepts in Social Policy

Whatever the source of ideals about welfare ends and means, there have emerged a number of middle-range **normative concepts** in the discussion and analysis of welfare states that merit discussion and clarification. These will appear in all or most welfare ideologies, and form the building-blocks of many debates between proponents of different positions. We will present four pairs of concepts that are central to many debates. It is interesting to notice how new social movements share the traditional left-wing position for some items, but very much the right-wing position for others. This confirms that in many respects they are different from the traditional left–right dimension, and deserve separate consideration on many issues.

It is difficult to encompass all these ideas in a neat classification. A particularly fundamental issue that runs through most of the following concepts is that of inequality. Equality and inequality have been at the heart of most social policy debates throughout the twentieth century. A major issue has been that the welfare state has been seen as a vehicle for egalitarian redistribution, welcomed by the left, and disliked by the right. In fact, however, the evidence is complex and not wholly supportive of this assumption. In recent decades income and health inequalities have grown, while educational and housing inequalities have probably not. However, it is difficult to come to a clear judgement when the units of measurement, such as health or educational needs, and the period of time over which they should be measured, can vary widely. It is also clear that interventions powerful enough to have a significant impact on inequality can have undesirable side effects. Against this view is the observation that too much inequality can also have undesirable side effects, on health needs, educational achievement, crime, and economic productivity. Nevertheless, for mainstream social policy writers the question of the extent of inequality, and what to do to reduce it, continues to be dominant. The intersection of this fundamental issue with other normative concepts will be presented in many points in the following sections.

Needs and Choice

The first concept is regarded as central to much classic social policy analysis, and is discussed in more detail in Chapter 6. **Needs** are regarded as the main underlying reason for developing social policies by traditional proponents who have occupied the middle ground between the left and the right. Those needs that should be met have generally been identified as those that alternative institutions, such as the market and the family, have failed to meet. Thus, where the labour market provides insufficient wages, or none at all, the need for income in order to buy food, clothing, shelter, and so on is identified as a moral imperative that should be met. The difference between left and right here centres on the means for meeting this need, and at what level it should be met. The left have traditionally favoured state provision at levels not too far removed from basic adequacy. The right have favoured compulsory insurance, or a very meagre state safety net at such low levels that if at all possible people would avoid it (such as the nineteenth-century workhouse).

The identification of needs remains at the heart of ideological differences over welfare. The newer ideologies use the same general argument, but in relation to specific groups such as women, ethnic minorities, disabled people, and older people. Evidence and arguments are assembled to demonstrate that these groups have been left out of provision for the population in general. In the case of environmentalists, the needs of future generations are a central focus in the concept of sustainability, where current needs should only be met where they do not render the meeting of future needs impossible.

Meeting needs is a complex problem, since they are difficult to measure unambiguously, and the means of meeting them can have unintended side-effects, some of which can render the original effort ineffective. For example, other than very basic needs for water, food, and protection from the weather, many needs are culturally relative. Thus the legitimate types of food, drink, clothing, and shelter which we need vary markedly over time, between regions, genders, ethnic groups, and so on. This suggests that the closely related concept of **choice** should be considered in parallel to need. Here the various ideologies differ more sharply than over need. The right champion the idea that individuals are best helped by being able to exercise choice as a major starting-point in arrangements for people's welfare. Since markets are the best way of providing choice, where people have the money to pay the right are very supportive of the use of markets and the minimum use of bureaucratic state provision. However, feminists argue that women very often do not have access to the money or the freedom to spend it as they wish, even in more affluent households, and environmentalists argue that too many of us exercise choices that will damage our own futures, let alone those of our children, through pollution, resource depletion, and genetic manipulation. In other words, choice only works where the consumer has the knowledge and capacity (which usually means money) to make choices.

The **empowerment** of welfare clients that has been proposed by social policy ideologies concerned with ethnic minorities, disabled people, or elderly people may or may not be accomplished through markets. The right tend to conflate choice and the market mechanism. In fact markets are difficult to control, and appear to have side-effects that can simultaneously restrict choice. For example, the establishment of **quasi-markets** for schools may increase choice for some parents initially; but if some schools select the more able pupils, and others slowly run out of pupils and funding and eventually close, parents with children in them, or who live near them, may well find their choices severely restricted. Quasi-markets in health may have the same effect; in addition, the costs of preparing complex contracts in health tends to drive up costs, and to quickly lead to **producer capture**, whereby purchasing is routinized and insulated from real consumer choice.

Rights and Obligations

If people have needs that are not being met, the welfare state in principle grants them the right to expect these to be met either directly, by the state, or under its jurisdiction financially or legally. **Rights,** then, are an intimate part of social policy. However, the meaning of 'rights' varies with the legal context of the welfare state, and *de facto* with the way in which welfare professionals and bureaucracies work in practice. For example, in Germany welfare rights are legally enshrined, whereas in the UK they are usually not (Box 4.4).

In the USA the Constitution guarantees US citizens equal rights whether they are black or white; yet even here, interpretation has varied. A famous example is the 1954 Supreme Court ruling in the Brown case that all black US children had the right to educational provision equal to that for white children. This was very nearly a hundred years after the civil war had been fought on the issue of slavery, and resulted in several constitutional amendments (numbers 13, 14, and 15) that tried to guarantee equal citizenship for black people in the US. Even after the 1954 ruling, however, education changed very slowly until the civil rights movement changed the political climate in the southern states ten years later.

An important discussion of the relationship between rights and social policy was set out in Marshall's seminal analysis of the growth of citizenship in the UK (see Chapter 3, Box 3.8). He suggested that the development of rights under the British state had taken place in three stages: in the first, civil rights were recognized in the eighteenth century; in the second, political rights were recognized in the nineteenth century; and in the third, social rights were recognized with the foundation of a mature welfare state in the UK in the twentieth century. As noted earlier, this was part of a wider characterization of the UK within a Middle Way ideology as a compromise mixture of democratic-welfare-capitalism.

Rights, then, are contested and struggled for. They are not permanent. For the ideology of the right, rights are negative rights about freedom from constraint, particularly meaning interference by the central or local state, and minimal guarantees that social rules such as those of the market operate fairly. Although these cost money to police they are felt to be relatively cheap. By contrast, the rights favoured by the left, such as

---

Box 4.4 Social security rights in Great Britain and Germany

Jochen Clasen's (1992) study of the comparative erosion of unemployment benefits in Great Britain and in Germany in the 1980s shows how much easier it was for a government to achieve this in Great Britain. Here, with a central ministry responsible for both insurance and means-tested benefits, and no particular legal entitlement for citizens to receive the equivalent of the amounts deposited from the insurance system, the British government was free to reduce unemployment benefits in favour of means-tested assistance.

By contrast, while the German government started to try to make the same kind of fiscal savings by reducing German workers' entitlements, the strategy failed because of three factors. First, unemployment benefits in Germany are legally insulated from other pressures on the social security system in a separate agency; second, they are funded by legally separate, earmarked contributions; third, there is by law an automatic consolidation of the accumulated fund, which can then be used to retain or finance improvements in benefits for the unemployed.

the positive rights to certain levels of welfare services, are much more expensive to provide. For ideologies associated with the new social movements, rights are about making sure that excluded groups get equal treatment. In this sense they share common ground with the left. Women, ethnic minorities, future generations, disabled people, and so on have, or should have, the right to a level of service commensurate with their needs. This may mean that in some circumstances they get a level of provision considerably in excess of that typically provided to other citizens.

In recent years **obligations** have come to be seen as an intimate corollary of welfare rights. Citizens, it has been argued, should be active not merely in their pursuit of rights for themselves, but also in their contribution to the social context on which we all depend in one form or another, from the richest to the poorest. For example, we should not only expect the state to help us if we are poor, but we should expect to take paid work if we can. If we have children, we will be helped through social policy, but we should also strive to be good parents; in state-provided education we should achieve our potential. In the health service we should co-operate with medical staff, and try to get better.

Such expectations are part of a fundamental aspect of social life, the process of reciprocity. This was a major theme of nineteenth-century social analysis. The spread of industrialization across Europe and America led to the contrast being drawn between the dense network of social relations in traditional communities and the open exchanges typical of industrial market societies. Toennies termed this the move from 'community' to 'society'; Durkheim, from 'organic to mechanical solidarity'; Main, from 'status to contract'. All these writers found the changes wrought by industrialization heightened their consciousness that, as Mauss (1967) described it, when a gift is offered between two parties a reciprocal obligation to repay it is set up in some sense, whether in markets, families, or governments. The move from reciprocal obligations central to the closely woven textures of pre-industrial communities to contract obligations typical of industrial society, however, had not eliminated Mauss's central observation that with a gift was given an obligation to repay it. Inability to repay left the recipient with reduced social power and lower status. This is the anthropological source of the stigma so often experienced by welfare recipients, and alerts us to the complexities that underlie the apparent selflessness of altruism that some have naively argued to be the basis of a good welfare state.

Such obligations, epitomized in the title of a book by Laurence Mead, *Beyond Entitlement* (1986), have increasingly been stressed within right-wing ideology. Active citizenship is not new, however; President Kennedy in his inaugural speech admonished us, 'Do not ask what your country can do for you, but what you can do for your country.' More recently, New Labour in the UK have also taken up the idea that welfare recipients should feel obliged to return such largesse in some way (see Box 4.5).

Thus the 'welfare to work' scheme obliges benefit claimants to undertake some activity in return for benefit, such as training or community service. The new social movement ideologies also stress such obligations. For example, feminists want men to undertake the obligations of fatherhood, but they are also concerned that typical family obligations have meant obligations for women rather than men, particularly to undertake unpaid social care. Such obligations do not, in fact, seem to arise out of

---

Box 4.5 New Labour's Green Paper on Welfare Reform

'At the heart of the modern welfare state will be a new contract between the Citizen and Government, based on responsibilities and rights.

Towards a New Welfare Contract

Duty of Government

- Provide people with the assistance they need to find work.

- Make work pay.

- Support those unable to work so that they can lead a life of dignity and security.

- Assist parents with the cost of raising their children.

- Regulate effectively so that people can be confident that private pensions and insurance products are secure.

- Relieve poverty in old age where savings are inadequate.

- Devise a system that is transparent and open and gets money to those in need.

Duty of Individual

- Seek training or work where able to do so.

- Take up the opportunity to be independent if able to do so.

- Give support, financial or otherwise, to their children and other family members.

- Save for retirement where possible.

- Not to defraud the taxpayer.

Duty of us All

To help individuals and families to realize their full potential and live a dignified life, by promoting economic independence through work, by relieving poverty where it cannot be prevented and by building a strong and cohesive society where rights are matched by responsibilities.'

Welfare Reform Green Paper (1998), 80.

---

reciprocal social exchanges, but out of expectations about the family duties of women. Other groups stress the obligations of polluters to pay, or the obligations of able-bodied people to others.

Justice and Merit

Meeting needs and fulfilling rights where resources are scarce raise questions of distribution and rationing. What is **justice** in social distribution? In principle a just provision of welfare implies the equal meeting of equal needs. However, as we have seen, it can be difficult to determine what needs are when cultural relativities influence judgements. Geographical peculiarities may also lead to territorial injustice. When we have to compare needs for very different services, such as medical intervention and educational provision, the possibilities for relative injustice are compounded. What is the relative welfare effort that should be devoted to education or healthcare?

One answer proposed by John Rawls (1972) is that, in principle, we could plan a society as if we were screened behind a veil of ignorance. What would we choose for ourselves if we did not know what lay in store for our own lives? He argues that we would choose a relatively equal society without large disparities of wealth and income. The rationalization for this is that it would be the safest way of ensuring that we were unlikely to suffer too much. However, there are other ways of answering this question. We might choose to risk poverty for the opportunity of greater wealth available to only a few. It can also be argued that a relatively egalitarian society is not, in fact, practicable. Inequality may be inevitable and necessary to motivate or reward the talented, or would otherwise only be possible through a suffocating blanket of state control. The fate of Eastern Europe in the forty years after the Second World War lends support to such a conclusion.

Another idea, developed by health economists, is that we should provide services in relation to the **quality of life** they can subsequently sustain (see Chapter 13). In health-care, for example, a medical intervention might be considered just where it can provide a greater increase in the quality of life for a patient than an equivalent intervention for an alternative patient. This can be refined to take into account the number of years over which the improvement in the quality of life is likely to last. Thus many years of modestly greater quality for a child might be preferable to a few years of a considerable increase in quality for an older person. This idea could be extended, in principle, to the calculation of the relative benefit and costs of different social policies, and hence the ideal just distribution of welfare effort. However, it would be difficult to do these calculations and plan social policy in sufficient detail.

Rawls's conception of justice as equality is really a popular or democratic approach to the rationing of scarce resources, whereas heath economists are trying to develop a technical solution. Either way, social justice has been associated most strongly with ideologies of the left and the new social movements, and arguments in favour of equality achieved through positive policy interventions. Equality is a simpler goal than the technical targeting of interventions very precisely where their benefit will be greatest. For the right justice is more concerned with civil equality under the law, with an otherwise *laissez-faire* approach to social planning, in which inequalities could be allowed to arise spontaneously.

Inequality is not necessarily incompatible with both justice and **merit**. If it motivated the talents of some for the good of all, would we choose to tolerate inequality from behind the Rawlsian veil? In the absence of detailed social welfare calculations, can we trust professionals such as doctors, planners, social workers, or teachers to provide services to those who deserve them most? What about functional effects for the whole community? These questions raise a classic issue in social policy of the extent to which policies should strive for equality of outcome or equality of opportunity.

Equality of outcome means that after social policy interventions, differences between people in terms of their welfare are diminished. Their incomes, housing space, educational qualifications, might all be more similar than before. This might be possible to achieve through the expansion of some kinds of welfare available to all, such as total income, total healthcare, or total housing. In such cases everyone gains, although at different rates, and this is less likely to cause political controversy. However, other welfare is not expandable in the same way. Education is the classic case. While it is designed to give everyone the skills they need for adult life, it also has a major function of identifying and stratifying people by ability. In this respect it is a **positional good** (Box 4.6), in that there are only so many top positions, for example in business, medical, legal, or academic life, that can be occupied, just as there are only so many geographical points that can provide a panoramic view. If educational qualifications are expanded, they tend to lose their exclusivity at the same rate—the result of educational inflation.

In reality many kinds of welfare cannot be expanded indefinitely either, and the question arises of who merits access in preference to others. The alternative to equality of outcome is **equality of opportunity**, whereby we are all given equal support and help; but that thereafter inequalities are allowed to multiply, as individuals make what they can of their opportunities, and education, employment, income, housing, and so on are distributed according to merit rather than justice. The left has had a very ambivalent attitude to the question of equality. In principle it has supported equality of outcome, but in practice it has adopted equality of opportunity in its policies. For example, in the 1960s the Labour government removed the strongly symbolic secondary/grammar-school divide and developed comprehensive secondary education in the state sector as a radical push towards equality in education, yet at the same time left the private ('public') schools in place and rapidly expanded university education for middle-class children.

The right has also been inconsistent on issues of equality and merit. In principle the Conservative government in the 1980s strongly supported equality of opportunities,

---

Box 4.6 Positional goods

In his book *The Social Limits to Growth* (1977), Fred Hirsch observed that we desire some goods and services that are valuable to us in part because they are not available to everyone. For example, not everyone can enjoy a beautiful countryside view from a commanding height above the potential viewing-points of others. While there is a limited technical solution to the problem of mass viewing (as in football stadia and theatres), in the end there will have to be an unequal distribution of the view. He described these goods and services as 'positional goods'.

In social policy educational achievement is such a good, since part of the function of education is to stratify people, regardless of their objective achievement: only some will get the highest grades, get to the best universities, and develop high-status careers. For some people the attractions of privatized social services (experienced as exclusive and only available to the few) are also in part because they are positional goods. There are many other such goods: traffic-free roads, empty beaches, unpolluted atmosphere, personal autonomy. Hirsch argued that there is a compelling myth that we can all have access to such goods if only economic growth can be sustained at a fast enough pace. This, sadly, is an illusion.

but not equality of outcome. Yet in housing it has enabled many millions of tenants of state-owned housing to become highly satisfied property owners, and in higher education it engineered such a major expansion of university provision that BA degrees have become widely within reach of working-class children in a more radical manner than ever before (see Chapters 12 and 16). For other ideologies, the relative emphasis on equality of outcome or equality of opportunity has tended to produce disagreements within the movement. Light greens, liberal feminists, and the Asian minorities favour equality of opportunities; dark greens, socialist feminists, and the African-Caribbean minorities favour equality of outcomes.

Citizenship and Status

In recent social policy analysis, the concepts we have discussed—need, choice, rights, obligations, justice, and merit—have been brought together under the term of **citizenship.** Marshall argued that civil, political, and social rights define the conditions for citizenship to exist. His key observation was that there had been a steady expansion of areas in which citizens had defined rights. Citizens, Goodin (1988) has argued, were gaining membership of a community, and as a result were gaining entitlements available to all members of that community. Community membership ensured that needs would be met if possible, but that there would be obligations too. Being a community member was thus the key to welfare citizenship, implying access to universal services and a sense of social inclusion.

However, the term 'community', while it might imply relative homogeneity when applied to small groups or pre-industrial societies, is misleading with respect to modern industrial societies. Class stratification, gender and ethnic differences can multiply within a community, and hence between formally equal citizens. Citizenship equality is affected by people's positions in the social and economic structure; hence the term tends to carry quite different meanings for the ideological positions we have considered in this chapter. For the left, citizenship is about the solidarity expressed through a relatively altruistic welfare state built on the common experience of the Second World War. Participation in the normal life of the community is the mark of the citizen, and indeed has been used by Townsend (1979) as a sociological method of defining poverty as that condition which prevents full social participation. But, for the right, citizenship is confined to formal equality in law and politics without any prescribed level of social support. The new social movements have also been critical of defining citizenship as community membership. Lister (1990) points out that membership can mean very different things for men and women, black and white people, able-bodied and non-able-bodied people. Greens have worried that animals have been denied rights to their own welfare, and are thus clearly not regarded as full members of the human community.

This critique of citizenship as community membership has highlighted the question of the **status** of people, and especially whether they are excluded or included in the life of the community. Weber famously argued that modern societies are stratified not only by social class and by political power, but also by social status, meaning by this the esteem in which people are held. Status can be quite varied within any community, and may systematically exclude certain groups. Where community values celebrate ideals of masculinity, white culture, work, or mobility, those who are unable to embody such values tend to have a lower status or social esteem, and may find themselves excluded from the goods and services commonly available in that community. With the growth of income inequality during the 1980s there has been increased concern among social policy analysts that large sections of the UK community may have become excluded from the mainstream. While the left have expressed concern about this process, it has been the New Social Movements that have been particularly active in challenging the exclusion that results from low status. Feminists have challenged the male domination of public and private values which undervalues women; greens have challenged the celebration of continued economic growth and the dominance of paid work; anti-racists have celebrated ethnic diversity and dignity; and disabled people have affirmed the disabling effects for them of conventional architectural and technological arrangements.

Ideology, Ideologies, and the 'Good Society'

In this chapter we have observed that the major positions used in social policy debate are contested. Where there are attempts to persuade us of the inevitability or common sense of any particular policy, we should beware and consider the interests of those who support the policy. These interests are often organized into ideological positions which spill over into a range of issues. In recent years the previously simple choice between left and right has been complicated by new social movements and religious ideas which cut across the traditional political spectrum. The search for the 'good society' has become more uncertain.

Debate about social policy will always be inherently ideological. Nevertheless, we can identify many of the middle-range, normative concepts that form the building blocks of any particular ideological position. All ideologies use ideas such as needs, choices, obligations, merit, and status. Indeed, much policy debate consists of teasing out where a particular policy stands on these issues. This is because the policy goals and means that different sections of society would prefer to see, and think of as right and just, are determined both by their interests and their ideals. This chapter shows how interests and ideals combine particular normative principles into coherent sets of ideas constituting the competing ideologies that ultimately define the politics of welfare.

Glossary

choice Choice over goods and services can be established in markets through the act of buying. However, where these are distributed through administrative and professional means, the question of clients exercising choice can challenge received wisdoms about accepted welfare arrangements. It is difficult to increase choice for everyone, since the choices of some may restrict the choices of others.

citizenship The formal status conferred on a member of a national community. With it normally come a set of rights to equal treatment under the law, to vote, and to social support. It has famously been used by Marshall to analyse the twentieth-century welfare state (see Chapter 3, Box 3.8).

dominant ideology A term which comes out of a tradition of Marxist writing which argues that the economic relationships in a society determine the main social, political, and intellectual views of the day.

empowerment Recent developments in welfare debate have acknowledged that under the original 1948 arrangements, many clients of the welfare state were expected to be passive and grateful recipients of state handouts. There has now been a common criticism of this assumption on all sides in favour of clients having more power, dignity, respect, and autonomy through a process of empowerment.

equality of opportunity This means that citizens will be a given an equal start in life, but thereafter will be allowed to make what they can of their talents and opportunities.

equality of outcome This means that those with equal needs receive equal treatment. In turn this may mean that some disadvantaged people might receive more support than others.

explanatory ideals Social policy debate about the ideal goals of policies and the means of achieving them frequently includes discussions of the circumstances under which welfare states developed, and especially the way in which policies operate in the real world. Writers advocating particular policies may also have strong views about why welfare states exist and how they work. For example, 'defending' the welfare state makes assumptions about the circumstances under which welfare states exist or can be changed; or advocating a specific policy, such as to introduce market mechanisms or encourage professional change, will involve assumptions about how the policy will work in practice.

functionalist explanation A kind of explanation which views the social system as a whole, and which tends to argue that social arrangements exist because they work well to fulfil the functional requirements of the system. If those functions are not yet manifestly identified they are assumed to exist latently. This analysis thus tends to be circular, in that it both assumes functions and then uses them as an explanation. It is also teleological, in that it assumes that social development is evolving towards some kind of preferable end state.

grand narrative A term in post-modernist writing applied to wide-ranging and comprehensive schemes such as communism or fascism, designed to perfect human society.

Hippocratic oath The commitment, recorded from ancient Greece by Hippocrates, still traditionally given by medical doctors to work for the good of the patient, and to 'do the sick no harm'.

hyphenated society Marshall (1963) argued that by the middle of the twentieth century industrial society in the UK had developed to a balanced point that included a strong but not uncontrolled capitalist economy, and a comprehensive but not too intrusive welfare state brought about by democratic means. This balance, which he felt was a good one, was a mixture, or hybrid, whereby the various parts kept each other in check in a hyphenated society of democratic-welfare-capitalism.

justice A fair action in accordance with the rules. In social policy it has come to mean either the allocation of social services according to need, or, in the absence of our ability to actually measure all the many individual needs there are, it has been used to define an egalitarian society in which needs are most likely to be met equally. In complex societies it may be that an unequal distribution of services can increase the capacity of the whole system to meet needs, and simple egalitarian justice is thus difficult to operationalize.

merit Merit means that under the rules an individual receives what they deserve. For some writers this is an essential incentive for individuals to produce effectively for the whole system, and to deter others from non-production. For others the rules are seen to be devices for exclusion, such that the term 'merit' camouflages the systematic reproduction of inequalities.

needs The most central concept to social policy debate. Where goods and services are distributed outside the market, in which we can express our preferences through the act of buying, it is difficult to identify who should have what. What people need is established in relation to administratively or professionally defined norms, but these are inherently open to debate and challenge. In particular, beyond very basic needs for food and shelter, there is considerable cultural variation in social defined needs (see Chapter 6 for an extended discussion).

new social movements Social movements are collective attempts to change social arrangements through public campaigns. Traditional movements included the labour movement and the suffragette movement. Since the 1960s a number of new social movements have developed or renewed themselves as part of the general liberalization of social values at that time. These include movements focused on environmentalism, women, and anti-racism.

normative concepts Much debate in social policy between different major ideological positions, such as left and right, takes place at a middle range, or intermediate level, over particular concepts that are prescriptive—that is, they say what ought to or should be the case. The case for more or less state intervention, or equality, for example, is often made through appeal to these middle-range normative concepts, such as needs, choices, justice, merit, rights, and obligations.

normative ideals Social policy debate is not just about the scientific evidence for engineering social change, but also about the way society ought to be. This involves normative ideals, including both the desired end states we would like to push towards, and also the means with which we would like to get there. Many writers mix up ends and means in their writing, which we have to reflect on carefully in order to appreciate their views.

obligations In recent years most shades of ideological opinion have come to place increasing emphasis on the obligations that go along with the rights that individuals can acquire. This is in part a recognition of the anthropological observation of the central place of reciprocity in social life: exchanges are usually balanced, and in the case of a right the balance is an obligation. Thus an individual is expected to work hard, get better, or take employment in exchange for education, healthcare, and income support.

particular conception of ideology A concept used by Mannheim to indicate those ideas that an individual or group might express about particular circumstances, which are erroneous, and which may or may not be deliberately false, but which the proponent of the view has an interest in sustaining.

positional goods Some goods and services are valuable to us in part because they are not available to everyone. For example, not everyone can enjoy a beautiful countryside view from a commanding height above the potential viewing-points of others. Some social services, such as higher education, can be thought of in this way. While there is a limited technical solution to the problem of mass viewing (as in football stadia and theatres), in the end there will have to be an unequal distribution of the view. We can describe these goods and services as 'positional goods'.

post-modernism This is a new historical era, after the modern era, identified initially in architecture in the mid-1970s as a reaction to the functional designs of housing estates in the middle of the twentieth century all over the world. The term has since spread into social analysis through French intellectual work in the 1980s. An important part of this work has been to argue that there are no longer any grand ideas or schemes (see **grand narrative**) such as communism or fascism, that human society can follow to improve itself.

producer capture This occurs where the producer of a service is able to 'capture' and dictate the preferences of consumers and terms of service delivery. Professional groups such as doctors are accused of this control from time to time. Where consumer representatives or advocates have been set up, there is concern that in a more narrow sense they may also be captured and come to espouse the interests of the producers rather than the consumers.

quality of life The basis for one attempt at measuring medical need, and hence distinguishing between different medical cases where resources are limited and have to be rationed. The argument is that medical care should be used to maximize the number of years and the quality of life of the patient. In principle this allows a rational choice to be made, for example between a case where the quality of life will only be increased modestly but over many years, and a case where it may be increased substantially but for a short period only. This might favour the treatment of children over the treatment of older people, for example.

quasi-markets Markets in social services, such as schools and healthcare, set up administratively to encourage different providers to compete with each other in the hope that this will motivate them to increase quality, or at least cut costs, and that consumers will get greater choice as a result. They are not full markets, since there are many areas where natural monopolies operate, where real prices are difficult to set for complex services, or where it is not politically acceptable for services to be driven out of business. Experience to date suggests that the costs of inter-unit contractual development has been high, and that choice has not been greatly increased.

rights Constitutionally or legally defined capacities, such as the capacity to vote, usually conferred on members of the relevant community or society, often through the acquisition of citizenship. Where these involve freedom from constraint, such as the capacity to engage in religious worship, they are relatively simple to define and cheap to guarantee. Where they involve capacities that depend on the provision of services such as education, healthcare, or income maintenance, they are difficult to define and expensive to guarantee. The right have tended to argue for rights to freedom from constraint; the left have tended to argue for rights to services.

Seebohm Rowntree The Rowntree family owned the York-based chocolate business. Seebohm undertook several famous surveys of working families in York between 1898 and 1951. He showed in his early surveys that severe poverty was widespread, but that the post-war welfare state had all but eliminated it by 1951. There is a continuity of definition of the poverty line between his work, the Beveridge report, and current social security income support benefit levels. The Rowntree Foundation, which commemorates his work, now funds a wide range of social policy research into poor and disadvantaged people.

social administration The management of the production and distribution of social services in general. It was used to define the academic discipline of social administration from the late 1940s, when the first Chair in the subject was established at the University of Nottingham along with the national association which dealt with the subject, the Social Administration Association. In 1988 the title was changed to the Social Policy Association to reflect a wider academic interest in the sociological and political science analysis of the welfare state. 'Social administration' now connotes a rather limited and uncritical approach to the subject, dominant between the 1940s and the 1970s.

Social Darwinism In the nineteenth century the revolutionary biological ideas of Charles Darwin were applied to society and social relations by writers such as Spencer in the UK and Sumner in the USA. The main point taken from Darwin was the idea of the survival of the fittest, suggesting that state intervention to protect or support the weak was not only self-defeating, but might be positively harmful if it allowed the weak to flourish at the expense of the strong.

social reproduction The idea that in addition to the biological reproduction of human beings there is an equally important activity of reproducing the fundamental social relationships necessary to the continuity of human society. These include the capacity for relating to a group and responding appropriately to emotions, mostly learnt in families, and the capacity to learn and to work cooperatively, mostly learnt in schools.

status The esteem in which we are held in a community in relation to some of the central values cherished in that community. Max Weber argued that it was the third basic dimension that stratified societies alongside class and power. The new social movements have increasingly drawn attention to the way in which social values can divide people by esteem. Where maleness, whiteness, and physical and mental dexterity are esteemed, this can lower the status of women and black and disabled people.

total conception of ideology In this term Mannheim refers to the 'world view' of an individual or group, that is, their total way of looking at the world. It ranges across a number of social issues and may include erroneous ideas. It is bound up with their way of life and identity in such a way as to make it difficult for them to see issues from any other point of view. It has some similarity to the term **dominant ideology,** although Mannheim did not hold to the Marxist view that this was determined by prevailing economic relations in a society.

Guide to Further Reading

George, V. and Wilding, P., *Welfare and Ideology* (Hemel Hempstead: Harvester Wheatsheaf, 1994). This is the third edition of a well-known book on ideology and social policy, which tackles many of the issues very succinctly.

References

Abercrombie, N., Hill, S., and Turner, B. S. (1980), *The Dominant Ideology Thesis* (London: Allen and Unwin).

Bell, D. (1960/1965), *The End of Ideology* (New York: Free Press).

Beveridge, Sir W. (1942), *Social Insurance and Allied Services* (Cmd. 6404, London: HMSO).

Castles, F. G., and McKinlay, R. (1979), 'Public Welfare Provision, Scandinavia, and the Sheer Futility of the Sociological Approach to Politics', *British Journal of Political Science*, 9, 157–71.

Clasen, J. (1992), 'Unemployment Insurance in Two Countries: A Comparative Analysis of Great Britain and West Germany in the 1980s', *Journal of European Social Policy*, 2/4, 279–300.

Dale, J., and Foster, P. (1986), *Feminists and State Welfare* (London: Routledge & Kegan Paul).

Denny, D. (1985), 'Race and Crisis Management', in Nick Manning (ed.), *Social Problems and Welfare Ideology* (Aldershot: Gower).

Doyal, L. and Gough, I. (1991), *A Theory of Human Rights* (Basingstoke: Macmillan).

Ferris, J. (1991), 'Green Politics and the Future of Welfare', in Nick Manning (ed.), *Social Policy Review 1990–91* (Harlow: Longman).

Fukuyama, F. (1992), *The End of History and the Last Man* (London: Hamish Hamilton).

George, V. and Wilding, P. (1994), *Welfare and Ideology* (Hemel Hempstead: Harvester Wheatsheaf).

Goodin, R. E. (1988), *Reasons for Welfare: The Political Theory of the Welfare State* (Princeton University Press).

Hage, J. *et al.* (1989), *State Responsiveness and State Activism* (London: Unwin Hyman).

Harvey, D. (1990), *The Condition of Postmodernity: An Enquiry into the Origins of Cultural Change* (Oxford: Blackwell).

Hicks, A. and Swank, D. (1984), 'Welfare Expansion: A Comparative Analysis of 18 Advanced Capitalist Democracies, 1960–71', *Comparative Political Studies*, 17/1, 81–119.

Hicks, A., Swank, D., and Ambuhl, M. (1989), 'Welfare Expansion Revisited: 1957–1982', *European Journal of Political Research*, 17, 401–30.

Hirsch, F. (1977), *The Social Limits to Growth* (London: Routledge & Kegan Paul).

Kerr, C., Dunlop, John T., Harbison, F. and Myers, C. A. (1973), *Industrialism and Industrial Man* (Harmondsworth: Penguin).

Lister, R. (1990), 'Women, Economic Dependency and Citizenship', *Journal of Social Policy*, 19/4, 445–68.

Mann, M. (1970), 'The Social Cohesion of Liberal Democracy', *American Sociological Review*, 35, 423–39.

Mannheim, K., (1936/1968), *Ideology and Utopia: An Introduction to the Sociology of Knowledge* (London: Routledge & Kegan Paul).

Marshall, T. H. (1963), *Sociology at the Crossroads* (London: Heinemann).

Marx, K. and Engels, F. (1976), *The German Ideology* (Moscow: Progress Publishers).

Mauss, M. (1967), *The Gift: Forms and Functions of Exchange in Archaic Societies* (New York: W. W. Norton).

Mead, L. (1986), *Beyond Entitlement: The Social Obligations of Citizenship* (New York: Free Press).

Oliver, M. (1990), *The Politics of Disablement* (Basingstoke: Macmillan Education).

Pascall, G. (1997), *Social Policy: A New Feminist Analysis* (London: Routledge).

Rawls, J. (1972), *A Theory of Justice* (Oxford: Clarendon Press).

Stephens, J. D. (1979), *The Transition from Capitalism to Socialism* (London: Macmillan).

Taylor-Gooby, P. and Dale, J. (1981), *Social Theory and Social Welfare* (London: Edward Arnold).

Titmuss, R. (1974), *Social Policy: An Introduction* (London: Allen and Unwin).

Townsend, P. (1979), *Poverty in the United Kingdom: A Survey of Household Resources and Standards of Living* (Harmondsworth: Penguin).

Wedderburn, D. (1965), 'Facts and Theories of the Welfare State', in R. Miliband and J. Saville (eds.), *The Socialist Register* (London: Merlin Press).

Wilensky, H. L. (1981), 'Leftism, Catholicism, and Democratic Corporatism: The Role of Political Parties in Recent Welfare State Development', in P. Flora and A. J. Heidenheimer (eds.), *The Development of Welfare States in Europe and America* (London: Transaction Books).

Williams, F. (1989), *Social Policy: A Critical Introduction: Issues of Race, Gender and Class* (Cambridge: Polity).

Wilson, E. (1977), *Women & the Welfare State* (London: Tavistock Publications).

5 Economics and Social Policy

John Baldock

Contents

Introduction: The Relevance of Economics to the Study of Social Policy

Many social policy students are reluctant to spend their intellectual energy on understanding the economics of social policy questions. Indeed, one of the reasons people are attracted to the study of social policy is that they see it as being quite unlike economics: about social needs and compassion rather than about scarcity and competition. They do indeed see economics as a 'dismal science', and as one that tends to accept and even justify social conditions like poverty and inequality, the things that social policy seeks to remedy. However, social policy students cannot afford to avoid economics altogether, because without at least an awareness of the logical and practical realities that economic analysis can shed light on, all the social goodwill in the world may come to little. This chapter is therefore written for non-economists. It contains none of the graphical figures or algebraic formulae that are a frequent feature of economic textbooks, and seeks to explain some of the basic economic insights in plain English. In doing so it will inevitably offend some professional economists. However, its justification is that it is better that social policy students consider economic issues in a basic way than not at all.

One of the reasons for the tensions between social policy and economics is that they study very much the same phenomena, but from different points of view. They occupy the same intellectual territory, tackle the same problems. Both are essentially concerned with maximizing welfare, that is, getting the most benefit out of the resources available to us on this earth: producing as much as is sustainably possible and allocating what is produced in a fair and just way. Put more simply, they are both about the organization of production and consumption. Indeed, before the beginning of the twentieth century students of social policy and of economics would not have seen themselves as being in different disciplines, but as part of one that they would most probably have called **political economy.** Certainly Adam Smith, often seen as the father of modern economics and author of *An Inquiry into the Nature and Causes of the Wealth of Nations* in 1784 (published in a Penguin Classics edition in 1986), saw himself as a student of welfare. Equally people like Charles Booth, Seebohm Rowntree, Karl Marx, and Frederick Engels saw their research on poverty and employment as part of the study of economics.

Efficiency and Welfare

The central concern of economics is with efficiency. Adam Smith observed that although some nations are better endowed with resources, and some individuals have greater talents, none the less there remain huge differences in the wealth of nations that cannot simply be explained by these differences. A central determinant is how well a nation and its people organize their resources and labour to produce goods and services, and the efficiency with which that is done. Efficiency is fundamental to whether the welfare or standard of living of the people is high or low.

Two concepts lie at the heart of an economic understanding of efficiency: **marginal cost** and **marginal benefit**. Broadly speaking, economic efficiency is obtained when these are equal. One way of understanding this point is to consider an economy of only one person. This is why Robinson Crusoe features large in economic textbooks. Defoe's hero is a good example of the one-man economy. Initially Crusoe had only his labour and the resources available on the island out of which to construct his welfare, at least until Man Friday came along to help him. Crusoe could work at finding food and building shelter. At first the extra gain, the marginal benefit, he got from this work far outweighed the extra effort, the marginal cost. But there came a point where the additional labour (marginal cost) to improve his house and or to find more food outweighed the extra satisfaction (marginal benefit). At this point marginal cost exceeded marginal benefit and Robinson Crusoe's economy was slipping into inefficiency.

However, one of the obvious problems with the Crusoe analogy is that it is a great simplification of the real world we all live in. There is not just one of us and we do not just produce food and shelter. On the contrary, there are a very many of us working in different ways and desiring a huge range of goods in order to obtain our welfare. All the marginal costs of production and all the marginal benefits of consumption need to be compared in order to determine whether the economy is operating efficiently. Therefore economic theory constructs overall economic efficiency (what is called general equilibrium) out of three parts. **Efficiency in production** requires that labour and resources (what are called the factors of production) be combined in the optimal proportions producing as much as possible of each good. **Efficiency in product mix** requires that the combination and amounts of goods and services produced should be that most desired by consumers. **Efficiency in consumption** requires that output be divided amongst consumers in such a way as to maximize the sum of their satisfaction (or their utilities, as economists call them). Thus, to use the Robinson Crusoe analogy again, once Man Friday had appeared on the scene, efficiency in production required that he and Crusoe combine their labour and skills so as to produce as much as possible; efficiency in product mix required that they produce the combination of goods that maximized output in relation to their tastes, not too much of one and too little of another; and efficiency in consumption required that they divided their output between them so that their combined total utility was as high as possible. This would not necessarily mean they would consume equal amounts of everything; they would have different tastes, and they would prefer different amounts of different goods.

Two things become clear. First, even the simple two-person society on Defoe's island would face very complex choices in making the most of its resources. Second, whether Crusoe and Man Friday found ways to create an efficient island economy could have a profound effect on their material welfare and hence their senses of happiness and well-being. Economic efficiency is the key to optimizing welfare. It will be helped by good intentions, but not assured by them. Thus, for a complex modern society, while we can understand what economic efficiency would mean in principle, in practice we cannot calculate how near or far from it we are at a point in time. Indeed, this is an example of one of the key limitations of economics (and why social policy students are impatient with it); often it can tell us what in theory needs to be achieved, but it cannot tell us in practice whether we are succeeding or how we ought to go about it. Economic theory can show there is in principle a point at which the economy, in the sense of production and consumption, is organized in such a way that any change will make at least someone worse off without making any others better off. This point is called **Pareto efficiency**. The concept is named after its author, the French economist and sociologist Vilfredo Pareto (1848–1923), and it describes a state of equilibrium in an economy where all the marginal benefits of consumption are equal to each other, and are also equal to all the marginal costs of producing the goods and services that are being consumed. In fact, Pareto efficiency can be obtained at not just one point, but along a line of points, describing different but equally efficient arrangements of production and consumption. Because we cannot ever know whether an economy has achieved Pareto efficiency it is a concept useful only in principle. Of more practical use is the concept of a **Pareto improvement**. This is a change which takes an economy a step closer to the Pareto optimum. There is a Pareto improvement where a change in the organization of production or of consumption produces a net gain in welfare by making at least one person better off without making any others worse off. Taken together, the concepts of Pareto efficiency and of Pareto improvement can be used to test whether a social policy change is likely to make society better or worse off.

Two main areas of doubt have bothered economists and other social theorists in these respects. One concerns whether the pursuit of Pareto efficiency is likely to be fair and just; the other is what sort of system of economic arrangements is most likely to get closest to optimum economic efficiency. We will deal with each of these issues in turn. The first question is usually put by non-economists, such as moral philosophers, who find the definition of Pareto efficiency inadequate; their criticisms often revolve around the issue of how much inequality is acceptable in a society. The second tends to involve debates about the role of the market compared with other methods of economic organization.

Is an Efficient Economy a Fair Economy?

It might be assumed that an economy that was Pareto-efficient would be an equal society, that is, one in which all goods were allocated equally to all of us. However, because our needs and tastes differ (as well as the degrees to which we find work a **dis-welfare**) and because we do not all wish to consume the same goods in the same amounts, Pareto efficiency does not require equality. None the less, given that human beings are relatively similar in their abilities, needs, and desires, it is likely that Pareto-efficient economies would exhibit a great deal more equality than is seen in most countries. Why not then use social policy to take from the richer, whose total utility may be only slightly reduced, in order to give to the poor, for whom the gain in marginal utility would be much greater? This is the argument for **progressive taxation** in order to redistribute resources from the better-off to the less well-off. There is no doubt that this can create an increase in total utility in the immediate term. However, here we need to distinguish between **short-run efficiency**, a static condition in which the factors of production are conceived of as fixed, from **long-run efficiency**, in which **technical change** allows the productivity of labour and capital resources to be raised, so producing more with the same physical inputs. What would be the consequences for long-run efficiency if governments were always to intervene to reduce consumption inequalities by taxing the rich? (Note that these would not always be Pareto improvements, since they could make the rich less well-off in order to make the poorer better-off. A Pareto improvement would require that the rich valued the extra consumption of the poor more than their own use of the resources.) In the end this is a question that can only be answered by trying it and seeing what happens. Levels of taxation and redistribution do vary between countries, and there is always a continuing debate amongst politicians and economists as to how far these differences explain the range of national outputs and economic growth.

The trade-off between an immediate increase in equality, which would probably raise total utility in most economies, and the effects on future output due to economic growth cannot be calculated with any certainty: the number of variables to be taken account of are too many to answer the question historically and, anyway, the future is always different from the past. The debate therefore inevitably becomes one in which values and ideologies play a larger part than evidence. The concept of a Pareto improvement is essentially a conservative one, allowing change to current production and allocation only in so far as it makes some better off without making others worse off. Socialist ideologies and free-market ideologies are radical in that they are prepared to take a gamble on the future, arguing either that greater (enforced) equality will ultimately produce greater welfare, or alternatively that minimal or no government-led redistribution will make everyone better off in the long run (see Chapter 4).

An original contribution has been made to this debate by John Rawls, a moral philosopher, in his book *A Theory of Justice* (1972). Whereas all other theories of society (socialism, utilitarianism, libertarianism, etc.) prescribe a just society on the basis of estimates of the likely future development of the economy, Rawls's theory of justice is based entirely on a moral position independent of what may in fact occur in the real world. He asks what sort of a society we would regard as just were we not to know what our own position in that society would be. This is the famous 'veil of ignorance' from behind which his hypothetical society-makers would make their choice. Rawls suggests they would agree on a number of 'principles of justice' according to which society should be ordered. In particular, he argues that they would subscribe to a general principle of justice which required that 'all social primary goods—liberty and opportunity, income and wealth, and the bases of self-respect—are to be distributed equally unless an unequal distribution of any or all of these goods is to the advantage of the least favoured' (Rawls 1992: 303). The consequence for the economics of social policy is that no intervention should be made unless it can be shown to be to the benefit of the least well-off. This would not always be compatible with a Pareto improvement making no-one worse off.

However, the essential point here is about the primacy of values in any conception of efficiency. Economics can only test for efficiency in terms of some ultimate goal, be it a Pareto or a Rawlsian improvement or some other, which is in the last resort dependent on a value choice.

How Can an Economy Get as Close as Possible to Long-Run Economic Efficiency?

The pursuit of welfare through economic efficiency involves three levels of choice: first, the acceptance of a particular type of economic system; second, the management of that system; and third, the construction and implementation of particular social policies.

Pursuing Economic Efficiency 1: Choosing Between Economic Systems and Ideologies of Welfare

The concept of efficiency does not prescribe any particular economic system that will best achieve it. Economics is often associated by social policy students with a preference for free competition and a minimum of government interference in the operation of market forces. It may be true that most professional economists have concluded that competition is usually the best route to efficiency, but that is their judgement based on the evidence they see. There is no necessary link between markets and economic efficiency. In principle it is possible to conceive of a totally planned economy that gets closer to optimum efficiency than even the most efficient of existing market economies. Indeed, that is why for most of the twentieth century a substantial proportion of the world's population lived in societies that were experimenting with non-market economies. Communism and socialism had their roots in a huge body of historical and theoretical analysis, of which the writings of Karl Marx were a significant part, which suggested that market systems were inefficient, exploitative, and likely to collapse in on themselves. Setting aside the question of whether this view was right or not, it helped make the twentieth century one in which nations actually chose, sometimes through elections but more often through revolutions and political coups, their overall economic systems. A rationale which argues that one system of economic organization is best is essentially a political ideology. In this sense the twentieth century has been the century of ideology. Before that, governments and citizens had little concept of general systems of economic allocation which might be selected in preference to others. Rather, politics was focused on specific issues, and the general economic context was taken as given. Somewhat paradoxically, one of the chief gifts of economics to the modern world was not scientific pragmatism but the politics of ideology, whose central role in the evolution of social policy is discussed in more detail in Chapter 4. Suffice to say here that the notion that the main business of politics was to choose between whole economic systems led in the last 80 years or so to numerous conflicts and terrible suffering. There is nothing less likely to be an efficient source of welfare than war.

Pursuing Economic Efficiency 2: The Management of the Economy

With the collapse of the 'communist' systems of Eastern Europe and the former USSR, the market economy, moderated to varying degrees by state action, has become the general rule. In democracies citizens generally vote for politicians and parties that will increase their welfare by managing the economy effectively. In the 1992 presidential election Bill Clinton's campaign headquarters in Little Rock, Arkansas, had a big poster on the wall that said, 'It's the economy, stupid!' The point was to remind the campaign team that polls showed what voters most wanted was a president who would help the country out of the current economic recession. Throughout Clinton's presidency he remained a popular leader largely because he was seen by citizens as contributing to economic boom and the decline of unemployment.

The idea that political leaders are responsible for the successful overall management of the economy is another of the gifts of economics to modern politics. Economic management is a government's most fundamental welfare policy. Left to their own devices, economies tend to move between boom and recession. Until Maynard Keynes this phenomenon, called the **business cycle**, was generally thought by economists to be inevitable and a powerful constraint on the ability of governments to protect the welfare of their citizens. In industrial societies the main welfare consequence of the business cycle was mass unemployment in the depth of recessions. This became an increasing source of political instability as the proportion of a nation's population that was made up of urbanized wage-labour grew larger. In the years after the First World War, and particularly during the world industrial recession that was triggered by the Wall Street collapse of 1929, millions of workers and their families were cast into the poverty of unemployment, and existing social assistance schemes were overwhelmed. It was in the search for a solution to mass unemployment that the study of political economy separated into the more distinct academic subjects of social policy and economics. While economists sought to develop policy instruments that would control the business cycle, social policy, or 'social administration' as it was first called in Britain (see Chapter 2), emerged largely out of a search for systems which would provide for the welfare of those who found themselves out of work or unable to work. Economic policy became primarily concerned with the creation and maintenance of employment, and social policy came to be largely focused on meeting the needs of those outside or excluded from the job market. This is a distinction that remains today, despite governments' attempts to link welfare and work into a virtuous circle (see Chapters 7 and 11).

The unemployment rate in an industrial economy is a key indicator of both economic efficiency and social welfare. Economists recognize the inevitability of a degree of unemployment due both to the time it takes people to move from one job to another (frictional unemployment) and to the replacement of old industries with new ones (structural unemployment). However, beyond these, long-term mass unemployment is a symptom of production inefficiencies, a failure of the market to match available labour to demand; and it means that a country is producing less output, and is therefore arguably also producing less welfare, than it ideally could. High unemployment also indicates poor management of the economy, and the opportunity costs of lost output can be huge. During the period of high unemployment in the UK in the early 1980s the former Labour Chancellor of the Exchequer, Denis Healey, remarked that one 'cannot walk fifty yards down the road without seeing a job that needs doing and someone who could do it'. A core task of economic management is to find ways to match the two.

In 1936 John Maynard Keynes (1883–1946) published *The General Theory of Employment, Interest and Money*, in which he argued that governments could counter the business cycle by boosting the demand for goods during a downturn. When a recession looms people tend to save more rather than spend, and businesses tend to be cautious about investing. These rational responses at the individual level are counterproductive for the whole economy, tending to encourage an even deeper recession. Keynes showed how governments could encourage spending and investment by lowering the cost of borrowing through the central bank's influence on interest rates. A government could also create demand itself by spending more, financing the expenditure not out of balancing taxation but by borrowing, or even to a degree by printing money. Because of the availability of labour in a weakening economy, Keynes was able to show that such government expenditure would not be inflationary but would merely draw more labour into work, creating further demand and production. At the time of the publication of his General Theory Keynes had for some time been advising the British government to follow such a course, but so strong was the common-sense view (or conventional wisdom) that governments should reduce borrowing during a downturn in the business cycle that little heed was paid to his arguments in pre-war Britain. It was rearmament that pulled Britain and America out of recession. However, by the end of the Second World War Keynes's arguments, by now call **Keynesianism,** had been accepted by most political leaders, and a commitment to demand management and the maintenance of full employment formed the foundation of the post-war Beveridge welfare state. In May

1944, at the end of the war in Europe, the British wartime coalition government published a White Paper, *Employment Policy*, in which it promised:

The Government accept as one of their primary aims and responsibilities the maintenance of a high and stable level of employment after the war. This paper outlines the policy they will follow in pursuit of that aim.

A country will not suffer from mass unemployment so long as the total demand for its goods and services is maintained at a high level. But in this country we are obliged to consider external no less than internal demand. The Government are therefore seeking to create, through collaboration between the nations, the conditions of international trade that will make it possible for all countries to pursue policies of full employment to their mutual advantage.

If by these means the necessary expansion of our external trade can be assured, the Government believe that widespread unemployment in this country can be prevented by a policy of maintaining total internal expenditure.

(Cmd. 6527, 1944)

In this excerpt from the employment White Paper the central strength and the core weakness of Keynesianism are both captured. It was an invention as significant as any tangible product created by science or technology, providing a logic and a set of levers that governments could use to control the business cycle. Once a full employment economy was in place, the remainder of the welfare state—education, pensions, the National Health Service—could be financed out of the resources it would generate. But no nation could pursue these polices in isolation without pricing itself out of world markets. This was not too great a problem in 1944 and for the 30 years following, when Europe and the United States could match the productivity of most other nations. But since then the global mobility of capital, which allows almost any goods to be produced wherever labour is cheapest, has undermined the Keynesian logic in just the way the 1944 White Paper predicted.

In 1985 the British government published another White Paper, *Employment, the Challenge for the Nation*, that marked the demise of Keynesian demand management:

The world of work is changing fast in all the industrialized countries. Many of the older ones have found it difficult to cope with this, and the strains have shown in the unemployment that now casts a shadow over the whole of Western Europe . . . The United Kingdom has suffered along with others . . . Unemployment reflects our economy's failure to adjust to the circumstances and opportunities of today; to the changing pattern of consumer demand; to new competition from abroad; to innovation and technological development; and to world economic pressures . . . Improving the working of the labour market is particularly important. Jobs will be created to the extent that people are prepared to work at wages that employers can afford.

The key contribution of Government in a free society is to do all it can to create a climate in which enterprise can flourish, above all by removing obstacles to the working of markets . . . In short, Government must help set the framework for the nation's effort. But we shall never get enough jobs if we let ourselves imagine the effort can be left to Government.

(Cmnd 9497, 1985)

The difference in the commitments implied in these two White Papers, 41 years apart, demonstrates the most important post-war change in the social policy role of governments, particularly British governments: the abandonment of full employment as the fundamental social policy goal. The 1944 White Paper marked the beginning of what has been called a 'golden age' both for the economy and for people's welfare (Howlett 1994). The first level of choice in seeking economic efficiency appeared settled in favour of a social democratic combination of the market and the welfare state; the second level would involve governments managing economies by using Keynesian levers in order to obtain full employment and non-inflationary growth. However, by 1985 Keynesian economics had ceased to work. Running an economy at full employment generated unacceptably high levels of inflation, priced a country's goods too high in the global economy, and eventually forced governments to shift abruptly to high interest rates in order to finance public spending and support the currency. The economic management choices of governments everywhere became much more limited and routine, concerned with restraining public expenditure and limiting government borrowing in order to maintain international competitiveness. Research into the opinions of European politicians shows that traditional differences between left and right remain important in principle and at the level of political discourse, but that once in government politicians of all persuasions have during the 1990s agreed to relatively contractionist policies (George and Taylor-Gooby 1996).

Governments were left with only the third level of choice: to pursue relatively specific sets of social policies in so far as their budgets allowed. This shift was perhaps most revealingly demonstrated soon after the 1997 election when the new Labour chancellor of the exchequer, Gordon Brown, decided to hand over the management of interest rates to the Bank of England, guided by a special committee of appointed economic advisors, the Monetary Policy Committee. Instead of seeking to distinguish himself from the previous Conservative chancellor in terms of how he would manage the economy, Gordon Brown committed himself to the same economic targets. This reflects a growing consensus amongst economists that finance ministers now have relatively little freedom of manœuvre in the **macro-economic management** of their economies because of the effects of **globalization**. The British chancellor has therefore chosen to get involved in the more detailed determination of specific welfare policies, particularly those concerned with the social security system, issues that would not have been seen as important enough for a chancellor in earlier decades.

Pursuing Economic Efficiency 3: The Construction and Implementation of Particular Social Policies

Once the overall economic system has been decided and the parameters within which it will be managed have been taken outside everyday politics, economic criteria can still inform the design and implementation of discrete social policy initiatives. New policies can be considered in terms of their likely contribution to overall economic efficiency: are they likely to be Pareto improvements or not? Might a social policy be justifiable in terms of a set of ordered values, such as Rawls's principle of justice?

It is almost a universal axiom of economics that a government should not intervene in an existing economy unless doing so will produce an efficiency gain or achieve some other goal that is valued above efficiency, such as some criterion of social justice. It follows from this that any proposed state activity, such as a social policy, or even any continuing activity, should be carefully evaluated for its likely costs and outcomes.

Included in this evaluation should be some estimate of the **opportunity cost** of the proposed activity. That a social policy achieves its goals is not a sufficient reason to support it. The resources may have produced even more valued gains in some other area of government policy or had they been left to allocation by market forces. Economics provides a considerable armoury of concepts and analytical tools that can be used in policy evaluation, and it is a source of considerable frustration to economists that these are so rarely or so cavalierly used. For example, Nicholas Barr, in his book *The Economics of the Welfare State*, says firmly that:

The central argument of this book is that the proper place of ideology is in the choice of aims, particularly in the definition of social justice and in its trade-off with economic efficiency; but *once these aims have been agreed* the choice of method should be regarded as a *technical* issue rather than an ideological one. (Barr 1993: 100. Italics in original)

However, anyone with even a passing interest in the way in which social policies are initiated or changed will know that this simply does not happen. Technical questions, particularly the evaluations of economists, play very little part in the political processes that change social policy. One reason is to be found in the quotation from Barr itself. He writes, 'once these aims have been agreed'. Unfortunately they never are. There are always competing definitions of 'social justice and its trade-off with economic efficiency'. The politics of welfare, described in Chapter 3, are predominantly about competing values and interests and leave little room for technical questions. However, this should not stop social policy students from asking some of the more technical questions that economists would like to see posed.

   Market failure is the main economic justification for government intervention in societies where the market economy has been established and accepted as the dominant means of production and allocation. Market failure is essentially any fault that undermines the long-run matching of supply to demand (i.e. of marginal cost to marginal benefit). This can occur whenever any of the three types of efficiency mentioned earlier are not fully attained: production efficiency, product mix efficiency, and consumption efficiency. The most common signs of market failure are unmet demands, unused resources, excessive costs and prices, and the over-production of some goods and services. The sources of market failure are one of the main preoccupations of economic theory and occupy a substantial part of any standard economics textbook (e.g. Samuelson and Nordhaus 1992). The relevance of this to social policy is that market failures make the economy less efficient than it could otherwise be: it will therefore generate less welfare than it ideally could.

   There is considerable debate amongst economists and other interested social theorists as to when governments should intervene to try to correct market failures. Libertarians, such as Hayek (1944) and Friedman (1962) (see Chapter 4) often argue that intervention can make the problem worse and that it rarely constitutes a step towards greater efficiency. This is because in the short term it is difficult to calculate and remedy the inefficiency and, in the longer term, because state interventions tend to become institutionalized into large bureaucracies which are continued long after the imperfections they were designed to remedy have passed. Politicians and bureaucrats develop vested interests in sustaining and enlarging intervention in ways that will ultimately render the economy even less efficient than if the intervention had not happened in the first place. Interventions also often require funding through some form of general taxation. Economic analysis usually concludes that taxes make economies less efficient (because they raise the marginal cost of production at a given level of output) so there is a trade-off between the remedies for market failures and the efficiency costs of carrying them out.

Should governments choose to intervene, there are three main ways in which they can do so (see Chapter 1):

- Regulation, such as food hygiene standards; a requirement that motorists wear safety belts; or emission controls on vehicles and factories. Regulation can be relatively cheap for government because the costs generally fall on those who have to conform. However, it does require enforcement, with inspections to see if people are keeping to the rules, and prosecutions or other remedies if they are not.

- Taxes, subsidies, and one-off surcharges, such as taxes on smoking and drinking or subsidies to parents buying nursery education or to the rail network. Using taxes to discourage some activities and subsidies to encourage others does not require large bureaucracies, and the policies can be changed or withdrawn relatively quickly and easily. Subsidies are the more complicated, in that in order to subsidize a state must first obtain funds through taxation. One-off surcharges, such as the exceptional levy on the privatized utilities that the new Labour government imposed in 1998, appeal to economists. They can be calculated to extract just the right amount of extra-normal profit, and because they are one-off they do not have longer-term disincentive effects on investment and production.

- Provision, either in cash or kind, such as cash transfers like benefit payments (see Chapter 11) or the provision of education or health services (Chapters 12 and 13). However, in order to provide services in cash or kind, governments must first tax existing economic activities, and need to be sure that the value of state provision will outweigh the opportunity costs of the private consumption that may otherwise have taken place.

Box 5.1 gives some examples of the sorts of market failure that are commonly perceived as requiring government intervention which might be defined as social policy. The sources of market failure most relevant to social policy are the existence of what are

---

Box 5.1 Potential examples of market failure

Production inefficiency	Product mix inefficiency	Consumption inefficiency
Unemployment	Hospital waiting lists	Unbalanced access to higher education
Depletion of non-renewable resources	Too few nurses	High-risk surgical interventions
Environmental pollution by industry	Too many lawyers	Single-person car journeys
Unsafe foods	Too few children	Sheltered housing for relatively able people

called **public goods** and **merit goods,** the impact of **externalities,** and the consequences of **imperfect information.**

Public goods constitute the classic justification for government provision. They are those products and services which either would not exist at all without state intervention or of which too little would be produced and consumed. Common textbook examples are the provision of a lighthouse to warn ships of danger or of an army to defend a nation's borders. (Like many textbook cases, these examples may reveal the logic of the argument but are rarely crucial issues in the real world!) A public good is one for which people are willing to pay, but are unlikely to do so because such goods have the two characteristics of non-excludability and non-rivalness. **Non-excludability** means it is impossible to exclude those who have not paid for it from enjoying the good. If one ship owner were to set up a lighthouse, others could use it just as much but without paying. They would be what are known as **free-riders.** This does not necessarily mean that no lighthouses will be built: some shipowners may be wealthy and interested enough despite the free-riders. This is partly because of the characteristic of **non-rivalness;** others' use of the lighthouse does not diminish its benefit to the shipowner who built it. However, these two characteristics will together lead to market inefficiency, because fewer lighthouses will be built than the community as a whole would be willing to pay for. The same public-good characteristics apply to a defence force. If I live within the borders it defends I cannot be excluded from benefiting even if I am not paying (and neither if I am a pacifist can I reject the 'benefit'); and the benefit of one citizen does not lessen the benefit of another.

There are few examples of pure public goods (indeed, a standing army is probably the only widely accepted example), and one of their frequent characteristics is that, in addition to their defining characteristics, they are very expensive, far beyond the budgets of single individuals. They are what are sometimes called **lumpy goods:** too expensive for private purchase. It is this, possibly more than their non-excludability and non-rivalness, that actually makes them objects of public expenditure. Drinking fountains in market squares may effectively have performed as a public good, but because they were relatively cheap they were often paid for by a local benefactor. Indeed, the growth of local government has probably reduced rather than increased their supply.

Merit goods are more common than pure public goods. They are forms of private consumption which are thought to contain some additional social benefits as well; they contain the characteristics of both private and public goods. In part they are privately consumed in ways which diminish what is available to others (i.e. they exhibit rivalness), but they also possess a degree of non-excludable public benefit. Education and healthcare are the classic examples. Although the education of a child will be of advantage chiefly to that individual, everyone else in the economy may also gain to a degree from the benefits of having a more educated and productive member of the workforce. Education is also a 'lumpy good'. Many families could not afford the costs of even basic schooling. Left to the market, too little education would be produced and purchased; the marginal cost would be below the marginal value (which would include the individual utility and the social utility). Because citizens may not choose to consume the 'right' amount of a merit good, a feature of their provision is that they are both paid for by the state and made compulsory—for example, full-time education up to the age of

16 in the UK. It can be argued that the public-benefit element of higher education is not as great as it is for the provision of more basic skills in schools. Someone who trains to be a lawyer or accountant may personally consume most of the added value in enhanced lifetime earnings, and there may be little or no public benefit, particularly if there are more lawyers and accountants than there are jobs. To some extent this is the argument in favour of student loans, particularly schemes under which repayment only begins once the beneficiary has reached a certain level of earnings, as in the UK. In the case of healthcare, the merit-good argument can reach more uncomfortable conclusions. If we accept that the social benefit from health treatment is greater for younger people because they are likely to have more economically active years ahead of them, we might conclude that older people, particularly the retired, should either pay a larger proportion of their health costs or receive less expensive care. The public-benefit case might also lead one to conclude that those whose illnesses are curable should have more spent on them than those who are unlikely to survive.

Sometimes, the social value of a merit good takes a form which reduces a utility loss to members of the public rather than giving them added value. We might all feel uncomfortable about the prospect of elderly people getting poorer healthcare and be prepared to pay to reduce that moral discomfort. To take another example, there are merit-good aspects to the provision of forms of poor relief. Assume that we are all willing to pay to some degree to ensure that people do not live below a certain level—because we will derive value from seeing and knowing of less poverty around us. If provision is made voluntarily in the form of charitable giving, as it often was before the modern welfare state, all of us will benefit from the outcome, and the benefit of one does not exclude the benefit of another. But some will choose not to contribute and to be free-riders, and the amount of poor relief provided will be too low: less than the point where its marginal cost equals its marginal benefit. Similar arguments may apply to services to protect children from cruelty, to protect animals, and so on. The key point is that state provision financed by compulsory taxation may be a better way to ensure that a more efficient quantity of these goods is produced. But it does not guarantee that a government will tax and spend on them in a way that adequately reflects the utility that citizens are prepared to pay for. Governments are reliant on an imperfect political process to signal the nature and volume of demand for merit goods. Government may even seek to side with the free-riders, funding too little and hoping the charitable sector will fill the gap. However, if the demand for provisions which have substantial public-good characteristics is left to private and charitable purchases, supply will certainly be less than Pareto efficient.

Externalities have features that are closely related to public and merit goods and similarly can be used to argue for state intervention. External costs and external benefits are those that affect people who are not directly involved in the activities of the producer and consumer of a good. Many examples of **external costs** come from studies of the harmful environmental effects of market activities (see Chapter 18) and these are increasingly defined as social policy issues because of their long-term effects on a community's welfare. The production of electricity from oil or coal may impose pollution costs on those who live close to a power station; the use of pesticides on crops may ultimately damage people's health; the private use of the motor car may crowd the roads, pollute the atmosphere, and kill and wound pedestrians. In all these cases more of these goods may be produced and consumed than a perfect market would allow because their producers and consumers are not bearing the full costs of what they do. Costs are shifted to others who have not chosen to accept them. The standard economics answer is to tax the relevant producers and consumers with the cost of compensating those who are affected by the externality. While feasible in theory, this is very difficult to do in practice, because often the value and distribution of the external costs may be difficult to establish. Alternatively, many forms of consumption have **external benefits**. Indeed, merit goods are those where the external benefit is large and widely distributed enough to be used to justify public funding or even provision. But many more forms of private consumption have positive externalities. If I keep a nice garden there may be some benefit to neighbours, but probably not enough to justify public funding.

Imperfect information is a fundamental risk to the efficiency of all types of economy, but it is most particularly a threat to competitive markets. It is also used as a justification for some forms of state provision. Imperfect information refers to uncertainties about prices, quality, availability, and the future. In order for a market to work efficiently both producers and consumers must have good information (in principle, perfect information) about prices set by all the competing producers and of the quality of the goods and services they provide. Only in this way can true marginal cost be brought into equilibrium with true marginal benefit. A conscientious shopper for food in a town with several of the national supermarket chains represented might well be close to a position of perfect information. But a sick person searching for the most appropriate and cheapest medical care is likely to face a huge information deficit (see Box 5.2). This being so, a free market in healthcare is likely to be very inefficient and unfair. In practice there tends to be over-production of some forms of healthcare and under-production of others, and on a very large scale and leading to substantial opportunity costs for the economy (see Chapter 13). Similar arguments can be advanced to a lesser degree for education and social-care services. In all of these cases consumers are likely to be poor judges of their needs. However, public provision is not an automatic solution to the efficient allocation of products and services with high information costs. A public service may be equally poor in monitoring the quality of its services and discovering the needs of its users. The inefficiencies will still be there; they will just be of a different sort.

Uncertainty about the future is a key informational imperfection. For producers the costs of their raw materials, capital, and labour may change abruptly, such as the price of energy. Consumers may have poor information about their future needs in some areas, as a result of accidents, illness, and old age, for example. The miscalculation of risk is a source of economic inefficiency. Where the distribution of these risks is predictable across whole populations (i.e. in an actuarial sense) economic theory indicates that private insurance is the most efficient solution to uncertainty. If the uncertainty has no social implications and the costs of insurance are relatively low then the issue can be left entirely in the private sector. However, there are a number of limitations to private insurance that can lead to state intervention. Some risks are both very expensive and will lead to social costs if people have not troubled to take out insurance, such as acute medical care, long-term nursing care, and unemployment. Individuals left to their own devices will tend to underestimate the risk of future needs; they tend to discount future

---

Box 5.2 The problems of uncertainty facing the consumer of medical care

- Many consumers do not desire medical care.
- Many consumers do not know they need medical care.
- Consumers do not know how much medical care they may want or need in the future or how much it might cost.
- Consumers do not know what particular kinds of medical care will meet their needs: surgery, diagnostic tests, drugs, etc.
- Consumers do not often accumulate previous experience of particular medical interventions.
- Consumers cannot tell whether they have got good or bad medical care, either before, during, or after consumption.
- Consumers enter the doctor–patient relationship on an unequal basis, where both think the 'doctor knows best'.
- Medical care cannot be returned, exchanged, or discarded and its outcomes are often irreversible.
- Consumers can rarely exchange valid information about the use of 'good' or 'bad' medical care.
- It is difficult to change one's mind during the course of consuming an episode of medical care.
- There is no useable concept of the 'average consumer' to underpin marketed provision when there is such variety in illness and degrees of disability.
- Consumers from other cultures and systems of belief may also be very different to any concept of the 'average consumer'.

Source: adapted from Titmuss 1976: 146–7.

---

risk. Those who face the highest risks may be the least able to pay the contributions. In addition, insurers face the problem of **moral hazard**, people hiding information that reveals the true risks they face, for example of illness, or behaving in ways that increase them, for example not saving for old age. Insurers may respond by using **adverse selection** either not to ensure some groups or to charge them very high premiums. One answer is state regulation requiring **compulsory insurance** of a risk up to some minimum. Compulsory social insurance, particularly for unemployment and pensions, is the foundation of many welfare systems, particularly those of western Europe such as Germany, Austria, the Netherlands, and Switzerland. The main problem with social insurance funds is that, over time, the demands on them tend to exceed the accumulated value of the premiums (i.e. the social security contribution rates) that the state finds it politically possible to impose. State subsidies out of general taxation then become necessary, blurring the line between pure state provision and social insurance.

Overall, the main conclusion of this section on the economic justifications for specific social policy interventions is that they should be concerned with showing how the existing system, usually the market, is failing to achieve a desired outcome efficiently. They should demonstrate market failure. Economic analysis also tends to support the minimum possible intervention in the status quo, preferring regulation and taxation to subsidies and direct provision.

Introducing Market Disciplines into Public Welfare Systems

Over the last decade in the UK and elsewhere some of the large public welfare bureaucracies have been reformed in ways that attempt to introduce market disciplines into the way they work. There are two main ways in which this has been done. **Purchaser–provider splits** separate the bureaucracies into separate parts, one of which assesses the need for a service and then commissions the other part, consisting of the providers who are to supply it. The changes to the NHS and local authority social services took this form following the recommendations of reports from Sir Roy Griffiths and the implementation of the National Health Service and Community Care Act 1990 (see Chapters 13 and 14). As a result Local Health Authorities and GP fundholders purchased healthcare services on behalf of their patients from the hospital trusts and the community health trusts. Under this arrangement both purchasers and providers remained within the public sector and funds for these **internal markets** still came from the taxpayer. A further development of this model requires the purchasers to buy services from outside the public sector, from voluntary agencies, and from private for-profit agencies. This is known as **contracting out.** In spending on domiciliary care and nursing-home care for old people, the local authority social services departments were required from April 1994 to spend some two-thirds of public funds on contracting out the provision of services to agencies outside the state sector.

Overall these internal markets and contracting out arrangements are known as **quasi-markets.** This reflects the fact that they differ from real markets in a number of important ways. First, the ultimate consumer of the service, such as the patient or the user of home care services, is not the direct purchaser. This is done on their behalf by public professionals, such as GPs and case-managers. Thus one of the key elements of market efficiency—clear signals which match the utility of consumers to the costs of provision—is missing. Second, quasi-markets usually involve cash-limited spending by the purchasers. For example, the UK government allocates specific sums per year for the purchase of health services or nursing home provision. In a real market spending would tend to rise so long as the marginal benefit of the services exceeded the marginal cost. There is therefore a bias to inefficient underspending built into most quasi-markets in the public sector.

The main justification for quasi-market arrangements is that they will force service providers to be more cost-efficient. Because the providers will have to compete to win contracts and work from the purchasers they will be obliged to keep their costs as low as possible. But if cost-savings become the paramount goal they may put pressure on professional standards, and particularly on the distinctive qualities of the voluntary sector where welfare provision has traditionally been driven by moral imperatives. Trust, one of the key values of a welfare system, between service users and the providers may be undermined.

The relationship moves from a relatively informal model based on trust, verbal agreements and an assumed value commitment to 'do the best we can with the money', to a more formal model based on a culture of precise service-led agreements and legally binding contracts. But will the more formal approach remain compatible with widely accepted voluntary sector virtues of flexibility and innovation? Will voluntary organizations [and professionals] do less as they deliver only the level of service identified in the bid and the contract? (Kendall *et al.* 1997: 195)

Conclusion: The Relationship of Economics to Social Policy

Some readers will have noticed that this chapter has made no reference to money. Yet much of the debate about social welfare today is concerned with how it should be paid for and whether 'the money can be found'. It is safe to say that many students of social policy would expect to see 'economics' on the side of and amongst the arguments of those who would restrict public expenditure on welfare. The main aim of this chapter is to show that economics is not about money and that there is nothing in economic theory that is the enemy of the welfare state.

Economics is not about money, it is about resources—labour, knowledge, and real assets—and their allocation. A country will have higher standards of welfare if it finds ways to allocate its resources in a manner that best fits the long-run preferences of its citizens. Economics is not a guide to what those preferences should be but to how, in principle, they can be matched with work and production. The key question economic analysis would ask of any proposed social policy is not how much money it will cost, but what alternative uses of the resources are there to the one proposed, and whether they would generate more or less benefit. The economic cost of a social policy outcome is all the other potential outcomes that have been forgone: the opportunity cost.

Readers will also have observed that economic evaluation is more often used, if it is used at all, to test existing policies than it is to justify new ones. Welfare initiatives are generally driven by a combination of strong political support, such as the electoral commitments of a government, and a set of ideological beliefs, such as a view that competitive markets are best. Governments do not have the time or the political will to subject their welfare interventions, or reductions in them, to the testing that economic theory suggests they ought to use.

Glossary

adverse selection The exclusion from insurance cover or from an entitlement to a benefit of those who are most likely to need it, such as the exclusion of the sickest from hospital or of young drivers from motor insurance at a reasonable cost.

business cycle The tendency of an economy to move in waves between periods of growing output and employment and falling output and greater unemployment.

compulsory insurance When the government requires by law that people insure against a risk; for example, all workers must pay for social insurance and all drivers must cover against third-party harm in accidents.

contracting out When the responsible (state) organization contracts out the performance of a task (such as refuse collection) or the provision of a service (such as nursing-home care) to another, often private or voluntary, agency.

dis-welfare An experience, either unavoidable consumption (neighbour's noise) or a price paid (work, illness, taxes), that reduces total utility enjoyed.

efficiency in production Combining the factors of production (land and capital, labour and knowledge) in the proportions that produce a good or service as cheaply as possible.

efficiency in product mix Producing just that combination of goods and resources that most cheaply meets all the wishes of consumers.

efficiency in consumption Allocating the total available production of goods and services amongst consumers so that they are all satisfied equally and as much as possible.

externalities (external costs and external benefits) Either the costs or the benefits that economic behaviour bestows on those who are not parties to the bargain; for example, the damage done to a house by passing lorries, or the 'gain' from living close to a perfume factory.

free-riders Someone who benefits from some good or service without paying for it or contributing to its production, such as the student in a flat-share who never cleans or buys milk.

globalization In its economic sense: the tendency for the world to become one market, in which goods will be produced where costs are lowest and sold where prices are highest.

GNP and GDP Gross National Product is all of a country's output of goods and services (usually in a calendar year) plus income from assets abroad, but with no deduction (that is, gross, not net) for depreciation in the value of the country's assets. Gross Domestic Product is this, but excludes income from assets abroad.

imperfect information Not knowing entirely what is available in the economy, at what qualities and at what costs.

internal markets Pseudo- or quasi-markets within an organization or a service system where one part plays the part of purchaser and the other of provider. Real money transfers or merely shadow prices may be used.

Keynesianism Named after the political economist, John Maynard Keynes (1883–1946); a general theory of how a market economy works which emphasizes the role of total demand (aggregate demand) and the need to maintain it at a level which ensures high output and low unemployment.

long-run efficiency Obtaining economic efficiency over a variously specified longer term, usually several years, and contrasted with short-run efficiency. Long-run efficiency usually requires saving, investment, and innovation.

lumpy goods Those products that cannot be bought in small amounts, such as a house or primary education. This means that many people may not be able to afford them.

macro-economic management The management by a government of the overall performance of the economy using such controls as interest rates, taxes, and government spending.

marginal benefit The satisfaction or utility gained by the consumption of the last unit of a product, such as the last mouthful in a meal or the last day of a holiday.

marginal cost The cost, measured either in money spent or the effort of work, of obtaining or producing the last unit of output, such as the last car off the production line or the last working hour of the week.

market failure When the market fails to produce what is most wanted at the lowest possible price: usually reflected in unemployed resources, unconsumed output, or unmet demands.

merit goods Goods and services where individual consumption also produces a more general community benefit, such as a child's consumption of education.

moral hazard The unmeasurable risk of extra expense faced by a welfare system or by an insurance company because people may either fail to admit to risk factors or may be less careful once they know the risk is covered; for example, someone who leaves a job because there is income support, or who leaves doors unlocked because of cover against theft.

non-excludability In the economic sense: the impossibility of excluding someone from benefiting from or using some product, such as from a public good like a national defence force.

non-rivalness A situation where one person's consumption of a (public) good does not reduce what is available to another; for example, a television signal.

opportunity cost Refers to the value of all possible lost opportunities to consume resources in ways other than the current or proposed one.

Pareto efficiency A balanced position of production and consumption where any change will make at least one person worse off.

Pareto improvement A change in production of allocation of goods or services that makes at least one person better off while making no-one worse off.

political economy A term used to describe the study of, and the operation of, the combined arrangements of government and the workings of the economy in a society. It is typically a nineteenth-century term. David Ricardo (1772–1823) and John Stewart Mill (1806–73) saw their work as the construction of theories of political economy, while Karl Marx (1818–83) called his famous work *Capital: A Critique of Political Economy*.

progressive taxation Taxation, usually of income, that takes a larger proportion of whatever is taxed the more someone has of it, such as a tax rate that starts at 10 per cent of income and rises in stages to a higher rate such as 40 per cent.

public goods Products from which people cannot be excluded from consumption (such as fresh air) and where one person's consumption does not reduce what is available to another. There is no possible profit in the production and marketing of such goods.

purchaser–provider splits The separation of a state welfare bureaucracy into one part that commissions the provision and another part that 'contracts' to provide it.

quasi-markets Where internal markets or contracting out are limited by regulations that mean the arrangements are not fully exposed to market competition.

short-run efficiency Obtaining the maximum satisfaction at the lowest cost in the very immediate term. Unlike long-run efficiency, this is usually obtained by using up all resources as fast as possible; for example, in a war.

technical change Inventions and innovations that allow cheaper ways of producing existing goods or which create new goods.

Guide to Further Reading

The best book on the economics of social policy is Nicholas Barr's *The Economics of the Welfare State* (Oxford: Oxford University Press, 1998), now in its third edition. It is written for non-economists as well as those who have some grounding in the subject. Howard Glennerster's *Paying for Welfare: Towards 2000* (Prentice Hall/Harvester Wheatsheaf, 1997) provides in its opening chapters a particularly lucid account of the economic issues associated with social spending. Similarly accessible to many social policy students is Julian Le Grand, Carol Propper, and Ray Robinson's *The Economics of Social Problems* now in its third edition (London: Macmillan, 1993). More difficult, and more suitable for those with some preference for economics, is Anthony Culyer's *The Political Economy of Social Policy* (London: Martin Robertson, 1980). If you are prepared to read a whole book in order to grasp the economist's sceptical ways of looking at social issues, Fred Hirsch's *Social Limits to Growth* (London and Henley: Routledge and Kegan Paul, 1977) and James Meade's *The Intelligent Radical's Guide to Economic Policy* (London: George Allen and Unwin, 1975) are very stimulating.

References

Barr, N. (1993), *The Economics of the Welfare State* (2nd edn., Oxford: Oxford University Press).

Friedman, M. (1962), *Capitalism and Freedom* (Chicago: University of Chicago Press).

George, V. and Taylor-Gooby, P. (eds.) (1996), *European Welfare Policy* (Basingstoke: Macmillan).

Hayek, F. (1944), *The Road to Serfdom* (London: Routledge and Sons).

Howlett, P. (1994), 'The Golden Age, 1955–1973', in Johnson (1994), 310–39.

Johnson, P. (1994) (ed.), *Twentieth-Century Britain: Economic, Social and Cultural Change* (London: Longman).

Kendall, I., Blackmore, M., Bradshaw, Y., Jenkinson, S., and Johnson, N. (1997), 'Quality Services in Quasi-Markets', *Social Policy Review*, 9, 184–202.

Keynes, J. M. (1936), *The General Theory of Employment, Interest and Money* (London: Macmillan and Co.).

Rawls, J. (1972), *A Theory of Justice* (Oxford: Clarendon Press).

Samuelson, P. A. and Nordhaus, W. D. (1992), *Economics* (14th edn., New York and London).

Titmuss, R. M. (1976), *Commitment to Welfare* (London: Allen and Unwin).

6 Social Need and Patterns of Inequality and Difference

Mark Liddiard

Contents

Introduction: A Contestable Concept at the Heart of Social Policy

The concept of 'social need' lies at the heart of social policy. Arguably, the recognition and satisfaction of need distinguishes the welfare function of the state from its other roles and activities. Inseparably linked to the debates about the nature, effectiveness, and cost of the welfare state has been the issue of how far it meets which needs. Yet the concept of 'need' poses difficult conceptual and normative questions. How do we decide which are valid 'needs' and which are not? If some 'needs' are more or less legitimate than others, how do we decide which 'needs' are a priority, and which are not? Are there any needs which are so basic and fundamental that ensuring they are met may be part of an individual's rights and an obligation of the state? Even if one can establish a measure of 'basic needs', as some authors claim, should the meeting of these be the responsibility of the government, or rather the responsibility of others, such as families and charity?

These questions are fundamental to social policy, and the subject has long acknowledged the significance of 'need' as a rationing device, whereby resources of different kinds are distributed according to various criteria of entitlement. Different groups and individuals have radically different ideas about what should be defined as 'need', and which should not. Often, the concept of 'need' has seemed to be highly subjective and beyond 'objective' agreement. In the 1990s these dilemmas came to the fore in a number of areas, most publicly in the context of healthcare, where medical professionals have been in the unenviable position of having to decide upon the validity of some people's health needs over others.

The definition of social need is thus crucial to social policy, and the lack of consensus about which needs should take priority lies at the conceptual heart of welfare. Whilst it may be possible to justify state involvement in the provision of welfare in terms of meeting social need, if the needs which state welfare and ultimately state resources are supposed to be meeting are vague and ill-defined, so the arguments in favour of state welfare are weakened. Yet clarifying the nature of social need is more than simply a theoretical debate—it has real practical significance. Access to resources and the distribution of these resources are often heavily dependent upon notions of 'need'.

Defining 'Need'

A key characteristic of 'need' is the fact that it can be defined and measured from a variety of perspectives. Jonathan Bradshaw (1972) made this diversity the basis of his taxonomy of social need, in which he outlines four types of need.

Normative need is the name given to the way in which an expert or professional may define need in the context of a set of professional or expert standards. Welfare professionals reach judgements about what may or may not be legitimate need. They are active in the processes which decide whether or not a need exists and, if it does, how it may best be met within the confines of existing resources. The judgements of welfare professionals and the bodies of knowledge and standards that they use are clearly an important feature in defining 'need'.

Felt need is the name given to what a person or a group believe they 'need'. This conception relies upon the individual's own perception of need and any discrepancy between their situation, and what they believe it ought to be. However, this self-perception is likely to be subjective and may be better described as a 'want'. Felt need is necessarily affected by the knowledge and expectations of the individual, which may be unrealistic. Alternatively, researchers have shown that the poorest sections of society may be only marginally aware of their poverty and the extent of their need.

Expressed need is a felt need that has become a demand. Academics have argued that social need can be closely associated with either an effective economic or political demand. Yet it is important to acknowledge that just because people have the power to demand something, this does not necessarily imply that they need it. In this sense, it is important to distinguish between 'need' and 'demand'.

Comparative need is the name given to need defined by comparing the differences in people's access to resources. This approach recognizes that 'need' is a relative concept, and so any debate about it must take place in the context of a comparison between people. Need may be defined in terms of the average standards found within a community or society, or by comparing the resources available to some in contrast to others who are defined as similarly entitled. A comparative approach has, of course, been most widely employed in the context of debates about poverty.

Bradshaw's taxonomy is very helpful in setting out the range of ways in which 'need' can be approached and understood. A number of authors have developed these ideas further in a number of ways, one of whom was Forder (1974), with his concept of **technical need.**

Technical need is the name given to a need which arises when a new form of provision is invented, or existing provision is made much more effective. This in turn creates a need for a solution that previously did not exist. Once a new invention has occurred it can then lead to forms of felt, expressed, normative, and comparative need. Advances in medical technology are the most common example of this, and one of the most pertinent illustrations is the development of Viagra, the male anti-impotency pill.

There is a question as to the degree to which it is possible to reach any consensus about 'need', and whether or not there are any features of need which can be identified as essentially incontestable. Many social theorists have sought to establish basic needs

---

Box 6.1 Viagra and the NHS

The successful development of Viagra for the treatment of male impotence, and the ensuing debate about its availability on the NHS, is an excellent illustration of **technical need** and the issues it raises for considering need more generally. The publicity surrounding Viagra has certainly generated a **felt need.** Interestingly, however, it has also led to much more **expressed need** by legitimizing a request that had previously been highly stigmatized. There has also been a strong element of **comparative need** in this debate—people may have access to it in some countries or areas and not in others. The Government are certainly keen to avoid 'prescription by postcode', but whilst Viagra is currently not available on the NHS, it is none the less freely available to those able and willing to pay for a private consultancy. The debate here is also very much about **normative need,** and about who should be the arbiter of need, government, professionals, or consumers.

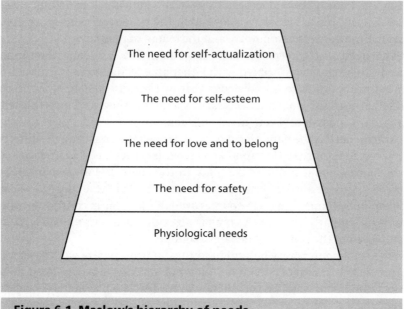

Figure 6.1 Maslow's hierarchy of needs

with which all would be likely to agree. The importance of trying to establish a list of basic needs should not be underestimated. If one can establish a concrete and agreed set of basic needs which really should be met in a society, it may be much easier to add legitimacy to the very existence of welfare states, whose objective is to meet need.

Attempts to produce a list of human needs have taken a variety of different forms, and one of the first to construct such a list was Maslow (1954), who set out a hierarchy of five basic needs, and argued that once the most basic need for survival (physiological need) is met, so further ones demand attention in succession.

Whilst Maslow's basic human needs are of some theoretical interest, it is immediately apparent that they present real practical difficulties. Not only are they difficult to measure, but they will also vary from individual to individual. Given the fluidity of such needs, it would evidently be impossible to expect state action to ensure that every citizen had them met.

David Harvey (1973) sought to move this debate on by identifying nine categories, goods, and services that people require in order to meet the human needs Maslow had set out: food; housing; medical care; education; social and environmental services; consumer goods; recreational opportunities; neighbourhood opportunities; and transport facilities. The real difficulty with such lists of need, however, comes when considering the relative importance of each of these categories. Clearly, not all forms of need carry equal significance and importance. According to Maslow, only the basic physiological needs are essential for sustaining life and must necessarily be met before higher needs. Yet how do we rank the remaining 'needs'? The real problem here is that what we perceive and define as valid and legitimate 'needs' may be little more than subjective judgements, relative to the society and time period in which they are being made. The implication is that whilst real and important steps may be taken in addressing various agreed needs in society, as social values and ideas about what is essential to living as a full member of society shift, so in turn may the notion of what people legitimately need. In short, the debate about 'need' can be seen to be inherently relative, and heavily influenced by time and social context. Some observers believe that the relative nature of social need means that attempts to measure and order forms of need are essentially misguided and ultimately doomed to failure. They argue that debate about need may ultimately be little more than a political one, in which different political positions succeed or fail in insisting on their particular conception of need.

Can we Establish a Level of Basic Needs?

Is it possible to say that there are any basic needs which, once they have been identified, really ought to be met? This is an important question, because if one can establish that there are certain basic needs the meeting of which are essential for any civilized human being, then this may begin to establish an argument in favour of the welfare state.

A starting-point for establishing basic needs is the notion that needs are related to ends; that is, in order to achieve certain ends in life, such as a high level of education, one may have first to fulfil a variety of needs—the need for financial support; the need for childcare; the need for adequate transport; and so on. Indeed, the distinction here is between **ultimate needs** and **intermediate needs**. Ultimate needs are the ends to which other activities are directed; in contrast, intermediate needs are not ends in themselves, but are rather a means to an end. For instance, we may need something, such as a basic education, in order to fulfil other needs, such as finding a job.

Yet we all have many different ends in sight, and we believe we need different things in order to achieve our ends. We could never say that everyone should have whatever they require in order to fulfil their ends in life—the list of potential needs is infinite. None the less, some writers, particularly Raymond Plant, have made some important progress here by attempting to identify what people need in order to achieve any ends in life at all.

These needs might be regarded generally as physical well-being and autonomy: an individual would have to be able to function efficiently as a physical entity and have freedom to deliberate and choose between alternatives if he is to pursue any conception of the good. (Plant 1985: 18)

In short, Plant (1985) suggests that it is possible to identify two basic needs in any society. First, there is a need for physical survival, without which we obviously cannot hope to achieve anything! Second, Plant argues that there is a basic need for autonomy, or freedom. In order to make genuine choices about our paths in life, we need to have autonomy and the freedom to make informed choices. These two basic needs are crucial, argues Plant, because unless they are met we cannot hope to achieve any ends at all in life.

These arguments seek to derive needs from basic human goals upon which we might all agree. None the less, there do seem to be a number of problems here, not least of which is the question of what rights to survival and autonomy actually justify in practice. Plant, for instance, interprets survival as effectively referring to health. In this sense one can argue that this justifies the provision of healthcare. However, the level and extent of healthcare being argued for remains very unclear. Does the argument that people need it to ensure survival really extend to saying that they should have as much of it as technically possible? If this were the case, it would place unacceptable and unachievable demands upon a health service. In which case, where does one draw the line between what is a justifiable need for healthcare which should be met, and what is not? Similarly, in order to guarantee physical survival one could argue that it is necessary to guarantee an income to ensure subsistence, thus raising again problems about what minimum of income is sufficient.

A further and very real problem with Plant's approach concerns the role of the state. Even if one can establish that there are indeed a number of basic needs which can and should be met, it does not simply follow that the state should be the vehicle for meeting these. Presenting a strong and coherent argument for the meeting of certain basic needs may be one thing, but deducing a state obligation—as opposed to those of individuals, families, or charity, for instance—may be quite a different matter.

Need in Terms of a Basic Minimal Standard

Much social policy debate about need takes place in terms of minima, or basic levels below which some individuals may be defined as being in real need. The difficulty is just how to decide upon the nature of any minimum. For example, some have argued that there is a minimum living standard which applies to all societies, below which one is evidently in need of assistance. Usually based upon various ideas of subsistence and the very minimum required for survival, this is the notion of **absolute poverty**. The measurement of absolute poverty generally limits poverty to **material deprivation**, and seeks to establish a price for the basic necessities in life. Those who are then unable to afford these necessities are deemed to be in absolute poverty, unable to afford to maintain even basic subsistence levels.

Seebohm Rowntree's (1871–1954) work was one of the first to attempt to define and measure need in this way and establish a basic minimum income below which subsistence was not possible. Applying his measure in 1899, Rowntree discovered that a third of the working-class households in York were in absolute poverty—and lacked the minimum income necessary for subsistence. In his third survey of York in 1950 this proportion had dropped to just 1.5 per cent of his total sample, leading some to argue that poverty in the UK had effectively been eradicated.

The concept of 'absolute poverty', however, is not a concrete and objective measure of need. On the contrary, it is very much open to debate and interpretation, and there have been a variety of differing attempts to operationalize this concept, or put it into a form which can be empirically measured. The problem comes in terms of what are defined as the minimum needs necessary for subsistence—do these only refer to physical needs, and the basic need for food, shelter, and good health? Or could we, indeed should we, include in this approach other needs which may be equally important for becoming a full and involved member of society—access to leisure, such as holidays, or to sources of cultural enrichment such as the theatre or opera?

Even when focusing exclusively upon nutritional requirements, it is unclear what basic nutritional requirements should be. Different individuals in different occupations, for instance, may have very different nutritional needs. This variety is even more pronounced in the case of other dimensions of need such as housing, clothing, or education.

Official Poverty

Despite these difficulties, the idea of need defined in terms of a basic minimal standard has proved to be pervasive. Many official definitions of poverty tend to be related in some way to an absolute or subsistence poverty line. In the UK, for instance, 'official' poverty has conventionally been measured in terms of benefit levels. Benefits such as Income Support are paid to those who can demonstrate a low income, and are intended to provide a basic minimum income for those experiencing material hardship. Those individuals whose incomes are at or below this level are deemed to be in poverty. In Britain until the 1980s the Government based its estimate of the extent of poverty and need in society on the numbers living at or below benefit levels. Those receiving an income of between 100 and 139 per cent of benefit levels were often defined as on the margins of poverty.

This approach, however, attracted some considerable criticism, not least because it implied that every time benefit levels were increased, this paradoxically increased the number of those defined as being in poverty! From 1985 the Government chose instead to publish figures on the numbers living below incomes which were 50 per cent of the average adjusted for household type. Those living on less than 80 per cent of the average income were deemed to be on the margins of poverty. This has been described as the **relative income standard of poverty**. Interestingly, the Government also modified the way in which it calculated its figures. Originally it sought to calculate the income for each household member separately. However, this was changed, and all members of a household were assumed to have an equal share of the total household income, which is evidently questionable. The result, however, was that this change actually reduced the numbers on low incomes by more than 1 million people. The problem with such a measure of need, however, is the arbitrary point at which one draws a poverty line.

Relative Poverty

Peter Townsend was a very vocal proponent of the idea that poverty must be related to the society in which it may be present. However, Townsend argued that the relative income standard of poverty is arbitrary—it is unclear why the poverty line should be drawn at 50 per cent of average income—70 per cent could have just as much validity. Townsend was therefore keen to establish a more objective and less arbitrary measure of poverty and need, but one which was necessarily relative to wider standards in society. After all, given economic and social change, standards and expectations may shift; luxuries may become comforts, and comforts in turn may become necessities. Townsend argued, therefore, that poverty had to be related to and defined by the standards of a particular society at a particular time and, moreover, reflect more than simply material impoverishment. With this in mind, he focused upon the concept of **relative deprivation**. Townsend suggested that any definition of poverty should include some measure of an individual's ability to participate in social activities which are generally customary in society.

Townsend's Definition of Poverty

Individuals, families and groups in the population can be said to be in poverty when they lack the resources to obtain the types of diet, participate in the activities and have the living conditions and amenities which are customary, or at least widely encouraged or approved, in the societies to which they belong. Their resources are so seriously below those commanded by the average individual or family that they are, in effect, excluded from the ordinary living patterns, customs and activities. (Townsend 1979: 31)

With this in mind, Townsend constructed what he described as a **deprivation index**. This covered some sixty types of household activity relating to diet, clothing, health, recreation, travel, and so on, from which he chose twelve items that he saw as relevant and necessary to the whole of society. He then calculated the proportion of the population deprived of these. Each household was given a score on a deprivation index, and the more respects in which a household was found to experience deprivation, the higher its score. Townsend then related deprivation to income levels. In particular, he related the average score of households to different levels of income, expressed as a percentage of basic benefit levels. From this, Townsend claimed to have identified a poverty threshold, in terms of a level of income below which the amount of deprivation suddenly increased dramatically—at approximately 150 per cent of benefit levels. He therefore argued that all households without this level of resources were suffering from poverty and in need. Importantly, he also felt that his figures and his definition of poverty were not arbitrary, but were ostensibly 'objective'.

Problems with this Approach

Townsend's approach to poverty, and hence to need, was groundbreaking. He developed a social measure in terms of household integration into the community around them, and so moved measurement on from arbitrarily chosen minimum standards. But his work also attracted criticism, not least from David Piachaud (1981), who makes a number of pertinent points:

Townsend claimed to have found an 'objective' point at which to draw a poverty line, below which deprivation increases very rapidly. In fact, Piachaud argues that a poverty line based on 150 per cent of benefit levels is as arbitrary as any other. Indeed, after examining Townsend's data, Piachaud disputes the suggestion that deprivation starts to rapidly increase below this level of 150 per cent of benefit levels.

It is also not clear why the items employed in Townsend's index have been selected. For instance, it is unclear why not eating cooked meals should necessarily be equated with deprivation, as Townsend claims. After all, some people may prefer to eat sandwiches and salads! This is a crucial point—namely, Townsend does not seek to establish whether scoring high points on his 'deprivation index' is actually a consequence of shortage of money, or a consequence of choice!

Mack and Lansley: Breadline Britain

Mack and Lansley (1985, 1991) follow Townsend's social approach to the measurement of need and poverty, defining poverty in relative terms, but attempting to improve it in two important ways.

First, they sought to clarify whether or not people lacked something by choice, or whether it was a consequence of financial pressure.

Second, they were concerned about the accusation that any items included in their deprivation index would be necessarily arbitrary. They therefore adopted a **consensual approach to poverty**, and asked their respondents what they considered to be necessities in contemporary Britain. An item became a necessity if a majority (or more than 50 per cent of the population) classified it as one. On the basis of this deprivation index, they then went on to measure the extent of poverty, which they defined as 'an enforced lack of socially perceived necessities'. Later surveys have used the same method.

The last survey using this 'consensual approach' to measure poverty in Britain in the 1990s (Gordon and Pantazis 1997) came up with some startling and disturbing results:

In the early 1980s, 14 per cent of households (approximately 7.5 million people) were living in poverty—this had increased to 20 per cent (approximately 11 million people) by the 1990s.

Roughly 10 million people in Britain today cannot afford adequate housing.

Some 7 million people go without essential clothing, such as a warm waterproof coat, because of a lack of money.

Approximately 2.5 million children are forced to go without at least one item needed, such as three meals a day, toys, or out of school activities.

About 6.5 million people cannot afford one or more essential household goods, like a fridge, a telephone, or carpets for living areas.

To summarize, it is evident that attempting to establish any measure of need in terms of a basic minimal standard is fraught with problems. Absolute or subsistence definitions of need and poverty are to a degree arbitrary or a matter of subjective judgement. In any event, many commentators argue that any attempt to measure deprivation and need must be relative to the standards and expectations of wider society. In other words, the nature of poverty necessarily varies over time and reflects the contemporary social circumstances in which it is experienced. In this sense, poverty and deprivation are related to social inequality—the poor are those whose incomes or resources are so far short of society's average that they simply do not have an acceptable standard of living. If poverty is measured and gauged in terms of average expectations and average incomes, then reducing poverty and meeting need may actually be impossible without attacking inequality. In the UK, inequality pervades many features of society, most notably in terms of income.

Need and Inequality

One of the most significant forms of inequality in the UK is in terms of income distribution. Data on income distribution have been used to chart changing patterns of poverty and need over time. Indeed, according to this measure there has been a considerable increase in the scale of poverty in the UK over the past 20 years or so. In 1979, for instance, 5 million individuals in the UK had incomes below 50 per cent of the average income; by 1991/92 this number had risen to 13.9 million, and 6 million of these had incomes below half the 1979 average (Hills 1995). While average income for the population as a whole rose by 36 per cent between 1979 and 1990/91, the real income of the bottom tenth actually fell by 14 per cent!

Whilst many industrialized countries experienced moves towards greater income inequality, this grew more rapidly in the UK than in any other country with the exception of New Zealand. The reasons for these increases in inequality are complex. In particular they reflect the fact that, during the 1980s, more people became dependent upon state benefits, not least because of increases in unemployment. Yet simultaneously the gap widened between the income of those dependent on benefits and the population with earnings. This was a consequence of the fact that, since the early 1980s, benefit levels have generally been linked to prices rather than income levels: changes in inequality which have affected some social groups more than others.

There are, for instance, important differences between ethnic groups. The incomes of some ethnic minority groups are well below the national average, and a significant percentage of their populations live in areas high in indicators of deprivation. Households where the head of household is from an ethnic minority group are much more likely to appear in the bottom 20 per cent (or quintile) of the income distribution than their white contemporaries. In 1995–6, for instance, two-thirds of Pakistani or Bangladeshi households were in the bottom quintile compared with just a fifth of the general population (Office for National Statistics 1998). This is, of course, partly related to unemployment and its high incidence amongst some ethnic minority groups. Throughout the 1980s and into the 1990s unemployment rates amongst ethnic minorities have consistently been twice the national average (Hills 1995).

There are also important differences between men and women here. Whilst men are much more likely to be in the professional and skilled manual groups, women are more likely to be in the skilled and unskilled non-manual groups, reflecting the dominance of women in some occupations such as clerical and secretarial work and their importance in some professions such as teaching and medicine. Women have been heavily concentrated in low-paid and low-status employment and, in the UK, women's average earnings are two-thirds those of men.

An important question for social policy concerns the extent to which the welfare state should seek to reduce inequalities. Which inequalities are the most damaging in the sense of reducing people's opportunities or in contributing to other needs such as poor health? Alternatively, there is also the risk that welfare allocations, or the taxes necessary to pay for them, may actually have been adding to forms of inequality.

The Welfare State and Inequality

It is clear that some households will pay considerably more in taxes than they receive in benefits, while others will benefit more than they are taxed. Overall, one can say that there is some redistribution of income from households on higher incomes to those on lower incomes. In 1995–6, for example, UK households in the bottom quintile group had an average original income (or income derived from various non-Governmental sources, such as employment or occupational pensions) of £2,430. Once redistribution through taxes and benefits had occurred, such households were left with a final income of £8,230. In other words, on average, these households had gained some £5,800 through redistribution (Social Trends 1998). In contrast, households in the highest quintile group (or the top 20 per cent) had an average original income of £41,260 and a final income of £29,200. In other words, on average, these households had made a net loss of some £12,060 through redistribution (Social Trends 1998). Chapter 11 includes discussion of these issues in the context of social security benefits.

However, the welfare state also has an important redistributional role in terms of welfare services which are provided 'in kind' rather than as cash benefits, such as the National Health Service, state education, personal social services, and subsidized and social housing. It has been argued that the provision of such services should be considered as a non-monetary form of income, or a **social wage**, which forms an important addition to cash incomes. However, there has been some intense debate about who actually benefits most from the provision of such services. Julian Le Grand, for instance, has argued that state welfare provision does not in fact enhance redistribution and reduce inequality. Rather, he has showed that state welfare services accentuate the divisions between those facing need and those who are comfortably provided for. In the use of transport, education, and possibly healthcare the better-off consume disproportionately relative to their needs (Le Grand 1982). It has been claimed by some commentators that the welfare state has increasingly been 'captured' by the middle classes.

In contrast, recent research by Tom Sefton (1997) has shown that the welfare state did go some way towards tempering the growing income inequalities that were witnessed in the 1980s. Whilst much attention was devoted to the widening income gap between rich and poor, most calculations failed to take into account the value of welfare services to different groups. In 1993, the 'social wage', or the value in kind of the main state services, was worth just over £800 each a year to the richest 20 per cent of the population by income, but worth almost £1,500 each a year to the poorest 40 per cent (Sefton 1997). However, there is considerable variety here between services—higher education, for instance, is certainly worth more to the better-off in society, while subsidized social housing and the personal social services strongly benefit the poor.

However, that income inequality has increased remains the basic fact. Average real incomes of the poorest fifth of the population rose only 6 per cent between 1979 and 1993, compared to more than 60 per cent for the richest fifth. The social wage has helped to offset this growing inequality of cash incomes, although it has still not prevented inequality from rising. Whilst one would anticipate that welfare services would mainly benefit lower income groups, the surprising reality is that the poorest half of the population receive just 60 per cent of the value of these services. Indeed, only in the context of social housing has there been a clear shift in the distribution of welfare spending towards the poorest individuals and families (Sefton 1997).

Demographic Change in the UK

Demographic trends are of fundamental importance for social policy and any debate about social need. Ultimately, demographic changes have a direct impact upon welfare provision, because they alter the size and composition of the population who contribute to and use the services provided by welfare states. One role of social policy (the subject) is to chart and follow demographic trends—both in the short and much longer term—and anticipate the needs that different patterns of population change are likely to imply for welfare provision. Demography lies at the heart of social policy because of its close relationship to need and, in turn, demand from the welfare state. (Table 8.1, p. 162, lists some of the main sources of data about the UK population that are available to social researchers and social policy-makers.)

Knowledge about the size and structure of the population is essential for understanding and anticipating demand for all kinds of welfare services, such as education, healthcare, and social security benefits. Demographic change provides the best basis available for estimating future needs, and can also be interpreted as an indication of wider social shifts in values and forms of behaviour which may have implications for the needs faced by future Governments and taxpayers.

Population Structure

This century there has been a huge growth in the total world population. Since 1900 the world population has more than trebled from around 1.6 billion to an estimated 5.8 billion in 1997. It is projected to rise still further, to more than 8 billion, by 2025. Yet within this pattern there are important differences. Less developed areas, for instance, have much lower life expectancies than do more developed regions. While North America has the longest life expectancy—74 for males, and 80 for females—this compares with just 52 and 55 respectively for Africa (Social Trends 1998).

Europe has also had a growing population; between 1961 and 1996 the total population of European Union member states increased by some 17 per cent, from 317 million to 373 million. Over the same period the population of the UK experienced an 11 per cent increase, and in 1996 stood at 58.8 million. Change in population is dependent on a number of variables—specifically, the number of births, the number of deaths, and migration in and out of the country.

	1800	1900	1950	1997
Asia	635	947	1,402	3,539
Africa	107	133	224	758
Europe	203	408	547	728
Latin America and Caribbean	24	74	166	492
North America	7	82	172	302
Oceania	2	6	13	29
	978	1,650	2,524	5,849

Table 6.1 World population
Source: United Nations.

Births and the Family

One of the most important factors affecting population structure is the number of live births. The UK has seen a number of changes to fertility patterns. More women are now delaying having their first child, and the average age of mothers for all live births rose from 26.4 in 1976 to 28.6 in 1996. Women are also choosing to have fewer children. There has also been a dramatic increase in the number of births outside marriage, particularly during the 1980s. Of live births in England and Wales in 1996, over a third were outside marriage—more than four times the proportion in 1971. However, it is important to remember that around four-fifths of births outside marriage are jointly registered by both parents (Social Trends, 1998).

The family is a central object of social policy intervention. However, the nature of the contemporary family is experiencing a variety of important changes, which in turn attract the attention of social researchers, politicians, and policy-makers. Many of these changes are linked and related in different ways and have consequences for both the goals and the design of social policies. The section in Chapter 8, 'Demographic trends in family life', covers some of the issues here, providing additional statistics and a different perspective.

Marriage, Divorce, and Cohabitation

One of the most striking areas of debate has been focused upon the question of marriage and its centrality to modern British society. Whilst politicians regularly proclaim the virtues of marriage and the benefits of dual-parenthood, the contemporary family is now considerably more diverse in its characteristics. Some researchers and politicians have not been slow to attach many of the ills of our modern society to changing family forms. Whilst the main changes involved may be reasonably clear in their nature, what is far from clear are the implications of these for social welfare. A number of developments are notable, one of which has been the declining marriage rate and the corresponding increase in cohabitation.

Marriage may be an institution, but it is one which growing proportions of the population are hesitant to subscribe to. In 1995 there were 322,000 marriages in the UK, the lowest recorded figure since 1926. Not only are fewer people actually marrying, but the average age of people getting married for the first time is increasing. The median age of first marriage has increased for women from 21.4 in 1971 to 23.3 in 1987 and, correspondingly, the number of teenage marriages have dropped dramatically. At the same time, there has been a sharp increase in the number of people cohabiting, together with a shift towards cohabiting for longer periods. For instance, the proportion of all non-married women aged 18 to 49 who were cohabiting in Great Britain has doubled since 1981, to 25 per cent in 1996–7 (Social Trends 1998).

At the same time as a rise in cohabitation there has been a dramatic increase in divorce. Since 1971 divorce has more than doubled. It is perhaps unsurprising that so many politicians and clergy claim that the institution of marriage in the UK is under threat. The rise in divorce has important and significant implications for social policy in a number of ways. The complexity of reconstituted families may have important consequences for the meeting of social need in the future. The provision of old-age care, for instance, has been the focus of concern. Traditionally a main source of informal care for the elderly has been by younger family members. Yet with the increase in divorce and, in turn, remarriage, it is less clear just how these family responsibilities may or may not be shared out (Finch and Mason 1993).

Lone Parents

A further shift in family form which has provoked concern amongst policy-makers and politicians has been the increase in the number and proportion of lone-parent families over the past 25 years. The UK has one of the highest rates of lone parenthood in the European Union. In 1996, lone parents headed around 21 per cent of all families with dependent children in Great Britain—almost three times the proportion in 1971—and nine out of every ten are lone mothers. This high rate of lone parenthood has been viewed by many as being inherently risky, and a number of authors have argued that there is something necessarily advantageous about two-parent households. (This issue is covered in greater depth in Chapter 8, particularly the section, 'Theoretical and policy perspectives on the family'.) The high rate of lone parenthood has also led to debates about the provision of benefits to this group. Do their greater needs require higher benefits and more assistance, or will these merely 'reward' lone parenthood? Indeed, the identification of lone parents as somehow being distinct and different from their contemporaries lies at the heart of many arguments about the emergence of an 'underclass' in the UK.

United Kingdom (Percentages)		
	Males	Females
Single	13	38
Separated	30	24
Divorced	43	33
Widowed	14	6
All lone parents	100	100

Table 6.2 Lone parents by gender and marital status, 1995–7
Source: Office for National Statistics (1998).

As with all social policy debates, the acknowledgement of demographic change is perhaps less important than the interpretation of such changes, and an assessment of the appropriate response by government. Certainly, many of the debates about lone parents in the UK have only selectively engaged with the demographic evidence. Whilst much is made of the high rate of lone parenthood in the UK by Charles Murray (1990) and others, it is important to clarify a number of points. Lone parenthood, for example, is not necessarily a permanent state. On the contrary, many lone parents go on to form new joint households fairly quickly. In the early 1990s, for instance, some 15 per cent of lone mothers each year ceased to be lone parents (Social Trends 1998). Such a rate implies that half of all lone mothers would have a duration of lone parenthood of around four years or less. Moreover, contrary to the pervasive image of the teenage mother attempting to jump the housing queue, the majority of lone parents are actually divorcees in their twenties or thirties.

In short, the nuclear family is undergoing substantial change in the UK arising from fewer marriages, more cohabitation, and more extra-marital births; increasing divorce and remarriage; declining fertility and smaller families; and a rise in lone parents and reconstituted families. The nuclear family may still be dominant, but it is none the less only one possible family form.

Household Change

The rise in divorce and the declining fashionability of marriage has led to other changes, all of which are important to social policy. The average size of households in Great Britain has almost halved since the beginning of the twentieth century to some 2.4 people per household in 1996–7 (Social Trends 1998). Of particular significance has been the rise in single-person households. More and more of us, it seems, are living on our own. In 1961 just 14 per cent of households were single-person households. By 1996–7 this had increased to some 27 per cent, and seems set to climb further as more of us live independently after leaving home and before marriage; as a consequence of divorce, or simply as a reflection of the growing proportion of the elderly, many of whom live in 'solo' households. The implications of this development may be profound, not least for housing policy. The growing number of single-person households—who in turn want somewhere to live—has figured strongly in recent debates about the need for 4.4 million new homes in the UK by 2016. Whilst the population of the UK may have remained

Number of people	Great Britain (Percentages)			
	1961	1971	1981	1991
One	14	18	22	27
Two	30	32	32	34
Three	23	19	17	16
Four	18	17	18	16
Five	9	8	7	5
Six or more	7	6	4	2
All households (=100%) millions	16.3	18.6	20.2	22.4
Average household size (number of people)	3.1	2.9	2.7	2.5

Table 6.3 Households: by size

Source: Office for National Statistics (1998).

reasonably static over the past few decades, it is important to remember that demand for housing can increase within a static population if new and smaller households are forming faster than old ones dissolve.

In short, demographic change has a very real and integral relationship with the issue of social need. However, it would be erroneous to assume that one can chart a clear and straightforward relationship between demographic change and the consequent needs faced by society. On the contrary, there may be common acknowledgement of a particular demographic pattern, but very different assessments of the implications for social policy. Nowhere is this more aptly illustrated than in the various debates about an ageing population and the consequences of this for welfare provision.

Ageing of the Population

The population age profile of industrialized societies is changing in important ways, not least of which has been the movement towards what is commonly described as an **ageing population**. The age structure of the population reflects variation in past births, increases in longevity, and the effects of migration. This is an important debate, reflecting concern about the welfare costs of an expanding **dependent population**—or the proportion of the population economically supported by those of working age. In other words, this is a crude measure of the number of people economically supported by those of working age—what is known as the **dependency ratio**. Those people aged under 16, and those over pensionable age, are often deemed to represent the dependent population and, importantly, many countries are experiencing an increase in the proportion of the population above pensionable age. In 1961, for instance, just 12 per cent of the UK's population were aged 65 or over, and only 4 per cent were aged 75 and over. By 1996 this had increased to some 16 per cent and 7 per cent respectively (Social Trends 1998).

The proportion of the population aged 65 or over is projected to rise further, as the post-Second-World-War 'baby boom' reach retirement age. By 2021 it is projected that some 20 per cent of the population will be aged over 65 (Social Trends 1998). Moreover, there will be a particular increase in the number of very elderly people. Whilst in 1961 there were nearly 350,000 people aged 85 and over, by 1996 this number had increased to nearly 1.1 million (Social Trends 1998). These developments clearly have profound implications in terms of future need for healthcare, social care, and pensions—and what this is likely to mean for national budgets, taxation, and welfare spending in the near future. Old people are higher users of health services than their younger peers. For example, patients aged 75 and over use approximately six times the average of NHS spending (Taylor-Gooby 1991). The stark implication is that a growing proportion of retired people will impose a burden of rising cost upon a shrinking population of working age. This has generated vigorous policy debate. Concern about the ability of the country to pay for growing pension costs in the future has led to a variety of reviews and changes to pension provisions in the UK, all of which claim to have at their heart a concern with this demographic trend.

However, even here, where the evidence about demographic change and its relationship to social need appears to be fairly uncontentious, all is not as clear as it initially seems. On the contrary, the impact of the ageing population upon welfare states into

	All ages (millions)	Under 16	16–34	35–54	55–64	65–74	75 and over
					United Kingdom (Percentages)		
Mid-year estimates							
1961	52.8	25	24	27	12	8	4
1971	55.9	25	26	24	12	9	5
1981	56.4	22	29	23	11	9	6
1991	57.8	20	29	25	10	9	7
Mid-year projections							
2001	59.5	20	25	29	10	8	7
2011	60.5	18	24	29	12	9	7
2021	61.1	18	23	26	14	11	8
2031	60.7	17	22	25	13	13	11

Table 6.4 Population: by age

Source: Office for National Statistics (1998).

the next century may be more complicated than it appears at first. Rather than representing a demographic timebomb, a number of competing points can be made.

Whilst it does seem likely that the ageing population will lead to greater costs in some areas, these are none the less likely to be matched by a reduction in other costs, such as childcare. Sefton (1997) shows that the effect of a smaller child population on education spending has already more than offset the effects of an ageing population on healthcare and personal social services spending. Indeed, those aged over 65 are not necessarily dependent. Far from being economically dependent, the elderly may make a number of important economic contributions to society—in terms of informal and unpaid childcare or care for other elderly people, for instance, and in terms of their important role as consumers of economic goods and services.

Certainly, those aged 85 and over are likely to increase as a proportion of the population, and to present a variety of needs in terms of health and social care. However, it is important to acknowledge that they still represent only a very small proportion of the entire population. The fact remains that economic growth could easily meet growing costs here. If current standards of provision are maintained, the cost of maintaining health and social services provision can be met by modest economic growth (Hills 1993). In other words, the issue here is not one of economic necessity, but of political priority. Who should benefit from increases in economic productivity: existing workers or the retired? Moreover, the costs of an ageing population are not necessarily borne by the state—the movement towards private provision in terms of health and social care, and particularly in terms of pensions, is likely to alleviate some of the projected welfare costs.

Concerns about the demographic ageing of the population also ignore the fact that old age is to an extent a social construct, rather than simply a physical or biological fact.

In other words, the current relationship between old age and physical dependency is changing. Old people in the future may be considerably healthier and more active than in the past because of improvements in diet and lifestyle.

Conclusion: Social Need, Demographic 'Facts', and Policy Judgements

A logical mind might consider that social policy should be determined by 'social need', and that need should be measured in terms of empirical 'facts' such as changes in the size and structure of a population (demography) and evidence about deprivation (such as measures of poverty). This chapter has sought to show that there can be no simple links made between facts about need and the necessary social policies. The very words we use to describe demographic change ('the ageing population' or 'lone parenthood') involve elements of judgement. All attempts to measure poverty have been criticized for the normative assumptions they inevitably have to make about either minima or the forms of social inclusion and exclusion that count. For this reason policy cannot follow directly from evidence of need. As Chapter 3 explains, a political process must intervene, determining which needs are recognized and the degree to which they are then to be alleviated by social policies.

Glossary

absolute poverty Poverty defined and measured in terms of the minimum requirements necessary for basic subsistence and survival. Those deemed to be in absolute poverty are unable to afford even the basic necessities in life. They exist below even 'subsistence poverty', the level at which people can just continue to survive.

ageing population A change in the age structure of the population, whereby the proportion of older people increases relative to the numbers of younger people. An ageing population is often used to refer to one in which the proportion over pensionable age is increasing, which in turn may imply more social spending on pensions and healthcare, and less revenue.

comparative need Need established by comparing the standards achieved by similar groups within one society, such as those living in different parts of the country; or in different societies, such as a comparison of the incomes of or provision for retired people in one nation compared with those in another. In other words, need is seen as an inherently relative concept, and any debate about need must be related to the wider context within which the debates are taking place.

consensual approach to poverty Attempting to establish a consensus about what the population consider to be necessities in that particular society, at that particular period in time, without which one could be defined to be in poverty.

dependency ratio Usually the ratio of those outside the labour force (for example 0–15 and 65 and over) to those defined as in the labour force or of working age.

dependent population The section of the population economically supported by those in employment.

deprivation index A list of items defined as essential to being a full member of society, without which one could be deemed to be experiencing deprivation.

expressed need Need that has become a demand. There is a close relationship between need and demand, but simply because someone demands or wants something does not necessarily mean that they need it.

felt need An individual or group's belief that they need something. This relies heavily upon an individual's own perception of their need, and their perception of any discrepancy between what their situation may be and what it should be. This definition is very similar to a 'want'.

intermediate needs Needs which are not ends in themselves, but are rather a means to an end. For example, we may need some things, such as a basic education, in order to fulfil other needs, such as finding employment, which in turn may answer the further need for income.

normative need How an expert, such as a doctor or welfare professional, may define need in a given situation or circumstance. Important because welfare professionals are closely involved in the identification of need, and how this may best be met within the confines of existing resources.

material deprivation Having insufficient physical or material resources—food, shelter, and clothing—necessary to sustain life in either an absolute sense or relative to some prescribed standard.

relative deprivation Deprivation measured by comparing one's situation to that of relevant others, or to standards accepted in a particular society at a particular time.

relative income standard of poverty A relative measure of poverty which relates it to average income levels within society. For instance, those found to be living at or below incomes which are 50 per cent of the average, may be defined as being in poverty.

social wage The value of welfare services which are provided 'in kind', rather than as cash benefits, such as the National Health Service, state education, personal social services, and subsidized social housing.

technical need Need arising when some new provision is invented or existing provision is made much more effective, creating a need for a solution that was not previously available.

ultimate needs Needs which are seen as ends in themselves, and to which other activities and needs are directed; for example, survival, autonomy, and self-fulfilment may be defined as ultimate human needs.

Guide to Further Reading

Bradshaw, J., 'A Taxonomy of Social Need', *New Society*, 496 (30 March 1972), 640–3. An important and influential exposition of the different forms that social need might take.

Coleman, D. and Salt, J., *The British Population: Patterns, Trends and Processes* (Oxford: Oxford University Press, 1992). A thorough and very comprehensive guide to the many debates surrounding the British population, drawing together a wealth of evidence and argument.

Doyal, L. and Gough, I., *A Theory of Human Need* (Basingstoke: Macmillan, 1991). A considered account of the key issues and dilemmas here, further developing the approach of Raymond Plant to the question of need.

Gordon, D. and Pantazis, C. (eds.), *Breadline Britain in the 1990s: The Full Report of a Major National Survey on Poverty* (Bristol: University of Bristol, 1997). The latest report on the extent and nature of poverty in Britain using the 'consensual method' pioneered by Mack and Lansley.

Hills, J., *The Future of Welfare: A Guide to the Debate* (York: Joseph Rowntree Foundation, 1993). A comprehensive guide to the wealth of evidence and debate about the future sustainability of welfare spending, drawing upon some rich sources of data.

Office of Population Censuses and Surveys, *Social Trends* (London: HMSO, 1998). An invaluable source of Government data on a range of topics, including the family, population change, and patterns of income and wealth.

Piachaud, D., 'Peter Townsend and the Holy Grail', *New Society*, 57 (10 September 1981), 419–22. An influential challenge to Peter Townsend and the claim that need and poverty can be objectively measured.

Townsend, P., *Poverty in the United Kingdom* (Harmondsworth: Penguin, 1979). Essential reading for any consideration of poverty in the UK, in which Townsend spells out his 'poverty threshold'.

References

Abel-Smith, B. and Townsend, P. (1965), *The Poor and the Poorest*, Occasional Paper in Social Administration, 17 (London: Bell).

Barry, N. (1990), *Welfare* (Milton Keynes: Open University Press).

Bradshaw, J. (1972), 'A Taxonomy of Social Need', *New Society*, 496 (30 March), 640–3.

Coleman, D. and Salt, J. (1992), *The British Population: Patterns, Trends and Processes* (Oxford: Oxford University Press).

Doyal, L. and Gough, I. (1984), 'A Theory of Human Needs', *Critical Social Policy*, 10, 6–33.

——(1991), *A Theory of Human Need* (Basingstoke: Macmillan).

Ermisch, J. (1990), *Fewer Babies, Longer Lives* (York: Joseph Rowntree Foundation).

Falkingham, J. (1989), 'Britain's Ageing Population: The Engine Behind Increased Dependency Ratios', *Journal of Social Policy*, 18 (2), 211–33.

Finch, J. and Mason, J. (1993), *Negotiating Family Responsibilities* (London: Routledge).

Forder, A. (1974), *Concepts in Social Administration: A Framework for Analysis* (London: Routledge and Kegan Paul).

Gordon, D. and Pantazis, C. (eds.) (1997), *Breadline Britain in the 1990s: The Full Report of a Major National Survey on Poverty* (Bristol: University of Bristol).

Harvey, D. (1973), *Social Justice and the City* (London: Allen and Unwin).

Hills, J. (1993), *The Future of Welfare: A Guide to the Debate* (York: Joseph Rowntree Foundation).

——(1995), *Inquiry into Income and Wealth* (York: Joseph Rowntree Foundation).

Jones, K., Brown, J., and Bradshaw, J. (1983), *Issues in Social Policy* (2nd edition; London: Routledge and Kegan Paul).

Joseph Rowntree Foundation (1995), *Inquiry into Income and Wealth* (2 vols., York: Joseph Rowntree Foundation).

Joshi, H. (1989), *The Changing Population of Britain* (Oxford: Blackwell).

Kiernan, K. and Wicks, M. (1990), *Family Change and Future Policy* (York: Joseph Rowntree Foundation).

Le Grand (1982), *The Strategy of Equality* (London: Allen and Unwin).

Mack, J. and Lansley, S. (1985), *Poor Britain* (London: Allen and Unwin).

——(1991), *Breadline Britain* (London: Unwin Hyman).

Maslow, A. (1954), *Motivation and Personality* (New York: Harper).

Murray, C. (1990), *The Emerging British Underclass* (London: Institute of Economic Affairs).

Office for National Statistics (1998), *Social Trends* (London: HMSO).

Piachaud, D. (1981), Peter Townsend and the Holy Grail, *New Society*, 57 (10 September), 419–22.

Plant, R. (1985), 'The Very Idea of a Welfare State', in P. Bean, J. Ferris, and D. Whynes (eds.), *In Defence of Welfare* (London: Tavistock).

Sefton, T. (1997), *The Changing Distribution of the Social Wage*, STICERD Occasional Paper 21 (London: London School of Economics).

Smith, G. (1988), *Social Needs: Policy Practice and Research* (London: Routledge).

Taylor-Gooby, P. (1991), *Social Change; Social Welfare and Social Science* (London: Harvester Wheatsheaf).

——and Dale, J. (1981), *Social Theory and Social Welfare* (London: Edward Arnold).

Townsend, P. (ed.) (1970), *The Concept of Poverty* (London: Heinemann).

——(1979), *Poverty in the United Kingdom* (Harmondsworth: Penguin).

7 Work, Employment, and the Production of Welfare

Sarah Vickerstaff

Contents

Introduction: Work and Welfare

We believe work is the best form of welfare for people of working age and that includes lone parents (Harriet Harman, speaking as the then Secretary of State for Social Security quoted in the *Financial Times* 3.7.97).

Employment is one of the best defences against poverty, unhappiness, and low self-esteem, which in turn are likely to adversely affect an individual's physical and mental health. In addition, paid work outside the home has traditionally been seen as a key mechanism of social integration, a person who 'works' is a full citizen, a useful and 'fully paid-up', taxpaying member of society. People who are in paid employment have higher rates of involvement in other social, political, and sporting activities. This is partly a question of money—having the income to enjoy leisure activities—and partly a matter of greater social inclusion or greater integration into public life. Thus, although we tend to conflate welfare with the welfare state and its policies, in fact work and employment are more fundamental producers of individual and societal welfare. In the first 25 years after the Second World War it was taken for granted in Europe and the USA that a key goal of government policy was the maintenance of **full employment**. The problem for many societies in Europe today is that there does not seem to be enough work to go round. Since the early 1970s, and especially in the 1980s, with the growth of persistent unemployment, this commitment to full employment, and the belief in its possibility, has been shaken throughout the advanced industrial (or increasingly **post-industrial**) world.

Unemployment tends to grab the newspaper headlines as *the* key employment issue, but since the 1960s many other developments have been occurring in the world of work. The sorts of jobs available and the skills and attributes they require have been transformed; access to work is changing (who gets what kind of job); and for many people their experience of work, especially in relation to job security, has fundamentally altered. Thus, in this chapter, in order to consider the connection between work and welfare we must first look at all of these features of the **labour market**. We can then go on to review and evaluate some of the policy responses to these issues and investigate contemporary debates on what to do about unemployment.

The Work Available

In the period since the 1960s the UK economy has witnessed a progressive decline in manufacturing industry and hence the number of jobs available in this sector. At the same time there has been an increase in **service sector** and office or white-collar work. This shift from industry to services and the related move from manual to non-manual work have radically changed the pattern of demand in the labour market.

The transformation of the British economy from a strong manufacturing base to a 'post-industrial' service base has brought with it a collapse in the demand for the labour of unqualified youths. (Ashton 1992: 186–7)

In addition to this shift in the pattern of activity in the economy, technological changes and new standards of customer service have also meant that the skill and competence requirements for jobs have changed.

Twenty years ago, almost all the manual workers in my operation were men and a lot of the work consisted of humping sacks of potatoes around. Today, it's all fiddly work, putting sauce on the bits of chicken for Marks and Sparks, and the assembly line is 90 per cent women. Mostly men don't apply for it—it's part-time and they see it as women's work. (Food factory manager, quoted in The Report of the Commission on Social Justice 1994: 187)

Even in the worst periods of unemployment since the late 1970s there have been simultaneous skills shortages and hard-to-fill vacancies. There is considerable debate about the overall trends in skill requirements for the jobs available in today's economy. Some argue that there is an upward trend in the skill levels required, pointing to the shift from manual to non-manual work and the impact of newer technologies such as computer applications. Others, on the other hand, indicate the growth of unskilled service-sector jobs which require few skills or personal attributes. Far from the old disciplines of assembly-line work in factories becoming a thing of the past, these work techniques are increasingly being applied to all kinds of other work, for example fast-food restaurants and telephone call centre workers. (One version of this argument is the McDonaldization thesis; see Box 7.1).

A major piece of research into the trends in job skills in the UK found evidence for a polarization of skills (for a discussion of this research and the wider debate, see Gallie 1991, 1996). In other words, the middle ground of semi-skilled jobs is disappearing, and instead skilled manual, managerial, and professional jobs are becoming more skilled, whilst many of the remaining jobs are becoming more routine and unskilled. In Britain at least, this polarization has not changed the fact that many of the unemployed do not have the abilities and skills that employers are looking for, whether these be specific skills or the more intangible quality of 'employability'. This mismatch in labour supply and labour demand is seen as one cause of unemployment. It is also in this context that debate about the role of education and training policy has taken centre stage in many European countries (see Chapter14).

Another feature of the way in which work has been changing is the growth of part-time and other forms of **flexible or casual work.** This growth is driven largely by the expansion of the service sector, but also by increasing economic competition, leading employers to seek ways to improve efficiency and reduce labour costs. The degree of growth of part-time and flexible work across Europe varies considerably (see Gregory and O'Reilly 1996), depending in large measure on the prevailing context of employment regulation. Where part-time workers enjoy substantially the same employment

---

Box 7.1 The McDonaldization thesis

George Ritzer, in a book entitled *The McDonaldization of Society*, has argued that the process typified by the way fast food restaurants are run is extending into many areas of contemporary life.

'First, a McDonaldized world is dominated by homogenous products. The Big Mac, the Egg McMuffin and Chicken Nuggets are identical from one time and place to another. Second, technologies like Burger King's conveyor system, as well as the french-fry and soft-drink machines throughout the fast-food industry, are as rigid as many of the technologies in Henry Ford's assembly-line system. Further, work routines in the fast-food restaurant are highly standardized. Even what the workers say to customers is routinized. In addition, the jobs in a fast-food restaurant are deskilled; they take little or no ability. The workers, furthermore, are homogeneous and the actions of the customers are homogenized by the demands of the fast-food restaurant (for example, don't dare ask for a rare burger). The workers at fast-food restaurants can be seen as a mass of interchangeable workers. Finally, what is consumed and how it is consumed is homogenized by McDonaldization.' (1993: 155)

Box 7.2 The pros and cons of part-time work

'Since part-time employment almost never pays enough to support a family (and perhaps not even a single person), part-time jobs can only be taken by those with another earner in the family—often in practice, women married to men in employment. For this group the tax and benefits system offers a substantial incentive to work part-time. . . . For women whose partners are unemployed or earning a low wage topped up by family credit, benefit withdrawal starts at a much lower point, creating effective disincentives for the woman to work.

Thus, it is argued, the rise in part-time working is helping to create a gulf between "work-rich" families, with more than one job, and "work-poor" families with no job at all, while offering little or nothing to the unemployed who need a full-time wage.' (Hewitt 1996: 44)

---

protection as full-time workers, some of the flexibility that employers may gain from being able to deploy part-time or casual workers as and when they want is lost. One thing unites the experience of part-time employment across Europe, however, and that is the fact that it is overwhelmingly women who work part-time. The growth of part-time work is seen as contributing to the growing income disparity between the rich and poor in society (see Box 7.2) which is another feature of the employment landscape in recent years, especially in the USA and Britain.

Employment Security

All of these changes to the work available and who has access to it raise issues about the experience of work and the impact this has on people's welfare. The growth of flexible and casual work has affected not only the unskilled but also white-collar, managerial, and professional workers. Many people in employment will have seen workforce reductions in their own workplace or have experienced job loss second-hand through friends and relatives. Many men may have had to change their jobs, perhaps losing the **occupational identity** they believed they would keep for all their working lives. In this context even the employed are likely to feel more insecure about their job prospects. In this respect the changes in the labour market over recent years may have gone some way to making men's patterns of working across the life-cycle more like women's: periods of work interspersed with periods of economic inactivity. Such broken career patterns and part-time or casual work obviously have implications for levels of income, and for any pension entitlement based on years of working service.

Gender and Access to Work

Although we talk about the period of post-war full employment, this is not really an accurate picture of typical **participation rates** in the past, as Pamela Meadows reminds us:

If we take the household as the unit, 50 years ago the head of the household, whether male or female, was likely to be economically active, with other household members other than lodgers and adult or adolescent children likely to be inactive. This model, which had persisted since the industrial revolution, was envisaged by Beveridge as unchanging and still forms the basis of our social security system. However, it does not match present social reality. (1996: 4)

Full employment meant that any man who wanted to find a job had a reasonably good chance of success. As Beveridge had defined it in 1944: 'Full employment . . . means having always more vacant jobs than unemployed men' (quoted in Rubery 1997: 63). The **male breadwinner model** of the family underlay definitions of full employment and the way in which social security provisions were framed, and also informed employers' and employees' notions of the suitable workers for particular jobs. In Britain 40 years ago the 'typical worker' (found in many sociological studies of the time) was a man, working full-time in industry in skilled or semi-skilled work. Today the average worker is more likely to be a woman working part-time in a service-sector job such as retail.

These facts have profound implications for how we understand 'work', and for the role of public and social policy in responding to labour market problems. As many writers have pointed out, the old view of 'work' as paid employment outside the home in the public sphere served to downgrade the unpaid work which went on, undertaken mainly by women, in the domestic sphere: childcare, cleaning, cooking, and so on. This led some feminists in the 1970s to develop a campaign for wages for housework. Women's access to paid employment outside the home was restricted by domestic responsibilities, especially childcare and the prevalent social belief that women's real place was in the home. One of the most dramatic trends in the labour market since the 1970s has been the steady increase in the numbers of women in paid employment outside the home, and in particular the **participation rates** of married women have

Year		1973	1979	1990	1992
Men	Employed	93.8	91.8	86.3	81.3
	Unemployed	2.1	3.8	6.3	11.5
	Inactive	4.4	4.4	6.3	7.2
Women	Employed	58.3	62.0	71.0	70.2
	Unemployed	0.3	1.3	2.0	3.2
	Inactive	41.7	36.7	27.0	26.6

Table 7.1 UK employment trends by sex: percentage of the population aged 25–54 years*

* These figures exclude the 16–24 age group who in the last two decades have become the age group most affected by unemployment (see Table 7.5).

The Report of the Commission on Social Justice 1994: 153.

	Males				Females			
	1978	1981	1991	1997	1978	1981	1991	1997
Distribution, hotels, catering, and repairs	15	16	19	20	24	25	25	26
Manufacturing	35	33	26	26	22	18	12	10
Financial and business services	9	10	15	16	11	12	16	19
Transport and communication	9	9	9	9	3	3	3	3
Construction	8	8	8	7	1	1	1	1
Agriculture	2	2	2	2	1	1	1	1
Energy and water supply	5	5	3	1	1	1	1	—
Other services	16	17	19	19	38	39	41	40
All employees (=100%) (millions)	13.4	12.6	11.5	11.5	9.4	9.3	10.7	11.3

Table 7.2 Employees by gender and industry, UK: percentages
Source: Office for National Statistics 1998: 78.

seen very significant rises in most European countries. Table 7.1 gives some indication of these developments. It also begins to reveal another feature of recent labour market changes noted above: as female employment has increased, so male unemployment has grown. This is not usually because of direct substitution (that would be women doing jobs that men once did) but rather because the kinds of jobs available have changed. Another important issue revealed in Table 7.1 is that the number has been increasing of inactive men, that is, those who are not in paid employment and are not available for work. This growing group is mainly composed of those who have retired early or have given up work for reasons of invalidity.

Although many more women are working outside the home the labour market is still gendered in the sense that, typically, men and women work in different kinds of jobs in different sectors. This is illustrated in Table 7.2. Women are concentrated in service-sector jobs, often in occupations such as nursing, teaching, catering, and cleaning, which mirror traditional domestic skills and tasks, or in jobs in retail, personal services, and tourism where women may be employed in part to attract the customers. The distinction between women and men's jobs are surprisingly enduring both in practice and in terms of the career expectations of young women and men. Such a gendered **division of labour** has implications both for women and men's employment opportunities but also for their relative average wages. This is often referred to by the notions of horizontal and vertical segregation, in which women are concentrated in certain industries and sectors and within those at the bottom of career ladders; and by the notion of a **gender pay gap,** in which women's average earnings are well below those of men (see Table 7.3). The number of women working part-time further strengthens the impact of these factors.

Lower earnings for women reflect their concentration in lower-paid sectors of

	Pence per hour	Pounds per week
Men (full-time)	939	391.6
Women (full-time)	750*	283.0
Pay gap (%)	80	72

Table 7.3 Average earnings of full-time employees in Britain, 1996

* Average hourly earnings for part-time women were 544 pence per hour.

Source: Equal Opportunities Commission 1996.

employment and at the bottom of career ladders, but they also reflect the ways in which skills are defined:

In manual work, 'skill' is socially constructed, so that jobs that involve tasks associated with masculine expertise—such as driving—are seen as more skilled than jobs that involve feminine dexterity—such as sewing. (Abbott and Wallace 1997: 195)

Women's relative lower earning power obviously has implications for their welfare in terms of their current standard of living, but also in respect of pensions, and hence the threat of poverty in older age. As Ginn and Arber comment:

Among elderly people, inequality in personal incomes is structured by class and gender, and occupational pensions are the main means by which a disadvantaged position in the labour market during working life is translated into a low income in later life. The concentration of poverty among women in later life is well established. (1993: 47)

The net effects of these changes in the labour market has been to reduce the numbers of traditional 'men's jobs' whilst at the same time increasing the numbers of jobs seen as suitable for women. However, many of the jobs which women are now doing are part time, poorly paid, and with few prospects of career advancement. Some commentators see these developments as irreversible: 'Men, both the young and the old, may be waiting for the return of an era which has gone for good' (Balls 1993: 23).

Unemployment and Social Exclusion

Relatively high rates of unemployment have come to characterize many European economies; however, patterns of unemployment vary considerably in terms of age, race, gender and geography (see Box 7.3 for the problems of defining unemployment). Unemployment rates are higher for young people, ethnic minorities, those with no, or poor, educational or training qualifications and generally higher for men than for women (see Table 7.4 for gender and age variations). In addition, there are regions of exceptionally high unemployment.

> **Box 7.3 The problems of defining unemployment**
>
> We need to be cautious when looking at unemployment statistics, especially when comparing across countries. Unemployment can be defined for data gathering purposes in a number of different ways, which have implications for the headline figure of unemployment, and hence public perceptions of the problem. Before April 1998 in the UK the main indicator of unemployment was the government figures based on the claimant count (that is, those unemployed and claiming benefits). This calculation was much criticized, as it did not include, for example, people on government training schemes. From 1998 the International Labour Office definition is used. This definition of unemployment is accepted as a more workable one for comparative purposes: someone is unemployed if they do not have a job but are available to start work within two weeks and have looked for work in the previous four weeks or have been waiting to start a job.
>
> However, even this measure is open to debate. Some people may regard themselves as unemployed even though they may not be officially defined as such, for example, someone who was forced to take early retirement but did not wish to give up work, or a disabled person not in work but who would actually like to work if suitable employment were available.
>
> Also defining someone as unemployed may not be strictly accurate; they may be engaged in work in the informal economy, doing voluntary work or unpaid caring in the home, thus actually 'working' if not part of the formal economy.

Youth Unemployment

Young people throughout Europe have been particularly affected by unemployment (see Table 7.5). This has led some to talk about the restructuring of the youth labour market and the prolonging of the transition from school to work (see Chapter 14). As a result, possible responses to youth unemployment have been a major focus for debate and policy reform (see below). The implications of a hard core of long-term unemployed young people have also fuelled the debate about the development of an **underclass**. A recent definition of the underclass underscores the potential relationship between unemployment and social exclusion:

a social group or class of people located at the bottom of the class structure who, over time, have become structurally separate and culturally distinct from the regularly employed working class and society in general through processes of social and economic change (particularly de-industrialisation) and/or through patterns of cultural behaviour, who are now persistently reliant on state benefits and almost permanently confined to living in poorer conditions and neighbourhoods. (Macdonald 1997: 3–4)

Many young people only experience unemployment for a short period before going into further education, training, or a job, and therefore we must not assume that unemployment alone causes social exclusion or the basis for an underclass. Nevertheless, in certain localities such as Liverpool in England, or amongst certain ethnic communities,

	United Kingdom (Percentages)						
	1991	**1992**	**1993**	**1994**	**1995**	**1996**	**1997**
Males							
16–19	16.4	18.6	22.0	20.9	19.6	20.6	18.2
20–24	15.2	18.9	20.3	18.3	17.0	16.2	14.0
25–44	8.0	10.5	10.9	10.2	9.0	8.7	7.0
45–54	6.3	8.4	9.4	8.6	7.4	6.4	6.1
55–59	8.4	11.2	12.3	11.6	10.2	9.9	8.0
60–64	9.9	10.2	14.2	11.6	9.9	8.9	7.6
65 and over	5.9	4.9	4.6	3.7	–	4.1	4.0
All aged 16 and over	9.2	11.5	12.4	11.4	10.1	9.7	8.1
Females							
16–19	12.7	13.6	15.9	16.0	14.8	14.6	14.0
20–24	10.1	10.2	11.8	10.7	10.6	8.9	8.9
25–44	7.1	7.3	7.3	7.0	6.7	6.3	5.4
45–54	4.6	5.0	5.0	5.0	4.5	4.1	3.8
55–59	5.5	4.5	6.0	6.5	4.7	4.2	4.8
60 and over	4.4	3.1	3.9	2.9	–	–	2.0
All aged 16 and over	7.2	7.3	7.6	7.3	6.8	6.3	5.8

Table 7.4 Unemployment rates:[a] by gender and age

[a] Unemployment based on the ILO definition as a percentage of all economically active.

Source: Office for National Statistics 1998: 87.

such as blacks in American inner-city ghettos, unemployment may be more persistent and intra-generational, leading to the kind of social marginalization implied in definitions of the underclass. (Roberts 1997: 45–7)

Lone Parents and Unemployment

Another group which has attracted special attention in the debate about unemployment, especially in the United States and the UK, are lone parents. In comparison with other European countries the UK has a high number of lone-parent households; they are less likely to be in paid employment, and are therefore more likely to be dependent on state benefits. Table 7.6 provides comparative data on unemployment and participation rates for lone parents.

In America the 'problem' of lone mothers has been seen as a key side-effect of earlier welfare systems: income support for lone mothers is thought to have reduced the incentive to marry and to work. Hence, conservative critics have pointed to the growth in the numbers of lone mothers as evidence that the welfare state has contributed to the breakdown of the family and the work ethic.

The ability of lone parents to go out to work is obviously dependent upon a range of

	Percentages	
	1991	**1996**
Finland	–	42
Spain	31	42
Italy	28	34
Greece	25	31
France	20	28
Sweden	–	22
Belgium	14	20
Irish Republic	23	18
Portugal	9	17
United Kingdom	14	15
Denmark	12	11
Netherlands	11	11
Germany	6	10
Luxembourg	3	9
Austria	–	7
EU average	17[b]	22

Table 7.5 Youth unemployment rates:[a] European Union comparison

[a] Unemployment of 15–24 year olds, except UK where figures are 16–24; ILO definition of unemployment.
[b] Excludes Finland, Sweden, and Austria because they did not join the EU until 1995.

Source: Office for National Statistics 1998: 88.

Country	ILO unemployment rate 1996 (%)	Activity rate 1996 (%)
UK	19.2	48.4
Ireland	28.0	53.9
Germany	16.6	74.1
France	22.2	84.5
Austria	11.3	85.2
European Union average (1995)	19.6	65.8

Table 7.6 Lone parent unemployment and participation rates

Source: TUC 1998: 22.

factors: for example, the accessibility of appropriate and affordable childcare; a supply of jobs that pay sufficient to sustain the household; and the skills and disposition of the individual.

Explanations of Unemployment

There is no single explanation of unemployment, and indeed we should not expect one, as unemployment itself is a varied condition, encompassing, for example, differences between short-term temporary job loss, long-term unemployment or 'voluntary' re-dundancy, or early retirement. However, debates about the causes of unemployment are important because they underpin different policy responses. It is generally agreed that the core of recent unemployment is structural, namely that declining employment in some sectors, such as manufacturing, is not compensated for by employment expan-sion in others. Unemployment may occur because more jobs are lost than are created, or because of constraints on mobility (that is, the new jobs are located somewhere different to the old jobs); or because people are not prepared or able, for a variety of reasons, to accept different kinds of work. Another cause of structural unemployment is technological development; in this case advances in process and methods means that less people are required to produce the same level of output as in the past. Thus, both the number and the kinds of people in demand in the labour market change.

In relation to policy discussions, we can draw a broad distinction between individual-ist and structuralist explanations of unemployment, and hence different approaches to its remedy. Neo-liberals see high unemployment as a consequence of the uncompeti-tiveness of Western economies in comparison to emerging economies in other parts of the world. This uncompetitiveness is seen in part as a result of the market distortions created by the welfare state: individuals for a variety of reasons have failed to adapt sufficiently to the new economic circumstances. This may be because they refuse to accept lower wages and change the kind of work they do; because they fail to acquire the new skills needed to get work; or because, in the context of welfare benefits which ameliorate the effects of unemployment, they have lost the incentive to get work. Structuralist explanations, on the other hand, see the unemployed as victims of global economic forces and changes, locked into cycles of social and economic disadvantage beyond their power as individuals to change.

All societies in Europe have to wrestle with the issue of unemployment, although the severity of the problem varies from country to country. The economic and social costs of high unemployment have led to employment/unemployment policy being a key site of debate on the future of the welfare state in the next century.

What Can Policy Do?

There are various ways in which public policy can have an impact on work and employ-ment. First, the demand for labour can be affected by the broad course of macro-economic policy, for example through the impact of monetary and fiscal policies on economic development and growth (see Chapter 5). Second, specific employment regulation such as collective labour laws regarding the conduct of industrial relations and trade unions and individual labour law regarding aspects such as discrimination and unfair dismissal can affect the experience of employment and issues such as wage determination. Third, education and training policies may have an impact on the supply of labour and hence the employability of individuals (see Chapter 14). Fourth, policy may be directed to what is often referred to as active labour market policy, which includes job creation and job subsidy policies. Fifth, welfare and benefit systems are used to try to ensure a safety net for the inactive, unemployed, low-paid, or retired. Social policy analysts have traditionally been concerned with the benefit systems, but in practice it is difficult to separate out policy in these different areas, as they inevitably impact upon each other.

Lying behind policy choices are political views about what government should and can do. We will consider three different broad approaches to the question of what policy can and should do: the deregulationist or neo-liberal approach; the regulation or social-democratic approach, which can take a number of different forms; and the radical alternatives, sometimes thought of as 'green' ideas (see, for example, Esping-Andersen 1996a: 10–21). In practice, as we shall see, real life policies are sometimes a mixture of these different perspectives.

Deregulation or the Neo-Liberal Approach

A liberal market approach of deregulation and minimal welfare is the approach that broadly characterized the US and UK in the 1980s and early 1990s.

The case for a deregulated labour market rests on the belief that regulation—in very broad terms employment protection and minimum wage legislation, plus adequate legal backing for trade unions—renders markets less flexible and less adaptable, thus driving up unemployment. (Philpott 1997: 12)

Simply put, the belief is that highly paid workers in the first-world economies have priced themselves out of jobs in the face of competition from low-wage economies in other parts of the world. The solution, in part, is to reassert market forces with the aim of depressing wages. The answer to unemployment is to concentrate on restimulating the economy, and free up the labour market so that labour can find its true price. Often combined with this kind of analysis is the argument that the welfare state and its benefit safety net has created a dependency culture in which even when there is work people lack the incentives to go out and get it. One approach, advocated by Charles Murray in the United States, for example, is therefore to withdraw benefits and force people back to work.

These arguments have found their strongest supporters in the United States, where policy has been directed towards the twin aims of creating a lower wage economy at the bottom end of the labour market, and making participation in employment or training a condition of benefit entitlement. The latter approach to unemployment benefits is usually called **workfare,** and typically carries with it a strong moral undertone:

Dispute over what can be expected of poor people, not lack of opportunity, is the main reason chronic poverty persists in America. (Mead 1997: 1; see Box 7.4 for a classic exposition of the case for work requirements as a condition of benefit)

Box 7.4 The case for work requirements in welfare policy

'To welfare advocates, mandatory work requirements appear severe. They charge that programmes 'force' or 'coerce' recipients to work. Conservative critics of welfare, on the other hand, see little point in trying to enforce work in the teeth of the disincentives to work that they think deter employment on welfare. Better to abolish aid so that the employable have no alternative to working. . . .

When asked, however, most welfare recipients and other poor people typically say that they want to work. If they do not actually work, the reason is that the practical difficulties seem overwhelming, not that they reject the idea. Not working, in fact, causes them shame and discouragement, since they are not living by their own values. This gap between intention and behaviour is what makes work enforcement necessary. . . .

While voluntary, service-oriented programmes realise some gains, these policies are sometimes not cost-beneficial. They cost too much for the work gains and welfare reductions they realise. It is the mandatory, work-oriented form of welfare employment programme that clearly delivers the goods. The impacts of such programmes are likely to rise as they are more fully implemented. . . .

While many investments might be made in the poor, a virtue of welfare enforcement is that it directly addresses non-work, the greatest economic problem of welfare adults. And it does so in a way that does not immediately deny them all support. The combination of aid with work-tests does more for the dependent than aid without expectations, the traditional liberal recommendation, or the denial of aid favoured by anti-government conservatives. This combination is also more politic. The voters want welfare adults to do more to help themselves, but not at the cost of putting children at risk. The only way to realise both goals is to enforce work *within* the welfare system.' (Mead 1997: 36–7, 41)

These ideas have travelled from America to the UK and were influential in the Conservative governments of the 1980s and early 1990s. They still inform current policy thinking, as will be seen below.

Of course, underlying such policy ideas is the assumption that there are jobs into which people can be forced, and in the American example the expansion of low-paid service-sector jobs has been considerable. In Europe it is not so clear that such a policy could work without some element of government-sponsored job creation.

Regulation or the Social-Democratic Approach

A 'regulation' or 'social-democratic' approach to unemployment and related employment issues starts from the premise that the difficulties are structural rather than individual, and therefore that state intervention of some sort to secure the welfare of disadvantaged groups is legitimate. Thus, policy is expected to combine employment protection measures, such as unfair dismissal legislation and directives on working hours, with social protection for those who are disadvantaged in the labour market. Esping-Andersen (1996a) sees Sweden as the archetype of such an approach: comprehensive and universalistic benefit systems combined with active labour market policies designed to create jobs, especially in the public sector, and to provide continuing education and training to enable people to take up job opportunities. The problem with such an approach, simply put, is that it is expensive and requires a degree of social consensus accepting high levels of taxation as the price for a developed welfare system.

In other countries in Europe a different variant of the social democratic approach has been tried, leading to what Esping-Andersen has characterized as the 'labour reduction route':

> While the Scandinavians have managed the surplus of 'deindustrialized', largely unskilled, masses with retraining and job creation, and the Americans with wage erosion, the continental European nations have opted to subsidize their exit, especially through early retirement. This has arguably produced an 'insider–outsider' divide, with a small, predominantly male, 'insider' workforce enjoying high wages, expensive social rights, and strong job security, combined with a swelling population of 'outsiders' depending either on the male breadwinner's pay or on welfare state transfers. (1996*a*: 18)

The growth in the numbers of inactive men, that is, the retired and those on invalidity benefits, has been considerable in countries such as Denmark, Germany, and France. Not unsurprisingly, those most likely either to be forced into early retirement through redundancy or to opt for an early end to work are those whose employment was unskilled and/or poorly paid (OECD 1994: 27–35). As a result the labour-reduction route is liable to increase the dependency of older groups on welfare benefits of one sort or another.

Due to the welfare costs associated with such approaches to the problem of unemployment, social democratic ideas have increasingly come under pressure from the arguments of the neo-liberals. However, in most Continental European countries the social costs of a deregulation approach as developed in America are seen as too high: unemployment may be reduced, but at the expense of growing poverty and social inequality. Social democratic or regulation perspectives have therefore increasingly argued for what Esping-Andersen (1996*a*: 3) has characterized as a 'social investment strategy'. This emphasizes the desirability of moving from passive (income support) benefits to active labour-market policies. Thus, in addition to the concern with social security through benefits systems, a regulation approach now typically also puts a premium on so-called supply-side measures: that is, policies on education and training designed to make people more employable.

In recent debates about the future of the welfare state in Europe, especially in Britain, there has been discussion of the possibilities of a 'middle way', that is, a basis for policy that borrows from both neo-liberal and social democratic ideas (see the discussion of recent policy below).

Radical Alternatives

Although debate about employment and unemployment policy is dominated by the dispute between deregulation and regulation perspectives, a third set of ideas has increasingly tried to inject radical alternatives into the argument. Such alternatives do not form a coherent whole, but rather come from a number of different perspectives. What unites them is often an anti-state, self-help approach, and for this reason they are sometimes characterized as 'green' ideas.

> ## Box 7.5 Reconceiving work
>
> 'But whatever employment levels pertain in the medium term, there are good reasons to recast the utopia from one of full employment to one (sometimes dubbed "full engagement") which provides access to income and to meaningful work, paid or unpaid as citizens.
>
> First, for the immediate future, the lead export sectors for the UK—such as financial services, tourism and manufacturing—will remain central to national employment levels and generating secondary employment and income. However, the evidence of "jobless" communities is on the rise. . . . So, in the face of mass unemployment there is a pressing need for alternative approaches to work within deprived neighbourhoods that meet people's needs and promote self-reliance.
>
> At the same time, there is a pressing social and economic need to reverse the low status and conditions of unpaid work, given the increasing stress and personal cost to those doing it. . . .
>
> Second, employment should be seen not as an end in itself, but as a means to achieving a better quality of life. This means distinguishing between forms of work, with the aim of promoting patterns of work that are socially useful and contribute to greater personal autonomy and fulfillment.' (Mayo 1996: 146–7)

These ideas revolve around a rejection of continued economic growth as an overarching aim for government policy, or simply see the possibility of a return to post-war 'full employment' as utopian (Mayo 1996). Thus, if it will be impossible to find paid employment for everyone, the focus must shift to finding alternatives to work or attempts to share work out more evenly (see also Marsh 1991). This might involve facing the question of why we should continue to see paid employment as a defining characteristic of citizenship or social inclusion. Instead participation through other activities such as voluntary or community work should rank equally as a contribution to society (see Box 7.5).

Another set of ideas suggests that in the face of continued high unemployment policy should focus on guaranteed incomes schemes. This would involve a universal guaranteed income for anyone who fell below an agreed acceptable threshold, whether they were in employment or not (Pixley 1993: 91–4). Critics of such an idea point both to the cost but also to the effect on incentives, arguing that no-one would take certain low-paid jobs if they were guaranteed an income regardless of whether they worked or not.

Recent Policy Initiatives in the UK

Up until the middle of the 1970s, full employment was an avowed aim of governments in the UK, and there was a broad political consensus on the role of the welfare state in supporting the unemployed. Since that time, and especially since the early 1980s and the period of Conservative government, the agreement on policy objectives has broken down and policy has moved progressively away from the full-employment ideal.

In the 1980s Conservative governments followed in the footsteps of Republican politicians in the United States in arguing that the welfare state had resulted in perverse incentives, discouraging the unemployed from seeking work and leading to welfare dependency. As a result policy shifted in a neo-liberal direction, reducing employment protection and the bargaining power of trade unions whilst simultaneously cutting levels of welfare benefits and increasingly moving to a more conditional system of entitlement to benefit.

Changes to social-security benefits were focused around two main perceived problems. First, there was the need to reduce public expenditure and second to restructure work incentives. Thus the targets for policy were to reduce the levels of benefit and require the unemployed to demonstrate their availability or willingness to work (see Chapter 11). As Evans summarizes:

Social security changed from concerns about coverage in the 1970s to concerns about fiscal constraint and labour market incentives. Targeting, economic incentives, and efficiency became the central concerns of policy in the 1980s. (1998: 263)

The Jobseeker's Allowance, introduced in 1996, marked the final point of these developments under the Conservative governments of the 1980s and 1990s. This marked the end of insurance-based unemployment benefit, replacing it finally with an allowance that required claimants to demonstrate that they were actively looking for work as a condition of receiving benefit. Critics of these developments viewed them as simply punitive:

With declining employment prospects for the unskilled, for black people and for working-class youth, who figure disproportionately among the unemployed, the measures introduced by the Jobseeker's Allowance serve only as a form of punishment. (Novak 1997: 106)

Welfare to Work

The new Labour Government of 1997 came into power committed to the reform of the welfare state; however, this was not heralded as a return to the ideas and policies of the 1960s and 1970s. Instead, the new government was keen to develop a new middle way which took up some of the ideas of the neo-liberals whilst maintaining the social democratic commitment to social justice. The centrepiece of this new approach is the New Deal, a raft of **welfare to work** policies announced in the first budget of the new Labour Government in 1997. The avowed aim of the policy is to get the long-term unemployed, especially younger people, back into work on the basis that work is the best guarantor of welfare. 18–24 year olds who have been claiming Jobseeker's allowance for 6 months or more will enter a 'gateway' to work, which involves job search and career advice and training before taking up one of four options (see Box 7.6).

Any young people who refuse to take up one of these options will have their benefit cut. Gordon Brown (Chancellor of the Exchequer at the time of announcing the policy) said that there would be no fifth option 'to stay at home in bed watching television' (quoted in the *Financial Times*, 26.6.97).

In addition to these measures focused on young people, the scheme will also apply to

---

Box 7.6 New Deal options

Young people enter a 'gateway' to the four options; this involves a period of one-to-one advice and guidance which may last up to 4 months. They then move onto one of the following options:

1. A job in the private sector: a job subsidy of £60 a week for six months will be paid to employers who employ an unemployed young person.
2. A job in the voluntary sector: on the same basis as (1) above.
3. A place on an environment taskforce: the young person will receive normal benefit plus £20 a week.
4. Full-time education and training.

---

pregnant women, lone parents, and the long-term disabled. To facilitate the re-entry of women with children into the labour market there is also a new national strategy on childcare. In June 1998 the New Deal was extended to the group of people aged 25 and above. The new policy is couched in terms of a new partnership between government and the private sector:

New Deal will close the gap between what young people have to offer, and the needs of employers, with an intensive programme of training, further education and work experience.

Employers have an important role to play in making New Deal a success, offering employment under the subsidised jobs option and providing training during that time. . . . In turn, the scheme benefits employers in a number of ways. It helps meet their manpower needs and it gives them a new source of potential recruits.

(Labour Party, undated)

In addition to the New Deal, the new Labour Government is continuing a range of training policy measures such as Modern Apprenticeships, designed to improve the skills of the workforce (see Chapter 14), and it is introducing new employment protection measures, most notably a minimum wage (see Box 7.7).

Writing in 1998 it is too early to assess these policies fairly; however, it is clear that the approach does borrow from what have here been characterized as the 'regulation' and 'deregulation' approaches. The commitment to a minimum wage and a degree of trade union recognition puts the policies firmly in the social-democratic camp, as does the emphasis on supply-side measures such as improved access to further education and training. However, there is no option for young people to opt out of the New Deal and still receive benefit. The policy introduced by earlier Conservative governments of making entitlement to welfare conditional on participation in work or training is maintained, and owes much to the American examples of workfare schemes. This aspect of the policy is more in the tradition of neo-liberal thought.

The New Deal scheme is inevitably controversial; neo-liberals point to the cost of the programme and argue that it produces no new jobs. Critics from the political left argue that it retains too much of the compulsion that characterized the neo-liberal policies which preceded it. At the time of writing, the scheme is very new but there are concerns

---

Box 7.7 The case for a minimum wage

'A national minimum wage, set with care, can be a force for social justice and economic efficiency in the UK. A minimum wage should be designed to banish exploitation in the labour market, encourage employers to invest in people, and prevent taxpayers paying a large part of employers' production costs.

- In a rich country like ours, no adult workers should be expected to work for £1.50 or £2 an hour;
- Without a minimum wage, the taxpayer ends up subsidizing low-paying employers through the social security system;
- Labour-market research shows that at the bottom of the labour market, where employers are most powerful, low pay undervalues the skills of workers;
- Low pay is a symptom of a cycle of low investment, high turnover, and low-quality production, which needs to be reversed.'

Source: Report of the Commission on Social Justice 1994: 204.

---

that policy will offer no solution to the lack of jobs in the economy: 'There is clearly a danger that in depressed local economies the lack of jobs will reduce the effectiveness of the New Deal' (Bill Callaghan, TUC quoted in the *Financial Times* 6.4.98). Nevertheless, the policy represents a new attempt at a social investment strategy with active labour-market intervention in the attempt to reduce unemployment.

Conclusions

Despite a number of decades of persistent unemployment and widespread popular fears about an emerging 'workshy', delinquent, and socially marginal underclass, work, or rather employment, seems to be as popular as ever. Most young people want to find a good job, many lone parents would like the opportunity to work, and many disabled people feel unfairly excluded from the world of paid employment. Employment is still seen by the majority as the ticket to full participation in society. The problem for the UK and other European societies is whether it is possible to produce both high levels of employment and social justice or equality. The American example of a low-wage, low-skills, high-employment economy is impressive in the number of jobs it provides but worrying with respect to the growing ranks of the working poor. This raises the question of whether any job is better for the individual's welfare than no job (see Box 7.8). The Swedish or German examples of high-wage, high-skills, high-employment economies have looked increasingly unsustainable as competition in the global economy heats up. The search for a 'middle way' between these two alternatives is bound to continue. Whether the UK is in the vanguard of such a new approach, or merely the test bed in which these ideas will prove unworkable, remains to be seen.

Box 7.8 Is any job better than no job?

Source: *Financial Times*, 8.10.96. Reprinted with permission.

Glossary

division of labour 'One of the most distinctive characteristics of the economic system of modern societies is the development of a highly complex and diverse division of labour. In other words, work is divided into an enormous number of different occupations, in which people specialise.' (Giddens 1993: 491)

flexible or casual work This refers to jobs which are not full-time and permanent, but rather temporary, on short-term contract, variable hours, or one-off contracts for a particular piece of work. Labour flexibility is the ability of a firm to modify the employment and utilization of its labour force in the face of changing labour and product market conditions. (Pass *et al.* 1991: 328)

full employment Usually defined either as more jobs available than people seeking employment, or a job available for anyone seeking one.

gender pay gap The Equal Opportunities Commission (1996: 2) offers a definition: 'The gender pay gap is defined as women's earnings as a percentage of men's earnings. The pay gap is said to be narrow as this figure approaches 100 per cent.'

labour market The labour market refers to the process whereby firms look for employees (the demand side of the market) and people offer their labour power in return for a wage or salary (the supply side of the market). In practice there can be said to be many different labour markets, such as local labour markets: the supply and demand for labour in a local area; or skilled and specialist labour markets.

male breadwinner model This model assumes a traditional nuclear family structure in which the man goes out to work and earns a family wage (enough for himself and his dependants), and the woman stays at home and works in the domestic sphere for no money.

occupational identity In the past a lot of men, especially skilled workers, could expect to stay in their industry or craft throughout their working lives, and as a result there were often strong occupational identities, for example in shipbuilding, mining, and the steel industry.

participation rates This refers to the percentage of a particular group, such as women, who are in or are seeking paid employment.

post-industrial As the share of employment in industry has declined, and advanced capitalist economies such as Britain are dominated by non-industrial employment, the term 'post-industrial' has been used to denote a new phase for these economies.

service sector It is typical to characterize the economy as divided into three main sectors: the primary sector, which includes activities such as agriculture, mining, and fishing; the industrial sector, which includes manufacture and construction; and the service sector, which includes retail, banking, teaching, health, and personal services.

underclass 'A social group or class of people located at the bottom of the class structure who, over time, have become structurally separate and culturally distinct from the regularly employed working class and society in general through processes of social and economic change (particularly de-industrialization) and/or through patterns of cultural behaviour, who are now persistently reliant on state benefits and almost permanently confined to living in poorer conditions and neighbourhoods.' (Macdonald 1997: 3–4)

welfare to work This term has been a specific and a general reference. Specifically, it has recently been used to refer to the Labour Government of 1997's policies designed to get the long-term unemployed off welfare benefits and into paid work. More generally, the term is sometimes used to refer to all policy ideas which see work as the best form of welfare and therefore argue that policy should be directed towards encouraging or forcing unemployed people back into work.

workfare This can be defined as any social policy in which participation in job search, training, or work is a condition of receiving benefits.

Guide to Further Reading

Esping-Andersen, G., 'After the Golden Age? Welfare State Dilemmas in a Global Economy', *Welfare States in Transition: National Adaptations in Global Economies*, ed. by G. Esping-Andersen (London: Sage, 1996). This chapter provides a good review of the problems facing welfare states in the post-full-employment period.

Macdonald, R. (1997) (ed.), *Youth, the 'Underclass' and Social Exclusion* (London: Routledge). This is a recent collection of articles reviewing the debate about whether an underclass is developing in the UK with particular reference to the position of young people.

Marsh, C. (1991), 'The right to work: justice in the distribution of employment', *Social Policy Review 1990–91*, ed. Manning (Harlow: Longman). This article provides an interesting discussion of the possibility of introducing a legally enforceable right to work.

Mead, L. M., *From Welfare to Work: Lessons from America* (London: Institute of Economic Affairs, 1997). This book provides an introduction to Mead's work, a leading American thinker on welfare reform along with commentaries from a number of British social policy writers and thinkers, including Frank Field, who was Minister for Welfare Reform for the first 15 months of the new Labour Government in 1997/8.

Meadows, P., *Work Out—Or Work In?* (Layerthorpe: Joseph Rowntree Foundation, 1996). This edited collection reviews the main trends and changes in patterns of access to paid employment and concentrates on the policy implications of these developments.

Philpott, J. (ed.), *Working for Full Employment* (London: Routledge, 1997). Contributions to this edited collection examine the nature and consequences of contemporary unemployment and examine different policy responses. A number of contributions compare an Anglo-American deregulation approach with the more European regulation approach.

Pixley, J., *Citizenship and Employment* (Cambridge: Cambridge University Press, 1993). This book reviews theoretical arguments about the centrality of work in our societies and in particular, the extent to which full employment is still a viable policy goal. She also undertakes a critical analysis of alternatives to paid work, such as guaranteed incomes schemes and communes.

References

Abbott, P., and Wallace, C. (1997), *An Introduction to Sociology: Feminist Perspectives* (London: Routledge).

Ashton, D. (1992), 'The Restructuring of the Labour Market and Youth Training', in Brown and Lauder (London: Routledge), 180–202.

Balls, E. (1993), 'Danger: Men Not at Work: Unemployment and Non-Employment in the UK and Beyond', in Balls and Gregg (1993), 1–30.

——and Gregg, P. (1993), *Work and Welfare: Tackling the Jobs Deficit* (London: Institute for Public Policy Research).

Crompton, R., Gallie, D., and Purcell, K. (1996) (eds.), *Changing Forms of Employment: Organisations, Skills and Gender* (London: Routledge).

Equal Opportunities Commission (1996), *Briefings on Women and Men in Britain: Pay* (Manchester).

Esping-Andersen, G. (1996a), 'After the Golden Age? Welfare State Dilemmas in a Global Economy', in Esping-Andersen (1996) 1–31.

——(1996b) (ed.), *Welfare States in Transition: National Adaptations in Global Economies* (London: Sage).

Evans, M. (1998), 'Social Security: Dismantling the Pyramids?', in Glennerster and Hills (1998), 257–307.

Gallie, D. (1991), 'Patterns of Skill Change: Upskilling, Deskilling or the Polarisation of Skills?', *Work Employment and Society* 5/3, 319–51.

——(1996), 'Skill, Gender and the Quality of Employment', in Crompton, Gallie, and Purcell (1996), 133–59.

Giddens, A. (1993), *Sociology* (Oxford: Oxford University Press).

Ginn, J. and Arber, S. (1993), 'Pension Penalties: The Gendered Division of Occupational Welfare', *Work Employment and Society*, 7/1, 47–70.

Glennerster, H., and Hills, J. (1998) (ed.), *The State of Welfare: The Economics of Social Spending* (Oxford: Oxford University Press).

Gregory, A., and O'Reilly, J. (1996), 'Checking Out and Cashing Up: The Prospects and Paradoxes of Regulating Part-Time Work in Europe', in Crompton, Gallie, and Purcell (1996), 207–34.

Hewitt, P. (1996), 'The Place of Part-Time Employment', in Meadows (1996), 39–58.

Labour Party (undated), *A New Deal for a New Britain* (London: Labour Party).

Macdonald, R. (1997) (ed.), *Youth, the 'Underclass' and Social Exclusion* (London: Routledge).

Manning, N. (1991) (ed.), *Social Policy Review 1990–91* (Harlow: Longman).

Marsh, C. (1991), 'The Right to Work: Justice in the Distribution of Employment', in Manning (1991), 223–42.

Mayo, E. (1996), 'Dreaming of Work', in Meadows (1996), 143–64.

Mead, L. M. (1997), *From Welfare to Work: Lessons from America* (London: Institute for Economic Affairs).

Meadows, P. (1996), *Work Out—Or Work In?* (Layerthorpe: Joseph Rowntree Foundation)

Novak, T. (1997), 'Hounding Delinquents: The Introduction of the Jobseeker's Allowance', *Critical Social Policy*, 17/1: 99–110.

Office for National Statistics (ONS) (1998), *Social Trends 28* (London: HMSO).

Organization for Economic Cooperation and Development (Brussels: OECD) (1994), *New Orientations for Social Policy*, Social Policy Studies 12 (Brussels)

Pass, C., Lowes, B., Pendleton, A., and Chadwick, L. (1991), *Collins Dictionary of Business* (Glasgow: Collins).

Philpott, J. (1997), 'Looking Forward to Full employment: An Overview', in Philpott (1997), 1–29.

——(1997) (ed.), *Working for Full Employment* (London: Routledge).

Pixley, J. (1993), *Citizenship and Employment* (Cambridge: Cambridge University Press).

Report of the Commission on Social Justice (1994), *Social Justice: Strategies for Renewal* (London: Vintage).

Ritzer, G. (1993), *The McDonaldization of Society* (Newbury Park, California: Pine Forge Press).

Roberts, K. (1997), 'Is there an Emerging British "Underclass"? The Evidence from Youth Research', in Macdonald (1997), 39–54.

Rubery, J. (1997), 'What Do Women Want from Full Employment?', in Philpott (1997), 63–80.

Trades Union Congress (TUC) (undated), *Jobs, Unemployment and Exclusion* (London).

8 The Family and the Production of Welfare

Jan Pahl

Contents

Introduction: A Changing Source of Welfare

'The family' is a controversial topic. There are some commentators who deplore the changes which are taking place in family life, while others applaud the end of what they see as damaging patterns of family relationships. Some argue that 'family policy' has gone too far and has created a culture of dependence that loads intolerable burdens on the welfare state, while others insist that 'family policy' in Britain has not gone far enough in supporting families and their members. Behind these debates lie deep ideological divides and a fundamental division between the private sphere of the family and the public sphere where social policy is made and implemented.

In this chapter we shall be looking at the facts behind the rhetoric. What changes are taking place in the lives of families and their members? What part do families play in the production of welfare? What are the principles which underlie family policy and what has been the impact of recent policy changes? And what does 'the family' mean in a world of cultural diversity and rapid social change?

Families and Households

Definitions

'Family' and 'household' are important terms for this topic, so we begin with some definitions. The **household** is a key unit in social policy, since it is the focus of a great many policy interventions. For example, means-tested social security payments are calculated on the basis of household income; the council tax is levied on households, not individuals; and many statistics are based on the unit of the household.

One definition of the household is given in *Social Trends*, the annual publication of the Office for National Statistics:

A household is a person living alone or a group of people who have the address as their only or main residence and who either share one meal a day or share the living accommodation. (Office for National Statistics 1998: 235)

So households are based on a common place of residence and some sharing of either food or accommodation. Of course, in many cases the 'household' contains a single 'family', but the concept of family is intrinsically much more complicated than the concept of household.

Many definitions have been suggested for the term **family**. In Britain it seems to be agreed that a married couple and their dependent children constitute a family, but when other social groupings and other cultures are concerned, definitions become less secure. The definitional possibilities can be explored by asking a range of different people whether, in their opinion, the following constitute 'a family':

- one parent and his or her children?
- a cohabiting couple and their children?
- an elderly person and an adult child?

- a lesbian couple and the children of one of them?
- a group of students living together and sharing meals?
- a father living apart from his wife and children but supporting them financially?

The answers suggest that the idea of the family is essentially subjective, reflecting each person's ideas about family life. The Family Policy Studies Centre, which produces many useful publications on this topic, concluded, 'There is no definition of a family. The UK Association of the International Year of the Family does not define a family, but aims to support families in all their possible forms' (Family Policy Studies Centre 1997: 1).

However, there do seem to be some characteristics which define a 'family' for most people. These include:

- marriage or a marriage-like relationship between adults
- the presence of children who are or have been dependent on the adults
- sharing of resources such as living space, money, and property
- continuity over time
- links with other kin

The official definition of the family, used in all government censuses and surveys, is that a family is:

a married or cohabiting couple, either with or without their never-married children (of any age), including childless couples or a lone parent together with his or her never-married child or children. (Office for National Statistics 1998: 235)

However, even this definition might be controversial, since it excludes households which some people would regard as 'families', such as lesbian or gay couples with children, and includes some households which might not be seen as 'families', such as cohabiting couples without children.

A useful distinction has been made between the nuclear family and the extended family. The **nuclear family** typically consists of one or two adults living together in a household with their dependent children. However, many nuclear families are embedded in larger kin networks, with whom they may from time to time share living space, money, and property, and which may include grandparents, aunts and uncles, cousins and so on. This larger kin network is described as an **extended family**, and though it is often described as being characteristic of more traditional societies, it also remains an important source of support in Britain.

Another useful distinction is between those who focus on 'the family', a term which implies that there is one, ideal type of family, and those who focus on 'families', a term which allows for the increasing diversity of family forms. The idea of 'the family' rests on the assumption that the most natural and desirable family is composed of two married parents and their children, with the father as the main breadwinner and the mother as the homemaker, who fits any paid work around her responsibilities for the home and children. The idea of 'families' underlines the point that family life and relationships can take many different forms, as we shall see, and that no one type of family should be privileged over the others.

Debates about 'Family Values'

All the changes taking place in family life throughout Europe and North America have produced fierce debates. On the one hand some people have argued that the 'breakdown of the traditional family' is to blame for a range of social problems, from unemployment and crime to violence and lone-parent families. On the other hand, other people have argued that the 'traditional family' is itself the problem. From this point of view, family violence and lone-parent families are symptoms of inequalities, and even exploitation, within the family, and the changes taking place in family life are to be welcomed rather than deplored.

The following quotations express these two different approaches to the changing shape of family life, both taken from Muncie *et al.* (1995: 59):

Despite attempts to subvert it, our laws and systems must acknowledge the family as the basic building block of the nation. Instead of simply calling for more money as the solution to every problem, or even trying to accommodate unconventional lifestyles, the nation's spiritual leaders should unashamedly extol the virtues of normal family life.
Gerald Howarth, Conservative MP, 1991

Family policy needs to recognize that families come in all shapes and sizes . . . to claim that one kind of family is right and others wrong can do considerable harm by stigmatizing those who live in non-traditional family settings.
Harriet Harman, Labour MP, 1991

These debates reflect profoundly different ideological approaches to families and family life. Since **ideology** will be a key concept for this chapter, it may be useful to begin with a definition.

Ideologies are sets of ideas, assumptions and images, by which people make sense of society, which give a clear social identity, and which serve in some way to legitimize power relations in society. (McLennan 1991: 114) (See also Chapter 4.)

This definition underlines the fact that ideologies not only influence the ways in which individuals think about themselves and their place in the world, but also shape the development of social policy and social action in the broader, political arena. One way of making sense of different ideologies about the family is to consider the theoretical perspectives which underlie them.

Theoretical and Policy Perspectives on the Family

Many theoretical explanations of the social world have been developed within the discipline of sociology. In thinking about families, three theoretical perspectives are particularly relevant.

Three Theoretical Perspectives

The functionalist analysis of the family was developed by the American sociologists Parsons and Bales (1956). They suggested that the nuclear family, consisting of a breadwinner/husband and a homemaker/wife, is the type of family which fits most easily with the requirements of industrial society. Lacking close ties to a wider kin network, the nuclear family is able to move from place to place following the demands of the labour market, and generally to perform the functions necessary for the stable continuation of an industrial society.

From this theoretical perspective the modern nuclear family has two main functions: the socialization of children and 'personality stabilization' or 'tension management' for the adults. Parsons and Bales made a clear distinction between the roles of the husband/father and the wife/mother. They saw the father's role as being instrumental, with his employment providing for the economic well-being of the family, while the mother's role was affective, being concerned primarily with the emotional well-being of the family. In Parsons' and Bales' analysis the tasks assigned to each sex arose out of biological differences, and in particular out of the mother's responsibility for child-bearing and child-rearing.

Functionalist theories were linked with ideas about modernity, which assume that societies progress towards greater uniformity, leaving behind dysfunctional, or even simply diverse forms of family life. There was an underlying assumption that the middle-class American family of the 1950s and 1960s was by definition a superior form of the family and one to which other groups should aspire. It was often described as the 'normal' family.

Even though the functionalist perspective is now seen as old-fashioned and ethnocentric, there are ways in which the ideologies which underpinned this work are still powerful. For example, the British Social Attitudes Survey includes a question which asks respondents whether they agree or disagree with the statement, 'A husband's job is to earn the money; a wife's job is to look after the home and family'. Every time that this question is asked there is a sizeable minority of people who agree: for example, in 1995 24 per cent of respondents said that they 'agreed' or 'strongly agreed' with the statement, with men more likely to agree than women (Jowell, Brook, and Taylor 1995: 302). The functionalist conception of the family is still widespread. However, a powerful critique of functionalism has been developed by feminists.

The feminist perspective sees the 'normal family' as essentially unequal; it argues that the dependence of women and children on the male breadwinner creates a damaging power imbalance within the family which is the source of many problems, especially for women and children. Far from being a building-block of society, this type of family has been described as 'anti-social':

The division of labour within the family is associated with the greater power of men. Despite the contemporary rhetoric of the 'egalitarian family' and the 'sharing marriage' . . . modern families are still deeply unequal affairs. The principle of the wage-earner and his dependants, or the husband who contributes cash while his wife contributes domestic labour, is not a division of labour between equals, but an unequal exchange in which the man's interests predominate. (Barrett and McIntosh 1982: 65)

Barrett and McIntosh went on to make links between this type of family and a variety of issues which have great policy relevance. These include childcare, violence within the family, social security policy, and the allocation of resources within families.

Other feminists have seen the family as the site of a particular type of exploitation:

(Families) are not just random sets of people united by bonds of affection and kinship who live together and share out the jobs that need doing so as to offer each other practical support in a joint endeavour to get along in the world. Rather they are . . . part of a system of labour relations in which men benefit from, and exploit, the work of women—and sometimes of their children and other male relatives too. (Delphy and Leonard 1992: 1)

To sum up, the feminist perspective on the family argues that:

- The 'normal' family is characterized by inequalities between women and men, and between children and parents, which continue despite the rhetoric of increasing equality.
- These inequalities are translated into inequalities in the allocation of resources, such as money, and in the work done within families, including childcare, domestic work, and caring for dependent members of families.
- These inequalities are maintained by the state, through social and economic policies which assume that families will contain a male breadwinner and a woman who is responsible for childcare and domestic work.

From the feminist perspective, the increases in cohabitation, divorce, and the numbers of lone-parent families are all symptoms of the dissatisfaction which women feel with the traditional form of the family.

However, from the New Right perspective the changes occurring in family life are evidence of a deterioration and decay which is damaging to all. The rise in births outside marriage, the increase in divorce initiated by women, and the failure of fathers to support their children are all symptoms of what is going wrong. The following quotation may be taken as an example of this perspective:

The normal family is threatened from three different directions. First, there are brands of feminism which are deeply hostile to the family, most especially to the role of fathers as breadwinners. Secondly, the responsibility of the family for children and young people is being subverted by the state itself and by professional bodies of doctors and teachers . . . the web of incentives and penalties set by the tax and benefit system is now firmly loaded against the normal family. Thirdly, modern technological developments such as new techniques of embryo fertilization threaten to dislocate traditional relations within the family. (Anderson and Dawson 1986: 11)

The Institute of Economic Affairs has been active in setting out the agenda of the New Right in relation to the family, in publications such as those by Dennis and Erdos (1993) and Morgan (1995); for a critique of this perspective see Abbott and Wallace (1992). Briefly, the New Right perspective can be summed up as follows:

- The 'normal' and most socially valuable form of the family consists of a married couple, with both parents committed to the care of their children, the father through his responsibility for the family's economic well-being and the mother through her responsibility for the home and family.
- This form of the family is currently under threat, because of demographic and ideological changes, which reflect the influence of feminism, individualism, and a more general moral decay.
- The state has played a part in undermining the normal family, by providing support for other types of families, by failing to reward marriage, and by tolerating high levels of unemployment among young males.

The State and Family Policy

There have been a number of attempts to produce a definition of **family policy.** Hantrais and Letablier concluded,

For a social policy to be described as family policy . . . the family would need to be the deliberate target of specific actions, and the measures should be designed so as to have an impact on family resources and, ultimately, on family structure. (Hantrais and Letablier 1996: 139)

However, definitions of family policy tend to founder against the rocks of national and cultural differences. In particular, states vary greatly in the extent to which it is seen as appropriate for governments to intervene in family life. For example, within Europe, Britain has never had an explicit family policy. By contrast, in Finland, France, Germany, Greece, Ireland, Italy, Luxembourg, Portugal, and Spain, the constitution recognizes the family as a social institution and undertakes to afford it protection. Some countries, such as Germany and France, have a designated Minister for the Family (Hantrais and Letablier 1996).

However, in Britain there has always been a debate about the extent to which the state should be involved in family life. This debate emerged again during the 1997 election, and was apparent in the election manifestos put out by the main political parties. The relevant section in the Conservative Party Election Manifesto was entitled 'Choice and Security for Families'. It began by expressing concern about state interference:

The family is the most important institution in our lives. It offers security and stability in a fast-changing world. But the family is undermined if governments take decisions which families ought to take for themselves . . . Conservatives believe that a healthy society encourages people to accept responsibility for their own lives. A heavy-handed and intrusive state can do enormous damage. (Conservative Party 1997: 15 and 17)

Despite the warning about state interference, the manifesto went on to promise new support for families where one parent was not in paid work because of caring for children or a dependent relative. The promised change took the form of allowing one partner's unused tax allowance to be transferred to an earning spouse, a change which would reward two-parent families with only one parent in paid work, but which would be irrelevant to one-parent families or to families where both parents were unemployed. As the manifesto explained, 'We believe our tax system should recognize and support the crucial role of families in their caring responsibilities' (p. 15).

The relevant section in the 1997 Labour Party Election Manifesto was headed 'Help Parents Balance Work and Family', and the text explicitly supported women's right to take paid work and endorsed the value of state involvement in family life:

Labour does not see families and the state as rival providers for the needs of our citizens. Families should provide the day-to-day support for children to be brought up in a stable and loving environment. But families cannot flourish unless government plays its distinctive role: in education, where necessary, in caring for the young; in making provision for illness and old age; in supporting good parenting; and in protecting families from lawlessness and abuse of power. Society, through government, must assist families to achieve collectively what no family can achieve alone. (Labour Party 1997: 24)

In November 1998 the Home Secretary Jack Straw took a first step in realizing the government's broad manifesto commitments by issuing a Green Paper, *Supporting Families: A Consultation Document* (Home Office 1998). This suggested a number of specific ways in which government could help families, particularly in their role in bringing up children:

- Advice and support for families, including a new national parent helpline and an expanded role for Health Visitors;
- Reducing child poverty;
- Balancing work and home priorities through family-friendly policies;
- Reducing the risks of family breakdown by providing a 'pre-marriage information package' to couples and encouraging pre-nuptial agreements;
- Tackling serious problems like domestic violence, truancy and school-age pregnancy, with a major publicity campaign to raise awareness of domestic violence issues.

The consultation document was met with immediate criticism from many sides of the political spectrum, illustrating the political risks inherent in government statements about family policy. The Conservative Party warned of state intrusion into private lives as did representatives of lone parents, and gay and lesbian people, for different reasons. It remains to be seen whether the consultation paper marks a shift in the traditional reluctance of British governments to pursue explicit family policies.

Whether or not Britain has an explicit family policy, there is still an enormous amount of policy-making which is relevant to family life. This may take the form of tax and social security policy, legislation related to marriage and divorce, provision for children and dependent adults, and policies relating to health, housing, and employment. Later in this chapter we shall consider some of these in more detail.

Demographic Trends in Family Life

Information about the changing patterns of family life comes from a variety of different sources, including the ten-yearly national Census of Population, the General Register Office, which collates certificates for births, marriages, and deaths, and a variety of quantitative and qualitative surveys. The annual review *Social Trends* presents a great deal of quantitative data in a very accessible form, and is an essential source of information about all areas of social policy in Britain (Office for National Statistics, 1998). In this chapter it is only possible to summarize a few of the most important trends in family life. Table 8.1 outlines some of the large-scale, quantitative surveys which have produced the data on which this chapter is based.

Changes in Birth Rates and in Fertility

In 1996 the population of the United Kingdom was 58.8 million, of whom just under 6 per cent identified themselves as belonging to an ethnic minority. The **age structure** of the population is a consequence of variations in the annual number of births and deaths. The population pyramid shown in Fig. 8.1 shows that these variations can be quite substantial. The bulge in the pyramid in the late 1940s represents the 'baby boom' which followed the Second World War, while the even bigger bulge among people now

Survey	Frequency	Sampling frame	Type of respondent	Location	Sample size to nearest 1000	Response rate (%)	Reference
British Household Panel Survey	Yearly from 1991	Postcode address file (PAF)	All adults in household plus teenagers in 1994	GB	10,000 (first wave)	74 (1991)	Buck et al. (1994)
British Social Attitudes Survey	Annual	Electoral register PAF	One adult in household	GB	5,000	67	Jowell et al. (1994)
Census of Population	Every 10 years	Local address lists	Household 'head'	UK	58,000,000	98	Office for National Statistics (1997)
General Household Survey	Continuous	PAF	All adults in household	GB	12,000	82	Office for National Statistics (1997)
Labour Force Survey	Continuous	PAF	All adults in household	GB	60,000	83	Office for National Statistics (1997)
National Child Development Study	Five sweeps since 1958	All children born in one week in 1958	Children, parents, adult 'children'	GB	11,000	73 (1991)	Ferri and Smith (1998)
New Earnings Survey	Annual	Inland Revenue PAYE records	Employers supply data on employees	GB	210,000 (employers)	94	Office for National Statistics (1997)
Social Change and Economic Life Initiative	Interviews in 1985 and 1987	Electoral register	All adults in household	Six areas of GB	6,000	75	Anderson et al. (1994)

Table 8.1 Major social surveys in the United Kingdom

in their 30s is a result of the fashion for large families in the 1960s (Office of National Statistics 1997: 29).

Figure 8.1 suggests that individual experience can be strongly affected by the age cohort into which a person is born. Those born in the late 1940s, or during the 1960s, will be competing throughout their lives with a larger number of peers for school places, jobs, housing, healthcare, and so on. By contrast, the relatively small cohorts born during the 1930s and the 1970s will face less competition in all these areas. However, when the 'bulge' generations reach old age there will be a relatively small population of working age to support them financially or to care for them. There has been some concern about the effects of these changes in the **dependency ratio**, that is, in the ratio of those who are dependent to those who are economically active.

The **total period fertility rate** (TPFR) measures the average number of children born to each woman if birth rates in the specific period persisted throughout her child-bearing life. In the United Kingdom the TPFR peaked at 2.95 in 1964 and then fell to a low point of 1.69 in 1977. The fall in the birthrate is partly a consequence of smaller family size, but it is also a result of the increase in the proportion of childless women. The percentage of women who were still childless at the age of 30 rose from just under a fifth among women born in 1947 to a third among women born in 1962. Changes in

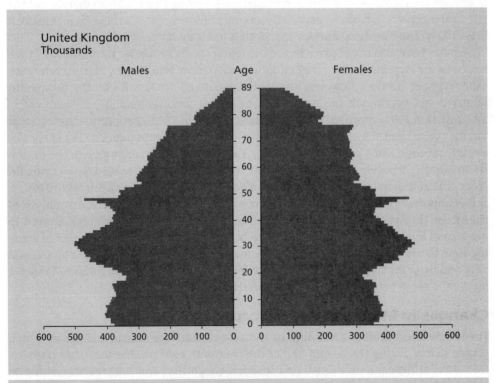

Figure 8.1 Population pyramid by gender and age, 1995
Source: *Social Trends* no. 27 (Office for National Statistics, HMSO, 1997).

the TPFR are thought to have been influenced by more women receiving higher education, by an increase in female participation in paid work, and by greater control over
fertility because of the contraceptive pill (Office for National Statistics 1997: 32).

Changes in Households and Families

Information about demographic changes is sometimes presented in terms of 'households' and sometimes in terms of 'families': when using this sort of data it is important
to notice which term is being used.

The average size of households in Great Britain has almost halved since the beginning of the twentieth century and in 1995 stood at 2.4 people per household. However,
this figure conceals large variations in household type. There has been a decrease in the
proportion of 'traditional' family households. So in 1961 38 per cent of households
consisted of married couples with their dependent children, while 26 per cent of all
households consisted of couples with no children. However, by 1995 only 24 per cent of
households consisted of the 'traditional' family, while couples without children made
up 29 per cent of all households (Office for National Statistics 1997: 40).

One-person households increased from 11 per cent of all households in 1961 to 28 per
cent in 1995. This reflects a number of different factors, including the increasing numbers of young people who are financially able to leave the parental home but who delay
marriage, the increases in divorce and separation among those who do marry, and the
rise in the expectation of life, especially among older women. All these factors make it
more likely, and more possible, for individuals to set up homes of their own.

Changes have also taken place in the demography of the family. In particular, there
has been an increase in the proportion of **lone-parent families**, by comparison with
other types of families. However, despite the alarms of the New Right, the two-parent
family is still very much the norm. So lone-parent families made up 23 per cent of
all families in 1994 compared with 8 per cent in 1971. In 1994 52 per cent of lone-parent
families were headed by a mother who was either divorced or separated, 35 per cent by
a single mother, and 4 per cent by a widow. Lone fathers were very much in the minority, making up 9 per cent of all lone parents, and in general they tended to be caring for
older children than lone mothers (Office of Population Censuses and Surveys 1996).

It is important not to regard being a lone parent as a permanent state. An analysis of
the British Household Panel Survey found that in the early 1990s, on average, around 15
per cent of lone mothers per year ceased to be lone parents, usually as a result of forming new partnerships. If such a rate were maintained, half of all lone parents would
only remain so for around four years (Office for National Statistics 1997: 43; see Table 8.1
for details about the British Household Panel Survey).

Changes in Marriage and Divorce

There have been profound changes in the rate of marriage and in the age at which
people marry during the second half of the twentieth century. The marriage rate rose
from 1931 to 1971 and then fell dramatically: between 1981 and 1992 the marriage rate
per 1000 of the population fell from 7.1 to 5.4. However, it has been argued that the
period from 1950 to 1980 represented an anomaly, in that marriage rates were unusually high, and that rates in the 1990s represented a return to normal. The age at

which individuals married rose by about two years between 1961 and 1994, to 28 years for men and 26 years for women, though this figure masks social class differences in which those of higher social class tend to delay marriage even longer. Similar patterns are found in other European countries, though the United Kingdom has one of the highest marriage rates in the European Union.

There has also been a change towards more cohabitation before marriage, and to the substitution of cohabitation for marriage, at least in the early years of marriage. So 48 per cent of women marrying for the first time in 1987 had cohabited before marriage, compared with only 7 per cent of those marrying at the beginning of the 1970s (Kiernan and Wicks 1990: 8). This means that more children are being born outside marriage, though in the majority of cases these births are registered by both parents who are living in a stable relationship in the same house. Attitudes towards cohabitation vary greatly with age. In 1994 the British Social Attitudes Survey asked people whether they agreed or disagreed with the statement that 'living together outside marriage is always wrong'. Forty per cent of men born before 1930 considered that it was always wrong, compared with 7 per cent of those born between 1960 and 1978; slightly lower percentages of women said that they thought that living together outside marriage was wrong (Jowell *et al.* 1994; see Table 8.1 for details about the British Social Attitudes Survey).

The other important trend is the increase in divorce. The United Kingdom has the highest divorce rate in the European Union, and it has been estimated that four out of ten new marriages will end in divorce. In 1994, over one half of all divorces were to couples with children under 16, with wives much more likely to initiate divorce than husbands. Reasons for the divorce also varied, with women more likely to seek a divorce because of the unreasonable behaviour of their partners, and husbands more likely to cite adultery as the reason for the breakdown of the marriage (Haskey 1996).

The cumulative effect of these changes is that **reconstituted families** are becoming more common: these are families in which one or both of the adults have been married before. In 1991 8 per cent of all families with dependent children contained one or more step children (Office of Population Censuses and Surveys 1991). The children in

---

Box 8.1 Recent changes in families and households

- lower fertility, older age at childbearing and increasing childlessness;
- smaller household and family sizes;
- growth in single-person households and in living alone;
- decline in adoption and a growth in lone parenthood;
- decline in first-marriage rates;
- rise in the prevalence of cohabitation and a growth in divorce;
- increase in remarriages, reconstituted families, and stepfamilies;
- growth in the ethnic minority population, resulting in greater diversity in family sizes, composition, and kinship patterns.

(See Haskey 1996: 8)

these families may have two parents and two step-parents, they may move between two different 'homes', and they may have up to eight grandparents. Some of the complexities involved in living in a re-constituted family have been described by Robinson and Smith (1993) and Ferri and Smith (1998). The evidence suggests that re-marriages, and therefore stepfamilies, are at greater risk of breakdown than first marriages (Burgoyne *et al.* 1987).

The main changes which have taken place in families and households are summarized in Box 8.1.

Changes in Employment Patterns

Changes in the labour market over the past few years have made a profound difference to the ways in which families are able to provide for the welfare of their members. There is only space here to outline the main changes, which are discussed in more detail in Chapter 7 of this book: see also Grint (1991), Gallie (1988), the publications coming from the Social Change and Economic Life Initiative, and the journal *Labour Market Trends*. Important changes in patterns of paid work are highlighted in Box 8.2.

Box 8.2 Recent changes in patterns of paid work

- a decline in manufacturing industry and a growth in service-sector jobs;
- a decline in the numbers of full-time, secure jobs and an increase in part-time and insecure jobs;
- an increase in unemployment, which has particularly affected unskilled male workers and those from minority ethnic groups;
- an increase in women's employment, especially in part-time work and among younger women and women with children;
- a growing divide between 'work-rich' households, with two or more earners, and 'work-poor' households where no-one has a paid job.

All these changes affect the extent to which families are able to provide for the welfare of their members and for the particular mix of strategies which they use in making that provision.

The Production of Welfare Within Families

One theme of this book is that the welfare of individuals is produced not only by the welfare state, but also by the market and by the family. This next section considers the ways in which families produce welfare for their members.

Types of Welfare Provided Within Families

There are four general points which have to be made at the outset. First, for many people the family is a first line of defence against the 'five giant evils' which Beveridge saw as the targets for the welfare state: want, disease, ignorance, squalor, and idleness (Beveridge Report 1942: para. 8). When all goes well, families provide a means of redistributing income from those who earn to those who do not, in order to ensure that individual family members have enough food and clothing, and a roof over their heads; people with minor illnesses and long-term disabilities are usually cared for at home, and home is the place where children are nurtured and where their education begins. Of course, other types of welfare can also be provided within the family, from loving relationships to opportunities for leisure and pleasure of different sorts. However, for the purposes of this chapter the focus will be on the welfare associated with being fed and clothed and housed, and being cared for in childhood and times of physical dependence.

Second, it is important to remember that 'families' do not produce anything: it is the individuals within families who produce, and consume, any welfare which may be created. So in this section we shall have to move the focus from the family itself to the individuals which make up the family. This change of focus reflects a move between disciplines. Traditionally economists have used the household/family as the key unit of analysis, while sociologists have been concerned about the different perspectives of individuals within households: the idea that there can be profound differences between 'the husband's marriage' and 'the wife's marriage' was first introduced by the American feminist sociologist, Bernard (1982).

Third, creating welfare at home is work. This point was made vividly by John Masefield in the following poem:

> To get the whole world out of bed
> And washed, and dressed, and warmed, and fed,
> To work, and back to bed again,
> Believe me, Saul, costs worlds of pain.
> (Masefield 1946: 61)

Work at home may be unpaid, but it is still work, according to the definition suggested in a recent sociology textbook:

Work is the carrying out of tasks, involving the expenditure of mental and physical effort, which have as their objective the production of goods and services catering for human needs. An occupation is work which is done for a regular wage. (Giddens 1997: 491)

One of the concomitants of the development of a welfare state is the move of many sorts of work out of the home: this has particularly affected women, as they have moved into paid work as nurses, social workers, teachers, nannies, and care assistants, doing the sorts of tasks which women have traditionally performed as part of their family duties.

Fourth, there is a trade-off between different ways of producing welfare, which relates to the shifting boundaries between paid and unpaid work. A mother who does not have paid employment is able to look after her children herself, cook for the family, and clean the house, and she may produce goods such as soft furnishings and home-made clothes. If the same woman has a full-time job she is likely to have to pay for childcare and to buy more pre-prepared meals; she may employ another woman to clean the house, and she will probably buy ready-made soft furnishing and clothes.

There have been a number of attempts to classify the different types of work which are done within families. One approach has been to list all the different tasks for which family members may be responsible and to sort them into groups. So, for example, one study divided work within the household into 'house maintenance' (such as painting and decorating), 'home improvement' (alterations and building work), 'routine housework' (shopping, cooking, washing up, and cleaning), 'domestic production' (gardening, knitting, and sewing), 'car maintenance' (washing and repairing), and 'childcare' (Pahl 1984: 214). In the traditional, conventional household some of these tasks were typically done by women and some by men. The conclusion of the study was that women's employment was crucial in determining who did what work within the household: the more hours the woman spent in paid employment, the less conventional was the division of labour within the household (Pahl 1984: 275).

Another approach has been to consider work within the household in terms of the time household members spend on different tasks. For example, the Social Change and Economic Life Initiative used time-budget diaries to investigate the relative amounts of time which men and women spent on 'childcare', 'shopping', 'odd jobs', and 'routine domestic work' such as cleaning, cooking, and washing up. The results showed that, despite increases in women's employment, they continued to spend more time than men on childcare, shopping, and routine domestic work, while men were likely to spend more time than women on odd jobs around the house. However, between 1974 and 1987 there was a tendency for men to do more routine housework and shopping and for women, especially those in full time employment, to do less (Anderson, Bechofer, and Gershuny 1994; see Table 8.1 for details about the Social Change and Economic Life Initiative).

In the following pages we shall consider three different types of work, each of which produces welfare for individuals within families; we begin with the work of childcare and with the social policies which are most relevant to the support of children within families.

Childcare and Child Support

In 1994 children under 15 made up 19 per cent of the British population, with more boy children than girl children being born in every year. The proportion of the population under 15 is approximately the same as in the rest of Europe, but is in marked contrast to the world as a whole, where one-third of the population is aged under 15 (Botting 1996: 25). On average women are having fewer children than they did in the past, and children are growing up in smaller families: in Britain the average number of children in families with dependent children was 1.8 in 1993 (Ferri and Smith, 1998).

Four-fifths of children live in a family home with both their parents. However, in 1993 19 per cent of children lived with their mother alone and a further 2 per cent with just their father. This can be compared with 1971, when just 7 per cent of children lived with only one parent. The increase in the proportion of families headed by only one parent is due both to the increased incidence of births outside marriage and to the increases in marriage and divorce. There has also been a rise in the numbers of children living in poverty. The Child Poverty Action Group has calculated that in 1992 29 per cent of all children were living in poverty, defined as on or below the income support level; this represents about three and a half million children. Over three-quarters of children growing up in lone-parent families lived in poverty, compared with just under one-fifth of children in two-parent families (Oppenheim and Harker 1996: 30).

Having children involves both expense and hard work. One study calculated that a child reaching his or her seventeenth birthday will have cost around £50,000 (Middleton *et al*. 1997). However, this calculation included only direct costs and did not take account of the lost income of the person who took the prime responsibility for childcare, usually the mother. An estimate of the amount involved concluded that the total could be as high as £202,000 (at 1990 values), of which 40 per cent represented being out of employment during the child's early years, 36 per cent represented working shorter hours in order to fit in with childcare, while 25 per cent represented lower rates of pay because of loss of work experience (Joshi 1992: 121).

Mothers still carry the main responsibility for children, despite much rhetoric about the increased commitment of many fathers to their children. A study of the division of household tasks, carried out in 1991, showed that looking after a sick child would be the responsibility of the mother in 60 per cent of families and shared between both parents in 39 per cent of families; fathers took responsibility in just 1 per cent of families. The study showed that the situation had changed very little since 1983 (Central Statistical Office 1995: 32).

There are a number of different reasons why childcare has become an important issue in social policy. The first reason has been concern about the welfare of children, in a society in which many children live in poverty, in which some parents are divorced or separated, and in which a proportion of parents are failing in their parental responsibilities. For many years the law about caring for, bringing up, and protecting children from abuse had been inconsistent and fragmented. The Children Act 1989 aimed to bring about radical changes and improvements in the law and to provide a single and consistent statement of it.

The Children Act was a long and complex piece of legislation, which was generally welcomed when it came into force. It provided a single and consistent statement of the law that applies to the welfare of children. The introduction to the Act set out the underlying beliefs:

The Act rests on the belief that children are generally best looked after within the family with both parents playing a full part and without resort to legal proceedings. That belief is reflected in:

- the new concept of parental responsibility
- the ability of unmarried fathers to share that responsibility by agreement with the mother
- the local authorities' duty to give support to children and their families

(Department of Health 1989: 1)

A guide to the Act, and a discussion of the ideologies which are reflected in it, has been provided by Freeman (1992). He suggested that the Children Act expressed ideologies from both the right and the left. On the one hand, it presented the two-parent family as the ideal and warned of the dangers of too much state intervention. On the other hand, it gave new and stronger powers both to local authorities and to children.

The principles which underpinned the Children Act were the basis for its many and complex provisions. The first principle was that the welfare of the child should be paramount. This principle applied to any issue related to the upbringing of the child, the administration of a child's property, court proceedings, or disputes between parents.

The second principle was that there should be as little delay as possible, since delay was likely to prejudice the welfare of the child, because of the uncertainty which this creates and also because of the damage which delay may do to relationships.

The third principle was incorporated into a checklist which courts should consider in any contested cases. The checklist included such issues as the child's physical, emotional, and educational needs, the likely effect of any change in circumstances, the capacities of the parents to care for the child and the implications of the child's age, sex, and background. The child's 'background' included his or her religion, racial origin, culture, and language, and this principle reflected the increasingly multicultural nature of the British population.

The fourth principle was concerned with minimal intervention. The Act stated that a court should not make an order 'unless it considers that doing so would be better for the child than making no order at all' (section 1(5)). In this the Act reflected the then Conservative government's suspicion of state interference into family life.

Finally, the Act laid stress on the principle of **parental responsibility,** marking a shift of emphasis from parental rights to parental responsibilities. The aim was to stress that parents, rather than the state, have the prime responsibility for children. Mothers, and the fathers of legitimate children, automatically have parental responsibility, while fathers who are not married to the mother of the child can acquire parental responsibility in a number of different ways. In differentiating between married and unmarried parents in this way, the Act seemed to confirm the value attached to traditional family forms.

The second reason for childcare becoming a focus for social policy has been the rise in the numbers of lone-parent families. This has led to growing concern about the provision of financial support for dependent children. The key issue is whether children living in lone-parent families should be financially supported by the state, through the social security system, by the earnings of the caring parent, usually the mother, or by contributions from the absent parent, usually the father. Compared with other European countries, in Britain a relatively high proportion of lone parents depend on the social security system. Concern about the financial burdens which this laid on the state led to the passing of the Child Support Act 1993.

The aims of the Child Support Act were to:

- Ensure that parents accept financial responsibility for their children whenever they can afford to do so
- Strike a fair and reasonable balance between 'first' and 'second' families
- Maintain parents' incentives to take paid work rather than depending on social security

(Secretary of State for Social Security 1995: 10)

The Child Support Act led to the setting up of the Child Support Agency. This organization undertook to develop a system for ensuring that money would be transferred from the 'absent parent', usually the father, to the 'parent with care', usually the mother. A formula was developed for calculating the amount which should be paid, with an upper limit set at 30 per cent of the absent parent's net income.

When it was first set up the Child Support Agency was criticized from a variety of different positions. Some men's groups considered that the payments to parents with care were set too high and that the formula did not take adequate account of the cost of supporting second families. Some women's groups resented the pressure that was put on women to name the fathers of their children, and argued that the focus on lone mothers living on social security meant that the Treasury, rather than women and children, was the main beneficiary of the Act (Clarke, Glendinning, and Craig 1994; Bennett 1997).

There are a number of other ways in which social policy recognizes the work of childcare and the need for the support of children and those who care for them. These include:

- **child benefit,** the social security benefit paid to all mothers to help with the costs of bringing up children.
- **maternity pay, maternity allowance,** and **maternity leave,** which recognize the need of mothers for financial support and time off paid work when a new baby is born. Some other countries provide **paternity and parental leave,** but this is not yet the case in the United Kingdom (Hantrais and Letablier 1996).
- **childcare** provided by local authorities, either in the form of day nurseries or foster care: this tends to be restricted to children with 'special needs', either because they have a disability or because the care they receive within the family is considered to be inadequate.

In general the UK government has followed the principle that having children is a private decision undertaken by the couple and that public agencies should only become involved when parental care breaks down. It is assumed that the costs and work of childcare are a private matter.

Domestic Work

Under the heading of domestic work we shall consider such activities as cleaning, preparing meals, washing up, and shopping for food and household necessities. All these activities produce welfare for the members of the household and carrying them out involves an enormous amount of time and effort. It has been calculated that the time spent in productive work in the home is equal to the time spent in paid work (Rose 1989: 124). Attempts to estimate the value of domestic work have indicated that including unpaid work in national income would add between a quarter and more than a half to measured income, depending on the methods used for the calculation (Hyman 1994: 63).

When the first path-breaking study of housework was carried out it was initially considered to be a frivolous topic and one not worthy of academic study (Oakley 1974). However, there is now an enormous literature documenting the changing patterns of domestic work (for a review, see Morris 1990). Women still carry the main burden, though there is some evidence of men increasing their involvement; a study comparing the situation in 1991 with that in 1983 concluded that the allocation of domestic tasks was as follows:

- Household shopping: 8 per cent of men were 'mainly responsible' for this in 1991 compared with 5 per cent in 1983.

- Cooking the evening meal: 9 per cent of men were 'mainly responsible' for this in 1991 compared with 5 per cent in 1983.
- Doing the evening dishes: 28 per cent of men were 'mainly responsible' for this in 1991 compared with 17 per cent in 1983.
- Traditional gender differences continued, with women being 'mainly responsible' for washing and ironing and men being 'mainly responsible' for repairing household equipment. (Central Statistical Office 1995)

Despite the importance of domestic work in terms of the welfare it creates, there is very little explicit social policy related to the topic. This probably reflects the fact that, until recently, domestic work was taken for granted as something which women did, unpaid, as part of their roles as wives and mothers. Only since 1973 have judges been encouraged to take the unpaid work done at home into account in making the financial settlement when a marriage ends.

However, implicitly the welfare state still tends to assume that women will be responsible for domestic work and childcare. Welfare providers often take for granted that one parent will be free to take children to and from school, to accompany them to the doctor and the dentist, and to stay in for the health visitor and the social worker. Women who fail to carry out domestic work in the way expected of them risk being considered 'bad mothers' by those with responsibility for the welfare of children.

Caring for Sick and Disabled People

'Caring' is another type of work which was taken for granted until the late twentieth century: it was seen as something that wives and mothers did naturally, as part of their domestic responsibilities. So 'caring about' someone was assumed to involve 'caring for' them, to use the distinction first made by Graham (1983). The word 'carer' came into use during the 1980s, as feminists and pressure groups argued that caring for sick and disabled people was real work and that it reduced the costs of health and social services.

What sorts of people require, and give, care within the family? Besides those with ordinary short-term illnesses, care may be needed because of mental or physical disabilities, or long-term illness, either mental or physical. Most elderly people are fit and well, but there is a tendency for both physical and mental infirmities to increase with age. Care may be given by spouses to each other, by parents to their disabled children, by adult daughters and, less often, by adult sons to their parents; increasingly it is also being recognized that some quite young children provide care for their disabled parents (Parker 1990; Twigg, Atkin, and Perring 1990; Twigg 1992).

In 1985 the General Household Survey asked about caring and produced the first national data about people who give and receive care. Respondents were asked whether they were 'looking after, or providing some regular service for, someone who was sick, elderly or handicapped'. When the results were applied to the whole population it was estimated that there were six million people who were doing some sort of caring for others (Green 1988; see Table 8.1 for details about the General Household Survey).

However, the figure of six million has to be treated with some caution. Only about half these people said that they were the sole or main carer, and only about a fifth spent more than 20 hours per week on caring activities. Nevertheless, this still amounted to a great deal of work done and welfare provided. The study showed that the different sorts of care included:

- Personal help with dressing, bathing, going to the toilet, and feeding;
- Physical help with activities such as walking, getting in and out of bed, going up and down stairs;
- Practical help, such as preparing meals, doing housework or shopping, or doing household repairs and gardening;
- Other sorts of help, such as giving medication, changing dressings, taking the person out, or simply keeping him or her company.

The survey showed that needing personal and physical help tended to be associated with very long hours of work for the carer. Some carers, most of them women, were providing 100 or more hours of care per week, far more than any paid worker would undertake.

Caring is costly in a number of different ways. First, there are costs in terms of lost earnings. The rate of paid employment is lower for all adults providing care. However, the effect is greater for women than men, and greatest in the case of a mother caring for a disabled child (Arber and Ginn 1995; Baldwin 1985). Second, there are the additional costs of disability. These may include additional heating, when someone is at home all day, adaptations to the house, special equipment such as wheelchairs and other aids, extra clothes and bedding, and higher transport costs when a person is unable to use public transport. Third, there are likely to be costs to the carer in terms of stress and strain (Glendinning and Millar 1992; Pahl and Quine 1987).

Social policy is now beginning to recognize the contribution which carers make to the welfare of individuals within families. The National Health Service and Community Care Act 1990 outlined a system of community care in which social services departments were responsible for providing care for disabled people and support for carers. The White Paper which preceded the Act said:

> The Government acknowledges than the great bulk of community care is provided by friends, family and neighbours. . . . But it must be recognized that carers need help and support if they are to continue to carry out their role . . . practical support for carers should be a high priority. (Secretaries of State for Health 1989: 4-556)

In 1985 the Carers (Recognition and Services) Act imposed an obligation on local authorities to assess the needs of carers as well as of those who are cared for. However, the support which carers can expect remains very limited: one study of people looking after a relative with Alzheimer's Disease at home found that most carers had less than 16 hours away from caring each week, out of a total of 168 hours in the week (Levin, Moriarty, and Gorbach 1994).

Financial support is provided by the Social Security system. The rules of eligibility change constantly, but the position at any one time can be checked in the handbooks produced by the Child Poverty Action Group (see, for example, Child Poverty Action Group 1998). At the time of writing the main benefits are:

- Disability Living Allowance for people under 65 who have a long-term disability which prevents them taking paid employment

- Attendance Allowance for people over 65 who need someone to help them with activities of daily living

- Invalid Care Allowance for those who provide care for someone who is receiving the higher rate of the Disability Living Allowance. To qualify for this allowance the carer has to be caring for at least 35 hours per week. The current rate is £37.35 per week, so the maximum that anyone can be 'paid' is £1.00 per hour: if caring at home is work, it is very badly paid work indeed.

The question of the boundary between **public and private spheres** is central to any discussion about the production of welfare within the family. Are looking after children, doing housework, and caring for sick and disabled people essentially private matters, carried out because people love and care for each other? Is it appropriate for the state to become involved, through social policies focused on the work done within families? And if these issues become a matter of public as well as private concern, what forms should state intervention take, given that, historically, care and control have tended to advance together? These are likely to be central questions in any discussion of social policy as it relates to families.

Disadvantage Within Families

However, families can be sources of disadvantage or 'dis-welfare' as well as of welfare. Many people are ambivalent about their families, even when things are going well, but for some individuals the family becomes the place where they experience inequality, unhappiness, and even danger. In this section we consider three aspects of family life which can create problems for individual family members.

Financial Inequalities

Throughout much of social policy the household is regarded as an economic unit. When a man and a woman live together, especially if they are married, it is assumed that they will share the income which enters the household. This assumption underlies the idea of the household means test. Being eligible for a means-tested benefit implies that the income of the household as a whole is below the minimum considered necessary: it is assumed that an individual cannot be poor if he or she lives within a household which has an adequate income.

However, it has become apparent that there can be considerable financial inequalities even within quite affluent families. In particular, women and children have been found living in poverty in households with adequate incomes (Pahl, 1989). Most of the research on this topic has focused on married or as-married couples, with or without children, so in this context the word 'family' usually means a nuclear family living together in a household.

Over the past few years many typologies have been devised with the aim of making sense of the complexities of money management within families (see, for example, Buck *et al.* 1994; Morris and Ruane 1989; Pahl 1995; Wilson 1987). One much-quoted typology was developed for the Social Change and Economic Life Initiative (Vogler and Pahl, 1993 and 1994; see Table 8.1 for details of the survey). Respondents were asked to

> ## Box 8.3 Systems of money management
>
> - the 'female whole-wage system', in which the husband hands over his whole wage packet to his wife, minus his personal spending money; the wife adds her own earnings, if any, and is then responsible for managing the financial affairs of the household (27 per cent of the couples in the sample);
> - the 'female-managed pool', which involves the pooling of all or nearly all of the income, usually in a joint account: so both partners have access to the household income, but the woman has the main responsibility for managing and controlling finances (15 per cent of couples);
> - the 'joint pool', which involves the pooling of all or nearly all the income, usually in a joint account, with both partners sharing the management and control of the pool (20 per cent of couples);
> - the 'male-managed pool', which involves the pooling of all or nearly all of the income, usually in a joint account: so both partners have access to the household income, but the man has the main responsibility for managing and controlling finances (15 per cent of couples);
> - the 'male whole-wage system', in which the husband has sole responsibility for managing and controlling finances, a system which can leave non-employed wives with no personal spending money (10 per cent of couples);
> - the 'housekeeping allowance system', which involves separate spheres of responsibility for household expenditure. Typically the husband gives his wife a fixed sum of money for housekeeping expenses, to which she may add her own earnings, while the rest of the money remains in the husband's control and he pays for other items (13 per cent of couples in the sample).

identify which of several systems of money management came closest to the way in which they organized their finances. The researchers then went on to create a typology of allocative systems, which divided couples according to who managed and who controlled household finances. The allocative systems are summarized in Box 8.3.

Other studies have also identified an 'independent management system', with each partner keeping his or her income separately and taking responsibility for particular bills. It has been suggested that this system is characteristic of couples who are cohabiting or who are at an early stage in the relationship. Anecdotal evidence suggests that independent management of finances may also be more common in same-sex couples, but so far no research has been published in Britain on this topic.

There is now a considerable body of research showing that the system of money management adopted by a couple has significant implications for the lives of individuals within the household. These differences can be summarized as follows:

- When money is scarce women tend to get the job of making ends meet, since it is usually they who are responsible for finances in low income households (see also Kempson 1996);
- Men tend to spend more than women on personal interests and leisure pursuits. Access to personal spending money reflects both total household income and the management of

money within the household. However, gender inequalities are greatest in households with male-controlled systems of money management and least in households with joint pooling of money (Pahl 1989).

- Women are likely to bear the brunt of financial cutbacks. When money is short women are more likely than men to cut back on such things as food, heating, social life, and entertainment. Again, these gender inequalities seem to be greatest in households with male-controlled systems of money management and least in households with joint pooling systems (Vogler and Pahl 1994).

- Women are more child- and family-focused in their spending. Money which is controlled by women is more likely to be spent on children, on food, and on collective expenditure for the household, while men tend to hold more back for their individual use. If the aim is to benefit children, women make more efficient use of household income (Blumberg 1991; Dwyer and Bruce 1988).

- Individuals can be poor in households with adequate incomes. This finding has important implications for policy initiatives aimed at the relief of poverty (Kempson 1996).

Financial inequalities within families often seem to occur when one family member, typically a male breadwinner, uses money as a way of exercising power and of controlling other family members; another source of power and control is violence.

Violence against Women Within the Family

Violence seems to be an enduring characteristic of family life, with women and children being the main victims. Throughout most of history this has been taken for granted, to the extent that in 1792 Judge Buller confirmed that husbands had the right to beat their wives, so long as the stick that was used was not thicker than a man's thumb. What is now described as 'wife abuse' or 'domestic violence' was then considered to be a private matter, lying outside the public domain and not amenable to legislation (Dobash and Dobash 1980).

Violence against women became a public issue in the 1970s, largely as a result of the growth of the Women's Movement and the work of feminists in documenting the nature and extent of the problem. The first refuge for abused women was set up in London in 1971, and refuges, or shelters, can now be found in most parts of the world. Male violence within the family has become recognized as a threat to the physical and mental health of women and children and as a major cause of morbidity and mortality (Kingston and Penhale 1995).

Domestic violence is also a crime. About half of all homicides of women are killings by a partner or ex-partner; one in five of all murder victims (male or female) is a woman killed by a partner or ex-partner; one-third of all reported crimes against women, and one-quarter of all reported assaults, are the result of domestic violence (Victim Support 1992: 4). The 1992 British Crime Survey showed that 11 per cent of women who lived with a partner had experienced some degree of physical violence (House of Commons Home Affairs Committee 1993). Men can also be the victims of domestic violence, but the evidence suggests that the injuries which they suffer are in general less severe than those inflicted on women by men, and the violence is less enduring.

Despite the seriousness of much domestic violence, the appropriate agencies have often been reluctant to provide help for the victims. One problem is that so many different agencies are potentially involved. If a woman has injuries she may need medical and nursing care. She has been the victim of a crime, so the police can be involved, and she may have to go to court to get an injunction to prevent her husband from assaulting her again. Many husbands are not deterred by legal action, so she may decide to leave home to protect herself and her children. She may go to a refuge, or to the local authority housing department: if she has dependent children the 1985 Housing Act gives her the right to temporary accommodation. Lacking an income, she is likely to apply to the Benefit Office for income support. There is now ample evidence of the ways in which policy-makers and professionals have failed to meet the needs of abused women (Edwards 1989; Mullender 1996; Pahl 1985).

The law relating to violence in the family was changed by the Family Law Act 1996. Previously the legal position was quite complicated, with different legislation applying in the case of married and unmarried couples. The 1996 Act consolidated existing legislation and set out the position with regard to the occupation of the family home and the right of individuals to protection against violence. More specifically, the Act:

- Widened the scope for occupation and non-molestation orders, which now apply to 'associated persons', such as ex-partners, as well as to currently married and cohabiting people;
- Increased the rights of courts to attach a power of arrest to court orders;
- Simplified the position with regard to the different courts in which cases involving domestic violence can be heard.

Separation and Divorce

Unhappy marriages are the root cause of much dis-welfare within families, while separation and divorce tend to create inequalities between the different members of families. When a couple separate the result is typically a reduction in household incomes for women and children and a modest increase in the household incomes of men. The most effective route out of poverty for women in this situation is remarriage, a fact which reflects the greater earning power and job security of men, and the responsibility of women for childcare (Burgoyne *et al.* 1987).

The state has had an interest in marriage ever since the Marriage Act 1836. However, throughout the nineteenth century divorce was only available to the very rich. This led to a situation in which many individuals were trapped in unhappy marriages, while those who had gone on to make new relationships were forced to do what was then called 'living in sin', being unable to divorce or to legalize the new relationship.

Attempts to remedy this situation produced the 1937 Divorce Law, which made divorce possible, but only when a 'matrimonial offence' had been committed: one partner had to prove that the other was guilty of adultery, cruelty, or desertion. Though this made divorce accessible to ordinary people for the first time, the idea that one partner must be to blame for the breakdown of the marriage made divorce procedures essentially adversarial.

Concern about the adversarial nature of the divorce process led to the Divorce Reform Act 1969. The main provisions of this Act were:

- The only ground for divorce was the 'irretrievable breakdown' of the marriage;
- Breakdown could be established by reference to one of five 'facts', which included adultery, desertion, unreasonable behaviour, two years' separation if both consented to the divorce, or five years' separation if one partner did not want the divorce;

- Unreasonable behaviour included financial irresponsibility, violence, alcoholism, and constant criticism.

Those who did not want to wait two or five years for a divorce still had to rely on fault-based facts to prove that the marriage had broken down, so bitterness and blame continued to surround divorce proceedings.

At this time legal aid was made available to those who did not have enough money to obtain advice and take the case to court. Since the granting of legal aid was dependent on a means test on individuals, not couples, many wives qualified for legal aid and this made it possible for them to obtain a divorce. After the 1969 Act the divorce rate rose quite sharply, and continued to rise throughout the next 20 years, with about three-quarters of all divorces being granted to women.

Concern over the fact that four in ten marriages were ending in divorce, and that couples were continuing to use fault-based facts to prove breakdown, led to a demand for a new law relating to divorce. This reached the statute book as the Family Law Act 1996. The aims of the Act were set out by the government as follows:

- To support the institution of marriage;
- To include practical steps to prevent the irretrievable breakdown of marriage;
- To ensure that spouses understand the practical consequences of divorce before taking any irreversible decision;
- To minimize the bitterness and hostility between the parties and reduce trauma for the children;
- To keep to the minimum the costs to the couple and to the taxpayer.

The Act attempted to send a message that ending a marriage is a serious business. Mediation was not compulsory, unless the courts ordered it because the couple could not agree. The voluntary organization National Family Mediation was charged with providing mediation services, but was nevertheless underfunded. In addition, the spouse who had applied for the divorce had to attend an information meeting at the court about financial and other consequences, and then there had to be a three-month 'period of reflection' after the meeting (Bird and Cretney 1997).

The Family Law Act 1996 ended the concept of fault: the single ground for divorce was that the marriage had broken down. The aim was to make couples think more carefully about getting divorced, but if they decided to go ahead then the aim was to minimize bitterness and harm to children. Some commentators have argued that the ending of the concept of fault devalued the marriage vows, while others suggested that the focus on mediation reflected an outmoded view of the nature of family relationships (Lewis and Maclean 1997).

Social Policy and Families in the Future

Patterns of family life and the nature of family policy have changed greatly over the second half of the twentieth century. What do demographic trends tell us about the future shape of family life? As we saw earlier in this chapter, family policy reflects strongly held and often conflicting ideologies. What cultural and ideological forces will shape policy-making in the future?

Future Trends in Family Life

Predictions about the future must always be regarded with some scepticism. However, demographic trends provide a useful start. In general these involve taking current patterns and projecting them into the future.

In some respects the future is already unrolling. For example, the population pyramid shown in Fig. 8.1 can be used to predict important aspects of the future. The relatively large cohort of babies born during the 1960s will mean a relatively large population of elderly people when these individuals retire from employment in the years around 2030. After that there will be a decline in the numbers of elderly people, and in the population as a whole, because of the low birthrate in the 1970s and 1980s. Changes such as this have implications for social policy, and may have lay behind the government decision to equalize the retirement age for men and women at the age of 65 by the year 2020.

The annual review, *Social Trends*, has summarized some of the main demographic trends (Office for National Statistics 1997). These include the following:

- More people will remain single, either because they have never married, or because they have yet to marry. This reflects three trends: the rise in the age of marriage, the increase in cohabitation, and increasing scepticism about marriage itself.

- More marriages will end in divorce. Among both men and women 7 per cent were divorced in 1992, but this is expected to rise to 11 per cent of men and 12 per cent of women by the year 2020: the larger percentage among women reflects the fact that women typically outlive men.

- More people will live alone. This is partly because of the increase in divorce and partly because of greater longevity; but it also reflects the fact that young people are financially able to leave their parents' homes without having to marry.

- More people will live in re-constituted families. Increases in divorce will mean that more children spend more time living with a step-parent, or being shared between two parents who live apart; some children may effectively find themselves with four parents and eight grandparents.

- Grandparenting will change. The rise in the employment rate of mothers with young children will make grandparents, and especially grandmothers, an important source of childcare; at the same time the increase in life expectancy will mean that grandparents will be fitter and more active than in the past, and indeed many will still be in employment themselves when their grandchildren are growing up.

Another view on the future is provided by cultural theorists. Here the focus is on the development of post-modernity, and on the transformations which are said to be taking place in intimate relationships. One approach has been to argue that the focus is shifting 'from institution to relationship', that is from the institution of marriage, with its structures of age and gender, to the individually chosen relationship, which can be broken when it ceases to satisfy (Giddens 1992). A key concept has been the idea of **individualization**:

Individualization means that men and women are released from the gender roles prescribed by industrial society for life in the nuclear family. At the same time, and this aggravates the situation, they find themselves forced, under pain of material disadvantage, to build up a life of their own by way of the labour market, training and mobility, and if need be to pursue this at the cost of their commitments to family, relations and friends. (Beck and Beck-Gernsheim 1995: 6)

Whether or not the cultural theorists will prove to be right in their predictions for the future, it is likely that families will continue to be controversial. The struggle will continue between those who think that change has gone too far and those who think that it has not gone far enough.

European Perspectives on Family Policy

Debates about family policy will increasingly take place in the context of the European Community. However, the different countries involved have very different approaches to family policy.

Nation states differ greatly in the extent to which family policy is explicit or implicit. In many European countries the constitution explicitly recognizes the importance of the family, and the state undertakes to afford it special protection. In some countries, such as France, Germany, and Luxembourg, this commitment is translated into institutional structures for formulating and implementing policy. Other states, such as Greece, Italy, Portugal, and Spain, pledge themselves in their constitution to support the family, but do not have central institutions equipped to carry out family policy-making. Some countries, such as Denmark, Finland, the Netherlands, and Sweden, do not identify the family as an explicit area of policy; instead individuals, and particularly children, are the focus of policy. In others, such as Ireland and the United Kingdom, official government policy has not generally directly targeted the family as a policy area because of the concern of governments to avoid interfering in the private lives of individuals (Hantrais and Letablier 1996).

The tension between policies which support family life and those which encroach on family privacy is revealed in many of the documents which have shaped family policy in Europe. The European Convention on Human Rights (1950) stipulated that:

1. Everyone has the right to respect of his [sic] private and family life, his home and his correspondence.

2. There shall be no interference by a public authority with the exercise of this right except such as is in accordance with the law.

The main treaties of the European Union have not been explicitly concerned with family policy, despite growing pressure that the EU should be concerned with the welfare of families. However, many European initiatives have affected families, most notably in the areas of childcare, working hours, and maternity, paternity, and parental leave. Legislation in these fields has been presented in terms of equal opportunities or health and safety at work. The principle of **subsidiarity**, according to which actions should be taken at the lowest appropriate administrative level, has inhibited the making of substantive family policy at supra-national levels.

At national levels there are great variations in terms of family formation and structure and in the nature and extent of family policy. These variations have been documented by the European Observatory on National Family Policies (Ditch *et al.* 1996: 5). Total Period Fertility rates are declining throughout the continent and every country now has a fertility rate below replacement level: it is argued that this may have beneficial social, economic, and environmental consequences. Most European countries are experiencing increases in cohabitation and divorce and in the numbers of lone-parent families, with a consequent increase in step and other relationships.

Policy responses to these changes in family life will reflect long-standing ideological and cultural differences between individuals and between nations. In the future social policy will continue to be a sensitive indicator of the current state of opinion on the changing nature of family life.

Key Legislation and Policy Documents

Children Act 1989: see page 169.

Child Support Act 1993: see page 170.

Divorce Reform Act 1969: see page 177.

Family Law Act 1996: see pages 177–8.

Housing Act 1985: see page 177.

National Health Service and Community Care Act 1990: see page 173.

Glossary

age structure This term is used to describe populations in terms of the relative numbers of people of different ages. The age structure of the population reflects variations in the past number of births, together with increased longevity and changes arising from migration (Office for National Statistics 1998: 32).

child benefit This is a universal benefit, paid to the mother of a child under 16, or under 19 if the child is still in full-time education. At the time of writing there are higher rates of benefit for the first child and even higher rates for the first child of a lone parent (Child Poverty Action Group 1998: 187).

childcare This term is often used to refer to the support available outside the family to help parents to care for dependent children. It includes day nurseries and playgroups, as well as care by childminders and nannies. However, as much care is provided by grandmothers as is provided by all other sources of childcare put together (Brannen *et al.* 1994: 44).

dependency ratio This term was coined by economists to describe the ratio between those who are 'economically active', in that they earn their own living in the labour market, and those who depend on other earners for their financial support. The definition does not, of course, recognize the fact that those who are economically active are often dependent on those who are 'economically inactive' for the provision of domestic services, childcare, and other supports, and that 'economically inactive' people can be contributing valuable unpaid work to their family or community.

extended family This term was coined by sociologists to describe the wider kin group, in contrast to the 'nuclear family'. An extended family may link three or more generations, including people whose relationship is that of grandparent/grandchild, brothers and sisters, uncles and aunts, nephews and nieces and cousins.

family The official definition of the family, used in all government censuses and surveys, is that a family is a married or cohabiting couple, either with or without their never-married children (of any age), including childless couples or a lone parent together with his or her never-married child or children (Office for National Statistics 1998: 235).

individualization This term refers to the process by which the individual, rather than the group, becomes the key unit in society. The idea implies the breaking down of the structures of class, occupation, locality and gender. As one commentator said 'The individual himself or herself becomes the reproduction unit for the social in the lifeworld' (Beck 1996: 130).

household A household is a person living alone or a group of people who have the address as their only or main residence and who either share one meal a day or share the living accommodation. (Office for National Statistics 1998: 235)

family policy For a social policy to be described as family policy . . . the family would need to be the deliberate target of specific actions, and the measures should be designed so as to have an impact on family resources and, ultimately, on family structure (Hantrais and Letablier 1996: 139).

ideology Ideologies are sets of ideas, assumptions and images, by which people make sense of society, which give a clear social identity, and which serve in some way to legitimise power relations in society (McLennan 1991: 114).

lone-parent family A lone-parent family consists of a lone parent living with his or her never-married dependent children, provided these children have no children of their own (Office for National Statistics 1998: 235).

maternity allowance This is a contributory benefit paid to women who are pregnant or who have recently given birth, who have paid sufficient contributions but who do not qualify for Maternity Pay, either because they have changed jobs during pregnancy or because they are self-employed (Child Poverty Action Group 1998: 84).

maternity leave This term refers to the right for women to take paid leave from employment around the time of the birth of a baby (Ditch *et al*. 1995: 47).

maternity pay This is a contributory benefit paid to women who are pregnant or who have recently given birth. Entitlement to the benefit depends on women having been employed for at least 26 weeks and to have satisfied certain other conditions (Child Poverty Action Group 1998: 77).

nuclear family This term was coined by sociologists to describe the social group consisting of parents and their children; it is particularly contrasted with the 'extended family', which includes members of the wider kin group, such as grandparents, uncles and aunts, cousins, nephews and nieces, and grandchildren.

paternity and parental leave The first term refers to the right of a man to take paid leave from employment when he becomes a father. The second term refers to the right of parents to take leave when a child is ill. Currently neither are state policy in the United Kingdom, though some other European countries do give limited rights to such leave (Ditch *et al*. 1995: 47).

parental responsibility The Children Act 1989 used this term to sum up the collection of duties, rights, and authority which a parent has in respect of a child. The aim was to stress that parents, rather than the state, have the prime responsibility for children. Mothers, and the fathers of legitimate children, automatically have parental responsibility, while fathers who are not married to the mother of the child can acquire parental responsibility in a number of different ways (Department of Health 1989: 1).

public and private spheres The separation of public and private has a long history in Western European thought, deriving from the Ancient Greek distinction between the *polis*, meaning the sphere of public life, and the *oikos*, meaning the private household. The involvement of the state in the private life of the family has been criticized as interference and control, or it has been welcomed as a support to the work done in this sphere and as a check on the tyranny which the strong can exercise over weaker members of families.

reconstituted families These are families in which one or both parents have been married before, so at least one parent–child relationship involves a step-parent and a stepchild.

subsidiarity This idea originated within the Roman Catholic Church and has been adopted as a central principle of the European Community. It expresses the idea that actions should be taken at the lowest appropriate administrative level. So actions should not be undertaken by nation states if they can be carried out by regional bodies, and public agencies should not take on responsibilities which can be undertaken within the family (Hantrais and Letablier, 1996: 45).

total period fertility rate (TPFR) The TPFR measures the average number of children born to each woman, if birth rates in the specific period persisted throughout her childbearing life (Office for National Statistics 1997: 32).

Guide to Further Reading

Anderson, M., Bechofer, F. and Gershuny, J., *The Social and Political Economy of the Household* (Oxford: Oxford University Press, 1994). Results from the Social Change and Economic Life Initiative used to illuminate important areas of family life.

Bernades, J., *Family Studies: An Introduction* (London: Routledge, 1997). An introduction to the sociology of the family.

Brannen, J., Meszaros, G., Moss, P., and Poland, G., *Employment and Family Life: A Review of Research in the UK* (London: DoE, 1994). A comprehensive review of the literature and of policy in this area, produced by the Employment Department.

Fox Harding, L., *Family, State and Social Policy* (London: Macmillan, 1996). A useful introduction to family policy in the UK.

Hantrais, L. and Letablier, M., *Families and Family Policies in Europe* (London; Longman, 1996). A comparative study of family policy in the European Union.

Gittins, D., *The Family in Question* (London: Macmillan, 1992). A re-issue of a classic text on family life and family ideologies.

Morris, L., *The Workings of the Household* (Cambridge: Polity, 1990). Covers employment and unemployment, the domestic division of labour, household finance, and young people in the household, with comparative material from the UK and the USA.

References

Abbott, P. and Wallace, C. (1992), *The Family and the New Right* (London: Pluto).

Anderson, D. and Dawson, E. (1986), 'Popular but Unrepresented: The Curious Case of the Normal Family', in Anderson, D. and Dawson, E., *Family Portraits* (London: Social Affairs Unit).

Anderson, M., Bechofer, F., and Gershuny, J. (1994), *The Social and Political Economy of the Household* (Oxford: Oxford University Press).

Arber, S. and Ginn, J. (1995), 'Gender Differences in the Relationship Between Paid Employment and Informal Care', *Work, Employment and Society*, 9/3, 445–71.

Baldwin, S. (1985), *The Costs of Caring: Families with Disabled Children* (London: Routledge).

Barrett, M. and McIntosh, M. (1982), *The Anti-Social Family* (London: Verso).

Beck, U. and Beck-Gernsheim, E. (1995), *The Normal Chaos of Love* (Cambridge: Polity).

Bennett, F. (1997), *Child Support: Issues for the Future* (London: Child Poverty Action Group).

Bernard, J. (1982), *The Future of Marriage* (New Haven: York University Press).

Bernades, J. (1997), *Family Studies: An Introduction* (London: Routledge).

Beveridge Report (1942), *Social Insurance and Allied Services* (Cmd. 6404, London: HMSO).

Bird, R. and Cretney, S. (1997), *Divorce: The New Law* (Bristol: Bristol Family Law).

Blumberg, R. L. (1991), *Gender, Family and Economy* (London: Sage).

Botting, B. (1996), 'Population Review: Review of Children', *Population Trends*, 85, 25.

Brannen, J., Mezaros, G., Moss, P., and Poland, G. (1994), *Employment and Family Life: A Review of Research in the UK* (London: Department of Employment).

Buck, N., Gershuny, J., Rose, D., and Scott, J. (1994), *Changing Households* (Colchester: University of Essex).

Burgoyne, J., Ormrod, R., and Richards, M. (1987), *Divorce Matters* (Harmondsworth: Penguin).

Central Statistical Office (1995), *Social Trends, no. 25* (London: HMSO).

Child Poverty Action Group (1998), *Rights Guide to Non-Means-Tested Benefits* (London: Child Poverty Action Group).

Clarke, K., Glendinning, C., and Craig, G. (1994), *Losing Support: Children and the Child Support Act* (London: Child Poverty Action Group).

Conservative Party (1997), *You Can Only Be Sure With The Conservatives* (London: Conservative Party).

Delphy, C. and Leonard, D. (1992), *Familiar Exploitation: A New Analysis of Marriage in Contemporary Western Societies* (Cambridge: Polity).

Dennis, N. and Erdos, G. (1993), *Families without Fatherhood* (London: Institute of Economic Affairs).

Department of Health (1989), *An Introduction to the Children Act 1989* (London: HMSO).

Ditch, J., Barnes, H., Bradshaw, J., Commaille, J. and Eardley, T. (1995), *A Synthesis of National Family Policies in 1994* (York: University of York).

Dobash, R. and Dobash, R. E. (1980), *Violence against Wives* (Shepton Mallet: Open Books).

Dwyer, D. and Bruce, J. (1988), *A Home Divided: Women and Income in the Third World* (Stanford, CA: Stanford University Press).

Edwards, S. (1989), *Policing Domestic Violence* (London: Sage).

Family Policy Studies Centre (1997), *Putting Families on the Map* Factsheet 1 (London: Family Policy Studies Centre).

Ferri, E. and Smith, K. (1998), *Step-parenting in the 1990s* (London: Family Policy Studies Centre).

Ferri, E. and Smith, K. (1998), *Parenting in the 1990s* (London: Family Policy Studies Centre).

Fox Harding, L. (1996), *Family, State and Social Policy* (London: Macmillan).

Freeman, M. (1992), *Children, their Families and the Law: Working with the Children Act* (Basingstoke: Macmillan).

Gallie, D. (1988), *Employment in Britain* (Oxford: Basil Blackwell).

Giddens, A. (1997), *Sociology* (Cambridge: Polity).

——(1992), *The Transformation of Intimacy* (Cambridge: Polity).

Gittins, D. (1993), *The Family in Question* (Basingstoke: Macmillan).

Glendinning, C. and Millar, J. (1992), *Women and Poverty in Britain—the 1990s* (Hemel Hempstead: Wheatsheaf).

Graham, H. (1983), 'Caring: A Labour of Love', in Finch, J. and Groves, D., *A Labour of Love: Women, Work and Caring* (London: Routledge).

Green, H. (1988), *Informal Carers* (London: HMSO).

Grint, K. (1991), *The Sociology of Work: An Introduction* (Cambridge: Polity).

Hantrais, L. and Letablier, M. (1996), *Families and Family Policy in Europe* (London: Longman).

Haskey, J. (1996), 'Population Review: Families and Households in Great Britain', *Population Trends*, 85 (Autumn), 7, 13.

Home Office (1998), *Supporting Families: A Consultation Document* (London: The Stationery Office).

House of Commons Home Affairs Committee (1993), *Domestic Violence: Third Report* (London: HMSO).

Hyman, P. (1994), *Women and Economics* (Wellington, New Zealand: Bridget Williams Books).

Joshi, H. (1992), 'The Cost of Caring', in *Women and Poverty in Britain: The 1990s*, ed. C. Glendinning and J. Millar (Hemel Hempstead: Wheatsheaf).

Jowell, R., Curtice, J., Brook, L., and Ahrendt, D., with Park, A. (1994), *British Social Attitudes: the 11th Report* (Aldershot: Gower).

Jowell, R., Curtice, J., Park, A., Brook, L., and Ahrendt, D. (1995), *British Social Attitudes: the 12th Report* (Aldershot: Gower).

Kempson, E. (1996), *Life on a Low Income* (York: Joseph Rowntree Foundation).

Kiernan, K. and Wicks, M. (1990), *Family Change and Future Policy* (London: Family Policy Studies Centre).

Kingston, P. and Penhale, B. (1995), *Family Violence and the Caring Professions* (London: Macmillan).

Labour Party (1997), *New Labour: Because Britain Deserves Better* (London: Labour Party).

Levin, E., Moriarty, J. and Gorbach, P. (1994), *Better for the Break* (London: HMSO).

Lewis, J. and Maclean, M. (1997), 'Recent Developments in Family Policy in the UK', in *Social Policy Review 9*, ed. May, M., Brunsdon, E., and Craig, G. (London: Social Policy Association).

McLennan, G. (1991), 'The Power of Ideology', *Society and the Social Sciences* (Milton Keynes: Open University).

Masefield, J. (1946), *Poems* (London: Heinemann).

Middleton, S., Ashworth, K., and Braithwaite, I. (1997), *Small Fortunes: Spending on Children, Childhood Poverty and Parental Sacrifice* (York: Joseph Rowntree Foundation).

Morgan, P. (1995), *Farewell to the Family?* (London: Institute of Economic Affairs).

Morris, L. and Ruane, S. (1989), *Household Finance Management and the Labour Market* (Avebury: Gower).

Morris, L. (1990), *The Workings of the Household* (Oxford: Polity).

Mullender, A. (1996), *Rethinking Domestic Violence: The Social Work and Probation Response* (London: Routledge).

Muncie, J., Wetherell, M., Dallos, R., and Cochrane, A. (1995), *Understanding the Family* (London: Sage).

Oakley, A. (1974), *The Sociology of Housework* (Oxford: Martin Roberts).

Office of Population Censuses and Surveys (1991), *Social Trends 21* (London: HMSO).

——(1996), *Living in Britain: Results from the 1994 General Household Survey* (London: HMSO).

Office for National Statistics (1997), *Social Trends 27* (London: HMSO).

——(1998), *Social Trends 28* (London: HMSO).

Oppenheim, C. and Harker, L. (1996), *Poverty: The Facts*, (London: Child Poverty Action Group).

Pahl, J. (1985), *Private Violence and Public Policy* (London: Routledge).

——(1989), *Money and Marriage* (London: Macmillan).

——(1995), 'His Money, Her Money: Recent Research on Financial Organisation in Marriage', *Journal of Economic Psychology*, 16/3, 361–76.

Pahl, J. and Quine, L. (1987), 'Families with Mentally Handicapped Children', in *Coping with Disorder in the Family*, ed. J. Orford (London: Croom Helm).

Pahl, R. (1984), *Divisions of Labour* (Oxford: Basil Blackwell).

Parker, G. (1990), *With Due Care and Attention: A Review of Research on Informal Care* (London: Family Policy Studies Centre).

Parsons, T. and Bales, R. (1956), *Family Socialisation and Interaction Process* (London: Routledge).

Robinson, M. and Smith, D. (1993), *Step by Step: Focus on Stepfamilies* (Hemel Hempstead: Harvester Wheatsheaf).

Rose, R. (1989), *Ordinary People in Social Policy: A Behavioural Analysis* (London: Sage).

Secretary of State for Social Security (1995), *Improving Child Support* (London: HMSO).

Secretaries of State for Health (1989), *Caring for People: Community Care in the next Decade and Beyond*, Cm. 849 (London: HMSO).

Twigg, J. (1992), *Carers: Research and Practice* (London: HMSO).

Twigg, J., Atkin, K. and Perring, C. (1990), *Carers and Services: A Review of Research* (London: HMSO).

Victim Support (1992), *Domestic Violence* (London: HMSO).

Vogler, C. and Pahl, J. (1993), 'Social and Economic Change and the Organisation of Money in Marriage', *Work, Employment and Society*, 7/1, 71–95.

——(1994), 'Money, Power and Inequality Within Marriage', *Sociological Review*, 42/2, 263–88.

Wilson, G. (1987), *Money in the Family* (Aldershot: Avebury).

Part Three

Planning, Financing, and Implementing Welfare Policies

9 Professions, Bureaucracy, and Social Welfare

Andrew Gray and Bill Jenkins

Contents

Introduction: White Coats and Grey Suits

Do you remember the harrowing case of Child B? She came to public attention critically ill with leukaemia. After a series of chemotherapy regimes without any change in her underlying condition and yet causing great suffering, the purchaser of her healthcare, Cambridgeshire Health Authority, took advice from a consultant specializing in child cancer on the efficacy of further treatment. The consultant recommended in effect that the disease should be allowed to run its course without further intervention and that the child should be spared the suffering of the treatments and allowed to end her life with dignity. The health authority accepted the advice and ended the treatment.

Child B's father, however, was upset by this decision and took the case to the newspapers. In effect he accused the health authority of taking the decision on financial grounds (each course of treatment was costing the NHS about £75,000). Although the authority denied this, the news coverage gave the impression of challenging this bureaucratic valuation of a child's life. An anonymous benefactor then paid for a further round of treatment in a private clinic. But after a short period of remission and a display of considerable bravery (of the sort that often surprises parents), Child B died.

Is this a case of invidious bureaucracy threatening the professional imperative of patient care? Or is it a demonstration of the intrinsic tensions and dilemmas often thrown up in social policy decisions?

This idea that professionals are under threat from bureaucracy and managerialism is represented in Box 9.1. Drawn from a campaign by the Royal College of Nurses against the Conservative health service reforms of the 1980s, the tableau pitches Florence Nightingale—lamp holder for the values of healthcare—against Sir Roy Griffiths—chairman of a 1983 report championing more general management in healthcare, doyen of private sector retail management (he was a senior executive with Sainsbury's) and fixated on nostrums of management mantra which, stereotypically, he is unable to express in continuous prose! It is a powerful image of the tensions between essential professional values of service and the deadening hand of bureaucratic management. The implication is that the white coats are losing out to the grey suits.

For the Conservative Government of 1979–97, for whom Griffiths was a totem, the imperative was to bring resource issues to bear on social policy decisions. Its campaign was designed to break up restrictive practices perpetrated by monopoly providers with little regard to public costs or desires. The 1980s and 1990s were thus punctuated by a series of reforms of education, healthcare, housing, police, social services, and related public services. In a piece of early 1990s jargon, the intention was to *re-invent* the professions as *providers* of public services committed to comprehensive management.

For the advocates of reform the benefits have been both welcome and visible: greater efficiency and more responsiveness. For its detractors, schemes such as deregulation, competitive tendering, internal markets, devolved budgeting, and quality and consumer initiatives have not only subordinated professionals but built up powerful and expensive new bureaucracies with the public as the loser.

Professionals themselves have adopted a variety of positions in relation to these changes. Some have been hostile:

I did not join the profession to push paper but treat patients (hospital consultant resisting pressure to be a clinical director, i.e. manager of clinical colleagues in a department).

Others have been more accommodating:

If the senior police officers of (this area) don't get stuck in and learn to manage our resources and operations more efficiently and effectively, then head quarters, or even worse some berk in the Home Office, will take over (chief superintendent).

All have had to deal with changing contexts and relationships in the practice of their professions.

> ### Box 9.1 White coats and grey suits: Florence Nightingale *vs.* Sir Roy Griffiths
>
>
> "THE FIRST AIM OF A HOSPITAL SHOULD BE TO DO THE SICK NO HARM."
>
> *Florence Nightingale.*
>
> "CENTRAL INITIATIVES... MANPOWER TARGETS... EFFICIENCY SAVINGS... PERFORMANCE INDICATORS."
>
> *The Griffiths Report.*

It would be easy to engage in a knock-about on the gains and losses in all this. Our aim, however, is to elaborate the changing nature of professional life in public and social policy and the relationship of professionals to organizational arrangements and others in the delivery of services. We may begin with Socrates, who asserted that:

Interference by the three classes [businessmen, auxiliaries, and guardians] with each other's jobs and interchange of jobs between them, therefore, does the greatest harm to our state and we are entirely justified in calling it the worst of evils. (Plato, *The Republic*, 434)

By extension, we might suggest that attempts to turn professionals into bureaucratic managers or invite the bureaucrats to take professionals' decisions may be counter-productive. Yet the past couple of decades in British government have been predicated on precisely this notion; mixing up the 'classes' and bringing their functions closer together has been regarded as exactly what the state needs.

Has it worked? What do we mean by 'bureaucracy' and 'profession'? How have public management reforms affected the relationship between bureaucrats, politicians, professionals, and publics in a new mixed economy of public service? As these are all significant questions, this chapter presents some conceptualizations of bureaucracy and professionalism, offers a comparative analysis of relationships over the past thirty years or so, and draws out some issues.

Models of Bureaucracy and Profession

Bureaucracy

Bureaucracy is a word with a myriad of meanings, many malign. Certainly it does not take much inflection in calling someone a bureaucrat to cause offence. Like other social science terms used extensively in social and political debate (like 'democracy'), it has become attached to particular ideologies and has suffered from conceptual vandalism.

Social science itself has compounded the difficulties in that, as Beetham notes (1996), there are at least two major conceptualizations of bureaucracy: those in the sociology of organizations, and political economy. Moreover, any elaboration of a model of bureaucracy has to deal with the term 'model' as a defining, explaining, or prescribing device. Our purpose is limited to helping you to recognize bureaucracy, or more exactly bureaucratic characteristics, as a prelude to an examination of how well professional practice fits in with this traditional organizational arrangement in public services. Thus we seek to elaborate the defining characteristics of bureaucracy and provide some explanation of their effects in practice.

Weber's Characterization of Bureaucracy For most of the twentieth century, any discussion of bureaucracy has begun with the work of Max Weber, a German sociologist (1864 to 1920). The son of a liberal politician and a dominating and puritanical mother, Weber took up an academic career and rose meteorically to become a professor at the tender age of 31. Following a decade of emotional and mental disorders, he began to readjust to life and in this period until his death he wrote much of the work by which we now regard him as a leading sociologist, such as *The Protestant Ethic and the Spirit of Capitalism* (written in 1904–5) and *The Theory of Economic and Social Organization* (1910–18). In these we can see ideas about society and bureaucracy underpinned by an interest in the origins, manifestations, and exercise of authority. His sources are eclectic in time and across societies, drawing on ancient civilizations such as China, Egypt, and Greece as well as industrial Europe.

Authority, for Weber, is legitimate power. The basis of legitimation has three distinctive forms. *Traditional authority* is derived from the customs and practices of a particular social group as they pass through generations. Typical are the dynastic traditions of rulers. *Charismatic authority*, on the other hand, is derived from the possession of leadership characteristics. Originally a term used to describe fanatical religious leaders, it has come to embrace qualities such as oratory and vision. Of course, Weber died before the twentieth century provided its most graphic examples of such authority at work through dictators and their cult-generating machines. Had he experienced these he might have taken a less historical view of the decline of this authority in preference to his third category, *rational-legal authority*. For Weber regarded this type as the distinguishing vehicle of legitimate power in the organizations of industrial society. This is

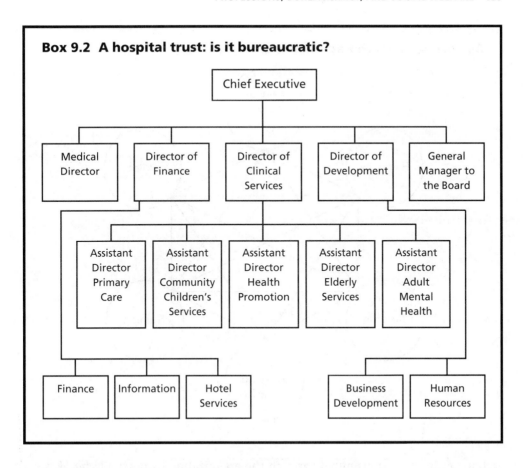

Box 9.2 A hospital trust: is it bureaucratic?

the authority which comes from the rights and responsibilities of office, appointment to which has followed laid-down procedures, and which is recognized by subordinates. Thus the authority does not derive from the individual or the traditions of the office but from the designated responsibilities and procedures of the position itself.

The striking feature of rational-legal authority for Weber was the way it had become institutionalized in modern industrial society. In contrast to organizations and societies governed by élites and citizens (autocracy and democracy), he described this as bureaucracy (government through office). Bureaucracy is thus the organizational arrangement through which rational-legal authority is institutionalized.

Box 9.3 is an abstraction of Weber's ideas for, despite his central concern with this defining form of industrial organization, Weber nowhere systematically codified his elements of bureaucracy in a single framework. Rather, they emerge from fragmented elaborations. As a result, different commentators may present as few as four main features while others list a dozen or so (see Beetham 1996). However, most agree on a core set of defining characteristics.

First, bureaucracies are characterized by a division of labour into *formal jurisdictional areas*; that is, functions are allocated to specified units (sometimes called departments or sections) and the designated responsibilities and authorities are limited by boundaries.

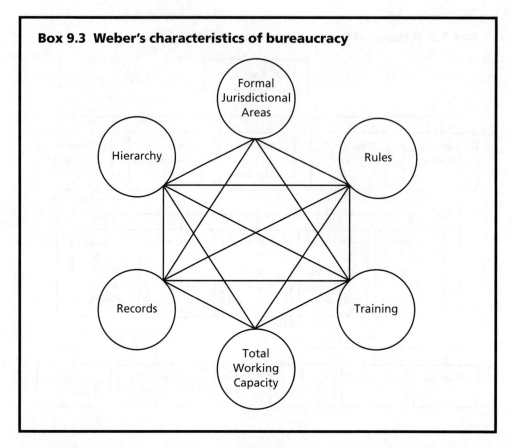

Box 9.3 Weber's characteristics of bureaucracy

Second, authority is transmitted through the organization through a *hierarchy*, i.e. a scalar chain in which the authority of one superior is then subordinate to another. Third, the activities of bureaucracy are carried out according to *rules*, i.e. laid-down regulations and procedures for the conduct of activities, whose rationality lies in their promotion of functions. Of particular note here is, fourth, the *recording* of activities against these rules, thereby creating file-based narratives of transactions which subsequent officials may follow.

If these characteristics apply to structure and process, others relate to the bureaucrats themselves. Their performance of tasks according to the distinct jurisdictional areas requires organizational *training*. In the English medieval military, soldiers were part-timers, usually commandeered by their landowners under an obligation to the monarch. When the monarch summoned they just turned up. When such an arrangement became a shaky basis on which to conduct campaigns against increasingly sophisticated enemies who, in a very un-British-like way, practised beforehand, a standing bureaucratic army developed in which training was a distinguishing feature for soldiers who also devoted full working capacities to the organization.

These elements taken together have been described as constituting bureaucracy as an ideal type. A word of caution here: by ideal type we mean belonging to ideas rather than to states of idyll. Weber's characteristics of bureaucracy are abstractions of what he observed. Thus it may be more useful to treat them as frameworks for analysing the bureaucratic tendencies in organization rather than prescriptions for or descriptions of actual organizations.

Bureaucracy Today: Empirical, Theoretical, and Ideological The empirical pervasiveness of bureaucratic tendencies in the modern world is well documented. Much of it, but by no means all (consider the giant commercial corporations), is found in public service provision. Highly developed and formalized division of labour, extensive hierarchies of command, rules, and procedures, with transactions duly noted and recorded by specifically trained dedicated officials, are dominant features of the organizations through which our public services are provided.

For Weber, the growth of bureaucracy was associated with the growth of legal and technical rationality as a response to arbitrary governance and the industrial revolution. In today's world, developments in the technology of work and the increasing pressure by publics for standardized services demand organizational characteristics which combine specialization (to combat the technical complexity) and integration (to give effect to co-ordinated direction often determined by political masters). Bureaucracy has the potential to provide these and its predominance in government (and private organizations too) is testament to its power to deliver.

Bureaucratic tendencies, however, are not without their problems. Many researchers have identified the contrast between the formalism of Weber's model and the paradox of the pervasive informal features in organizations which sustain them. Much of this informal behaviour, i.e. that which is not prescribed by the organization, arises as a way of handling the inherent contradictions of different bureaucratic characteristics.

Box 9.4. Pensioner refused mature student's grant

In the early 1970s, there lived a pensioner in Staffordshire who had retired from work three years earlier and was becoming bored with doing nothing. As with many of his generation, he had missed out on the developing opportunities for further and higher education but had heard about the brave new world it offered. With a 'I'll have some of that' response, he duly applied for and was accepted at his local university (Keele—but then we all have our crosses to bear!). His place secure, the next stop was his local educational authority to obtain one of these mature student full grants he had also heard about. To his surprise he was turned down. Why? Apparently on the grounds that the eligibility rules at the time stated that an applicant for such an award had to be gainfully employed for three years prior to the application. Our pensioner had not been so; he had been retired. A nonsense? Certainly, but it had arisen because the rules had been drawn up to prevent young people (perhaps encouraged by their parents, who were reluctant to fork out for their share of the grant) from making an application with the appearance of independence from their parents. However, in this case an official in the education authority applied the rules ritualistically to a situation to which they could not adapt. (Fortunately, rules can be changed—though it can be difficult—and our hero got his money!)

Rule use is a particularly graphic area. Rules are shown to be greatly functional to the provision of public services. In processing large numbers of transactions rules help to promote standardized outcomes (like cases being treated alike). Moreover, they execute this with considerable efficiency as they obviate the need for decision criteria to be invented on each occasion. But at least 50 years of research has identified three informal 'Rs' of rule use (and, unlike the three 'Rs' of education, they actually do all begin with that letter!).

The first two are often found together. *Ritualism* is the habitual use of a rule even in circumstances for which it is no longer appropriate. Box 9.4 provides an illustration of this. It would not be surprising if in this case officials justified their actions by reference to a literal interpretation of the rule and a 'don't blame me, I did not make the rules' disclaimer. This would constitute *retreatism*, i.e. the use of rules to protect or defend oneself.

Reductionism is more subtle: it is the perverse way rules can reduce as well as enhance standards of behaviour. Imagine a situation in which a lack of rules has been identified as contributing to poor performance, perhaps even discrimination in the provision of public services. The remedy, the setting out of a rule, makes explicit the standard of behaviour required. This has the desired effect in obliging poor performers to raise their level. However, for those who are performing above the standard and perhaps being innovative and progressive, the precise elucidation of this standard will not only make them aware of the extent to which they have been performing unnecessarily above it, but will make such future performance public (see Box 9.5).

A further consequence is *bureaucratic politics*. You will know that political activity derives from differentiation. All differentiation in an organization (as in society) has the potential to lead to political activity, but it takes specific challenges to the interests arising from the differentiation to translate into politics. As we have seen, a central bureaucratic characteristic is division of labour reflected in the differentiation into sections and units. The formal functionality of these arrangements is again evident: effectiveness through the specialization, concentration of effort, and discipline. The organizational units thereby created develop group loyalties. In circumstances where the interests of the units are supported (as in resource or policy growth), this differentiation remains tacit politically; however, when these interests are threatened units

---

Box 9.5 A reductionist tendency of performance indicators

Sources in some local authorities report that the Audit Commission's annual publication of league tables of local authority performance in selected services is anticipated with decidedly mixed feelings. For a service to be at the top of a list is by way of an invitation for resources to be taken away and redeployed in favour of the much more public worst-performing services. In other words, the publication of the standard and performance can help to bring unacceptable performance up to the standard (a formal and desired effect) but also promote reduction of standard amongst the highest performers (an informal, and presumably undesired effect).

may engage in political competition which may not only divert resources in themselves but undermine the concentration of effort towards formally prescribed activities.

Bureaucracy as a theoretical construction (rather than as an empirical reality) is based on certain premises about society and human behaviour and the way in which these are expressed in organizations. Weber conceived bureaucratic characteristics as value-free, i.e., neutral instruments or mechanisms amenable to the promotion of any ordained values irrespective of context. However, this denies the value of bureaucracy itself. After all, an instrument for embodying or promoting a rational-legal authority (or any other) cannot by definition be value-free. Second, for bureaucratic mechanisms to be culturally neutral would imply that the norms and values of organizational members displaying bureaucratic characteristics have no influence on its realization. This seems illogical, given that most of our predictive theories of society are based on exactly the opposite notion.

So, bureaucratic characteristics are intrinsically value-laden. This makes them ideological, and many have been quick to challenge bureaucracy on this ground. You may have noticed that these challenges come from both the right and left of the political spectrum. First, there have been arguments against the conservatism of bureaucracy, that is, its inbuilt protection through formal and rigid structures and rules of the status quo or, put another way, its resistance to change. Second, there have been protestations of the inherent undemocratic quality of bureaucratic life. On the other hand, others have advocated bureaucratic characteristics as effective command structures in circumstances where consistency and predictability are a requirement, and as accountability structures through which officials are accountable for not only the quality of public goods and services but also the means by which they are provided. Jaques (1990), for example, described how:

At first glance hierarchy may be difficult to praise. Bureaucracy is a dirty word even among bureaucrats, and in business there is a widespread view that managerial hierarchy kills initiative, crushes creativity, and has therefore had its day. Yet 35 years of research have convinced me that managerial hierarchy is the most efficient, the hardiest, and in fact the most natural structure ever devised for large organizations. Properly structured, hierarchy can release energy and creativity, rationalize productivity, and actually improve morale.

Interestingly, as Box 9.6 shows, members of public service professions have been amongst the most vociferous complainants of the deadening hand of bureaucracy on their ability to provide services to their clients. But what is a profession and what are the characteristics of professional life? The next section seeks to elaborate these prior to a comparison with those of bureaucracy.

Profession

Weber saw professionalization in society as a manifestation of the same force as that driving bureaucratization—rationality. Indeed, for classical sociology many of the characteristics of **profession** are similar to bureaucracy: formal jurisdictions, specialization, training, and full-time commitment. However, we have seen that professionalization is often represented as conflicting with bureaucracy. We shall examine the extent and nature of this conflict in the next section. But first, we must seek some understanding of professionalism.

Box 9.6 The deadening hand of bureaucracy?

'Joyce Brand, a social worker for 25 years (and incidentally the mother of Jo Brand the comedi-
enne), feels that professionals have been forced to submit their values to a bureaucratic norm.
She attributes the loss of social service departments "rooted in humanity and professionalism"
in part to the "relentless march of the market". But she adds: "it is from within the organization that the greatest threat comes. We now have MBA managers so preoccupied with *systems, recording and checking*, that they have stopped valuing their most precious resource,
their staff . . . These managers have devised sophisticated and time-consuming *assessment
procedures* . . . They have set up *procedures and instructions* . . . while they translate human
distress into *recordable statistics*." '

(*The Independent*, 10 April 1997, bureaucratic emphases added)

Does this strike a chord with you? Is the deadening hand of bureaucracy thwarting
professional effectiveness?

Profession as a Victim of a Conceptual Tug-of-War Unfortunately, profession as a concept is no easier to elucidate than bureaucracy. Perhaps because in industrial society
the status of professional has been prized (with or without financial gains), the concept
has become elastic. In fact, not all of its connotations are favourable (consider 'the oldest
profession' and the 'professional foul'), and some are selective (profession in contrast to
amateur). But, in an occupational sense, the concept has been at the centre of a tug of
war between those who regard their vocations and marketplace positions as protect-
able through a professional label, and others who aspire to this status and position
without attracting widespread public recognition (see Box 9.7). Thus it is hard to deny
that profession is 'an intrinsically ambiguous, multifaceted folk concept, of which no
single attempt at isolating its existence will ever be generally persuasive' (Freidson
1994: 25). Nevertheless, as with bureaucracy, our analysis requires some elaboration.

During the 1950s and 1960s there was a concerted interest in defining the characteristics of professions. In an early expression, Greenwood (1957) sought on the basis of a
functional analysis to provide a taxonomy of professions. In this the 'established' professions (medicine, law, clergy, and academia) were seen as possessing a set of attributes
including specialist knowledge, autonomous judgement, self-regulation, codes of ethics,
and a distinctive culture (see Box 9.8). This set of attributes was cited in many subsequent collections of readings on professions, and proved useful in empirical studies in
establishing the extent to which different occupational groups could be classified as

---

Box 9.7 Public recognition of social policy professions

In a poll of 2,000 people in the UK, 71 per cent of respondents placed doctors first as
professions, 15 per cent police officers first, 6 per cent teachers, 3 per cent nurses, and
1 per cent social workers.

Source: Community Care, 3 March 1987.

Box 9.8 Attributes of a profession: a functionalist analysis

1. **systematic body of theory:** 'the skills that characterize a profession flow from and are supported by a fund of knowledge that has been organized into an internally consistent system';

2. **professional authority:** 'the layman's comparative ignorance' leaves the client 'no choice but to accede to professional judgement';

3. **sanction of the community:** 'by granting or withholding accreditation' a professional body is authorized by the state to control entry to and training in the profession;

4. **regulative code of ethics:** an 'explicit, systematic, and binding' code 'which compels ethical behaviour on the part of its members' in relation to clients and colleagues;

5. **the professional culture:** 'a social configuration unique to the profession' which 'consists of its *values, norms* and *symbols*'.

Source: Greenwood 1957.

---

professions or, indeed, as semi-professions, a term used to encompass emerging public-service groups which nevertheless lacked one or more of the defining attributes.

From such studies specialized knowledge and autonomy emerged as critical defining qualities of professionalism and became the basis of a search for absolute classes of professional groupings. However, it soon emerged that professionalism might be relative. Specialization, for example, was seen to be limited by situation and time while autonomy appeared as at least two-dimensional (i.e. autonomy from client and from the employing organization). Further, it became fashionable to ask how far social behaviour was constructed in situations rather than determined by social forces. Thus there developed an increasing recognition of the importance in understanding the way in which the term 'professional' is actually made and used by practitioners in their everyday interactions.

Partly in sympathy with this approach, a Durham University team recently set out to observe professionals working together in local government to ascertain their defining characteristics as professionals and ask professionals about their work.[1] In adopting a list of self-defining professional groups (i.e. accountants, engineers, environmental health officers, librarians, planners, social workers, solicitors, and so on), the team sought to establish from each respondent what it meant to be a professional. The responses revealed that professionalism meant one or more of the following: a specialist knowledge and expertise, a position, and an ethos promoting the values of professionals (including against corporate bureaucratic managerialism).

---

[1] *Professionalism and the Management of Local Authorities*, a research and development project financed by the Local Government Management Board and carried out by Dr Sarah Banks, Professor John Carpenter, Professor Andrew Gray, Elizabeth Green, and Dr Tim May. References to the Durham study are to this work.

Profession as Specialist Knowledge and Expertise In the Durham study, as in earlier work, individuals identified the professing of specialist knowledge or expertise as a central element of being a professional. Thus for one social worker:

the purpose of being a professional is to ensure that comprehensive knowledge is available to be applied to various presenting issues.

Moreover, specialism remains central, even though the circumstances of how, when, and where this specialism is used varied between different groups and contexts, while public service reforms are seen as eroding professionals' rights to exclusive exercise of the specialism. For example, local authority architects resent others less qualified taking on an increasing share of their tasks:

Clients like housing don't want to pay our fees . . . They try to cut corners by employing some-one themselves who's a . . . jack of all trades, who thinks he can do it.

Yet practitioners also take on parts of other roles in order to help out and get work done as part of a flexible team approach or because of staff shortages elsewhere.

Profession as Position Professionals see the way this knowledge and expertise is used as furnishing them with a distinctive position. In essence this is about autonomy, that is, the freedom from both clients and employing organizations to define and determine the application of their work. As we have seen already, autonomy has long been regarded as another central element of professionalism. However, practitioners recognize that its practice is related to context. Indeed, professionals employed in public service organizations have to manage an inherent tension between their obligations to clients, the profession at large, and their employing organization's objectives.

How this tension is managed is clearly set within the democratic process in general and the statutory obligations of public agencies and their professions in particular. After all, professionals in public service have to recognize that ministers and councillors are at liberty to ignore the soundest of their professional advice and to accept that legislation (e.g. in community care and housing) shapes the demands on and limits of their professional practice. This suggests that the exercise of autonomy is set by an internal political process of its own. Moreover, this process encompasses collaboration (an increasingly common term in the New Labour dictionary) across disciplines in order to provide services. Thus for a social worker:

Co-operation with other professional groups is vital in order to give good service to users . . . Health and social services must work more closely together. District nurses, health professionals must 'trust' each other more and understand where they stand.

The position of professionals will also depend on how they are structured in their organizations. Professional groups may be self-contained within discrete units to provide cohesion for professional discipline or, as is increasingly the case, merged with others to give effect to the need to collaborate and focus activities on specific client groups or sets of services. Thus, in bringing together, say, housing and social services into one new department, new professional positions may be forged which, although still dependent on specialist knowledge and expertise, may structure a particular position from which it may be applied.

Profession as Ethos To profess a specialist knowledge and expertise is also to espouse a set of values which is to be promoted for the benefit of the profession and its clients. There is a moral element here which, as Weber noted, is a source of political power and thus subject to opposition by those opposed to the professionals' claim to status. Yet what are its elements? Certainly this ethos imposes a hierarchy of duty on the professional: priority is given to client and profession over other claimants. Thus the specific client is the consumer and client relationships are sacrosanct. Relationships with other professional practitioners are collegial rather than hierarchical. This collegial and client-oriented ethos is realized through service, professional maintenance, and innovation.

Of course, this ideal of the professional ethos tends to reflect original sole practices, that is, individual professionals acting directly with clients without outside mediating influences, perhaps as you might find if, as a private individual, you sought professional advice from a lawyer or accountant. This situation is relatively rare in the context of today's industrial and collectivized society. Moreover, we are concerned with public service professions. These may have a broader conception of the commitment to the client which incorporates obligations to the service department and the employing organization as a whole (e.g. hospital, school, or local authority).

If this commitment to client well-being is a defining element of a professional ethos, so is its obligations to the profession as a whole. The codification of specialist knowledge and expertise is set out by the profession through its corporate body (usually an institute or association such as the British Association of Social Work or the Chartered Institute of Public Finance and Accountancy). This explication will usually be supported by codes of conduct and ethical practice which guide members' relations with clients and employing organizations. Such professional associations gain the allegiance of members, if only through their control of registration, i.e. the award (or removal) of a licence to practice as a professional. But such bodies are also seen by members as standard-bearers of the values of the profession, so much so that members may be as critical of them for not protecting the profession against external challenges as they are of those challenges themselves.

One set of such threats to professional ethos comes from the bureaucratic tendencies of large organizations. As we shall see in the next section, public sector reforms have intensified these for many public service professions. As one housing officer explained:

The increased emphasis on performance targets, pleasing political masters to obtain finance etc., have all served to decrease the emphasis and value placed on professional work; professional views/opinions are often not appreciated or welcomed by senior management or members.

Health professionals and social workers have also expressed concern that 'having customers, not clients' (that is, paying punters with sets of service demands rather than recipients of a professionally determined treatment) has undermined their professional ethos.

From the literature on the conceptualization of profession and the reflections of professionals themselves we can draw out elements of the professional experience. At its heart, profession appears to be about the professing of specialist knowledge and expertise, a distinctive autonomous position from which to practise them and a culture or ethos which emphasizes the commitment both to clients and the collegiality of professional colleagues at large. However, some of these elements coincide with bureaucratic characteristics and some are in direct conflict with them. The next section attempts to provide a comparative framework before providing a history of their relationship in the post-1945 public services in the UK.

Command and Communion

We have so far established something of the defining elements of both bureaucracy and profession. Yet how can we compare them so that we are clear of the distinctive qualities and modes of governance? The following paragraphs provide a framework of comparison based on three dimensions: legitimation, accountability, and integration.

By *legitimation* we refer to the basis on which the actions of those in bureaucratic or professional contexts are justified. This is, in effect, the source of the authority by which bureaucratic or professional decisions are made and taken. Etzioni, in a seminal contribution on semi-professionals, argued that 'the ultimate justification for an administrative [i.e. bureaucratic] act is that it is in line with the organization's rules and regulations, and that it has been approved directly or by implication—by a superior rank', while the justification for a professional act is that 'it is, to the best of the professional's knowledge base, the right act' (1969, pp. x–xi). It should be noted that the importance of this distinction is that the legitimation of the bureaucratic act is internal to the organization, with not only the codification of authorized and unauthorized activity, but the allocation of praise and blame conducted hierarchically. The legitimation of the professional act is external; the codification of appropriateness and the allocation of praise and blame is carried out externally by a collegial body. Clearly the potential for conflict is high, as professionals working through public bureaucracies face different sources of authority and different mechanisms by which their actions will be judged.

This brings us to the second comparative dimension: *accountability*. Professionals see themselves as accountable to at least three sets of accountees: the client, the profession, and the organization through which they practise (see Box 9.9). Thus for the professional there is an accountability in any one set of actions which is subject to these three sets of forces, some of which are external to the organization. For any individual professional the immediacy of these forces varies. Doctors and social workers, for example, may have day-to-day contact with the public, while others, such as accountants and lawyers in public organizations, may have greater contact with their employing organization or even other public agencies, including central government departments. In bureaucracy, however, accountabilities are resolved through the managerial hierarchy within the organization.

These differing accountability patterns are a pointer to another distinction: *integrating mechanisms*, i.e. the means by which differentiated organizational activities are co-ordinated. Bureaucratic characteristics, such as the formal rules, lead to co-ordination through the *standardization of work* tasks. With the hierarchical internal authority, these provide a strong integrating capability. The professional organization, however, leaves much of the decision-making and -taking to the professional operators on the ground, relying on the *standardization of the skills* of the professionals. As Mintzberg notes in a

Box 9.9 Accountabilities in professional modes of organization

Client

Profession

Employing
Organization

useful discussion of different co-ordinating mechanisms available to organizations (1979), this is a loose instrument dependent on external agents to provide the necessary capability. It also can run into difficulties as attempts by the organization to impose unity on a myriad of individual decisions are resisted by professionals seeking to protect their freedom of action. In these circumstances the integration is a negotiated political process rather than one of command.

We can now summarize the contrasts between the bureaucratic and professional organization by elucidating the dominant mode of governance in each, that is, the mechanisms which regulate interactions and relationships. First, bureaucratic characteristics of organization are associated with a **command mode of governance.** This mode is based on the rule of law emanating from a sovereign body and delivered through a scalar chain of superior and subordinate authority. Legitimacy for public service decisions and behaviours lies in their being within the bounds prescribed through due process by the institutions charged with the provision. The strength of the command mode of governance lies in the efficiency and effectiveness of control and accountability; its weakness is in rigidity and conservatism in the face of changing environments.

Professional characteristics are associated with a **communion mode of governance,** that is, a set of shared values and creeds. Thus in the delivery of a service the legitimacy for actions lies in their consistency with the protocols and guiding values of the group's shared frame of reference. The strength of communion lies in the guidance afforded by its shared values through different environments; its weakness is its insularity from those environments and a consequent failure to adapt its normative order.

Thus command is associated with the line management of traditional bureaucracy, communion with service decisions in professionalized sectors. As we wish to know whether the public service reforms have effected changes in these modes of governance and the issues raised for social policy and its beneficiaries and providers, the next section provides an account of these reforms.

Changing Patterns of Service Delivery[2]

Bureaucracy and Professionals in Traditional Public Administration

Traditionally, the organization and delivery of government services in the UK has been characterized by the development of a career-based public bureaucracy and the organization and delivery of services by established professionals. Established by the reforms of the Victorian Northcote Trevelyan Report, the neutral career service developed into a foundation of British central government. In a different way UK local government has also been based on a career service but, in this case, one of professional groups in associated departments (e.g. engineers, social work, housing, and education).

In this traditional system of public administration, politicians (ministers, members of parliament, and local councillors) were separated from service delivery by an administrative cadre that neutrally implemented their policies and, in many instances, acted as a conduit between politicians and the professional groups who delivered services to the public. Thus, in broad terms, education was left to educators, healthcare to health professionals, policing to police officers, and social work to social workers. In traditional public administration, therefore, professional, political, and administrative domains were relatively segregated (see Box 9.10). **Command** was the dominant mode of relationship between politicians and administrators, while **communion** was a strong element in the professional domain (including in the relations with service beneficiaries such as patients).

Bureaucracy and Professionals in Public Resource Management

From the 1960s but especially in mid-1970s a number of factors undermined this traditional model. Long-held criticisms of UK central administration, not least the lack of

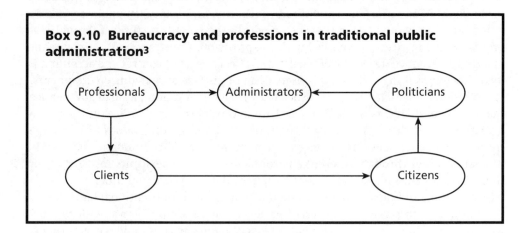

Box 9.10 Bureaucracy and professions in traditional public administration[3]

Professionals → Administrators ← Politicians

Professionals → Clients

Citizens → Politicians

Clients → Citizens

---

[2] This section develops Gray and Jenkins (1995).
[3] Boxes 9.10–9.12 are based on an idea in Richards (1992).

co-ordination in public expenditure planning and control, and campaigns for more rational strategic planning, decision-making and policy evaluation, were exemplified in the Fulton Committee on the Civil Service (Cmnd. 3638, 1968). This was a time of interest by both politicians and administrators in introducing more rational criteria into the allocation of expenditures: interests which were given political momentum by the election of Mr Heath's government in 1970, whose commitment to rational management in government led to the introduction of reforms such as a think tank, the Central Policy Review Staff, designed to assist the Cabinet's strategic thinking. In local government there were also attempts to co-ordinate and integrate local authorities via systems of corporate management and the creation of policy and resource committees to develop council strategies, while in the health service planning systems also became fashionable.

By the middle of the decade, however, attention shifted sharply in response to a public expenditure crisis. The Treasury's view was that generalist administrators and professionals alike left financial management to others; as a consequence the use and consumption of resources was neglected. The solution was not some complex planning system but rather firm financial *control*. As a result, systems of cash limits introduced from 1976 were followed after the election of the Conservatives in 1979 by efficiency reviews, financial management initiatives, and resource management regimes. Hence it can be argued that from the mid-1970s resource management replaced traditional public administration, with a consequent shift in the relationships between politicians and professional groups (see Box 9.11).

The characteristics of this model clearly vary between and within areas (civil service, local government, health services) but the overall logic of the reforms was undoubtedly to effect a change in the political control of public services. Politicians sought to extend command into professional domains by empowering the administrators (now managers) to effect more line management into their relations with professionals. In some professionalized services such as police and social work, this proved possible within the existing structures (in some local authorities, for example, generalist managers became directors of social services and social workers took on management responsibilities in

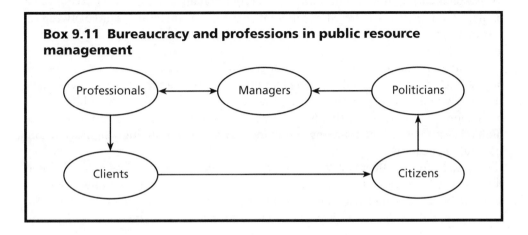

Box 9.11 Bureaucracy and professions in public resource management

the area teams). In health and higher education, however, this proved more difficult, and gave rise to the development of parallel structures: general management in health and a structure of planning, resource, and other committees to bypass the senate–faculty–department professional authority in universities.

The emphasis on resource management shared with traditional public administration a set of value-free arrangements for delivering public services. Resource management, however, was seen as appropriate to the more complex economic and social environment. It emphasized economy, efficiency, and effectiveness, delegated financial management, decentralized personnel management systems and a strengthening of audit (through the new National Audit Office and Audit Commission).

The first of these strategies was established in 1979 with the prime minister's Efficiency Unit and its oversight of departmental efficiency reviews (still called Rayner scrutinies after the first efficiency adviser, Derek Rayner, Chief Executive of Marks & Spencer plc). Rayner's ambition was not just to make savings. His wider brief was to initiate a cultural change amongst administrators where management in general and resource management in particular would become seen as a valued activity, if not part of the golden road to the top. His schema was later transferred to the NHS and higher education and spawned an altogether more ambitious programme known as the Financial Management Initiative (FMI). Driven by the logic of management accounting, the FMI was a reform programme that set out to make managers at all levels (the word *managers* was deliberately used in its publicity) accountable for the resources they used, and to develop and instal systems through which performance could be measured. In giving managers devolved budgets and operational targets, the new accountable management sought on the one hand to install greater control and accountability over resource use, and on the other to liberate entrepreneurialism.

These changes also introduced a new system of decentralized and results-driven personnel management. Traditional public administration was organized as a career service, with rewards tied to the position of individuals on hierarchical grading structures linked to incremental pay spines. For professionals, advancement was generally on the basis of criteria elaborated and even applied directly by professional peer groups. Any resulting distortions on the pay bill (e.g. as a result of high numbers of merit awards for hospital consultants) would have to be accommodated. The world of accountable management, however, ushered in different possibilities, including a link between reward and performance (as measured by meeting targets) and the local setting of pay and conditions.

Practitioners responded with varying degrees of enthusiasm. If some were sceptical, others, including some professionals, had no difficulty adapting (such as veterinary surgeons who had experienced such regimes in private practice). Most public service professions, however, found themselves having to reconcile their traditional communion relations with an encroaching command regime and increasingly significant contractual implications.

If in terms of its effects on Whitehall the FMI may be regarded as only a limited success, the influence of the philosophy that drove it was considerable. Forms of accountable management quickly spread throughout the public sector. In education, healthcare, police, and social work, budgets were delegated, targets set, and professionals designated as 'managers', with responsibilities for delivering activities and services within them. More importantly, these changes made a change in the discourse of administration and professional life inevitable, with the language of financial management colonizing that of administrative and professional groups.

Bureaucracy and Professions in Today's Mixed Economy of Public Management

For the reformers these consequences did not reach far enough. The Conservative government, supported by protagonists of the New Right, was becoming more committed to raising the status and profile of management (and a concept of business-style management at that) as a valued activity in its own right. This determination provided the political impetus to drive through further reforms which embraced increasing enthusiasm for privatization and competition, deregulation, and a commitment to customers. Above all it entailed a subjection of the private world of public service professional monopolies to competition, however that could be contrived. Since the last years of the 1980s there has been a concerted development of mixed economies in public services; and meeting its challenge has required a new culture of public management, one now endorsed by a new Labour Government.

The public sector has certainly been through a transformation in a decade marked not only by a change of language but also by developments of public management that have complicated the interaction of the political, professional, and managerial worlds even further (see Box 9.12). These new developments are represented by structural reforms that have sought to institutionalize the separation of service provision from political decision-making, the creation of markets and competition, and consumer-focused initiatives to orientate services outwards to their clients as well as, in certain circumstances, empowering customers themselves. These aims are often entwined rather than separate, but they also find practical expression in a series of reform

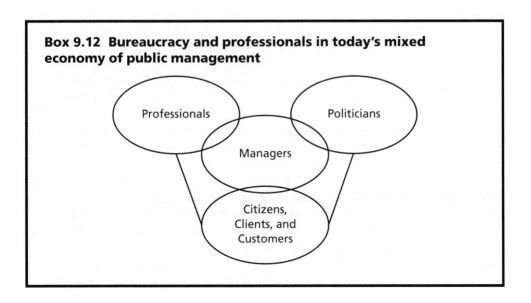

Box 9.12 Bureaucracy and professionals in today's mixed economy of public management

Professionals

Politicians

Managers

Citizens, Clients, and Customers

initiatives that have affected social policy throughout central and local government and the NHS.

In central government the main structural strategy to develop public management has been the creation of executive agencies to provide discrete services within central departments. Since the original Efficiency Unit Report (1988) over four-fifths of the home civil service has been converted to agency form, a considerable organizational achievement. Headed by chief executives on short-term contracts and performance-related reward systems, these agencies are intended (*pace* the Prison Service and the Child Support Agency) to be run at arm's length from ministers under quasi-contractual framework documents of operational targets and budgets agreed with departments and the Treasury. Many, especially those in health and safety or research and development, are essentially professional services. Others depend on considerable professional inputs (not least the Meat Hygiene Service!).

To this has now been added the impetus of the Citizen's Charter in all its forms (Cm. 1599, 1991) and market testing (known since Cm. 1730 1991 as 'competing for quality'). Free-market critics, including the Adam Smith Institute and the Institute of Economic Affairs (IEA), argue that public services are monopolies with no incentives to care for their customers. Part of the case for decentralizing public organizations is the need to rectify this by empowering clients and drawing them more closely into the policy process. But this desire to enhance the customer focus (in the broadest sense of the term) is also behind the construction of markets of purchasers and providers within a service (e.g. in health, education, and community care) and the various mechanisms by which many services (including professional) are tested against private-sector competition. These markets and variants of market testing bring with them explicit contractual procedures and obligations. So too, though in a less legal but perhaps more visible way, do patient, student, and other variants of citizen's charters.

The experience of agencies, markets, and charters illustrates a number of key aspects of today's public management. First, there is a new political environment where policy and management are seen as distinct and separate activities. Second, there is a corresponding new internal managerial environment where managers are given freedoms within pre-set frameworks and held accountable against agreed targets. Third, new organizational arrangements are designed to facilitate employees' identification with their organizational purposes, a concern with quality and customer needs. This is a new order of decentralized management within an overall system of central control. For its supporters it offers scope for the liberation of organizational energy, encouraging local initiative and entrepreneurship and enhancing greater customer or client awareness. It provides a complex overlap and set of interactions between the political, professional, managerial, and customer environments and spheres of responsibility. This, in turn, has led to new sources of legitimation in service delivery and new sets of relationships between politicians, providers, and authorizers.

Perhaps most significant in these relationships is the way the managers, initially at least, have derived unintended power and influence from their pivotal position at the interface of the participants both representing and communicating with them. Moreover, further government reforms, most notably the recent delegation to health trust chief executives of the responsibility for clinical assurance, have become more interventionist in professional areas. It is also noticeable how the client and citizen have become fused with the customer, each with sets of distinctive rights which makes it difficult for traditional professional–client relationships to be maintained.

If this account is valid, it portrays a world not only considerably removed from that of traditional public administration (Box 9.10) but also from the simple model offered by market theorists. In this a number of characteristics are clear. First, the professional nature of many public services is often seen in a wholly negative light, or as something that needs to be controlled or managed by enhancing the contractual nature of relationships and diminishing the force of communion. Second, any form of decentralization or empowerment changes the nature of power and politics in the system. The consequences depend on the sources of advantage and disadvantage within the new regime. If it is managers who have gained most influence in this new regime, the reasons are not hard to determine: they arise from the centrality of contract and the managers' ability to act as brokers to it. Politicians and professionals still wish to maintain some discreteness to their domains; they prefer to deal with each other and the (paying) customers through intermediaries. This is reinforced by the development of contracting as the managers' stock in trade to the relative disadvantage of other parties.

From Command and Communion to Contract

How have the public sector reforms described in the previous section affected the bureaucratic characteristics of public service organizations and the professions which work through them? The remaining task of this chapter is to provide an answer to this question.

We have conceptualized *bureaucracy* as characterized by *formal jurisdictional areas* of function, *hierarchy* of authority, *rules* for governing decisions and activities, *records* of transactions conducted under these rules, dedicated *training* to assist performance and the commitment to the organization of *members' full working capacities*. These characteristics were defined as associated with a command mode of governance. Professionals have been conceptualized as distinguished by their *specialist knowledge and expertise*, their *position* (or autonomy) in relation to clients and employing organizations, and *ethos* (the values which vocation demands are to be promoted for the benefit of the profession and its clients). These characteristics were seen as associated with a communion mode of governance.

Both 'models' of bureaucracy and profession are ideal types, abstractions belonging to the world of ideas rather than expressions of actual organizations. However, the previous section suggests that in traditional public administration the distinctiveness of the domains of bureaucracy and professional meant that the elements of each ideal type were likely to be visible in actual organizational contexts, and that the association of bureaucracy with command and profession with communion was empirically observable.

But what of the effects of the public sector reforms since 1970 on bureaucracy and profession? We suggest that the bureaucratic character of public organizations has been moderated by the extension of discretion in the management of service delivery (for example, by more freedom to allocate resources and choose alternative forms of service provision), but that this discretion has been governed increasingly by more formal contractual arrangements encompassing both service and financial targets. Thus jurisdictions are a little less rigid, hierarchies a little flatter, and regulations have shifted their emphases. Interestingly, one traditional professional group, accountants, has found its position within public organizations significantly enhanced as the managers of these contractual regimes.

At the same time the reforms have brought an increase in the bureaucratic tendencies of public service professions. Specialist knowledge, for example, is increasingly determined by the context of practice. This was always true for some professions which grew up indigenously with the welfare state (including social work), but now others, including teachers and accountants, find that the elements of their expertise are defined not only through their organizational situation but often by it. One professional response to this trend has been for professional associations to increase the extent to which acceptable professional practices are elaborated in formal statements (such as codes of ethics) which can guide the conduct of members in the new contractual and regulated regimes (see Banks 1995, 1998).

Similarly, professional position and ethos have been affected. If in more traditional models of professional practice (such as health) the autonomy from employing organizations was regarded as extensive, nowadays professionals have increasingly to reconcile their professional judgements with the organization's priorities. Thus, in a famous televised case, a hospital chief executive warned that clinical consultants who continued to disregard the directions of their clinical director 'would feel the organization's full force' (Channel 4, 1993). As we saw earlier, such challenges to professional position have met some restatement of a professional ethos endorsing professional values against the developing power of managers. In the Durham study of local authorities there was a tendency for social workers and others to express a reinvigorated professional ethos against the 'men in grey suits'. However, some had clearly accommodated the new order with a professional vocation:

(my profession provides) a challenging position in an agency constantly in the 'eye' of the public [social worker];

a fact recognized by at least one councillor:

I see local government officers as having a more independent and impartial role than colleagues in private practice; making decisions on behalf of the community, i.e. quality of life, needs the highest level of professional/democratic partnership. Maybe the local authority has and needs a special kind of professional?

These changes to bureaucracy and professions suggests that the intensification of contract arrangements has weakened both the command mode of governance of traditional bureaucracy and the communion mode of traditional professionalism. Instead, interactions in the new mixed economy of the public service delivery have been governed increasingly by a **contract mode of governance**. Here relationships are effected through an inducement–contribution exchange agreed by both parties. Legitimacy for actions under such a mode lies within the terms of the agreed exchange, that is, the contract, or at least its interpretations. The strengths of contract lie not only in the predetermined life of the contract but, more significantly, the motivation to perform up to contract expectation (in order to gain the rewards) and the consequent high probabilities that planning assumptions will be acted on. Weaknesses can be traced to the reductionist tendency of contracts (see Box 9.5), that is, in the absence of other inducements the parties will limit their actions to those explicitly elaborated in the contract, and the difficulty in the face of changing circumstances in effecting alterations to specification without undue cost.

Are the Reinvented Professions the Worst of Devils?

In practice, public service management inherently relies on combinations of all three modes of governance. But the balance has altered without much chance of a return to the old order, for good or ill. This would imply a definitive change in the role of public service professionals, even their reinvention in the new contracting (perhaps in both senses of the term) state. What can we conclude on the relations of professionals and bureaucracy in the present context of public policy?

First, to recapitulate, there has been *a shifting emphasis in the modes of professional relations with public service delivery* from differentiated command and communion to more integrative contract. The increasing emphasis on contract as the basis of organizational relationships (purchasers and providers, departments and agencies) is affecting not only the macro-relationships of professional organizations with its other agencies in the service supply chain, but even relationships within public service organizations (e.g. the development of internal markets in local authorities, hospitals, universities, and even the BBC). The consequent increase in the transaction and opportunity costs of managing such service relationships has led to expressions of considerable professional resentment. But more significant, perhaps, is the implicit shift in the basis for service rationing and related choices ('is it in the contract?'), the drawing of accountability away from general notions of conduct to explicit terms and conditions which accounts must address, and the professions' tendency to generate more codes of ethics rather than concentrate on providing the conditions for ethical behaviour.

Second, within this general shift, the *reforms have met with differentiated rather than uniform responses in the professionalized public services*. Logically, there are distinctions to be drawn both between the different services and between different practitioners within the same profession. How and why these distinctions arise, however, is as yet not properly understood.

Third, the *public service professions are increasingly fragmented*. Some public service professions have traditionally been characterized by differentiated internal organization (such as specialities in medicine and their institutionalization in the Royal Colleges), and have found the reforms reinforcing this. Others appear to have reached a desired integration, only to find that the transition from public administration to today's public management has undermined it (from social work to child protection, community care, and so on, each with different levels of self-regulation).

Fourth, some reforms, notably the increase in external audit and evaluation, have brought *a shift from opaque to transparent professional work*. Perhaps combined with the decline of a deferential culture in today's society, there is a notable questioning of the value of the professional contribution and more access to the answers. Schoolteaching seems particularly to have been affected by this, with even public statements by OFSTED on the numbers of unsatisfactory practitioners.

Fifth, *some deskilling is in train*. The contract and framework regimes are reinforced by increasingly detailed professional and management protocols. In some areas, including health and social services, the effect is to narrow the areas of professional discretion, with the result that non-professionals may be employed at the margins of hitherto professional work. This may not universally lead to a proletarianization of professional work, but challenges professional hegemony.

Sixth, *professionals have reacted to the reforms with different degrees of engagement with the management process*. At one extreme are those who have sought to maintain a segregation of their activities from those of management. Thus a sensitive complaint of clinical directors in health trusts can be that they become more management than clinical. But even in medicine, perhaps the most reluctant collectively to embrace the management process, there are those who argue that the management of resources and activities is an extension of professional vocation. And other professionalized services, notably those based in local government, have clearly taken or been obliged to take this view.

Seventh, some of the reforms, notably the development of service charters, have brought *more attention to service processing at the expense, certainly as measured by effort if not quality, of service content and substance*. Entering some district general hospitals, for example, one is bombarded with phosphorous electronic screens informing you how many accident and emergency patients were triaged within five minutes of reception, the average wait in the fracture out-patient clinic, and so on. Perhaps the exception is policing, in which the emphasis on targeting crime patterns appears to have changed the substance of detection, although only at the expense of more public complaints about lack of police attention to reported minor offences. However, even here this may force police authorities to focus more on clear-up rates than on the general enhancement of pubic security.

Finally, but only in the context of this list, the professions' responses display characteristics both of *strategic choices and contingent responses to strategic imperatives*. We would have thought that in 1979 Ladbrokes would have given short odds for social work being at the top of the incoming Conservative Government's hit list of public service professions. Yet it took at least a decade and a half before social work found itself threatened, and parts of it, such as child protection, managed to secure at least some moral high ground, despite continuing public concern with child abuse cases. Perhaps social work has shown adaptive behaviour, responding where it has had to and influencing its environment where it could. Schoolteaching, on the other hand, has responded to each assault (regardless of merit) as though it was a pay and conditions issue, and through this failure to distinguish between imperative and choice has forfeited much of the professional discretion it formerly enjoyed.

These conclusions seem to raise even more questions than they provide answers! You may like to consider at least the following as you continue your reading of this text and other studies:

- Are professions reacting differently to these changes depending on their relationships with different client groups (for example, individual members of public compared to a local authority as client)?
- Is the problem in the professional–bureaucracy relationship one of maximizing effectiveness and efficacy versus efficiency?
- Are professionals inevitably being drawn into managerial and bureaucratic roles by the purchaser–provider split (for example, by the need to market themselves, including informing purchasers and finding out their needs, to find finance, and so on)?
- Can bureau-managers be professional as well as professionals be managerial?
- Is it inevitable that if professionals wish to succeed to the strategic and most senior positions they will have to cease practising as professionals (in which they may still be needed) in order to become managers?

We need to know much more about current developments before we can answer these questions fully. However, in the new order we may certainly identify members of professions as managers, marketers, and entrepreneurs as well as practising providers. These roles undoubtedly fuse rather than keep separate the elements of the state (after Socrates), but do they threaten the public weal? We note that in the increasing contractual nature of relationships between the professionals and their services there has been a diminution of traditionally espoused (even if rarely realised) values such as equity of treatment and public accountability. Indeed, in so far as the public management reforms have produced a struggle between the reformers and the professions, there is a sense in which the 'public' in public services is often forgotten in a rush to impose or resist 'good business practice'. In this sense Socrates has a point.

Glossary

bureaucracy An abstract organizational form characterized by formal jurisdictional areas of function, hierarchy of authority, rules for governing decisions and activities, records of transactions conducted under these rules, dedicated training to assist performance, and the commitment to the organization of members' full working capacities.

command mode of governance Interactions and relationships regulated through the rule of law, emanating from a sovereign body, and delivered through a scalar chain of superior and subordinate authority with legitimacy for public service decisions and behaviours defined by the bounds prescribed through due process by the institutions charged with the provision.

communion mode of governance Interactions and relationships regulated through a set of shared values and creeds, under which legitimacy for service actions is defined by their consistency with the understandings, protocols, and guiding values of the group's shared frame of reference or way of interpreting and managing the world.

contract mode of governance Interactions and relationships regulated through an inducement–contribution exchange agreed by both parties. Legitimacy for actions under such a mode lies within the terms of the agreed exchange, that is, the contract, or at least its interpretations.

profession Occupational groups distinguished by their specialist knowledge and expertise, their position (or autonomy) in relation to clients and employing organizations, and ethos (that is, the values which vocation demands are to be promoted for the benefit of the profession and its clients).

Guide to Further Reading

For further discussion of bureaucracy, a good general text is provided by Beetham (1996). Remember that it is always useful to go back to original sources such as Weber (plenty of edited collections include extracts of his writings). For further discussion of professionals in the context of public service, see Laffin and Young (1990) and Banks (1995). An excellent general review of professions, including a review in relation to social policy, is Freidson (1994), but it is written in the context of the USA and is not an easy read. For general accounts of public service reforms in the UK see Flynn (1997), in local government see Wilson and Game (1997), and for those in welfare policy in particular, see Taylor-Gooby and Lawson (1993).

References

Banks, S. J. (1995), *Ethics and Values in Social Work* (Basingstoke: Macmillan).

——(1998), 'Codes of Ethics and Ethical Conduct: A View from the Caring Professions', *Public Money and Management*, 18/1, 27–30.

Beetham, D. (1996), *Bureaucracy* (Milton Keynes: Open University Press).

Channel 4 (1993), *Operation Hospital*.

Cm. 1599 (1991), *The Citizens' Charter: Raising the Standard* (London: HMSO).

Cm. 1730 (1991), *Competing for Quality* (London: HMSO).

Cmnd. 3638 (1968), *Report on the Committee on the Civil Service* (Ch. Lord Fulton, London: HMSO).

Efficiency Unit (1988), *Improving Management in Government: The Next Steps* (London: HMSO).

Etzioni, A. (1969), *The Semi-Professionals and their Organization* (New York: Free Press).

Flynn, N. (1997), *Public Sector Management* (3rd edn., Hemel Hempstead: Harvester Wheatsheaf).

Freidson, E. (1994), *Professionalism Reborn: Theory, Prophecy and Policy* (Chicago: University of Chicago Press).

Gray, A. G., and Jenkins, W. I. (1995), 'Public Management and the National Health Service', in J. J. Glynn and D. A. Perkins (eds.), *Managing Health Care* (London: Saunders), 4–32.

Greenwood, E. (1957), 'Attributes of a Profession', in *Social Work*, 2/3, 44–55.

Griffiths, R. (1983), *NHS Management Inquiry* (London: Department of Health and Social Security).

Jaques, E. (1990), 'In Praise of Hierarchy', *Harvard Business Review*, Jan–Feb, 127–33; repr. in Thompson, G., Frances, J., Levacic, R., and Mitchell, J. (eds.), *Markets, Hierarchies and Networks* (London: Sage, 1991).

Laffin, M. and Young, K. (1990), *Professionalism in Local Government* (London: Longman).

Mintzberg, H. (1979), *The Structuring of Organizations* (Hemel Hempstead: Prentice-Hall).

Plato, *c*.380 BC, *The Republic*, transl. with an introduction by H. D. P. Lee (Harmondsworth: Penguin Books, 1955).

Richards, S. (1992), *Who Defines the Public Good? The Consumer Paradigm in Public Management* (London: Public Management Foundation).

Taylor-Gooby, P. and Lawson, R. (1993), *Markets and Managers: New Issues in the Delivery of Welfare* (Buckingham: Open University Press).

Wilson, D. and Game, C. (1997), *Local Government in the United Kingdom* (2nd edn., London: Macmillan).

10 Public Expenditure Decision-Making

Andrew Gray and Bill Jenkins

Contents

Introduction: Political Incrementalism or Rational Planning?

In June 1998 the Labour Chancellor of the Exchequer Gordon Brown addressed the House of Commons on the subject of the reform of public finance and to extol 'prudence' in her various guises. There would be prudence in public finance (and no imprudence in public spending), public debt would be kept at a prudent ratio, while prudence and investment in reform would create a strong and fair Britain. Such actions would bring their rewards. In particular they would permit Mr Brown to escape from the tight public spending regime he had adopted voluntarily from the previous Conservative government and, more specifically, they would allow public spending, in current terms, to grow by 2.25 per cent for the next three years, while capital spending and investment would also rise.

But what were the problems that Mr Brown sought to address, and what were the solutions proposed? The difficulties, he argued, were that for over thirty years public spending in the UK had been focused on an annual spending round rather than long-term planning, and had been dominated by a 'year-to-year bidding culture'. The consequence was a system fixated to current spending and characterized by 'muddling through' and incrementalism. The results of this included a neglect of the outcomes of governmental programmes, and too little attention to investment and reform.

Mr Brown's solutions to these problems were that, in future, UK public spending would be governed by firm rules and, within these rules, a new regime would be established to reform public spending in Whitehall. This new approach would be 'prudent and responsible', while government would be 'enabling' and 'empowering' rather than centralizing and controlling. There would be a focus on investment, and a commitment to assessing public sector assets (and if necessary disposing of these to release resources), and departmental spending would be linked to outputs and investment for reform. More specifically, a new public spending framework was required. To break with the old culture the annual spending round would be abolished and departments would be given fixed three-year budgets. To facilitate investment, capital and current departmental spending would be disentangled. Finally, in the place of incremental budgeting, departments would be set targets for efficiency and performance that they would be expected to meet. This new approach, coupled with other changes arising out of the Government's **Comprehensive Spending Review** (see further below) would allow short-termism to be replaced by a strategic focus. This would, in turn, permit the sensible redirection of resources within a controlled system of public expenditure allocation (Cm. 3978, 1998).

When Mr Brown sat down his opposite number on the Conservative benches, Francis Maude was less than complimentary. He first questioned Mr Brown's reputation for caution ('Good bye Iron Chancellor, may he rust in peace'), adding that, in fact, 'Prudence' had been dumped: 'she was just another photo-opportunity'. In contrast, the *Financial Times* welcomed the Chancellor's proposed fiscal reforms as 'bold and innovative', praising his determination to move from a discretionary system to one based on rules, his plans to link spending to the meeting of efficiency and quality standards, and his moves to create a regime that emphasized investment: 'no-one could complain at a chancellor who sets out to stop the absurdity where investment is the first casualty in any squeeze on spending' (12 June 1998).

Mr Brown's plans for a new financial framework and public spending regime (Cm. 3978, 1998) were followed rapidly by the detailed results of Labour's **Comprehensive Spending Review** (Cm. 4011, 1998) which announced the redirection of resources towards areas such as health and education and away from activities such as defence. This review was presented as part of a wider programme to identify and provide 'money for modernization' by investing in reform within government departments and reallocating resources according to the Government priorities and its 1997 election pledges. Yet are such moves important other than at a technical and managerial level? For some they clearly are. For some they represent the defining event in the Blair government, proclaiming 'the continuing existence of a project that might be called, after all, social democratic: a belief in public good attainable by public means, without any nonsense about the minimal state, or flirtations about private health provision' (Hugo Young, *The Guardian*, 15 July 1998).

The debate over the UK New Labour government's 1998 public spending reforms indicate that public expenditure is both a political and economic product. Moreover, its management is played out before a variety of audiences, ranging from the immediate political community (parliament and parties), through the wider public (interest groups and the electorate), out into the global economic marketplace. Politically, it appears that voters favour the products of public expenditure (health, education, roads, defence) but have an aversion to paying for them. Economically, the needs of the domestic economy and the predisposition of the international community have come to embrace fiscal prudence rather than largesse, despite the pressures on public expenditure, especially in recessions, and other technical difficulties in the way of controlling both its totals and distribution between programmes.

But what is public expenditure, where does it come from, where does it go, and why is it apparently so difficult to control? The remainder of this chapter will deal with these questions in turn. The first section will examine the significance of public expenditure and some of the definitional problems that surround it. From there we proceed to explore the growth of public expenditure historically and comparatively. We then examine the search for public expenditure control and the mechanisms developed by UK governments to deal with this problem. Finally, we discuss the main issues in the public expenditure debate at the turn of the millennium, especially as these relate to public expenditure policy and management and desirable and feasible future developments in the face of what some see to be a **fiscal crisis** of the welfare state.

The Significance of Public Expenditure

Public expenditure may appear both esoteric and complex, best left to economists and those few politicians who understand it. On the contrary! As citizens we subscribe to public expenditure when we pay income tax, buy a drink in a pub (paying value added tax, or VAT, and excise duty) or fill up with petrol (paying petrol tax as well as VAT). We are affected as recipients when we attend school, use a university library, or visit a doctor. More specifically, most welfare and social programmes depend on public financial support, with government either acting directly as provider, or perhaps indirectly, as purchaser of services on behalf of its citizens. These factors, and its growth and scale in recent times, have made it difficult to separate public expenditure from the role of the state. Debates over public spending thus focus on the scope of governmental activities as well as the range and impact of taxing and spending powers. This can be seen historically in the rise and fall of Keynesian economics, the emergence of the New Deal in the USA, the Beveridge Report in the UK and, more recently, the rise of New Right thinking (see Chs. 1 and 2). Like it or not, public expenditure reflects the priorities in government.

The range and type of services provided by governments has, of course, changed over time, influenced by factors such as shifting emphases on individualism and collectivism, changing needs (such as those of an ageing population), or new ways of delivering services (such as information technology). The case for public expenditure is thus based on *political*, *economic*, and *strategic* criteria. Political fairness and equity encompass issues such as democratic accountability over the service delivery and community action. If hard-nosed economists reject such arguments, they still opt for public provision on the grounds of market failure and inefficiency, necessitating the provision of **public goods** (such as defence and police) and the management of **externalities** (such as pollution). In addition, markets may fail to provide strategic direction and investment or offer economies of scale (as in areas such as transport or healthcare).

Such views held sway in the UK following the Beveridge reforms of the 1940s, and were reinforced in the 1960s and early 1970s by an enthusiasm for planning and rational decision-making. However, they came under pressure from alternative political and economic arguments, such as the liberal economic philosophy of the **New Right**, which challenged monopolistic public provision of services for eroding individual liberty, stifling entrepreneurial spirit, encouraging dependency on the state, and enhancing the power of public sector unions. The practical response to such arguments can be seen in the Conservative government's withdrawal after 1979 from some traditional social policy areas (like public housing provision), the deregulation of others (such as care for the elderly), and changes in healthcare (quasi-markets) and pensions (proposals for personal provision).

What Is Public Expenditure?

But what *is* public expenditure? If voters often see it as what governments extract from them as taxation, departments tend to think of it as what they spend on services and occasionally as the outcomes of this spending, such as health gain. These views suggest links between revenue raising, spending, and the outcomes of government activities. Public expenditure is indeed the result of money raised by the state to further its objectives. In any country, however, public spending hides a complex history of values and commitments shaped by political ideology, economic theory, interest-group pressure, and changing political and social forces.

Where does the money come from and where does it go? Box 10.1 shows the variety of sources of UK public expenditure as it was in 1997–8 and its application to services. Note the relatively low proportion that income tax constitutes of total revenue, the massive nature of the expenditure sums involved (the committed total of spending is £315bn) and the dominance in these of social security, personal social services, and education, as well as the cumulative debt interest. Perhaps more important, however, is how and why these spending totals have changed and, on the revenue side, how the 'burden' of taxation is distributed. First, however, we turn to the problem of defining public expenditure.

It is an unfortunate fact of political life that UK public expenditure can be defined and measured in a variety of different ways (see, for example, Corry 1997b; Likierman 1988; Mullard 1993) and, as we will see, significant changes to both definitions and measurements were an integral part of Gordon Brown's 1998 reforms (Cm. 3978, 1998). As Watson notes, 'Most of the definitions of public expenditure are biased, in one way or another, to suit the objectives of those who seek to promote them.' This is because 'public expenditure policy bridges the gap between politics, economics and social policy. It links the government's involvement with social policies with the resource cost of this

Box 10.1 Planned receipts and expenditure of UK government 1997–8

Public money 1997–98 – where it comes from and where it goes

(£ billion)

where it comes from		where it goes
Income tax	72	22 Defence
		38 Education
Social security contributions	49	53 Health and personal social services
Corporation tax	27	15 Housing, heritage and environment
Value added tax	51	17 Law and order
Excise duties	34	100 Social security
Council tax	11	
Business rates	15	13 Industry, agriculture and employment
Other taxes	24	9 Transport
Other financing	13	23 Other spending
Borrowing	19	25 Debt interest
Total 315		315 Total

Source: Treasury (1996a).

approach, as well as indicating the wider cost to the economy' (Watson, 1997, 41–2). Yet to understand the debates over public expenditure we need to know how the government calculates and presents its accounts, and what the important features of these are.

The UK Government's spending plans for 1998/9 and beyond are shown in Tables 10.1 and 10.2. The important terms that emerge are:

- The *Departmental Expenditure Limit* (formally known as the *Control Total*): a sum agreed by the Cabinet in advance for Departmental spending particular year (and post-1998 over a three year period) effectively setting a ceiling on public expenditure;

- *Totally Managed Expenditure (TME)* (formally known as **General Government Spending (GGE)**): the actual planned public expenditure total for a particular year or at least one version of it;

- *Annually Managed Expenditure (AME)*: a new category introduced from 1998 on to indicate spending that the Government considers cannot be given multi-year limits and is subject to annual review e.g. social security benefits, debt interest etc.

£million	1998–99	1999–00	2000–01	2001–02
Education and Employment (DfEE)*	14,170	15,470	17,290	18,610
Health	37,170	40,230	43,130	45,990
of which: NHS	36,510	39,580	42,410	45,180
DETR Environment – and Transport	9,370	9,730	10,580	12,000
DETR – Local Government and Regional Policy	32,770	34,250	35,510	36,980
Home Office	6,890	7,730	7,810	7,990
Legal Departments	2,640	2,760	2,800	2,720
Defence	22,240	22,290	22,830	22,990
Foreign and Commonwealth Office	1,040	1,090	1,110	1,130
International Development	2,330	2,440	2,910	3,220
Trade and Industry	3,110	3,340	3,710	3,720
Agriculture, Fisheries and Food	1,420	1,280	1,220	1,260
Culture, Media and Sport	910	990	1,000	1,040
Social Security (administration)	2,880	3,330	3,410	3,490
Scotland	13,120	13,850	14,510	15,130
Wales	6,670	7,040	7,410	7,780
Northern Ireland	5,680	5,950	6,160	6,310
Chancellor's Departments	2,900	3,160	2,980	3,200
Cabinet Office	1,310	1,420	1,360	1,320
Welfare to Work	1,170	1,330	1,280	1,280
Invest to Save budget		20	60	80
Capital Modernisation Fund			1,000	1,500
Reserve[1]	1,000	1,500	2,000	2,500
Departmental Expenditure Limits[1]	**168,800**	**179,200**	**190,100**	**200,200**
(*Education spending in UK[1]	38,200	41,200	44,700	47,800)

Table 10.1 Public spending plans for departments 1998–2002: departmental expenditure limits

1. Figures rounded to nearest £100 million.

Source: Cm. 4011, 1998.

£million	1998–99	1999–00	2000–01	2001–02
Social Security Benefits	95,500	100,500	103,000	108,900
Housing Revenue Account Subsidies	3,800	3,600	3,600	3,600
Common Agricultural Policy	2,600	2,500	2,500	2,700
Export Credit Guarantee Department	100	100	0	100
Net Payments to EC institutions	3,500	2,900	2,900	3,200
Self-Financing Public Corporations	–200	–400	–400	–500
Locally Financed Expenditure[2]	15,700	16,700	17,800	19,100
National Lottery	1,600	2,500	2,500	2,300
Central Government Gross Debt Interest	28,100	27,600	27,300	27,200
Accounting and other adjustments	13,400	15,300	18,800	20,000
AME Margin	800	1,000	2,000	3,000
Annually Managed Expenditure	**164,800**	**172,400**	**179,900**	**189,500**
Total Managed Expenditure[3]	**333,600**	**351,600**	**370,000**	**389,700**

Table 10.2 Public spending plans for departments 1998–2002: annually managed expenditure[1]

1. Rounded to nearest £100 million.
2. Includes local authority self-financed expenditure and Scottish non-domestic rate payments.
3. Total managed expenditure is equal to the sum of the Departmental Spending Limits and Annually Managed Expenditure, and is also equal to the sum of the public sector current expenditure and public sector net investment.

Source: Cm. 4011, 1998.

Two points are important here: first debates over the actual totals of public expenditure in the UK over time have often involved consideration of General Government Spending (GGE) (now TME) or some variant of this; second crucial indicators for successive UK governments have been historically less the absolute total of public spending but either the relation of this total to the **Gross Domestic Product (GDP)** or the **Public Sector Borrowing Requirement (PSBR)**, the amount the government needs to borrow to balance revenue and expenditure (in 1998 this was retitled **the Public Sector Net Cash Requirement**). Indeed, for many years the PSBR took on an almost totem-like status, with the test of almost all policy initiatives being 'will it increase the PSBR?'. This obsession assumed that the PSBR provided an indication of the fiscal stance of a government, and that it gave important signals to international financial markets. However, it was often argued that PSBR was flawed as an economic indicator, and its use as a guide to government finances was out of step with most other European countries (see Appendix A). The Labour government's reforms of 1998 made some effort to address such criticisms.

These terms are set out in an appendix to this chapter (see Appendix A). Although the changing terminology seeks to clarify what is and is not included in calculating public expenditure totals, it is still dealing with a situation of considerable complexity. For example, for many years the *cash* totals made no distinction between *capital* spending such as on the building of roads, *current* spending (such as on teachers' salaries), and *transfer payments* (such as welfare benefits). As a consequence, cuts in capital expenditure were often made to counter short-term fiscal pressures elsewhere. The 1998 reforms sought to address this by making a sharp distinction between current and capital spending. Second, the accounting process is based on Treasury rules regarding what may be included in the accounts and how they are treated. As will be discussed later, the Treasury has historically seen its role as the guardian of the public purse, and it has therefore sought to define public expenditure in such a way as to protect government and taxpayers from what it perceives as overcommitment now and in the future. Such a role may be laudable, but unbalanced if it contributes to a system of public accounts that fails to deal adequately with changes in the way the public sector operates and discriminates against particular types of activities (such as public sector investment). Again, the changes made by Gordon Brown in 1998 sought to address part of this problem.

But is the growth of public expenditure by national governments something to be welcomed, or viewed with suspicion and horror? Two economists from the **International Monetary Fund (IMF)** have charted public expenditure growth and its consequences for a selection of industrial economies over a period of 125 years (Tanzi and Schuknecht 1995). Their findings (see Box 10.2) show similar patterns, especially after 1945. Thus, by 1990, most major industrialized nations committed over 30 per cent of their Gross Domestic Product to public expenditure, with some (France, Germany) spending in the region of 50 per cent.

Have such increases delivered important social and economic gains such as declines

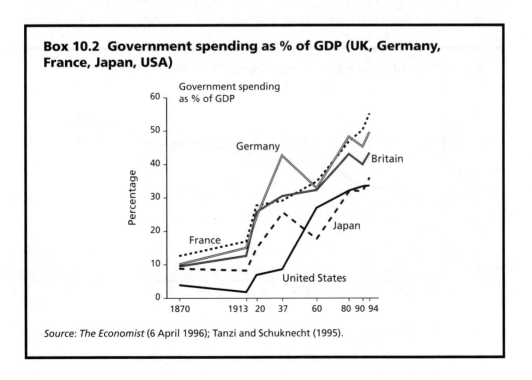

Box 10.2 Government spending as % of GDP (UK, Germany, France, Japan, USA)

Source: The Economist (6 April 1996); Tanzi and Schuknecht (1995).

in infant mortality and increases in life expectancy, educational achievement, and economic growth? Tanzi and Schuknecht argue that before 1960 increased public spending delivered appreciable results; subsequently, however, achievements have been more modest, and economies with lower increases have been more innovative. They argue further that smaller-scale government (as in the 'tiger' economies of South East Asia) does not necessarily perform worse when compared with nations with larger social programmes. This analysis needs to be treated with caution, not least as it neglects causation and overlooks the difficulties of comparing different social and political systems. Yet it indicates both the almost inexorable growth in public expenditure in industrial countries (including those with a small state welfare system, such as the USA) and some of the puzzles surrounding these developments.

Even if definitional difficulties and the need to take into account changes in the value of money imply that long-term analysis of public expenditure trends should be viewed with caution, it appears that the trend of public expenditure growth in the UK has been steadily upwards. Hogwood (1992), for example, offers evidence of a pattern of increasing expenditure up to and including the Second World War, and even more so thereafter. In the immediate aftermath of 1945 increases in social expenditure were balanced by declining defence spending, but after 1950 social expenditure rose both in absolute terms and relative to GDP under all governments.

These trends can be analysed. Using Treasury figures for General Government Expenditure GGE(X) it is possible to plot the rise in public expenditure since 1963 both in real terms (Box 10.3) and as a percentage of Gross Domestic Product (GDP) (Box 10.4). This data shows that the general level of public expenditure rises steadily, although there is a sudden cutback in public spending in the late 1970s, minor checks in the mid-1980s, and a slowing down of increases predicted for the late 1990s. Public expenditure

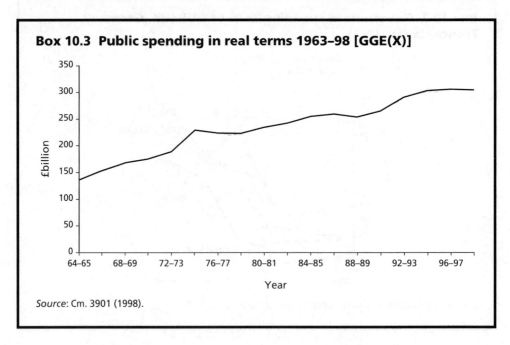

Box 10.3 Public spending in real terms 1963–98 [GGE(X)]

Source: Cm. 3901 (1998).

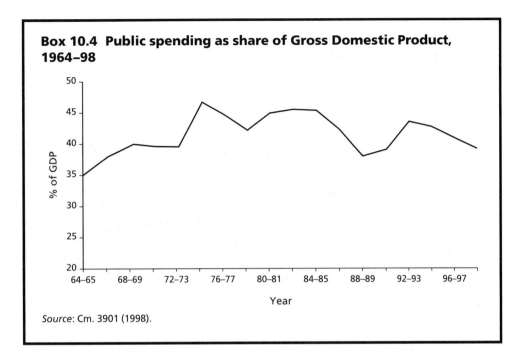

Box 10.4 Public spending as share of Gross Domestic Product, 1964–98

Source: Cm. 3901 (1998).

as a share of GDP fluctuates more sharply, falling in the late 1970s and again between 1982 and 1987, after which it rises until 1991 to decrease thereafter. However, in all of this time it has rarely been significantly lower than 40 per cent of GDP.

How does one explain this? Some commentators point to a lack of political will against the power of bureaucratic self-interest. Yet, whatever one's view of Mrs Thatcher's administrations of the 1980s, a failure of political will could hardly be numbered amongst their faults. So were events out of government control or unanticipated? Corry and Gray (1997) argue that what remains unrecorded is the effect of the economic cycle, especially on unemployment and its financial consequences for benefits paid and tax revenue forgone. We might add to this developments such as the widening of income distribution and the consequent triggering of other benefits (such as those in housing). Certain unanticipated consequences of social policy initiatives hence impact significantly on public expenditure.

Growth of UK Public Expenditure: Winners and Losers

The above commentary suggests that the overall trend conceals shifting patterns within public expenditure totals. To explore these we will track departmental spending over a period of years, since Whitehall tends to account by departmental activities. However, even this has classificatory and definitional problems. Housing benefit, for example, has been classified in the public accounts sometimes as housing expenditure and at other times as social security expenditure (Hogwood 1992). Even disaggregated data therefore need to be taken as indicative rather than definitive.

Box 10.5 shows the relative expenditure changes in social security, health, education, defence, housing and public order as a percentage of GDP. The 'winner', taking up to 15

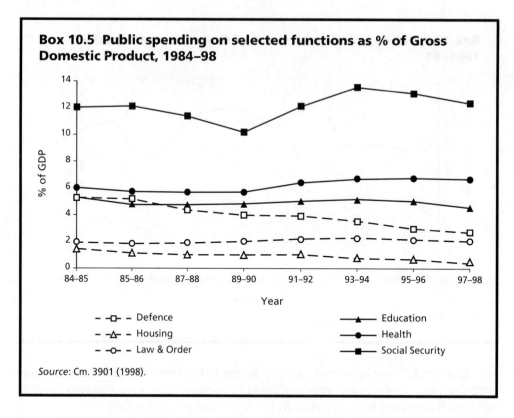

Box 10.5 Public spending on selected functions as % of Gross Domestic Product, 1984–98

Source: Cm. 3901 (1998).

per cent of GDP, has been social security. In contrast, housing and defence have been on a downward path, the latter in the wake of the Cold War and fundamental reviews of Britain's role in the new world order. Meanwhile education and health have remained stable, a point often proudly referred to by successive Conservative governments who claimed, when accused of expenditure cuts, that they had in fact increased spending in these areas in real terms.

Different ways of painting this disaggregated picture reveal more subtle overtones and raise further puzzles. Box 10.6 traces the growth and decline of various policy areas against the background of change in total public spending (General Government Expenditure) and public sector debt interest. This figure indexes data to 1978/9 prices and examines the emerging changes. Total public expenditure tracks upwards, finishing 39 per cent higher in 1995/6 than twenty years earlier. However, this conceals large increases in law and order and protective services (up by over 100 per cent), social security (up 84 per cent), and health (up 69 per cent), a significant decline in housing (down 65 per cent), fluctuations for defence (eventually down 7 per cent) and government debt interest moving cyclically with the economy. Again the reader should view this data as indicative rather than definitive. As Heald notes (1997), technical strategies such as 'substitution' (the classification of housing benefits as social security rather than housing spending, for example) may distort the figures. Nevertheless, Heald's own further analysis of expenditure in real terms carries a similar message (Box 10.7).

Do these changes reflect deliberate policy choices? In part, certainly, but not in

Box 10.6 Real expenditure by function 1977/8–95/6 (1994 prices; index 1978–9 = 100)

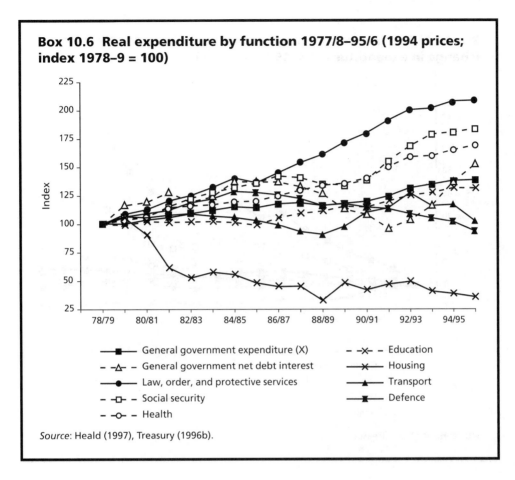

Source: Heald (1997), Treasury (1996b).

whole. Social Security spending, for example, has been influenced by the rise in eligible claimants (such as pensioners), casualties of downturns in the economic cycle (such as the unemployed), and changes to eligibility (such as housing benefit). Similarly, health spending has been affected by the upward pressure of demography (an ageing population), increased sophistication and cost of medical technology, and greater expectations of and demands for services. However, for critics such as Cooper (1997), the main problem with successive Conservative Chancellors was that in their public spending plans and polices they continually choose to spend far less on *investment* than *consumption*: more on benefits, for example, and less on education and training. This was a serious problem:

low levels of investment . . . are brewing up problems in the long term. Across the board from physical infrastructure to teenagers, from council houses to social insurance, money that could have been invested to give a return has been diverted to current expenditure instead. Sooner or later that was bound to cost us more. (Cooper 1997: 97)

In 1997 Ms Cooper (an economist) was elected as a new Labour Member of Parliament in Mr Blair's government and, in 1998, was no doubt heartened to hear Gordon Brown commit the Government to a public expenditure system where public investment was to be given a high (if not the highest) priority.

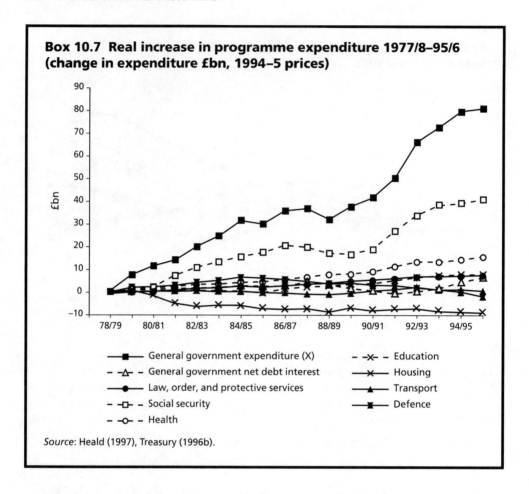

Box 10.7 Real increase in programme expenditure 1977/8–95/6 (change in expenditure £bn, 1994–5 prices)

Legend:
- General government expenditure (X)
- General government net debt interest
- Law, order, and protective services
- Social security
- Health
- Education
- Housing
- Transport
- Defence

Source: Heald (1997), Treasury (1996b).

Growth of Public Expenditure: Some International Comparisons

Yet how do the UK's patterns of public expenditure compare with other countries? As was noted earlier, in historical terms the growth of public expenditure in the UK has a similar cyclical profile to several other major industrial countries (Tanzi and Schuknecht 1995). Data covering a more recent period (Box 10.8) indicates the relative movement of General Government Expenditure over the last eighteen years for the UK compared with an average for the European Union (EU) and countries who are members of the **Organization for Economic Co-operation and Development (OECD)** (this group includes the USA, Canada, most West European countries, and Japan). Table 10.3 is a snapshot of relative public expenditure by functional area in EU countries.

Box 10.8 gives some indication of why Conservative governments in the 1990s often proudly boasted that they were doing better in economic terms than other European counties and did not wish to be burdened with 'socialist policies' such as the **EU social chapter.** During this period the UK moved close to the average for OECD countries, a figure kept low by economies with low social policy budgets (relative to GDP), in particular

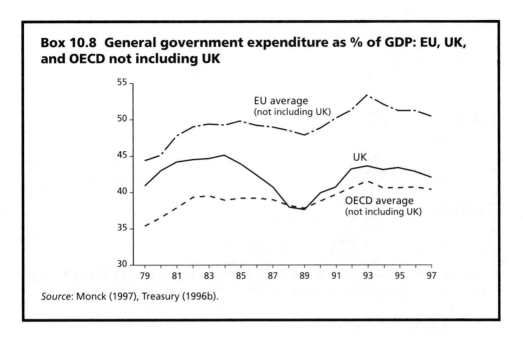

Box 10.8 General government expenditure as % of GDP: EU, UK, and OECD not including UK

Source: Monck (1997), Treasury (1996b).

the USA and Japan. For advocates of deregulation and a smaller British state, the message was 'doing better, but could do better still'—by, for example, further liberalizing of the economy and policies to keep public expenditure less than 40 per cent of GDP, if not lower. Interestingly, Mr Blair's New Labour government has maintained this stance, committing itself to a 'sustainable investment rule', where new public debt as a proportion of GDP will be held, over the economic cycle, at 'a sustainable and prudent level' (Cm. 3978, 5). This is projected to fall below 40 per cent of GDP from 2000/01 onwards.

What of the UK compared with its European partners? Table 10.3 compares spending by policy area for EU countries in 1992 and demonstrates that, at that point, the UK spent in comparison with the EU:

- 20 per cent less on social security;
- 10 per cent less on education;
- 50 per cent less on general public services;
- up to EU average on health but 10 per cent less than the four largest EU countries—Germany, France, Spain, and Italy; and
- more than the median on defence (40 per cent) and public order (33 per cent).

With all their potential flaws, these data agree with others charting the UK's record in social policy spending (Hills 1993; Hogwood 1992) in illustrating the relative public expenditure preferences of recent UK Conservative governments: a strong commitment to spending on law and order, a scepticism with regard to governmental intervention, and a preference for social polices that lean towards safety-net provision and targeting of benefits. Whether this reflects the characteristics of various expenditure control mechanisms or the explicit policy choices is a question we address later. Again, Mr Blair's New Labour government has sought to change elements of this by redistributing

Country	General	Public order	Defence	Education	Social	Health
Belgium	3.3		2.7	7.3	22.4	
Denmark	4.0	1.1	2.1	7.2	26.0	5.6
Germany	4.8	1.6	2.2	4.1	19.7	5.9
Spain	1.8	1.3	1.6	4.2	18.4	5.1
France	3.9	0.9	3.2	5.4	23.5	7.5
Italy	4.2	1.8	1.9	5.4	18.7	6.5
Netherlands	na	na	2.7	5.3	na	na
UK	1.9	2.0	4.2	4.9	15.8	5.9
EU Median	3.9	1.5	2.5	5.4	19.7	5.9
UK – EU	–2.0	0.5	1.7	–0.5	–3.9	0.0
Big 4 EU*	4.1	1.5	2.1	4.8	19.2	6.5
UK – Big 4	–2.2	0.5	2.1	0.1	–3.4	–0.6

Table 10.3 Expenditure as percentage of GDP by functional area for EU countries with broadly comparable data (1992 or nearest year)

* 'The Big 4' are Germany, Spain, France, Italy.

Source: Hulme 1997; European Commission 1996.

resources to areas such as health and education and away from areas such as defence and foreign policy. However, the commitment to tight fiscal constraints and a reluctance to intervene remain, while social security spending is considered a policy area in need of tight fiscal control and reform.

Public Expenditure: The Search for Control

All governments have to balance spending with the revenue to finance this and its willingness and capacity to borrow. As we shall see, the process for making the necessary decisions was traditionally conducted annually, yet the provision of facilities such as hospitals, schools, and roads have long-term expenditure implications. The logic implies the planning of public expenditure. Different countries approach this in different ways. In the UK the management and control of public expenditure is the responsibility ultimately of the Cabinet and specifically the Chancellor of the Exchequer, who, with the Chief Secretary of the Treasury, another cabinet minister, stand as guardians of economic policy against the spending claims of departmental ministers (Thain and Wright 1995). This system is mirrored at the administrative level by Treasury officials who are in constant dialogue with civil servants in spending departments. In this small, closed community, public expenditure policy is forged and fought over on a continuous basis.

Plowden and the Public Expenditure Survey (PES)

The present system of managing UK public expenditure has its origins in the recommendations of the 1961 Plowden Committee. This Committee, established to explore a perceived failure in public expenditure planning, argued that in the annual public expenditure round the long-term implications of many programmes were ignored, and commitments entered into by ministers were often not linked to the development of the economy. Plowden therefore proposed the introduction of a system, the **Public Expenditure Survey (PES)**, to allow spending to be determined and assessed in an integrated way.

The intention was to establish a process in which departments engaged in annual discussions with the Treasury, first at official and then ministerial level, to agree their spending plans in the short (annual) and longer term (of between three and five years) consistent with planned economic policy. The outcome of these discussions would be agreed by Cabinet, which would be able to consider the integrated package and then make informed choices over priorities in line with economic plans and performance. This would lead to a Public Expenditure White Paper published in the beginning of a year (January/February) prior to the Chancellor's annual Spring Budget. This annual cycle (see Box 10.9) was the cornerstone of the public expenditure process for decades, although as we shall see, there were significant changes both in procedure and emphasis from its initiation in the 1960s on, while in 1998 Gordon Brown introduced further significant changes, perhaps in an effort to restore the long-lost strategic vision that Plowden had sought to impose.

In its first decade PES evolved into a set of regularized and systematic routines, yet public expenditure continued to rise. Initially this was thought to be due partially to inaccurate projections of economic performance, and partially to the fact that there was little evaluation of the effects of public spending. The Heath government (1970–4) sought to remedy the latter by introducing the Central Policy Review Staff (CPRS), a 'think-tank' to assist ministers to think strategically (Blackstone and Plowden 1988), and Programme Analysis and Review (PAR), intended to give PES an evaluative cutting edge (Gray and Jenkins 1982). Both survived the change to a Labour government in 1974, but were marginalized after that date by a severe crisis of public expenditure control. It was this crisis rather than the arrival in 1979 of Mrs Thatcher's first administration which marked the shift over the next twenty years from planning to controlling public expenditure.

One cause of this crisis of the mid-1970s was thought to be the inflationary effect of PES's planning in volume terms (for example, the numbers of doctors and teachers) rather than in real costs of public programmes. **Cash limits** were introduced in 1975 and refined in the period up to 1979 to set ceilings on departmental budgets, including a fixed limit for inflation as reflected in price increases and wage rises. If circumstances pushed costs up then departments faced an effective resource cut. If these brought greater financial discipline and ensured departments kept to published economic projections, they could not be applied to areas where spending was demand-led (such as social security).

After 1979 the new Conservative Government extended the cash controls of PES in conjunction with policies to cut inflation and reduce public sector manpower. By 1982 **cash planning** replaced the old volume planning of the original PES process and a succession of initiatives, such as efficiency scrutinies (1980) and the **Financial Management Initiative (FMI)** (1982), focused administrative attention on the more efficient use of

Box 10.9 Main stages in the PES process

January/February:	Treasury post-mortem on previous survey. Similar exercise in departments. Treasury begins work on *Guidelines* for next survey.
March:	Draft *Guidelines* agreed by departments and approved by Cabinet. MTFS and Budget documents published confirming spending totals agreed in the previous Autumn Statement. MTFS provides the basis for the overall 'expenditure judgement'.
March/April:	Treasury and departments revise and agree baseline expenditures for the next three years.
May/June:	Departmental ministers bid to Chief Secretary for resources additional to that provided by base-line. Period of 'shadow-boxing' as Treasury and departmental officials clear the ground for negotiations between Chief Secretary and ministers on their bids.
July:	Cabinet decides whether or not to confirm planning total for coming year as set out in the previous Autumn Statement, and charges the Chief Secretary with reaching agreement with departments on their bids within the envelope. Formal decision on setting up of Star Chamber, Prime Minister decides its chairman.
September/October:	Ministerial bilaterals.
October/November:	Star Chamber convened if necessary to deal with outstanding differences between Treasury and departments.
November:	Cabinet meets and hears reports from Chief Secretary and/or Chairman of Star Chamber on results of deliberations. Cabinet approves settlements made in Star Chamber; resolves outstanding differences; and agrees survey figures.
November:	Results of survey exercise published in Autumn Statement.
February:	Departmental public expenditure plans published in separate volumes jointly presented to Parliament by the Chief Secretary and the relevant minister. These provide a detailed breakdown of the outline plans previously presented in the Autumn Statement and incorporate unavoidable changes in programmes since the autumn. The Treasury produces a Statistical Summary to accompany the 19 individual departmental volumes.

Note: MTFS: Government 'Medium Term Financial Strategy'.
'Bilaterals': Discussions to fix departmental budgets between spending ministers and Chief Secretary of the Treasury.

Source: Thain and Wright (1992a).

public resources; while the threat of appearing before a special cabinet sub-committee, often referred to as the Star Chamber, concentrated the political minds of spending ministers on settling within agreed totals.

The development of PES in the 1980s resulted in a process unrecognizable from the immediate post-Plowden era. The government's aim was now to 'design and maintain a system that provided for tight control of monetary aggregates while bearing down simultaneously on costs' (Thain and Wright 1992a: 22). So while the form of the bargaining process remained relatively unaltered, PES's overall focus abandoned almost entirely any form of medium or longer-term planning, and concentrated on short-term cash control.

Thain and Wright (1992b) also argue that the effectiveness of PES in this period can be assessed in terms of its capacity as a regulatory system for the interests of the main players in the public expenditure game, achieving the public-expenditure objectives of successive governments, and aiding collective political decision-making. They found that the reformed PES system was indeed effective in maintaining the cohesion of the Whitehall network, but added that 'effective is not optimal' (1992: 196), as PES succeeded by maintaining itself as a closed and opaque system from which many interested parties (such as local authorities) were excluded.

As a mechanism for achieving public expenditure objectives, Thain and Wright found PES more patchy. The original ambitious plan to reduce public expenditure in real terms failed because defence and law and order spending were committed to grow while social security spending rose with the recession. But, from 1983 onwards, the aim changed to that of reducing public spending (General Government Expenditure, or GGE) as a proportion of GDP. This strategy was achieved (see Box 10.4) between 1984 and 1989 as GDP grew, allowing 'more public expenditure to be accommodated without increasing the ratio' (Thain and Wright 1992b: 198). However, this objective in turn was replaced by the target of holding the GGE/GDP ratio constant and, from 1990, to achieving 'stability over a medium term period, an admission that in some years the ratio might rise' (Thain and Wright 1992b: 198). This explains why governments of the 1980s can make some claim to have constrained public expenditure while in real terms GGE in 1990 was about 19 per cent higher than in 1979 (see Box 10.3 above).

Yet part of the Plowden vision was to impose some economic rationality on political decision-making, to encourage ministers through PES to take a collective view, and assist them to prioritize programmes. Here Thain and Wright echo the views of many before them in arguing that in spite of many changes PES continued to be less about setting priorities than a way of balancing bids and savings within preset spending limits. They add:

In a formal sense, it is obviously true that the Cabinet collectively decides the relative priority of both the total and the different kinds of public expenditure. . . . But that prioritization is arrived at *ex post facto*. The order of priorities they now agree to are the sum of a number of *ad hoc* decisions, each determined on-its-merits, programme by programme, department by department in bilateral negotiation with the Treasury. (1992b: 213)

Thus PES by the 1990s had become a device for achieving 'improved financial discipline and tighter short-term control. Planning and allocation for a period ahead have become less important functions' (Thain and Wright 1992b: 218). At the same time there had developed a more positive attitude to efficiency and value for money and, politically, more attention to the role of the state (in terms of privatization, contracting-out, and the advance of quasi-markets). However, Conservative governments found themselves under pressure to allocate more real resources to programmes such as health and education, and to improve service quality. These, together with other pressures on the economy, were to place continuing and sustained demands on public expenditure in the 1990s.

Public Expenditure Control and Reform in the 1990s

In spite of continued political rhetoric on the need to keep public spending down, the GGE/GDP ratio and the Public Sector Borrowing Requirement (PSBR) climbed sharply between 1988 and 1992. Partly in response, the Conservative government embarked on a further set of reforms to PES. These included:

- a new *Control Total* to limit the overall amount of public spending for the three-year public sector planning projections;
- a new Cabinet Committee *EDX* (Economic and Domestic Expenditure) to replace the Star Chamber;
- a programme of expenditure programme reviews (known as *Fundamental Departmental Reviews*, or *FDR*) in which each Whitehall department was forced to assess the totality of its activities and expenditure against current needs and objectives and to propose savings;
- the production of a *unified budget* to integrate revenue raising and spending decisions; and
- a change from cash accounting to an accruals based system of *Resource Accounting and Budgeting (RAB)*.

Some of these changes represented an effort by the Treasury to reassert control over spending, which it considered to have been hijacked by departmental ministers. As former Treasury official Nick Monck observed, by 1992, while 'the Cabinet ritually endorsed weasel words about the aims of the Survey [i.e. PES] . . . in practice new plans were not constrained by the totals published a year earlier' (1997: 280). Control Totals were intended to change this, as each year's total was now set *before* the PES negotiations, and any changes in expenditure could take place only within it. Moreover, the new Cabinet Committee EDX was intended to resolve disputes between spending ministers and the Treasury. Chaired by the Chancellor, the function of this committee was to neutralize political influence by making recommendations to Cabinet, after discussion with spending ministers but without negotiation with them (Hulme 1997: 109), thus attempting to impose a degree of consistency on spending decisions.

The other elements in this quintet fell outside the PES process, but are intended to relate to it. The FERs represented serious efforts to cut departmental running costs and to reduce and rationalize central government departments in terms of assessing what activities are necessary to deliver government objectives. By the general election of 1997 most departments had passed though this process, some with quite remarkable results. Indeed, even the Treasury was not immune from the cold wind of change, with its own FER resulting in a redefinition of its mission and aims, a major structural reorganization, and the culling of 25 per cent or more of its senior staff (Parry *et al.* 1997; Wright 1995).

Meanwhile the Treasury announced in 1994/5 that it intended to recast departmental accounts into a system known as Resource Accounting and Budgeting (RAB). Something similar had already been introduced into New Zealand government, with major consequences for departmental management and ministerial decision-making (Pallot and Ball 1997). The official rationale for these changes was to bring Whitehall departments into line with business accounting practices, including the production of a wider range of financial statements such as balance sheets. The Conservative government of John Major claimed that a resource-based PES would help determine public spending priorities more rationally and assist choices, while giving departments greater control over their financial management (Cm. 2929, 1995). As Wright has observed, the successful introduction of RAB could have far-reaching consequences, since its adoption by departments implies 'identifying outputs and the ways that these are produced; charging for all resources consumed, including the use of capital assets; classifying and valuing all assets; publishing a balance sheet and reconciling resource flows and cash funding' (1995: 580). He notes also that the hidden agenda could be to force down departmental spending by changing the incentives for managerial behaviour.

Yet RAB is but the latest of a wave of structural and processual reforms that have swept though the public sector since the late 1980s. These include the restructuring of the majority of government departments into Next Steps Agencies, the reorganization of the National Health Service into 'trusts', changes in education such as local financial management in schools, and formula funding and civil service reforms, including more decentralized departmental financial management (see Gray and Jenkins 1997). What binds these together is the belief that greater efficiency, cost control, and quality of service can be achieved in public organizations through delegated systems of financial management involving a much clearer degree of cost specification and the delegation of responsibility. But has all this delivered increased efficiency, reduced public expenditure, and improved quality? As Corry and Gray note, it is difficult to assess from available data whether any gains in efficiency have been achieved, or whether changes will lead to lower public expenditure in the future (1997). It was these and other important issues that Gordon Brown's 1998 public expenditure reforms sought to address, as discussed further below.

Public Expenditure at the End of the Twentieth Century

What of the state of public expenditure in the UK today? We have observed that by the mid-1990s the principal machinery of expenditure decisions, the PES, had shifted from the ambitions of the Plowden Report (1961) to more pragmatic and short-term arrangements in which the cash function predominated. The preceding pages have also noted a variety of demographic and political factors influencing public expenditure at the end of the century. This final section of the chapter will bring these considerations together to ask whether public expenditure is in good order.

Assessing the history of PES, Hulme (1997) and Thain and Wright (1995), among others, argue that it exhibited a number of strengths and weakness. The former include:

- responsiveness to political leadership;
- the capacity to agree budgets on time;
- sufficient control over expenditure totals to contain inflation;
- containment of public spending as a proportion of GDP equal to if not better than other European Countries; and
- an increased focus on efficiency and value-for money.

In contrast weakness include:

- frequent failure to meet public expenditure targets;
- too much emphasis on short-term factors;
- a lack of 'transparency' regarding information provided by the system and a lack of open debate over choices; and
- a lack of objective evaluation of existing policies or new initiatives.

Was further reform desirable and feasible? The issues here are both managerial and political. Managerially, a case could be made for alterations to both the structure and processes of PES. Monck, for example, has argued that a successful system for the management, planning, and control of public expenditure would be one that offered 'timely statistics about expenditure, realistic forecasts, information and analysis on the intended and actual results of programmes and a culture that ensured cash limits and financial control were taken seriously' (1997: 282–3). Yet such processes are often poorly developed within British government: the information is often impenetrable, there is little enthusiasm for programme evaluation, and there are few incentives to drive financial and programme managers (see Hulme 1997). Reforms such as Resource Accounting and Budgeting, or devolved departmental financial management, clearly have the potential to improve public expenditure management and planning; but to shift PES away from short-termism and towards evaluation requires significant reforms in both political and administrative cultures that would go directly against the grain of changes in the 1980s and early 1990s.

These problems were recognized in part, if not in whole, by the incoming Labour government of 1997. Hence one of the first actions of Mr Brown when becoming Chancellor of the Exchequer was to suspend the annual round on the PES process and to introduce into Departments and across the totality of government a series of comprehensive spending reviews. While these were proceeding the Chancellor accepted the tight public expenditure control totals imposed by the previous Conservative Chancellor, Kenneth Clarke.

The outcomes of the Comprehensive Spending Reviews were revealed in the summer of 1998 (Cm. 4011, 1998) after the Chancellor had announced his overall strategy to reform the public expenditure process (Cm. 3978, 1998). As indicated earlier, Mr Brown's emphasis here was the prudent management of public finance, a phased programme of higher public investment, the more effective use of public assets, and the modernization of public services. Furthermore, all this was to be underpinned by long-term plans and strict financial rules, in particular:

- 'the golden rule': that over an economic cycle the government would only borrow to invest;
- 'the sustainable investment rule' that net public debt as a proportion of GDP would be held at a stable and prudent level.

More specifically, Mr Brown signalled the replacement of PES as an annual cycle by three-year plans for Departments which would be given greater flexibility in return for justifying expenditure against targets and objectives previously agreed. Furthermore, this process would involve a 'contract' (known as a Departmental Public Service Agreement) between the Department and the Treasury that would be monitored by a Cabinet Committee which would review a department's performance in terms of both efficiency and quality. The Chancellor argued that these structural reforms would allow the Government to be 'more strategic' while other changes such as a focus on investment, a distinction between capital and current spending, and the adoption of the RAB reforms (see above) would move the planning of public expenditure onto a more informed, organized, and planned footing. Certainly in many ways these proposals, in contrast to what preceded them, appear to return, in spirit if not substance, to the ideals of the Plowden reforms of the 1960s, albeit within a framework of tight and stringent, Treasury-directed cash controls developed in the 1980s and 1990s.

Public expenditure control is indeed of fundamental importance. As Heald (1997) argues, what has characterized public expenditure under governments prior to 1998 has often been policy drift itself, a consequence of a closed and opaque system in which a select few political and administrative actors operate with little or no direct input from many important players in the game, conducting business according to a restricted set of parameters and rules. His argument for reform is therefore to build transparency into the process, something that would require both technical skill ('providing information that is intelligible') and political will. Do the changes of 1998 meet these criticisms? Certainly the literature accompanying Mr Brown's reforms are peppered with commitments to 'transparency', but how these commitments will be interpreted and what effects the changes will have remain to be seen.

Public Expenditure in the Millennium: Crisis? What Crisis?

In January 1997 Andrew Dilnot questioned whether the Labour Party could stand by the principles of the National Health Service (NHS) if it meant what it said about keeping to the Conservatives' publicized spending totals. He argued that this was impossible, and that the NHS would be in crisis within years. This assessment was based on the fact that public expenditure plans for the NHS envisaged spending growing by 0.6 per cent in real terms in 1997/8 (about £1bn less than normal), by 0.8 per cent in 1998/9, a cut of 0.7 per cent in 1999/2000, and then zero in 2000/1. Thus, over four years there would be a cumulative growth of less than 1 per cent in real terms, compared with 15 per cent in the previous four. Dilnot claimed that it was impossible to deliver the current standard of NHS provision on this basis, and 'hard choices had to be made between higher taxes and changing the ambition and role of the public sector'. In this fiscal climate efficiency savings would be no more than a drop in the ocean, and the future could only be preserved by some explicit system of rationing (Dilnot 1997).

To some extent Mr Brown may have countered the Dilnot arguments with his announcement in the summer of 1998 that, having kept the lid tightly on NHS spending in the first two years of the new Labour government, he was now able, as a consequence of the Comprehensive Spending Review, to put an extra £5billion into the NHS in the period 1999/2001. However, even sums of this magnitude may not be sufficient to combat the claims that, as the NHS reached its fiftieth anniversary in 1998, costs may be on an upward spiral that will be difficult to control without extreme measures, such as the introduction of a new system of charges or explicit rationing criteria, to exclude either classes of treatment or even patients from a comprehensive service free 'at the point of use' (Willman 1998).

Such crisis scenarios are not restricted to the UK and, indeed, have gained in intensity as politicians in many industrial countries develop a fixation on a magic ratio of public spending to GDP which they believe will ensure economic success and political vitality. But, *is* there some natural level to public spending, beyond which disaster follows, and above which promises economic salvation? Careful analysis is required, as it is clear from much of the data presented earlier that no great difference in national performances in inflation, growth, and investment can be attributed to the public expenditure–GDP ratio.

Nevertheless, there are:

genuine and binding political constraints on how much the state can tax and spend; many people do not want to pay so much towards certain types of state activity. The supply of public spending . . . is therefore heavily constrained. But it is constrained by political legitimacy rather than any law of economics. (Cooper 1997: 91)

This is the nettle that Dilnot fears that politicians will not grasp. Yet the issue must be finance and taxation. The political instinct is to presume that individuals are wedded to service levels, but do not wish to pay more tax to sustain them. To suggest lower services or higher taxes is therefore seen as tantamount to electoral suicide. However, recent attitude studies demonstrate that this problem is more complex. In the first instance, many individuals perceive little connection between what they pay to the state and what they receive from it. Thus studies indicate that Labour lost votes in the 1992 election less for suggesting tax rises than the perception that it would squander them if it came to power (Heath *et al.* 1994). Extensions of this argument lead to suggestions of hypothecating taxation so that identifiable inputs are spent on specific services (such as the Liberal Democrats' commitment to increase income tax by 1p for education). However, such a move flies in the face of a lifetime's tradition by successive governments and the Treasury of how public finance should be managed. Hence even if cracks in this stance are appearing in the late 1990s (such as a willingness by the Labour government to consider hypothecating taxes or charges in a policy area such as road transport) it must be doubted if moves in this direction will be any more than marginal.

A different line of argument, based on recent research (Hall *et al.* 1997; Taylor-Gooby 1995), indicates that while many individuals claim to support increased public spending, they favour some forms more than others (health, education, and pensions), while levels of support vary with age, income level, and gender. To understand attitudes towards public spending it is therefore important to disaggregate issues in terms both of policy areas and the public at large. This argument is taken further by Cooper (1997) who observes that, while those who fear suggesting higher public expenditure funded by higher taxation might be over-cautious, what appears clear is that public support for such moves may be selective. For example, people may demand better and higher-quality services for themselves and be willing to fund these, but still be reluctant to contribute to the funding of universal provision of this quality.

The supply of public spending is thus subject to political and economic factors. In economic terms, the rhetoric of the UK being over-taxed and hence needing to reduce public expenditure to bring down tax levels is questionable: international comparisons of the average tax burden over the past twenty years—34 per cent to 36 per cent for the UK compared with 57 per cent in Sweden (Hills 1996)—suggest taxpayers can afford to pay more. Politically, however, they may not want to pay, or at least not for all services, or to bodies they do not trust. Hence the public spending problem becomes essentially one of **political legitimacy** fuelled by a history of governmental mechanisms which have failed to control public expenditure or to make any serious effort to evaluate its outcomes.

Conclusion

In 1995 the Conservative Chancellor, Kenneth Clarke, claimed that 'the share of national income taken by the state in public expenditure must be reduced to below 40 per cent (of GDP) if we are to remain competitive in today's world'. To some extent, even with all its reforming zeal, Mr Blair's New Labour government appears to support this view (Cm. 3978, 1998). As previously noted, this assumption may be contentious. It has been argued that international comparisons of economic performance do little to establish whether there was any 'ideal share' of GDP for government services. Rather, the appropriate level of such services 'will vary between countries and, over time within each country'. Consequently, demographic differences result in the demand for services such as education, healthcare, and pensions varying hugely while, as a country becomes more affluent, it is likely to spend a bigger proportion of its GDP on health, education, and other services. Thus in Britain 'it may make political sense for the government to try to push public spending below 40 per cent of GDP, but doing so at the cost of services does not obviously make economic sense' (*The Economist*, 2 December 1995, 37).

Perhaps, then fixations on public expenditure/GDP ratios and the Public Sector Borrowing Requirement (PSBR) lead down blind alleys. What is important is not some magic figure or ratio but a clarification of policy objectives and some reasoned assessment of whether the composition of spending and the means by which programmes are delivered are effective. However, taxation remains important, since there are clearly levels of taxation that might discourage economic activity and inhibit electoral survival.

The difficulty for UK politicians is that they are caught between a rock and a hard place, by the apparent successes of public expenditure control in the past decade and the political forces of rising and changing expectations. This explains the fiscal rectitude of Chancellor Gordon Brown and his assumption that public expenditure needs to be effectively contained relative to other major industrial economies. Yet rectitude has its costs for the responsiveness of health spending and other major areas of social policy. Hence the independent Institute of Fiscal Studies (IFS) has argued strongly that 'a constant level of taxation and public spending will not deliver health, education and social security in a way that will work . . . without either higher taxes or a redistribution of public spending and more private spending' (*The Economist*, 23 November 1996, 31–2).

Balancing the demand side of the public expenditure equation with the supply of resources to sustain services remains a classic dilemma accentuated by rising inequality, the reconstruction of the labour market, and expectations in society. These developments leave future governments with stark choices: 'to arrange for the state to do less; or force up taxes beyond the level that voters are prepared to support; or to curb social provision' (Kellner 1997: 133). Yet the problem may be less public expenditure *per se* as the system and policies that it seeks to sustain. This is what Corry terms the argument of effectiveness, in that while public expenditure is 'not necessarily a bad thing' it can be spent inefficiently 'and on things that nobody really wants or that add nothing either to economic strength and social cohesion' (1997a: 4). Thus, regardless of whether it is affordable in the long term, one of the major faults of the welfare state is that it might be badly designed, in that the same goals might be achieved just as effectively, but at lower cost.

In the light of such choices, politicians may seek to keep public expenditure pressures in check through liberalizing expenditure provision, delivering social programmes via alternatives, and opening up the system to give it greater transparency and legitimacy. Liberalizing capital finance is especially attractive as a remedy for under-investment in areas such as education, health, and housing. Public sector investment fell from 12 per cent of total government expenditure (GGE(X)) in the mid-1970s to a level of between 4 and 5 per cent in the mid-1990s (Corry and Gray 1997). This was the result of strict controls applied by the Treasury to constrain public sector borrowing (the PSBR problem).

Since 1992 the **Private Finance Initiative (PFI)** has sought to provide opportunities for private investment in public services. Under the PFI private organizations and consortia are encouraged to enter into contractual relations with public sector bodies to provide facilities such as hospitals, student accommodation, and so on. The incentive for private sector participation is to allow access to the revenue stream accruing from the capital project in return for a sharing of the risk. The attraction of such strategies is that via them some of the public expenditure constraints on delivering public services is avoided. This approach has been accepted and adopted by the New Labour government, a major element of the 1998 reforms being the proposals to develop new public–private partnerships as well as a programme of public sector asset disposals to release funds for investment (Cm. 3978, 1998). However, such strategies are not without cost. They may have long-term financial implications where losses may outweigh gains, and they may lead to the loss of overall control of public sector facilities. Indeed, the possible danger of such public/private arrangements is that they might change the shape and character of public services (Corry 1997b: 29–32; Gray 1997).

Alternative service delivery also opens up other possibilities of public–private partnership, as in the greater use of private insurance in areas such as pensions and long-term care for the elderly. Further alternatives include targeting welfare services more specifically, and greater use of means testing. Such ideas, discussed in detail by

Glennerster (1992) and Hills (1993), are fundamental to the debate on the mixed economy of welfare discussed elsewhere in this book. These strategies focus on improving the efficiency and effectiveness of existing services either by redesigning them (the benefit system, for example, or pensions) or by placing them in a competitive environment. However, as with the PFI, market-type mechanisms may limit government's capacity to plan and allocate public expenditure and thus aggravate problems of control and accountability in the contract state.

For these reasons it appears doubtful that the bind in which politicians find themselves can be simply solved by creative financial strategies, greater efficiency and effectiveness, or even by the redesign and retargeting of welfare systems—at least not without the rethinking and reshaping links between the politicians and the public. As previously noted, many of the major problems bedevilling public expenditure concern political rather than economic legitimacy. Some of the former can be traced to a public distrust of the political process, especially regarding the use and effectiveness of tax revenues. 'How can anyone expect people happily to pay their taxes when they have no clue what government is doing with their money and why, and whether it is good value for money?' (Corry 1997a: 8).

The case for greater transparency in the public expenditure process is therefore not simply a call for more information to be released to the public (such as league tables and performance indicators) but for a greater opening up of the system, starting with the decision-making process itself and including, perhaps, an active public involvement in shaping options in social policy areas such as healthcare and community care. One of the most crucial issues in public expenditure policy is therefore that of trust. At present we exist in a low-trust system, where voters do not trust politicians and politicians do not trust the public either to participate in the policy-making process or cope with difficult decisions. Politicians fear the voters and the electoral consequences of higher taxes or decisions that cut into popular services such as health and education; voters in turn distrust politicians either to use their taxes effectively or to design services on which they are rarely consulted. This cycle of distrust needs to be broken, otherwise some of the crucial problems in social and public policy are likely either not to be addressed at all or to be addressed in a sub-optimal and ineffective manner. Transparency and openness in public expenditure policy are thus crucial not only for accountability, effectiveness, and legitimacy, but for better public policy formulation and evaluation of decisions concerning the scope and extent of social policy provision, and the mechanisms through which it is delivered (Corry 1997b; Heald 1997).

Appendix A: Defining and Measuring Public Expenditure

As Likierman (1988) notes, UK national financial statistics published on behalf of the government by the Treasury do not use a measurement termed 'public expenditure'. Instead, the main terms in use before and after the 1998 reforms are outlined below. Further, see Heald (1995) on changes from the old to the new system in the early 1990s. Some of this terminology is explained in the annual Public Expenditure Statistical

Analysis issued by HM Treasury (for example, see Cm. 3901, 1998) while the latest proposals for defining and measuring public expenditure are set out in the Labour Government's 1998 White Papers (Cm. 3978, 1998; Cm. 4011, 1998).

The Control Total includes all government expenditure excluding cyclical social security expenditure (spending on unemployment benefit and income support), all local authority expenditure, financing requirements of public corporations, and any money drawn down from reserves. In 1998 this was renamed *Departmental Expenditure Limits* and set out in the form of three-year plans rather than annual allocations.

The Conservative governments of the 1990s expressed Government expenditure in terms of General Government Expenditure (X) (known as GGE(X)). This was the *Control Total* plus cyclical social security and government debt interest. *GGE(X)* was then reduced by a number of adjustments such as privatization receipts (counted as negative expenditure) to give a final total of *General Government Expenditure (GGE)* (see Cm. 3901, 1998, Appendix B). In 1998 *GGE* was replaced as the key aggregate by *Totally Managed Expenditure (TME)* (see Tables 10.1 and 10.2), this being the sum of public sector current spending and public sector net investment.

General Government Expenditure less *Government Receipts* (taxes, duties) gives *the General Government Borrowing Requirement (GGBR)*, which, when added to the borrowing of public corporations, gives the *Public Sector Borrowing Requirement (PSBR)*. In 1998 this was retitled the *Public Sector Net Cash Requirement*.

As Corry and Gray (1997) and Watson (1997) observe, the method of calculating expenditure as outlined above is particular to the UK. It is also crucial to the calculation of the *PSBR*, having implications both for international comparisons and internal fiscal management. Hence:

- Most other countries, in particular in the European Union, exclude the borrowing of public corporations and privatization receipts from the calculation of public expenditure. Thus in the EU member countries a different measure from the *PSBR*, known as the *General Government Financial Deficit (GGFD)*, is used to measure deficits. This is important in terms of the Maastricht convergence criteria.

- Furthermore, the *PSBR* as calculated in this way measured the balance in public finances in one year on a cash basis. One weakness in this was that current and capital spending were treated similarly, thus offering a perverse incentive to contain the *PSBR* by squeezing capital or investment expenditure (Watson 1997). Similarly, the treatment of privatization receipts as 'negative expenditure' has been a matter of some controversy both in accounting terms (Likierman 1988; Watson 1997) and in its capacity to act as a perverse incentive to promote asset disposal.

- In an effort to answer some of these criticisms, the Labour government's proposals of 1998 sought to offer a new format for the public finances. In particular these proposals stressed the importance of distinguishing between current and capital spending, and attempted to move the accounts more clearly in line with internationally accepted, accruals-based measures of financial accounts. As a consequence the Chancellor decided that a greater prominence be given to a new measure, the *Public Sector Net Borrowing (PSNB)*, defined as the extent to which net investment was not financed by surplus on the current account. This was considered a more sensible definition for assessing the fiscal position consistent with the new system of national accounts than the *PSBR* (Cm. 3978, 1998: 39).

Sources: Corry and Gray 1997; Watson 1997; Cm. 3901, 1998; Cm. 3978, 1998; Cm. 4011, 1998.

Glossary

cash limits Term used in central and local government budgeting to indicate the monetary ceiling on expenditure for particular activities or categories of expenditure in any one financial year.

cash planning Linked with a system of cash limits, this is a system of planning brought in by UK governments in the 1980s where public expenditure planning is done in cash terms, for example service level is determined by money available (such as, how many books can we get for £10,000?) rather than the volume planning system previously used, that is, we will plan to purchase 1,000 books (whatever they cost).

collectivism A system that favours collective or common provision and ownership in contrast to system of individual provision and reliance on free markets.

Comprehensive Spending Reviews (CSR) Introduced by the 1997 Labour Government of Tony Blair, these are the latest of several efforts by recent British governments to review public provision item by item asking whether any particular service needs to be provided by the state and, if the answer to this is yes, to explore whether it might be possible to deliver it in alternative ways (more economically, efficiently, and effectively, say). The CSR is seen as a mechanism through which public expenditure can be redistributed between departments to further the government's priorities (see further Cm. 4011, 1998).

European Union(EU) Social Chapter An initiative taken by European Community members in 1989 to begin to harmonize social policy, in particular in the area of labour market and employment relations due to a concern that workplace conditions and arrangements might suffer as a result of the competitive single market. The Conservative government of John Major secured the UK an 'opt out' from this arrangement; however, one of the first acts in the EU of Mr Blair's Labour Government in 1997 was to waive this 'opt out' and accept the Social Chapter's terms.

externalities Term used in economic theory to indicate second-order effects of economic activities often not directly costed in market terms (such as industrial pollution).

fiscal crisis Term used to indicate a projected crisis for states with large public expenditure programmes, especially in areas such as health, welfare benefits, and pensions, where it is argued (but also disputed) that a combination of rising public demand, entitlements, and falling tax revenue will place governments under an increasing, if not intolerable, economic strain.

Financial Management Initiative (FMI) Initiative introduced into UK government departments by HM Treasury in 1982 aimed at improving the management of resources by a variety of strategies, including delegated budgeting and increasing the accountability of individual managers for the management of resources.

general government spending (or expenditure) The international definition of general government expenditure (or public expenditure) includes the spending of central government, of local authorities, and, in the case of most counties, of regional government.

Gross Domestic Product (GDP) The value of goods and services produced by UK residents, including taxes on expenditure of both home-produced and imported goods and services and the effects of subsidies.

International Monetary Fund (IMF) International body established (together with the **World Bank**) as a result of the 1942 Bretton Woods meeting of forty-four countries to create and stabilize the world monetary order, including exchange rates, balance of payments deficits, and the operation of the system as a whole. The IMF can advance credit to countries with serious balance of payments deficits, but has the right to demand economic compliance with its suggestions. Hence the IMF has the power to intervene in the domestic policy-making of countries it assists.

individualism In contrast to collectivism, a set of beliefs that puts paramount importance on the rights and freedoms of individuals and the power of free-market mechanisms.

Keynesian economics An approach to national economic management named after the British economist and political adviser John Maynard Keynes that places strong emphasis on governmental intervention in economic management and, traditionally, on an associated goal of full employment.

New Right Term used in the 1980s to describe the intellectual and political influences on conservative-inclined governments such as those of Margaret Thatcher in the UK and Ronald Reagan in the USA. The intellectual basis of New Right thinking is often associated with writers such as the political economist and philosopher Friedrich Hayek and the economist Milton Friedman and the development of free-market or 'public choice' economics. New Right thinking is also heavily influenced by ideas of individualism, and advocates social and governmental systems based on this.

Organization for Economic Co-operation and Development (OECD) A Paris-based international organization financed mainly by the leading international industrial countries set up in the wake of the US Marshall Plan of the 1940s. The OECD is engaged in a variety of research and similar activities in areas ranging from economic forecasting and studies of comparative economic performance to science policy, environmental policy, and the growing importance and effects of information technology.

political legitimacy Term used to indicate the likely necessity that policy initiatives and spending decisions should match the values and expectations both of voters and those making such proposals. For example, while the economic case for reforming the welfare state may be strong, the political legitimacy of many proposals for this may be challenged by the public.

Private Finance Initiative (PFI) A scheme introduced by John Major's Conservative government and continued with by Mr Blair's Labour government that seeks to finance public sector projects (such as bridges, hospitals, and student accommodation) by schemes that involve the injection of private-sector capital in return for an income stream from such investments to the financing organization (through tolls, rents, and so on).

Public Expenditure Survey (PES) Annual system of public expenditure planning in UK government involving bilateral bargaining between the major Whitehall spending departments and HM Treasury, culminating in cabinet agreement on public expenditure objectives over the next (and subsequent) financial years. Formally conducted on an annual basis, this process was moved to a three-year cycle from 1998/9 (see further Cm. 3978, 1998).

public goods Goods and benefits that groups and individuals who do not contribute to their provision cannot be prevented from benefiting from (such as national defence and public order services).

Public Sector Net Cash Requirement/Public Sector Borrowing Requirement (PSBR)
The amount the government needs to borrow at any one time to bridge the gap between income and expenditure. In 1998 this was retitled the **Public Sector Net Cash Requirement** in line with other changes to the organization and operation of the public expenditure planning system introduced by the Labour government (Cm. 3978, 1998).

Guide to Further Reading

A clear and detailed, if somewhat dated, account of the debate on public expenditure in the UK is that by Andrew Likierman (1988), formerly of the London Business School, and now the Head of the UK Government's Accountancy Service. A good discussion of the public expenditure implications of social welfare programmes can be found in Glennerster (1992) and, in a different way, in Hills (1993). The story of the early years of the Public Expenditure Survey (PES) are well detailed in Heclo and Wildavsky (1974), while a definitive account of PES's development in the 1980s and early 1990s is that by Thain and Wright (1995). For some views by serving politicians of these events and the difficulties of public expenditure control, see the accounts of Joel Barnett (1982), Chief Secretary to the Treasury in the Callaghan Labour Government, and of Nigel Lawson (1992), Mrs Thatcher's Chancellor of the Exchequer in the 1980s. For a discussion of some of the main issues in the public expenditure area prior to the 1997 election of Mr Blair's Labour government, see Corry ed. (1997), while for details of the Labour government's public expenditure reforms and the outcomes of its programme of Comprehensive Spending Reviews see Cm. 3978 (1998) and Cm. 4011 (1998). For further information on topics covered in this chapter readers should also look at recent issues of the journals *Public Administration*, *Public Money and Management*, *The Journal of Social Policy*, and *Talking Politics*. The weekly journal *The Economist* also often carries short news articles on public expenditure issues. In addition it should be noted that HM Treasury (www.hm-treasury.gov.uk) and, indeed, most government departments can be accessed by the Internet/World Wide Web, as can many other organizations of relevance in this area (such as the Institute of Public Policy Research, the Institute of Fiscal Studies, and so on).

References

Barnett, J. (1982), *Inside the Treasury* (London: Andre Deutsch).

Blackstone, T. and Plowden W. (1988), *Inside the Think Tank* (London: Heinemann).

Clarke, K. (1995), 'The Future of Conservatism', Speech: Conservative Party Central Office.

Cm. 1867 (1992), *Budgetary Reform* (London: HMSO).

Cm. 2929 (1995), *Better Accounting for Taxpayers' Money: The Government's Proposals—Resource Accounting and Budgeting* (London: HMSO).

Cm. 3901 (1998), *Public Expenditure: Statistical Analysis, 1998–9* (London: Stationery Office Ltd.).

Cm. 3978 (1998), *Stability and Investment for the Long Term: Economic and Fiscal Strategy Report 1998* (London: Stationery Office Ltd.).

Cm. 4011 (1998), *Modern Public Services for Britain: Investing in Reform: Comprehensive Spending Review and New Public Spending Plans 1999–2002* (London: Stationery Office Ltd.).

Cooper, Y. (1997), 'The Key Public Expenditure Issues of the Future', ch. 4 in D. Corry (ed.), *Public Expenditure: Effective Management and Control* (London: The Dryden Press).

Corry, D. (ed.) (1997), *Public Expenditure: Effective Management and Control* (London: The Dryden Press).

——(1997a), 'Introduction: Improving Public Expenditure', in D. Corry (ed.), *Public Expenditure: Effective Management and Control* (London: The Dryden Press).

——(1997b), 'The Role of the Public Sector and Public Expenditure', ch. 1 in D. Corry (ed.), *Public Expenditure: Effective Management and Control* (London: The Dryden Press).

——and Gray, S. (1997), 'Recent History of Public Spending', ch. 3 in D. Corry (ed.), *Public Expenditure: Effective Management and Control* (London: The Dryden Press).

Dilnot, A. (1997), 'Magic Required', *The Guardian*, 23 January.

Donaldson, C., Scott, T. and Wordsworth, S. (1996), *Can we Afford the NHS?* (London: Institute of Public Policy Research).

Glennerster, H. (1992), *Paying for Welfare: The 1990s* (London: Harvester Wheatsheaf).

Gray, A. G. (1997), 'Editorial: The Private Finance Initiative', *Public Money & Management*, 17(3), 3–4.

——and Jenkins, W. I. (1982), 'Policy Analysis in British Central Government: The Experience of PAR', *Public Administration* 60(4), 429–50.

——(1997), 'The Management of Central Government Services', in Jones, W. D. A., Gray, A. G., Kavanagh, D., Moran, M., Norton, P. and Seldon, A., *Politics UK* (3rd edn., Hemel Hempstead: Prentice Hall), ch. 20.

Hall, J., Preston, I., and Ridge, M. (1997), 'How Public Attitudes to Expenditure Differ', ch. 7 in D. Corry (ed.), *Public Expenditure: Effective Management and Control* (London: The Dryden Press).

Heald, D. (1997), 'Controlling Public Expenditure', ch. 9 in D. Corry (ed.), *Public Expenditure: Effective Management and Control* (London: The Dryden Press).

Heath, A., R. Jowell, and J. Curtice (1994), *Labour's Last Chance* (Aldershot: Dartmouth).

Heclo, H. and Wildavsky, A. (1974), *The Private Government of Public Money* (2nd edn., London: Macmillan).

Hills, J. (1993), *The Future of Welfare: The Guide to the Debate* (York: Joseph Rowntree Foundation).

——(1996), 'Tax Policies: Are There Still Choices?', in D. Halpen *et al.* (eds.), *Options for Britain* (Oxford: Nuffield College).

Hogwood, B. (1992), *Trends in British Public Policy* (Buckingham: Open University Press).

Hulme, G. (1997), 'How Public Expenditure Priorities are Determined', ch. 5 in D. Corry (ed.), *Public Expenditure: Effective Management and Control* (London: The Dryden Press).

Kellner, P. (1997), 'What does the Public Think?', ch. 6 in D. Corry (ed.), *Public Expenditure: Effective Management and Control* (London: The Dryden Press).

Lawson, N. (1992), *The View from No. 11* (London: Corgi Books).

Le Grand, J. (1996), 'The Thinkable', *Prospect*, July.

Likierman, A. (1988), *Public Expenditure: Who Really Controls It and How?* (London: Penguin Books).

Monck, N. (1997), 'The Need for a Strong Treasury, and How to Make it Work', ch. 16 in D. Corry (ed.), *Public Expenditure: Effective Management and Control* (London: The Dryden Press).

Mullard, M. (1993), *The Politics of Public Expenditure* (London: Routledge).

Office of National Statistics (ONS) (1996), *United Kingdom National Accounts* (London: HMSO).

Pallot, J. and Ball, I. (1997), 'What Difference Does Resource Accounting Make?', ch. 13 in D. Corry (ed.), *Public Expenditure: Effective Management and Control* (London: The Dryden Press).

Parry, R., Hood, C., and James, O. (1997), 'Reinventing the Treasury: Economic Rationalism or an Econocrat's Failure of Control', *Public Administration*, 75(3), 395–416.

Tanzi, V. and Schuknecht, I. (1995), *The Growth of Government and the Reform of the State in Industrial Countries* (International Monetary Fund (IMF) Working Paper, Washington DC: IMF).

Taylor-Gooby, P. (1995), 'Comfortable, Marginal and Excluded: Who should Pay Higher Taxes for a Better Welfare State?', in R. Jowell *et al.*, *British Social Attitudes* (Aldershot: Gower).

Thain, C. and Wright, M. (1992a), 'Planning and Controlling Public Expenditure in the UK, Part I: The Treasury's Public Expenditure Survey', *Public Administration*, 70(1), 3–24.

——(1992b), 'Planning and Controlling Public Expenditure in the UK, Part II: The Effects and Effectiveness of the Survey', *Public Administration*, 70(2), 193–224.

——(1995), *The Treasury and Whitehall: The Planning and Control of Public Expenditure 1976–93* (Oxford: Oxford University Press).

Treasury (1995), *Better Accounting for the Taxpayers Money: The Government's Proposals—Resource Accounting and Budgeting* (Cm. 2929, London: HMSO).

——(1996a), *The Budget 1996: In Brief* (London: HMSO).

——(1996b), *Public Expenditure Statistical Analysis 1997–8* (Cm. 3201, London: HMSO).

——(1998), *Public Expenditure: Statistical Analysis 1998–9* (Cm. 3901, London: Stationery Office Ltd.).

Watson, S. (1997), 'What should Count as Public Expenditure?', ch. 2 in D. Corry (ed.), *Public Expenditure: Effective Management and Control* (London: The Dryden Press).

Willman, J. (1998), *A Better State of Health: A Prescription for the NHS* (London: Profile).

Wright, M. (1995), 'Resource Accounting and Budgeting and the PES System', *Public Administration*, 73(4), 580–90.

Part Four
Delivering Welfare

11 Cash Transfers

Tony Fitzpatrick

Contents

Introduction: Cash, the Welfare State's Most Disputed Territory

The benefit system attracts perhaps more controversy than any other welfare institution. One of the reasons for this is obvious: as we enter the next millennium benefits will cost more than £100 billion per year, representing one-third of all government spending, or about 12 to 13 per cent of **Gross Domestic Product** (twice the amount spent on healthcare). On one level, then, we are required to analyse the economics of the subject, such as looking at issues relating to cost and redistribution. However, this kind of analysis does not by itself reveal why the subject of cash transfers attracts such controversy. The real reason lies in the essential difference between this system and the others which are dealt with throughout Section 4. With goods such as health and education we are dealing with services in kind. As will become clear in the following chapters, these services have generated a great deal of debate and disagreement. Nevertheless, when we examine services in *cash*, by comparison, we have to take account of a level of normative and prescriptive commentary which arguably exceeds that of any other welfare institution. There are several reasons for this greater intensity of debate, but the most significant concerns the fact that a cash transfer can be spent in whatever way the benefit claimant chooses: in other words, in-cash services offer a degree of freedom, and demand a degree of self-responsibility, which surpasses that of in-kind services.

The Origins of Modern Social Security Systems

When we discuss cash transfers we are referring to the benefits which are paid out by the system of social security, but the meaning of the term **social security** changes depending upon your location. Ginsburg (1992: 101–2) notes how in the United States a distinction is made between welfare and social security: the former refers to the means-tested assistance for the very poor which carries a considerable social stigma; the latter refers to the non-means-tested benefits which are more highly esteemed. In continental Europe, however, social security has a very broad meaning which may encompass healthcare and which sometimes even substitutes for terms such as the 'welfare state' and 'social welfare'. In Britain we tend to occupy a midway point between these two extremes. Therefore, we can define social security as referring to the benefits and cash transfers which are provided, financed, and regulated by the state for the purpose of income maintenance in particular and social welfare in general.

The history of social security as such can be traced back to the Germany of the 1870s. Rimlinger (1971) has observed how Chancellor Bismarck responded to the rising influence and importance of the industrial working class by trying to reduce the appeal of socialist ideas. He introduced various benefits inspired by the **social insurance principle** where people contribute to a collective 'pool' during their periods of economic activity and draw benefits from that pool when they become economically inactive. Social insurance benefits are therefore intended to provide the individual with a collective form of protection, and Bismarck imagined that such benefits would therefore make the working class less likely to challenge the existing order. Over the course of time, however, the German socialists came to adopt the social insurance principle as their own, as something which could empower the powerless. The social insurance principle has therefore been of central importance to twentieth-century welfare systems, because it has offered conservatives a means of defending the existing order and has offered socialists and reformist liberals a means of changing that order.

In Britain the reformist Liberal government of 1905–15 became converted to the principle of social insurance, partly under the influence of William Beveridge, and so laid the foundations for the benefit schemes of the inter-war years. As we shall see below, the insurance system offers various advantages and disadvantages. On the publication of the Beveridge Report (1942), however, at the height of the Second World War, it was the advantages which were stressed, setting the tone for the widespread post-war belief that the welfare state was a benign institution which was here to stay.

More recently a number of commentators have challenged this pro-Beveridgean consensus. From the right, those such as Corelli Barnett (1986) have condemned what they see as the anti-capitalistic elements of the post-war welfare state, and have insisted that Beveridge helped to send the British economy down a self-destructive road where the country's social expenditure would always outstrip its ability to finance such spending. Meanwhile, some on the Left have argued that Beveridge managed to *save* market capitalism from itself without threatening its basic functions. For instance, Cutler *et al.* (1986) have accused Beveridge of performing the Bismarckian trick of legitimating existing capitalist society.

Direct and Indirect Forms of Transfer

One of the earliest and still the most influential analyses of the post-war social security system was provided by Richard Titmuss (1958). According to Titmuss, the Beveridge system enshrined a 'social division of welfare' where we fail to appreciate the extent and the generosity of an indirect and hidden welfare state. Firstly, Titmuss distinguished between state welfare and **fiscal welfare**: the former refers to the attempt to improve well-being by delivering goods and resources *to* people; the latter refers to the well-being which derives from a deliberate failure to collect resources *from* people. Cash transfers may therefore be classified as state welfare, whereas tax reliefs and allowances can be classified as fiscal welfare. Titmuss's distinction is important because the former is defined as expenditure, and of course governments worry when expenditure begins to rise, while the latter is merely foregone revenue which tends not to attract the same kinds of attention and does not appear in the public accounts. In short, our reactions to state welfare are different from our reactions to fiscal welfare: we easily become obsessed with the costs and the 'burdens' of the poor because they are seen as draining the public purse, whereas the fiscal welfare state, from which the non-poor benefit, is conveniently overlooked. As Dee Cook's (1989) study has shown, this division is reflected in the different responses which society makes to benefit fraud and tax evasion, with the former receiving much more attention, disapproval, and government action than the latter.

Titmuss also drew attention to **occupational welfare,** or the advantages which people may derive from their employment, including subsidized canteens, housing, and gyms, company cars, life assurance policies, and private health insurance. These can be thought of as 'indirect wages' because they help to boost employees' disposable incomes, thus securing their loyalty, but are more tax-efficient for the employer than simply raising salaries. State and occupational provision now interact in ways which are more complex than when Titmuss was writing due to the introduction of such things as Statutory Sick Pay, which is administered by employers, and the growth of occupational pension schemes. For millions, the latter are gradually replacing the state pension as the main source of post-retirement income; these schemes are administered by employers, but they also relate to fiscal transfers, since people paying into a scheme pay fewer insurance contributions to the state, and benefit from certain tax advantages.

Titmuss argued that once all of these forms of provision are taken into account the transfer system is far less redistributive and egalitarian than it might at first appear. Later research by Julian Le Grand (1982) seemed to confirm Titmuss's worst expectations about the non-poor benefiting disproportionately from welfare provision, because according to Le Grand fundamental, class-based inequalities have remained more or less intact. However, Le Grand's findings have themselves been subject to criticism: Powell (1995), for instance, insists that the welfare state was always concerned with a more modest form of citizenship which did not necessarily require the massive transfer of wealth and income to the worst-off.

An important revision of Titmuss's categories has been provided by Hilary Rose (1981). According to Rose, although Titmuss showed far more sensitivity to the social position of women than most of his contemporaries, he too neglected what she called the 'sexual division of labour'. This sexual division refers to the fact that because it is women who still perform most of the unpaid work in the home, and because it is men who gain the highest wages, as well as the wage-related benefits which go with them, then women could be thought of as being net contributors to the well-being of men; that is, women help to boost men's disposable incomes. Indeed, the research of Jan Pahl (1989) demonstrated how the distribution of income within the household is skewed in favour of men. Women, for instance, are more likely to spend their money on their children, while men are more likely to spend their money on themselves.

Titmuss's distinctions have been further refined by Kirk Mann (1992), who insists that the social division of welfare exists because both policy-makers and the affluent have observed and exploited social divisions within the working class. He finds that the organized labour movement failed to address racial discrimination, and sometimes exacerbated it, ensuring that poverty would have a substantial racial dimension and so giving rise to what Mann calls the 'racial division of welfare', where black people are more likely than their white counterparts to experience the most draconian and least generous aspects of welfare provision. For some reason there has been far less research conducted into race and social security than into any other welfare institution (Amin and Oppenheim, 1992; Craig and Rai, 1996; Law, 1996); nevertheless, what research has been performed would seem to bear out Mann's thesis, as summarized in Box 11.1.

The distinctions drawn by Titmuss suggest that any discussion of cash transfers has to be receptive to the indirect forms of welfare which he and those following him have identified, as illustrated in Fig. 11.1.

Box 11.1 The racial division of welfare

- Black people are two to three times more likely than white people to experience poverty;
- Black people are twice as likely to be unemployed;
- Black people are more likely to be in low-waged jobs, with the average hourly pay of black employees being 92 per cent that of white employees;
- Black people are less likely to qualify for insurance benefits, due to factors such as low and irregular earnings, short working lives in the UK, and absences abroad;
- Black people are twice as likely to be dependent upon means-tested benefits and less likely to claim benefits to which they are entitled in the first place;
- There is evidence of direct and indirect discrimination within the benefit system, both in the conditions imposed on benefit eligibility, such as the fact that not relying upon public funds is a condition of immigration into the UK, and in the administration of transfers, such as the racism of many benefit officers;
- No recognition on the part either of the Department of Social Security or the Benefits Agency of the need for racial equality strategies and ethnic monitoring.

Throughout the rest of this chapter we shall be mainly discussing the direct cash transfers of the social security system, but we shall have to bear in mind the fact that the nature and significance of this system is fundamentally affected by the existence of these other forms of indirect transfer.

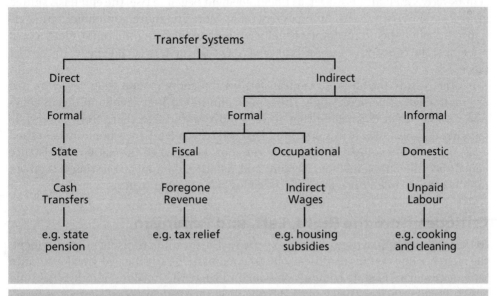

Figure 11.1 Transfer systems

The Objectives and Functions of Social Security

What are the objectives of social security? What should the objectives of social security be? The first question is empirical in that it deals with what *is* the case; the second is normative in that it deals with what *ought* to be the case. These questions are further complicated by research findings that show how cash transfers may function according to objectives which are implicit and covert.

The basic aim of Beveridge's (1942) system was the prevention of 'want', or poverty; and the insurance-based system that he recommended would do this, he believed, by guaranteeing a decent minimum income for those who either lost their earning capacity, due, say, to unemployment, sickness, and accident, or lacked an earning capacity, due, say, to retirement. However, as well as insuring the incomes of earners, the Beveridge system was concerned to meet the needs of households that depended upon them: in particular, the costs of a family and of important events that might affect it, like birth, death, and marriage. The prevention of poverty, argued Beveridge, would be brought about by reducing to a bare minimum the numbers of people relying upon means-tested assistance, and he anticipated that a scheme of compulsory social insurance, in the context of a full-employment economy, would be sufficient to achieve this. However, in addition to benefiting from a full-employment economy, there was also the expectation that social security would contribute to the creation of such an economy. Jose Harris (1997) records how enthusiastic Keynes was for Beveridge's proposals because he believed that they would assist in the management of the demand for goods and services and, consequently, for employment (see Chapter 5).

The politicians and policy-makers who followed Beveridge throughout the next few decades held to this expectation that an insurance model of social security would prevent poverty. Gradually, however, as unemployment began to rise, the emphasis shifted away from poverty prevention to poverty relief. More and more households either exhausted their rights to insurance benefits or, because of rising unemployment, could not amass the contribution records needed to entitle them to such benefits in the first place.

In other words, the aims of cash transfers became more modest than Beveridge had originally envisaged: increasingly, the explicit aim was to 'keep claimants' heads above water' rather than to imagine that social security could free them from poverty altogether. By the 1960s it was admitted that a large-scale reliance upon means-tested assistance was not going to disappear in the short term, when the National Assistance benefit became Supplementary Benefit; and reliance upon means testing has grown rapidly ever since (see the section on the categories of cash transfer).

Critiques from the Right, Left, and Feminism

As the post-war welfare state began to experience the pressures of rising unemployment, the right became ever more critical. Milton Friedman (1962) criticized social insurance schemes as forms of state compulsion which infringe the freedom of individuals and which are less efficient than a market-based insurance system. As an alternative he advocated that social security should become a purely means-tested system which aims to relieve the proven need of those whose income falls below a certain level. Also on the right, F. A. Hayek (1976: 87) argued that there was a need for an 'assured minimum income' to be provided outside of the market and he was not averse to the principle of social insurance (Hayek 1960: 285–97). However, he was opposed to the monopolization of such schemes by the state which, he thought, should provide only for those who experience absolute destitution.

By contrast, many on the left have interpreted social security not so much as a system for poverty prevention or relief as one of social control. Marxists have argued that cash transfers function according to wider socio-economic requirements: they help to camouflage the exploitative nature of capitalism, and they enforce the values and behavioural norms which enable capitalism to function more effectively. For instance, according to Norman Ginsburg (1979), the social security system can be charged with having three repressive functions. First, it depresses wage levels because benefits are so low that people are effectively forced into low-paid jobs. Second, it maintains the labour supply: in order to claim benefits people are expected to be capable of, and actively looking for, employment, so providing a cheap pool of labour where they can be hired and fired at will. Also, since eligibility for insurance benefits requires the kind of long-term employment histories which women are less likely to have, they are thrown back onto their domestic roles as carers, 'reproducing' the present and future generations of predominantly male workers. Finally, the system disciplines claimants and workers alike: the former are 'individualized' and denied a collective voice, the latter are effectively disciplined into their roles as employees because that, at least, is better than being a claimant. According to Marxism, then, because capitalism's ultimate objective is the exploitation and control of non-property-owners, the benefit system must be interpreted in the same light.

Some feminist theorists have argued, along similar lines, that social security reinforces gender divisions. Beveridge may have talked about equality between men and women, but this did not square with his assumption that most women would be dependent upon a husband so that their entitlements to benefits could reasonably be determined by the employment records of their spouses. What this has done, feminists argue, is to weaken women's independence within marriage and to restrict their freedom to leave an unwanted partnership. The research of Glendinning (1992) and Millar (1996; Glendinning and Millar 1992), for example, draws our attention to the ways in which social security makes women more vulnerable to poverty than men. Gender-based discrimination manifests itself particularly in the experience of lone mothers. Cary Oppenheim and Lisa Harker (1996: 36) have shown that 58 per cent of lone parents (90 per cent of whom are women) were in poverty in 1992/93.

Of the above critiques it was those from the political right which were to be the most influential in actual policy-making. By the 1980s the Thatcher government was explicit in its belief that social security should aim to relieve destitution rather than prevent poverty—a concept which they disputed anyway. The Green Paper of 1985, *Reform of Social Security* (Cmnd. 9517, 1985) set out three objectives for cash transfers: first, the system must meet genuine need; second, it should be consistent with the general aims of the economy; third, it must be simple to understand and administer. These aims were interpreted by the Thatcher government as requiring more means-testing, targeting, discretionary provision, and the enforcement of the work ethic, and these are the aims of the reforms which were subsequently introduced in 1988.

Overall, the experience of the last fifty years has shown that the basic and fairly simple aims of the Beveridge social security system need to be understood in the context of the more complicated realities that emerged in trying to fulfil those aims. Barr and Coulter (1990: 274–6) summarize the strategic aims of the social security system as: *income support*, which encompasses poverty relief, the protection of living standards, and redistributing an individual's income throughout the life-cycle; *the reduction of inequalities*, that is, class, racial, and sexual inequalities; and *social integration*, so that benefits permit social participation without stigma. However, they argue that these will only be achieved if a transfer system can adhere to certain operational principles: *efficiency*, so that incentives to work and save are not adversely affected; *equity*, which implies providing an adequate minimum income to those who need it the most; and *administrative simplicity*.

We can see, then, that the aims of the actual cash transfer system are complex and even contradictory. In some respects it seems to have a benign aspect, fulfilling basic needs and either preventing or relieving poverty; in others it may appear less than benign, controlling behaviour and reproducing underlying social disadvantages.

Universalism and Selectivism

A debate about the relative merits of universalism and selectivism has shadowed the last fifty years of social policy research, although many authors have come to dismiss it as redundant; for example, Spicker (1993: 94) insists that the 'debate is moribund and has been for years.'

The principle of universalism is relatively easy to define. According to Titmuss, the principle of universality refers to

the aim of making services available and accessible to the whole population in such ways as would not involve users in any humiliating loss of status, dignity or self-respect. There should be no sense of inferiority, pauperism, shame or stigma in the use of a publicly provided service; no attribution that one was being or becoming a 'public burden'. (Titmuss 1968: 129)

The difficulty arises when we attempt to contrast this principle with that of selectivism which, at its simplest, refers to non-universalist measures for directing the greatest amount of resources towards those whose needs are greatest. However, for some commentators selectivism implies means-testing whereas for others it does not.

David Collard (1971) is one of those who has insisted that selectivism is equivalent to means-testing. If a person is in need, he says, then according to the universalist principle this need is enough to trigger an entitlement to a welfare service regardless of that person's income. By extension, the selectivist provision of a welfare service requires not only evidence of need but also proof that the individual lacks a level of income sufficient to provide for that need themselves. In short, selectivism implies means-testing or charging at the point of use, whereas universalism implies the absence of means-testing and charging.

However, others have argued that this kind of interpretation is simplistic and that, although selectivism can imply means testing, the two are certainly not equivalent. For instance, Seldon and Gray (1967) maintain that it is the prior test of *need* which makes a service selectivist, even if that service is then provided free of charge and without reference to income. According to this interpretation, universalism refers to a blanket form of provision which is designed to cover everyone, whereas selectivism refers to the provision of those needs which universality fails to incorporate.

Why, then, do some regard the debate as 'moribund'? After all, the distinction does seem to apply to many benefits. Child Benefit is a universal benefit, not because it is provided to absolutely everyone—obviously, childless couples do not receive it—but because entitlement to it is triggered by the birth of a child. By contrast, Housing Benefit is selective because the amount which an individual does or does not receive depends ultimately on his or her level of earnings, savings, or other forms of income. However, the reason why some regard the debate as outdated is because many cash transfers are both universal and selective. Unemployment Benefit, for example, is universalist in that it is payable on an 'interruption of earnings', and yet it is also selectivist because it is payable only to those who have previously amassed the required level of contributions through wage-earning activity.

Commentators point out, therefore, that the defenders of one principle invariably make room for the other. Titmuss (1968), for instance, recognizes the need to combine both universalist and selectivist provision. The problem with universalist benefits is that they may be spread so thin across the entire population that the amount of cash they actually provide is too low to fulfil basic needs; the problem with selectivist benefits is that they may have a stigmatizing effect because those who receive them have been judged as incapable of looking after themselves. These points are pursued in the next two sections.

However, the debate has revived in recent years, although its terms have altered. First, this is because the Thatcher government of the 1980s placed a great emphasis upon means-testing, or 'targeting', forcing the defenders of universality to retreat. Second, the emerging literature of global social policy makes it clear that the debate is far from dead. Bob Deacon *et al.* (1997: 17–19) point out that the distinction between universalism and selectivism has reappeared on the supra-national stage, and continues to fuel a large amount of controversy and argument. With the death of the communist project, global capitalism is being challenged to secure universal legal, political, and social rights. However, given their commitment to free market forces, there is relatively little support for universal *social* rights within the chief supra-national agencies that currently oversee global capitalism: the International Monetary Fund, the World Bank, the Organization of Economic Co-operation and Development.

Fiona Williams (1992) is one of those who has taken the debate into new areas, making a connection between social welfare issues and post-modernism. The latter refers to the importance of difference and diversity when it comes to people's needs and identities. Post-modernism therefore relates back to an earlier, pre-Thatcher meaning of selectivism: non-stigmatized provision for those whose needs are not met by universal services. According to Williams, if selectivism is detached from the idea of means testing and targeting, then we can see how the principle of universalism can be combined with that of selectivism/diversity, the former being that which meets everyone's basic needs, the latter suggesting a subjective, bottom-up approach to diversity, where we are sensitive to issues of gender, race, age, disability, and sexuality in addition to class. Williams therefore places the old debate about universality and selectivity into a new context, and has inspired research into post-modern social policies.

Six Categories of Cash Transfer

The six types of benefit are illustrated in Table 11.1 and are explained in the following sub-sections.

Social Insurance Benefits

In order to qualify for insurance benefits in the event of unemployment, sickness, or retirement, employees must previously have paid a certain amount of contributions into a compulsory state-managed fund (Child Poverty Action Group [CPAG] 1997a). Such benefits, therefore, are 'earned entitlements' which go to workers rather than to citizens *per se*. In 1995/6 contributory benefits cost £42 billion. Social insurance was once the foundation of social security in the form of Unemployment Benefit and the State Pension. However, the former, which was previously payable for 12 months, has been incorporated within the Jobseeker's Allowance and is now payable for a maximum of 6

Type of transfer	Principles	Examples
Social insurance benefits	Contributory	Contribution-based Jobseeker's Allowance
		Retirement Pension
Social assistance benefits	Means-tested	Income-based Jobseeker's Allowance
		Housing Benefit
Categorical benefits	Non-contributory and non-means-tested	Child Benefit
		Disability Living Allowance
Discretionary benefits	Rules and judgements	Social Fund
Occupational benefits		
Statutory	Employment status	Statutory Sick Pay
Non-statutory	Employment record	Occupational Pension
Fiscal transfers	Tax concessions	Personal allowances
		Mortgage Interest Tax Relief
		Working Families Tax Credit

Table 11.1 Six categories of benefit

months, while the relative value of the latter has been steadily eroding, because since 1980 it has been uprated annually in line with inflation rather than earnings. Relative to average disposable incomes (or general living standards), the basic state pension is worth slightly less than it was in 1948 while the relative value of unemployment benefit is 72 per cent of its 1948 value (Hills 1997: 45, 51). At present the basic pension is worth approximately 15 per cent of average earnings, and if it continues to be indexed to inflation then by the year 2040 it will be worth just 7.5 per cent of average earnings. In 1996 ten and a half million people were receiving a retirement pension, at a total cost of £29.9 billion (DSS 1997).

Hills (1997: 44) identifies five problems with the insurance system:

- The link between contributions and entitlement is obscure.
- Beveridge assumed an economy of full-time full (male) employment, but women (and other disadvantaged groups) have always been less likely than men to accumulate the necessary contributions, and Beveridge's ideal economy no longer exists anyway.
- Insurance benefits have been so low that many more people than Beveridge anticipated have had to rely upon means-testing.
- The insurance fund is more symbolic than real, since contributions are really a *de facto* form of taxation.
- Widening the coverage of insurance benefits means that certain groups have to be 'credited' into the system, which undermines the contributory principle.

However, there are also four main advantages:

- There is both a real and a perceived link between contributions and entitlements, even if the link is somewhat obscure.
- Insurance contributions can be thought of as a 'hypothecated tax', that is, tax revenue which is earmarked for specific purposes.
- The take-up of insurance benefits is high because, as earned entitlements, there is far less stigma than with means-tested benefits.
- Social insurance contributes to the functioning of the labour market, by reducing the costs associated with risks, for example.

Social Assistance Benefits

These benefits provide a residual safety-net for those who do not qualify for insurance benefits, and they are paid out to those whose income and assets have fallen below a prescribed amount, the level of which depends upon family size and other circum- stances (CPAG 1997b). Entitlement to assistance benefits is basically worked out by calculating the amount the claimant is assumed to need, and the income, savings, or capital assets which the claimant has access to, and then subtracting the second from the first. The main assistance benefits are: Income-based Jobseeker's Allowance; Income Support (which used to be the main means-tested benefit, but which can now be claimed only by those who do not need to look for work in order to qualify for benefit); Housing Benefit; Family Credit; and Council Tax Benefit. In 1995/6 these social assistance benefits cost £28 billion. In 1948 2 per cent of the population were claiming National Assistance, whereas in 1995 10 per cent were claiming Income Support, with half of that increase having occurred since 1980. This means that approximately 22 per cent of the population were in households receiving either Income Support or Housing/Council Tax Benefit. Jonathan Bradshaw (1993) found that in 1992/3 Income Support provided both couples with two children and lone parents with only about three-quarters of the amount needed for even a 'low-cost' budget.

According to Spicker (1993: 141–2) the main arguments for means-tested assistance are that it enables resources to be targeted upon those most in need and that, because it is financed out of taxation, resources are 'vertically' redistributed from rich to poor (see the penultimate section of this chapter). However, there are also three problems with means-tested benefits: first, they create a poverty trap where any increase in earnings is largely cancelled out by the withdrawal of benefit (see the next section below); second, they do not reach everyone in need because the take-up of such benefits is typically lower than for insurance benefits (see 'Stigma, Take-Up, and Fraud' below); finally, because they are not provided on a universal basis they are complex and expensive to administer.

Categorical Benefits

These are paid to specific groups, or categories, so long as certain criteria are met. The most obvious example of a categorical benefit is Child Benefit, which is provided on behalf of all children under the age of 16. In 1996/7 13 million children received Child Benefit at a total cost of £6.7 billion (DSS 1997). Also, there exists a Disability Living Allowance, which goes to those who either find it difficult or impossible to walk, or who require constant supervision and care from another person. The Invalid Care Allowance is paid to the carers of those in receipt of the Disability Living Allowance (CPAG 1997a). In 1995/6 categorical benefits cost £16.4 billion.

Discretionary Benefits

This refers to the Social Fund which was created in 1988 and provides help for those on means-tested assistance who have urgent or exceptional needs (CPAG 1997b). Strictly speaking, the Social Fund is not entirely discretionary, since it contains a regulated element which provides a legal entitlement for maternity expenses, funeral expenses, and cold weather payments to those who satisfy the eligibility conditions. However, there is also a substantial discretionary element to the Fund: each benefit office has an annual budget which it must not exceed; there is no legal entitlement to payment, as DSS officials decide who receives money and who does not; most payments are in the form of loans which have to be repaid to the Benefits Agency; and there is no right of appeal to an independent tribunal.

Occupational Benefits

These benefits can be either statutory or non-statutory. The former refers to Statutory Sick Pay and Statutory Maternity Pay, both administered by employers (CPAG 1997a). The category of non-statutory occupational benefits now refers largely to the occupational pension schemes which are run by employers, and into which employees contribute a certain percentage of their earnings. Occupational pensions are an increasing source of income for elderly people as the value of the state pension dwindles.

Fiscal Transfers

Governments have always used tax allowances and reliefs, such as Mortgage Interest Tax Relief, for this purpose, but recent years have seen the increased co-ordination of fiscal transfers within the benefit system. In America the Earned Income Tax Credit boosts the income of low-earning families and is generally popular because it is regarded as a hand-up and a reward for work rather than a hand-out. In Britain, means-tested Family Credit is to be replaced with a Working Families Tax Credit (WFTC) in 1999. Details have yet to emerge at the time of writing, but according to Dilnot and Giles (1998: 27–31) there would be considerable problems in fully integrating the WFTC with the tax system, whilst if it were not to be fully integrated—if, for instance, it were to be nothing more than a 're-badging' of Family Credit—then there is a question-mark over whether it is worth the administrative upheaval of introducing the WFTC in the first place.

Unemployment and Poverty Traps

The **unemployment trap** and the **poverty trap** should not be confused, although they both occur because of the ways in which social security interacts with the labour market.

The phenomenon of the unemployment trap was noted by Beveridge in his 1942 Report:

it is dangerous to allow benefit during unemployment or disability to equal or exceed earnings during work.... It has been experienced in an appreciable number of cases under unemployment benefit and unemployment assistance in the past. The maintenance of employment ... will be impossible without greater fluidity of labour ... than has been achieved in the past. To secure this the gap between income during earning and during interruption of earning should be as large as possible for every man. (Beveridge 1942: paras. 411–12)

Michael Hill (1990: 104–5) describes the unemployment trap as the disadvantage which arises when a person's income in employment is not significantly greater than, and may even be less than, their income when on benefit. This is known as a narrow **replacement ratio** and describes the situation where benefits establish a 'wages' floor' below which paid work is either not financially worthwhile or only marginally so. A narrow gap between earnings and non-earnings provides the unemployed claimant with a significant disincentive against looking for a job. We can therefore define the unemployment trap as the situation where a move into paid employment leads to no significant increase in overall income due to a narrow replacement ratio, that is, when there is a narrow gap between earnings and benefits.

In his history of the period Hill notes how the unemployment trap became of increasing concern to policy-makers in the 1960s. The National Assistance scheme had a provision known as the 'wage stop' to prevent individuals from receiving benefits which were more generous than the wages they were likely to earn when in work: the gap between earnings and non-earnings was maintained by reducing benefits under certain circumstances. However, by the 1960s policy-makers preferred to pursue an alternative route, introducing benefits which people could receive whilst in employment in order to tackle the disincentive effect of the unemployment trap. This kind of approach involves a system of earnings' disregards, where a person can earn a certain amount without it affecting their benefit entitlement, thus boosting their overall income. It was decided to introduce a scheme of income-tested rent and rate rebates for the lower-paid and Family Income Supplement (FIS) for families with children. However, while this approach went some way to tackling the unemployment trap, it had the additional effect of creating a poverty trap. This refers to the situation faced by the low-paid worker claiming in-work benefits: as their earnings increase that person not only has to pay tax and insurance contributions but also experiences a withdrawal of their benefits. For instance, an increase of £1 in earnings might lead to £0.80 of that £1 being effectively taken away again due to taxation and benefit withdrawal; this would imply a 'marginal tax rate' (the amount of income lost for every extra pound earned) of 80 per cent. We can therefore define the poverty trap as the situation where an increase in earnings leads to no significant increase in overall income, due to the combined effect of taxes and transfers.

This poverty trap was first described by Frank Field and David Piachaud, and received an extended analysis by Alan Deacon and Jonathan Bradshaw (1983). They found that in the early 1980s the low-paid could face marginal tax rates of more than 100 per cent so that an increase of earnings could actually leave people worse off than before. Therefore, although those on low wages had slightly higher incomes than they would otherwise have had on benefits alone, they were effectively trapped at this level of income unless their wages rose significantly. The social security reforms of the 1980s were partly designed to address the poverty trap: Housing Benefit was introduced in 1982, and Family Credit replaced FIS in 1988. The explicit intention of the Conservative government was to improve the incentives of the low paid (without the affluent having to pay more tax), but to what extent has this happened?

According to the research of David Piachaud (1997), the incentives for large numbers of people are now actually worse than they were in 1979. The main reason for this is the increased reliance upon Income Support which, as we saw in the last section, has risen dramatically since 1980. The problem with marginal tax rates reaching 100 per cent or more *has* been dealt with: in 1985, 70,000 people faced rates of 100 per cent plus, whereas by 1995/6 this had fallen to 10,000. However, the numbers facing rates of 60 per cent or more has risen from 450,000 to 630,000 over the same period, and the numbers facing rates of 80 per cent or more has risen from 290,000 to 420,000. Some, like Frank Field (1995), have therefore identified a new 'poverty plateau', where families can remain on low incomes for an extremely long time.

Piachaud illustrates this disincentive effect using the example of a married couple with two children who live in council housing. In April 1995 gross earnings of £50 per week would have left this family with a net income of £127 once transfers had been taken into account; however, if their **gross earnings** were to rise to £210 per week then, because of the combined effects of taxation and benefit withdrawal, their net income would only be £137, so they would just be £10 better off than previously! In short, they would face a marginal tax rate of 94 per cent; and in 1995 one-quarter of all employees were earning less than £210 per week. Using similar examples, the Commission on

Social Justice (1994) found that such a family would have to be earning a gross of approximately £270 per week, or £14,000 per year, in order to be free of the poverty plateau.

Pete Alcock (1997: 229) points out that this increase in means-testing has also introduced another form of trap: a savings trap. Because most means-tests now take into account both the capital holdings of claimants and the interest that collects on savings (above a specific amount), then those with savings can either lose their entitlement to means-tested support altogether or have their level of benefit reduced. This savings trap particularly affects those pensioners who are on low incomes but who have saved or invested money 'for a rainy day'.

As things stand at present, the Labour government is keen on introducing a WFTC (as discussed in the previous section), one of the reasons being that it would supposedly enable people to take up low-paid jobs more effectively than the present system, with its heavy reliance upon means-testing. We shall have to wait and see, but the evidence from those countries which already have a tax credit system is not encouraging. According to the Joseph Rowntree Foundation (1998), Canadian tax credits were abandoned when it was found that the system reduced the incentive to work in twice as many cases as it improved them. Tax credits were also found to have a disincentive effect in both Australia and the USA. It is unlikely, therefore, that the problems associated with the unemployment and poverty traps are going to be solved overnight.

Stigma, Take-Up, and Fraud

Stigma implies the possession of a low status in the eyes of society: to occupy, and to be seen to occupy, an inferior social rank. According to Paul Spicker (1984) five forms of stigma can be identified: first, the stigma engendered by poverty and social exclusion; second, that which a physical disability or a disease can lead to; third, there are mental stigmas associated with such matters as mental illnesses and drug addictions; fourth, there are moral stigmas which certain actions or patterns of behaviour can give rise to, such as criminal behaviour. Finally, there is the stigma which dependency upon welfare services can create.

An important question to ask is why this final form of stigma has continued to exist. Is it due to a failure of the welfare state? As the quotation from Titmuss on page 260 suggests, he believed that the universalization of social rights would eliminate the sense of inferiority which accompanied, and was intended to accompany, the use of public services under the Poor Law. People would be able to use and to claim welfare services as of right, without experiencing shame or dishonour. On this reading, the continuance of stigma might be attributed to the failure of modern policy-making. However, such universalism was not the only objective of state welfare. For T. H. Marshall (1981) one of the aims of the welfare state should be to eliminate stigma without thereby eliminating social inequality *per se*: to create a society of equal citizens who could possess unequal amounts of wealth and income. Yet could this maintenance of social inequality undermine attempts to eliminate stigma? If inequality is needed to make people respond to incentives, then perhaps those who do not respond properly may be legitimately stigmatized. Such was the conclusion of Beveridge himself:

Assistance . . . must be felt to be something less desirable than insurance benefit; otherwise the insured persons get nothing for their contributions. Assistance therefore will be given always subject to proof of needs and examination of means; it will be subject also to any conditions as to behaviour which may seem likely to hasten the restoration of earning capacity. (Beveridge 1942: para. 369)

So, although Beveridge desired the gradual reduction of means-testing, he believed that it must always be 'felt to be something less than desirable'. These arguments suggest, therefore, that some of the architects of state welfare effectively saw a valuable and continued role for stigma in maintaining people's incentives to better themselves.

One way or another, stigma has always been most closely associated with cash transfers. The association is weakest in the case of insurance benefits, since these are defined as earned entitlements, and strongest in the case of assistance benefits. Carol Walker (1993: 146–68) notes how, as Beveridge's goal of reducing means-testing has been abandoned, successive governments have tried to make assistance benefits look more attractive, while those who depend upon them have been simultaneously demonized as scroungers. She argues that this 'mixed message' has led to a poor record on the **take-up** of assistance benefits, with significantly fewer people applying for them than are actually entitled. There are undoubtedly other factors at work with the non-take-up of benefits, such as a general lack of knowledge about entitlements, or a wariness at the complexity of the benefit system; but Walker insists that the take-up of assistance benefits is lower than it should be largely because potential claimants can see the stigmatizing effects. These effects can be difficult to quantify, however. For instance, the Social Security Advisory Committee (1997: 7) notes that 70 per cent of those who apply to the Social Fund are successful in their application, but this figure takes no account of those who do not apply in the first place for what is the most discretionary and stigmatizing form of cash transfer.

According to the findings of the Department of Social Security (1997) the most recent figures for the take-up of means-tested benefits are shown in Box 11.2.

By and large, governments tend to be more concerned with the amount of benefit being defrauded than they are with the amount going unclaimed. There are two aspects to this issue: the economic and the moral. First, how much is being defrauded? Claim and counter-claim is made in answer to this question. For instance, in 1996 the Social Security Select Committee (1996: paras. 46–51) estimated that around £1 billion a year was being lost as a result of Housing Benefit fraud, but that the figure could be as high as £2 billion. This figure of £2 billion was widely publicized in the press and media at the time, but it is one for which the government itself claimed there was 'no clear evidence' (DSS 1996: para. 4). However, even the lower figure would be a justifiable cause for alarm; and yet researchers cast doubt on this kind of official estimate. Roy Sainsbury (1998) points out that the estimates of how much is being defrauded correspond closely to the amount of fraudulent activity which the Benefits Agency claims to have terminated. Is this because the Agency is remarkably efficient, or is it because estimates regarding fraudulent activity and detection are systematically over-estimated in an institution where performance-related pay is so important? Since the National Audit Office found

---

Box 11.2 The take-up of benefits

- In 1995/6 a total of somewhere between £2.2 billion and £3.5 billion of income-related benefits went unclaimed. The take-up of these benefits was between 78 and 85 per cent, so that between 2.9 million and 4.5 million people were not claiming benefits to which they were entitled.

- The take-up of Housing Benefit was between 89 and 94 per cent, with between £410 million and £760 million going unclaimed.

- The take-up of Income Support was between 76 and 82 per cent, so that between 1.17 million and 1.68 million people were not claiming that to which they were entitled, with between £1.2 billion and £1.8 billion going unclaimed.

- The take-up of Council Tax Benefit was between 74 and 82 per cent, with between £370 million and £620 million going unclaimed.

- The take-up of Family Credit was about 70 per cent, with £300 million going unclaimed and 240,000 people not claiming although they were entitled to do so.

---

that local authorities had over-estimated the amount of fraud of Housing Benefit and Council Tax Benefit by 30 per cent, Sainsbury insists that it is 'difficult to lend any credence at all to official measures'.

Second, why do people engage in fraud? The popular image of the defrauder is of a selfish, criminally motivated individual stealing resources from those who genuinely need them. Research by Hartley Dean and Margaret Melrose (1996, 1997), however, found that this image bears little correspondence to reality. People were often motivated out of sheer desperation, genuine confusion (about what they were and were not entitled to), a sense that they had been betrayed by the welfare state, or economic necessity in response to a system which seemed to want to keep them in poverty. Equally, the government could be said to derive an advantage from fraud: because fraud assists the operation of a flexible, low-wage economy, because people who work unofficially in the 'informal' economy are contributing to national output, and, finally, because politicians can make political capital out of condemning fraud at periodic intervals.

Dependency Culture and the Underclass

The debate concerning the underclass is a very old one which continually reappears in new guises. Lydia Morris (1994: 10–32) traces its roots from the nineteenth century, finding a succession of theorists expressing concern about the undeserving poor who were believed to threaten the stability and prosperity of society. For Malthus they were the 'redundant population'; for Marx they were the semi-criminal lumpenproletariat; for Mayhew, Booth, and Stedman-Jones they were the residuum of decent society. Therefore, Morris argues that when we discuss the underclass we are merely continuing a debate which has lasted on and off for two centuries.

In our day the debate has been revived on two separate occasions. In the America of the 1960s Oscar Lewis (1968) published the findings of his research into poor Puerto Rican families. Lewis had concluded that these families had successfully adapted to their poverty and deprived social environments by repressing their expectations of better times to come, by abandoning any hope of secure, well-paid employment, and by developing a culture which enabled them to cope with being poor in an affluent society. Lewis had merely set out to describe what he called a 'culture of poverty', but his thesis was picked up by those who were critical of the recent expansion of social security and welfare programmes. Some of these criticisms focused upon the poor as victims of a welfare system which trapped them in poverty, while others identified the poor as responsible for their own social conditions due to a failure of moral character on their part. Daniel Moynihan (1965: 5), for instance, attributed poverty amongst black Americans to the 'disintegration of the negro family'. From a Marxist perspective, Piven and Cloward (1971) interpreted these debates as a camouflage for America's unwillingness to abolish poverty and as an attempt further to regulate the poor.

Concerns about the underclass and what came to be called the 'culture of dependency' revived in the early 1980s, and flourished in a fertile political climate with the Reagan administration in America and the Thatcher government in Britain. The right-wing commentator, Charles Murray (1984), alleged that over-generous benefits in America had led to the emergence of a significant underclass of several million people. By encouraging neither marriage nor independence within the labour market, the American equivalent of assistance benefits had created a generation of unemployed and unemployable black youths, as well as a generation of lone mothers who expected to be 'married to the state'. Murray's empirical research was subsequently challenged by many, but the gist of his argument proved to be highly influential. Lawrence Mead (1986) argued that in the future the welfare state in general and the benefit system in particular would have to stress the obligations rather than the rights of citizenship. These kinds of argument have given a theoretical justification for the expansion of **workfare** programmes in the USA, where claimants are compelled to work or train in return for their benefits.

Murray (1990) later applied his ideas to the British context and found that here, too, a dependent underclass was in the process of developing as a result of increased illegitimacy, single parenthood, and youth unemployment. For those such as Murray, therefore, the term 'underclass' does not refer to an extreme of poverty, that is, the poorest of the poor, but to a different *type* of poverty: the value-system (the culture) possessed by those who expect society and the state to do everything for them without having to contribute anything in return. Murray's thesis has come to wield a certain amount of influence in this country, certainly on the right wing, but also on the left: Dennis and Erdos (1992) argued that the benefit system had helped to break up the traditional family with catastrophic social effects. Frank Field (1989) was initially sceptical regarding Murray's account of the dependent underclass, arguing that he had ignored 'structural' factors beyond individual control. More recently, however, Field has combined a critical analysis of means-testing with an interpretation which sees human nature as inherently selfish and as something which post-war welfare provision has pandered to:

Means tests sanction inaction, non-saving and lying. These powerful messages, relayed through the system which gives basic income support to the poorest, play a part in cutting the poorest off from mainstream Britain. (Field 1996: 17)

Field's recommendations for a new 'socially authoritarian' benefit system have wielded some influence on the Labour government elected in 1997.

The research of Dean and Taylor-Gooby (1992) still represents the most extended analysis of these issues. They conclude that terms such as 'underclass' and 'dependency culture' do not reflect objective phenomena out there in the real world; rather, they are 'mythical constructions' which indicate a widespread tendency to blame the victims for the very disadvantages (unemployment, social exclusion) which have been perpetrated against them. Claimants are not culturally separate from 'normal' society: if anything, claimants cope with their situation by adopting and internalizing what they see as the norms and values of non-claimants—a characteristic which Dean and Melrose (1997) refer to as 'conservative resistance'. Edwards and Duncan (1997) found that lone mothers who rely upon state benefits, a group often vilified as irresponsible, hold views broadly in line with dominant British norms about motherhood. According to Dean and Taylor-Gooby, far from requiring additional motivation to work, claimants might actually have unreal expectations about what the job market can deliver. What the underclass debate does is to stigmatize state dependency in order to make dependency upon employers/wages and upon the traditional family look natural, moral, and inevitable. As a consequence, even more pressures are now being loaded upon benefit recipients than in the past. The underclass debate shows no signs of abating, however. In fact, it may well have entered popular consciousness to an extent which is difficult to dislodge and could have become a self-fulfilling prophecy. Nick Davies has argued from the left that

When the government cut into the weekly income of the poorest, when they ensured that there was nothing there for them to fall back on in the event of a crisis, they guaranteed . . . the creation of an alternative economy, based on crime and drugs and prostitution. (Davies 1997: 293)

Set against this view, however, is the continued insistence of conservatives such as Lawrence Mead (1997) that social problems are due to a decay of values and of morally correct behaviour, thereby justifying benefit reform which is based upon obligations, that is, workfare, rather than rights and entitlements.

Redistributive Effects of Taxes and Transfers

There are basically two main forms of redistribution: vertical and life-cycle. **Vertical redistribution** implies redistribution from net losers to net gainers. Assistance benefits, for instance, are intended to redistribute from high-income to low-income groups. **Life-cycle redistribution** implies the redistribution of resources from one part of a person's life-cycle to another: most people of working age pay taxes and contributions to fund the services, such as pensions, which they expect to receive during the non-working periods of their lives.

A Snapshot of Redistribution

What happens if we look at the figures on taxes and transfers for any one year? Fig. 11.2 has been adapted from John Hills (1997: 15) and shows the distribution of cash benefits amongst households (and after allowing for the greater needs of bigger households) grouped in deciles by **final income,** once transfers and income tax have been taken into account.

Households in the bottom half of the income distribution receive 2.4 times as much from cash benefits as those in the top half. It can be seen that the poorest decile, or the poorest tenth, receives four times as much as the richest decile, and, because the poorest derive less of their income from the market, cash transfers make up 69 per cent of their gross income whereas they account for only 2 per cent of the gross income of the richest. Hills notes that means-tested benefits are most concentrated on the poorest, but that even universal benefits, like the basic state pension, account for a high proportion of the income of the poorest households. In addition, the reason why the poorest decile receives less than the next two groups is either because they are not entitled to benefits or because they fail to claim those to which they are entitled.

Direct income tax takes a greater proportion of higher incomes than of lower ones, but once all taxes, including indirect ones like VAT, are taken into account, then the effects of taxation are evened out. In fact, those in the poorest decile actually pay out more of their gross income in the form of taxes than any of the other nine income groups (Hills 1997: 85). Fig. 11.3, which has been adapted from Hills (1997: 17), compares original incomes (before taxes and transfers have been taken into account) with final incomes (after taxes and transfers).

Overall, it can be seen that the bottom five deciles are net gainers from the tax and transfer system, whilst the top five are net losers. However, this does not necessarily

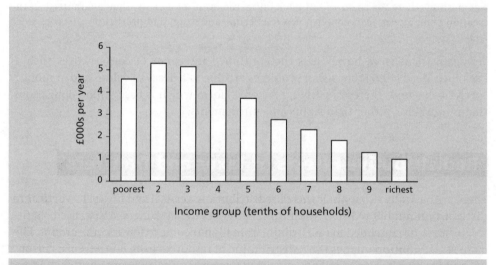

Figure 11.2 Average value of cash benefits received by households, 1995–6
Source: adapted from Hills (1997: 15).

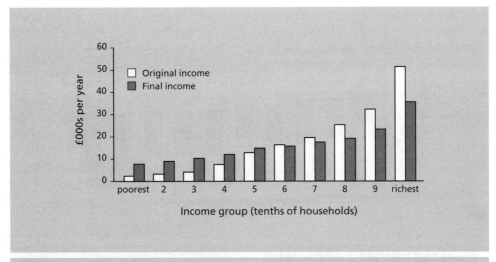

Figure 11.3 Household incomes: effects of taxes and transfers, 1995–6
Source: adapted from Hills (1997: 17).

mean that vertical redistribution has taken place, that is, that what the poorest receive has been transferred from the richest, since it might well be that people in the bottom five deciles are basically funding their own benefits:

Even if the poor in any given year benefit from the welfare state while the rich pay for it, there might still be no redistribution at all between different people, when everything is totalled over complete lifetimes. (Hills 1997: 19)

Life-Cycle Redistribution

This form of redistribution is extremely difficult to measure, but Hills's research reveals that the combined effect of taxes and transfers does redistribute income from those parts of our lives when our earning capacity is greatest (early twenties to late fifties) to those when it is weakest. Basically, cash transfers and direct taxes reduce incomes during the former period, but boost them during retirement. This improvement is especially pronounced once services in kind are also taken into account. Therefore, living standards across the life-cycle are 'smoothed out': 'People "pay into" the system at times in their lives when incomes are relatively high, but "draw out" from it when they are relatively low' (Hills 1997: 19). Now, in order to compare vertical with life-cycle redistribution we have to look at the total redistribution between the lifetime rich and the lifetime poor. In Fig. 11.4, adapted from Hills (1997: 20), those with the lowest average lifetime living standards, the 'lifetime poorest', are represented on the left with the 'lifetime richest' on the right.

Each bar shows the value of the benefits (health and education are included) which each decile derives from public provision, but is split between the amount (the self-financed benefits) which each income group effectively finances for itself through the taxes which it pays, and the amount (net lifetime benefits) which it 'receives' from the

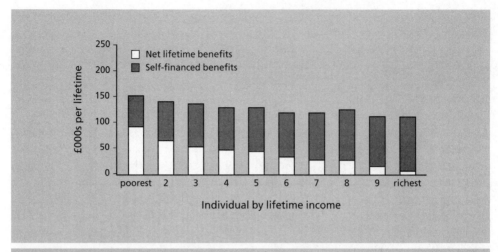

Figure 11.4 Lifetime benefits 1991

Source: adapted from Hills (1997: 20).

taxes paid by others. What Fig. 11.4 shows is that the distribution of gross benefits is very flat; the average person, whatever their income, can expect to receive gross benefits over their lifetime of approximately £133,000 (at 1991 prices). The difference is in the distribution of self-financed benefits, with those in the bottom deciles less likely than those in the top to pay for their own benefits out of their own taxes. Hills concludes as follows:

> The system does therefore redistribute quite successfully from 'lifetime rich' to 'lifetime poor'. However . . . *most* benefits are self-financed over people's lifetimes, rather than being paid for by others. Of the £133,000 average gross lifetime benefits from the system, an average of £98,000 is self-financed. Nearly three-quarters of what the welfare state does looked at this way is a 'savings bank'; only a quarter is 'Robin Hood' redistribution between different people. (Hills 1997: 19)

In other words, when we look at the total amount of redistribution effected by the welfare state, 75 per cent is of the life-cycle form and 25 per cent is vertical, and Hills's research would suggest that this is also representative of the cash transfers part of the welfare state. Hills also finds that most of those who are in the poorest 20 per cent of society remain there for extended periods of time (Browne, 1998). In short, the cash transfer system contributes to the immobility of the poor, providing a safety-net which is also something of a spider's web, and trapping those whom it is designed to help.

European and Global Dimensions

A useful overview of the changes in European cash transfer systems between 1985 and 1995 has been provided by Mary Daly (1997). In terms of social security expenditure, absolute cutbacks occurred in Belgium and Ireland, spending held steady in France,

Greece, Luxembourg, and the Netherlands, whilst there was a considerable rise in spending in Denmark, Finland, Italy, Portugal, Spain, Sweden, and the UK. For the most part these increases in benefit expenditure were due to growth in unemployment and to an ageing population rather than to the expansion of benefit programmes, although some expansion did occur in Southern Europe.

Daly (1997: 133) identifies four trends in European reform over this period: a restriction in the access to benefit through a tightening-up of eligibility criteria; the increased use of means-testing; movement towards privatization; and a shift towards more active employment measures where benefits are closely tied to things such as job search and training. Overall, European countries have tried to reduce the costs of transfers to employers, to emphasize taxation rather than contributions as the source of funding and to alter the division of responsibility for funding between national, regional, and local levels.

Daly discusses three areas where reform is tending to occur: pensions, unemployment benefits, and benefits related to caring. She detects something of a convergence in European pension systems in recent years. First, there has generally been a lengthening in the period which people have to spend in employment: the statutory age of retirement is being, or has been, raised in Austria, Germany, Greece, Italy, Portugal, and Britain, whilst the period during which contributions have to be paid in order to qualify for a state pension has been lengthened in France and Spain. In fact, whereas in 1960 13 years was the average contribution period, by 1985 this had risen to 26 years, and today the period runs from a minimum of 35 years in Spain and Greece to a maximum of 48 years in Ireland. Second, there has been an increased use of means-testing and earnings-testing in addition to changes in the rules which mean that the pension levels are now more likely to be calculated on the basis of a person's entire working-life rather than the years in which earnings, and therefore contributions, were highest. Daly (1997: 134–6) concludes that people now have to work longer in order to qualify for less generous pensions, although the basic structure of pension systems remains largely unchanged.

Unemployment benefits have been reformed to more closely reflect labour market incentives and disincentives. Eligibility rules have been made more restrictive in many countries, and the level of benefits made less generous in Austria, Finland, France, Germany, Spain, and Sweden; waiting periods have been introduced or lengthened in Sweden and Belgium; there has been a tightening of the rules about looking for and accepting employment in Finland and Britain; the required period of labour market participation has been lengthened in the Netherlands and Britain. In general, therefore, unemployment benefits have been made less generous and more stringent in the face of rising unemployment although, as with pensions, the basic structure of provision remains intact (Daly 1997: 136–8).

Finally, with benefits associated with caring for children, the most significant development has been in the area of parental leave, with greater subsidization forthcoming from the state. Only in Ireland, Spain, and Britain were there no new policy developments. By 1995 10 out of 16 European nations were prepared to make payments towards parental caring. There has also been a trend towards state subsidization of private and personal care for the elderly, the ill, and the disabled. New cash benefits were

introduced in Austria, Denmark, Finland, Germany, Ireland, and Luxembourg, with
Belgium, Italy, Sweden, and Britain all extending existing provision (Daly 1997: 140–2).

The one area which Daly neglects is that of social assistance, but extensive research
across all countries belonging to the Organization for Economic Co-operation and
Development has been provided by Ian Gough *et al.* (1997). Table 11.2, adapted from
Gough *et al.* (1997: 24–7), provides a summary of their findings.

We can see from the first three columns that assistance benefits are of most importance in Australia, Canada, Ireland, New Zealand, the UK, and the USA: the countries
which can be termed 'neo-liberal' (see Chapters 1 and 2). In most of these countries the
group which is largely dependent upon assistance is that of elderly people, whereas in
other countries they are largely catered for through insurance benefits. Lone parents
also make great demands on these nations' assistance schemes, whereas elsewhere

	Social Assistance recipients as % of population (1992)	Social Assistance expenditure as % of GDP (1992)	Social Assistance expenditure as % of social security expenditure (1992)	Change in Social Assistance recipients as % of population (1980–92)	Change in expenditure on Social Assistance as % of GDP (1980–92)
Australia	17.8	6.8	90.3	4.2	1.4
Austria	4.8	1.3	6.7	–0.4	0.3
Belgium	3.6	0.7	3.0	1.7	0.2
Canada	15.1	2.5	18.9	4.1	0.9
Denmark	8.3	1.4	7.8	N/A	N/A
Finland	9.2	0.4	N/A	5.7	0.3
France	2.3	1.8	6.4	1.5	0.2
Germany	6.8	1.6	11.9	2.9	0.6
Greece	0.7	0.1	N/A	N/A	0.0
Iceland	3.7	0.2	1.2	N/A	N/A
Ireland	12.4	5.1	41.2	3.7	2.2
Italy	N/A	1.5	9.1	1.2	0.4
Japan	0.7	0.3	3.7	–0.5	–0.1
Luxembourg	2.7	0.4	1.4	N/A	N/A
Netherlands	N/A	2.2	10.9	1.1	0.5
New Zealand	25.0	13.0	100.0	–5.7	4.4
Norway	4.0	0.7	4.8	2.5	0.5
Portugal	2.1	0.4	3.8	1.2	0.2
Spain	2.7	1.2	8.4	N/A	1.0
Sweden	6.8	0.5	6.7	2.7	0.3
Switzerland	2.3	0.8	1.8	0.5	–0.1
Turkey	N/A	0.5	N/A	N/A	N/A
UK	15.3	6.4	33.0	6.7	1.2
USA	17.5	1.3	39.8	1.0	0.2

**Table 11.2 An international comparison of the costs and incidence of
social assistance benefits**

Source: Gough *et al.* (1997: 24–7).

there are either fewer lone parents or they have greater entitlements to non-assistance benefits. Although information is lacking, unemployment has led to a greater demand for assistance benefits, and women tend to be more dependent upon these benefits than men except in the Nordic countries. As Table 11.2 shows, assistance benefits are of least importance in the Benelux countries, Greece, Iceland, Japan, Portugal, and Turkey.

In columns 4 and 5 we can see that in Australia, Canada, Finland, Ireland, and the UK the *numbers* of recipients has risen significantly, and that in Australia, Canada, Ireland, New Zealand, Spain, and the UK *spending* on assistance benefits has risen considerably. Gough *et al.* (1997: 33) find that, after housing costs, the most generous benefits are in Austria, Italy, Luxembourg, the Netherlands, the Nordic countries, and Switzerland; the least generous are in the USA (with the exception of New York state) and southern Europe. Overall, and with one or two exceptions, there has been an increased emphasis given to assistance schemes within the social security systems of the above countries.

Finally, how might these changes have affected the distribution of income? Research shows that in the mid-1980s income inequality across a range of countries was as represented in Fig. 11.5, adapted from Hills (1995: 64).

The **Gini Coefficient** is a way of measuring income inequality: basically, the closer a country is to zero then the more equal is the distribution of its income across the population. In Fig. 11.5, therefore, Finland is the most egalitarian country and the USA the least.

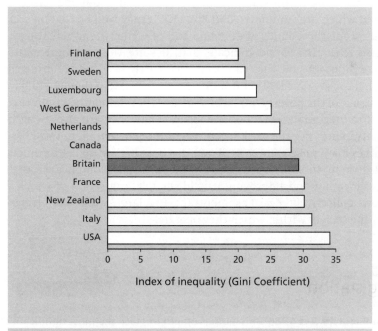

Figure 11.5 Income inequality in the mid-1980s
Source: adapted from Hills (1995: 64).

Since the mid-1980s inequality has actually fallen in Finland, Ireland, Italy, Portugal, and Spain; it has been rising slowly in Belgium, France, (West) Germany, Japan, and the USA, and has risen most significantly in Australia, Britain, the Netherlands, New Zealand, Norway, and Sweden. Indeed, Hills (1995: 65) reports that because income inequality rose so rapidly in Britain between 1977 and 1990, a pace matched only by New Zealand between 1985 and 1989, it is now one of the most unequal countries in the developed world. In terms of cash transfers, taxes, and their relation to the labour market Hills (1995: 72) draws five conclusions about the period from the mid-1980s to the early 1990s:

- In France and Canada the distribution of disposable incomes remained stable due to the changes in taxes and transfers cancelling out a rise in labour-market inequality.
- In Australia and Germany taxes and transfers slowed the effects of growing market inequalities.
- In the UK and Sweden taxes and transfers failed to slow the growth of market inequalities.
- In the Netherlands, changes in taxes and transfers contributed to a rise in the inequality of disposable incomes.
- In the USA, taxes and transfers accelerated the widening inequalities of market incomes.

Conclusion

The cash transfer system embodies a number of contradictions and tensions, the most important of which are summarized in Box 11.3. It may well be that no social security system can escape these kinds of dilemma and that they are inherent features of any system. If so then this would indicate that, despite the technical nature of these tensions, decisions on how they can be at least partly resolved are primarily political and ethical. If society decides that it wants a targeted system then it will have to accept the continuance of the poverty trap, which means that claimants should be condemned and subject to draconian social policies far less than they are at present. If, however, society wants to improve the work incentives of the poorest, then it will have to accept that resources may consequently 'spill over' to those higher up the income ladder who do not need them. In short, as technically complex and complicated as the transfer system is, reforming and improving it is ultimately a question of which values and principles we collectively regard as important. To a large extent, cash transfers mirror and reflect the society within which they operate.

Key Legislation

The Social Security Act 1986 This legislation put in place the most significant social security reforms of the 1980s and represented the biggest upheaval in the system since the Second World War. The principles behind the Act were set out in the White Paper, Cmnd. 9517 (1985), Reform of Social Security.

Box 11.3 Tensions within the transfer system

- Targeting *versus* incentives
  There is a need to both target resources on the poorest whilst maintaining their incentive to work. The problem is that if resources are to be targeted then this implies withdrawing benefits quickly as the incomes of the poorest begin to rise; yet if benefits are withdrawn too quickly then people are caught in a poverty trap and their incentive to earn higher wages is consequently reduced. But if, to maintain incentives, benefits are withdrawn less rapidly as incomes rise then this might imply providing benefits to those who do not, strictly speaking, need them and so make the system less targeted than it might be otherwise.

- Redistributive *versus* solidaristic aims
  As the system becomes more vertically redistributive some of the more affluent members of society become less willing to fund it. By contrast, the more 'solidaristic' the system is—the more it benefits all groups within society—then the less redistributive it is likely to be.

- Equality *versus* inequality
  There is also a tension between egalitarian outcomes and inegalitarian means. The most vertically redistributive benefits are means-tested ones, and yet these are the benefits which have the greatest divisive and stigmatizing effects, with those who receive them feeling that they are the undeserving poor, subsisting at the bottom of the income ladder. Consequently, such benefits tend to have low take-up rates, thus reducing the pro-equality effects which they are intended to have and which are their greatest justification.

Glossary

fiscal welfare Refers to the distribution of welfare which comes through the deliberate policy of not collecting revenue from people, for example due to tax reliefs and allowances.

final income Final income refers to the income which is left once taxes and benefits have been taken into account, as opposed to 'original income', which is income before taxes and transfers have been accounted for.

Gini Coefficient A method of measuring income inequality on a scale from 0 to 100. The closer a country is to zero the more equal the distribution of income within it; the closer a country is to 100 then the less equal the distribution of income within it.

Gross Domestic Product The value of all goods and services which are produced in Britain excluding net property income from abroad.

gross earnings The value of earnings before taxes and transfers are taken into account.

life-cycle redistribution Also known as 'lifecourse' redistribution, this refers to the redistribution of resources from the more affluent periods of a person's life, that is, the years of labour market activity, to the less affluent periods, such as childhood and retirement.

occupational welfare The benefits which a person receives by virtue of their occupation or career, for example from employers, trade unions, or other workplace associations; sometimes known as 'perks'.

poverty trap The situation where an increase in earnings does not leave an employed individual much better off, and possibly leaves him or her even worse off, due to the combined effects of taxes and benefit withdrawal.

replacement ratio The difference between earnings when in work and benefits when out of work.

social insurance principle The principle that individuals should be collectively insured against risks such as unemployment which they face within the labour market, through the payment of contributions into a fund during periods of employment.

social security The system of benefits and transfers for income maintenance which are funded out of taxation and insurance contributions.

stigma The feeling of shame and rejection which is felt and/or attributed because of low status, such as the lack of self-respect which long-term dependency upon benefits may induce.

take-up Refers to the percentage of those who receive the benefits out of those who are entitled; for example, a take-up of 80 per cent indicates that 8 out of 10 of those eligible for a benefit actually receive it.

unemployment trap The trap faced by the unemployed and those in low-waged jobs where, due to a combination of benefit withdrawal, taxation, and low wages, the earnings received while in work are hardly greater than, and may even be worse than, the income received while out of work.

vertical redistribution Typically refers to redistribution from rich to poor, but can also imply redistribution from poor to rich.

workfare A system whereby claimants are required to engage in some form of employment or training scheme in order to qualify for benefits.

Guide to Further Reading

Baldwin, S. and Falkingham, J. (1994) (eds.), *Social Security and Social Change* (Hemel Hempstead: Harvester Wheatsheaf). A comprehensive examination of the Beveridge model and why it has come to be challenged by wide-reaching changes in modern society.

Beveridge, W. (1942), *Social Insurance and Allied Services* (London: HMSO). The original report itself, which should be read not only for its historical significance but because it still represents an insightful analysis into social security issues.

Child Poverty Action Group (1997a), *Rights Guide to Non-Means-Tested Benefits* (20th edn., London: CPAG). Published every year, this provides the most up-to-date guide to such matters as insurance and categorical benefits.

Child Poverty Action Group (1997b), *National Welfare Benefits Handbook* (27th edn., London: CPAG). Published every year, this provides the most up-to-date guide to the entire range of means-tested benefits in Britain.

Dean, H. and Taylor-Gooby, P. (1992), *Dependency Culture: The Explosion of a Myth* (Hemel Hempstead: Harvester Wheatsheaf). Drawing upon both empirical and theoretical research, this book offers a highly critical analysis of the debate concerning welfare dependency.

Hill, M. (1990), *Social Security Policy in Britain* (Aldershot: Edward Elgar). A well-written introductory text, but one which is now somewhat dated.

Hills, J., Ditch, J., and Glennerster, H. (1994) (eds.), *Beveridge and Social Security: An International Retrospective* (Oxford: Oxford University Press). Provides an expert analysis of the Beveridge reforms, their contemporary relevance, and the influence which they have had internationally.

Hills, J., with Karen Gardiner and the LSE Welfare Programme (1997), *The Future of Welfare: A Guide to the Debate* (rev. edn., York: Joseph Rowntree Foundation). An indispensable source of information for those interested in welfare issues generally. A revision and updating of the text originally published in 1993.

Spicker, P. (1993), *Poverty and Social Security* (London: Routledge). An entertaining and sometimes controversial examination of the interaction between poverty and social security.

Walker, C. (1993), *Managing Poverty: The Limits of Social Assistance* (London: Routledge). Focuses upon assistance benefits and assesses their adequacy or otherwise for relieving poverty.

References

Ahmad, W. and Atkin, K. (1996) (eds.), *'Race' and Community Care* (Milton Keynes: Open University Press).

Alcock, P. (1997), *Understanding Poverty* (2nd edn., London: Macmillan).

Amin, K. and Oppenheim, C. (1992), *Poverty in Black and White* (London: CPAG).

Barnett, C. (1986), *The Audit of War* (London: Macmillan).

Barr, N. and Coulter, F. (1990), 'Social Security: Solution or Problem?', in Hills (1990), 274–337.

Beveridge, W. (1942), *Social Insurance and Allied Services* (London: HMSO).

Bradshaw, J. (1993) (ed.), *Housing Budgets and Living Standards* (York: Joseph Rowntree Foundation).

Browne, A. (1998), 'Most Poor Stuck in Poverty Trap', *The Observer* (8 February).

Bull, D. (1971) (ed.), *Family Poverty* (London: Gerald Duckworth & Co.).

Child Poverty Action Group (1997a), *Rights Guide to Non-Means-Tested Benefits* (20th edn., London: CPAG).

——(1997b), *National Welfare Benefits Handbook* (27th edn., London: CPAG).

Cmnd. 9517 (1985), *Reform of Social Security* (London: HMSO).

Collard, D. (1971), 'The Case for Universal Benefits', in Bull (1971), 37–43.

Commission on Social Justice (1994), *Social Justice: Strategies for National Renewal* (London: Vintage).

Cook, D. (1989), *Rich Law, Poor Law* (Milton Keynes: Open University Press).

Craig, G. and Rai, D. K. (1996), 'Social Security, Community Care—and "Race": The Marginal Dimension', in Ahmad and Atkin (1996), 124–43.

Cutler, T., Williams, K., and Williams, J. (1986), *Keynes, Beveridge and Beyond* (London: Routledge & Kegan Paul).

Daly, M. (1997), 'Cash Benefits in European Welfare States', *Journal of European Social Policy* 7/2, 129–46.

Davies, N. (1997), *Dark Heart: The Shocking Truth about Hidden Britain* (London).

Deacon, A. and Bradshaw, J. (1983), *Reserved for the Poor: The Means-Test in British Social Policy* (Oxford: Basil Blackwell & Martin Robertson).

Deacon, B., with Hulse, M., and Stubbs, P. (1997), *Global Social Policy: International Organisations and the Future of Welfare* (London: Sage).

Dean, H. and Melrose, M. (1996), 'Unravelling Citizenship: The Significance of Social Security Benefit Fraud', *Critical Social Policy* 16/1, 3–31.

——(1997), 'Manageable Discord: Fraud and Resistance in the Social Security System', *Social Policy and Administration*, 31/2, 103–18.

Dean, H. and Taylor-Gooby, P. (1992), *Dependency Culture: The Explosion of a Myth* (Hemel Hempstead: Harvester Wheatsheaf).

Dennis, N. and Erdos, G. (1992), *Families Without Fatherhood* (London: IEA).

Department of Social Security (1995), *Social Security Statistics 1995* (London: HMSO).

——(1996), *Housing Benefit Fraud: Reply by the Government to the Third Report from the Social Security Select Committee, Session 1995–96* (London: HMSO).

——(1997), *Social Security Statistics 1997* (London: HMSO).

Dilnot, A. and Giles, C. (1998) (eds.), *The IFS Green Budget: January 1998* (London: IFS).

Edwards, R. and Duncan, S. (1997), 'Supporting the Family: Lone Mothers, Paid Work and the Underclass Debate', *Critical Social Policy*, 17/4, 29–49.

Evans, M. (1998), 'Social Security: Dismantling the Pyramids?', in Glennerster and Hills (1998), 257–307.

Field, F. (1989), *Losing Out* (Oxford: Blackwell).

——(1995), *Making Welfare Work: Reconstructing Welfare for the Millennium* (London: Institute of Community Studies).

——(1996), *Stakeholder Welfare* (London: IEA).

Friedman, M. (1962), *Capitalism and Freedom* (Chicago: University of Chicago Press).

Ginsburg, N. (1979), *Class, Capital and Social Policy* (London: Macmillan).

——(1992), *Divisions of Welfare* (London: Sage).

Glendinning, C. (1992), *The Costs of Informal Care: Looking Inside the Household* (London: HMSO).

——and Millar, J. (1992) (eds.), *Women and Poverty in Britain: The 1990s* (2nd edn., Hemel Hempstead: Harvester Wheatsheaf).

Glennerster, H. and Hills, J. (1998) (eds.), *The State of Welfare: The Economics of Social Spending* (2nd edn., Oxford: Oxford University Press).

Gough, I., Bradshaw, J., Ditch, J., Eardley, T., and Whiteford, P. (1997), 'Social Assistance in OECD Countries', *Journal of European Social Policy*, 7/1, 17–43.

Hallett, C. (1996), *Women and Social Policy* (Hemel Hempstead: Harvester Wheatsheaf).

Harris, J. (1997), *William Beveridge: A Biography* (2nd edn., Oxford: Clarendon).

Hayek, F. A. (1960), *The Constitution of Liberty* (London: Routledge & Kegan Paul).

——(1976), *Law, Legislation and Liberty: vol. 2, The Mirage of Social Justice* (London: Routledge & Kegan Paul).

Hill, M. (1990), *Social Security Policy in Britain* (Aldershot: Edward Elgar).

Hills, J. (1990) (ed.), *The State of Welfare: The Welfare State in Britain since 1974* (Oxford: Oxford University Press).

——(1995), *Joseph Rowntree Inquiry into Income and Wealth*, 2 (York: Joseph Rowntree Foundation).

——with Karen Gardiner and the LSE Welfare Programme (1997), *The Future of Welfare: A Guide to the Debate* (rev. edn., York: Joseph Rowntree Foundation).

Joseph Rowntree Foundation (1998), *The Working Families Tax Credit: Options and Evaluation* (York: Joseph Rowntree Foundation).

Law, I. G. (1996), *Racism, Ethnicity and Social Policy* (New Jersey: Prentice Hall).

Le Grand, J. (1982), *The Strategy of Equality* (London: Allen & Unwin).

Lewis, O. (1968), *La Vida* (London: Panther).

Mann, K. (1992), *The Making of an English 'Underclass'? The Social Divisions of Welfare and Labour* (Milton Keynes: Open University Press).

Manning, N. and Page, R. (1992), *Social Policy Review*, 4 (London: SPA).

Marshall, T. H. (1981), *The Right to Welfare* (London: Heinemann Educational Books).

Mead, L. (1986), *Beyond Entitlement* (New York: Free Press).

——(1997), *From Welfare to Work: Lessons from America* (London: IEA).

Millar, J. (1996), 'Women, Poverty and Social Security', in Hallett (1996), 52–64.

Morris, L. (1994), *Dangerous Classes: The Underclass and Social Citizenship* (London: Routledge).

Moynihan, D. (1965), *The Negro Family: The Case for National Action* (Washington, DC: Department of Labor).

Murray, C. (1984), *Losing Ground: American Social Policy 1950–80* (New York: Basic Books).

——(1990), *The Emerging British Underclass* (London: IEA).

Oppenheim, C. and Harker, L. (1996), *Poverty: The Facts* (3rd edn., London: CPAG).

Pahl, J. (1989), *Money and Marriage* (London: Macmillan).

Piachaud, D. (1997), 'The Growth of Means-Testing', in Walker and Walker (1997), 75–83.

Piven, F. and Cloward, R. (1971), *Regulating the Poor: The Functions of Public Welfare* (London: Tavistock).

Powell, M. (1995), 'The Strategy of Equality Revisited', *Journal of Social Policy*, 24/2, 163–85.

Rimlinger, G. (1971), *Welfare Policy and Industrialization in Europe* (New York: John Wiley & Sons).

Rose, H. (1981), 'Re-reading Titmuss: The Sexual Division of Welfare', *Journal of Social Policy*, 10/4, 477–502.

Sainsbury, R. (1998), 'Putting Fraud into Perspective', *Benefits*, 21, 2–6.

Seldon, A. and Gray, H. (1967), *Universal or Selective Benefits* Institute for Economic Affairs, Research Monograph 8 (London: IEA).

Social Security Advisory Committee (1997), *Eleventh Report 1997* (London: HMSO).

Social Security Select Committee (1996), *Housing Benefit Fraud, vol. 1: Report Together with the Proceedings of the Committee* (London: HMSO).

Spicker, P. (1984), *Stigma and Social Welfare* (Beckenham: Croom Helm).

——(1993), *Poverty and Social Security* (London: Routledge).

Titmuss, R. (1958), *Essays on the Welfare State* (London: Allen & Unwin).

——(1968), *Commitment to Welfare* (London: Allen & Unwin).

Walker, A. and Walker, C. (1997) (eds.), *Britain Divided: The Growth of Social Exclusion in the 1980s and 1990s* (London: CPAG).

Walker, C. (1993), *Managing Poverty: The Limits of Social Assistance* (London: Routledge).

Williams, F. (1992), 'Somewhere over the Rainbow: Universality and Diversity in Social Policy', in Manning and Page (1992), 200–19.

12 Education and Training

Sarah Vickerstaff

Contents

Introduction

In most industrial societies state involvement in education predates the development of other comprehensive services such as healthcare. As it is a universal state service, education has always been a core interest of social policy students and researchers. Their central concerns have been with inequalities in access to education and with educational outcomes, particularly social differences in educational attainment. Simply put, social policy has been centrally concerned with questions of equity in access and equality of outcome. It has been much less typical for standard social policy texts to consider the structure of training provision and the policy implications of access to training opportunities. However, this is changing: in addition to the traditional concern with the social impact of education, policy debates since the 1970s have focused primarily upon the economic effects of education and training provision such as employment and earnings. In practice it is very difficult to divorce the social functions of education from its potential economic functions.

It has been argued with increasing force since the late 1970s that the quality and capacity of a country's Education and Training systems (these will be referred to by the acronym ET, the accepted term in the literature) are a critical element in the performance of whole economies. The distinctive differences in ET from one country to the next are thought to be a factor which helps to explain the differential performance and success of national economies. It is argued further that this economic effect of ET may be becoming more significant in the rapidly changing economic and technological environment that prevails at the turn of the new century.

The Social and Economic Functions of Education and Training

The fact that governments typically became involved in mass education before the development of other comprehensive services of the welfare state poses the question of why **education** was thought to be so important. Education has always been seen as providing individual, social, and economic benefits. For the individual, education is supposed to provide opportunities for personal development and growth, scope to realize our potential and hence the basis for progress into our chosen careers. On a more social level education is characterized as a civilizing force, with the potential to reduce social inequality and contribute to social unity. A traditional liberal view of education has tended to stress the value of education for its own sake, eschewing the idea that education should perform an explicitly preparatory function for employment. However, it has always also been argued by some that education should fulfil a role in preparing each generation for employment, by inculcating habits of timekeeping and discipline and providing abilities and skills relevant for the world of work.

What the functions of **training** should be have been much less debated. Traditionally, there has been both a philosophical and an institutional split between education and training. They have been seen as fulfilling distinct functions, and in Britain they have historically been provided by different institutions and agencies. For much of this century training has been viewed as primarily providing economic benefits for particular employers, and therefore something best left to private individuals to provide. Although training is typically seen in this more instrumental light, as providing specific skills and abilities for, or in, employment, it is also recognized as providing advantages to the individual in terms of their employability, their earning potential, and their future career prospects. More recently it has been argued that a highly skilled workforce is also a more flexible, creative, and innovative one, so that in addition to the immediate benefits of enhancing someone's specific skills there is the broader advantage of a more adaptable pool of labour for the economy as a whole.

For these reasons it is difficult in practice to separate the individual, social, and economic advantages and disadvantages of access to ET. Levels of ET contribute to an individual's and, it seems, a nation's earning capacity, and hence make a great contri-

---

Box 12.1 A vision for the future development of education and training

1. In all countries knowledge and applied intelligence have become central to economic success and personal and social well being.

2. In the United Kingdom much higher achievement in education and training is needed to match world standards.

3. Everyone must want to learn and have ample opportunity and encouragement to do so.

4. All children must achieve a good grasp of literacy and basic skills early on as the foundation for learning through life.

5. The full range of people's abilities must be recognized and their development rewarded.

6. High-quality learning depends above all on the knowledge, skill, effort, and example of teachers and trainers.

7. It is the role of education both to interpret and pass on the values of society and to stimulate people to think for themselves and to change the world around them.

Source: *Learning to Succeed*, the Report of the National Commission on Education (London, 1993), 43.

---

bution to welfare. It is not surprising, therefore, that debates over the 'proper' function of education and the right balance between the individual, social, and economic functions of ET has been a linking thread of policy reform since the 1970s. From that time the view has grown that schools are failing to provide young people with the basic education and kind of skills they needed for the world of work. (See Box 12.1 for a recent vision statement for the future of education and training in Britain.) This has raised anew the issue of the role of government in overseeing and providing an 'appropriate' ET system.

The Role of Social and Public Policy

Much recent debate on ET in Britain (as with other areas of social policy) has been dominated by arguments about the relative roles of the state and the market in delivering the quantity and quality of services needed. The case for state intervention in ET is usually built around two main lines of argument: economic arguments about market failure, and social arguments about equity and equality of opportunity. The economic justification for state involvement in ET revolves around an assessment of the relative benefits that accrue from ET to society as a whole (the public good), to individuals and to employing organizations (the private good); the argument being that the balance of gains should determine who pays. The question immediately becomes complicated,

---

Box 12.2 What are skills?

'**Core Skills.** These are very general skills needed in almost any job. They include basic literacy and numeracy, and a range of personal transferable skills, such as the ability to work well with others, communication skills, self-motivation, the ability to organize one's own work and, often, a basic capability to use information technology.

Vocational Skills. These are needed in particular occupations or groups of occupations, but are less useful outside these areas. While these skills are less general than core skills, they are none the less highly transferable between jobs in a given field. An example is a basic ability to use common computer packages, such as a broad understanding of computer-aided design packages.

Job-Specific Skills. The usefulness of these is limited to a much narrower field of employment. Often these are forms of knowledge rather than skills as traditionally defined. They could be specific to individual firms. An example could be using a specific computer-aided design package to produce designs to a style and format required by an employer.'

Source: *Labour Market and Skills Trends 1996/7* (Department for Education and Employment, London, 1996), 40.

---

however, because, of course, not all education and training have the same benefits or advantages. It is necessary to distinguish between **basic or foundation education** and **higher education,** and to analyse the nature of different skills gained through training (see Box 12.2). It is apparent that the more general the education or training, the more difficult it is to apportion the relative benefits to society, to the individual, and to employers. It is now taken for granted that the state should provide access to education, funded through general taxation, and that a basic level of education should be compulsory. Although the individual is the prime beneficiary, the public goods or gains are also clear: the democratic, cultural, and creative benefits of an educated citizenry and the economic advantages, in terms of productivity, flexibility, and innovation of a well-educated workforce.

The same argument is less transparent for other aspects of ET. Box 12.3 shows that whereas the public good argument is relatively easy to make for compulsory education, it becomes progressively more difficult with training. The more firm-specific training is (that is, the extent to which the training is not transferable to other work situations) the less justifiable it appears to be to finance it from the public purse through general taxation. In response to these issues we can distinguish theoretically between three ideal types of ET regulation; these are the **market model,** the **social partnership model,** and the **state model** (Sheldrake and Vickerstaff 1987: 55; see also Finegold and Crouch 1994: 276).

Paying for ET

The market model argues that if individuals or firms perceive a commercial advantage in acquiring skills or skilled employees they will undertake training. For example, the

Box 12.3 Benefits accruing to different aspects of education and training

Aspect of ET	Provider	Public Good	Individual Benefit	Employer Benefit
Foundation and core skills	Compulsory education in schools	Social and cultural benefits; flexible workforce	Access to further and higher education; foundation for life; career opportunities	Core skills of workforce; trainability of employees
Vocational preparation	Schools, further education (FE) colleges and employers	School to work transition facilitated	Access and entry to workforce improved	Work-role socialization; pre-recruitment screening
Intermediate vocational skills	Employers/FE colleges	Skills base for the economy; economic competitiveness	High market value of transferable skills; earnings/career prospects	Vocational skills provision; impact on productivity, innovation, and quality
Higher education	Universities and FE colleges	Cultural and creative life; research and development	Career prospects; individual development	Preparation of future managerial and professional staff; research and development
Job-specific skills	Employer	Healthy economy	Career progress within the company	Return on training investment in terms of employee retention; quality; productivity and innovation

return on the investment in adding skills will be recouped either in higher wages for the individual or in higher productivity for the employer. The role of policy here is to ensure the smooth operation of the market, but to allow the quantity and quality of training provided to be market-driven. However, for various reasons the market may produce sub-optimal outcomes in terms of the quantity and quality of training desirable for the economy as a whole. For the employing firm the problem is that, in a free labour market, the trained employee can take her skills to the highest bidder. This is usually known as the 'poaching' problem, and has often been used by companies as a justification for not investing in training: they spend money on training someone only to see that employee poached by another firm which free-rides on the benefit. There are thus incentives either for firms to poach already trained labour or to restrict training to firm-specific skills which have less value in the labour market. In practice, however, it may be very difficult for training to be sufficiently firm-specific. In the case of many vocational and job-specific skills the obvious beneficiary is the individual whose employment prospects are enhanced. None the less, from the individual's perspective there is a risk that investing in skills, either by not earning or by taking lower wages whilst undergoing education or training, will not be repaid by a better-paid job in the future. In addition, there is also an information problem for the individual in knowing which skills would make a sound investment. It may also be the case that the individual cannot currently afford to acquire desirable skills. (For a full discussion of these market incentives and failures, see Layard 1994 and Finegold 1991).

Another way of looking at these issues, which has become prominent in education policy debates, is by reference to **rates of return** on spending on ET. By calculating the cost of education and training, to an individual in terms of foregone earnings and for society in respect of public expenditure, we can attempt to determine the rate of return to the individual and to society as a whole in terms of extra earnings and output (see Glennerster 1998: 54–7). This approach has been very significant in the 1990s in the debates about higher education. The proven pay premium for graduates (in the form of expected extra earnings as a result of having a degree) has been seen as a justification for expecting students to contribute more to the direct costs of their education:

The costs of higher education should be shared among those who benefit from it. We have concluded that those with higher education qualifications are the main beneficiaries, through improved employment prospects and pay. As a consequence, we suggest that graduates in work should make a greater contribution to the costs of higher education in future. (National Committee of Inquiry into Higher Education (NCIHE), Summary Report 1997: 28–9)

Nevertheless, the social rate of return in the form of social, economic, and cultural benefits are seen still to justify continued, and even expanding, public expenditure in higher education (NCIHE, Summary Report 1997: 29).

These problems of quantifying who benefits from ET, and the market failures and perverse incentives that result, imply that public policy must seek solutions either by providing ET directly (the state model) or by developing mechanisms for sharing the costs of training amongst the main beneficiaries (the social partnership model). In practice, many countries use a combination of approaches depending upon the particular area of ET.

Access to ET?

In addition to the policy issue of who pays for ET, there is also the question of whether governments should become involved in determining its structure and contents to ensure that its benefits are evenly spread and that curricula are 'appropriate'. If ET can have an impact on an individual's welfare in terms of earning capacity and participation in the cultural and social life of the society, then public policy faces questions of equality of access to ET opportunities. In practice evaluations of educational opportunities and outcomes show that the experience of education varies significantly from one social group to another. Rather than being a force for liberation, many writers have argued that schooling reinforces social divisions and serves to perpetuate or reproduce class, race, and gender divisions (see Box 12.4 and, for further discussion, Halsey *et al.* 1997). Access to education and rates of success, as measured by qualifications, are highly correlated with socio-economic background (see Table 12.1). It is also the case that those with the poorest education are least likely to receive substantial post-compulsory

---

Box 12.4 Social class and education

'If the industrial working class was the driving force behind social change in the nineteenth and early decades of the twentieth century, it is the middle class who are now seen to determine the destiny of post-industrial societies. During the period of economic nationalism [1945–72] the burgeoning middle class benefited most from the expansion of the welfare state, employment security, and the opportunities afforded by comprehensive education and the expansion of post-compulsory provision. Accordingly, within the sociology of education it was the question of working-class access and opportunity which dominated debates . . . Now, it is not working-class resistance to education which represents the primary sources of class conflict as predicted by neo-Marxist analysts, but the exclusionary tactics of the middle classes at a time of profound personal and social insecurity. With the breakdown of economic nationalism, the demise of bureaucratic careers and the attendant risks of downward mobility have led the middle classes to reassert their vested interests in an attempt to maximise the reproduction of their class advantage.

. . . cultural capital in the form of academic credentials is essential to the reproduction of middle-class privilege. This, it can be argued, has led to intense class conflict over the question of educational selection, when concerns about ensuring "equality of opportunity" have been superseded by primarily (although not exclusively) middle-class claims for greater "choice" over the education of their children. . . .

This is clearly reflected in buoyant demand for access to higher education. Therefore, at the same time that the "new" middle class have been demanding increasing access to higher education for their children, the "old" professional middle class is concerned to preserve its monopoly of access to élite universities.'

Source: 'The Transformation of Education and Society: An Introduction', by P. Brown, A. H. Halsey, H. Launder, and A. Stuart Wells, in *Education: Culture, Economy and Society* (Oxford University Press: Oxford, 1997), 14–15.

	Degree	Higher Education	GCE A level	GCSE grades A–C[c]	GCSE grades D–G[d]	Foreign, other	No qualifications	All
Professional	66	16	7	5	1	4	2	100
Employers and managers	24	19	16	20	6	2	12	100
Intermediate non-manual	26	25	12	20	6	3	8	100
Junior non-manual	5	6	14	37	16	2	20	100
Skilled- manual and own account non-professional	2	9	14	25	14	2	34	100
Semi-skilled manual and personal service	1	5	9	23	12	3	47	100
Unskilled manual	—	1	5	16	11	2	65	100

Percentages

Table 12.1 Highest qualifications held:[a] by socio-economic group,[b] United Kingdom 1996–7

[a] People aged 25 to 69 not in full-time education.
[b] Excludes members of the armed forces, economically active full-time students, and those who were unemployed and had never worked.
[c] Or equivalent.
[d] Or equivalent, includes commercial qualifications and apprenticeships.
Source: Social Trends 28 (1998), 67.

education and training, being confined to unskilled work in which little or no training is offered (see Table 12.2).

Since the beginning of the 1980s the pressures on public expenditure (see Chapter 10 this volume), the growth and persistence of unemployment, changes in the abilities and skills needed in the economy, and growing fears about the social implications of a poorly educated and increasingly unemployable underclass have put all the issues of the role of government in overseeing and providing an 'appropriate' ET system into sharp relief. Before we go on to explore some recent policy developments and debates in Britain, it is necessary to consider the legacy of ET policy from the past.

The Education and Training Legacy

The capacity of national ET systems to respond to the rapidly changing social and economic conditions at the turn of the century is obviously built, in part, upon the education and training legacy in each country. Britain's education and training system is often seen as inferior to those of her competitors.

Britain's failure to educate and train its workforce to the same levels as its international competitors has been both a product and a cause of the nation's poor relative economic performance: a product because the ET system evolved to meet the needs of the world's first industrialized economy, whose large, mass-production manufacturing sector required only a

	On-the-job training only	Off-the-job training only	Both on- and off-the-job training	Percentages All methods of training
Professional	5.8	14.9	3.7	24.4
Associate professional and technical	5.0	13.8	5.3	24.2
Managers and administrators	3.7	10.2	2.6	16.4
Personal and protective service	4.8	8.2	2.9	15.9
Sales	3.6	8.8	1.5	13.9
Clerical and secretarial	3.9	8.0	1.8	13.7
Craft and related	3.3	4.7	2.5	10.4
Plant and machine operatives	2.3	2.8	0.8	5.9
Other occupations/no answer	1.9	3.9	0.7	6.5
All occupations	3.9	8.5	2.4	14.8

Table 12.2 Employees[a] receiving job-related training:[b] by occupation and method of training, United Kingdom, Spring 1996

[a] Employees are those in employment excluding the self-employed, unpaid family workers, and those on government schemes.
[b] Data are for people of working age (males aged 16 to 64 and females aged 16 to 59) receiving job-related training in the four weeks prior to interview.

Source: Social Trends 27 (1997: 68).

small number of skilled workers and university graduates; and a cause, because the absence of a well educated and trained workforce has made it more difficult for industry to respond to new economic conditions. (Finegold and Soskice 1988: 21–2)

A national system of mass schooling developed relatively late in England in comparison with other European countries. Throughout the nineteenth century the development of education was characterized by **voluntarism,** and provision was neither directed nor co-ordinated by government. The model for the curriculum was derived from the traditional independent **public schools,** in which a classical education was prized over science or anything of a vocational or practical bent. As Green comments:

One of the principal casualties of the tradition of *laissez-faire* in education was scientific and technical instruction. With the exception of pure science, which developed largely independently of formal educational institutions, England was, by the mid [nineteenth] century, incomparably backward in most areas of scientific and technical education. For the working class, elementary education was largely absent. State-organized trade schools for artisans and engineers, which were common in Europe, had not developed in England where received opinion regarded the workshop as the only fit place for learning a trade. (1990: 292)

This tradition of élite education left vocational and practical education and training to industry, and has continued to have effects on the ET system to the present day. With the development in this century of a national education system, the split between education and training was rigidly maintained, and resulted in the failure to develop a comprehensive and integrated system that catered not merely to the needs of an academically oriented minority, but also to the mass of people destined for skilled and unskilled manual and routine clerical work. The 1944 Education Act recommended the creation of a schooling system composed of three types of secondary school catering for different abilities and aptitudes: the grammar school for a traditional academic curriculum, technical schools for more practical or vocational studies, and secondary modern schools for a less academic route. The Act also provided for some compulsory education for the post-school 15 to 18 age group. In practice, however, the technical schools were never widely introduced, and provision for post-compulsory-school education was weak. The failure to create the system outlined in the 1944 Act was due in part to the decentralized nature of education administration, in which local government had practical management control over education. (Aldcroft 1992: 30–1)

Industrial Training Policy

Until the end of the 1970s the apprenticeship system was the mainstay of industrial training in Britain. Originally a legally regulated system dating back to the medieval guilds, over the long haul of industrialization the apprenticeship had become a self-regulated system administered by the two sides of industry. The apprenticeship system was built on work-based, practical, hands-on learning, as much a process of socialization into a trade as a process of skills acquisition. Divorced from education this system reinforced the gulf between theoretical learning in education and practical training in industry.

The lack of a national framework for the regulation of training also meant that the apprenticeship model was never systematically extended to cover the broad range of emerging occupations in the new modern industries and services, but remained concentrated in traditional industries and manufacturing such as shipbuilding, construction, and engineering, reinforcing the split between education and training. A by-product of this differentiation was the higher status and desirability of education and the identification of vocational education or training as a second best option.

Prior to the 1960s British governments were willing to intervene in training matters only in times of war, or as part of what have been called elsewhere poor-law measures to provide training for the unemployed. However, by the 1960s wider concerns about economic performance and the pressures of foreign competition put the industrial training issue back on the political agenda. Skill shortages and the then current vogue for economic planning and tripartism led to the first major attempt to reform the training system, through the 1964 Industrial Training Act. The French example of an apprenticeship tax was an important model, and the 1964 Act introduced a levy on firms administered by tripartite Industrial Training Boards (ITBs) representing employers and trade unions. Firms paid the levy to the ITBs and then could be reimbursed if they had undertaken appropriate training. The aim was to spread the costs of training more equally across industry (Vickerstaff 1992: 250). Subsequently, the tripartite Manpower Services Commission (MSC) was created in the early 1970s to co-ordinate policy in the training and employment areas. This was the first time that a single body was commissioned with a strategic capability to oversee and plan policy.

Although these developments were a departure from the voluntarist past, it was still relatively weak regulation by European standards; there was no individual legal entitlement to training as a right; the MSC in practice had very little power to change what happened at the level of the individual firm, and the separation of education and training remained largely intact. These changes did move Britain closer, however, to other models of ET provision in Europe. With the change of government in Britain in 1979 the previous period of reform towards a more interventionist approach, in which the role of the social partners (trade unions and employers) were institutionalized in agencies like the MSC, began to be challenged.

Education Policy

In education, meanwhile, over the long period from the end of the Second World War to the middle of the 1970s, change in policy was gradual. As Taylor-Gooby has argued, the period can be characterized by four key features, namely the decentralized nature of education management in the hands of local education authorities; the dominance of teachers and other education professions in defining and determining the content of education; the gradual replacement of the division between grammar schools and secondary moderns with the extension of the comprehensive schooling model; and lastly, the persistent primacy, culturally and in resource terms, given to academic curricula and qualifications over more vocational education (1993: 102–3). This pattern met with increasing criticisms from both left and right of the political spectrum as the 1970s progressed.

This brief overview of ET in the last century in Britain indicates the specific legacy of institutions and approaches from which current policy reform has had to build. The effect of developments up to the 1970s was a hybrid system with a bias towards keeping government's role confined to one of broad overall direction rather than detailed intervention or control. Today ET is offered by five main groups of providers in Britain: the school system (both public and private), further education colleges, higher education in universities, government-sponsored schemes based on work experience and training with employers, and on-the-job training in employment. This mixed system of provision has tended to be poorly integrated, with the status of academic qualifications and routes overshadowing the vocational stream; movement between academic and vocational streams has traditionally been limited.

Schooling

Much has been done since the early 1980s to try to upgrade vocational education and provide a coherent system in which the traditional academic routes and the newer vocational schemes are integrated. Governments have taken a far more centralized approach to the development of both the academic and vocational curricula, and this has been part of a wider debate about the extent to which schools were accountable for their methods, were delivering acceptable standards, and were meeting the needs of industry (Dale *et al.* 1990: 13). Thus, the development of government policy had two dimensions: the desire to change the content of education, to make it more vocational and hence 'relevant' to the world of work; and the urge to change the processes of educational reform by taking tighter centralized control. The key piece of legislation in the process of change was the 1988 Education Reform Act.

Country	Percentages
Germany	62
France	66
Japan	50
England	27

Table 12.3 16-year-olds in certain countries reaching equivalent of GCSE grades A–C in mathematics, the national language, and one science, 1990–1
Source: Green and Steedman (1993).

The Government, through this Act, instituted a **National Curriculum** for the first time for all schools in England and Wales. This continued a trend for more central government control over the school curriculum and the breaking up of the teaching professions' monopoly over curriculum design. An earlier policy, the Technical and Vocational Education Initiative (TVEI), created in 1982, had begun this trend by aiming to involve business people more in the development and delivery of school education. TVEI provided extra funds for schools to develop projects in different subject areas, which gave students experience of how industry worked and skills relevant to work and new technologies.

This focus on the curriculum also reflected the growing belief that educational standards in Britain were falling and, as has often been the case in the history of ET policy, comparisons with other countries were influential in seeming to prove that Britain was not educating its children as well as some other countries. (For an example of such comparisons, see Table 12.3.)

However, evidence on Britain alone suggests that standards as measured by examination results have been improving (see Table 12.4). Interpretation of such data raised the question of how to define standards in education, which, as we will see, has been a major focus of educational policy debate in the 1980s and 1990s.

	1987	1988	1991	1992	1993	1994	1995
English	46.2	48.9	55.2	55.3	57.1	58.2	56.9
Maths	37.1	41.9	43.7	44.7	45.3	45.9	44.8

Table 12.4 Percentage of entrants gaining GCSE grades A–C or O level/CSE equivalents in English and Maths
Source: Torrance 1997: 322.

The Education Reform Act of 1988 allowed schools to opt out of Local Education Authority (LEA) control and become **grant maintained** from central government; those remaining under LEA control moved to local school-level management. The development of **Local Management of Schools** introduced five new elements to the management of schools: delegated responsibility for the school budget; formula funding, in which most of a school's delegated budget is based on pupil numbers; new admissions regulations; and devolved responsibility for staffing matters and performance indicators in the form of league tables of pupil performance (Thomas and Bullock 1994: 41). The Act attempted to increase parental choice by open enrolment, in which parents could 'choose' schools for their children outside their local authority area; some choice had been available before the Act, but had been hindered by the operation of local authority quotas on admission numbers. The aim of these reforms was to create a managed market system of education, which encouraged schools to compete for pupils.

The 1988 Act has been a controversial intervention in education, not least for its particular definition of educational standards as something that can be measured primarily by examination results and performance indicators such as rates of truancy. Under the Act such results are published nationally in the form of league tables, information which is supposed to help parents in making a choice of school for their children. Critics of the Act have argued that the league tables merely measure the social class backgrounds of the children and do not give any indication of **value-added,** that is, the extent to which the school has had an impact on individual pupils' progress and achievements during their schooling (see Box 12.5). At the time of writing the new Labour Government which came to power in 1997 remained committed to the publication of league

---

Box 12.5 What do the league tables measure?

'. . . the position of a school in a league table of this kind is influenced by many factors which have little to do with whether it is a good school. A selective school will normally show up well, just because it is selective. . . . It is well established, for example, that the children of parents with post-compulsory schooling are likely to do well at schoolwork. Conversely poverty is liable to impact on a home in a way that holds a pupil back. Accordingly, it is not surprising if a school which draws many of its pupils from a relatively prosperous neighbourhood figures higher in a league table than one in a deprived working-class area. . . . There is no telling, however, whether it is a better school on that account.

   . . . if schools come to believe that their position in a league table is vital to their prestige and to their future success, they may adopt practices, which are not in the best interests of children, in order to maintain or improve their position. If more children apply for places than are available, schools may be tempted to select covertly on ability or on the basis of parental attitudes. They may be wary of accepting pupils who they fear will prove hard to teach, and too ready to exclude those who prove disruptive.'

Source: Learning to Succeed, the Report of the National Commission on Education (London, 1993: 64–5).

tables, but discussion continued as to whether measures of value-added could be incorporated in some way.

The 1988 Act has also been challenged for its vision of parental choice. Research by Ball, Bowe, and Gewirtz (1997) has indicated that, in practice, the degree of choice may be profoundly circumscribed by parents' social circumstances:

In the case of the working-class respondents choice of secondary school was a contingent decision rather than an open one. . . . School has to be 'fitted' into a set of constraints and expectations related to work roles, family roles, the sexual division of labour and the demands of household organization . . . it is not simply a matter of education being of less importance for working-class families, our interviewees were very concerned that their children get a good education. Rather the competing pressures of work and family life made certain possibilities difficult or impossible to contemplate. (Ball, Bowe, and Gewirtz 1997: 411)

In addition, the cost of travel and the difficulties of resourcing childcare may make the local school the only real 'choice' for the poor family.

The Labour Government which came to power in 1997 had fought the election campaign with education policy as one of its main priorities. Policy proposals of the new Government included measures to reduce class sizes for 5- to 7-year-olds; a new framework of community, foundation, and voluntary schools, and action to raise the status and morale of the teaching profession. The focus on raising standards, publishing school results, and targeting poorly performing schools which had been developed by the previous government remained a central plank of policy. Given the cost of schooling to the public purse (see Chapter10 this volume) the debates about how public policy can best ensure value for money and provide the kind of schooling which people desire for their children will inevitably continue, as will debates about the balance between the social and economic functions of education.

The Transition from School to Work

There have been major changes since the late 1970s in the traditional routes from full-time education into work. In the past many school leavers went straight into employment at 15 or 16 (the school-leaving age was raised to 16 in 1973) and some into apprenticeships, the latter mainly young men. In the middle 1970s youth unemployment began to rise and there was a debate about the role of education, with employers arguing that schools were failing to meet the needs of industry and many educationalists arguing that schools were still failing the majority of students who were not destined for higher education (Blackman 1992). In addition, during the 1970s the old apprenticeship system was beginning to collapse through a combination of declining employment in traditional industries, where apprenticeship was the accepted route into skilled trades, and the continuing recession, which was causing a reduction in employers' expenditure on training. Both factors speeded up the decline in apprenticeship that had been apparent for some time (see Table 12.5).

A long-held criticism of the British ET structure was the complicated qualification system, which had developed incrementally and in an uncoordinated fashion over a long period. A major set of developments in the 1980s attempted to overcome this problem

Year	Number of apprentices
1970	218,000
1975	155,300
1980	149,500
1981	147,600
1982	123,700
1983	102,100
1984	82,000
1987	58,000
1990	53,000

Table 12.5 The decline in apprenticeship numbers in Great Britain

Keep 1994: 310.

by establishing frameworks for the ET system as a whole; in addition to the National Curriculum for schools there was the development of National Vocational Qualifications (**NVQs**), and the framing of National Targets for Education and Training (**NTETs**). In 1986 the Government established the National Council for Vocational Qualifications (NCVQ) to institute a framework of qualifications to cover all occupations in England, Wales, and Northern Ireland. Scotland is covered by parallel developments overseen by the Scottish Vocational Education Council (SCOTVEC). This was the first major attempt this century to create a unified system of vocational accreditation linked to academic qualifications. The standards for NVQs in each industry have been established and accredited by the Industry Lead Body for that sector. A General National Vocational Qualification (GNVQ) has also been developed as a vocational qualification for those not in training or employment.

A contrast is often made between a state-led system of ET provision, such as is found in Sweden, where initial vocational education and training is provided in the education system and the **dual systems** typical of Germany, Austria, and Switzerland. In the dual systems vocational education and training is primarily provided by employer-based apprenticeships, with requirements for off-the-job training, and restrictions on firms employing school-leavers without providing further ET. In Britain there is a hybrid system. This is shown in Box 12.6, which illustrates the connections between the traditional educational qualifications and the new S/NVQs, the institutions that provide them, and the typical labour-market expectations associated with different levels of ET. On the right-hand side of the pyramid are the corresponding NTETs.

Britain has traditionally had a low rate of 16- and 17-year-olds staying on in full-time education, and a low proportion of 16- or 17-year-olds undertaking any further education compared with other industrial countries (see Table 12.6). However, the situation has been improving over the last decade for a number of reasons; the introduction of the Youth Training Scheme (YTS) meant that a majority of school leavers received some

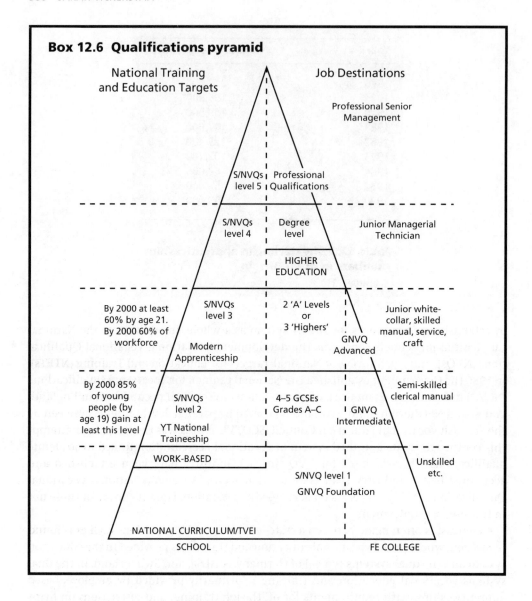

Box 12.6 Qualifications pyramid

National Training
and Education Targets

Job Destinations

Professional Senior
Management

S/NVQs level 5 | Professional Qualifications

S/NVQs level 4 | Degree level — Junior Managerial Technician

HIGHER EDUCATION

By 2000 at least 60% by age 21. By 2000 60% of workforce — S/NVQs level 3 | 2 'A' Levels or 3 'Highers' — Junior white-collar, skilled manual, service, craft

Modern Apprenticeship — GNVQ Advanced

By 2000 85% of young people (by age 19) gain at least this level — S/NVQs level 2 | 4–5 GCSEs Grades A–C — Semi-skilled clerical manual

YT National Traineeship — GNVQ Intermediate

WORK-BASED

S/NVQ level 1 — Unskilled etc.

GNVQ Foundation

NATIONAL CURRICULUM/TVEI

SCHOOL   FE COLLEGE

further training and education and youth unemployment encouraged young people to stay on at school or go to college (see Table 12.7).

However, the significance of the figures is affected by the relatively low rates of qualification of these young people. The aim that a YT place should lead to a qualification of at least NVQ Level 2 is substantially lower than typical apprentice training for the 16 to 19 age group in other countries (Prais, Jarvis, and Wagner 1991: 139).

The YTS was introduced in 1983 as a publicly funded one-year scheme for school leavers. Most YTS places were with employers, but they had to include some off-the-job training. In 1986 the scheme became two years in duration, and in 1987 a change in policy meant that young people who refused a YT (the scheme had also changed its name

Country	16-year-olds	17-year-olds	18-year-olds	16–18-year-olds
UK (1988)	50	35	20	35
W. Germany (1987)	69	43	33	57
France (1986)	78	68	52	66
USA (1986)	94	87	55	79
Japan (1988)	92	89	50	77

Table 12.6 Staying-on rates in full-time education and training, %

Finegold *et al.* 1990: 50.

Year	1985	1986	1987	1988	1989	1990	1991	1992	1993	1994	1995
%	66.7	69.1	72.7	74.8	75.7	77.1	80.6	81.7	83.6	83.6	82.7

Table 12.7 Participation of 16- and 17-year-olds in education and training: England

Source: DfEE 1997: 52.

by now to Youth Training, or YT) were ineligible for unemployment benefit. In some industries the YT scheme took over as the first year and then two years of an apprenticeship. However, it is generally agreed that the relatively low level of most YT schemes did not compensate for the loss of traditional apprenticeships. Thus, intermediate and technician-level skills have been identified as some of the key areas of skill shortages (Skills and Enterprise Network 1993: 51; Ryan (ed.), 1991).

Experience of the YTS has been very varied across a number of dimensions (see Box 12.7). Some schemes have provided good-quality training and access to jobs; others have provided brief employment with limited training content or employment prospects; some have been characterized as merely providing 'warehousing' for unemployed young people, keeping them off the streets and out of the unemployment figures (Roberts 1995: 71–2). In addition to these variations, distinct gender and race differences have been identified, young women typically being channelled into traditional 'female' areas of work such as retail and carework, and young blacks concentrated in schemes with the lowest subsequent employment prospects (Roberts 1995: 73–4). In September 1997 the new Labour Government introduced National Traineeships for school and college leavers aged 16 and above. These are employer-based training programmes leading to NVQ level 2 or its equivalent.

In autumn 1993 the Government announced the introduction of a new programme of **Modern Apprenticeships** in partial recognition of the intermediate skills gap. Modern Apprenticeships are designed to achieve NVQ level 3, and the training has to

Box 12.7 Experiences of YTS

YTS trainees in their own words:

'I said I'd never go on one but YTS is the only way into things now. Everyone at school said it was slave labour and that you got treated like rubbish but when it came to it I didn't have much choice really. There wasn't much else available.'
(Kath, clerical trainee)

'For me the YTS has just been a way into an apprenticeship, if I hadn't have got taken on (as an apprentice) I wouldn't have stayed for the second year.'
(Harinder, construction trainee carpenter)

'I help with digging, planting and laying lawns . . . loading the van with turf or trees or whatever, and helping the gaffer get on with what he's got to do.'
(Adam, at a landscape gardeners)

'Most of the time involves supervising the clients, keeping them occupied or entertained, making sure they can feed themselves properly and sometimes cleaning and bathing them . . . but once you get into the swing of things and you've learnt the ropes, the training doesn't really come into it.'
(Lucy, community care scheme)

'Working with state of the art CNC (computer numerically controlled) lathes and the installation, servicing and application of cutting machines using laser technology across manufacturing industry.'
(Bob, engineering)

'It's been a good opportunity to get some work experience . . . at least on the YTS you get good experience which is better than being on the dole.'
(John, horticulture trainee)

'Youth training is about giving employers cheap labour for a couple of years, so there's no reason for them to take you on. It's not about giving kids jobs . . . it's not really helping that much.'
(Frances, retail trainee)

'Everyone says you've a better chance of finding work when you leave YTS than if you had not been on one in the first place. I don't think so . . . You're seen as not as good as the other person if you've been on a YTS and they haven't. In a way it's work experience but that's all it is.'
(Joe, maintenance and construction trainee)

'No way, I won't stay here for two years! I'll leave and get a job anywhere if I have to, a shop or something, and maybe go to night school. Or I could get work in an old people's home, you don't need any qualifications to work in an old people's home.'
(Anne, community care trainee)

All quotations taken from Phil Mizen *The State, Young People and Youth Training* (London, 1995).

conform to a model for each sector developed by the relevant **Industrial Training Organizations** (ITOs) (replaced by National Training Organizations in 1998) and **Training and Enterprise Councils** (TECs). There is a 'pledge' or training contract between the apprentice and the employer, overseen by the TEC. The reintroduction of apprenticeships has the potential to improve significantly the quality and quantity of post-compulsory education and training that the average young person who is not going on to higher education receives. However, considerable complexity still confronts the young school-leaver trying to choose the best likely path into work; the 1980s and 1990s have seen the proliferation of different routes and qualifications. Nevertheless, far fewer British school-leavers now go straight into employment or unemployment than was the case in the 1970s. While over three-quarters of 16-year-old school leavers went into work in 1978, for most young people at the turn of the millennium the transition from school (or college) to work has been prolonged, and no longer typically occurs at 16.

Higher Education and Training for Adults

The funding and role of higher education became major policy issues in the 1980s and 1990s. An influential committee chaired by Sir Ron Dearing was commissioned in May 1996 to make recommendations on 'how the purposes, shape, structure, size and funding of higher education, including support for students, should develop to meet the needs of the United Kingdom over the next 20 years' (NCIHE, Summary Report 1997: 3). The Report indicated that more young people were going into higher education than ever before: 32 per cent of the 18+ age cohort in 1995, compared to just 12.4 per cent in 1980 (NCIHE, Report 6 1997: 40).

This expansion in the numbers of people in higher education resulted in a change in intake, with increasing numbers of mature students, growth in the number of part-time students, and a greater diversity of educational background and experience among undergraduates. None the less, young people from the upper and middle classes are still far more likely to go on to university than their working-class peers. The Dearing Report recommended the continued expansion of higher education and, most contentiously, that students should be expected to contribute more to the cost of their education by paying a proportion of the tuition fees. It thus adhered to a traditional liberal view of the functions of education whilst acknowledging the rate-of-return arguments discussed above:

Over the next 20 years, the UK must create a society committed to learning throughout life. That commitment will be required from individuals, the state, employers and providers of education and training. Education is life-enriching and desirable in its own right. It is fundamental to the achievement of an improved quality of life in the UK. (NCIHE, Summary Report 1997: 8).

The argument is that, as individuals who undertake a degree and the organizations which employ them benefit most from university education, they should be expected to contribute more to the cost of it.

Despite the growth in the number of mature student entrants into universities in the 1990s (NCIHE, Report 5 1997: 12), the wider continuing education and training for adults has traditionally been the weakest area of ET. Government funds considerable initial training for young people and schemes for the adult unemployed through general taxation, and in addition there is a range of training, education, and enterprise programmes. However, in Britain there are no specific taxes levied for training. The majority of job-related training is paid for by private industry. Governments have been prepared to intervene with schemes for the long-term unemployed, but continuing training and retraining for employed adults has generally been seen to be industry's responsibility, and thus has been subject to the market failures and perverse incentives described above. The Labour Government of 1997 introduced a 'New Deal' for 18- to 24-years-olds as part of the wider programme of Welfare to Work policies (see Chapter 7 in this volume). The **New Deal** is aimed primarily at young adults who have been unemployed for six months or more, and involves four options, each of which includes an element of continuing education and training. The options are: a subsidized job with an employer; full-time education or training; work on the Environment Task Force; or work with the voluntary sector (DfEE 1997: 2). In the summer of 1998 the scheme was extended to unemployed adults.

As with other areas of ET provision, international comparisons of employers' policies and expenditure on training for adults have been influential in the policy debate in Britain. Studies in the middle 1980s argued that British employers spent significantly less than their German, American, French, and Japanese competitors. However, it is difficult to compare adult training expenditure, either within Britain or across economies, because of the problems of how training has been defined and measured from case to case (Ryan 1991). In addition, it has also proved difficult to quantify the volume of training actually done, as companies are not obliged to record their expenditure on training.

Most of this in-work training is of relatively short duration, undertaken either on employers' premises or at a college of further education (Skills and Enterprise Network 1993: 60; Department of Employment 1993: 23–58). More adults are returning to education and training, either because of unemployment or because of employers' demands for new skills. Nevertheless, there are still concerns about the skills and qualification levels of the British workforce in comparison to other countries. As a government publication concluded:

the task is not just one of training, but of constant updating and improvement of skills to meet the demands of the jobs of today and tomorrow. There is also clear evidence of deficiencies in the qualifications of people across the whole economy and, most notably, in the key intermediate level occupations. (DfEE 1996: 55)

This suggests that in the future more and more people will have to learn new skills in order to keep their jobs, and that adults will be an increasingly significant group within ET provision. Some commentators have heralded this as the need for a 'learning society' in which people expect, and are enabled, to continue updating their education throughout life (see, for example, the Report of the Commission on Social Justice 1994: 141–5; DfEE 1996: 69–82). The creation of a learning society would challenge the traditional focus of ET public policy and funding on schooling, higher education, and the unemployed, and raise anew the issue of whether the social return on investment in continuing education and training for adults justifies support from the public purse.

Conclusions

This chapter has provided an introduction to some of the key policy issues and debates in the area of education and training (ET). It is clear from the discussion that the pace of change in British ET has quickened considerably since the early 1980s, and that the state role in terms of funding, regulation, and provision has come under increasing public scrutiny. Belatedly, the ET system is encouraging more young people to stay on in education and more school leavers to continue in some further education and training than ever before. Compulsory education must be the foundation for any strategy to improve the skills profile of the workforce as a whole. Training in employment has to build upon the base which education has laid down and often, in the past, too many young people left full-time education bored, poorly qualified, and thoroughly ill-disposed towards the idea of education. Not only for economic but also for social reasons, a continuing increase in the number of young people staying on in education must be desirable, assuming that the curriculum is able to meet all their needs, aspirations, and aptitudes.

Recent policy developments in Britain have gone some way towards mitigating the historical legacy of a weak and fragmented ET system. Moves to develop a national framework of academic and vocational qualifications offer the promise of upgrading the image of training, and of facilitating moves between vocational and academic streams which were so difficult in the past. Nevertheless, academic qualifications remain the 'gold standard' against which the new S/NVQs and GNVQs are measured.

In the twenty-first century most young people will continue with some education and training after compulsory schooling. It may also be that employers taking on school leavers are increasingly expected (or even required) to provide some further ET. There is much rhetoric about the desirability of a 'learning society' in which everyone is enabled to continue with the education and training necessary for work or simply to pursue their own interests and development. It is now much more accepted that ET should be a continuing process throughout life. However, a key problem for policy debate is how expansion and improvements can be financed and, in particular, how public financing should be spread more evenly across different parts of ET provision. The policy developments discussed above suggest an increasing recognition of the need for some kind of social-partnership model of funding for ET, in which the costs are shared more equally among those who benefit. A mixed economy of ET provision, combining public expenditure, individual finance, and employers' contributions has always existed, but the relative costs to the different sectors are likely to remain centre stage, as are concerns about the balance between the social and economic functions of ET.

Glossary

basic or foundation education These terms usually refer to the basic skills of literacy and numeracy that should be acquired during compulsory schooling. In recent years, especially since the development of the National Curriculum (see below), there has been considerable debate over what constitutes these basic elements of education, for example whether physical education and music are as much a part of foundation education as are English and Mathematics.

dual systems This is a system of vocational ET which combines work-based training with school or college-based education. The German apprenticeship system is one example.

education This can refer both to institutions, such as schools, colleges, and universities, and to the process. That is, what is learnt in educational institutions or, indeed, in other contexts. The issues of what education is for or what it should contain are much debated, as was seen in this chapter.

grant maintained Under the 1988 Education Reform Act, schools were enabled to opt out of Local Authority control and become self-governing, run by their head teachers and governors, funded (grant-maintained) directly by Central Government.

higher education This refers to degree-level and post-degree-level education.

Industrial Training Organizations (ITOs) ITOs were established as voluntary, sector-based training organizations when most of the statutory Industrial Training Boards (ITBs) set up under the 1964 Industrial Training Act were abolished in 1981. These in turn were replaced by National Training Organizations (NTOs) in 1998.

Local Management of Schools Under the 1988 Education Reform Act, the budgets for schools were devolved from the local authority to individual schools. The Board of Governors for each school became responsible for managing the budget.

market model The market model of training provision is where government provides little or no direct training provision, nor any requirement of companies to train. The amount of training is left to the market to decide. In theory, if the company needs a particular skill in order to compete, it will acquire it either through training or recruitment. An individual may invest in their own training because they can see a future labour-market advantage in doing so.

Modern Apprenticeships These were announced by the then Government in the autumn of 1993. Modern Apprenticeships have now been established in many different sectors of employment and are designed to achieve a NVQ level 3 qualification according to a model of training for each sector developed by the relevant ITOs and TECs.

National Curriculum This was introduced by the 1988 Education Reform Act, and applies to all children of compulsory school age in state schools, with a few exceptions such as Hospital Schools. The curriculum specifies subjects to be taken and levels of attainment to be achieved at different ages.

National Vocational Qualifications (NVQs) In 1986 the National Council for Vocational Qualifications (NCVQ) was set up to establish a system of national vocational qualifications (NVQs). These NVQs are work-based assessments of competence and skill at 5 levels. The standards for each level were developed by lead bodies in industry, the public sector, and commerce.

national training and education targets (NTETs) Such targets were first suggested by the Confederation of British Industry in 1989. The idea was supported by government and a National Advisory Council for Education and Training Targets was established (a separate body, the Advisory Scottish Council for Education and Training Targets, has established specific targets for Scotland). The National Targets apply to the United Kingdom, and are a voluntary aim to which business organizations, trade unions, and professional bodies pledge support.

New Deal A raft of welfare-to-work policies initiated by the Labour Government in 1997 to get young people and the long-term unemployed into work.

public schools These are independent schools which charge fees and which do not have to provide the National Curriculum.

rates of return This refers to extra earnings gained by an individual who invests in extended education. For example, a university student may forgo some earnings now in expectation that a degree will subsequently increase earnings. This is a private rate of return, but there can also be social rates of return, although there is more debate about these. In the latter case it is argued that, for example, the extra earnings accruing from extended education translate into a measure of the society's economic gain overall.

social partnership model This refers to joint public and private funding of training provision through tripartite (government, industry, trade unions) delivery systems within a framework of nationally agreed procedures and standards.

state model This model of training is when public funding via taxation and delivery through public institutions predominates, within a context of legal training rights and duties.

training There is no single agreed definition of training. A definition used by the Department of Employment in 1993 is not untypical: training is an 'intentional intervention to help the individual (or the organization) to become competent, or more competent, at work' (Department of Employment 1993: 8).

Training and Enterprise Councils (TECs) TECs are a network of locally based employer-led organizations which promote, plan, and deliver training and enterprise initiatives in their local area. In Scotland, Local Enterprise Companies (LECs) fulfil a similar role.

value-added In relation to education, this refers to the extent to which schooling has affected the rate of learning or improvement of an individual child. Whereas league tables measure outcome in terms of examination or test performance, a value-added measure would need to assess how much a child had progressed whether or not they achieved a particular test outcome.

voluntarism This is the belief that industry is best left to manage its own employment affairs free from government intervention or legislation.

Guide to Further Reading

For a history of the British education system, see A. Green's *Education and State Formation* (1990). A good edited collection of readings on education, covering the history, sociology, and politics of the educational process, policy, and practice is A. H. Halsey, H. Lauder, P. Brown, and A. Stuart Wells (eds.), *Education: Culture, Economy, and Society* (1997). Two books which look at the impact of ET on young people, their experiences, and the effects of ET on employment prospects are P. Mizen, *The State, Young People and Youth Training* (1995) and K. Roberts, *Youth Employment in Modern Britain* (1995). A standard social policy approach to education can be found in H. Glennerster 'Education Reaping the

Harvest', in H. Glennerster and J. Hills (eds.), *The State of Welfare* (1998). There is a wide-ranging literature on training policy; a volume edited by R. Layard, K. Mayhew, and G. Owen, *Britain's Training Deficit* (1994), provides a good overview of current issues, and the article in it by D. Finegold and C. Crouch, 'A Comparison of National Institutions', introduces some of the key themes in cross-national comparisons of training policy.

References

Aldcroft, D. H. (1992), *Education, Training and Economic Performance* (Manchester: Manchester University Press).

Ball, S. J., Bowe, R., and Gewirtz, S. (1997), 'Circuits of Schooling: A Sociological Exploration of Parental Choice of School in Social-Class Contexts', in Halsey, A. H. *et al.* (eds.), *Education: Culture, Economy, and Society* (Oxford: Oxford University Press), 409–21.

Blackman, S. (1992), 'Beyond Vocationalism', in Brown, P. and Lauder, H. (eds.), *Education for Economic Survival* (London: Routledge), 203–25.

Brown, P., Halsey, A. H., Lauder, H., and Stuart Wells, A. (1997), 'The Transformation of Education and Society: An Introduction' in Halsey, A. H. *et al.* (eds.), *Education: Culture, Economy, and Society* (Oxford: Oxford University Press), 1–44.

Dale, R., Bowe, R., Harris, D., Loveys, M., Moore, R., Silling, C., Sikes, P., Trevitt, J., and Valsecchi, V. (1990), *The TVEI Story* (Milton Keynes: Open University Press).

Department for Education and Employment (DfEE) (1997), *Design of the New Deal for 18–24 Year Olds* (London: DfEE).

Department for Education and Employment (DfEE) (1996), *Labour Market and Skills Trends 1996/7* (London: DfEE).

Department of Employment (1993), *Training Statistics 1993* (London: HMSO).

Finegold, D. and Soskice, D. (1988), 'The Failure of Training in Britain: Analysis and Prescription', *Oxford Review of Economic Policy*, 4/3, 21–50.

Finegold, D., Keep, E., Miliband, D., Raffe, D., Spours, K., and Young, M. (1990), *A British Baccalaureate* (London: Institute for Public Policy Research).

Finegold, D. and Crouch C. (1994), 'A Comparison of National Institutions', in Layard, R., Mayhew, K. and Owen, G. (eds.), *Britain's Training Deficit* (Aldershot: Avebury), 251–81.

Glennerster, H. (1998), 'Education Reaping the Harvest', in Glennerster, H. and Hills, J. (eds.), *The State of Welfare* (Oxford: Oxford University Press), 27–74.

Green, A. (1990), *Education and State Formation* (Basingstoke: Macmillan).

Green A. and Steedman, H. (1993), *Educational Provision, Educational Attainment and the Needs of Industry: A Review of Research for Germany, France, Japan, the USA and Britain* (London: National Institute of Economic and Social Research).

Keep, E. (1994), 'Vocational Education and Training for the Young', in Sisson, K. (ed.), *Personnel Management* (Oxford: Blackwell), 299–333.

Layard, R., Mayhew, K., and Owen, G. (eds.) (1994), *Britain's Training Deficit* (Aldershot: Avebury).

Manpower Services Commission (MSC)/National Economic Development Office (NEDO) (1985), *A Challenge to Complacency* (Sheffield: MSC).

Mizen, P. (1995), *The State, Young People and Youth Training* (London: Mansell).

National Commission on Education (NCE) (1993), *Learning to Succeed* (London, Heinemann).

National Committee of Inquiry into Higher Education (1997), *Summary Report*.

NEDO/MSC (1994), *Competence and Competition* (London: NEDO).

Office for National Statistics (ONS) (1997), *Social Trends 27* (London: HMSO).

Office for National Statistics (ONS) (1998), *Social Trends 28* (London: HMSO).

Prais, S. J., Jarvis, V., and Wagner, K. (1991), 'Productivity and Vocational Skills in Services in Britain and Germany: Hotels', in Ryan, P. (1991) (ed.), 119–45.

Report of the Commission on Social Justice (1994), *Social Justice Strategies for National Renewal* (London: Vintage).

Roberts, K. (1995), *Youth Employment in Modern Britain* (Oxford: Oxford University Press).

Ryan, P. (ed.) (1991), *International Comparisons of Vocational Education and Training for Intermediate Skills* (London: The Falmer Press).

Sheldrake, J. and Vickerstaff, S. (1987), *The History of Industrial Training in Britain* (Aldershot: Gower).

Skills and Enterprise Network (1993), *Labour Market and Skills Trends* (Sheffield: Employment Department).

Taylor-Gooby, P. (1993), 'The New Educational Settlement: National Curriculum and Local Management', in Taylor-Gooby, P. and Lawson, R. (1993), *Markets and Managers* (Buckingham: Open University Press), 102–16.

Thomas, H. and Bullock, A. (1994), 'The Political Economy of Local Management of Schools', in Tomlinson, S. (ed.), *Educational Reform and Its Consequences* (London: IPPR/Rivers Oram Press), 41–52.

Torrance, H. (1997), 'Assessment, Accountability, and Standards: Using Assessment to Control the Reform of Schooling', in Halsey, A. H. *et al.* (eds.), *Education: Culture, Economy, and Society* (Oxford: Oxford University Press), 320–31.

Vickerstaff, S. (1992), 'Training for Economic Survival', in Brown, P. and Lauder, H. (eds.), *Education for Economic Survival* (London: Routledge), 244–67.

——(1993), 'The State and Industrial Training in the United Kingdom', in J. Sheldrake and P. D. Webb (eds.), *State and Market Aspects of Modern European Development* (Aldershot: Dartmouth), 142–56.

13 Health and Health Policy

John Butler and Michael Calnan

Contents

Introduction: Ill Health, Society, and Healthcare

Ill health and disability are regarded in most modern societies as undesirable conditions. Not only do they cause personal pain and distress, they may also affect the well-being of society as a whole. Infectious diseases are an obvious example: because they threaten communities as well as individuals, societies are justified in taking steps to ensure that people are properly immunized and treated. Disease and disability can also harm the economic interests of a society, for example by causing people to take time away from work when they are ill. More days of productive labour are lost because of illness among the workforce in industrialized nations than through strikes or action in the workplace.

Since the effects of disease and disability are social and economic as well as personal, most societies have accepted some degree of collective responsibility for the care of those who are ill, and they have developed institutionalized ways of treating them. In Biblical times, disease was seen as the result either of sin or of possession by devils, and sufferers were cast out of normal society until they had been ritually cleansed. With the advent of a more scientific approach to the study of disease in the western world in the sixteenth and seventeenth centuries, the task of treating the sick began to be assumed by specially trained people (physicians, surgeons, and apothecaries) whose claim to expertise was recognized and protected by the state, and who consequently acquired a monopoly position in the business of healing. During the course of the ensuing three centuries, medical practice—that is, the whole process of diagnosing and treating disease—has evolved into an elaborate social institution as well as a personal service.

Today, the western style of medicine has become an international activity in which knowledge and techniques are known and followed in almost every country. Subject to language abilities, a doctor trained in Japan can receive specialist surgical training in Germany and go on to perform operations in America. The methods, equipment, and drugs involved will be readily recognized in each country. The companies that manufacture the drugs and equipment which determine the scope of modern medical practice are operating in global markets, and advances in diagnosis and treatment are reported in medical books and journals which are read throughout the world.

This chapter provides an introduction to healthcare in the United Kingdom, recognizing that the practice of medicine is not just a technical matter of interest to doctors and others who work in the National Health Service (NHS), but is of much wider significance. The problems that people bring to their doctors are sometimes simple to treat, but they often have multiple causes resulting from the complex stresses and strains of modern life. The patterns of ill health in a society are intimately related to its culture and its social and economic organization as well as to its geography and climate, and an important key to understanding the task that is faced by the NHS is to understand the social context of ill health in modern Britain.

Similarly, the way in which a society addresses the problem of ill health is deeply reflective of its history, political traditions, and social values. The health problems faced by the UK and America, for example, are broadly similar, but the healthcare systems of the two countries are markedly different. Reflective of its relatively short history as a dynamic and entrepreneurial country, the American system sets a high value on the delivery of good quality personal medical care to individual consumers through competitive markets. The UK, by contrast, with its long history of collective responsibility for people's well-being, has placed rather more emphasis on the prevention of disease through social action and on ensuring a measure of equality in people's access to healthcare. Not only patterns of ill health but also systems of healthcare are rooted in the particular histories of particular societies; and it is this that makes them of such great interest to the social scientist.

Health and Illness in Society

To analyse the development, shape, and focus of health policy it is important to have an understanding of the assumptions about health, illness, and disease and their determinants which are inherent in policy initiatives. Hence, this first section focuses on outlining different definitions and conceptualizations of health and then examining how the distribution of health, illness, and disease is influenced by social and economic position.

Concepts of Health, Illness, and Disease

Despite considerable discussion over the past twenty years, defining health remains problematic. Certainly, there is a vast array of different approaches to defining and conceptualizing health and illness, although it is possible to distinguish at least two different classifying continua. The first is the extent to which it is based on 'objective' knowledge derived from experts, or the extent to which it is derived from 'subjective' knowledge such as lay perceptions. The second criterion is the extent to which the concept of health focuses on the individual or how far it is more collectivist or population-oriented and focuses on the community or specific social groups.

One of the more common definitions portrays health in terms of the presence or absence of disease and draws on 'objective' or expert knowledge derived mainly from biomedical or epidemiological models. This approach is now outdated, and has in some respects been replaced by the more behaviourally oriented multiple-risk-factor model, which emphasizes the interaction between behavioural (so-called lifestyle) risk factors and biological and genetic factors in the causation of diseases (mainly chronic diseases such as coronary heart disease). Finally, in contrast to the previous two essentially individualistically oriented approaches, there is the collectively oriented social and environmental model, which emphasizes the social patterning of disease and its social, economic, and environmental determinants.

It is possible also in the alternative approach which is based on subjective definitions of health and illness to distinguish the individualistically related holistic definition, which involves the interaction between mind (cognition/emotion) and body, and emphasizes the more biographical elements in the way individuals have experienced and interpret health and illness. The more collectivist definition highlights the multidimensional nature of concepts of health and shows how they vary between cultures and groups. These studies have shown that health consists of both positive (physical and mental well-being) and negative aspects (illness, dysfunction, disability). This multi-dimensional definition of health has been adopted by agencies such as the World Health Organization, and in their holistic definition health is seen as a resource for realizing physical, mental, and social potential.

This 'subjective' approach has emphasized the both contrasting and complementary nature of lay perspectives compared with the biomedical model of health. However, while there have been attempts to incorporate multi-dimensional aspects of health into measures of health status (Jenkinson 1994) there is still a tendency to focus on negative aspects, particularly morbidity and mortality. Hence the following debate about health and social inequalities has tended to use rather limited socio-epidemiological indicators of health or, more accurately, disease.

Social Position and Health

Social epidemiologists are increasingly presenting evidence of a relationship between patterns of ill health and disease and social and economic position as well as other cultural or environmental factors. The approach highlights the vulnerability of certain social groups to disease in general rather than specific disease. Hence there are discussions about the relationship between patterns of ill health and social class; income; housing status; gender; marital status; ethnicity; religious affiliation; and geographical location. The major focus of the debate in the United Kingdom, and more recently in Europe, has been on inequalities or variations in health in relation to socio-economic position, that is, social class, income, and housing tenure. It is difficult to judge why the relationship between socio-economic position and patterns of ill health has received the most attention. It may be that it is the most important of the range of social, cultural, and economic determinants, and that it can also account for patterns of relationships between other social factors and ill health; that is, that there is an interrelationship between socio-economic position and gender. Alternatively, it may be that social and economic inequalities in health have been over-estimated to the neglect of other cultural factors. Whatever the explanation, the focus of the policy debate has been on the relationship between social and economic position and ill health, and thus this will be the focus of the more detailed discussion in the following section.

Social and Economic Position and Ill Health

The relationship between socio-economic circumstances and ill health has been well documented, although it was the publication of the *Black Report* followed by *The Health Divide* (Townsend, Davidson, and Whitehead 1988) which produced the most comprehensive evidence and generated a wider debate. The following quote from Wilkinson (1996) clearly illustrates the evidence of socio-economic differences in death rates:

imagine two people, each with a similar-sized circle of friends and relatives—let us say fifteen personal contacts but living in separate rich and poor areas—for every death that occurs among the circle of friends of the person in the rich area, the person in the poor area will know of two, three or even four times as many deaths among his or her circle of friends.

More specifically, Fox and Benzeval (1995) map the social variations in mortality and morbidity. They show that people in unskilled occupations and their children are twice as likely to die prematurely in comparison to professionals, and that gradients in mortality by social class are apparent for nearly all causes of death to a greater or lesser extent. Men in social class 5 lost 114 years of potential life per 1,000 population, against 39 years for men in class 1, with women in unskilled occupations losing 34 years compared with 16 years for women in professional occupations. Social-class differences in mortality are not so marked amongst the elderly, although men over 75 in social class 5 still have a more than 50 per cent higher death rate than those in social class 1.

The problem with using occupation as an indicator is that it can misrepresent the position of women. More effective discriminators than social class, according to Fox and Benzeval (1995), are housing tenure and car ownership. For example, between 1976 and 1981 women and men in owner-occupied accommodation with access to a car had a Standardized Mortality Ratio of 78 against that of 138 for women and 129 for men in local authority rented accommodation without a car. This evidence is particularly important because it demonstrates that a strong socio-economic gradient exists for women as well as for men.

Data on social variations in patterns of morbidity show similar gradients (Fox and Benzeval 1995). For example, general household survey data shows that age standardized morbidity ratios for chronic illness are approximately 40 per cent higher for people in local authority accommodation without a car than for owner-occupiers with two or more cars. Age-standardized long-standing illness rates for people who are unemployed are over 70 per cent higher than those of individuals who are employed. Data from a range of other sources (Fox and Benzeval 1995) also shows that various indicators of health such as height, body mass index, lung function, and blood pressure vary by social class. Finally, there is evidence (Fox and Benzeval 1995) that morbidity resulting in consultations with general practitioners can also be shown to vary between socio-economic groups. For example, age standardization consultation rates with GPs for serious conditions are significantly higher among local authority tenants, people who were unemployed, and people both from the Caribbean or Indian subcontinent, than in the general population.

In summary, the UK experience is mirrored in other European countries, the USA, and Australia, in that the more disadvantaged people's socio-economic circumstances are the worse is their health status. But, as Benzeval and colleagues (1995) point out, economic inequality appears to be growing more quickly in Britain than in any other advanced industrial society.

Explaining Socio-Economic Inequalities in Health

There seems to be some consensus that social and economic status is related to health status, although there is less agreement about why such a relationship exists. The obvious explanation is that adverse social and economic circumstances determine ill health, although this has been contested and some commentators say the explanation lies elsewhere. It is possible to identify three other alternative explanations to this materialist or structuralist approach which will be discussed before looking at the argument that poor social and economic circumstances cause ill health.

The Role of Health Services The idea here is that, as the role of health services and healthcare is a major benefit for health, and because the middle and affluent classes make more use of it, this explains the socio-economic variations in health. However, both these sets of assumptions have been contested.

First, the evidence is that modern medicine is not the key determinant of health in modern populations (Wilkinson 1996). For example, Bunker *et al.* (1994) estimate that the total benefits of all existing forms of professional medical interventions (preventions and treatment) added at most five years to the life expectancy of Americans, which constitutes only 20 per cent of the gain in American life expectancy during the twentieth century.

Second, given this relatively small contribution of medical services to the health of the population, it is doubtful whether differences in medical care have a major influence on health inequalities. Certainly, the evidence suggests that there are variations in the use of preventive services such as cervical screening by social class, although it is difficult to pinpoint any social class variations in the use of treatment services because of the difficulty of distinguishing 'need' from 'demand'.

Artefact Explanation   Another explanation which has also received little support is that the differences in mortality by social class are an artefact of the way the statistics are devised; that is, the meaning of social class itself is unstable over time. However, as Fox and Benzeval (1995) indicate, the size and consistency of evidence suggests that this explanation can be discounted. They point to the equally strong socio-economic gradients in mortality and morbidity which have been found in both longitudinal and cross-sectional studies where all the data are collected from the same source.

Social Selection   The third explanation, which of the three discussed so far has received the most support, is the social selection one, where social variations in health arise as a result of social mobility. Healthy individuals tend to be promoted, whereas those in poor health find it difficult to obtain employment, or have to take less demanding jobs. Thus, health determines social position rather than social circumstances determining health status. The social selection explanation is multidimensional in that it refers to both mobility between and within generations, both between social classes and into and out of the labour market. There seems to be some supportive evidence for the health selection argument, although it appears to explain only a small proportion of the mortality differential between social groups. For example, West (1991) suggests that health-related selection is most likely to occur between childhood and early adulthood, that is, as people move from their parents' class to their own achieved class. The most frequently quoted example of this effect is that taller women tend to marry into social classes higher than their father's more often than shorter women do. The infant mortality rates and the birthweight of their babies were then better than those of their peers who remained in the original social class (Fox and Benzeval 1995). However, more recent research provides a mixture of evidence, some of which supports the social selection hypothesis and some other which raises doubts about it. For example, a recent analysis (Power *et al.* 1996) using data from the 1958 cohort study (NCDS) examined explanations for social inequalities in health with respect to health-related social mobility and cumulative socio-economic circumstances over the first three decades of life. They found that social mobility varied by health status, with those reporting poor health at age 23 having higher odds of downward mobility than of staying in the same social class. Men with poor health were also less likely to be upwardly mobile. However, prevalence of poor health at age 33 increased with decreasing social class, from 8.5 per cent in classes 1 and 2 to 17.7 per cent in classes 4 and 5 among men, and from 9.4 per cent to 18.8 per cent among women. Moreover, these marked social class differences remained significant after adjustment for effects of social mobility. Thus this led the authors to conclude that 'lifetime socio-economic circumstances accounted for inequalities in self-reported health at age 33, while social mobility did not have a major effect on health inequalities.'

A different approach to this issue involved an analysis (Bartley and Owen 1996) of the relationship between socio-economic status, employment, and health during economic change (1973–93). Using data from the General Household Survey over this period they focused on men aged 20 to 59 years. They found that men in socio-economic classes 1 and 2 with no long-standing illness experienced little decrease in their chances of being in paid employment as the general unemployment rate rose. Those most affected were men in manual groups with limited long-standing illness. The likelihood of paid employment was affected far less by such illness in non-manual than in manual categories. In social class 1 about 85 per cent of men with such illnesses were in paid employment in 1979, and 75 per cent by 1993; in class 4 the equivalent proportions were 70 per cent and 40 per cent. In addition, amongst men in manual categories with long-standing illness there was no sign of employment rates rising again as the economy recovered.

The authors conclude that socio-economic status makes a large difference to the impact of illness on the ability to remain in paid employment, and this impact increases as unemployment rises, but does not diminish as unemployment falls. This suggests that manual occupations have become more 'health selective' over the past 20 years, and according to the authors contradicts the theory that people in poor health are more likely to enter manual occupations with low status. The authors also suggest that measures of intervention and prevention should be implemented early in life to resist accumulation of adverse social circumstances.

Social and Economic Position Determines Health Status This explanation contains what some commentators (Townsend, Davidson, and Whitehead 1988) have, at least until recently, identified as two distinct arguments. One of them emphasizes the direct effect on health of living and working in poor conditions and having a low income. The other explains the relationship between social and economic position and health status by the fact that people living in poor social circumstances are also more likely to engage in health-damaging behaviour such as smoking, having a poor diet, or having a low level of exercise. For example, Blaxter (1990) shows that those who were smokers, drinkers, had a poor diet, and carried out a low level of exercise were more likely to be men, to be unskilled manual workers, to be unemployed if among the young age group, and living alone if elderly.

One explanation for this relationship between socio-economic position and health-related behaviour was believed to be due to the poorer knowledge of groups from unskilled occupations or with low incomes, because these groups tend to have a lower level of formal education or live in a sub-culture which has a different set of values.

However, there is little evidence to support this argument, and it is now accepted that the two explanations are interrelated: that social structural factors shape or modify beliefs or attitudes, or create social circumstances which encourage certain patterns of behaviour or 'lifestyles'. More recent evidence suggests, however, that it might be more useful to concentrate on the explanation that places greater emphasis on the direct impact of the material circumstances in which people live and work, on their patterns of health-damaging behaviour. Not only is there some doubt about whether health beliefs vary by socio-economic position, but also whether and how health beliefs influence health-related behaviour (Calnan 1994). For example, Calnan and Williams (1991), in their examination of the salience of health in the lives of households from professional and unskilled occupations, found that matters of health rarely surfaced in people's descriptions of their daily lives, nor did a concern with health in the context of health-related behaviour.

The more favoured explanation which places greater emphasis on the direct impact of the material circumstances is well illustrated in the work of Graham (1989), who showed how the interrelationship between socio-economic circumstances and gender influenced individuals' attitudes to smoking. Graham (1989) shows that at both household and individual levels the evidence points to substantial spending on tobacco by low-income households. For example, low-income households with two adults and two children devote an average of 5 per cent of the weekly household income to tobacco, compared with 2 per cent in all households with two adults and two children. In addition, they spend absolutely more on tobacco than other households. Also spending among low-income households with children is higher than among those without children. The highest expenditure on tobacco, calculated on a per capita basis, is among one-adult households with children: 90 per cent are headed by women. Studies have also shown that there are higher levels of spending on tobacco among households with a disabled child at all income levels.

Through her qualitative investigations, Graham (1989) also provides an explanation for this pattern. In her study of 57 women she showed how in some families smoking was associated with breaks for care when mothers rested and refuelled. She showed that cigarettes were also associated with breaks in the pattern of care when the demands of the children were too much to cope with. In the context where women had to cut back any luxury goods for themselves such as shoes, haircuts, and so on, cigarettes could be a woman's only purchase for herself: thus smoking reflects the social isolation and stress of caring for children in poverty. In these situations the social benefits of habits such as smoking outweigh the known costs, and even if some of these women would like to give up smoking, changing their health habits is difficult given the barrier of lack of resources such as time, energy, and finance.

Another area where there is a relationship between social position and health-related behaviour is in patterns of food consumption. Evidence (Calnan 1994) has shown how diet is most commonly referred to in the context of health maintenance, implying that food choice may be strongly shaped by health knowledge. However, there are other constraints on food choice related both to the internal structure and organization of the family and external to the family. One of these is cost, and there is evidence in the United Kingdom (see Calnan 1991) that many of those from households living on low incomes do not eat their preferred diet mainly because prices of 'healthy' foods are higher than those of 'unhealthy' foods. In addition to cost, there are other factors that influence choice. One of these is availability. Recommended foods for a healthy diet are less likely to be available in deprived areas than in more affluent areas. Costs of an individual diet not only include the costs of food but also the expenses incurred in buying foods, such as transport costs to and from shops. Local shops or the mobile shop tend to be used not because of quality but because of convenience. The costs of time and money (many do not have cars) outweigh the benefits of shopping in a supermarket where the food may be better-quality and cheaper.

This approach examines the interaction between socio-economic circumstances and health-related behaviour, and how health-related behaviour provides the link between socio-economic position and poor health outcomes. However, the importance of this explanation must not be exaggerated. For example, studies examining the inverse relationship between socio-economic position and the incidence and prevalence of coronary heart disease show that smoking and other health-related behaviours only partly account for this relationship (see Calnan 1991), and it is necessary to look to other determinants within the socio-economic environment for an adequate explanation. This leads on to the approach that highlights the direct effect of poor material and physical environments, including adequacy of housing, working conditions and pollution, and social and economic influences such as income and wealth, levels of unemployment, the quality of the social environment, and, particularly, levels of support. For example, as Fox and Benzeval (1995) state, there are strong and statistically significant positive correlations between measures of deprivation such as the proportion of unemployed, overcrowding, and various health indicators. Census data from 1991 show that the mortality ratio is 1.95 higher in the most deprived areas compared with the least deprived areas.

Two aspects of the relationships between material and physical circumstances and health will be considered in more detail: housing and poverty. It is possible to identify the link between housing and health (Best 1995) through homelessness, damp and cold housing, poor housing design which can lead to fires, accidents, and infestations, and the impact of housing on individuals' mental health. Homelessness is related to higher rates of hospital in-patient stay, and a higher prevalence of conditions such as chronic chest conditions or breathing problems. Families living in temporary accommodation of the bed-and-breakfast kind face a range of hazards such as poor hygiene and associated illnesses. However, the clearest evidence of the relationship between poor housing and health is through the effects of inadequate heating and dampness. Inadequate warmth and dampness in the home clearly contributes to respiratory illness, and can cause hypothermia (Best 1995).

Housing design is a major influence on level of accidents in the home, and households in disadvantaged circumstances are likely to be the worst affected by such accidents: those living in high-rise buildings are most prone to serious accidents such as falling from windows and balconies. Statistics are less helpful in establishing a clear link between housing and stress-related illness; nevertheless, there are good grounds for believing that poor sound insulation between neighbouring houses, a lack of privacy, and overcrowding are all likely to contribute to mental health problems (Best 1995).

Low income and poverty has a variety of causes including unemployment, lone parenthood, low wages/high outgoings, and self-employment. There is evidence of a consistent association between low income and ill-health (Benzeval and Webb 1995). For example, in an analysis of data from the Health and Lifestyle Survey Blaxter (1990) found that groups with low incomes reported the highest rates of morbidity and disability.

How does low income affect health? Three distinct but interacting processes are important and these are physiological, psychological, and behavioural. From a physiological point of view, low income increases individuals' exposure to harmful environments. Psychologically, living with limited access to resources creates stresses and reduces individuals' ability, choices, and support to solve problems, and stress and poor social support have been shown to have a detrimental effect on health. The behavioural explanations of how poverty may result in health-damaging behaviours have been discussed earlier.

Finally, a slightly different approach to explaining inequalities has been put forward by Wilkinson (1996). He argues that it is income inequality rather than low income which is the key determinant of poor health, in that relative income is more important than absolute income in rich developed countries. He argues too that income inequalities influence national mortality rates primarily by determining the strength of the impact of relative deprivation on health. Narrowing health inequalities give rise to faster improvements in national mortality rates. The reason for this effect is that psychosocial problems such as stress, weak self-esteem, and feelings of low social status are more important than the physical effects of poverty. If this is true then more rapid reductions in national mortality rates will be achieved by reducing the degree of income inequality in a society than by simply raising the incomes of the poor.

In summary, evidence has been presented which has shown how disease and ill-health are associated with social position. Much of the discussion in the UK has focused on the relationship between socio-economic position and health outcomes. In an overview of the Black Report's explanations for socio-economic differentials in health, MacIntyre (1997) introduced the distinction between 'hard' and 'soft' versions. She argues that the debate about the relative importance of the different explanations, that is, 'selection versus causation', became polarized, each explanation was seen to be mutually exclusive, and there was a tendency to confuse the 'hard' and 'soft' versions of the explanations. She suggests also that instead of seeing the explanations as opposing one another, they should be treated as complementary in that their relative importance in different social contexts should be examined, as should their possible interactions or additive effects. The policy response to this evidence will be discussed later in the chapter.

The National Health Service

The Values of the NHS

Sometimes described as 'the jewel in the crown of the welfare state', the **National Health Service** (NHS) came into being on 5 July 1948. From the outset it was organized and financed in ways designed not only to provide health and medical care to the people, but also to reflect and promote the values of equity and fairness in a nation coping with the aftermath of a debilitating war. The NHS is not unique among healthcare systems in the values it displays, but it has preserved and developed them over fifty years with a constancy that marks it out as an exemplar of publicly provided healthcare.

At the heart of the NHS is the belief that, since good healthcare is a fundamental determinant of people's capacity to succeed in life, it should be equally available to all who need it, not just those who can afford it. This is not an inevitable belief: it is perfectly possible for health services to be bought and sold in private markets, just like any other goods and services. Where this happens, however, the best care is most likely to go to those who can best afford it, and the less well-off are left with care that is offered by charities, or residual care provided as a safety-net by public authorities.

The NHS was consciously designed to avoid such inequalities by removing healthcare in the UK from the distribution of goods and services that typically results from market forces. From the outset two features of the service have been vital in maintaining the quest for equity and fairness. First, the NHS has always been financed largely, though never exclusively, from public funds rather than private fees or charges. In most years since 1948, between about 80 and 90 per cent of the total cost of the NHS in the UK has been met by the Treasury from government revenue (taxation and borrowing). Much smaller proportions have been taken directly from individuals through National Insurance contributions and through charges paid by those using the services offered by the NHS. Since taxation in the UK is broadly progressive over a limited range of income (that is, those who are better-off generally pay more in taxation than those who are less well-off), the cost of financing the NHS is borne roughly in proportion to people's ability to pay for it.

The second vital feature of the NHS, which together with the public funding base provides the equitable foundation of the service, is that access to care has always been determined by medical need rather than financial contribution. In principle, though not always in practice, people in equal need of care should have similar access to the services of doctors, hospitals, **community health services,** and so on, however much or little they have contributed to the cost of their treatment. Central to the principle of equal access is that most of the services offered by the NHS are free at the point of use: they are available to patients as taxpayers, not to consumers as customers. With the exception of charges for prescriptions and some other services, the ability of people to pay for their own care, which is a distinctive feature of the private market, has been eliminated as a criterion of access to the NHS.

An important consequence of the commitment to equality of access has been the conscious pursuit of geographical equality in people's access to care. Since its inception in 1948, the NHS has tried to ensure that people receive a similar service wherever they live in the UK, and subsequent policies (notably controls over the movement of general practitioners and the introduction in 1976 of a fairer way of **allocating resources** to different parts of the country) have reinforced the goal. Not only this, it has also been an explicit aim of the NHS to offer a comprehensive range of services for people of all ages ('from the cradle to the grave'). The service was launched in 1948 on the promise that nothing would be excluded from the menu of treatments it offered, and although the promise has come under great pressure in recent years, and some relatively minor treatments are not always available on the NHS, the principle of comprehensiveness still remains the formal position of the government.

The outworking of these principles has meant that, on its fiftieth birthday in 1998, the NHS would in some respects be broadly recognizable to those such as Aneurin Bevan and William Beveridge who had shaped its conception and enabled its birth. It is still largely a public service that is accountable to Parliament through the government of the day. It is still funded mainly through taxation, and is still free for most patients at the time of use. People still register with a general practitioner of their choice and gain access to secondary and tertiary services only through the referral system. The wholly private market in healthcare, which has always run in parallel with the NHS, still accounts for no more than about 10 per cent of all health-service activity in the UK.

The Cost of the NHS

Rather more surprising to the founding fathers would be the current cost of the NHS. In 1950 the service cost £447 million, and there was every expectation that, when the back-log of untreated illnesses had been cleared, the cost would actually decline. With the introduction of free treatment and a range of innovative preventive services, there seemed good reason to expect the amount of illness in the community—and therefore the cost of the NHS—to diminish. That quite the reverse has happened is now well understood. The complexity and cost of medical technology have increased at a rate unimaginable in the 1940s; the numbers of people living through to extreme old age have risen far above those predicted; and people's expectations of care when they are ill have soared. By 1998 the cost of the service is likely to have risen to £45 billion—a five-fold increase since 1950 even allowing for the effects of inflation, which have always been higher in the NHS than in the general economy (Table 13.1).

Year	Spending as % of gross domestic product (GDP) at market prices	Index of health spending as % of GDP (1960=100)
1960	3.9	100
1965	4.1	106
1970	4.5	115
1975	5.5	140
1980	5.6	144
1985	5.9	150
1990	6.0	154
1995	6.9	177

Table 13.1 Total healthcare expenditure in the UK as percentage of Gross Domestic Product at market prices, 1960–95

Source: Office of Health Economics 1997: 2.11.

Country	Total healthcare expenditure per person (£)	Spending as % of gross domestic product (GDP) at market prices
Australia	1,021	8.5
Austria	1,559	9.7
Belgium	1,199	8.0
Canada	1,183	9.5
Denmark	1,214	6.5
Finland	1,041	8.2
France	1,449	9.9
Germany	1,552	9.6
Greece	315	5.3
Ireland	746	8.0
Italy	967	7.7
Japan	1,695	7.2
Netherlands	1,249	8.8
New Zealand	712	7.5
Norway	1,348	7.3
Portugal	435	7.7
Spain	592	7.6
Sweden	1,126	7.7
Switzerland	2,286	9.7
United Kingdom	787	6.9
United States	2,285	14.5

Table 13.2 Total healthcare expenditure per person and as percentage of Gross Domestic Product at market prices in OECD countries, 1994

Source: Office of Health Economics 1997: 2.9, 2.11.

Even so, the UK still spends a lower proportion of its income on healthcare than most other industrialized countries, particularly through the private sector (Table 13.2). Whereas the USA, for example, spent some 14 per cent of its national product on health-care in the mid-1990s, the proportion in the UK was only about 7 per cent. Of course, it cannot be inferred from this that healthcare in the US is twice as good as in the UK, much less that Americans are twice as healthy as Britons. A lot depends on the efficiency of the two systems in getting the maximum amount of healthcare from each dollar or pound spent, and in any case the relationship between the volume of healthcare provided and the levels of health in a community is highly complex. Important differences may also occur in the ease of access that different groups of people have to the system. In contrast to America, healthcare policy in the UK has generally taken the view that superb care for the few may be less desirable socially than good care for the many.

Nevertheless, international comparisons of healthcare spending do point towards a major weakness of a tax-based system like the NHS: governments are always under pressure to restrain the growth in public spending. The view is pervasive in the UK that too much public spending will fuel inflation, erode investment in manufacturing and service industries, and reduce the scope for reductions in personal levels of taxation. In consequence, healthcare systems such as the NHS, that are funded largely from tax revenue, are usually more squeezed for resources than those where people pay for their own care through some form of **insurance.** Through insurance people are usually prepared to pay more for better healthcare for themselves and their families, but the British government can only increase the proportion of national income spent on the NHS if it is prepared to raise taxes, increase public borrowing, or cut back on other programmes such as education, defence, or social security. None of these options is politically easy.

The Structure of the NHS

Even more surprising to the founding fathers of the NHS, were they to return today, would be the changes that have occurred in the structure of the service. The organizational structures created in 1948 reflected the current views about the nature of healthcare and the relationship between central government and local administration. Under the political control of the Ministry of Health, the NHS was organized into three largely unco-ordinated sectors: the hospital service, run by regional hospital boards and local hospital management committees; the general practitioner services, run by executive councils; and the community health services, run by local government. Policy was promulgated by the Ministry of Health and implemented by the local committees and councils.

Although the structure worked well for many years and was able to bring about some fundamental changes in the way that hospitals worked, the inflexibility of the three-pronged structure became increasingly problematic. People's needs did not fall neatly into each of the three sectors: in the course of a single episode of illness, a patient might need the services of the GP, the hospital, and a community nurse. The difficulty of providing unified packages of care from managerially separated sectors led to the first major restructuring of the NHS in 1974, when the community health services were removed from local government and merged with the hospital services under the control of regional and area health authorities and district management teams. The general practitioner services remained apart and unreformed, and GPs retained their traditional freedom to refer patients anywhere in the NHS.

The Management of the NHS

Further major revisions to the structure of the NHS took place in 1982, with the replacement of the area health authorities and district management teams with new district health authorities, and in 1985, with the introduction of **general management.** In retrospect the importation from the private sector of the ethos and attitudes of general management, together with the creation of new mechanisms for putting them into practice, can be seen as the single most important shift occurring in the first forty years of the NHS. By the mid-1980s a new approach to the management of the public services was dominant in Westminster and Whitehall. Increasingly, the services were seen as inefficient, unresponsive to the needs of those they served, and dominated by the self-serving interests of the professionals who controlled the technology. The almost God-like status and autonomy of the hospital consultants, caricatured by Sir Lancelot Spratt, was an obvious manifestation of a deeper structural malaise.

In 1983 Mr (later Sir) Roy Griffiths, then the managing director of Sainsbury's, was commissioned by the government to 'advise on the effective use and management of manpower and related resources in the NHS'. His unpublished report to the government, which took only eight months to complete, highlighted the lack of a clear management structure in the service in which those responsible for getting things done could be identified and held to account. As Griffiths put it in a memorable phrase, 'If Florence Nightingale were carrying her lamp through the corridors of the NHS today, she would almost certainly be searching for the people in charge.' Griffiths's recommended solution, which was accepted immediately by the government, was the appointment at all levels of the NHS of general managers charged with implementing the policies of the government and the health authorities and accountable for their performance. It did not matter whether they came from a medical, nursing, commercial, financial, or military background: it was their managerial skills and experiences that counted.

By the late 1980s, with general management extending its influence throughout the NHS, the time was ripe for the next phase in the government's quest for the modernization of the public services, particularly the NHS. Although the background to the **internal market** had been developing throughout the decade, with the introduction of such innovations as the contracting-out of hospital domestic services to private contractors and the encouragement given to health authorities to sell their products in commercial markets, it was the publication of the influential White Paper *Working for Patients* early in 1989 that crystallized these trends into a single project of staggering ambition: to open the NHS to market forces.

The Internal NHS Market

The background to the internal NHS market is complex, though certain landmarks stand out clearly. One was the work in the early 1980s of an American economist, Professor Enthoven, who identified the lack of competitive stimulus as a major source of inefficiency in the NHS. As a remedy Enthoven proposed that, instead of automatically using their annual budgets to maintain their 'own' hospitals, the **district health authorities** (DHAs) should be free to shop around among all the hospitals within a reasonable geographical distance and 'spend' their budgets where they felt they could get the best value for money. Hospitals would then be forced to compete against each other for the 'custom' of the DHAs, giving them market-type incentives to enhance the quality of their services while minimizing their production costs.

Enthoven's ideas were clearly visible in the 1989 White Paper *Working for Patients*, setting out the vision of a new NHS in which the district health authorities would be the major purchasers of services, and the hospitals (including private hospitals) would be the providers. Set in an administrative context which mimicked that of the market, the purchasers and providers would stand in a commercial relationship with each other. Every DHA would contract with the hospitals of its choice for the provision of a specified quantity and quality of care that would be available to its resident population. Contracts could, of course, be placed with a DHA's 'own' hospitals, but they could also be placed with provider hospitals in neighbouring (or even more distant) districts, and also with private hospitals.

Two of the key proposals in the White Paper, however, went far beyond anything that

Enthoven envisaged. One was the idea of giving general practices their own budgets from which to buy a limited range of care required by their patients when they went to hospital, with the cost of some in-patient and out-patient treatments to be charged back to the practice's budget. Not only would this devolve the purchasing function to the level at which the true needs of patients were best known, but it would also bring the GPs themselves into the ambit of the market by giving them the incentive to reduce unnecessary referrals. In future, **budget-holding general practices** would themselves bear the cost of the referrals they made, but as an incentive to refer patients only when it was really necessary they would retain any end-of-year savings on their budgets for investment in their practices.

The other key proposal in the White Paper was that of releasing some of the larger hospitals from managerial control by the district health authorities and allowing them to become self-governing players in the internal market. Their income would no longer take the form of a management budget from the DHA, but would be dependent solely upon the volume of business they could attract. Though they would remain publicly owned hospitals within the NHS, they would acquire a set of freedoms similar to those enjoyed by commercial hospitals competing in the private market. They would control their own assets, employ their own staff, develop their own business plans, and generally be responsible for their own destiny in the new competitive environment. Conversely, of course, they would also assume the risks of market failure, including the possibility of merging with rival hospitals or even, in extreme circumstances, going out of business if they failed to attract sufficient contract income.

The proposals in *Working for Patients*, though bitterly opposed by almost every interest group in the NHS, became law with the passage of the National Health Service and Community Care Act 1990, and they came into effect in 1991. From the outset, however, the internal NHS market was a dynamic structure, continuing to evolve and metamorphose even as it was establishing its viability. The number of budget-holding general practices and the range of services they could purchase expanded year by year; by the mid-1990s almost half the population was registered with them, and experiments were afoot to extend the scope of budget-holding to embrace the totality of services offered by the NHS, including emergency hospital care. The number of self-governing hospitals (or **NHS trusts** as they came to be called) likewise developed on a scale unanticipated in the White Paper, until by the time of the 1997 general election every provider unit in the country had become a trust, including not only hospitals but also community health services and ambulance services.

Yet precisely because the internal market was continually changing and evolving, it was also moving steadily away from the purity of its original conception. Seen by its originators as a way of opening up a large public service to the bracing breezes of market competition, it largely failed to behave in this way. Issues that should in principle have been left to the market to resolve were often determined by the central control mechanisms that were characteristic of the earlier decades of the NHS. The rationalization of hospital provision in London following a national enquiry was one example. Moreover, far from being freed from the intrusive inquisitiveness of the health authorities, the hospitals continued to have their futures planned for them by the purchasers. When it became clear in the late 1990s that East Kent had too many acute hospitals and an unsustainable number of beds, it was the fiat of the health authority rather than the invisible hand of the market that identified the hospitals which were to contract.

The internal market and the inequalities that it had supposedly generated was a prominent topic in the 1997 general election campaign, and the changes which the Labour Party had promised in its manifesto were unveiled in a White Paper entitled *The New NHS: Modern, Dependable*, published in December 1997. Building upon the transitions that were already under way, the White Paper set out the long-term vision of a 'third way' between the 'command and control' of the 1970s and the 'fragmentation and bureaucracy' of the 1990s. It was to be the way of 'integrated care' founded on partnerships. The divide between planning and providing was to remain, but competition and contracts were to be replaced by co-operation and service agreements. The quality of care would be enhanced by the introduction of national standards and guidelines. Management costs were to be capped. Most far-reaching of all, fundholding in general practice was to be replaced by a new system of commissioning, based on localities of about 100,000 people, in which representatives of *all* GPs and community nurses would participate, working closely with social services. Health authorities would continue to be accountable for the care provided in each locality, but they would lose many of the planning powers they had acquired under the 1990 Act.

Whether the proposals of the Labour government will change the NHS for the better, or whether they will merely rearrange the familiar and fading furniture of the service, remains to be seen. It is a long-term project, designed to take effect over ten years. The incoming Labour government in 1997 made it clear that no new resources were to be made available to the NHS, at least in the short term, and no new ways of funding it were to be tried. The challenges that have propelled the NHS to the forefront of national concern and consciousness are likely to remain, and the White Paper's objective of once again making the NHS the envy of the world is perhaps better understood within the abstracted ethos of public relations than in the real world of practical reform.

Challenges in Healthcare 1: Controlling Costs

The Rising Costs of Healthcare

Perhaps the most pressing challenge is posed by the global phenomenon of the rising costs of healthcare. In the United Kingdom, total expenditure on the National Health Service (NHS) rose from about 3.5 per cent of the gross domestic product in the mid-1950s to about 5 per cent in the mid-1970s and about 7 per cent in the mid-1990s. Other countries have experienced a similar increase in spending, and although the structural reasons differ from one to another the underlying dynamics are similar in all western countries. The striking increase in life expectancy throughout the twentieth century has led not only to substantial increases in the numbers of elderly people, who typically consume more healthcare than any other age group except very young children, but also in the dominant patterns of disease in modern societies. Long-term chronic illnesses and disabilities requiring extensive care over substantial periods of time now account for a large share of the health budget: about 20 per cent of the total cost of the NHS is spent on the care of people with mental illness, and 10 per cent on those with strokes, compared with only about 7 per cent on the treatment of cancer.

The spectacular growth of medical technology has also fuelled the growth in health expenditure. Transplant surgery was unknown and unperformed before the 1970s, CAT scanning before the 1980s, and keyhole surgery before the 1990s. It has been estimated that the amount of spending on the NHS needs to increase by about 1 per cent each year simply to keep pace with the rising cost of medical technology. The dawning of the exciting but costly era of genetic therapy will only serve to intensify the trend.

The rising cost of healthcare is a challenge to governments largely because of the impact it has on other sectors of the national economy. However desirable it may be to have a comprehensive and up-to-date healthcare system, its cost must always be balanced against other claims on the national income; and the point will be reached at which any extra spending on healthcare is judged politically (and perhaps even medically) not to be worth the benefits it produces. This is as true for countries which finance most healthcare through the private sector as for those, including the UK, in which more than 80 per cent of healthcare spending is through the public sector. In the former case the cost is borne to a considerable extent by private companies through the health insurance plans of their employees, adding to the price of goods and services and adversely affecting their competitiveness in world markets. It is said, for example, that the cost of health insurance for American automobile workers added almost $900 to the price of a basic Ford car in 1993.

In countries where healthcare systems are funded substantially from public resources, the concerns of governments about increasing costs are even more understandable. If the increase exceeds the rate of economic growth in the country, it can be funded only by raising taxes, increasing public borrowing, or reducing expenditure on other public programmes. None of these options is politically attractive, and UK governments have repeatedly found themselves in the paradoxical situation of persuading the electorate that they are generously spending ever-increasing sums of money on the NHS, while trying to avoid the actions that would give substance to the claim.

Controlling Costs in the NHS

On the other side of the coin, however, the method of funding the NHS in the UK makes the challenge of cost control much easier than elsewhere. Healthcare can basically be financed in one (or a combination) of three ways: from central government revenues raised through taxation and borrowing, from social insurance contributions paid by employees and employers, or by payments from patients (or their insurers) purchasing the care they need in private markets. In the case of the UK and other countries in which more than 80 per cent of the cost of healthcare is provided by central government, increases in spending on health services can be very effectively controlled by the national budgetary process. Indeed, this is seen by many foreign observers, particularly those from the USA, to be one of the greatest strengths of the NHS.

The procedure is reasonably transparent. Each year the UK government presents its annual budget to parliament containing its plans for both raising revenue (through taxation and borrowing) and spending it. Included in the spending plans is an allowance for the cost of the NHS in the forthcoming financial year and, tentatively, for a few years beyond that. Once parliament has approved the budget, the maximum spending on the NHS is fixed, and it will normally be exceeded only in exceptional circumstances (for example, to fund a particular new initiative that has become politically contentious during the year). In short, the funding of the NHS is determined by parliament and is controlled through the supply of public funds. This is not to say the government is immune from pressures to increase the level of spending: far from it. But it is to say that the mechanisms do exist for ensuring that no more is spent each year on healthcare than the government deems at the time to be politically and economically manageable.

This approach contrasts quite sharply with countries in which healthcare is financed largely through the private market, for the volume of trade in markets is driven by the demands of customers, not by externally imposed constraints on the producers. If, as in the USA, individuals and companies choose to spend part of their income on healthcare rather than other goods or services, then the market will try to provide enough doctors, nurses, and other resources to deliver the care for which people are prepared to pay. It will also try to persuade them to purchase care that they may not want or even need. This is one reason why spending on healthcare in the USA is higher than in any other country, and also why there is great concern there about the rapidly rising costs.

Challenges in Healthcare 2: Balancing Supply and Demand

The Problem of Rationing

A problematic effect of the rising costs of healthcare across all developed countries is reflected in the second major challenge facing governments, that of finding acceptable ways of bringing the supply of, and demand for, healthcare into balance. Increasingly, the problem is being described explicitly as that of rationing. If people's needs for healthcare are running ahead of the system's capacity to satisfy them, it follows necessarily that some needs will not be dealt with adequately, or even not at all. In extreme cases people may die because they cannot get access to the care that could have saved them.

There is nothing new in the phenomenon of people wanting more of something than they can afford: it is a fundamental fact of human nature and is a basic assumption in economics. In the case of healthcare, however, ethical questions intrude into what in other circumstances might be an unexceptionable observation about supply and demand. It is one thing for some people to be unable to afford luxury goods like jacuzzis and foreign holidays; it is seen as different in the case of medical treatments that might save or enhance their lives. Who is to decide which patients should and should not be treated, and on what grounds? Such questions are receiving increasingly prominent coverage in the media in the United Kingdom, generating an informed and emotional public debate without arriving at a set of universally acceptable criteria.

One such case was that of Jaymee Bowen, an 11-year-old girl who, in 1995, suffered the recurrence of a cancer for which she had already received one transplant. Her local health authority (Cambridge) declined to fund a second transplant for her on the grounds that it was not in her best interests: a second transplant was an experimental treatment that would involve Jaymee in 'great suffering' with only a small chance of success. Her father refused to accept the health authority's decision and sought a judicial review. The matter eventually went to the Court of Appeal, which found in favour of Cambridge Health Authority—not for the reason that it would not be in the child's best interests, but because the Authority was justified in claiming that its limited resources could be used to better effect in other ways.

Rationing in the NHS

In private markets the job of bringing the supply of and demand for healthcare into balance is performed by price: if the potential demand for care exceeds the available supply, prices will rise and either demand will fall or else new producers will enter the market. The basis for rationing is clear, even if not always socially acceptable: healthcare goes to those who can afford it and are willing to pay the market price.

In the NHS, by contrast, where the conditions of the private market do not prevail, other ways must be found of distinguishing between those who will and will not have their needs for healthcare fully met. For much of the lifetime of the NHS such mechanisms have been largely concealed beneath the cloak of clinical freedom: it has been left to the doctors and other clinicians to make these decisions on behalf of the community in the course of their everyday work. For the most part it is they who have decided how much of which treatments will be given to which patients, and they have used a variety of rationalizations to justify their inability to meet all the needs of all their patients all the time.

For the first thirty years of the NHS such covert rationing went either unnoticed or unremarked, and it was never a public issue. Since the late 1970s, however, the continuing pressure on successive UK governments to limit the growth of public spending has gradually exposed the extent to which care is rationed in the NHS; and as the evidence has steadily accumulated, an ethical debate has grown up about the proper basis for rationing in the NHS. The case of Jaymee Bowen was merely one of a number of well-publicized cases in the 1990s of patients being denied potentially life-preserving treatment in part because of a judgement by doctors and managers that the costs of such treatment could be better spent elsewhere.

By the mid-1990s it was clear that society's capacity to pose the ethical and clinical questions surrounding the rationing of care was running well ahead of its ability to provide acceptable answers. Some simple attempts were made by health authorities to impose rationing by exclusion (that is, to make certain treatments such as cosmetic surgery, in-vitro fertilization and dental implants unavailable on the NHS), but otherwise little had changed. The bold experiment in the state of Oregon in the USA, in which attempts were made to elicit community values about the treatments which could and could not be afforded from the public funds allocated to the Medicaid programme, attracted a great deal of attention in the UK but led to no substantive action. The status quo was preserved in which the rhetoric remained of an NHS providing comprehensive care from the cradle to the grave while the reality rebutted it a thousand times a day.

Challenges in Healthcare 3: Strengthening the Scientific Base of Healthcare

The Issue of Effectiveness

A third challenge is that of improving the scientific basis of healthcare to ensure that the treatments which patients receive are clinically effective and appropriate to their needs. The challenge is intrinsically independent of the problem of rationing, but it has been emphasized in recent years by the rising costs of healthcare. A treatment is appropriate if it can be shown to be effective in tackling the patient's particular problem, if its cost is broadly commensurate with the benefits it produces, if the doctors who use it are properly trained in its application, and if systems are in place to monitor the quality of the care the patient receives. Medicine has, of course, had a strong scientific base for a long time; but it necessarily encompasses elements of art as well as science, and it is still capable of doing things that are ineffective and inappropriate. In recent years, however, the realization has grown of the importance of strengthening the scientific basis of medical practice, not only to reassure patients but also to gain the maximum benefit from the resources used.

Known commonly as **evidence-based medicine,** the quest for a stronger scientific basis has a number of distinct elements. An important one is that of effectiveness—the extent to which treatments change the natural history of disease for the better. It was Professor Cochrane in the early 1970s who first drew systematic attention to the unproven effectiveness of many clinical procedures. Some, such as the use of insulin in diabetic patients and of penicillin in the treatment of infections, have been shown to be so obviously valuable in clinical practice that the formal testing of their effectiveness is unnecessary. But many other treatments whose benefits are far from obvious have gradually crept into the doctor's armoury through custom, bias, or familiarity even though they have never been subjected to rigorous testing. In his book, Cochrane pleaded eloquently that no new treatments should be allowed until they had been scrutinized through the standard experimental procedure of the **randomized controlled trial.**

Another strand in the quest for a stronger scientific basis, which has built upon Cochrane's work, is that of **the cost-benefit** and **cost-effectiveness** of treatments. Treatments should not only be demonstrably effective in clinical terms but should also represent good value for the money they cost. Unsurprisingly, this is an argument that has been steadily elaborated by economists with an interest in healthcare policy, and it has spawned the introduction of a range of different techniques for measuring 'value for money'. Some try to ascertain whether the gains for patients and for society are 'worth' the resources they consume (cost-benefit approaches); others, having decided or assumed that the gains are worth having, try to establish the least costly way of attaining them (cost-effective approaches). The challenge in these approaches lies not only in the design and implementation of research studies that will produce sensible conclusions, but also in persuading doctors and managers to act upon them.

Evidence-Based Medicine in the NHS

Throughout the 1990s several initiatives have been taken in the UK to encourage a better use of resources by sharpening the scientific basis of healthcare. One initiative has been the development of a national research and development (R&D) programme in health. It began in 1991 with the creation of a central Research and Development Committee charged with identifying the most pressing issues confronting the NHS, determining the information needed to address them, and then commissioning the research required to supply the information. Central to the programme is the idea that doing research and implementing the results should be two sides of the same coin.

The R&D Committee, supported by a Director drawn from the ranks of academia, began by identifying six priorities, including the evaluation of expensive medical technologies, the way in which the NHS is managed, the treatment of accidents, and the care of people with complicated disabilities. Academic centres were established at Oxford and York to assemble and disseminate up-to-date information about effective treatments and good management practices, and all researchers taking part in the programme were required to publish their findings as widely as possible. The R&D programme is an innovative attempt to achieve appropriate care (and hence to increase the value that the NHS gives for the money spent on it) through strengthening the scientific basis of medical practice.

Another initiative of the 1990s designed to enhance the appropriateness of care by assuring its quality has been that of **clinical audit**—that is, the regular and systematic scrutiny of all aspects of clinical care to ensure that required standards are being met and that corrective action is being taken to eliminate sub-standard practices. Audit is not a new phenomenon: every case of maternal death in the UK has been audited since 1957 to discover the cause of death, to identify avoidable factors that may have contributed to the death, and to ensure that mistakes are not repeated. But clinical audit was given prominence in the government's 1989 White Paper, *Working for Patients*, and since then it has steadily gained more widespread acceptance. Many audit studies are now conducted regularly throughout the NHS, some of them large and formal, others small and informal. Audits are also made of the management of the NHS, notably by the Audit Commission, whose sharply critical reports have become a valuable source of independent assessment of the workings of the NHS.

Challenges in Healthcare 4: Health Promotion and Disease Prevention

Health Promotion and Disease Prevention: UK Experience

Doubts about the effectiveness and benefits of scientific medical treatments and concerns about their costs coupled with the increasing evidence of the importance of behavioural and environmental factors in the causation of diseases, such as cancer and cardiovascular disease, were some of the reasons why the UK government began to formulate a policy for Health Promotion and Disease Prevention. The emphasis in early government policy which emerged in the 1970s was on disease prevention, and the approach to disease causation evident in this policy was the multiple risk-factor model. The focus in the 1976 government White Paper on prevention was on attempting to influence 'lifestyle' risk factors and health-damaging behaviour with particular emphasis on the health hazards of smoking. The following illustrates the general approach adopted.

Probably the most important single factor which men from their youth onwards should ponder is cigarette smoking, with exercise and obesity next in order of importance. To the extent therefore that coronary heart disease is determined by a man's lifestyle the prime responsibility for his own health falls on the individual.

Government policy during the 1970s and 1980s focused mainly on smoking control. The general approach taken by the government involved a mixture of measures primarily aimed at influencing the consumption as opposed to the production of tobacco. These measures included educational programmes mainly through the mass media, pricing through increasing tax (although this was rarely initiated for public health reasons), and regulation through controls over availability of tobacco for young people and a ban on TV advertising. Tobacco advertising and promotion was regulated through a series of voluntary agreements with the tobacco industries. Also, voluntary controls on smoking in public places and in public institutions increasingly became popular as cigarette smoking became a habit for only a minority of the population. Bearing in mind the difficulties in enforcing and regulating the legislative measures and the voluntary agreements, and the uncertainties about the effectiveness of the education campaigns, the statistics on changes in cigarette consumption during the 1970s and 1980s suggest that this piecemeal package of measures may have had some success. For example in 1972, 52 per cent of the male and 41 per cent of the female population in Great Britain were smokers. In 1986 the proportions had reduced to 35 per cent and 31 per cent for men and women respectively and by 1996–7 they had further dropped to 29 per cent and 28 per cent. The social class difference is still marked, with higher levels of smoking found amongst those with manual occupations; but the gender difference has been much reduced. All age groups have experienced a marked fall apart from women between 16 and 19, where there has been an increase. There are a range of possible reasons for the reduction in smoking other than the effect of the smoking-control measures. Why did the policy take this piecemeal approach? It has been argued that the major obstacles to the development of a coherent policy lie with the political strength of vested interests in tobacco manufacture and promotion in this country (the 'Smoke Ring') and the confusion of interests within the government itself, particularly the Treasury's dependence on revenue from tobacco tax. Hence, 'more interventionist' policy, such as a government 'ban' on tobacco advertising and promotion, were absent from the policy agenda because of vested interests in the Smoke Ring. However, given the strength of the pro-smoking lobby, why was there any smoking control policy at all? The major reason probably lies in the increasing support given by sections of the medical profession through the publication of a series of authoritative reports and through the political strength of the BMA.

During the 1980s the UK government also became involved with other aspects of prevention, particularly in relation to food and health, control over alcohol consumption, and attempts to encourage regular exercise. The overall approach still concentrated on the prevention of disease through the control of behavioural risk factors. However, the government's interest in and commitment to prevention received impetus from the emergence of the so-called 'epidemic' of AIDS. The 'moral panic' about AIDS led to a major House of Commons debate and the unique measure, at least in this context, of the setting up of a Cabinet Committee. The only long-term protection against the spread of AIDS was believed to be a change in the population's sexual habits, and consequently the government initiated a traditional public health education campaign aimed at the population as a whole.

The policy response of the government to AIDS provided the impetus and foundation for what was seen at that time as the most significant development in government policy in health promotion and disease prevention, that is, the publication of the White Paper for England, *The Health of the Nation*. Before that there had been an initiative which had targeted general practitioners and the primary healthcare teams. The enthusiasm for anticipatory care in general practice which was generated in the early 1980s has been supported by the government in the new contract for general practitioners implemented in 1990 and a key role is prescribed for the primary healthcare team in the *Health of the Nation* documents (Dept. of Health, 1992). Thus, the introduction of the new GP contract provided financial incentives for general practitioners to be more involved in health promotion and disease prevention. Since then the method of reimbursement for GPs for this prevention work has been modified on two further occasions because of doubts about its effectiveness.

The *Health of the Nation* White Paper was published in July 1992 and proposed a broad strategy for improving the health of the population. It emphasizes its concern with the 'pursuit of health in its widest sense', and the phrases 'adding years to life' and 'adding life to years' are taken from the WHO Health for All initiative. Stress is laid on the importance of distinguishing a health strategy from a healthcare strategy. Five key areas were chosen: Coronary Heart Disease and stroke, Cancer, Mental Illness, HIV/AIDS and sexual health, and Accidents, although recently there has been discussions about the addition of a sixth which relates to the environment. The five areas were chosen because they were major causes of premature death or avoidable ill-health; they were ones where effective interventions should be possible, offering significant scope for improvement in health; and it was possible to set objectives and targets in the areas and monitor progress towards them.

The key areas, the main objectives, and their associated targets are tools for achieving the wider strategic aim of the Health of the Nation. The strategy also identifies a number of settings such as schools, homes, and workplaces where health promotion could be focused to good effect, and it emphasises the value of joint working, 'healthy alliances', and intersectoral action. In each key area the Department of Health set out action plans and proposals for meeting the targets they had set, including co-ordinating action by other government departments; and it also established a framework for monitoring and reviewing progress towards the targets through the use of a variety of indicators.

The Health of the Nation has also been a key strategic goal for the NHS since the launch of the White Paper in 1992, has attempted to influence health authorities' plans to purchase healthcare to meet the needs of local people, and is reflected in local programmes carried out by hospitals, community health units, and primary healthcare teams. Regional health authorities were also to encourage District and Family Health Services Authority to shift the focus towards health promotion, including changing the balance of resources as necessary.

A recent National Audit Office report (NAD 1996) assessed the progress of the Health of the Nation. It concluded that many targets show encouraging progress; some have been met already, although with others progress towards some targets cannot be monitored at present. The lack of the availability and limits in the quantity and quality of data available suggests that it is very difficult to make a meaningful assessment of progress, and also that the timescale for measurement is too long, as some indicators will not respond quickly. However, there were areas where progress had been limited, such as with obesity, saturated fatty acids and total fat in the diet, drinking more than the sensible level of alcohol, and smoking among children aged 11 to 15 years.

More recently, the government through the Health of the Nation strategy has responded to the problem of inequalities in health. After the attempted suppression of *The Black Report* there was a more formal response, with the setting up of the Health of the Nation subcommittee on Variations in Health, which reported in October 1995.

The report accepted that cumulative differential exposure to health-damaging or health-promoting physical and social environments is the *main* explanation for the observed variation in health and life expectancy. The report identifies a role for the NHS at the local level to undertake a more systematic identification of health variations and to design and implement measures to tackle them. More specifically, they recommend that health authorities and GP purchasers should have a plan for identifying and tackling variations and for evaluating interventions. This plan should include provision for working in alliance with other relevant bodies and health authorities, and GP purchasers and Trusts should take steps to monitor access to services to safeguard equitable access. Overall, a role for the Department of Health was prescribed, particularly to promote health alliances at both national and local level and to ensure that the NHS implements recommendations for a coherent programme of research, particularly in evaluating health interventions.

The Labour Government in its White Paper on the NHS (DH 1997) and its Green Paper on *Public Health and Health Promotion* (DH 1998) has also emphasized the need to reduce inequalities and to promote health. The Green Paper (DH 1998) building on the *Health of the Nation* disease-oriented strategy identifies its priority areas as accidents, cancers, mental health, and coronary heart disease and stroke. Schools, the workplace, and neighbourhoods are seen as the settings in which policy should be focused, although deprivation is also to be tackled through the development of Health Action Zones. More recently, the government commissioned independent inquiry into inequalities in healthcare has reported (HMSO, 1998).

Challenges in Healthcare 5: The Need to Tackle Inequalities

Critical analysis of health promotion policy can be divided into two distinct approaches. First, there are those who can see the benefits of health promotion policy but criticize the approach adopted in the United Kingdom. Secondly, there are those that are critical of health promotion's role and function irrespective of the policy adopted. Those who adopt the former approach have criticized the Health of the Nation on a number of counts. First, while emphasis in *The Health of the Nation* is placed on developing a strategy for 'health', the concept of 'health' which is employed is limited to a biomedical or epidemiological one (reducing avoidable mortality and morbidity, and changing behavioural risk factors) and is disease-led. Any broader or holistic definition of health is neglected.

The second criticism focuses on the overall strategy which is claimed to be strong on setting targets and weak on specifying exactly what policies will be adopted to meet these targets. Also, doubts have been raised about the value of numerical targets which, it is claimed, are biased towards areas where quantification and measurement is straightforward. Some of these targets may have also been achieved if current trends in mortality, morbidity, and changes in risk factor persist irrespective of the interventions generated through the Health of the Nation (Baggot 1994).

The third criticism focuses on the need to tackle the social and economic factors that determine patterns of health and illness, and the fact that *The Health of the Nation* has rather belatedly attempted to examine these issues. At least in the early *Health of the Nation* documents, emphasis was placed on the influence on health of a wide range of social, structural, and environmental factors as well as individual behaviours. A key element in the strategy was that responsibilities for improving health lie far beyond those of the National Health Service. However, despite this emphasis there is no reference to the impact of poverty or inequality, or other socio-economic factors. References are made to 'variations' in health status in relation to geographic region, ethnicity, and occupational class, but these are rejected as a main focus for action because they are 'complex' and 'largely unexplained'. General discussion of the determinants of health in *The Health of the Nation* tend to emphasize behavioural factors and give secondary status to environmental factors such as food safety, air and water quality, and workplace and housing conditions—a range of physical environmental 'threats to individuals from the external world which they cannot themselves control', and for which the government and other agencies have a responsibility. Behavioural influences are conceptualized in epidemiological terms and divorced from their social context. More important, behaviours are seen as lying within the responsibility of the individual, although the government's task is to provide necessary information and education to enable the individual to exercise 'informed' choice. Thus, as with previous government policy documents on disease prevention and health promotion, there is concern with behavioural change but with minimal government intervention.

Those that have criticized the *Health of the Nation* policy for neglecting social and economic influences on health and illness do not, however, agree on the most appropriate policies for tackling inequalities (Davison and Davey Smith, 1995). Those who adopt the perspective of the 'new public health' which appears to have its roots in social democratic principles also emphasize the importance of environment and lifestyle, although they argue that these act as mediators between social and economic circumstances and health. This approach suggests that, rather than directly 'targeting' health-damaging behaviour, policy should focus on the environmental and cultural context in which it is created and maintained by looking at issues such as 'stress' or housing conditions. However, in contrast to the 'top-down' prescriptive policies associated with the traditional public health measures, this new public health trend emphasizes the need to encourage the 'empowerment' of both individuals and communities.

Benezeval *et al.* (1995), working within the tradition of the 'new public health', sets out a programme for the government to tackle inequalities. Four levels of policy intervention are proposed: 'strengthening individuals', 'strengthening communities', 'improving access to essential facilities and services', and 'encouraging macro-economic and cultural change'.

'Person-centred' initiatives focus on dealing with people's lack of knowledge or skills and abilities to manage stress among people experiencing disadvantage. The emphasis is on encouraging people to have the skills and resilience to handle adverse circumstances: that is, 'to be a survivor'. Emphasis is placed on empowerment, although it is not exactly clear how the activities suggested, such as 'counselling', will actually enhance empowerment.

The general aim of strengthening the community through community development is to bring the members of a neighbourhood together to provide mutual support, and to take collective action to improve their position and conditions. This usually involves local initiatives to create a 'safe' community or improve the quality of life of people living in deprived neighbourhoods.

The third level focuses on improving access to essential facilities and services. Top of the list of recommendations is universal access to a clean water supply and subsidized contraception. Improvement of the psycho-social environment is also recommended, by reducing the causes of stress both at work and in isolated housing estates. Specific measures include involving workers in managerial problem-solving and the provision of recreational facilities. Family poverty is addressed by a return to progressive taxation and more specific proposals for childcare provision, job training, and the replacement of universal child benefit with means-tested income support and family credit. Housing policies are directed to improving the quantity and quality of 'public housing', and involve abolition of universal tax relief on mortgages in order to fund means-tested mortgage benefits for the poor, transferring council housing to local housing companies and tax concessions to private landlords to encourage expansion of the private rented sector.

The final level involves encouraging macro-economic and cultural change. The policies prescribed are economic policies to benefit people living in poverty, investment in public-health measures, investment in schooling, and the promotion of the rights of women, particularly their protection from abuse. One cultural issue which does receive attention is smoking cessation where there is an emphasis on an increase in taxes on tobacco and a ban on advertising.

In contrast to the 'new public health' there are those who argue from a structural position which emphasizes the direct influence of material circumstances and working conditions on ill health. According to this approach, priority should be placed on social policies aimed at social justice and material improvement, with the assumption that equality in health should follow. In other words, this is a stronger version of the type of social and economic policy options described in Level 4 of Benzeval and colleagues' approach (1995).

Another criticism of the *Health of the Nation*'s approach, and of health promotion policy in general, comes from those at the individualistic and libertarian end of political philosophy, who emphasize the importance of individual choice, freedom, and the free market, with minimal state intervention. Individuals should be free to choose health or ill health, and should be free to decide whether they wish to consume healthy or unhealthy products or take part in risk-taking or health-damaging activities. Examples of this perspective can be found in the pro-smoking groups, who are dismissive of evangelical attempts to dictate how people should comply with 'healthy' lifestyles.

Finally, there is the perspective which is critical of 'health promotion' as a whole as it is seen as a covert method of controlling or regulating the population or certain groups within it. Some commentators see health promotion not only as encouraging people to take responsibility for their own health but as a form of surveillance which monitors people's lifestyles and defines some as less worthy of treatment. A slightly different approach suggests that health promotion is a form of social marketing, and that consumption of 'healthy' commodities and services should be seen in terms of the wider consumer culture. Diet, sport, and health clubs, are part of the consumer's concern with 'body maintenance' and 'image', which in turn is tied to the notion of individual responsibility and the ideology of consumer sovereignty in the marketplace (Nettleton and Bunton 1995).

Challenges in Healthcare 6: Developing Appropriate Organizational Structures

The New Public Management

The sixth major challenge dominating the contemporary debate about healthcare policy in the last decade of the century is that of the appropriate organizational structures for delivering care to those who need it. There are a number of strands to the challenge. One is the question of the role of government in the provision of healthcare. For reasons discussed above, modern governments have a legitimate interest in ensuring the availability of good healthcare; but how should that interest be expressed? As we have seen, for much of the post-war period in the United Kingdom, central government had direct responsibility for almost all aspects of the NHS and was accountable to parliament for its day-to-day working. The Service was financed very largely from public funds (that is, central government revenue); the buildings and equipment were publicly owned; the staff were public employees; and those who ran the NHS were accountable for their stewardship to the Ministry (later the Department) of Health. In the command-and-control economies of Eastern Europe the grip of the state on the healthcare system was even tighter.

But conventional wisdom about the involvement of government in the day-to-day working of public services has moderated appreciably since the 1970s. Most developed countries have experienced the phenomenon of 'government overload' in one form or another—that is, the inability of central governments to retain effective day-to-day control over complex public services in the face of the vast and swift changes going on around them in the management and technology of care. Instead, alternative ideas have emerged in which responsibility for the management and delivery of care is passed to semi-independent (or, in some cases, independent) agencies and organizations working within a regulatory framework set by government but not directly managed by it. Giving expression to these ideas has been far from easy, involving massive upheavals in many countries in the traditional ways of providing public services, and placing great strains on those responsible for managing the transition to newer, less monolithic and more flexible structures.

The Split Between Purchasers and Providers

The response to the challenge has led to radical change in the NHS following the White Paper *Working for Patients* in 1989. The 'internal market' has come of age. The functions of buying and selling services (or, to use the contemporary language, of commissioning and providing them) have been separated out and entrusted to different agencies. The health authorities which purchase services out of the budgets they receive from central government have become organizationally and managerially separate from the hospitals, the community health services, and the ambulance services that provide them. If some of the more explicitly commercial and competitive language of the New Right in the early 1990s has been moderated by the gentler language of New Labour in the late 1990s, the ideas have remained essentially the same.

So, too, have the aspirations. New Labour shares the hopes of the New Right that, with the passage of time, the separation of purchasing and providing will enhance the quality of services, increase the efficient use of resources, make the service more responsive to the needs and wishes of the patient, curb the power of self-serving professional interests, improve the availability of useful information about the workings of the service, and augment the inflow of private capital and revenue money.

The magnitude of the change, however, is such that any attempt at a balance sheet would be at best simplistic and at worst misleading. Many other large-scale changes occurred in the NHS at the time the internal market was being set up. Patients' charters were introduced, setting targets for many aspects of care in the NHS, including hospital waiting times. Spending on the service was raised in the early 1990s to ease the wheels of change; the terms and conditions under which GPs work for the NHS were altered; and research studies to plot the impact of the change were positively discouraged by the government. Moreover, any benefits the market might produce must be offset against its costs, particularly the sharp increase in the cost of managing the market.

From the patient's perspective, little may seem to have changed. The responsiveness of the NHS may, with the passage of time, be felt to have improved (though public satisfaction with the service has always been high), and the flashy logos of the new NHS trusts may catch the eye. The political brilliance of the NHS internal market, however, lies precisely in its claim to have enhanced the quality of care without disturbing the founding principles of the NHS. The service has not been privatized, and the purchasers in the internal market are not the patients but the health authorities and the general practices that are buying on their behalf. As in 1948, the NHS still purports to offer comprehensive care, it is still funded largely from taxation, it is still free for most patients at the point of use, and it is still committed formally to the principles of equity and fairness.

Convergence, Diversity, and the Continuity of Change

These, then, are among the dominant challenges facing western nations in developing their healthcare policies towards the end of the twentieth century: controlling the rising costs of healthcare, balancing supply and demand through the management of the rationing process, strengthening the scientific basis of healthcare, preventing disease and maintaining good health, tackling inequalities in health, and developing appropriate organizational structures. The ease with which ideas about healthcare policy can now be shared among politicians and policy-makers from different countries is leading to a degree of conformity in the ways they are responding to these challenges.

For example, the European member states of the World Health Organization, meeting in Ljubljana in 1996, pledged themselves to a Charter setting out a series of principles governing the reform of healthcare policy in Europe. Among the principles enunciated in the Charter were: that healthcare reforms must be governed by principles of human dignity, equity, solidarity, and professional ethics; that healthcare reform must aim for continuous improvement in the quality of care, including its cost-effectiveness; and that governments must regulate the financing of healthcare systems to ensure that good healthcare is delivered to all citizens in a sustainable way.

Yet in spite of a shared set of challenges facing the developed countries and the consequential trend towards convergence in healthcare policy, national systems and policies are by no means uniform. The World Health Organization does not, so to speak, produce an annual catalogue of standard health service systems from which governments can select and implement the one that gives them the features they want for the price they can afford. Systems are organic: they grow out of the political, social, and economic history of each country, and they adapt and change in ways that reflect contemporary national conditions and values. The particular responses of successive governments to the challenges described above have defined the main strands of British policy towards the NHS in the late twentieth century.

It is tempting to regard change as a process of transition from one state to another: that is, from one position of stability in which something is wrong to another position of stability in which the fault has been corrected. If this ever was a valid way of understanding change in complex organizations, it is no longer so. The speed of technological progress and the endemic nature of social and political change requires organizations to operate in an environment of permanent transformation. There is no longer a vision of the next stable state, only a memory of the current transient state that is about to be lost. The antithesis of change is no longer stability but stagnation. The six challenges around which this chapter has been built cannot properly be seen as finite (albeit immensely complex) problems that are capable of being resolved. They are intrinsically irresolvable.

It is therefore pointless to speculate about the future direction of healthcare policy even in the UK, much less on a wider international canvas. At the time of the British general election in 1987, none could have foreseen the radical innovation of the internal NHS market only four years later. All that can be predicted with confidence is that the future will be different from the present, and that the intervening period between the present and the future will therefore be characterized by mutation. The policy issues will have a greater or lesser durability, and the search for better ways of doing things will have more or less enduring features. But those who pretend that policy changes are directed towards a known, finite, and stable end are, perhaps, the alchemists of the late twentieth century.

Glossary

allocating resources Mechanisms that exist for sharing out the financial resources of the NHS between different parts of the country, between different fundholding general practices, and between different groups of services (acute hospitals services, mental illness, children, public health, etc.).

budget-holding general practices General practices that met certain criteria and that wished to do so could apply to hold their own annual budgets from which to meet the costs of various types of care that their patients received. These included many forms of in-patient and out-patient care, diagnostic testing, and the drugs that were prescribed for them.

clinical audit A generic description of various methods aimed at measuring and improving the quality of the work of doctors and other clinicians. An audit study compares the quality of a doctor's work against a pre-set standard of acceptability and, by feeding back the results, tries to bring about an improvement in the way that doctors work.

community health services Healthcare services other than those provided by general practitioners and hospitals. They include child health, health visiting and district nursing, and many services for the care of the elderly, the mentally ill, and those with learning difficulties.

cost-benefit An economic concept indicating which of two or more different activities or programmes is likely to give the best value for money. The expected benefits of each activity, discounted over an appropriate period of time, are expressed in commensurate terms and compared to their costs. One activity is likely to produce more benefit for each pound spent on it than another.

cost-effective An economic concept indicating which of two or more different methods is likely to achieve a predetermined goal at the least cost. It does not indicate whether the goal itself is worth achieving, merely the least costly way of doing so.

district health authority Created in 1982, district health authorities are the major purchasers of services through the internal market. Comprising both executive and non-executive directors, their core task is to assess the healthcare needs of their districts and to contract with a range of suppliers to provide services of a high quality at reasonable cost.

evidence-based medicine A generic description of various initiatives taken during the 1990s to increase scientific understanding of the effectiveness of different types of medical procedures and forms of care, and to ensure that effective procedures are adopted as widely as possible throughout the NHS.

general management A way of managing organizations in which managers are appointed for their managerial expertise rather than their professional qualifications. General managers in the NHS can come from medical, nursing, administrative, commercial, military, or financial backgrounds, and they may be managing people from very different backgrounds.

insurance A method of funding healthcare in which people pay regular contributions (premiums) to an insurer and the insurer pays all or part of the cost of any healthcare for those who are insured. Insurance can be publicly or privately organized, and people can usually choose to have more extensive benefits in return for larger premiums.

internal market A structure for providing public services in which the agencies (such as health authorities) which are responsible for deciding the availability of services and using their annual budgets to purchase them are managerially distinct from the organizations which actually produce the services and deliver them to patients. Purchasers and providers may relate to each other through the normal market mechanisms of price and competition, or they may be linked through service agreements that are negotiated between them.

National Health Service (NHS) The publicly funded healthcare system in the United Kingdom that came into being in 1948. It is funded from government revenue and provides a full range of healthcare services that are largely free at the point of use.

NHS trusts Created by the National Health Service and Community Care Act 1990, NHS trusts are public but semi-independent providers of healthcare, contracting with district health authorities and primary healthcare groups to provide services in return for income. The concept of the NHS trust was originally limited to larger hospitals, but since the mid-1990s all NHS providers other than general practice have become trusts.

randomized controlled trial A method widely used in medical research to test the effectiveness of a drug or procedure. Patients who are recruited into the trial are allocated, entirely at random, to either an experimental group that receives the test drug or to a control group that receives an inert drug. Where possible, neither doctors nor patients know which group they are in. The outcome is compared between the two groups over an appropriate period of time.

standardized morbidity rate The annual incidence of illness (usually expressed as a number per thousand or as a percentage) in a section of a population—such as smokers—adjusted to make it as though the age structure of that population was the same as that of the whole population.

standardized morbidity ratio This is the standardized morbidity rate (see above) of a group expressed as a ratio of the whole population rate, where that whole population rate is expressed as 100.

standardized mortality rate The annual rate of death (usually expressed as the number per thousand or as a percentage) in a section of a population—such as those in a particular occupation—adjusted to make it as though the age structure of that section was the same as for the whole population.

standardized mortality ratio The standardized mortality rate (see above) of a group expressed as a ratio of the whole population rate, where that whole population rate is expressed as 100.

Guide to Further Reading

Benzeval, M., Judge, K., and Whitehead, M. (1995) (eds.), *Tackling Inequalities in Health*, The King's Fund (London). An account of the major dimensions of inequalities in health in the UK, their causes, and the policy initiatives that are required to minimize them. The book considers not only the impact of the NHS on causing and reducing inequalities in health, but also the wider impact of lifestyle, community influences, living and working conditions, and broader socio-economic, cultural, and environmental conditions.

Klein, R. (1995), *The New Politics of the NHS* (London: Longman). An account of the political context of the NHS in the UK and the political processes that have shaped its development from its origin in the post-war period to the new era of the internal market.

Klein, R., Day, P., and Redmayne, S. (1996), *Managing Scarcity* (Buckingham: Open University Press). A research-based account of the dominating problem of rationing in the NHS, including discussions of the nature and history of rationing, the mechanisms by which it is done, and the likely ways forward in a context where the demand for care will continue to grow and the resources to provide will continue to be in short supply.

Powell, M. A. (1997), *Evaluating the National Health Service* (Buckingham: Open University Press). A general text that attempts not merely to describe the structure and functioning of the NHS but to evaluate how well it is doing. It does this by contrasting the achievements of the NHS against its objectives, comparing the NHS with the healthcare systems of other countries, and assessing the impact of the recent reforms of the NHS.

Ranade, W. (1997), *A Future for the NHS? Health Care for the Millennium* (London: Longman). An introductory text to the study of the NHS in the UK, including the changes introduced in 1991 and the plans of the incoming Labour government in 1997.

References

Baggott, R. (1994), *Health and Health Care in Britain* (London: Macmillan).

Bartley, M. and Owen, C. (1996), 'Relation between Socio-Economic Status, Employment and Health during Economic Change, 1973–93', *British Medical Journal*, 313, 445–9.

Benzeval, M., Judge, K., and Whitehead, M. (1995), *Tackling Inequalities in Health: An Agenda for Action* (King's Fund).

Benzeval, M. and Webb, S. (1995), *Family Poverty and Poor Health*, ch. 5, in Benzeval, M., Judge, K., and Whitehead, M. (eds.), *Tackling Inequalities in Health: An Agenda for Action* (King's Fund).

Best, R. (1995), 'The Housing Dimension', ch. 4, in Benzeval, M., Judge, K., and Whitehead, M. (eds.), *Tackling Inequalities in Health: An Agenda for Action* (King's Fund).

Blaxter, M. (1990), *Health and Lifestyles* (London: Routledge).

Bunker, J. P., Frazier, H. S., and Mosteller, F. (1994), 'Improving Health: Measuring Effects of Medical Care', *Millbank Quarterly*, 72/2, 225–58.

Calnan, M. (1991), *The Prevention of Coronary Heart Disease: Prospects, Policies and Politics* (London: Routledge).

Calnan, M. and Williams, S. (1991), 'Style of Life and the Salience of Health', *Sociology of Health and Illness*, 13/4, 506–29.

Calnan, M. (1994), 'Lifestyle and its Social Meaning', in Albrecht, G. (ed.), *Advances in Medical Sociology*, iv (JAI Press).

Cochrane, A. L. (1972), *Effectiveness and Efficiency: Random Reflections on Health Services* (London: Nuffield Provincial Hospitals Trust).

Davison, C. and Davey Smith, C. (1995), 'The Baby and the Bathwater: Examining Socio-Cultural and Free-Market Critiques of Health Promotion', in Bunker, R., Nettleton, S., and Burrows, R. (eds.), *Sociology of Health Promotion* (London: Routledge), 91–103.

Department of Health and Social Security (1976), *Prevention and Health: Everybody's Business* (London: HMSO).

Department of Health (1992), *The Health of the Nation: A Strategy for Health in England* (London: HMSO).

Department of Health (1997), *The New NHS: Modern, Dependable* (Department of Health, London).

Department of Health (1998), *Our Healthier Nation: A Contract for Health* (Department of Health, London).

Enthoven, A. C. (1985), *Reflections on the Management of the National Health Service* (London).

Fox., J. and Benzeval, M. (1995), 'Perspectives on Social Variations in Health', ch. 2, in Benzeval, M., Judge, K., and Whitehead, M. (eds.), *Tackling Inequalities in Health: An Agenda for Action* (King's Fund), 10–21.

Graham, H. (1989), 'Women and Smoking in the UK: The Implications for Health Promotion', *Health Promotion*, 4, 371–82.

Independent Inquiry into Inequalities in Health (1998), (London: HMSO).

Jenkinson, C. (ed.) (1994), *Measuring Health and Medical Outcomes* (London: UCL Press).

MacIntyre, S. (1986), 'The Patterning of Health by Social Position in Britain', *Social Science and Medicine*, 31, 831–7.

MacIntyre, S. (1997), 'The Black Report and Beyond: What are the Issues?', *Social Science and Medicine*, 44/6, 723–46.

National Audit Office (1996), *Health of the Nation: A Progress Report* (London: HMSO).

Nettleton, S. and Bunton, R. (1995), 'Sociological Critiques of Health Promotion', in Bunton, R., Nettleton, S., and Burrows, R. (eds.), *Sociology of Health Promotion* (London: Routledge), 41–59.

Power, C., Matthews, S., and Manor, O. (1996), 'Inequalities in Self-Rated Health in the 1958 Birth Cohort: Lifetime Social Circumstances or Social Mobility', *British Medical Journal*, 313, 449–53.

Ranade, W. (1994), *A Future for the NHS?* (London: Longman).

Secretaries of State for Health, Wales, Northern Ireland, and Scotland (1989), *Working for Patients*, Cmnd. 555 (London).

Townsend, P., Davidson, N., and Whitehead, M. (1988), *The Black Report and the Health Divide* (Harmondsworth: Penguin).

West, P. (1991), 'Rethinking the Health Selection Explanation for Health Inequalities', *Social Science and Medicine*, 32, 373–84.

Wilkinson, R. (1996), *Unhealthy Societies: The Affliction of Inequality* (London: Routledge).

14 Social Care

Julia Twigg

Contents

Introduction: The Uncertain Boundaries of Social Care

This chapter discusses social care. By this we mean the support of people with a disability, illness, or frailty, usually living in the community. The term thus overlaps considerably with community care. To a large extent, social care is defined in opposition to medical care: it is about those aspects of life that are not normally thought of as falling under the remit of medicine. The boundary of the medical and the social is, however, uncertain and contested and, as we shall see, where it is deemed to lie has become a political issue, and one that has considerable financial implications for individuals and government. The ambiguous position of **personal care** illustrates this (Twigg 1997).

In the chapter we start with the situation of various client groups themselves and then discuss the role of services in their support. The first sections cover older and disabled people and their carers; the middle section discusses the development of community care in relation to these groups; and two final sections explore the particular issues raised by the situations of people with mental health problems and learning disabilities.

Older People

The majority of people over 65 live independently and have no major care needs. For many, retirement opens up a period of leisure and new opportunities that is sometimes termed the Third Age. Not tied to chronological age, it is generally regarded as running from the mid-fifties to the mid-seventies. Most people in this age group do not suffer from health problems that limit their independence: a significant minority, however, do have problems with physical functioning or mental health, and the likelihood of these increases with age. For example, 9 per cent of people over 65 have difficulties getting up and down stairs, 2 per cent with getting in and out of bed, and 8 per cent with bathing or washing all over. Among those who are over 75, 13 per cent have difficulties with bathing/washing, and a similar proportion with stairs (*Living in Britain* 1994). Some mental health problems are associated with age. Senile dementia (whether caused by Alzheimers disease or multi-infarct dementia) affects about one in ten of the population under the age of 80, and about one in five after 80 (Marshall 1990). Though such difficulties present real problems for some older people, and ones with consider-able cost implications (older people are the largest consumers of public welfare services), it is salutary to consider the figures in reverse: 80 per cent of those over 80 do not have dementia, and 87 per cent over 75 manage their own personal care.

Problems with health and functioning are often exacerbated by the circumstances in which many older people live, particularly poor housing and poverty, both of which become more common with age. The importance of material and social factors in structuring the experience of old age is the basis of the **political economy perspective**, exemplified in the UK in the work of Townsend, Phillipson, and Walker. Their central assumption is that:

the process of ageing and the experience of old age cannot be understood without reference to the elderly person's location in the social structure and their relation to the economy. (Walker and Phillipson 1986: 2)

These connections they term the 'structured dependence of old age': it is economic and social forces rather than individual functioning that determine the circumstances of older people both as a group (their relative poverty and social marginalization) and as individuals, people carrying into old age the economic, social, and cultural resources that they built up and enjoyed in earlier life.

Ageism

Ageism is a form of social prejudice comparable with racism and sexism. Bytheway de-fines it as a set of beliefs that:

legitimates the use of chronological age to mark out classes of people who are systematically denied resources and opportunities that others enjoy, and who suffer the consequences of such denigration, ranging from well-meaning patronage to unambiguous vilification . . . Ageism gen-erates and reinforces a fear and denigration of the ageing process [stereotyping] presumptions regarding competence and the need for protection. (Bytheway 1995: 14)

Women suffer more from such ageist assumptions than do men. The fact that the old are predominately female subtly detracts from the status of the group as a whole.

Gender

On average, women live longer than men: life expectancy at birth for men is 72 and for women 77, and the gender differential has widened this century. 'The gender imbalance is most marked in advanced old age; over the age of 85, women outnumber men by three to one'(Arber and Ginn 1995: 11). Women suffer from greater material disadvantage, and old women are generally poorer than old men (largely because of the gendered na-ture of pension provision). The financial dependence of older women is socially created earlier in life by traditional expectations of financial dependence in marriage, so that inequalities in old age are related to the domestic division of labour earlier in life. Arber and Ginn argue that gender is as important as class in determining the situations of people in old age. Building on the political-economy approach, they point to the way in which:

a person's role in production and reproduction during working life has a profound influence on the material and health resources they have at their disposal in later life . . . the prejudicial images of older people that underlie discrimination derive from a dominant ideology in which only certain kinds of work are highly valued: production is given priority over reproduction . . . elderly women have been doubly devalued by combined ageism and sexism. (Arber and Ginn 1991: 178)

Disabled People

Disabled people under pensionable age, although often treated for planning purposes as a single group (the **younger physically disabled,** or **YPD**) in fact form a heterogeneous category that includes people born with an impairment (such as spina bifida or cerebral palsy); those whose disability results from trauma (such as spinal injury or loss of limb); and those suffering from degenerative conditions increasingly common in later life (such as arthritis or heart disease). This range affects not just the nature of the impairments, but also their meaning and significance for the individuals and society. The politics of disability have largely been driven by the concerns of the first two groups.

The Politics of Disability

In Britain the disability movement arose in the 1970s and 1980s, spearheaded by individuals who were themselves disabled (some who had formerly lived in institutions, like Cheshire homes) determined to challenge what they saw as the demeaning and oppressive accounts of disability presented by researchers, policy-makers, and practitioners. It is a civil rights approach that draws on the experiences of other radical social movements. Oliver, one of its main theorists, argues that the dominant account of disability in the West is one of personal tragedy, in which the central problem is located in the individual and his/her impairment rather than the socially constructed barriers that create that disability (Oliver 1990). This **social model of disability** sees disabled people not as individual victims of tragedy, but as collective victims of an uncaring and oppressive society. Environmental barriers—lack of lifts, steps, narrow doors—are the

---

Box 14.1 Terminology

Oliver and others in the disability movement make a distinction between

impairment: lacking part or all of a limb, or having a defective limb, organism, or mechanism of the body, and

disability: the disadvantage or restriction caused by a contemporary social organization which takes no account of people who have physical impairments and thus excludes them from the mainstream of social activities (Oliver 1990: 11)

In general the disability movement refer to 'disabled people', rather than the more humanistic 'people with disabilities', arguing that these are indeed people who have been 'dis-abled'.

clearest example of this social construction of disability: they are what handicaps people with functional impairments, not the impairments themselves. But it extends also to assumptions about what is normal or valued. Much medically based rehabilitation, Finkelstein argues, rests on stereotypical ideas of normality, for example forcing disabled people to walk upright, however badly or painfully, rather than accepting that for some people a wheelchair may be their normal mode of mobility just as shoes or a car are for others (Oliver 1990).

Recently the social model has itself been subject to critique within the disability movement from theorists who argue that the emphasis on the social construction of disability has consigned impairment to the theoretical shadows, leaving significant aspects of the experience of disability conceptually invisible (Shakespeare 1994; Hughes and Paterson 1997). The new emphasis on the body in social science has also put impairment back on the agenda (Twigg 2000).

Informal Care

Informal carers are people who give substantial amounts of practical and emotional help to frail or disabled people, usually members of their family, on an unpaid basis. Though often simply called 'carers', the term 'informal' is used to distinguish them from paid carers working in the formal service sector. The popularization of the term 'carer' since the 1980s marked a further stage in the debate about community care, one in which the involvement of families and of the informal sector assumed new visibility.

The Rediscovery of Family Obligation

Although the word 'carer' was new in the 1980s, the reality that underlay it was not. Family care has always been the predominant form of care. That fact, however, was obscured within academic and policy debate by a series of assumptions about the modern family. Sociologists in the 1950s and 1960s—reinforced by popular prejudices—assumed that extended family responsibility had withered away with the rise of modern industrial society and the nuclear family, and that modern families did not 'care' in the way that they had in the past. These assumptions began to be challenged in the 1970s, by feminist scholars in particular, who sought to expose the normative assumptions that underlay the old sociology of the family, particularly in regard to women. No longer exclusively focused on the nuclear couple, researchers were able to explore the range of household forms in which people increasingly lived, and this included the households of older people. The conceptual separation of 'family' and 'household' made it possible to see the ways in which households were linked in wider **kin networks** that could involve significant transfers of help. An explosion of research on carers in the 1980s and 1990s explored the nature of these transfers and their importance, particularly in the lives of older people (Finch and Mason 1993; Qureshi and Walker 1989).

As a result the earlier picture of disengagement and neglect by the family was shown to be wrong. Most help that comes to older and disabled people continues to come from their families, and this applies across households as well as within them. Most older people in Britain do not live with their offspring, but this does not mean that they do not receive substantial amounts of help from them when they are in need.

Carers: The New Client Group?

The forces that create caregiving derive from the family and kinship obligation, but their operation is shaped by the context of formal provision. What the state does and does not provide affects what families do, and failure to provide alternatives and making assumptions about involvement represent an implicit policy by default. In practice, community care could not continue were it not for the activities of family carers. Their input greatly exceeds that of the formal service sector, a fact that has increasingly been recognized by policy-makers. The government guidance literature around the NHS and Community Care Act 1990, which governs the current provision of social care, refers repeatedly to 'users and carers', treating carers almost as a new client group. This process was reinforced with the Carers (Recognition and Services) Act 1995, which gave carers the right to a separate assessment of their needs.

The new emphasis on carers arose in part from a recognition of the heavy burdens that many of them bear. Caring can be a stressful, lonely, and exhausting task, and carers are people who deserve public recognition and support. But the desire to support carers arose also from more instrumental motives on behalf of government. Supporting carers was seen as a cost-effective strategy, with small amounts of formal enabling the continuance of large amounts of informal support. Considerations of this sort suggested to government that the state should aim to incorporate carers more effectively into its activities. Exactly on what basis is less clear. In responding to carers, service agencies have to juggle between three models of their relationship with them: carers as resources (people whose involvement can be assumed and who form part of the background to formal provision); as co-workers (people with whom the agencies must co-operate and work in order to maximize the input going to the client); and as co-clients (people who have needs in themselves that social care agencies have an obligation to recognize) (Twigg 1989). This means that they cannot focus exclusively on either the disabled person or the carer, but hold their interests in balance. It also means recognizing that at times there are significant conflicts of interest between the carer and the disabled person.

The popularization of the word 'carer' in the 1980s, vigorously encouraged by the Carers National Association, created conceptual space for the recognition of carers' needs. Some carers have benefited from this terminology, being able to recast their activities in that light and becoming more confident in asserting their needs to service providers (Twigg and Atkin 1994). But it has also arguably enabled the state to formalize private responsibilities. Carers are now routinely included in care plans, and that recording and formalization of responsibilities has been interpreted by some as a retrograde step, part of a process of co-option that marks the growth of the surveillance state, in which more and more of life is made subject to the gaze of the state and its officials.

Caring as a Feminist Issue

Caring emerged as a women's issue very clearly in the 1980s. Initially it arose from a concern with the unequal burdens of men and woman in society and the assumptions made by the welfare state about the responsibilities of women for family care. Whereas women had little option but to care, men could discharge their family obligations through the labour of their wives. This pattern of inequality was reinforced by the state. For example, the **Invalid Care Allowance (ICA)**, a benefit developed in 1975 to support carers who would otherwise be in paid work, was originally only awarded to men and unmarried women under pensionable age, with the assumption that married women were always 'available' to care and did not merit compensation. This gender bias was later removed after threat of a judgment in the European Court in 1986, but the lobbying that preceded it provided an important focus for the emerging feminist concern over informal care in the late seventies and early eighties.

The feminist interest in informal care was never an isolated one, but was always part of a larger project of making the unpaid work of women conceptually and politically visible. In the 1970s this had applied to housework and childcare, but in the eighties it was extended to the responsibilities for elder care that many feminists of the second wave were starting to experience in their own lives. Seeing caring as a form of labour, often hard physical labour, undertaken in unrewarding circumstances with little public recognition, was of great strategic importance. It counteracted sentimentalizing discourses of love and family, and showed how caring at home in the private sphere limited women's lives and restricted their access to socially valued roles in the public (Hooyman 1990).

Caring also raises questions about the meaning of care itself. Though feminist work tended to conceptualize caring as labour, the aspect of love was never absent. As Ungerson (1987) and Graham (1983) showed, though caring *for* and caring *about* were conceptually different, they were also often linked. Caring was rarely simply a matter of physical tasks; it also involved feelings, both in that caring takes place in the context of intimate relationships which themselves involve strong feelings, and in that the activity of caring requires the direct deployment of feelings. **Emotional labour**—a term developed by Hochschild (1983) in relation to flight attendants, and extended by James (1989) in relation to hospice work—involves close personal attention to the needs of another in which feelings are manipulated and used to support and maintain the well-being of that person. Emotional labour characterizes much of woman's work, whether in the paid sector of the formal economy—typically the service sector—or the unpaid world of the family. Caring, whether informal and located in family relationships or formal and paid, is clearly part of this.

Criticism from the Disability Movement

The new emphasis on recognizing the needs of carers has been much criticized by the disability movement. Morris argues that rather than underwriting dependence through an emphasis on supporting carers, policy should encourage the independence of the people they 'care for'. The emphasis on the needs of carers that developed in the eighties threatens to divert attention and resources away from the real issue, which is the needs of disabled people. In addition, Morris criticized early feminist research on caring for failing to incorporate the subjective experiences of the recipients of care—in many cases themselves women—and this in a literature that emphasized the ways in which the personal is political. She argues that feminists constituted their subject—women—in ways that excluded disabled women (Morris 1991).

The disability movement has its roots in the experiences of younger, physically disabled people. This is not to say that its arguments do not also apply to older people; indeed, these ideas forged in relation to younger people have contributed much to the debate on community care for older people, particularly in relation to ideas of user empowerment and the articulation of choice. There are, however, ways in which the arguments need to be modified in the circumstances of some older people. For example, it is not easy to encompass the situation of people with dementia within this disability framework: far from transcending the need for a carer, having one such offers the best chance for people with dementia of continuing to live in the community.

It is also not the case that all disabled people wish to be freed of caring relationships. Some disabled and older people want to be looked after by family members. Caring takes place in a relationship, often one of long duration, and the dynamics of family and personal life are complex. Though some disabled people may indeed be oppressed by their 'carers', forced into a secondary position in relation to service providers, the reverse can sometimes also be true, and the needs of carers can sometimes be obscured behind those they care for (Twigg and Atkin 1994). Twigg has argued that so long as carers feel that they are under an obligation to care, whether enforced by the cared-for person or deriving from internalized social norms, there should be some recognition of their needs in their own right. It is the fact that carers are obligated by family relationships that means that caring is not simply a voluntary act. Many carers care against their own interests and are not able to give up at will. The issue, therefore, is how far it is proper in these circumstances to have regard for their needs, *in their own right*, and how these should be balanced against the needs of those they care for.

Inheritance and Family Care

Caring is predominately about practical and emotional rather than financial support. Since the coming of the welfare state in the early twentieth century, older people expect to be financially independent of their children. Caring and money are still linked, however, through the issue of inheritance. Most carers of older people can expect to inherit their assets, and policy-makers have sometimes used this fact to justify the burdens they bear, asserting that in time they will eventually get their reward. However, as Finch and Wallis (1994) found, there is little evidence to suggest that this is an important motivation for caring, or that older people use inheritance differentially between their children to reward caregiving. However, when people use their assets (be it their home or their savings) to buy a place in institutional care, this can have considerable financial implications for the family and their expectation of inheritance. This was always so in relation to local authority residential care, which has historically been means-tested, but in the past it was not so in relation to long-term care in hospitals. Increasingly, however, as we shall see, such care has been transferred out of the free-at-the-point-of-use health sector and into that of the means-tested social care sector.

As a result older people are more and more being required to use the value of their homes to fund long-term care. This is in conflict with expectations that developed in the 1980s, when the expansion of home ownership through public subsidies was based

---

Box 14.2 Who are the carers?

In 1985 a series of questions concerning carers were added to the General Household Survey, and in 1990 and 1995 some were repeated or new ones added (Green 1988; *Social Trends*, 1995; Rowlands 1998). Together these studies have provided reliable basic facts about the numbers involved in caring and the tasks they carry out. They have revealed that more than 6 million people, or one in seven of the adult population, were involved in caring at any one time. For those providing more than twenty hours a week of care, the figures are 1.4 million, or 3 per cent of the adult population. Caring cannot be seen as a marginal phenomenon, but something that most people will be involved in at some stage of their lives.

One of the surprising aspects of the data is that the gender difference is not as great as might have been expected: in the population 17 per cent of women were carers and 13 per cent of men (1990 figures). Partly this reflected the presence of spouse carers, where gender differences are not significant. It is among offspring caring for a parent that the gender imbalance is marked. Intimate care is also more strongly associated with women. Caring is thus **gendered,** but not in the blanket way that is sometimes asserted.

---

on an understanding that most people, and not just the well-off, would now be able to pass on significant sums to their children, and that wealth would 'cascade down the generations'. Work on public attitudes by Parker and Clarke (1997) suggests that there is wide support for the right to pass on wealth as opposed to using it to fund care. As a result governments have moved cautiously in this area, increasing the amounts of capital that older people are allowed to retain while still receiving state support for the costs of their residential care, but at the same time increasing the emphasis on self-funding. The issue is how far should people be expected to spend down, or to pauperize themselves, to fund their care. Should intergenerational inheritance be privileged? What is to be the fate of couples where one member goes into institutional care? Currently the survivor is able to retain possession of the house and some of the pension, but future governments, seeing the example of America, may cease to ringfence these personal assets.

Community Care for Older and Disabled People

What we now term 'social services' grew out of a disparate range of provision: district visiting, mother and baby clinics, maternity help. This had developed piecemeal from the 1880s across the voluntary and local authority sectors, and in the post-war era services for children, mothers, and older and disabled people were scattered across a number of local authority departments. In 1971, following the Seebohm Report, most of these were brought together under the aegis of the new **Social Services Department (SSD)**. The aim was to provide a 'single door' for all seeking help. SSDs were to offer a

generic social work service to all clients, thus overcoming the previous fragmentation and giving expression to a new professionalism and confidence in social work.

In practice informal **specialization** soon developed. The political and professional dominance of child protection work (see Chapter 15)—intensified by scandals involving the deaths of children under the supervision of social services—meant that work with older and disabled people was mostly relegated to social workers who were not formally qualified. Though social work has dominated the ethos of social services, only a minority of staff in fact have ever been qualified social workers.

During the nineties, major changes were introduced into social service departments. Their work was increasingly divided into child protection, governed by the new Children Act 1989, and community care, governed by the NHS and Community Care Act 1990.

The Reform of Community Care and the 1990 Act

Community care—enabling people to live as far as possible in the community—had been official policy since the 1960s. As we shall see below, for people with learning disability or mental health problems this implied a radical shift in the model of care away from the asylum and towards community-based provision, and one that was not fully embarked upon until the 1980s. For older people, however, it was more a question of ensuring that their widely expressed preference for continuing to live at home was actively supported by service provision.

During the 1980s a number of criticisms developed of the forms of public provision available for older and disabled people:

- too many resources were going into institutional rather than community care. Changes in relation to the funding of private residential care had resulted in a massive expansion of institutional provision
- the Audit Commission in an influential report of 1986 referred to the 'perverse incentives' created by such funding, whereby public money was available to support residential care but not to sustain people living at home
- the services provided were limited and inflexible, and often did not address people's real needs, for example for personal care or for support at night or at weekends
- services were poorly targeted. Too many allocations were at a low level of need, and it was hard for people with complex needs to receive adequate support
- management was poor in the sense that there was little strategic control over allocation and insufficient attention paid to whether people were actually made any better off by the services (outcomes) they received
- there were rarely mechanisms to assess cost effectiveness. For example, the Kent community care experiments suggested that it was possible to maintain many frail older people at home at lower cost than in a residential home. Social services did not have the information or organizational mechanisms that would allow them to assess and act upon such possibilities
- the views of users of services were rarely heard. Service providers were sometimes keener on following their own professional agendas than responding to the actual wishes of users.

A head of steam built up behind reform. The catalyst for change, however, was the rapid escalation of public expenditure on people in private residential care and the concern of government to put a stop to this. Sir Roy Griffiths was charged with reviewing community care, and his report of 1988 laid the foundations of the 1990 Act.

The NHS and Community Care Act 1990

This established the framework for the new community care (which was established in parallel with major changes in the NHS). Local authorities were made the **lead agencies** for community care. The following three concepts were central in the new community care.

The Purchaser–Provider Split The purchaser/provider split separates the functions of social welfare into purchasing, or defining what is needed in the locality and contracting for it, and providing, or supplying services. SSDs are now responsible for the first, though increasingly not for the second. Services can either be provided in-house by the SSD, or by the private and voluntary sectors. Government has tended to favour the latter two. The aim has been to create a **mixed economy of welfare,** in which suppliers compete against one another. The separation of purchasing and providing has been influenced by **public choice theory** which views public service providers, particularly professionals, as vested interests, aiming to maximize the scope of their enterprise and promote their own concerns. Social services were seen as provider-dominated and complacent. Forcing them to face competition would drive down costs and clarify objectives.

Care Management (or case management, as it was known in the earlier American-influenced work) involves a single worker taking responsibility for assessing, commissioning, and coordinating, and sometimes purchasing, support for a client. Care management in the UK is particularly associated with the work of the Personal Social Services Research Unit (PSSRU) and the Kent community care projects. Though this work was highly influential in the development of the 1990 Act, the devolvement of budgets to frontline workers that was a feature of the more successful projects has only rarely occurred. In most authorities budgets have remained at managerial level, and most contracts are for large blocks of service.

Needs-Led Provision As the critics of the eighties had shown, in making assessments social workers did not explore the nature of the client's situation and resources and then make a tailor-made response, as the textbooks suggested, but rather, provided fairly predictable and standard packages in which clients were fitted into whatever services were available locally. Such poor and routinized allocations were consistently criticized by the Audit Commission and the Social Services Inspectorate (SSI). Some criticized the dominance of professionals', as opposed to users', views of problems and how they should be tackled. The emphasis on needs-led provision in the 1990 Act was an attempt to move away from standard responses towards more flexible, individual, and innovative ones. It promised that people needing care would all receive needs-based assessments in which their views would be taken into account. Care management, particularly where budgets were devolved, was part of this, since care managers, it was argued, would not be restricted to a limited set of services but would be able to commission across a range of public, private-for-profit, and voluntary services.

Problems arise, however, from the lack of any sustained philosophical discussion of the nature of the needs that were to be recognized. In practice the 'needs' that social care agencies recognize have always been defined by the services they provide. Furthermore, an emphasis on needs introduced an open-ended quality to the discussion. Social

Box 14.3 PSSRU and the Kent community care experiments

During the 1970s and 1980s the Personal Social Services Research Unit at the University of Kent under the direction of Bleddyn Davis undertook a series of demonstration projects that aimed to show how case managers, particularly if they held their own budgets, could provide better and more closely tailored packages of support, maximizing the effectiveness of resources and ensuring the best mix of services at the keenest prices. It appeared from the Kent experiments that frail older people on the brink of admission to residential care could, on average, be supported in their own homes at less than two-thirds the cost of a residential place with a case-management approach (Challis and Davis 1986).

The intellectual roots of PSSRU are in economics. Its central analytic framework, the 'Production of Welfare Approach', models welfare activity in terms of various inputs (formal as well as informal) and a range of welfare outcomes. It thus addresses directly the issues of efficiency and effectiveness that have become increasingly central in the community care debate. For example, Davis makes a useful distinction between **horizontal target efficiency** (the degree to which individuals in the target category receive the intervention) and **vertical target efficiency** (the degree to which individuals who receive the intervention fall within the target definition of need). This enables him to assess one aspect of the effectiveness of an authority's provision, that of the number of people who deserve to get the service who are not getting it because, for example, they are unknown to the agency or have been refused in error, as well as assessing the number who do who are not in the target category because, for example, they have been wrongly assessed or have recovered from their previous illness.

care has always been rationed, and the primary means whereby this has been achieved is by limiting the level and availability of services. Needs-led assessment threatens this mechanism. For these reasons the radical implications of the needs-led element in the reforms were soon circumvented.

The new community care as it was finally implemented in the mid-1990s was severely constrained in terms of resources. Banding systems (describing differing levels of need) have been introduced to enable departments to prioritize clients. In many authorities, forms of services that that had been publicly provided for decades, like help with domestic cleaning, are no longer so.

Local Government Reorganization and the Future of Social Services Departments

The restructuring of local government in the 1990s brought further changes to social services. SSDs in England had either been organized at the county level (Dorset, for example) or, in the metropolitan areas, at district level (for example, Lambeth). Under reorganization most of the counties survived, though they lost some of their territory to create 47 new unitary authorities (such as Medway, separate from Kent). In Scotland 12 regional councils (each of which had had a Social Work Department) were replaced by 32 new unitary authorities, and in Wales 22 unitary authorities were created. Social services thus tend to be organized in much smaller population units than before. This should ideally make them more locally responsive, but anxieties have also been expressed at potential lack of expertise, particularly in relation to more specialist client groups, and a weakening of social work values. In some cases social services departments have been merged with housing, and sometimes the new director does not have a social work background.

Direct Payments

One of the themes that emerged in the debate about the new community care was the potential role of direct payments. The disability movement has long advocated the replacement of care services by cash payments that would enable disabled people to purchase their own assistance. Services in the state and voluntary sector, Morris and others argue, have been dominated too long by the interests and views of professionals, providing limited and patronizing services with a rigid and over-complicated division of labour.

> When the allocation of resources was placed in the hands of social services organizations and those working for them, [professionals] chose to spend large sums of money on segregated provision—which meant that disabled people had to live restricted and impoverished lives that the professionals concerned would *never* have chosen for themselves. (Morris 1997: 59)

Giving money directly to disabled people would free them to exercise choice over the sort of help they receive, from whom and when. The preferred model within the disability movement is that of the personal assistant (PA), employed and trained by the disabled person and directly accountable to them.

During the late eighties, the state-financed Disabled Living Fund did provide some money on this basis, though its scope was limited and government was cautious about its extension (Kestenbaum 1996). By the mid-nineties, however, with the development of the purchaser/provider split, the use of direct payments began to be looked on with greater favour by policy-makers: such payments fitted in with the emphasis on the mixed economy of care and the personal responsibility of individuals for their own care. The Community Care (Direct Payments) Act 1996 allows local authorities to make direct cash payments to certain individuals under the age of 65 in lieu of the community care services that they have been assessed as needing.

Though some anxieties have been expressed about leaving individuals to organize and pay for their own care (mostly in terms of exploitation of either workers or disabled people), from the perspective of government the real issue has always been one of cost, and the fear that such payments, particularly if based on objective criteria of need, would escalate out of hand. The specific exclusion of people over 65 from the remit of the 1996 Act reflects this fear, since they constitute the majority of people with disabilities. The social care budget, as we have seen in the discussion of needs-related provision, has always been severely rationed, with social services staff acting through their assessments as gatekeepers. Direct payments threaten such a mechanism. From the perspective of disabled people wanting to move assistance away from a discretionary and on to a rights basis, this is a highly desirable development.

Residential Care

The great majority of older people continue to live at home, and this applies even to severely incapacitated people, three to four times as many of whom live at home as do in institutions. Among the population of those aged between 65 and 74, only about 1 per cent live in some form of institutional setting, whether residential or nursing home or hospital; among those aged 85 and over the figure is about 26 per cent (1994 figures by Laing, quoted in Peace *et al.*, 1997)

Certain factors increase the likelihood of going into residential care: living alone is one of the strongest predictors. Cognitive impairment, particularly dementia, is also associated with institutional care, and most residents in residential or nursing homes have some level of confusion, even if slight. Of those with severe cognitive impairment in the general population, about one-third are estimated to live in residential or nursing homes (note that this means that about two-thirds do not).

Since the 1960s government policy has endorsed community care as the preferred option, and research supports the view that the overwhelming majority of older people would prefer to stay in their own homes. For those who do go into residential care, it is rarely a positive choice: most make the transition perforce, and few are consulted or have the opportunity to review the options or the provision (Allen *et al.* 1992). Hospital discharge is often a point of transition when older people move into residential care. This can be because of new levels of impairment, but it is often argued that in their attempt to increase turnover and avoid **bed blocking** hospitals rush older patients into residential care as the easiest course for them without a proper review of the options. Families play a key role in initiating and negotiating the transition; equally, they can play an important role in enabling the older person to remain at home. Carer breakdown or withdrawal is an important cause of institutionalization.

The Debate about Residential Care Residential care raises issues about the wider treatment of older people in society. As Peace and her colleagues argue:

if social policy is one of the important ways in which society is both constructed and managed, then residential care for older people, as a form of social policy, shapes attitudes towards and beliefs about older people and old age. (Peace *et al.*, 1997: 69)

This view is particularly associated with the work of Peter Townsend:

residential homes for the elderly serve functions for the wider society and not only their inmates. While accommodating only a tiny percentage of the elderly population they symbolise the dependence of the elderly and legitimate their lack of access to equality of status. (Townsend 1986: 32)

The Expansion of Private Residential Care in the 1980s Despite the long-established policy of supporting community rather than residential provision for older people, the 1980s saw an astonishing expansion of residential care funded by the public purse. Changes in the regulations concerning board and lodging payments in 1980 meant that social security would meet the costs of private residential care for older people who had very limited personal means. Previously only the better-off could choose to go into a private residential home; and those without means had to rely on local authority provision, which was scarce and required an assessment of care needs. Now individuals could choose to enter a private facility and the state would pay. There was no cap on the budget. From about £6 million in 1978, the cost to the social security budget rose to £200 million by 1984, peaking in 1993 at £2500 million (Peace *et al.* 1997).

Though the policy that lay behind the extension was unclear (and probably un-intended), once embarked upon it was hard to stop, partly because the option appeared to be popular with the public, and partly because it was linked to the Thatcherite projects of privatization and support of small businesses. Private residential homes were classic family businesses, typically started by a nurse with her/his partner in a large house bought with a mortgage or family savings. Profitability was closely linked to the capital and property markets, and availability was uneven geographically, clustered in decaying resort towns and other places where property was cheap.

The 1990 Act capped the open-ended commitment. Since 1993 local authorities have the responsibility for assessing an individual's need for care and for contributing to the purchase of appropriate provision, whether residential care or help in the home. Money was transferred from the social security budget to local authorities in recognition of these new responsibilities.

The quality of residential provision has been a persistent issue. Quality of care is itself an elusive concept. Research suggests that what matters most to residents is the charac-ter of the care regime—how staff talk to them, how much choice they can exercise over their daily lives—but most assessments focus on material factors—number of bathrooms, absence of shared bedrooms, wheelchair access—that may contribute to the experience of being cared for, but do not address its central reality. This bias towards physical matters has been reinforced by the responsibilities of local authorities for inspecting and registering private homes. It is easier to defend objective criteria regarding the physical environment against challenge or appeal than more subjective assessments of care.

Sheltered Housing

Sheltered housing is sometimes presented as a preferable alternative to residential care. It was encouraged in the 1960s partly in reaction against the bleak care regimes revealed in Townsend's classic study of 1962, *The Last Refuge*, which showed how poorly post-war old people's homes had lived up to Bevan's dream of hotel style accommo-dation for all classes. It has expanded greatly in the decades that followed, so that by the late eighties it housed nearly 5 per cent of older people (Mackintosh *et al.*, 1990). Very sheltered housing or close care, with meals and care facilities on the premises, has been a recent area of growth, particularly in the private sector.

Sheltered housing has been criticized by others, among them Butler, Oldman, and Greve (1983), for not being the panacea that is sometimes suggested. Social care needs, they argued, can be provided in the original home of the older person and do not require a move to sheltered housing, which largely solves a housing rather than a social need (many older people are poorly housed). There is little evidence that sheltered housing alleviates loneliness, and it can reinforce a ghetto mentality towards the old. Although people in sheltered housing receive more domiciliary care than those at home (largely as a result of the proactive work of wardens), sheltered housing does not appear to prevent eventual admission to residential care. It is, however, widely popular with families, who value the security it offers.

Domiciliary Care

The home help service (later home care) was the mainstay of community care of older people in the post-war period. Originally created for maternity cases, its use expanded greatly in the 1960s and 1970s to meet the needs of older people. At its peak in the late 1980s, 18 per cent of those over 75 received its support. A widely familiar and popular service, it was, after residential care, the largest item in the social services budget.

Home help has traditionally been modelled on housework—washing, cleaning, shopping—and that was predominantly what home helps did. Some, however, gave support that went beyond the official duties: making birthday cakes, offering companionship, taking the person out. The basis for this was a quasi-familial one, and behind the official model was another implicit one, that of the caring daughter-in-law. This extra support, however, was only offered on a personal and discretionary basis (*some* home helps to *some* clients), and it was not paid for: social services effectively 'extracted' extra labour beyond the official contract by being able to draw on the implicit gender contract that underlay home care, as it does so much 'women's work'.

One of the issues in the 1980s was the desire to extend the scope of home help to include personal care tasks such as washing, dressing, and putting to bed. Behind this was a perception that there were many heavily dependent people who could live at home if services were more flexible (traditionally home help only covered limited hours, often mornings only) and included personal care.

The debate was overtaken in the nineties, however, by a cost-cutting agenda in which the focus was not on increasing support for the most needy but on cutting out low levels of domestic assistance. Housework—the mainstay of the post-war service—is increasingly not provided by social services. Older people in need of such help are referred to the private (or, where it exists, the voluntary) sector. In the former case they have to pay the commercial rate. In the past home help was means tested, though the price to the client was low and in some authorities it was free. Changes in home care thus fit a general trend towards shifting the costs of social care for all but those on the lowest of incomes onto the individual.

Funding Long-Term Care

During the nineties a debate emerged about the future funding of long-term care. It arose from a number of factors:

- increasing numbers of older people. Though the figures are relatively stable at the moment, between 2011 and 2041 the number of over-85s will double (from 1.15 to 2.21 million)

- the apparent growing reluctance to pay income tax. This means that the costs of long-term care can no longer be met out of taxation on a pay-as-you-go basis. In the past, tax has been used as a means of redistributing income over the life cycle and between the generations. The political will to do this appears to have weakened

- distrust of government and its willingness to deliver the promises of the welfare state has meant that individuals increasingly look to personal rather than collective means to secure their futures. Only a minority, however, will have the income and the stability of employment to enable them to take out private long-term care insurance. Private-sector solutions are unlikely to be able to meet the needs of the majority

- the costs of long-term nursing care are considerable (between £300 and £400 per week in the 1990s), though only a minority of people will need it

- the shifting medical/social boundary. Healthcare has traditionally been provided free at the point of use. Social care, by contrast, has always been means-tested in some degree, so that most people are expected to pay all or part of the cost themselves. Health authorities have been increasingly reluctant to provide long-term as opposed to acute healthcare. Long-term care, even where it involves nursing, is increasingly defined as 'social care'. Older people have to meet these costs, and this, as we have seen, affects their capacity to pass on an inheritance to their children.

These issues are not unique to Britain, but have occurred across Western welfare states. Germany, for example, implemented long-term care insurance in 1995, integrating it with the system of social insurance that pays for healthcare. Insurance-based proposals have been made in Britain also. The influential Joseph Rowntree Foundation Inquiry, *Meeting the Costs of Continuing Care* (1996), recommended the establishment of a national care insurance scheme. This was to be a funded scheme that would build up a capital base independent of government; contributions would be compulsory and related to income. Benefits would be the same for all, and would cover the costs of care, which would become free at the point of use, while accommodation costs would be met from the individual's own resources. Those without such resources would be supported by the state, and those whose contributions over their employment history were insufficient would be supported from the general assets of the fund. Though the scheme would be insurance-based, it is **social insurance** rather than private insurance.

The majority report of the Royal Commission on the funding of long-term care, reporting in 1999, endorsed the separation of personal care costs (to be funded by the state) from housing and living costs (to be funded by the individual, or on a means-tested basis). Costs were to be met from general taxation. A minority report questioned this expansion of public funding and argued that resources should be targeted on the poorest.

Mental Health Problems and Social Care

The meaning and status of mental illness is subject to dispute. Within the medical model it is an illness that, like any other illness, can be diagnosed and classified according to objective symptoms and measurable criteria. It is best treated or managed by a medical approach, in which physical treatments like drugs (and, in the past, ECT) play a central role. This mental illness model is most commonly applied to psychotic conditions like schizophrenia, or to severe depression. Opposed to this is an alternative interpretation that stresses the subjective and meaningful nature of mental health problems, which are regarded as the product of interpersonal, social, and environmental pressures, and as existing on a continuum with the ordinary difficulties of life. This approach is most commonly applied to neurotic disorders like depression, obsessional behaviour, or substance abuse. Some who espouse this second model go beyond looking for social factors in the causation of mental health difficulties to deny the existence of mental illness itself, regarding it as a social construct, the product of medical discourse, or other forms of social **labelling.** This view is most commonly associated with the anti-psychiatry movement of the 1960s and the work of R. D. Laing, D. G. Cooper, and, from a different perspective, Thomas Szasz. Most current writers and practitioners adopt a mixed position, accepting some elements of the illness model, at least in relation to schizophrenia, at the same time as recognizing the importance of the subjective experience of difficulties and of social and environmental factors in the causation and exacerbation of mental health problems.

Prevalence of Mental Health Problems

These can broadly be divided into **psychotic conditions,** such as schizophrenia, where the individual lacks insight into his/her condition and where grasp of reality is significantly disturbed (hearing voices, visions), and **neurotic conditions,** such as depression and anxiety, where the individual, although distressed, remains broadly in touch with reality. Estimates of prevalence suggest that about one in seven adults aged between 16 and 64 living in the community have some sort of neurotic health problem. For those with functional psychosis (schizophrenia, manic depressive psychosis, and schizo-affective

---

Box 14.4 Mental health professionals

Psychiatrists are medical doctors who have specialized in mental illness. They emphasize an illness model and drug-based treatment, though many now operate in an eclectic way. They work predominately with more severe cases.

Clinical psychologists are not medical doctors, but have an academic background in psychology, augmented by a professional training. Their practice varies, but many use either **behavioural approaches,** in which the aim is to modify outward behaviour (rather than inner thoughts or feelings) through the use of incentives such as token economies within hospitals or self-generated rewards, or **cognitive approaches,** where the aim is to modify maladaptive thought processes, such as irrational, negative ideas about yourself or life that may support depression.

Psychoanalysts draw on the work of Freud and Jung and stress the role of the unconscious mind and the experiences of childhood in the formation of later difficulties. Analysis centres on talking, and may last for several years. The majority of analysts are in private practice.

Psychotherapists also use talking as the core of their practice, but their involvement tends to be shorter and more focused on particular forms of change in the patient's life. They draw on a variety of approaches, including psychoanalysis, and many are influenced by the humanistic psychology of Carl Rogers. They practise in a variety of settings.

Approved social workers (ASW) have a statutory role in relation to compulsory admission to hospital under the Mental Health Act 1983. Their practice is based on the techniques of social work.

Community psychiatric nurses (CPNs) are psychiatric nurses who are based in the community. They sometimes operate an outreach service from the hospital.

disorders) the rates are four per thousand, though this needs to be supplemented to include those living in long-stay institutions. Alcohol dependency is estimated at 47 per thousand, and drug dependency at 22 per thousand (Meltzer *et al.* 1995). In addition there are various forms of dementia, including Alzheimers, which are associated with ageing and differ from other psychiatric problems in that they have an unequivocal physical base in the form of organic deterioration of the brain. Although they are managed within the psychiatric (often psychogeriatric) service, they are more usefully considered in terms of the general difficulties of older people.

Women and Mental Health

The links between women and madness have received much attention. Writers like Showalter (1987) and Ussher (1991) have focused on the cultural representations of madness, exploring the ways in which women have been presented as unstable, irrational, nearer to madness than the 'rational' dominant male. They point to the preoccupation in this essentially misogynistic discourse with women's physiology—reproduction, sexuality—as the key to their mental instability. Hysteria becomes the metaphor for all that is ungovernable and threatening in women. As with other radical critiques, definitions of madness are seen as based on value-judgements and prescriptions of normality that support existing power structures, in this case those of patriarchy. Anger, misery, and frustration are recast and re-experienced as illness and depression.

Women appear to suffer more from mental health problems than men. They are more likely to be admitted to a psychiatric ward, to be prescribed psychotropic drugs for depression and anxiety, to consult a GP for minor mental health problems, or to identify themselves as having such in community surveys. This greater tendency to mental health problems applies, however, only to depression and anxiety: the rate for schizophrenic-type illness is the same for men and women (Meltzer *et al.* 1995). Men, by contrast, are more likely to suffer from problems of alcohol and drug dependence.

Box 14.5 Brown and Harris and the social origins of depression

Brown and Harris's study of working-class women in London in the early 1970s identified four factors that made women vulnerable to depression: loss of their own mother before the age of 11, the presence at home of three or more children under fourteen, absence of a confiding relationship, particularly with a husband, and the lack of a full- or part-time job. The study was important and influential because of the evidence it gave for the *social* origins of depression and—despite not being in any sense a feminist study—for its identification of features of traditional domesticity as detrimental to women's mental health. It also has implications for intervention. As some feminists have pointed out, if the sources of vulnerability are being at home with children, what is needed is support with childcare, not a prescription for Valium. The identification of the lack of a close relationship was also important in relation to arguments put forward by Eichenbaum and Orbach (1983) that women within traditional gender relations suffer from lack of nurture: men look to and receive emotional support from women, but are not socialized to give it in return.

Some writers explain this pattern in terms of women's socialization into dependence and passivity, resulting in behaviour that turns inwards as depression or self-harm rather than outwards as anger. Others, such as Payne (1991), point to material and social factors, for example women's greater likelihood to be in poverty or a lone parent. Being at home with a young child and without a job, as Brown and Harris showed, is associated with depression. There is some evidence of a closing of the gender gap in recent years, again pointing to the significance of social factors such as labour market participation.

Race and Mental Health Services

People from ethnic minorities (including the Irish) are over-represented in psychiatric admissions. Afro-Caribbeans are detained under the Mental Health Act 1983 at a rate of two and a half times the local white population (Rogers and Pilgrim 1996). The pattern with regard to people of Asian decent is mixed, with evidence of both greater and lesser involvement (Bhui and Christie 1996).

Some psychiatrists argue that this pattern is simply a reflection of higher rates of mental illness in certain populations, and some—contentiously—have suggested a genetic link with schizophrenia. Others point to the impact of poverty, deprivation, and the social difficulties—including pervasive racism—that black people face. These commentators have also exposed the racial stereotypes that lie behind the differential responses of mental health workers, including doctors, in which black people are presented as less in control and more threatening. Once within the orbit of psychiatry, black people do appear to be treated differently. They are more likely to be given major tranquillizers or antidepressants, more often as a depot (injection), in higher doses, and accompanied by less in the way of psychotherapy or counselling (Bhui and Christie 1996). The context in which black people receive treatment is thus a highly coercive one, and there are parallels with their treatment in the criminal justice system, where there is a similar pattern of over-representation and of harsh and punitive treatment:

psychiatry forms part of a larger social control mechanism which regulates and oversees the lives of black people. Since black people, particularly young black men, are over-represented in all parts of the criminal justice system, both the 'criminalisation' and 'medicalisation' of black people may be closely connected processes. (Rogers and Pilgrim 1996: 139)

The Closure of the Asylum

In the 1950s and 1960s policy shifted away from the long-stay hospital in favour of community care. The gaunt Victorian asylums, isolated and custodial, no longer seemed appropriate places in which to treat or care for people with mental health problems. New drugs played a part by controlling people's behaviour, though their role has been exaggerated (Rogers and Pilgrim 1996). Long-stay hospitals were increasingly perceived to be expensive and oppressive; and there was a growing desire in psychiatry to re-position acute psychiatric services with other acute specialisms on the main hospital site. Though the policy of running down the long-stay hospitals was established in the sixties, it was not until the eighties that the process of closure got under way (Korman and Glennerster 1990). Between 1980 and 1990 thirty-five large long-stay hospitals were closed, and the process accelerated in the nineties (Rogers and Pilgrim 1996). Although community care is now the policy, the shift in provision is not always as complete as might seem: many new 'community' facilities are on the sites of the old hospitals. Furthermore, in a critical report in 1994 the Audit Commission pointed out that two-thirds of the £1.8 billion spent on mental health in 1992/3 still went on in-patient facilities, despite the clear evidence of the cost-effectiveness of community provision and its popularity with users and relatives (Audit Commission 1994).

Some of the difficulties in making the transfer related to money. The full gains of hospital closure come only at the final stage: until then there is the added burden of running a parallel service. New community services did not always make up for lost hospital provision—this was particularly true in relation to the accommodation function that hospitals had provided. Money that should have been available to build up services in the community was allowed to leach across into the acute sector.

Mental Illness and the New Community Care

The Thatcher government in the run up to the NHS and Community Care Act 1990 was reluctant to accord lead agency status to the local authorities. This reluctance was all the stronger in relation to mental illness. Local authorities had only a limited tradition of work in this field, and psychiatrists were loath to lose their clinical responsibility for patients in the community. Moreover, the group who were the focus of planning concern were not people with mental health problems in general, but a distinct sub-category of these—those who are severely mentally ill (in practice, those with schizophrenia). It is their management in the community that drives the policy agenda. Though the 'severity' of their problems might—to politicians and the public—suggest medical dominance, many of the difficulties they face are social rather than medical: the need for housing, for purposeful activity, for friendship and rewarding social contact. This suggests the importance of a joint approach between health and social care.

In 1991 the government introduced the **Care Programme Approach (CPA)** (DoH 1996). This offers an integrated and co-ordinated framework for care, in which DHAs and SSDs are required to collaborate. Services are provided by a multidisciplinary team that includes professionals from both health and social care. CPA rests on four stages: assessment, care plan, appointment of key worker, and review of plan. It is thus very similar to the process of care management, and confusion has arisen in some authorities over the parallel nature of the structures.

New funding to support the development of social care facilities in the community was provided by the Mental Illness Specific Grant, introduced in 1991. It is a revenue grant and paid to the local authorities, who have to find matching funds to those provided by central government to the extent of 30 per cent. Unlike the other monies transferred under the community care legislation, it is ringfenced for mental illness—itself a measure of the sensitivity of the issue.

A Crisis in the Nineties?

As the nineties progressed it became increasingly clear that mental illness services were in trouble. Psychiatric services, particularly in the inner city, have come under acute pressure. A series of critical reports by the Audit Commission (1994), the Mental Health Foundation (1994), the Ritchie Report (1994), the House of Commons Select Committee (1994), and others detailed the failings of the system.

Lack of joint working across the health/local authority divide is recurringly identi-fied as a problem. One proposal suggested by the Conservative government in the 1997 Green Paper was a new and separate commissioning body for mental illness, the Mental Health and Social Care Authority (DoH 1997). The problem with such responses is that the real difficulties arise out of long-seated barriers to co-operation and good working at the front line. It is here that the different professional cultures of psychiatry and social work clash, with tensions over differential status and rewards, over the meaning and interpretation of mental illness or mental health problems, and over issues of treatment. It is unclear how far structural changes at the level of commissioning would address these.

Treatment in the Community The transfer to community care raised new issues around treatment, or rather exposed ones that had previously been hidden. While patients were living in hospital it was relatively easy to cajole or force them into receiving medication, even where that were not compulsorily detained and had the legal right to refuse. It was also easy to keep track of and control their movements: that was part of the coercive character of the hospital. However, once they were living freely in the community such surveillance and control became more difficult. Many now drift away from the orbit of the community mental health services—themselves often overloaded and unable to pursue active outreach work—and many patients have no wish to remain in contact, their experiences of psychiatric services being so negative. Some ex-patients in the user movement adopt the term 'survivor' of mental health services to express these feelings. Rejecting medication and help can be a symptom of the mental illness, but this is not always so. Many psychiatric drugs have significant and unpleasant side-effects. They impair concentration and willpower, and their long-term prescription can cause brain damage, producing disfiguring involuntary movements of the body that are distressing and stigmatizing. People in the user movement object in particular to the impersonal and over zealous manner in which drug therapy has been applied.

The dilemma of how to manage severely mentally ill patients who refuse medication was made more acute by a series of high-profile cases that involved killings (the Clunis case) or suicide (one man climbed into the lions' cage at London zoo). In response, in 1994 the government introduced **supervisory registers** to identify and keep track of mentally ill people who were most at risk to themselves or others and, in 1996, **supervised discharge** for patients who had been compulsorily detained at some point. Under this, the supervisor—usually the key worker—can require the patient to live in a particular place and to attend for treatment (Department of Health 1996). As yet there is no provision for compulsory treatment, though the issue continues to be aired.

Learning Disabilities and Social Care

Learning disabilities (previously termed mental handicap) are lifelong impairments, usually present from birth, involving incomplete development or damage to the brain or nervous system. In the past they were primarily defined in terms of level of IQ, but social development is increasingly recognized as significant, and some individuals with low IQ manage very successfully socially. About 1 per cent of the population, or about half a million people, are estimated as have learning disability at a level that will require some support. About 0.03 to 0.04 per cent have severe learning disabilities. In many cases these are accompanied by physical impairments, some of them profound (Mental Health Foundation 1996).

The vast majority of people with learning disabilities (89 per cent) either live with their families or in some form of independent supported accommodation. In the 1991 census about 4 per cent lived in hospital and 6 per cent in community-based residential accommodation.

Normalization

The key concept informing service development in the last three decades has been **normalization** (Brown and Smith 1992). Originally developed in Scandinavia and extended in the US through the work of Wolfensberger, normalization aims to ensure that people with learning disabilities share the same lifestyles and choices as non-disabled people. In the Scandinavian work this is rooted in ideas of social rights and citizenship; in Wolfensberger's, it is related to sociological concepts of deviance and labelling, whereby people with learning disabilities are socially devalued and excluded (Emerson 1992).

According to the principles of normalization, people with learning disabilities should be integrated with the rest of society—using the same facilities, living in ordinary housing, taking part in social and community life. Their surroundings and clothes should not be marked out as different—second-best, shabby, or demeaningly childish. They should be allowed to progress through the life cycle with all the normal expectations of adolescence, adulthood, and old age, including personal relationships, marriage, and parenthood. The rhythm of the day, week, and year should be the same: getting up and going to bed, enjoying work, leisure, weekends, and holidays, just as other people do.

In Wolfensberger's work particular emphasis is placed on **social role valorization**, whereby the negative and demeaning stereotypes projected onto disabled people by society are rejected and reversed through their positive involvement in socially valued activities. Wolfensberger has at times been criticized for a conservative emphasis on what is socially normative, which can involve a denial of individual choice. There is an authoritarian streak in his work; for example, faced with disabled people choosing a devalued option he is willing to coerce them into taking the valued one. Individual choice is thus made secondary to challenging the social status of the devalued individual or group (Emerson 1992).

Within UK service development, O'Brien's reformulation of normalization has been widely influential. This identifies five accomplishments that services should attempt to achieve (Emerson 1992).

Deinstitutionalization and Community Care: People with Learning Disabilities

Until the 1960s responses to people with learning disabilities were dominated by the Victorian asylum—large, grim, isolated institutions where people with learning disabil-

---

Box 14.6 O'Brien's five service accomplishments

- Ensuring that service users are **present** in the community by supporting their actual presence in the same neighbourhoods, schools, workplaces, shops, recreational facilities, and churches as ordinary citizens.

- Ensuring that service users are supported in **making choices** about their lives by encouraging people to understand their situation and the options they face, and to act in their own interest both in small everyday matters and in such important issues as who to live with and what type of work to do.

- Developing the **competence** of service users by developing skills and attributes that are functional and meaningful in natural community environments and relationships.

- Enhancing the **respect** afforded to service users by developing and maintaining a positive reputation for people who use the service, ensuring that choice of activities, locations, forms of dress, and use of language promote the perception of people with learning disabilities as developing citizens.

- Ensuring that service users **participate** in the life of the community by supporting people's natural relationships with their families, neighbourhoods, and co-workers, and, when necessary, widening each individual's network of personal relationships to include an increasing number of people.

---

ities were expected to spend the whole of their adult lives. Though a series of scandals in the 1960s and 1970s that exposed the squalid and neglectful conditions in these hospitals were the catalyst for change, the shift in policy away from institutions was part of a larger movement of **deinstitutionalization** and decarceration across Western societies (closures also took place in North America and Europe) that encompasses both mental-illness and mental-handicap hospitals.

The policy of hospital closure only began to take effect in Britain in the 1980s, with the Care in the Community Demonstration Projects, which aimed to transfer patients, many of whom had spent decades in hospital, to a new life in the community. Informed by the principles of the *Ordinary Life* report produced by the Kings Fund in 1980, the care in the community strategy was as much about developing new models of community provision as resettling ex-hospital patients. The new community-based models of care have been overwhelmingly popular with users.

Despite the success of the policy, a number of criticisms have been raised, particularly concerning recent trends. Collins (1995) found that the resettlement programme was haphazard and depended too much on the personal commitment of individual managers. Since central government has left to local and health authorities the power to determine models of care, this has resulted in purchasing of variable quality. The full transfer of monies from hospital to community has not always taken place, and institutional values have continued to operate. In some cases NHS Trusts have resisted the continuing process of resettlement and closure, choosing instead to develop facilities on the hospital site for commercial reasons—the profits from the care regimes being used to fund new developments. The Ordinary Life Movement of the eighties envisaged provision in small houses where individuals could choose their companions and use local facilities. Funding pressure in the nineties has led to homes getting larger (housing between 10 and 25 residents) and the increasing use of centralized facilities like laundry and catering. The transfer of staff from hospital to the new community facilities has reinforced this trend towards micro-institutions.

Ward (1995) argues that, far from facilitating individually tailored responses as its rhetoric might suggest, the NHS and Community Care Act 1990 has undermined it. Competitive contracting reduces rather than encourages innovative services. Collaboration between the NHS and social services has become more difficult, reinforced by the demise of the Community Mental Handicap Teams, a multidisciplinary structure that, where it worked well, acted to bridge the gap. Some NHS trusts are retaining responsibility for people with learning disabilities, though the reforms designated social services as the lead agency, for reasons of business viability. Finally GP purchasing adds a new 'wild card' in service development, and one where there is little established expertise (Ward 1995).

At the same time as service planning appears to be moving in the direction of larger and more impersonal units, progressive thinking has increasingly abandoned the concept of the group home in favour of **supported living,** whereby individuals choose where and how they live, with a range of supports built around those choices. Supported living separates housing from support—the agency is no longer the landlord—and allows for genuine exploration of how the individual would like to live his/her life and the assistance needed to enable this.

Much of the most effective service planning has been for those with less severe disabilities. One group who have posed problems for the new models of care have been those with **challenging behaviour.** These are a diverse group: some with mild or borderline learning disability but diagnosed as mentally ill who may become involved with the criminal justice system through, for example, arson or sexual offences, others with profound difficulties who may injure themselves (head-banging) or behave in ways that pose a challenge to those that care for them. Thirty years ago such individuals were largely in long-stay hospitals. Now many remain living with their families, and this can impose considerable strains upon them, often made all the harder by the unwillingness of services to take them on. In many authorities the solution has been one of seeking specialist placements out of the area. The Mansell Report (1993) suggests that local, community-based provision is possible and affordable if close attention is given to individual assessment and contracting.

Conflict with Parents

At times the new approaches to service provision have run into conflict with parents and with organized parents' groups who are influential lobbyists in some localities (Grant, Nolan *et al.*). Parents can be over-protective and can underestimate the capacity of their child to develop into greater independence. In the past many people with learning disabilities remained in an enforced state of childhood, denied the expression of adult choice or of sexuality. Girls were particularly protected and limited.

For some parents, however, the issue is less one of their child's capacity or potential than of the capacity of service provision. Many parents have had a long history of contact with social services in which social workers and models of care have come and gone (Twigg and Atkin 1994). They can be particularly anxious about securing the future of their offspring, especially beyond their own life, and many lack confidence in the stability of the new services and the agencies that provide them. This is one of the reasons why parents are often attracted to the village community model. These seem to offer an enduring and, above all, a safe environment. That they are also isolated, segregated, and assume that the countryside is the preference of all, is to them of lesser consideration.

Parents have lost out in the new models in terms of respite. Weekday attendance at a specialist day centre (the old ATCs, Adult Training Centres) did at least offer regular relief to parents that might also allow them to engage in paid work. The new forms of day provision, using the local swimming pool or adult education centre, for example, are more individually tailored and flexible, but they do not offer the same secure respite for parents. For some progressive service providers that idea of respite is itself suspect, suggesting an improper focus on the interests of the parents rather than the disabled person. For those looking after someone with severely challenging behaviour, however, regular respite may be vital to their ability to continue caring.

Abuse

One of the central anxieties expressed by parents concerns abuse. Though this can be a symptom of the overprotectiveness of parents, and while there is no evidence that individuals are more at risk in the new models of service provision, research has revealed that people with learning disabilities are exposed to alarming levels of physical and sexual abuse. Hilary Brown's work estimated that there are about 900 new reported cases a year. Men and women are both at risk, and abusers are mostly men known to their victims—other service users, family members, and staff. It is not a question of stranger danger. However, prosecution is rare. It has often proved difficult to persuade the courts to accept the evidence of people with learning disabilities, and too little attention has been given to supporting victims through the criminal justice system.

Self-Advocacy

The growth of the self-advocacy movement, in which people with learning disabilities are encouraged and supported in expressing their views and preferences, has been one of the single most significant developments of the last decade (Ward 1995). Through organizations like People First, users have increasingly been involved in service planning and purchasing.

Conclusion

Since the 1960s the field of social care has been dominated by a single policy, that of community care. This crosses all the client groups and is advocated by all political parties. It commands wide public support (at least in relation to groups whom the public regard as unthreatening).

And yet the reality of community care is more fragile. Social care remains caught in a secondary relationship with medical and acute hospital provision. To a considerable degree, its services are defined against what the health services do (as troubles around hospital discharge make plain). It has a residual quality, picking up the aspects of care not covered by the medical model. Social care never commands the same status as medical care. Politicians and the public have remained reluctant to recognize professional expertise in these areas, which are assumed to rest on merely commonsense knowledge. Community-based services may be praised in theory, but they are often starved of resources (this is particularly true of mental health services). Their character of being 'out there', provided in the privacy of people's own homes, makes them less visible to planners and policy-makers. Services with a clear institutional base tend to have a higher profile in the minds of those who allocate resources. As a result, we have the paradox that although social care is governed by one relatively clear policy—community care—it remains one of the more unstable areas of social policy, subject to cuts and to short-term political change.

Key Legislation

NHS and Community Care Act 1990 This established the current arrangements for community care, introducing care management and according primary responsibility for community care—lead agency status—to social services.

Community Care (Direct Payments) Act 1996 This permitted local authorities to make direct cash payments to individuals aged under 65 in lieu of the community care services that they had been assessed as needing.

Carers (Recognition and Services) Act 1995 This gave carers the right within community care to a separate assessment of their needs.

Mental Health Act 1983 The Mental Health Act 1983 established the current arrangements for the compulsory detention of severely mentally ill people. It reflected a civil rights concern with what was seen as an overly medically dominated approach established by the 1959 Act. The 1983 Act introduced the Approved Social Workers (ASW), who have a role in compulsory detention. The act has been criticized for being over-concerned with detention and of little relevance to the needs of the majority of people with mental health problems who face considerable difficulties in living in the community.

Glossary

bed blocking A term used predominantly in the healthcare system to describe the situation where a person, usually an older person, remains in a hospital bed though medically ready for discharge, because there are difficulties in arranging their social care.

care management Introduced by the NHS and Community Care Act 1990, this involves a single worker—not necessarily a trained social worker—taking responsibility for assessing, commissioning, co-ordinating and, sometimes, purchasing support for a client.

Care Programme Approach (CPA) Introduced in 1991 to provide a framework for the care of mentally ill people outside hospital, the CPA requires DHAs in collaboration with SSDs to put in place specific arrangements for the care and treatment of mentally ill people in the community.

challenging behaviour Behaviour that challenges the resources of families or services. Particularly associated with learning disabilities, it can involve violent behaviour that threatens the physical safety of the person or those around them, or distressing and transgressive actions that limit access to ordinary community facilities.

community care The support of older and disabled people in the 'community', usually taken to mean their own homes, or in home-like provision. Defined in opposition to institutional care. Community care has been official policy since the 1960s, though its implementation has been variable.

deinstitutionalization The process of closure of large long-stay institutions established to care for and contain old people, the mentally ill, and those with learning disabilities.

emotional labour The deployment of emotion as part of paid or unpaid work.

generic social work Provision by an individual worker, or by a team of workers, who use the common core skills of social work to help meet all forms of individual need. Originally seen as a means of providing a single door for all problems, it is now often considered inferior to specialist social work.

horizontal target efficiency A term used in relation to service provision to evaluate the degree to which individuals in the target category receive the intervention. Contrasted with **vertical target efficiency.**

informal carers People who give substantial amounts of practical and emotional help to frail or disabled people, usually members of their family, on an unpaid basis. Often simply termed 'carers', the word 'informal' is used to distinguish them from paid carers working in the formal service sector.

Invalid Care Allowance (ICA) Benefit available to people of working age out of the labour market. Set at a relatively low level, it neither represents full compensation for wages forgone, nor payment for care. Few carers receive it, as it interacts with other benefits.

kin networks Networks of kin that extend beyond the nuclear family and include kin acquired by marriage as well as blood.

labelling A theoretical approach that suggests that people become deviant as a result of the social process of being labelled as such.

lead agency Status accorded to SSDs under the NHS and Community Care Act 1990, whereby they have primary responsibility for community care.

learning disabilities Lifelong impairments, usually present from birth, involving incomplete development or damage to the brain or nervous system. Previously referred to as mental handicap, and sometimes termed 'learning difficulties'.

mixed economy of welfare The way in which welfare is provided by a variety of agencies, including statutory, voluntary, for-profit, and informal (families and friends).

normalization Currently the guiding principle in relation to services for people with learning disabilities, but extended to other groups of disabled people, aiming to ensure that they share the same lifestyles and choices as non-disabled people.

neurotic condition Mental health problems where the individual, although distressed, remains broadly in touch with reality; for example, depression and anxiety.

political economy perspective Applied in particular to the situation of older people, it analyses inequalities in resources and life chances as resulting not from individual variation but from the power relations that structure society.

personal care Covers activities that adults normally perform for themselves, such as washing and dressing.

psychotic condition Mental illness where the individual lacks insight into his/her condition and where grasp of reality is significantly disturbed, such as schizophrenia.

public choice theory This theory argues that bureaucrats have an interest in expanding public welfare as a means of building a larger power base, and that politicians have similar interests in pleasing the electorate by expanding public welfare services. It provides a New Right explanation of the expansion of welfare services.

social services departments (SSDs) (Also known as LASSDs: local authority social service departments), established in 1971 to co-ordinate and provide a range of social care, both community-based and residential. Responsible for **personal social services (PSS)**, their main client groups are children and families, older and disabled people, people with learning disabilities and, to a lesser degree, those with mental health problems. They also have a remit to support carers.

social model of disability Approach that emphasizes the ways in which disability is created not by impairments themselves but by the expectations of society.

social role valorization Conscious attempt to ensure that negative and demeaning stereotypes projected on to disabled people are rejected through positive involvement in socially valued activities.

specialization In social work, the tendency for certain workers to specialize in particular care groups, such as children or people with learning disabilities.

supervisory registers Introduced in 1994 to identify and keep track of severely mentally ill people living in the community who are most at risk to themselves or others.

supervised discharge Introduced in 1996 for certain patients detained at some point under the Mental Health Act 1983, whereby the supervisor—usually the key worker—can require the patient to live in a particular place and to attend for treatment.

supported living Approach to service planning in which individuals with a disability are supported to live in the way that they choose, rather than in specialized and dedicated provision.

user A person in receipt of social services support, adopted in preference to the more traditional 'client' to reflect a less passive approach and one that emphasizes the importance of their interests and views.

younger physically disabled (YPD) People with disabilities between the ages of 18 and retirement. Covers a range of conditions including those born with an impairment (such as spina bifida); those whose disability results from trauma (such as spinal injury); and those suffering from degenerative conditions (such as arthritis and heart disease).

vertical target efficiency The degree to which individuals who receive the intervention fall within the target definition of need. Contrasted with **horizontal target efficiency.**

Guide to Further Reading

Arber, S. and Ginn, J. (eds.) (1995), *Connecting Gender and Ageing: A Sociological Approach* (Buckingham: Open University Press).

Brown, H. and Smith, H. (eds.) (1992), *Normalisation: A Reader for the Nineties* (London: Routledge).

Campbell, J. and Oliver, M. (1996), *Disability Politics: Understanding Our Past, Changing Our Future* (London: Routledge).

Finch, J. (1989), *Family Obligations and Social Change* (Cambridge: Polity).

Lewis, J. and Glennerster, H. (1996), *Implementing the New Community Care* (Buckingham: Open University).

Peace, S., Kellaher, L., and Willcocks, D. (1997), *Re-evaluating Residential Care* (Buckingham: Open University).

Rogers, A. and Pilgrim, D. (1996), *Mental Health Policy in Britain* (Basingstoke: Macmillan).

Ward, L. and Philpot, T. (eds.) (1995), *Values and Visions: Changing Ideas in Services for People with Learning Difficulties* (Oxford: Butterworth-Heinemann).

References

Allen, I., Hogg, D., and Pearce, S. (1992), *Elderly People: Choice, Participation and Satisfaction* (London: PSI).

Arber, S. and Ginn, J. (1991), *Gender and Later Life: A Sociological Analysis of Resources and Constraints* (London: Sage).

——(eds.) (1995), *Connecting Gender and Ageing: A Sociological Approach* (Buckingham: Open University Press).

Audit Commission (1994), *Finding a Place* (London).

Bhui, K. and Christie, Y. (1996), *Purchasing Mental Health Services for Black Communities* (London: HMSO).

Brown, G. and Harris, T. (1978), *The Social Origins of Depression* (London: Tavistock)

Butler, A., Oldman, C., and Greve, J. (1983), *Sheltered Housing for the Elderly* (London: Allen & Unwin).

Bytheway, B. (1995), *Ageism* (Buckingham: Open University Press).

Challis, D. J. and Davis, B. P. D. (1986), *Case Management: An Evaluated Experiment in Home Care of the Elderly* (Aldershot: Gower).

Collins, J. (1995), 'Moving Forwards or Backwards? Institutional Trends in Services for People with Learning Difficulties', in L. Ward and T. Philpot (eds.), *Values and Visions: Changing Ideas in Services for People with Learning Difficulties* (Oxford: Butterworth-Heinemann).

Department of Health (1996), *Building Bridges: A Guide to the Arrangements for Inter-Agency Working for the Care and Protection of Severely Mentally Ill People* (London: HMSO).

Eichenbaum, L. and Orbach, S. (1994), *What Do Women Want?* (London: HarperCollins).

Emerson, E. (1992), 'What is Normalisation?', in Brown, H., and Smith, H. (1992) (eds.), *Normalisation: A Reader for the Nineties* (London: Routledge).

Finch, J. and Mason, J. (1993), *Negotiating Family Responsibilities* (London: Routledge).

Finch, J. and Wallis, L. (1994), 'Inheritance, Care Bargains and Elderly People's Relationships with their Children', in Challis, D., Davies, B., and Traske, K. (eds.), *Health and Community Care: UK and International Perspectives* (Aldershot: Gower).

Graham, H. (1983), 'Caring: A Labour of Love', in Finch, J. and Groves, D. (eds.), *A Labour of Love: Women, Work and Caring* (London: Routledge).

Green, H. (1988), *Informal Carers: A Study Carried Out on Behalf of the Department of Health and Social Security as part of the 1985 General Household Survey* (London: HMSO).

Hochschild, A. (1983), *The Managed Heart: The Commercialisation of Human Feelings* (Berkeley, Calif.: University of California).

Hooyman, N. R. (1990), 'Women as Caregivers of the Elderly', in D. E. Biegel and A. Blum (eds.), *Aging and Caregiving: Theory, Research and Policy* (London: Sage).

Hughes, B., and Paterson, K. (1997), 'The Social Model of Disability and the Disappearing Body: Towards a Sociology of Impairment', *Disability and Society*, 12/3, 325–40.

James, N. (1989), 'Emotional Labour: Skill and Work in the Social Regulation of Feelings', *Sociological Review*, 1.

Joseph Rowntree Foundation (1996), *Meeting the Needs of Continuing Care: Report and Recommendations* (York: Joseph Rowntree Foundation).

Kestenbaum, A. (1996), *Independent Living: A Review* (York: Joseph Rowntree Foundation).

Kings Fund Centre (1980), *An Ordinary Life: Comprehensive Locally-Based Residential Services for Mentally Handicapped People* (London).

Korman, N. and Glennerster, H. (1990), *Hospital Closure: A Political and Economic Study* (Buckingham: Open University Press).

Lewis, J., and Glennerster, H. (1996), *Implementing the New Community Care* (Buckingham: Open University Press).

Living in Britain: Preliminary Results from 1994 General Household Survey (London: HMSO).

Mackintosh, S., Means, R., and Leather, P. (1990), *Housing in Later Life: The Housing Finance Implications of an Ageing Society* (Bristol: SAUS).

Mansell Report (1993), *Services for People with Learning Disabilities and Challenging Behaviour or Mental Health Needs* (London: HMSO).

Marshall, M. (ed.) (1990), *Working with Dementia: Guidelines for Professionals* (Birmingham: Venture Press).

Meltzer, H., Gill, B., Petticrew, M., and Hinds, K. (1995), *OPCS Surveys of Psychiatric*

Morbidity in Great Britain: Report I: The Prevalence of Psychiatric Morbidity Among Adults Living in Private Households (London: HMSO).

Mental Health Foundation (1996), *Building Expectations: Opportunities and Services for People with a Learning Disability* (London).

Morris, J. (1991), *Pride against Prejudice: Transforming Attitudes Towards Disability* (London: Women's Press).

——(1997), 'Care or Empowerment? A Disability Rights Perspective', *Social Policy and Administration*, 31/1.

Nolan, M., Grant, G., and Keady, J. (1996), *Understanding Family Care* (Buckingham: Open University Press).

Oliver, M. (1990), *The Politics of Disablement* (Basingstoke: Macmillan).

Parker, G. and Clarke, H. (1997), 'Will you Still Need Me, Will you Still Feed Me—Paying for Care in Old Age', *Social Policy and Administration*, 31/2.

Payne, S. (1991), *Women, Health and Poverty* (Hemel Hempstead: Harvester Wheatsheaf).

Peace, S., Kellaher, L., and Willcocks, D. (1997), *Re-evaluating Residential Care* (Buckingham: Open University Press).

Qureshi, H. and Walker, A. (1989), *The Caring Relationship: Elderly People and Their Families* (Basingstoke: Macmillan).

Rogers, A. and Pilgrim, D. (1996), *Mental Health Policy in Britain* (Basingstoke: Macmillan).

Rowlands, O. (1998), *Informal Carers: An Independent Study carried out by the Office for National Statistics on behalf of the Department of Health as part of the 1995 General Household Survey* (London: The Stationery Office).

Russell, D. (1995), *Women, Madness and Medicine* (Cambridge: Polity).

Shakespeare, T. (1994), 'Cultural Representations of Disabled People: Dustbins for Disavowal', *Disability and Society*, 9/3.

Showalter, E. (1987), *The Female Malady* (London: Virago).

Thornicroft, G. and Strathdee, G. (1996), *Commissioning Mental Health Services* (London: HMSO).

Townsend, P. (1962), *The Last Refuge* (London: Routledge).

——(1986), 'Ageism and Social Policy', in Phillipson, C. and Walker, A., *Ageing and Social Policy: A Critical Assessment* (Aldershot: Gower).

Twigg, J. (1989), 'Models of Carers: How do Social Care Agencies Conceptualise their Relationship with Informal Carers', *Journal of Social Policy*, 18/1.

——(1997), 'Deconstructing the "Social Bath": Help with Bathing at Home for Older and Disabled People', *Journal of Social Policy*, 26/2, 211–32.

——(2000), 'Social Policy and the Body', in G. Lewis, S. Gewirtz and J. Clarke (eds.), *Rethinking Social Policy* (Milton Keynes: Open University Press).

——and Atkin, K. (1994), *Carers Perceived: Policy and Practice in Informal Care* (Buckingham: Open University Press).

Ungerson, C. (1987), *Policy is Personal: Sex, Gender and Informal Care* (London: Tavistock).

——(1997), 'Give Them the Money: Is Cash a Route to Empowerment?', *Social Policy and Administration*, 31/1.

Ussher, J. M. (1991), *Women's Madness: Misogyny or Mental Illness?* (Hemel Hempstead: Harvester Wheatsheaf).

Walker, A. and Phillipson, C. (1986), 'Introduction', in Phillipson, C. and Walker, A., *Ageing and Social Policy: A Critical Assessment* (Aldershot: Gower).

Ward, L. and Philpot, T. (eds.) (1995), *Values and Visions: Changing Ideas in Services for People with Learning Difficulties* (Oxford: Butterworth-Heinemann).

Ward, L. (1995), 'Equal Citizens: Current Issues for People with Learning Difficulties and Their Allies', in Ward, L. and Philpot, T. (eds.) (1995).

15 The Care and Protection of Children

Derek Kirton

Contents

Introduction: The Child, the Family, and the State

As a public issue, the care and protection of children presents something of a paradox. For the most part it remains hidden and marginal, yet it has the emotive capacity to generate some of the most heated discussions in the field of welfare policy. Clearly, this applies most notably to child protection—where 'scandal' may arise either from a perceived failure to protect or the 'unnecessary' removal of children from their homes—but also to matters such as the quality of residential care or the suitability of adopters. It might be argued that this situation reflects a deeper paradox within the treatment of children, where general social neglect can live cheek-by-jowl with self-righteous indignation when things go wrong.

This chapter will look at various aspects of the 'childcare system' but it is perhaps appropriate at this point to highlight some of the key factors which help to shape it. The pivot around which the care and protection of children turns is the relationship between state and family. In principle the model is a fairly straightforward one, which sees childrearing as primarily the responsibility of parents, with the state providing certain supports, setting out certain requirements, and playing a monitoring role. The state is essentially concerned with the question of whether **good enough parenting** is being provided. If not, it should intervene, preferably to enable adequate care to be achieved or restored, or to provide alternative care for the child.

In practice, the model is rather more complex. Judgements of the adequacy of parenting raise questions as to whether there is a consensus on what is 'good enough' and what, to use the legal term, causes 'significant harm' to the child. Who is to make such judgements and upon what basis? When intervention does take place, how is the balance to be struck between offering support of various kinds to the family and effectively protecting the child? As we shall see, such matters are strongly influenced by views on the importance of the 'blood tie' between parents and children born to them. A related concern is how far the child's interests can be understood as separate from those of their family. Moves in recent decades to emphasize the 'rights of the child' imply a degree of separation which would have been unthinkable a century ago.

While the care and protection of children is generally perceived as a matter for those directly involved in working with families, it is also important to emphasize the wider social policy context. The focal point for debate is the well-established link between on the one hand, problems such as child abuse, family breakdown, and youthful offending and on the other, those of poverty, housing problems, ill-health, and school exclusion.

For some, this link points to the need for more extensive welfare provision which, by providing greater support to (poor) parents, will help reduce the incidence of 'care and protection' issues. For others, the link is largely coincidental, the problems individual, and the need is for targeted intervention to change parental behaviour or to remove the children. Supporters of this position will highlight the fact that only a fairly small minority of poor parents abuse their children and that to suggest a link with poverty is an insult to the majority.

Foundations of the Modern Childcare System

Although its origins can be traced to the nineteenth-century activities of **child-savers** such as Thomas Barnardo and Mary Carpenter, the modern childcare system took its shape following the Second World War. Responding to material and emotional problems associated with evacuation, and Sir Walter Monckton's report (1945) on the death through neglect and beatings of 13-year-old Dennis O'Neill at the hands of his foster carers, the Curtis Report (1946) led to the Children Act 1948 and the establishment of Children's Departments in local authorities. The new Departments were significantly influenced by the work of John Bowlby on **maternal deprivation and attachment**, which focused on the importance for children of a consistent relationship with a nurturing figure.

The major thrust of work was both to support families, in order to prevent children from requiring substitute care, and to ensure that, when required, such care would correspond as closely as possible to a family model. This entailed the promotion of foster care as the 'preferred option' (and which had the additional merit of being cheaper) and the reform of residential care. In particular, there were efforts to move away from the large so-called 'barrack homes' (described by John Stroud as 'mouldering bastions'), which often accommodated up to 200 or more children, and which appeared to embody all the problems of the institution. The drive to create more homely environments was typified by the **family group home,** with at most between 10 and 12 children, live-in houseparents, and the twin aims of stability and simulation of 'family life'.

Children's Departments expanded steadily during the post-war years before they were absorbed into the Social Services Departments (SSDs) in 1971. While the local authority SSDs have remained central to the provision of childcare, voluntary organizations, including long-established national organizations such as the NSPCC (National Society for the Prevention of Cruelty to Children), Barnardos, or NCH (National Children's Homes, now known as NCH Action for Children), and more recently private providers of foster and residential care, have also exerted a major shaping influence on services. In 1995 there were an estimated 18,420 local authority social workers working with children and families, of whom roughly 95 per cent were qualified (LGMB/CCETSW 1997: 91). The children's residential care workforce was estimated to number 14,400 (ibid.: 59). Local authority expenditure on children and families totalled £1.931bn in 1994–5, representing 26 per cent of all social services expenditure (ibid.: 47–9).

Protecting Children

As was noted earlier, it is perhaps with issues of abuse and protection that childcare issues come most prominently under the public gaze. This usually takes the form either, on the one hand, of death or serious injury which could have been prevented or, on the other, the unnecessary removal of children. Within these scenarios, the professionals (most commonly social workers) are cast somewhat contradictorily, either as 'naive woolly liberals' or as behaving 'like the Gestapo'. Beyond creating what can appear to be a no-win situation for social workers, media coverage and public debate have also had important influences over policy and practice, as we shall see.

It is customary to trace the origins of modern child protection to the late nineteenth century, highlighting the formation of organizations such as the National Society for the Prevention of Cruelty to Children in the 1880s and the first protective legislation dealing directly with parents, the Prevention of Cruelty to and Protection of Children Act 1889. The Act made cruelty, neglect, or abandonment of a child an offence and gave powers for the court to remove the child and place them with another appropriate adult.

While policy evolved quite gradually and unevenly, it is possible to locate its development within the context of changing views of childhood. During the nineteenth and much of the twentieth centuries there was a progressive separation of children from the adult world, with childhood seen as a period of natural innocence and vulnerability, requiring long and careful socialization in readiness for the adult world. An increasingly protected status can be seen as part of this process.

The Rediscovery of Child Abuse

Child abuse had concerned Victorian reformers such as Thomas Agnew and Ben Waugh, and was to an extent seen as having been dealt with by the legislation of that period. It re-emerged into the public domain in the 1960s as 'battered child (or baby) syndrome'. Numerous medical research studies, and especially the work of Dr Henry Kempe in the US, demonstrated (largely through the use of X-ray evidence) that injuries inflicted by parents on children were frequently going undetected. The use of the term 'syndrome' to describe both the patterns of injuries and parental behaviour was important in establishing a **medical model** for child abuse. Its principal effect was to heighten awareness of physical harm amongst the medical profession and child welfare agencies. In the UK the work of the NSPCC's Battered Child Research Unit contributed significantly to a higher public profile during the 1970s, described by Jean Moore (1985: 55) as 'the age of child abuse'. Arguably a greater influence arose from the death of Maria Colwell in 1973 and the public reaction to it. Seven-year-old Maria was returned to her mother and stepfather after several years with foster carers, and subsequently suffered extreme neglect before being battered to death by her stepfather. Nigel Parton (1985: 69–99) argues that Maria's death coincided with growing concern about violence in society and breakdown in law and order, permissiveness, and perceived decline in the family. Media coverage of the case saw the birth of the 'naive do-gooder' stereotype for social workers, and pressure rose for a more authoritarian approach to be taken towards child abuse. Formal measures included the establishment of committees to co-ordinate policy and liaison between different agencies; the requirement that case conferences should be held to bring all professionals together to discuss individual children; tighter procedures for investigation; and the establishment of a register for children 'at risk' of abuse. Informally, there was pressure towards greater use of legal powers to remove children, and the 1970s saw a significant rise in compulsory removal of children from their homes. 'At the beginning of the decade over two-thirds were in care voluntarily and one-third on some sort of statutory order. . . . By 1980 only a quarter of children in care were not on some sort of statutory order' (Parton 1985: 125).

Child Abuse Inquiries and Their Consequences

Since the death of Maria Colwell there have been over forty formal inquiries into other child deaths (Doyle 1997: 156–8). The media stereotype of the ineffectual social worker has remained strong—neatly if cruelly captured in a Daily Mirror headline (16 January 1980) 'Malcolm Died as He Lived: Freezing Cold, Starving and Surrounded by Social Workers'. Although the published reports of these inquiries led to increases in compulsory removal of children, it is a matter of some debate as to how useful they have been in improving child protection practice. In their favour, it can be argued that the death of a child provides the strongest possible force for change. Not only does it give far greater weight to any recommendations made, but it is also more likely to enter the consciousness of all those involved. On the other hand, it is questionable how representative any one case, however tragic, can be of practice in general. There is also a danger of hindsight—that *after* a child's death the circumstances leading up to it appear misleadingly 'obvious'. Worries have also been expressed about the overwhelmingly bureaucratic measures which have been prompted by inquiries. 'In the final analysis, when the parents and children are talking alone with the worker, no amount of procedural guidelines will guarantee that the right things are said and done' (Jones *et al.* 1987: 66).

Understanding Child Abuse

Grasping the nature of child abuse—its causes and effects—is not merely of academic interest. Such knowledge has the potential to aid the prevention and detection of harm, and decision-making following abuse. Apart from assisting judgements made by welfare, legal, and medical professionals, insights into child abuse can also inform wider policy-making—for instance decisions about the use of resources, or co-operation between agencies. Effective understanding, however, is rendered difficult by a number of factors, perhaps the most important of which is definition.

Official classifications identify four categories of abuse: physical, neglect, sexual, and emotional. In the following section we concentrate on physical abuse and neglect, while sexual abuse is dealt with in a later section. Emotional abuse is a rarely used classification and will not be discussed in this brief overview.

If abuse sometimes appears self-evident—as in the case of serious injury or young children being left alone at home while their parents go on a fortnight's holiday—at other times it is much less so. One well-known example of this is smacking. For some, it is inherently 'abusive' and should be banned, while for others it is considered a requisite for effective childrearing which should be used more widely! More generally, consensus is unlikely as to types and degrees of punishment, about age and duration for leaving children alone, their staying out, about suitable TV viewing, and so on. In deciding whether acts or practices constitute abuse, their seriousness, frequency, and likelihood of repetition must all be judged.

The Prevalence of Child Abuse

As for any identified social problem, there is an inevitable interest in the scale of child abuse. Measures, however, will depend on both the definition used and the accuracy of the measurement. Official data tell us that during the 1980s and 1990s there have usually been between 30,000 and 40,000 children (roughly, 3 or 4 per 1,000) on child protection registers at any one time (Health and Personal Social Services Statistics, 1996). Gibbon *et al.*'s study (for a useful summary, see DoH 1995) provides a snapshot of this process and the various filters involved. The researchers found that, during 1992, there were 160,000 child protection investigations, from which 40,000 led to the convening of a case conference, and subsequently 24,500 additions to the child protection register. Only 4 per cent of cases investigated resulted in the child being removed from home under a legal order.

The breakdown of reasons for investigation can be summarized in Table 15.1.

Thus, taken together, physical abuse and neglect still account for almost three-quarters of all child protection referrals. Any such figures must, however, be treated with great caution for a number of reasons. Referral for investigation, which will usually be from teachers, health workers, neighbours, or police officers, requires both that the 'abuse' is known about, and that someone regards it as sufficiently important to be reported. Inevitably, much abuse goes unrecognized and unreported. Passage through the various filters will then depend on the information available to professionals and the judgements they make. Wide local variations 'in the criteria used to decide whether child protection procedures were warranted in a particular case and in the actual headings under which children were registered' suggest that local authority practices are at least

	%
physical abuse	44
sexual abuse	28
neglect	25
emotional abuse	3

Table 15.1 Child protection investigations: categories of suspected abuse

Source: DoH (1995: 69).

as important in determining recorded levels of abuse as its 'real' incidence (DoH 1995: 68). A study by Dingwall, Eekelaar, and Murray, *The Protection of Children* (1983), gives valuable insights into the processes involved in professional judgements. The authors contend that a **rule of optimism,** in effect the benefit of the doubt, is usually applied to the many situations where abuse might be suspected. This rule tends to be suspended mainly for one of two reasons: either where the parents are judged to be behaving inappropriately (including failure to co-operate with the professionals), or where those professionals directly involved feel that they must refer the matter outside their immediate circle, usually to higher authority.

Child Abuse and Social Inequality

Information drawn from child protection registers indicates that reported child abuse (with the exception of sexual abuse) is overwhelmingly a phenomenon of poorer working-class families, and is closely associated with factors such as unemployment and lone parenthood. Observing also an association with incidence of domestic violence and mental illness in families, the Department of Health report concludes that 'it is the most vulnerable in our society who are most likely to become the object of a . . . (child protection) . . . enquiry' (DoH 1995: 25).

These associations have sparked considerable debate between those who take recorded abuse as an accurate measure and those who do not. Those who would question the statistics can point to a number of factors which may lead to under-representation of more affluent families. First, such families come to the notice of welfare agencies less frequently, being both less likely to seek help or to become objects of professional concern. Second, they are more likely to benefit from the 'rule of optimism', because they are viewed as more respectable and hence unlikely abusers, can communicate more easily with middle-class professionals, and are better equipped to contest decisions.

No-one would dispute that serious child abuse occurs in all social strata, and few would suggest that reporting and processing of abuse cases is entirely without bias. The key question is whether biases can account for the class differences in recorded abuse. One who believes they cannot is Pelton (1985), who strongly attacks what he calls **the myth of classlessness.** Apart from what he says is the consistent and overwhelming nature of the evidence linking abuse with poverty and deprivation, Pelton highlights three specific factors in support of his argument. They are, first, that increased awareness and reporting has done nothing to diminish the class gap in recorded abuse; second, that even within classes, levels of abuse correspond with those of deprivation; and third, that child abuse fatalities, which are extremely difficult to hide or disguise, also occur mainly in poor families. Gauging the 'real' incidence of abuse is always likely to remain elusive, but as Pelton has argued, it is difficult to believe that abuse is evenly distributed throughout society. As to why the myth should exist, Pelton suggests that apart from well-meaning concerns not to 'label' poor families, the myth serves the interests of the psychological and helping professions, whose prestige gains from portraying abuse as a disease requiring their diagnosis and curative intervention. Recognizing abuse as a product of poverty would undermine such ambitions and raise awkward questions for politicians and policy-makers. The latter are also, according to Pelton, only too glad to support the myth.

Child Abuse, Race, and Ethnicity

Summarizing studies in the United States on associations between race and child abuse, Corby (1993: 68) comments that they 'provide a mixed picture', with some finding over-representation of minority ethnic families, and others not. In the United Kingdom he notes that 'the amount of hard information is meagre', with little research and no systematic monitoring. Such data as exist tend to show no significant association (ibid.: 69). The apparent absence of any ethnic differences within the UK in recorded levels of abuse may reflect the balancing-out of two contradictory trends. Channer and Parton (1990: 110) observe how, on the one hand, Eurocentric norms may lead to 'inappropriate and heavy-handed treatment', and hence over-readiness to remove children. On the other, however, a belief in **cultural relativism,** the notion that 'cultural' norms and behaviours are equally valid and only to be understood by insiders, may lead white workers to 'hesitate to intervene at all and hence put children from black families in real and serious dangers' (ibid.: 111).

Theorizing Child Abuse: Why Does it Happen?

A wide range of psychological and sociological theory has been used to cast light on the causes of child abuse. An excellent review of the many and varied theoretical perspectives is provided by Corby (1993: 85–105). Within the professional mainstream there has been considerable interest in developing profiles of at-risk populations to aid prediction. Checklists have been developed with a view to identifying parents most likely to abuse and children most likely to suffer abuse. A well-known example is provided by Greenland (1987), who lists high-risk factors as shown in Table 15.2.

The quest for prediction is understandably controversial. Checklists clearly have the potential to improve the protection of children by alerting professionals and policy-makers to pertinent risk factors. Yet there are also dangers with the checklist approach. Notably, over-reliance upon it can impede rather than aid good judgement. Checklist factors may harden towards a stereotype, and lead to self-fulfilling prophecy, with abuse incorrectly identified among those who score highly on the list, and missed among those who do not.

Medical or Social Explanation?

The factor-based or checklist approach fits well with what is often termed the medical model of child abuse. Typified by the early references to a child-battering syndrome, the key assumptions implicit in the model are that abusive practices are symptoms of a disease, the causes of which must be diagnosed in order to effect a cure. The precise nature of the disease has numerous variants, depending upon the theoretical base utilized, such as attachment theory, the psychodynamic, behavioural, or cognitive schools of psychology, or family-based theories (see Corby 1993: 86–96), and the weight given environmental factors. What is common to all is a relatively narrow focus on individual or family pathology, with external factors serving only as triggers, rather in the way that over-exertion may trigger a heart attack where there is already weakness. As with other medicalized social problems, a central role is given to the professionals in diagnosis

Parents	Child(ren)
1 Previously abused/neglected as a child	1 Previously abused/neglected
2 Age 20 or less at birth of first child	2 Under 5 at time of abuse/neglect
3 Single parent/separated Partner not biological parent	3 Premature/low birth weight
4 History of abuse/neglect or deprivation	4 Now underweight
5 Socially isolated, frequent moves, poor housing	5 Birth defect, chronic illness, developmental lag
6 Poverty, unemployed/unskilled worker, inadequate education	6 Prolonged separation from mother
7 Abuses alcohol and/or drugs	7 Cries frequently, difficult to comfort
8 History of criminal assaultive behaviour and/or suicide attempts	8 Difficulties in feeding and elimination
9 Pregnant, post partum, or chronic illness	9 Adopted, foster- or step-child

Table 15.2 Child abuse and neglect high-risk checklist

and treatment, while their patients or clients are offered the **sick role** as an alternative to direct culpability.

A rather different approach is offered by the **social model** of abuse. Again, there are several variations (Corby 1993: 97–104), but their common ground rests with the claim that social analysis offers better prospects for understanding child abuse than does the individualized medical model. Two rather different strands can be detected within the social model. The first relates to sources of stress. Writers such as Pelton (1985), Parton (1985), and Gil (1970) have underscored the importance of poverty, unemployment, and housing problems, while the 'ecological' theories of Garbarino and others (see Parton 1985: 154–8 for discussion) have pinpointed social isolation and lack of neighbourhood supports in the generation of abuse. These sources of stress are given much greater weight than in the medical model. Rather than simply providing triggers for underlying pathology in individuals or families, they can be seen as creating enormous pressures, under which the parenting in some families will buckle. The second strand involves locating child abuse in a wider social context. This can include examination of the ways in which the notion of abuse is socially constructed—for example, varying views about appropriate punishment, age-related responsibilities, or sexual knowledge—and is thus far from self-evident, as implied in the medical model. It may also highlight the links between violence against children and a wider incidence and 'acceptability' of violence in families or society. Strauss *et al.* (1980: 72) conclude that 'children are injured and abused because we as a society are committed to norms which approve of and legitimize using violence as a frequent form of training and punishing children'. This wider focus may also facilitate the posing of different questions, such as whether abuse of children reflects their lack of rights *vis à vis* parents/adults, and whether those in power who permit child poverty and deprivation are not at least as abusive as those who are labelled child abusers.

Among theorists of child abuse it is widely accepted that no single perspective comes close to offering all the answers. Child abuse undoubtedly reflects a complex mixture of psychological and social factors, and much depends on what type of explanation is being sought. If we are trying to understand abuse as a 'private trouble', then clearly the individual and family-based explanations may have more to offer than a broad-brush social theory. If, however, the aim is to cast light on child abuse as a 'public issue', its levels, patterns, and trends, then the reverse is likely to be true. Ideally, both medical and social perspectives can make significant contributions.

Child Sexual Abuse

If the 1970s could be described as the 'age of child abuse', then it is probably fair to say that the 1980s were 'the age of sexual abuse'. It emerged strongly as a public issue in the early to mid-1980s, an emergence which is widely taken to have come from work from within the women's movement. In particular, awareness of the family as a site for violence and the use of sexuality as a form of male domination, as in rape or harassment, for example, paved the way for greater recognition of child sexual abuse within families. This was further bolstered by the voice given to those who had suffered and survived sexual abuse. Greater recognition was reflected in a sharp rise in detection, and whereas the category of sexual abuse accounted for only 5 per cent of those on the child protection register in 1983, by 1987 the figure was 28 per cent (Creighton 1989). In 1986 Childline, a free telephone helpline, was established in the UK to give children experiencing abuse a channel to gain confidential counselling and support. Though not exclusively concerned with sexual abuse, recognition of its particular difficulties for telling and being believed was a major moving force. By 1994 Childline had counselled nearly 400,000 children and was receiving many more calls than the 3,000 it was able to answer every day. A vital element in these developments has been a cultural shift towards believing children when they make allegations of abuse.

Events in Cleveland during 1987 were to bring child sexual abuse dramatically to the attention of a wider public and seemed to symbolize the struggle over its recognition (Campbell 1988). When an unexpectedly large number of children were taken into care largely on the basis of a controversial medical diagnosis known as reflex anal dilatation, opinion was sharply divided between those who were inclined to see this as further uncovering of abuse, and those, led by the local MP Stuart Bell, who believed that certain doctors and social workers had 'gone mad'. The ensuing enquiry (DHSS 1988) was highly critical of many of the professionals involved, both for their knee-jerk reactions to medical diagnosis and flawed investigative techniques. However, if there was some evidence of a fall-off in referrals for child sexual abuse following the Cleveland affair, there was to be no return to the days when sexual abuse was rarely reported. This was despite other well-publicized cases of 'authoritarianism' and too great a readiness on the part of social workers and police to remove children from their homes, notably in Orkney and Rochdale, where subsequent reports found much of the intervention to have been heavy-handed. In the understated style of official reports, the Social Services Inspectorate commented that 'it is essential that any intervention should be undertaken in the least disruptive fashion, in order to ensure that it does not of itself do more damage to the child than taking no action at all' (SSI 1990: 14).

Understanding sexual abuse presents many of the same difficulties as for other forms of child abuse, though with the added problems of secrecy and, commonly, a lack of any physical evidence to support allegations. The struggles over whom to believe and questions of proof and children's testimony in legal cases are among the most distressing aspects of sexual abuse. On definitions and judgements, while serious forms of abuse present little difficulty, consensus can be much more elusive around the margins as to what is or is not 'sexual', what is harmful or abusive, what is appropriate to different ages, and so on. As the work of Smith and Grocke (DoH 1995: 81–3) demonstrates, there is wide variation in families' treatment of sexual matters and what is considered 'normal'. Perhaps their most thought-provoking findings relate to perceived signs of abuse. 'Excessive masturbation, over-sexualized and extensive sexual curiosity or sexual knowledge and genital touching are thought to be indicators of abuse. But since these behaviours were found to be common within a community sample, they were not in themselves sufficient to suggest abuse' (DoH 1995: 83). Definitions of sexual abuse can also be drawn narrowly or broadly. The former tend to concentrate on serious sexual assaults, rape, intercourse, or forced masturbation. The latter may additionally encompass experiences of indecent exposure, unwanted touching, verbal abuse, and inappropriate watching of sexual activity.

Prevalence figures depend very much upon the breadth of definition used. Kelly, Regan, and Burton (1991) found that 4 per cent of women and 2 per cent of men reported having experienced serious sexual abuse as children, these figures rising to 59 per cent and 27 per cent respectively when the wider definitions were used. The markedly higher rate for abuse of girls has been a consistent finding in both official records and self-report studies. Studies also show that between 80 and 90 per cent of sexual abuse, of both girls and boys, is carried out by men (Corby 1993: 66).

Causes of Sexual Abuse: Family Dysfunction or the Unacceptable Face of Patriarchy?

As for other forms of abuse, there has been a range of theoretical perspectives focused on sexual abuse, examining the characteristics of individual perpetrators, family dynamics, or broader social factors. In relation to child sexual abuse, tensions between medical and social models have revolved around gender rather than class (it being more widely accepted that sexual abuse is loosely, if at all, associated with social class).

Within the mainstream of professional intervention in cases of child sexual abuse, family models come closest to an 'orthodoxy'. In general terms, such models focus on relationships and communication within families, the analysis informing therapeutic intervention. In the case of sexual abuse there is particular concentration upon (step) father–daughter incest. This is generally taken to arise as a response to difficulties in relations between parents, whereupon the (step)father 'turns' to his daughter(s) for sexual gratification. Family models often claim or imply that mothers collude in this process to varying degrees, but are rarely entirely unaware of the abuse.

Not surprisingly, feminists have mounted a very strong critical challenge to this model and its assumptions. For them, the central point is to locate child sexual abuse within a patriarchal society, where both women and children may be seen as male 'possessions', over whom they have rights, and in particular to sex. For feminists, the family-based orthodoxy rests on gender assumptions which ignore the context of power and allow the logic of responsibility for abuse to be turned on its head. 'Male sexuality is seen as driven and uncontrollable,' observe MacLeod and Saraga, continuing ironic-ally, 'Poor men! It is up to women not only to nurture and care for their men adequately, and to control their own desires, but also to control men's sexuality' (1988: 34). Further-more, women are also cast as the natural protectors of their children, transforming abuse from male perpetration to female failure to protect. Thus, a mother becomes guilty of failing both her partner and children. Feminists also challenge the ortho-doxy's implication that if only women performed their roles as wives and mothers better, the problem of sexual abuse would disappear. Instead, they highlight the im-portance of gender and in particular the social construction of masculinity.

Feminist perspectives have had some success in arguing for the value of having women deal with the aftermath of sexual abuse, whether as police officers, social workers, or carers, and in promoting the removal of perpetrators rather than children from the family home. It is, however, also worth noting that greater recognition has been given in recent years to sexual abuse by women (Elliot 1993).

Beyond Sexual Abuse?

Following the emergence of child sexual abuse as an issue, there has been considerable, often intense discussion as to the existence of ritualized, sometimes satanic abuse. In some ways this has mirrored earlier debate on sexual abuse, with 'missionaries' preach-ing belated recognition of a major problem and others dismissing this as fanciful scare-mongering. An investigation carried out by La Fontaine found evidence of organized abuse, sometimes involving several families and/or paedophile networks, but only very rarely any links with ritualistic abuse. 'Evidence that adults had performed rituals of recognisably occult significance was virtually non-existent; there was even a scarcity of evidence of vaguer interest in the occult' (DoH 1995: 74).

Institutional Abuse

This term is used most frequently to describe abuse which takes place within the care system, and in particular within children's homes. In the 1980s and 1990s there has been a number of highly publicized cases, often involving many children and occurring over many years (Berridge and Brodie 1996). The irony of children, often removed from home for their own protection, then being abused by their protectors is a tragic one. Institutional abuse has taken a wide range of forms, including sexual abuse, physical abuse, or emotional abuse involving degrading treatment. Bullying by other residents has often been identified as a problem in residential care. On occasion, as with the case of 'Pindown' (a system of punishment based on isolation and humiliation), it may be the homes' regime itself which is deemed abusive (Levy and Kahan 1991). Though less well publicized, abuse within foster care is not uncommon, as is most clearly shown in the calls to Childline's dedicated 'Children in Care' line (Morris and Wheatley 1994). Sir William Utting's (1997) report into safeguards for children living away from home found continuing cause for concern throughout the care system and made wide-ranging recommendations to improve children's safety in residential care, foster care, boarding schools, hospitals, and prisons. The report highlighted the need to see safety in terms of the whole system for protecting children, and not simply as a matter of dealing with individual perpetrators.

Taken at its broadest, the concept of institutional abuse also alerts us to the possibility of interventions themselves being damaging, perhaps the result of numerous moves within the care system, or of poorly conducted child protection investigations. As Cleaver and Freeman observe, while an accusation of abuse might be 'all in a day's work' for the professional, its impact on families can sometimes be catastrophic. 'The disintegration of marital relationships . . . the movement of family members and the relocation of children were high prices to pay for a bruise or for the witnessing by children of an unsuitable video' (DoH 1995: 60).

Planning for Children who are being 'Looked After'

Research has found that the childcare system is often disorganized and slow in setting and achieving goals for the children it looks after. The higher priority given to planning within the childcare system over the past two decades and more can be traced back to Rowe and Lambert's (1973) landmark study, *Children Who Wait*. In examining the situations of children in long-term care, Rowe and Lambert identified the problem of **drift**, where children lived either in foster care or residential homes, often for many years, with no clear plan as to whether they would return home to their families, remain in care, or be adopted. The problems which were highlighted related both to planning for individual children, and planning services for children.

Concerns about planning were also boosted by a wider focus on the importance of long-term security for children, which came to be encapsulated in the term **permanence**. Maluccio *et al.* (1986: 5) describe permanency planning as 'the systematic carrying out, within a brief time-limited period, of a set of goal directed activities, designed to help children live in families that offer continuity of relationships with nurturing parents or caretakers and the opportunity to establish life-time relationships'. The philosophy of permanence placed particular emphasis on securing the futures of children decisively and relatively speedily. If parents could meet the children's needs adequately, without damaging delay, and with good long-term prospects, then permanence would be provided within the birth family. If not, then it should be provided through substitute care, most usually adoption, as quickly as possible. Good planning was to provide the means both for ensuring that decisions were soundly based, and that timescales did not allow drift to occur.

Adoption or Return to Birth Family?

The philosophy of permanence coincided in the 1970s with one of the periodic pendulum swings towards, or in this case away from, the importance of 'blood ties'. The death of Maria Colwell clearly contributed to this, but there were also theoretical influences, notably the emphasis on 'psychological parenting', with parent–child relationships seen to depend much more on the quality of care-giving than on biology (Goldstein *et al.* 1979). By the late seventies, with increasing removal of children from their birth families, many critics believed that, in practice, permanence policies had in effect become adoption policies. Countering what Fox Harding terms the 'state paternalism' lying behind permanence policies, organizations such as the Family Rights Group and, later, Parents Against Injustice emerged, to defend a **family rights** position. While in part this stance was based on giving greater weight to blood ties, it included an important political dimension. In particular, it was argued that at all stages of the process from children being removed from home through to their being adopted, the odds were stacked against birth families, who were for the most part relatively poor and disadvantaged. Not only were judgements often made on the basis of middle-class norms, but there was little acknowledgement of material deprivation and its effects. Furthermore, social work agencies were widely accused of making insufficient efforts to prevent children coming into care and subsequently to return them to their families. Fox Harding (1991: 59–154) provides a very good review of the arguments surrounding permanence and family rights, noting the dangers in both of idealizing families, whether substitute or biological.

In broad terms, the 1980s saw the pendulum swing back towards birth families. This is reflected by a falling 'in care' population, the broad outline of which can be seen in Table 15.3.

numbers in thousands	1975	1985	1995
children looked after	94.2	69.6	49.0
number in foster care	30.4	35.0	31.8
number in residential care	38.9	16.4	6.3

Table 15.3 Children looked after in England and Wales 1975–95
Source: Health and Personal Social Services Statistics (HMSO, 1996).

The change was partly due to the continuing efforts of the family rights campaign, which linked advocacy for individual families with lobbying policy-makers. The primary aims were to make social work practice more accountable—through greater openness and extending the legal protection of families—and to maximize efforts to keep or re-unite children with their birth families. Such efforts received significant support from research carried out in the early 1980s and summarized as *Social Work Decisions in Child Care* (DHSS 1985). Three major themes emerged from this research, the first being to show that contact between children and birth parents was vital both to prospects for return home and for the children's well-being. A second, however, was that much social work practice appeared neglectful or even obstructive of contact (ibid.: 5). The third theme was that of problems within the care system itself, where moves and instability were found to be common (ibid.: 10). In all, too many children were seen to be losing contact with their birth families, while not necessarily being offered the security implied by permanence policies. Social work agencies stood accused of being more concerned with intervention than what it might achieve. Echoing some of the earlier anxiety about drift, Millham *et al.*'s (1986) study *Lost in Care* found that if children did not return home within 5 weeks there was a strong chance of remaining in care for two years or more, and that levels of contact were the best indicator for return. Importantly, on leaving care the overwhelming majority of young people returned to or re-established contact with their birth families.

During the 1990s, following the report of a government-commissioned working party (Parker *et al.* 1991), efforts have been made to implement a more rigorous and standard-ized system of planning for 'looked-after' children. The impetus came from recognition that alongside planning over the major issues—such as return to birth family or adop-tion—more attention was needed in areas such as education, health, or social skills, where there was evidence of children's needs being neglected, with ultimately dam-aging consequences. The poor educational performance of many children in care has been of particular concern, given its consequences for later life (Fletcher 1996).

The Children Act 1989

Such acknowledgements coalesced during the 1980s into a greater emphasis on working constructively with birth families, and increased recognition was given to the import-ance of links with extended family and siblings. Boosted by the events of Cleveland, the Children Act 1989 (see Box 15.1) placed particular emphasis on the importance of support for birth families and the rights of parents, albeit couched in terms of parental responsibilities. The dominant theme was that of 'partnership'. At the same time, pres-sure for **children's rights** began to exert at least some influence on policy and practice, notably in terms of encouraging their participation in decision-making and attempts to give them a stronger voice (Fox Harding 1991: 155–200). Borrowing ideas from New Zealand in particular, some agencies began to experiment with **family group confer-ences,** in which family members were brought together and encouraged to draw up their own solutions to problems of childcare and protection with professional involvement being kept to a minimum (Family Rights Group 1996).

The thinking behind the Children Act is aptly described by Fox Harding (1991) as an 'uneasy synthesis', and many commentators have noted how the Act can be interpreted

---

Box 15.1 Key features of the Children Act 1989

- more active involvement of courts in decision-making about children
- welfare of the child to be paramount
- use of a welfare checklist for decision-making
- avoidance of delay
- no order to be made unless better than not to do so
- ascertaining and taking into account child's wishes
- specific orders to deal with residence, contact, and so on
- parental responsibility to be maximized, even when the child is in care
- bringing together public (local authority, police powers, and so on) and private (such as divorce) law
- due consideration to be given to child's religious persuasion, racial origin, and cultural and linguistic background

---

in quite different ways. For alongside the moves to empower birth families and children, there was to be no easing up on child protection nor a return to drift. Importantly, no additional resources were made available to implement the Act. In turn, this made it difficult to offer the promised support to families, and threatened to overload social work agencies and the courts as they grappled with competing demands.

Residential or Foster Care?

We will be looking at both residential and foster care in more detail below, but at this point it is useful to make some brief points about their respective places in providing public care for children. Since 1945, foster care has generally been the favoured option for most children, having, according to Packman (1981: 25), 'the blessing of Curtis, Bowlby and the Treasury' and, as can be seen from Table 15.3 (above), there has been a steady shift away from residential care. Colton (1988) summarizes the arguments from research which show that children and young people in foster care benefit from more extensive and personalized adult attention, and that this is generally reflected in their confidence, behaviour, and happiness with their carers. Research and testimony from young people themselves has also highlighted problems in residential care of lack of privacy, study facilities, or autonomy in everyday life, and bullying (Fletcher 1993). The move from residential to foster care and to smaller units has been repeated throughout Europe, although it has been taken much further in the UK than in any country except Sweden (Madge 1994).

Residential Care: A Positive Choice?

Apart from its dramatic reduction in size, residential care has also undergone significant change in its organization and rationale. With the modern emphasis on planning and permanence, residential care has largely ceased to provide long-term homes for children, and has become more 'task-focused'. Placements are likely to be time-limited, in principle at least relatively short-term, and aimed at some particular outcome. This may be return to the family, preparation for foster care, provision of a therapeutic environment, or, for older teenagers, readiness for life after leaving care. Homes, whether run by local authorities, private or voluntary organizations have often specialized around such functions, although the specialization has frequently been subverted by the need to find places urgently (Berridge 1985). Despite these developments, the perception of homes as 'dumping grounds', for adolescents perceived as troubled or troubling, has remained widespread (Utting 1991: s2.22). With foster care the preferred option, residential care is widely assumed to provide only for those too difficult to foster, whose foster placements are yet to be found or have broken down, or whose abuse is thought to make family life inappropriate. 'A child abused by his or her family may not be able to accept that he or she can be protected by care in another substitute family' (Utting 1991: s3.13). Even acknowledgement that 'many children prefer residential care' may be taken more as evidence of their problems than a positive choice. Residential care has thus been assumed to survive only because of its safety-net role *vis à vis* foster care.

Staffing has remained a consistent problem in residential care throughout the postwar years, with often high turnover and low pay and levels of qualification symbolizing a lack of expertise and status for residential workers compared with field social workers. In 1995, despite some improvements, 70 per cent of residential childcare staff remained unqualified (LGMB/CCETSW 1997: 93). This situation is often seen as increasing the potential for abuse, not only making it easier for abusers to gain employment, but also through lack of coping skills, awareness, or confidence to challenge bad practice. Considerable efforts have been made in the 1990s to iron out many of these difficulties (including the limits of legitimate restraint), with as yet mixed results (Berridge and Brodie 1996). However, if residential care appears to crystallize many of the difficulties inherent in parenting by the state, it remains both an integral part of the childcare system and appreciated by many of its residents. 'The best things about being in . . . residential care were getting "treated well" and there always being "someone to talk to or someone to listen" . . . young people referred to having more friends, activities, outings and "things" such as computers . . . to being safer and not being abused' (Fletcher 1993: 84).

Foster Care: The Ideal Method?

Looking after other people's children on a temporary basis has a long history, both as a formal practice, known as 'boarding out' under the Poor Law, and doubtless longer still as an informal one. As has been noted, foster care has been the favoured placement for children since 1945, and now provides for a clear majority of children 'looked after' (see Table 15.3 above).

Modern foster care has been shaped by the twin concerns of extending 'fosterability', and adaptation to the emphases on planning and permanence. Together, these have fuelled moves towards the 'professionalization' of foster care. The extension of fosterability entailed challenging prevailing beliefs about the impossibility of providing foster care for children with behavioural difficulties or disabilities, and the unsuitability of black and minority ethnic children for family placement. More recently, similar efforts have been made in relation to survivors of sexual abuse and children infected with HIV or AIDS. The extension of fosterability has been achieved through a combination of education, training, support, and financial inducements. Following the early examples, most notably of Kent, many agencies set up professional foster care schemes during the 1970s and 1980s (Shaw and Hipgrave 1983). Most dealt with teenagers, and, formally at least, mainly those who had been involved in crime. The schemes involved strong emphases on training and support and the payment of a fee to carers in addition to maintenance allowances, the fee being regarded as both a compensation for disruption to home life and reward for the carers' skills. Treatment rather than simply care was to be provided. However, maintaining a clear distinction between 'professional' and 'traditional' foster care has proved awkward, and more complex patterns have developed (Waterhouse 1997: 41–54). This was in part due to problems of distinguishing degrees of difficulty or skills, but also because many of the features of professional schemes, such as training and support, were soon extended to all foster carers. Many of the newly formed independent fostering agencies have a strong professional emphasis, including the payment of higher fees to carers and offering placements to more 'difficult' children or young people.

Foster Care, Permanence, and Planning

From the 1970s onwards, foster care, like residential care, has become increasingly 'task-focused'. The combined emphases on permanence and planning have served to underline the temporary nature of foster care and its role in working towards particular goals, whether return home, readiness for adoption, or independent living, perhaps entailing work on personal and family problems. The shift is well captured in Holman's (1975) distinction between a quasi-adoptive **exclusive foster care** and an **inclusive** model, where foster families can work constructively with birth parents and social workers and accept 'letting go' of the children.

While not attracting the negative publicity of residential care, foster care has not been without its own challenges. Many of these stem from the uneasy mix of 'professional childcare' and 'normal family life', the ambivalent status of foster carers between workers and volunteers, or even whether they are to be regarded as colleagues or clients of social workers. The tensions are difficult to resolve, and regularly surface in debates over payment and motivation, or what might reasonably be expected of foster carers in terms of opening up their homes. **Breakdowns** (some prefer the term 'disruption') of placements have been a worryingly common feature of foster care, with many investigations seeking to identify the factors relevant to success and failure. Perhaps predictably in view of the demands placed upon foster carers, problems of recruitment and retention of carers have also been a recurring theme. While a recent survey found the position surprisingly buoyant, there remained many localized shortages, including those relating to minority ethnic carers, while nationally, 'the most serious carer shortages identified . . . were for older children and sibling groups' (Waterhouse 1997: 47).

Adoption: A Service for Children?

Although, like foster care, it has a very long informal history, adoption as a legal concept in the UK dates only from 1926. It has been organized by both voluntary and statutory agencies, under regulations designed to prevent abuses (such as selling children for adoption), and to ensure children are appropriately matched with suitable adoptive parents.

Following the Second World War, adoption came to be based on the **clean break,** involving the severance of all legal links with the birth family and granting identical status to children born to the adopters (the one exception to this being that adoptees cannot inherit aristocratic titles!). This 'clean break' was thought to be in the best interests of all members of the **adoption triangle**—birth parent(s), child, and adoptive parents. During the 1950s and 1960s this was increasingly questioned, with recognition of the need for adoptees to trace their birth family in order to better understand their **identity.** Research was to show that total severance often increased the sense of loss experienced by those involved in adoption (Triseliotis 1973). The Children Act 1975 allowed adoptees access to their original birth certificate and knowledge of the circumstances surrounding their adoption.

By contrast with the clean-break philosophy, more recent thinking has placed greater emphasis on **openness in adoption.** Openness can be seen as a continuum from greater supply of information to all members of the triangle, or perhaps involvement of a birth parent in selecting adopters, through to continued face-to-face contact between the birth and adoptive families. Unlike many countries, the UK has no 'simple' adoption, involving a more limited transfer of parental responsibilities and therefore reversible. As well as developments in thinking on children's needs, moves towards openness have also reflected the changing nature of adoption. The transformation since the 1960s has been dramatic, with the overall scale of adoption falling sharply and affecting a very different group of children and families.

Having peaked at nearly 25,000 annually during the late 1960s, the number of adoptions has since dropped dramatically (see Table 15.4 below). This is despite various legal measures, including the introduction of adoption allowances under the Children Act 1975, to facilitate adoptions. The most striking aspect of the change has been the precipitous decline in baby adoptions, which is also indicated in Table 15.4 along with the proportionate growth in adoption of older children.

	1975	1985	1995
number of orders made	21,299	7,615	5,795
% of children under 1	21	21	6
% of children over 10	19	27	31

Table 15.4 Adoption orders 1975–95
Source: Marriage and Divorce Statistics, Office of National Statistics, 1997.

The drop in baby adoptions is generally explained as the result of greater use of contraception and termination, and the declining stigma attached to illegitimacy. Adoption is now much more likely to be from the care system, which often means that the children may be older, be the victims of abuse, or have special needs. Importantly, many more adoptions are now **contested,** or opposed by birth parents. Debates over contested adoptions crystallize some of the key differences between the advocates of permanence (and those who would wish to see adoption expanded) and family rights campaigners, both about the form of adoption and, indeed, its necessity or desirability. For Ryburn, adoption law still treats children 'as pieces of transportable personal property who can, by a legal fiction, have past links extinguished and join a new family as if they were born to it' (1993: 39).

Race, Ethnicity, and Adoption: Political Correctness?

Adoption has long been recognized as conferring social mobility upon children, as the majority of birth families are poor, while adopters are overwhelmingly middle-class. Far more controversial, however, has been the placement of black and minority ethnic children in adoptive (and foster) families. In 1965 the British Adoption Project (BAP) sought to challenge the prevailing view of the time that black children were unadoptable due to racial prejudice on the part of white families and the lack of availability of black families. The BAP was successful in placing over 50 children, most with white families. Thereafter, **transracial adoption** (TRA—in practice the adoption of black or minority ethnic children by white families) became established in many adoption agencies. The rise of black liberation struggles in the 1970s brought increasingly strong opposition to the assimilationist ideas underlying TRA. Its opponents argued that placement in white families had detrimental effects on children's sense of racial identity, knowledge of their culture of origin, and ability to cope with racism. It was also contended that the one-way traffic of black children into white homes was rooted in norms which devalued or even pathologized black families and assumed the inherent superiority of their white counterparts. Moreover, the long-standing notion that there were too few black adoptive families available for children was challenged, being blamed on the inadequate recruitment efforts of adoption agencies. This critique was very influential in the 1980s, and led many agencies to apply **same-race placement** policies which sought racial and ethnic matching between adoptees and adopters. The issue has, however, remained highly controversial, periodically erupting into the media spotlight, usually when a black child is removed from a white foster family who wish to adopt. The supporters of transracial adoption have argued that the fears expressed are not borne out by research and that the shortage of black families is real, thereby leading black children to remain in care for longer than necessary. They also tend to see the practice of transracial adoption as promoting racial integration and social harmony. By contrast, they characterize same-race policies as 'separatist' or even a form of apartheid (Gaber and Aldridge 1994). Hostile politicians and media pundits have targeted same-race policies, as well as adoption by lesbians and gays, as 'political correctness', and have threatened to clip the wings of those who support them. The latter, however, continue to see such measures as important both for meeting the needs of children and for wider moves towards social justice.

Children, Young People, Crime, and Welfare

During the 1990s, with its more punitive approach to young offenders, it may seem anomalous to include their treatment under the title of 'care and protection'. This would, however, be to misunderstand the history of what is now termed 'youth justice', and to assume that recent policy swings are irreversible. The last hundred years has seen a continuing debate about whether young offenders are criminals deserving punishment, or the victims of deprivation who need social care. (Some of the issues covered in this section are also discussed, from a more criminological perspective, in the section Welfare *vs.* Punishment in Chapter 17.)

The Rise of Welfarism

Interest in the 'welfare' of young criminals can be traced to the nineteenth century and the construction of childhood as a period of 'natural innocence', but also of vulnerability to corrupt influences. The programme of Victorian 'child-savers' rested on the twin pillars of separation from adult offenders and tutelage from appropriate adults for children involved in, or at risk of, offending. The mid-nineteenth-century creation of the Reformatory and Industrial Schools typified this process, with their emphasis on strict discipline and training for modest but respectable trades (usually domestic service, in the case of girls). More generally, children came to be imprisoned less and to have their own separate courts and prisons, the latter known from the early twentieth century as 'Borstals'. The trend towards seeing youthful offending as the product of deprivation continued. Initially cast in terms of poor socialization, the link was increasingly clothed in psychological garb. In the post-war years the work of John Bowlby was especially influential, especially the notion that maternal deprivation (see above) led to various forms of disturbed, anti-social behaviour, often including the criminal. His work also seemed to offer some explanation for the well-documented failure of institutions, approved schools, detention centres, and borstals, to curb offending (see Minty 1987 for a summary of the relevant research).

The 1960s are often taken to mark the high tide of welfarism, with the Children and Young Persons (CYP) Act 1969 its most potent symbol. Within the **welfare model**, offending was to be seen as a symptom of need, whether social or psychological. The Act sought to 'decriminalize', raising the age of criminal responsibility from 10 to 14, and envisaging a move to 17. Responsibility for young offenders was to be significantly relocated from the criminal justice system to welfare agencies. The Act's central measure was the **care order** where offending was one of the grounds for transferring parental responsibility to the local authority. The authority was then responsible for virtually all key decisions regarding the child, including where s/he would live.

The 1970s and a 'Return to Justice'

The 1969 CYP Act was born into a changed and hostile political climate. The incoming Conservative government in 1970 decided not to implement the raising of the age of criminal responsibility to 14. There was also opposition from magistrates and police, and more generally from the emerging 'new right', who saw welfarism as undermining both individual responsibility for crime and the workings of the criminal justice system. Above all, it was portrayed as 'soft' and thereby responsible for the rising crime rate. Magistrates appeared to respond by making greater use of custodial sentences in order to ensure punishment and to keep control over sentencing.

If welfarism attracted predictable fire from the political right, it was also subjected to considerable critique from the left, based primarily on civil liberties arguments. It was argued that welfarism had been grafted onto and extended the existing system—thereby 'widening the net'—rather than replacing it. Welfarist assumptions could lead to effectively indeterminate sentences (care orders once made lasting until 18) for often quite minor offences. Furthermore, the making of 'welfare-based' orders could have the effect of harsher sentences if the child should then reoffend. Above all, the growing harshness of the system was masked by a popular image that it was now hopelessly 'soft'.

These twin pressures led to the development of what was known as a **justice model**, which emphasized the importance of the offence and direct punishment according to its seriousness. This restoration of offending as an act of will, playing down any connection with social circumstances or psychological factors, was reflected in changes to social work and probation practice, with a stronger focus on 'offending behaviour' and less concern with the background of the offender.

The 1980s and the Paradox of Diversion

Conservative governments from 1979 to 1997, with law and order the dominant theme in criminal justice, endeavoured to make punishment more central to the treatment of young offenders. One of the earliest initiatives involved toughening the regimes in detention centres—to provide a **short, sharp shock**. Yet paradoxically, by the end of the 1980s the number of young people in custody had fallen sharply, as indeed had the number sentenced. These falls can be seen from the figures in Table 15.5, which also show the small but significant reversal of the trend on custody for boys during the early 1990s.

While the 1980s falls in sentencing and use of custody can partly be accounted for by a small fall in reported crime, they owe much more to the strategy of **diversion**. This

Year	Males (10–17) numbers sentenced (thousands)		Females (10–17) numbers sentenced (thousands)	
	Total	Custody	Total	Custody
1985	87.2	11.5	9.8	0.2
1990	40.8	3.6	5.1	0.1
1995	37.2	4.2	5.0	0.1

Table 15.5 Sentencing and custody rates for young offenders, 1985–95

Source: Criminal Statistics for England and Wales 1995, Home Office.

term could cover a range of measures, sometimes including community service or reparation, the common element being a desire to divert the young person away from the machinery of the criminal justice system. The use of police cautions rose dramatically— from 36 per cent of young male and 60 per cent of young female offenders in 1984, to 59 per cent and 80 per cent respectively in 1994 (Ruxton 1996). Despite declining support for welfarism, the idea that offending was often just a 'passing phase' remained strong, along with awareness that legal measures to 'label' an offender often made matters worse. Diversion was for the most part pursued away from the public gaze and stood in sharp contrast to the 'get tough' rhetoric of politicians. It was, however, sufficiently successful to underpin the Criminal Justice Act 1991's emphasis on custody only as a last resort, albeit with the quid pro quo of tougher 'punishment in the community' sentences.

The 1990s and (Really) 'Getting Tough'

Like the 1969 CYP Act, the 1991 Act was soon overtaken by events and a changing political climate. The years immediately following were to see the re-emergence of moral panic about young offenders and a pronounced shift in policy. Joyriding, 'bail bandits', and the 'persistent young offender' all emerged as important signifiers in public perceptions. Yet arguably the most powerful came from a single event, the murder of toddler James Bulger by two boys barely old enough to be legally responsible for their crime. Coinciding with wider concern over youth crime, this took on a wider resonance, appearing to herald the demise of 'childhood innocence'. As Jenks remarks (1996: 127), 'it was not just two children who were on trial for the murder of a third but childhood itself'. At the same time, the long-standing image of a system 'soft on crime' was revived, with stories of young offenders being sent on expensive safaris only to reoffend on their return. A series of 'get tough' measures followed, dramatically reversing the effects of the 1991 Criminal Justice Act. Existing custodial sentences for young offenders were extended both in length and scope, while new 'junior prisons', known as **Secure Training Centres,** were introduced for persistent offenders aged 12 to 14. Custodial regimes were to be toughened, with the introduction of US-style 'boot camps' and the use of the army's 'glass house'. The major political parties vied with each other for toughness in dealing with young offenders in the community, with proposed use of electronic tagging and blanket local curfews.

Following the 1997 election, the new Labour government seemed keen to fulfil their opposition slogan 'tough on crime, tough on the causes of crime'. Home Secretary Jack Straw attacked the 'excuse culture' surrounding youth crime, but also emphasized preventive measures. The Crime and Disorder Act 1998 included provisions to remove the presumption that children under 14 did not 'understand right from wrong', to replace cautions with a system based on two warnings only, to promote reparation, and to allow curfews for children under 10, either on an individual or area basis. The Act also introduced an order which would require parents of offenders to attend counselling or guidance sessions to improve their parenting. At the local level, youth offending teams, comprising social workers, probation officers, police officers, and education and health personnel were to be created, while a National Youth Justice Board was established to oversee developments.

Anglo-Saxon Youth Justice: The Only Way?

The approach to young offenders in the UK stands in marked contrast to most of continental Europe, being much closer in style to the US. The European model remains more rooted in welfarist ideas, with much lower rates of custody and higher ages of criminal responsibility (the European average being 14 to 16, against 10 in England and Wales, 8 in Scotland and Northern Ireland). A stronger emphasis on welfare is also evident in processes based more on investigative enquiry rather than prosecution, though the Scottish hearings system has elements of this approach. This system relies on Panels comprising lay volunteers, whose role is to consider whether any compulsory measures —such as statutory supervision or placement in residential care—are necessary to secure the effective care of the young offender. The hearings seek to provide a less formal atmosphere than court, and encourage the participation of the offender's family.

Conclusion

As the century draws to a close, the care and protection of children remains a challenging and contentious field, where long-standing tensions must continue to be managed with limited resources. Perhaps buoyed by eighteen years in opposition, the Labour government has been more than ready to acknowledge the 'failure' of the care system. The earliest signs of their own approach came from the 'Quality Protects' initiative which followed the formula of setting objectives for Social Services Departments and making additional funding available, dependent upon the meeting of specific targets. The latter included reducing the number of moves and time spent within the care system, and increasing the educational qualifications of those leaving it. The initiative also sought to emphasize more effective child protection and better support for care leavers and children with disabilities, with improved standards to be enforced by a more comprehensive and rigorous inspection regime. It remains to be seen whether these measures will, at long last, be those which decisively consign 'failure' to history.

Key Legislation

Prevention of Cruelty to and Protection of Children Act 1889 The Act's two key measures were, first, to make wilful cruelty or neglect a criminal offence, and second, to allow a child victim to be removed and placed with a relative or other 'fit person'.

Children Act 1948 The Act's main measures were the establishment of Children's Departments within local authorities and clarification of circumstances within which children could be received into care voluntarily or where the local authority could assume parental rights. The Act also placed a duty on local authorities to attempt to return children to their families where possible, and to place them in foster families where not.

Children and Young Persons (CYP) Act 1969 The Act is perhaps best known as the high point of welfare approaches to juvenile crime, with its various measures to decriminalize and to treat crime as a symptom of family problems. The main provision of the Act was the creation of the care order, which could be made by a court where parental care and control were regarded as inadequate and one of a series of conditions was met. These conditions were wide-ranging, from being a victim of abuse or being in moral danger, through being beyond parental control, to non-school attendance and offending behaviour.

Children Act 1975 The Act aimed to prioritize the welfare of the child, especially where this might be seen to conflict with the interests of their family. Its main measures related to facilitating adoption, allowing children to be legally 'freed' for adoption, strengthening the position of foster carers who wished to adopt, and introducing allowances for those who might not otherwise be able to afford to adopt. Adoptees were given rights to their original birth certificates and hence a route to tracing their birth parents.

Children Act 1989 Though the term is not used in the Act itself, 'partnership with parents' is widely taken to be its guiding principle. The Act emphasized the importance of parental responsibility and laid a duty on local authorities to support parents, including maximization of involvement when children are looked after by the state, even when subject of a care order. A greater role for the courts was seen as a way of strengthening the position of parents dealing with social work agencies. The Act also attempted to strengthen the rights of children to be involved in decisions affecting them, and to place greater emphasis on the extended family.

Criminal Justice Act 1991 For youth justice the main thrust of the Act was to consolidate the strategy of diversion, avoiding custody wherever possible while making the community alternatives as 'tough' as possible. The Act also attempted to make parents more directly responsible for their children's offending.

Glossary

adoption triangle This term, coined by Tugenhadt, refers to the relationships between child, birth parent(s), and adoptive parent(s). It serves to remind that adoption is always a triangular affair and can aid understanding of the relationships involved.

breakdowns Sometimes also known as disruptions, breakdowns describe those fostering and adoption situations where placements end sooner than planned or intended as a result of problems experienced within the foster or adoptive family.

care order A court order which transfers parental responsibility to the local authority, although it does not entirely extinguish the responsibility held by the child's parent. Care orders are made where the court believes this necessary to prevent significant harm to the child.

children's rights The term is used both to describe formal and substantive legal rights held by children but more broadly to a philosophy which seeks to maximize the involvement of children in decision-making. There are different approaches to children's rights, most notably those which see rights in a more paternalistic way, i.e. as rights to a certain treatment by adults and those tending more towards 'liberation', emphasizing that children should have greater powers.

child-savers A term coined by Platt to describe nineteenth-century reformers who sought to rescue children from life on the streets and its attendant deviance, and to provide homes which would offer a more constructive upbringing.

clean break An approach to adoption which involves complete severance of ties between the child and birth family, with its proponents arguing that this is in the best interests of the child, adopters, and usually, birth parents. See also **open adoption** (below).

contested adoption Refers to adoption applications where the birth parent(s) does not consent to the child's adoption. In this situation, courts can dispense with parental consent if they think it is being withheld 'unreasonably'.

cultural relativism The idea that norms and behaviour can only be judged in the context of their own culture and that those of different cultures are equally valid.

diversion A strategy in youth justice which seeks to avoid or minimize contact with the courts and custody.

drift This term describes a situation where there is either no clear long-term plan regarding a child's future, or where the plan is not being effectively implemented.

exclusive and inclusive foster care These terms are used to describe foster care, depending on whether the birth family (and sometimes professionals) tend to be excluded from or included in the foster family and actively involved in the foster child's life.

family group conferences FGCs attempt to maximize the possibility of (extended) families finding solutions to childcare problems, while professional intervention is kept to a minimum.

family group home A residential home modelled on 'family life', with relatively small numbers of residents and consistent parental figures among the staff.

family rights An approach to childcare issues which emphasizes the importance of birth family ties (or blood relationships).

good enough parenting A phrase used to indicate a threshold below which action must be taken to ensure that the child is able to receive appropriate parenting.

identity An important concept in modern adoption, which recognizes the importance of 'origins' or heritage (e.g. familial, social, cultural, racial, religious) in the adoptee's sense of self and well-being.

justice model An approach to youth crime which stresses the responsibility of young offenders for their crimes, that punishment is important and that it should be proportionate to the seriousness of the crime.

maternal deprivation and attachment A theoretical perspective deriving from the work of John Bowlby which emphasizes the importance of secure attachments between a children and their parental figures, and explores the consequences of attachment problems.

medical model An approach to understanding child abuse which treats it as a disease, with abusive behaviour as the visible symptoms.

the myth of classlessness A phrase coined by Pelton which attacks the view that child abuse occurs equally across all social classes and which highlights the importance of poverty and inequality in generating abuse.

openness in adoption Used to describe adoptions where contact (which may take a variety of forms) is continued between the adopted child and the birth family.

permanence A principle of childcare which seeks to avoid drift (see above) and resolve the long-term futures of children both decisively and fairly speedily.

rule of optimism A term used by Dingwall which suggests that professionals generally give parents the benefit of the doubt where there might be suspicions of child abuse.

same-race placements A policy under which children from particular racial or ethnic groups will be fostered or adopted by families from the same group.

Secure Training Centres Institutions introduced in the mid-1990s for 'persistent young offenders' aged 12 to 14, with an emphasis on discipline.

short, sharp shock A phrase used in the early 1980s to describe a toughened regime in Detention Centres, intended to deter young offenders from reoffending.

sick role A feature of the medical model (see above) which regards abusers as sick and hence less than fully responsible for their actions.

social model An approach to child abuse which emphasizes social factors both in its definition (or 'construction') and its causes.

transracial adoption Literally, the adoption of a child from one racial group by a family from another; in practice, almost invariably the adoption of minority ethnic children by white families.

welfare model An approach to youth crime which sees offending as a symptom of deprivation—whether psychological or social—and hence in need of social work intervention rather than punishment.

Guide to Further Reading

There is no recent historical overview of the childcare system, but Packman's (1981) *The Child's Generation* (Blackwell) provides a very readable account of post-war developments, while an earlier and more detailed history is provided by Heywood (1979), *Children in Care* (Routledge). Holman's (1996) *The Corporate Parent* (National Institute for Social Work) offers a sensitive and moving account of the work of Manchester Children's Department before reorganization in 1971. Other useful overview texts include Fox Harding's (1991) *Perspectives in Child Care Policy* (Longman) where she outlines four main influences— laissez-faire, state paternalism, birth family rights, and children's rights—on policy development. The collection of essays edited by Hill and Aldgate (1996), *Child Welfare Services: Developments in Law, Policy, Practice and Research* (Jessica Kingsley) provides good guides to a range of current childcare issues within a single volume.

Of the many texts on child abuse and protection, Corby (1993) *Child Abuse: Towards a Knowledge Base* (Open University Press) offers a good overview of definitions, debates about causes, and consequences. Though now somewhat dated, Parton's (1985) *The Politics of Child Abuse* (Macmillan) remains a classic in its application of wider social context to childcare. The essays within Waterhouse (ed.) (1994), *Child Abuse and Child Abusers* (Jessica Kingsley) also take a wider view, notably in some detailed research on abusers and gendered links between child abuse and domestic violence. Parton, Thorpe, and Wattam's (1997) *Child Protection: Risk and the Moral Order* (Macmillan) deals with some of the debates on risk management, placing them in a broader social context. As an overview text on child sexual abuse, Glaser and Frosh (1996), *Child Sexual Abuse* (2nd edn., Macmillan), is probably the most useful. The Department of Health (1995) *Child Protection: Messages from Research* provides an excellent summary of research projects undertaken during the

1990s and the key implications to be drawn from them. Among areas covered are the child protection system, partnership between professionals and parents, inter-agency cooperation, defining and researching abuse, and organized and ritual abuse. Reder, Duncan, and Gray (1993), *Beyond Blame: Child Abuse Tragedies Revisited* (Routledge) considers the place of child abuse enquiries in child protection work.

Utting's (1991) *Children in the Public Care: A Review of Residential Child Care* (HMSO) provides a good summary of developments and issues in residential care, while for foster care Berridge (1997), *Foster Care: A Review of Research*, offers a comprehensive guide to the relevant literature. Triseliotis, Sellick, and Short (1995), *Foster Care: Theory and Practice* (Batsford) gives a wide coverage of relevant issues and is an excellent textbook for foster care. Along similar lines and equally good for coverage of adoption is Triseliotis, Shireman, and Hundleby's (1997) *Adoption: Theory, Policy and Practice* (Cassell).

Although now rather dated, Pitt's (1988) *The Politics of Juvenile Justice* (Sage) provides a good overview of long-standing issues in the field of what is now termed youth justice. The most up-to-date text is provided by Haines and Drakeford (1998), *Young People and Youth Justice* (Macmillan).

For issues relating to childcare in Europe, Ruxton (1996), *Children in Europe* (NCH Action for Children, London) provides a very useful introductory overview.

References

Berridge, D. (1985), *Children's Homes* (Oxford: Blackwell).

Berridge, D. and Brodie, I. (1996), 'Residential Child Care in England and Wales: The Inquiries and After', in Hill, M. and Aldgate, J. (eds.), *Child Welfare Services: Developments in Law, Policy, Practice and Research* (London: Jessica Kingsley).

Campbell, B. (1988), *Unofficial Secrets* (London: Virago).

Channer, Y. and Parton, N. (1990), 'Racism, Cultural Relativism and Child Protection', in Violence Against Children Study Group, *Taking Child Abuse Seriously: Contemporary Issues in Child Protection Theory and Practice* (London: Unwin Hyman).

Colton, M. (1988), 'Substitute Care Practice', *Adoption and Fostering*, 12(1), 30–4.

Corby, B. (1993), *Child Abuse: Towards a Knowledge Base* (Buckingham: Open University Press).

Creighton, S. (1989), *Child Abuse Trends in England and Wales 1983–87* (London: NSPCC).

Curtis, M. (1946), Report of the Care of Children Committee, Cmnd. 6922 (London: HMSO).

Department of Health (1995), *Child Protection: Messages from Research* (London: HMSO).

Department of Health and Social Security (1985), *Social Work Decisions in Child Care* (London: HMSO).

——(1988), *Report of the Enquiry into Child Abuse in Cleveland (Butler-Sloss)* (Cmnd. 412, London: HMSO).

Dingwall, R., Eekelaar, J., and Murray, T. (1983), *The Protection of Children: State Intervention and Family Life* (Oxford: Basil Blackwell).

Doyle, C. (1997), *Working with Abused Children* (Basingstoke: Macmillan).

Elliot, M. (ed.) (1993), *Female Sexual Abuse of Children: The Last Taboo* (Harlow: Longman).

Family Rights Group (1996), *Family Group Conferences: Messages from UK Practice and Research* (London: FRG).

Fletcher, B. (1993), *Not Just a Name: The Views of Young People in Foster and Residential Care* (London: National Consumer Council).

——(1996), *Who Cares About Education?* (London: Who Cares? Trust).

Fox Harding, L. (1991), *Perspectives in Child Care Policy* (London: Longman).

Gaber, I. and Aldridge, J. (eds.) (1994), *In the Best Interests of the Child: Culture, Identity and Transracial Adoption* (London: Free Association Books).

Gil, D. (1970), *Violence Against Children* (Cambridge, Mass.: Harvard University Press).

Goldstein, J., Freud, A., and Solnit, A. (1979), *Beyond the Best Interests of the Child* (New York: Free Press).

Greenland, C. (1987), *Preventing CAN Death: An International Study of Deaths due to Child Abuse and Neglect* (London: Tavistock).

Holman, R. (1975), 'The Place of Fostering in Social Work', *British Journal of Social Work*, 5(1), 3–29.

Jenks, C. (1996), *Childhood* (London: Routledge).

Jones, D., Pickett, J., Oates, M., and Barbor, P. (1987), *Understanding Child Abuse* (Basingstoke: Macmillan).

Kelly, L., Regan, L., and Burton, S. (1991), *An Exploratory Study of the Prevalence of Sexual Abuse in a Sample of 16–21 Year Olds* (Child Abuse Studies Unit, University of North London).

Levy, A. and Kahan, B. (1991), 'The Pindown Experience and the Protection of Children', Staffordshire County Council, Stafford.

LGMB/CCETSW (1997), *Human Resources for Personal Social Services: From Personnel Administration to Human Resources Management* (Local Government Training Board/Central Council for Education and Training in Social Work).

MacLeod, M. and Saraga, E. (1988), 'Challenging the Orthodoxy: Towards a Feminist Theory and Practice', *Feminist Review*, 28, 16–55.

Madge, N. (1994), *Children and Residential Care in Europe* (London: National Childrens Bureau).

Maluccio, A., Fein, E., and Olmstead, K. (1986), *Permanency Planning for Children: Concepts and Methods* (London: Tavistock).

Millham, S., Bullock, R., Hosie, K., and Haak, M. (1986), *Lost in Care: The Problems of Maintaining Links between Children in Care and their Families* (Aldershot: Gower).

Minty, B. (1987), *Child Care and Adult Crime* (Manchester: Manchester University Press).

Monckton, Sir W. (1945), *Report on the Circumstances which led to the Boarding Out of Dennis and Terence O'Neill at Bank Farm and the Steps Taken to Supervise their Welfare* (Cmnd. 6636, London: HMSO).

Moore, J. (1985), *The ABC of Child Abuse Work* (Aldershot: Gower).

Morris, S. and Wheatley, H. (1994), *Time to Listen: The Experiences of Young People in Foster and Residential Care* (London: Childline).

Packman, J. (1981), *The Child's Generation: Child Care Policy in Britain* (2nd edn., Oxford: Basil Blackwell).

Parker, R., Ward, H., Jackson, S., Aldgate, J., and Wedge, P. (1991), *Looking After Children: Assessing Outcomes in Child Care* (London: HMSO).

Parton, N. (1985), *The Politics of Child Abuse* (Basingstoke: Macmillan).

Pelton, L. (1985), 'Child Abuse and Neglect: The Myth of Classlessness', in Pelton, L. (ed.), *The Social Context of Child Abuse and Neglect* (New York: Human Sciences Press).

Rowe, J. and Lambert, L. (1973), *Children Who Wait* (London: Association of British Adoption Agencies).

Ruxton, S. (1996), *Children in Europe* (London: NCH Action for Children).

Ryburn, M. (1993), 'The Effects of an Adversarial Process on Adoption Decisions', *Adoption & Fostering*, 17(3), 39–45.

Shaw, M. and Hipgrave, T. (1983), *Specialist Fostering* (London: Batsford).

Social Services Inspectorate (1990), *Inspection of Child Protection Services in Rochdale* (Dept of Health, London: HMSO).

Strauss, M., Gelles, R., and Steinmetz, S. (1980), *Behind Closed Doors: Violence in the American Family* (New York: Anchor Books).

Triseliotis, J. (1973), *In Search of Origins: The Experiences of Adopted People* (London: Routledge & Kegan Paul).

Utting, W. (1991), *Children in the Public Care: A Review of Residential Child Care* (London: HMSO).

——(1997), *People Like Us: The Review of the Safeguards for Children Living away from Home* (London: HMSO).

Waterhouse, S. (1997), *The Organisation of Fostering Services* (National Foster Care Association).

Housing and Housing Policy

Chris Pickvance

Contents

In this chapter we examine the development of the institutions through which housing is provided in the UK, the changing pattern of housing policy, and the present housing situation. It is shown that historically housing policy responded very slowly to housing conditions, and that it was political changes which were the stimulus to advances in housing policy. Similarly, today housing policy is as much concerned with political goals, such as securing votes and expanding the scope for market activity, as with meeting housing need. It is thus argued that housing policy is only partly a social policy. The distribution of households across the housing stock is discussed, and the effects of processes such as the expansion of owner-occupation and the residualization of council housing are outlined.

What is Housing?

Housing patterns and ways of thinking about housing vary between countries reflecting their different national housing traditions. As every visitor to continental Europe—east or west—knows, flat-dwelling there is a much more common pattern than in England and Wales (see Table 16.1). On the other hand, in Scottish cities in the nineteenth century the 'continental' pattern of flat-dwelling took root rather than the pattern of terraced housing south of the border. The explanation for this is to do with industrialization, wage levels, patterns of land ownership, land prices, the organization of the building industry, and architectural influence. For example, in Scotland in the nineteenth century working-class wage levels were lower than in England while land prices and building costs were higher, and architects were able to press the flat-dwelling solution more successfully.

A second difference concerns **housing tenure,** which refers to the legal relationship between household and dwelling. As Table 16.1 shows, Spain and Greece, two of the poorest countries in the EU, have the highest level of owner-occupation, and West Germany, the richest country, has the lowest level. This flies in the face of the traditional British idea that owner-occupation is associated with high income. The country in the world with the highest level of owner-occupation is in fact Bangladesh (87 per cent). Clearly this raises questions about the value and quality of what is owned and how it is built (whether self-built, commercially built, and so on). It also emphasizes the contrast between agricultural societies, where owner-occupation is the norm, and urban industrial societies, where industrialization leads to the growth of rented housing. Like any other single characteristic of housing, tenure therefore conceals as much as it reveals.

Table 16.1 also draws attention to contrasts in the role of social and non-profit hous-

	% owner-occupation	% social rented or non-profit	% private rented	average floor space (sq.m.)	% flats
Spain	78	2	18	83.6	63
Greece	77	0	23	—	57
UK	66	24	9	79.7	19
Scotland	54	40	6	—	45
France	54	17	20	85.4	42
Sweden	43	21	21	92.0	54
West Germany	38	15	43	86.6	50

Table 16.1 European housing patterns, 1987–92
Source: McCrone and Stephens (1995, Tables 2.2, 2.3, and 2.4).

ing between countries. This refers to housing whose construction is subsidized. Not only does it vary from nil to 24 per cent, but how it is provided varies greatly. In the UK, apart from Northern Ireland, non-profit housing is provided by local councils and, to a small extent, by housing associations. In Germany for a long time a trade union organization was the largest social provider. In France subsidies have been given to private providers. Once again the British experience of local political control of subsidized housing provision is very unusual. Within the UK, Scotland has a very high level of council housing—which is linked to its weaker economy and strong working-class tradition.

Average dwelling size does not vary greatly between the countries listed in Table 16.1, but size in square metres is a much more common matter of discussion about housing in continental Europe than in the UK. This is a product of post-war housing shortages and rent controls which were based on rents per square metre. French estate agents advertise the precise area of the land on which a house is situated perhaps because, as a relatively recently urbanized country, the idea of buying land still has as much significance as buying a house. In Eastern Europe households are likely to know the precise size of their dwelling, as rent levels were set on the basis of size.

In the UK thinking about housing centres on housing tenure and the following four categories of tenure will be used throughout the chapter:

- owner-occupiers, who own outright or are buying their house or flat with a loan (which is known as a mortgage);
- private tenants, who rent their house or flat from a private landlord;
- council tenants, who rent their dwelling from the local council; and
- housing association tenants, who rent from housing associations.

The latter two categories are often referred to as 'social tenants'. More information on each will be given below; but it should be remembered that tenure gives only a partial picture of a housing situation.

Every country, then, has its own way of thinking about housing which relates to a tradition of housing provision, policy debate, and intervention, and, in turn, to the country's particular economic, social, and political history. In this chapter we explore these in the British case. We examine the development of the main types of tenure and of housing policy, analyse the present housing situation, and show in detail how the owner-occupation and council-housing sectors work. The emphasis is on how far housing policy should be seen as social policy and how the housing 'system' works in practice.

The Emergence of Different Housing Tenures and the Evolution of Housing Policy up to 1939

We have already introduced the four main types of tenure. We now examine how and why these have changed over time. This historical account will also explain the emergence of housing policy and will allow us to introduce the question of how far housing policy is about meeting housing need and how far it has other objectives.

In the nineteenth century the vast mass of urban households were private tenants, and their landlords were middle-class business people and professionals who invested in housing as a safe way of saving. Income levels for most meant that anything beyond renting a room or a house was out of the question. Owner-occupation was restricted to the very well-off. It was in this situation that two types of initiative developed which were to have long-term consequences for housing provision in the UK: building societies and state action. There were others, such as philanthropic housing and employer-provided housing, but these had no long-term effects.

Building societies started as a self-help solution to housing conditions which developed independently of the state. They subsequently became one of the most important institutions of the UK housing scene.

Building societies were created in the early nineteenth century by people who earned enough to be able to save, and who formed societies to enable them to build houses for themselves. The principle was that the members would commit themselves to making regular savings which would be used to build houses once a sufficient amount had accumulated. This meant that once the first house had been built and the first member obtained a house, the members would continue to make payments into the society until a house had been built for the last member. The society would then 'terminate'.

Terminating building societies only worked if members trusted each other to keep up their payments until they all had houses. In practice they were vulnerable to members losing their jobs or falling ill. A second variety was the 'permanent' building society, in which savers did not need to be borrowers, and this became the basis for the building society familiar to us today, though until the 1930s they lent mainly to private landlords. Unlike public companies owned by their shareholders, building societies were and are mutual organizations owned by their members.

In the nineteenth century building societies could not be a widely used solution to housing provision, since they were restricted to the small minority with high enough incomes to be able to save. However, in the inter-war period they expanded considerably. They became a convenient place for investors to save—replacing houses in this respect—and as average incomes rose the fraction of the population which could afford to buy a house with a long-term loan increased. The inter-war rise in owner-occupation was thus facilitated by the growth of the building societies. As Table 16.2 shows, by the late 1930s owner-occupation was established as a significant form of housing tenure. The growth of building societies up to the Second World War happened with minimal government support. Governments established a regulatory framework to prevent fraud and provide security to savers, but did not provide financial support to them.

The other main development in the nineteenth century was the gradual growth of pressure for state intervention in housing, which led ultimately to council housing.

As the quotation from Engels in Box 16.1 shows, housing conditions in the nineteenth century were atrocious and aroused moral outrage among observers. If there was a simple connection between housing conditions and housing policy this would have been a time of dramatic advances in housing policy. In fact it was not. The slow emergence of housing policy shows how ideology, self-interest, and politics are far more important than housing need.

The nineteenth century was a period of *laissez-faire* in the economic sphere: the market

	Home-owner	Public rented*	Private rented	Other*
1914	10.0	1.0	80.0	9.0
1938	25.0	10.0	56.0	9.0
1951	29.0	18.0	45.0	8.0
1961	43.0	27.0	25.0	6.0
1971	50.5	30.6	18.8*	
1981	57.1	30.6	10.1	2.1
1991	66.0	21.3	9.6	3.2
1996	66.9	18.7	9.8	4.6

Table 16.2 Housing tenure in Great Britain, 1914–96

* 'Public rented' includes new towns as well as local councils. The 1971 figure does not distinguish between 'Private rented' and 'Other'. From 1981 'Other' includes housing associations only, and other tenures are included with 'Private rented'.

Source: Forrest *et al.* (1990: 57), Department of Environment (1998), Table 9.3.

was supposed to work best with minimal state involvement. Those who owned property resented state intrusion into their rights, and in particular central interference in the running of localities. Since only the propertied had the vote until the later nineteenth century they were able to control local policy. Most local councils were made up of landlords who were unlikely to initiate action that would affect their own housing or increase the local taxes they paid. They therefore did little—until the 1840s, when cholera struck. The desire of the propertied class for self-preservation overcame their resistance to legislation, and an exception to *laissez-faire* was allowed. Local and central state action on sanitation and urban infrastructure took place where the benefits to the propertied classes were clear. This paved the way for further state action.

Public health professionals were at the forefront of pressure for reform and had some support from politicians. But the rights of landlords to run their houses as they chose, whatever the resulting housing conditions, were strongly defended. The second half of the nineteenth century saw a gradual acquisition of powers by local councils to regulate new and existing housing in their areas. For example, they gained powers to set minimum standards of lighting, ventilation, sanitation, and structural stability in new houses, and powers to close houses unfit for human habitation and to demolish them. They were also obliged to rehouse the tenants and to compensate owners of such housing. These powers were given under public health legislation. It was only in the 1880s that government realized that housing issues needed to be addressed directly. In 1890 councils were allowed to build working-class housing as long as it was sold within ten years, a restriction later removed.

However the strength of *laissez-faire* ideology meant that Parliament would not pass **mandatory legislation,** laws that required action to be taken. Instead it passed **permissive legislation,** which allowed councils who wished to apply these measures to do

Box 16.1 Urban housing conditions in 1843

'These streets are often so narrow that a person can step from the window of one house into that of its opposite neighbour, while the houses are piled so high, storey upon storey, that the light can scarcely penetrate into the court or alley that lies between. In this part of the city there are neither sewers nor other drains, nor even privies belonging to the houses. In consequence, all refuse, garbage and excrements of at least 50,000 persons are thrown into gutters every night, so that, in spite of all street sweeping, a mass of dried filth and foul vapours are created, which not only offend the sight and smell, but endanger the health of the inhabitants in the highest degree. Is it to be wondered at, that in such localities all considerations of health, morals, and even the most ordinary decency are utterly neglected? On the contrary, all who are intimately acquainted with the condition of the inhabitants will testify to the high degree which disease, wretchedness, and demoralization have here reached. Society in such districts has sunk to a level indescribably low and hopeless. The houses of the poor are generally filthy, and are never cleansed. They consist in most cases of a single room which, while subject to the worst ventilation, is yet usually kept cold by the broken and badly fitting windows and is sometimes damp and partly below ground level, always badly furnished and thoroughly uncomfortable, a straw heap often serving as a bed, upon which men and women, young and old, sleep in revolting confusion.' (A report in an English magazine, *The Artisan*, 1843), quoted in Engels (1969: 69).

so, but which had no effect on the remainder (Gauldie 1974). Despite these obstacles to public action, a few councils did take a pioneering role and built council houses.

State intervention in housing became more acceptable in the late nineteenth and early twentieth century because of changes in the political situation. The political strength of the working class increased considerably after the vote was given to working-class men in the 1870s, and working-class political parties formed. The embryonic Labour Party made winning control of local councils its first objective on the way to gaining power nationally, and this reinforced the importance of local councils as a means of achieving policy goals. Public mobilization over the state of working-class housing increased, and governments were afraid of disorder. Lastly, government grants to local councils increased so that the financial obstacle to public action was partly lifted.

The culmination of this pressure for a new direction in housing policy did not occur until 1919, when councils became legally obliged to build houses to meet housing need, subject to central government approval, and were given a government subsidy. This dramatic step was partly due to government concern about house-building levels: the private sector had been failing to build enough houses before 1914, and war had meant a halt to house-building. But again the crucial stimuli were changes in political conditions:

- the continued growth of the labour movement as a political force (and fear that the Russian revolution might incite workers in the UK);

- the Glasgow rent strike in 1915, which caused government to introduce **rent control** to keep down rent levels; and

- the experience of war, with the huge contribution of the mass of the population and the feeling of solidarity that it created, which led the government to believe that a new policy was necessary. Hence the name for the first council housing programme, 'homes fit for heroes' (Gilbert, 1970).

It was this policy that gave councils their prominent role as direct providers of housing and helped maintain the tradition of strong local council action. In other countries subsidies were channelled to private building firms or specially created housing organizations.

This historical background reveals the three main types of state intervention in housing.

- The first is state regulation, mostly of private sector activity. This includes the legislation already referred to concerning overcrowding and the closure of unfit housing, building standards, rent controls and the regulation of building societies. These all remain important and have been elaborated in the post-war period. For example, detailed planning regulations now exist to improve the appearance and orderliness of the built environment and achieve social goals, and building regulations have been altered to reflect the new concern with energy efficiency.

- The second is state subsidization, when the state provides financial support to private actors such as households, landlords, financial institutions, or building firms. Subsidies increase the resources of private actors and take the form of payments, or reductions in taxes. They include tax relief to house purchasers on the interest paid on mortgages, and housing benefits to poor households to enable them to pay higher rents than they otherwise could.

- The third is direct provision. In the case of housing the clear example of this is council housing. Here, instead of regulating and subsidizing or taxing private agents to achieve policy aims, government acts directly.

The first and third types of state intervention are mainly the work of local councils (or the 'local state'), while the second involves central government and local branches of ministries too. It should be noted that in the case of housing the contrast between 'state' and 'market' provision is particularly unhelpful. The concept of state provision, i.e. council housing, is clear enough. But all private provision, whether by private landlords or owner-occupation, is highly regulated by the state and, in the case of owner-occupation, subsidized too. Hence there is no such thing as a pure market form of housing provision.

Post-War Tenure Patterns and Housing Policy

In the post-war period, as Table 16.2 shows, there have been three tenure trends: the continuing growth in owner-occupation, the continuing decline in private renting, and the rise and subsequent decline in council renting. These changes are connected with changes in housing policy which have made it far more varied in its aims. In particular it is now less of a social policy and favours middle- and high-income groups as well as low-income groups. This is because housing policy has become an explicit means of winning votes for the main political parties, and housing policies which attract votes from the better-off have become as important as policies aimed at the badly off. Let us examine policies towards the various housing tenures.

Council Housing

From 1945 housing policy concentrated on reconstruction, and council housing played an important role in this task. Subsequently the massive slum clearance programme of the 1950s and 1960s created space for further building of council houses and flats, including the much-criticized high-rise blocks. The council share of the housing stock continued to rise until a peak in 1977/8 in Great Britain, after which it went into a slow decline. We may examine the political and economic reasons for this evolution.

The rationale for council housing is that it is a way of meeting housing need for those whose ability to pay is so low that they could not afford a reasonable quality of housing on the private housing market. To perform this function council-housing rent levels need to be low enough to make it affordable. The difficulty of achieving this had emerged in the 1920s, when the rent levels of the first council houses placed them out of reach of the lowest-income groups in the working class. Whether council housing is affordable to poor households depends partly on rent levels and partly on social security benefits (such as housing benefits) designed to help with housing costs. The topic of housing benefits will be referred to briefly below, but generally the impact of social security benefits on households' ability to pay for housing is not considered here.

There are three reasons why rent levels have been lower in council housing:

- because the government subsidizes the production of council housing. For example, the rate of interest the government pays when it borrows money to build council housing is a special below-market rate;
- because until 1990 councils could subsidize rents from rates (the forerunner of council taxes); and
- because council housing operates outside the housing market. This difference between council and private rented housing is explained in Box 16.2.

Policy towards the council housing sector has changed considerably since the war. Initially there was agreement between the Labour and Conservative parties on its importance. But in the mid-1960s the Labour government argued that the job of post-war reconstruction was completed and that slum clearance should give way to individual house improvement: hence the level of council house building was reduced. The Conservative Party took this further and felt it should cater only for a small minority of households, while Labour continued to give it a broad role. These debates fed into conflicting positions about the level of government subsidy, rent levels, and the desirability of selling council housing.

In 1972 the Conservative government's Housing Finance Act introduced a major reform which reduced the subsidies paid on council housing. The aim was to force councils to raise rents which the government considered excessively low. Its motivation was to encourage households in the council sector to move into private rented or owner-occupied housing and to discourage demand from new applicants for council housing. The new rents were called 'fair rents', which meant 'closer to private sector rent'. The

---

Box 16.2 Council and private rent levels: how being outside the market helps keep council rents low

Rent levels in council housing depend on original building costs (and also on repair/modernization costs and subsidy levels), whereas rent levels in private rented housing depend on current market values.

In a period of rising house values the current market value of a house may be far higher than its original building cost. In the private sector successive owners each make a capital gain as the house is sold at successively higher prices, and landlords base their rents on the current value. Council houses do not go through this process, but remain outside the market. (They do have a market value, but this is irrelevant as long as they remain council houses. Only when they are privatized is this market value relevant.) It is because council house rents are based on original building cost, not current value, that they can be much lower than private-sector rents. Additionally, since most councils own houses built at different periods, they generally engage in 'rent-pooling' which spreads the advantage of the low building costs of the oldest houses over the whole stock.

---

change was an attempt to reverse the traditional advantage of low rents in the council sector by aligning rents with those in the private sector. This measure was reversed by Labour in 1975, but was reintroduced by the Conservatives in 1980. The effect was that between 1980 and 1989 council rents rose from £13 to £20 per week in constant prices. Over the same period, subsidies per council tenant fell by two-thirds, while they increased by one-third per owner-occupier household. By 1995 council rents were at a level which required housing benefit to be paid to two-thirds of tenants in England. On average this benefit reduced rents for those receiving it from £40.60 to £18.80, and fuelled an increase in spending on housing benefits—see Table 16.3 on p. 420. Paradoxically, therefore, the price of raising council rents to make the sector less attractive was an increase in housing benefits expenditure which more than made up for the reduction in subsidies paid to councils. This example of the dependence of a market solution on increased government spending emphasizes the obstacles to market solutions in the housing of poorer households.

The second major policy change affecting council housing has been the right to buy (or council-house privatization) policy introduced by the Conservative government in 1980. This policy gave council tenants the right to buy (or 'privatize') their council house or flat at a discount. Whereas previously councils had had the right to sell housing, only a minority of them had used it. The new act thus gave tenants a new right. The size of the discount was between 33 and 50 per cent initially, the maximum later being raised to 60 per cent for houses and 70 per cent for flats. There were several motivations behind this policy:

- the pursuit of a property-owning democracy as a political goal;
- the belief that councils have too much power, too many assets, and are inefficient landlords; and

- the belief that the scope for market solutions in housing should be expanded because they are more efficient.

The Right to Buy policy worked in tandem with the policy mentioned above of reducing subsidies and increasing rents in the council sector to make it less attractive to remain in.

The policy achieved its aims. It was the main factor in the reduction of the stock of council (and New Town) dwellings in Great Britain from 6.5m in 1979 to 4.5m in 1996, a reduction of 31.1 per cent. As a proportion of all housing, the size of the sector shrank from a peak of 31.7 per cent of all housing in 1977 and 1978 to 18.7 per cent in 1996. At the same time the level of new council building fell to below 10,000 houses per year. Councils were only allowed to use a small proportion of the proceeds of the sale of council housing for new building. The result was that the capacity of the council sector to provide housing for the groups most in need in the future has declined.

What were the detailed effects of the policy? Research by Forrest and Murie (1988) shows that:

- houses were much more likely to be bought than flats. Between 1981 and 1985 only 5 per cent of sales were of flats whereas they made up 30 per cent of the stock;
- attractive houses, such as post-war houses with two or more bedrooms and a garden in attractive areas, were most likely to be bought;
- council housing in areas with higher levels of owner-occupation, higher income levels and under Conservative control was more likely to be bought. In London sales levels in outer boroughs were far higher than in inner boroughs;
- the households most likely to purchase were those with a head in employment, with multiple earners, which owned a car, which were in the 30 to 59 age group, which had school-age children, and which were white rather than black.

Conversely, there was a low rate of sales in areas with high unemployment and high social deprivation.

This led to two important outcomes:

- Changes in the quality of the council-housing stock. As the most attractive council housing is purchased the housing remaining in the council sector is less attractive, more likely to be in unpopular areas, and more likely to be made up of flats.
- Changes in the social composition of households in the council sector. Council tenants become more homogeneous and increasingly share characteristics associated with poverty, such as having no earners or being female-headed households. This is known as the **residualization** of council housing. For example, between 1962 and 1993 the proportion of households in council housing in England with no earners (that is, whose members are unemployed or pensioners) rose from 7 to 63 per cent, while in the owner-occupier sector it rose only from 19 to 28 per cent. There is therefore a growing gulf between the two tenure sectors, which is discussed further below.

Owner-Occupation

The continuing rise of owner-occupation, from 29 per cent in 1851 to 66.9 per cent in 1996, has been the most striking trend of the post-war period (see Table 16.2). Successive governments have adopted policies favouring owner-occupation, the type of housing tenure favoured by middle- and high-income groups. In 1963 the tax on the imputed rent on the investment value of the house was abolished; in 1965 owner-occupied houses were exempted from capital gains tax; and in 1974 tax relief on mortgage interest was left untouched when it was abolished for most other types of borrowing. Additional government support for owner-occupation has taken the form of tax concessions to building societies to enable them to offer higher rates of interest to savers, guarantees to savers in the case of a building society bankruptcy, and the discreet encouragement of takeovers of failing building societies. Support for owner-occupation through tax relief reached a peak in 1988 and has since declined. The limit of tax relief has not been raised in line with inflation: it was raised once from £25,000 to £30,000 in 1983, and from 1988 it was restricted to one taxpayer per house, to prevent unmarried couples claiming relief on mortgages of £60,000. By comparison, the average house price in 1998 was £78,000. Since then the value of tax relief has been further diminished by reducing the tax rate to which it applied. By 1998 this had fallen to 10 per cent, and it will end in 2000.

The strong growth of owner-occupation has led to a debate about whether this growth is entirely due to the government policies outlined which make it more attractive than other tenures. There are two counter-arguments to this. The first is that in a period of inflation of the type experienced since 1970 any asset which provided a hedge against inflation would be very popular. Since the value of houses rose faster than inflation until 1988, there is evidence to support this argument. Calculations by Saunders (1990) based on surveys in three towns in 1986 showed average net capital gains of £20,000 per owner-occupier household in 1986 prices. (Net capital gain is gross capital gain less the value of the outstanding mortgage.) The net capital gain was highest in Slough (£26,000) and lower in Derby (£19,000) and Burnley (£13,000). Taking into account the number of years people had been owner-occupiers, the net real capital gains per year were £2,800

Box 16.3 Tax relief on mortgage interest as an incentive to owner-occupation.

This tax relief means the house-buyer pays and the government receives less income tax. By cheapening the cost of houses and thereby increasing demand, this tax relief has the effect of keeping house prices higher than they would otherwise be, since the supply of houses responds very slowly to changes in prices. The effect of abolishing it would be to raise government tax receipts and to lower house prices.

The incentive effect depends on the size of the tax relief, which depends on the rate of interest prevailing, the level of income tax to which the relief applies, and any ceilings in operation. The lower the rate of interest the lower the income tax rate, and the lower any ceiling the smaller the advantage to the house-buyer of tax relief on mortgage interest (and correspondingly the less the cost to the government). At present the size of this tax relief to the individual purchaser is at an all-time low. In 1995/6 the total 'tax expenditure' on this tax relief (which depends on the number of house-buyers with mortgages) was 2.8bn. (For trends, see Table 16.3 on p. 420.)

in Slough, £800 in Derby, and £900 in Burnley. For most households these gains are paper gains, in the sense that they are hard to realize; though this can happen, through inheritance or over-mortgaging, for example. (The latter happens when a house-buyer moves house and takes out a larger mortgage than needed, releasing cash in the process.) Capital gains may nevertheless act as incentives to owner-occupation alongside government policies. Interestingly, in Germany, where owner-occupation is low, it is not regarded as a hedge against inflation, and house prices rose only 0.4 per cent per year between 1972 and 1989, compared with 2.2 per cent per year in the UK between 1948 and 1988 (McCrone and Stephens, 1995: 53).

The second counter-argument is also put forward by Saunders, who argues that owner-occupation offers greater security and scope for freedom, control, and self-expression than any other type of housing. He goes further, and suggests that it may be rooted in a 'natural' desire for possession. Others have argued that rented housing can offer the same attractions, and that what is important is that the dwelling is self-contained.

These counter-arguments are not, of course, mutually exclusive. Hence, for example, from Saunders's point of view the different national levels of owner-occupation indicated in Table 16.1 do not imply that there are national differences in the 'natural' desire for owner-occupation. They could equally be due to government policies and to differences in economic incentives to households.

One effect of the rising share of owner-occupation has been the increased significance of owner-occupiers as a bloc of voters. The very success of policies favouring owner-occupation has meant that housing policy is increasingly identified with policy which meets the needs of owner-occupiers. The effect of the rise in owner-occupation on the composition of households in the sector is discussed in the next section. Its wider effects on attitudes to private and public provision are considered in Ch. 20.

Finally trends in three other fields of housing will be referred to briefly: the private rented sector, housing associations, and homelessness.

Private Renting

The long-standing decline of private renting can be attributed to a number of factors:

- the encouragements to owner-occupation and subsidies for council housing which have not been paralleled by favourable treatment for landlords;
- the attraction to landlords of converting rented housing to owner-occupation;
- the stigma attached to private landlords due to abuses;
- legislation which gave certain tenants security against eviction in the 1960s and discouraged landlords; and
- the existence of rent controls and fear that even when removed they might be restored.

However, by the late 1980s the size of the sector had fallen so much that the government introduced new policies, such as new types of tenancy which gave tenants fewer rights, incentives to householders to rent rooms, and the removal of regulation of rents in new rented housing (1980) and in new rental contracts, except where the tenant receives housing benefit (1989). But the effects have been negligible. The shortage of housing in this sector has meant that tenants cannot always enforce their rights against landlords, and that rents are high. The level of rents in the private sector has been a factor in the rise in spending on housing benefits, since the private rented sector is one which houses a minority of poorer households, as will be seen in the next section.

Housing Associations

The Conservative dislike of council housing was accompanied by support for housing associations. These are non-profit organizations which generally provide rented housing to groups with particular needs, such as the elderly or young people. Originally they were largely funded by government money on condition that they kept rents below certain levels in order to appeal to low-income households. Their great attraction to the government in the 1980s was that they were not councils. By 1991 they were building more new housing in England than councils, although it amounted to under 10 per cent of all new housing. Their difficulties increased after 1988, when they came under government pressure to expand but also to rely less on government funding and more on private funding. The effect is that they have had to charge higher rents to pay back the higher interest rates on private-sector loans. This either prevents them providing housing to the groups they serve, or else requires the government to pay higher housing benefits so that low-income households can afford the rents being charged. In 1995/6 two-thirds of housing association tenants in England were receiving housing benefit, and this cut the average rent they paid from £49.50 to £21.30.

Homelessness

Last but not least, there has been a considerable increase in homelessness and a number of government responses to it. The definition of homelessness is a difficult one. The narrowest definition is 'rooflessness'—meaning those sleeping rough. Wider definitions include those who are squatting, and those living in hostels for the homeless run by charities or by local councils. Even wider definitions include those living in insecure private housing at risk of eviction, and those who are concealed because they are living as parts of other households. Clearly the reality is much more complex than the single word 'homeless'. Government responses have been twofold. In 1977 local councils were given the responsibility of housing 'unintentionally homeless' people, a label which implies a distinction between the 'deserving' and the 'undeserving'. This was the culmination of a long campaign by squatters drawing attention to empty council housing (Bailey 1973) which finally found support from a Labour government. In 1985 the obligation was clarified, and only those unintentionally homeless people who fell into a priority need group, such as households with children, pregnant women, or 'vulnerable' persons were eligible for housing. Single homeless people and couples without children are generally outside this category (Malpass and Murie 1994). Since 1997 councils have been required to provide temporary accommodation for two years only, and to make homeless households apply for permanent housing through the council waiting list (Peace *et al.* 1997). In 1978, 53,000 people were accepted by councils as unintentionally homeless. This figure reached 175,000 in 1992 before falling to 144,000 in 1994. A similar number was refused because they failed to meet the eligibility criteria. In the early 1990s the government provided funding for a number of shelters for homeless people run by charities.

Public Spending on Housing

One way of understanding the overall character of housing policy is to examine the pattern of public expenditure on housing. Table 16.3 shows the main categories involved. (The figures are at constant prices, so they are comparable.) Column 'a' shows the decline in subsidies on existing social housing. Column 'b' reflects the fall in social house-building, and column 'c' the rise and fall of receipts from the sale of social housing. Column 'd' shows the net cost of social house-building to the public purse. Column 'e' shows the dramatic growth of spending on housing benefits. Finally, column 'g' shows the rise and fall of mortgage interest relief.

Ideally one would like to read each column of figures as a yardstick of policy aims. Whether this is possible depends on whether the spending is under government control or is influenced by factors beyond housing policy. Columns 'a' and 'b' do reflect the explicit policies of reducing subsidies to social housing, and cutting the rate of council housebuilding which are largely within the government's control. But column 'c' reflects tenants response to the right to buy social housing, and hence the evolution of spending is partly outside government control. Column 'e' is even less influenced by government policy, and hence cannot be read as meaning that the government wanted to devote more and more spending to housing benefits. Rather, the growth of spending on housing benefits is an unintended effect of another housing policy, namely the raising of social housing rents towards market levels and the reduction of regulation of private-sector rents, with the result that two-thirds of social tenants cannot afford to pay the rents they face. It is also due to continuing low incomes of the tenants concerned. Housing benefit spending has expanded to facilitate the shift to market rent levels, an interesting example of how government subsidy underpins private-sector housing. Finally, the rise and decline of mortgage interest relief in column 'g' is partly

	current	gross capital	capital receipts	net capital	housing benefits	total spending	mortgage interest relief
	a	b	c	d	e	f	g
1976/7	5292	12504	1152	11352	2947	17314	4659
1981/2	3960	6277	2387	3889	4087	12399	4569
1986/7	2321	6988	3748	3250	5974	12063	7218
1991/2	1406	7795	2658	5138	8513	15342	6823
1996/7	−115	4996	2279	2717	12423	15267	2634

Table 16.3 Public spending on housing, UK, at 1995/6 prices (£ million)

Notes:
1. Col b − col c = col d;
2. Col a + col d + col e + N. Ireland spending = col f;
3. Cols a–d are for Great Britain; cols e–g are for UK.

Source: Hills (1998), Table 5A1.

due to the changing policy (where the incentive value of the interest relief peaked in the mid-1980s), but is also influenced by interest rates which are a matter of general economic policy. Paradoxically, then, the largest form of public spending on housing in 1996/7, spending on housing benefits, was not the intended result of housing policy, but was due to the social security lifeboat needed to rescue tenants who could not afford market rents. This is a measure of the obstacles to introducing market mechanisms where people's ability to pay is very low.

Conclusion: Housing Policy and Social Policy

It has been shown that housing policy is not simply or even primarily aimed at those in greatest housing need. Housing policy was very slow to develop in the nineteenth century and the driving forces then and since have been political. Only by the 1920s did it gain a strong 'social' strand. For twenty years after 1945 housing policy was the subject of an inter-party consensus and went ahead on the 'two legs' of council housing and support for owner-occupation. Since the 1960s it has been increasingly used to pursue party political objectives even when this meant helping the better off more than those in greatest housing need. The promotion of owner-occupation, especially until the mid-1980s, the demotion of council housing, and the attempt to introduce market rents for social tenants are clear illustrations of this. This could happen because the voices of those in housing need and those representing them are often very weak compared with the voices of financial institutions and builders and the voting strength of the majority. Governments calculate the votes to be won and lost before introducing new policies. Since governments have numerous policy goals it should not be expected that policy in an area such as housing is driven by a single goal such as meeting housing need.

The Present Housing Situation in the UK

To understand the present housing situation we first need to understand what is meant by a household and the housing stock. This will help us to answer the question of whether there is a housing shortage. We then investigate the distribution of households across the different tenures.

The **housing stock** refers to the available housing in the country. This is partly a physical fact, since there are a certain number of physical dwellings available: the number increases if one includes caravans. However, it is also a social fact. The existence of 215,000 second homes means that not all the housing stock is available to those seeking housing: some is also necessary to facilitate movement, and to allow repair in both private and social sectors. Some housing is unfit, and some council housing is empty because it is 'hard to let' (for example, because it lacks lifts or is located in a very unattractive neighbourhood).

Turning to **households,** the census definition refers to 'a single person or group of people who have the address as their only or main residence and who either share one meal a day together or share a living room'. (The pre-1981 definition required that household members were catered for at least one meal a day by the same person, a requirement which was abandoned in the face of variability in eating habits.) The number of households depends partly on the size and age structure of the population. But there is no constant relation between the size of the adult population and the number of households. The ratio between the number of households and the adult population is known as the 'headship rate'. This depends on customs regarding young and elderly people living independently, rates of cohabitation, marriage, separation and divorce, women's participation in the labour force, preferences for living alone rather than with partners, and so on. For example, in southern Europe it is still unusual for young people to leave home before marriage or setting up home as a couple. In northern Europe the opposite is the case. Between 1971 and 1996 in Great Britain there was an increase in the number of households as the mean household size decreased from 2.9 to 2.4.

However, some households contain other potential households. For example, a single adult or young couple sharing with their parents is known as a **concealed household** because potentially they would like to live as a separate household. Whether they can do so depends on the housing situation itself. When the supply of housing increases, or its affordability improves (either because incomes rise or housing costs fall), the number of households increases. For example, young people leave home earlier, or young couples who are living in the parental home can afford to live on their own. For all these reasons the number of households is not simply a demographic fact. It follows that the scale of housing needed by the population is always open to debate.

One estimate is that in 1991 in England and Wales there were 20.3m households and 20.9m dwellings. However, if one allows for concealed households, second homes, the need for vacancies, and unfit dwellings, it is clear that the housing problem measured in these terms is far from solved. Hills (1998) argues that in 1991 there was an overall shortage of 517,000 dwellings. In addition, local variation means that shortages will be proportionally greater in some places than others.

Tables 16.4 to 16.7 show the distribution of households of different social characteristics among the different types of housing.

Table 16.4 shows that 25 per cent of under-25s are owner-occupiers, a very high figure by European standards, and that this figure rises to 76 per cent in the 60 to 64 age group. Below 60 owner-occupiers are more likely to have a mortgage than not, but this reverses in the 60+ age groups. Council renting is relatively constant across the age range. This reflects the fact that young households can enter the sector and, once within it, are likely to stay—unless they buy the dwelling. Of the other tenures, private renting is extremely important for the under-25s: it reflects young people's lower incomes, lower priority on housing compared with work, and greater mobility.

Table 16.5 shows that higher-income households are more likely to be buying a house, and low-income households are more likely to be social or private tenants. However, there are two unexpected patterns. First, social housing is not restricted to the very lowest income deciles. This may be because while access depends on need there is no continuing check on household income and no obligation on a household to leave social renting if its income rises. Households with multiple earners may stay in a council dwelling rather than move out. Second, the likelihood of being an outright owner (having no outstanding loan) is actually higher for lower-income groups. This is

	Outright owner*	O/O with mortgage	Council rented	Housing assn.	Rent with job	Private renting unfurnished	Private renting furnished
under 25	1	24	24	9	2	15	26
25–29	1	55	21	5	3	6	8
30–44	4	65	18	4	2	4	3
45–59	21	56	15	2	2	2	1
60–64	49	27	20	2	1	2	0
65–69	57	10	25	4	1	3	1
70–79	57	6	27	4	1	6	0
80+	54	2	27	7	0	8	1

Table 16.4 Age of household head and tenure, Great Britain, 1994 (horizontal percentages)

* An outright owner is someone without a mortgage.

Source: Office for Population Censuses and Surveys (1996), Table 11.9b.

partly because of the relation between income and age. On retirement, when most owner-occupiers have paid off their mortgages (see Table 16.4), their household income will fall and they will move to a lower-income decile as they rely on pensions. It is also because of ownership of low-value houses among low income households.

The main changes in the tenure patterns of different income groups between 1980 and 1992 can be seen by comparing Tables 16.5 and 16.6. They show an increase in house purchase at every point in the income range, and therefore its spread to lower income groups. Conversely there is a sharp decline in council renting across the board, but particularly in the upper six income deciles, where the proportion has halved. In

Income decile	1 Lowest	2	3	4	5	6	7	8	9	10 Highest
Outright owner	23	27	33	36	30	27	18	18	17	15
In process of purchasing	5	8	14	24	37	45	63	78	72	79
Local authority rented	51	44	38	24	19	17	10	7	5	2
Housing assn.	6	7	5	5	3	3	2	1	1	0
Other rented unfurnished	6	6	5	4	4	3	3	3	3	1
Rented furnished	6	6	4	4	5	3	2	2	2	3

Table 16.5 Housing tenure and household income, Great Britain, 1992 (vertical percentages)

Source: Central Statistical Office (1993), Table 6.

Income decile	1 Lowest	2	3	4	5	6	7	8	9	10 Highest
Outright owner	20	33	34	27	20	16	15	14	16	17
In process of purchasing	1	3	8	18	28	40	51	56	59	64
Local authority rented	60	52	43	37	41	33	27	22	18	15
Other rented unfurnished	13	9	7	9	5	6	3	4	3	1
Rented furnished	4	1	4	4	4	3	2	2	2	1

Table 16.6 Housing tenure and household income, United Kingdom, 1980 (vertical percentages)

Source: Department of Employment (1982), Table 5.

other words, as those purchasing have become more heterogeneous in income terms, the council sector has become more homogeneous. The decrease in the two private rented-sector categories has been more even across the income range; finally, there has been an increase in outright ownership among the three middle-income deciles.

Table 16.7 confirms outright ownership as being very high among the economically inactive (pensioners, with possibly some unemployed too). Owner-occupiers with mortgages show the expected gradation by socio-economic group. The fact that even in the

	Outright owner	Owner with mortgage	Council renting	Housing assn.	With job	Private renting unfurn.	Private renting furnished
Economically active							
Professional	11	78	1	1	3	2	4
Employers and managers	13	74	3	1	3	3	3
Intermediate non-manual	11	68	7	2	2	4	5
Junior non-manual	12	57	14	6	1	5	4
Skilled manual and own-account non-professional	14	60	17	3	1	4	2
Semi-skilled manual and personal service	12	42	29	4	4	5	4
Unskilled manual	11	32	42	7	0	5	3
Economically inactive	45	11	31	5	0	6	2
Total	25	42	20	4	1	4	3

Table 16.7 Tenure by socio-economic group and economic activity of household, Great Britain, 1994 (horizontal percentages)

Source: OPCS (1996), Table 11.11b.

unskilled manual group one-third or more have a mortgage shows how far owner-occupation has spread. (These figures may be misleading, however, since the classification is by the occupation of the head of household, whereas ability to take out a mortgage depends on the incomes of both partners in the case of couples.) Council tenancy shows a concentration of low-status socio-economic groups which parallels that of low incomes shown in Table 16.5.

Council Housing and Owner-Occupation in Practice

As we have seen, the major political debates over housing have concerned the degree to which it should be provided by the state or by the market, and the degree to which it should be subsidized and regulated. To go beyond the ideological debates about market and state alternatives of access to housing, we need to understand how different housing tenures work in practice. The focus here will be on owner-occupation and council housing, and how households gain access to them. It will be shown that the normal functioning of both tenures leads to some undesirable results.

It is useful to think of access as controlled by **gatekeepers** and to see households as possessing varying characteristics and resources which affect their chances of successful entry. In owner-occupation the gatekeepers are the staff of estate agents, banks, and building societies. In council housing they are council officials. The term 'gatekeeper' is appropriate because these groups operate **rules of access** which determine the chance that a household will be able to obtain access via the channel concerned. In owner-occupation access depends on ability to pay and the security of the house as an asset. In council housing it depends on meeting rules of eligibility which are mostly non-financial.

Owner-Occupation in Practice

The first step in considering owner-occupation is to recognize that, for the vast majority, owner-occupation is only possible with the help of a mortgage provided by a building society or bank. It is true that a small minority of people inherit houses or can afford to buy them for cash. It is also true that the mortgage will not cover the whole cost of purchase, and that some reliance on savings or a family loan will be necessary. The extent of inheritance of houses and family financial help and their correlation with social class are discussed in Boxes 16.4 and 16.5.

The primary concern of banks and building societies—the main source of mortgages —is profit (or 'surplus'). This means they need to match the investments they receive from savers with loans to house purchasers. Originally building societies borrowed only from individuals. Today, like banks, they also borrow on the money markets, but they remain restricted to lending money on housing. To operate effectively financial institutions need to maintain public confidence and control risk. Banks and building societies risk losing their money if borrowers prove unable to maintain their repayments. Building societies are subject to an additional constraint. Because their savings

---

Box 16.4 Inheritance of housing

This refers to the inheritance of a house or of the proceeds of the sale of a house. A survey by Williams *et al.* (1991) found that 9 per cent of respondents lived in households where a member had inherited a house or part of the proceeds of the sale of a house. Sixty-seven per cent of recipients were aged 40 or over. Those who were owner-occupiers at the time of inheritance were 6 times as likely to inherit as council tenants (13 per cent *versus* 2 per cent), and there was a strong correlation with social class: 17 per cent of households with professional or managerial heads had inherited compared with 5 per cent of semi-skilled and unskilled manual heads. Inheriting on more than one occasion was even more strongly correlated with class than inheriting on one or more occasions. Since the probability of inheriting housing depends on the ownership patterns among the parental generation, the degree of inequality in this respect may diminish in the future due to the increased proportion of all households in owner-occupation. However, inequalities in the value of inherited houses are likely to remain.

---

are taken in on a short-term basis but are lent out in long-term (25-year, for example) house mortgages, they are less able to withstand a 'run on the bank', when savers descend demanding their money back, a familiar phenomenon in Russia or Latin America. Hence the creation of public confidence in their operation is a prime concern. Their success in achieving this is a reflection of the high degree of social stability in the UK and trust in institutions generally. One form of government support for building societies is that it guarantees the protection of 90 per cent of a person's savings (up to a certain maximum) in the case of a collapse. In passing, it may be added that competition from banks in the provision of mortgages, and the greater reliance of building societies on the money market for funds (a means of avoiding the instability and high cost of collecting savings from individuals), were major influences in the conversion of many building societies into public companies in the 1990s. What had started as self-help mutual organizations became fully fledged market institutions.

The need of mortgage lenders to maintain confidence and control risk has practical effects on access to housing, since it is translated into a concern for the security of the loan. This means that they examine carefully the capacity of the borrower to repay and the value of the house, since they want to be confident about the regularity and level of income of the household. And since the mortgage is secured against the house (that is, the lender holds the deeds of the house as long as the occupier has an outstanding loan) they are selective about what houses they lend on.

This has three consequences.

Red-Lining In some cities whole neighbourhoods are considered risky and are 'red-lined', which means no loans are obtainable for purchase in them from the main lenders. (The term 'red-lining' refers to the line drawn round such neighbourhoods on a map.) For example, in the 1960s Islington, an Inner North London district well known today for its affluent population, was an area in which the main building societies were

---

Box 16.5 Family help with finance for housing

It is difficult to research how much financial help a household has had from its family, since finance may not have been given explicitly for housing. A study of 16- to 35-year-olds in South-East England in 1991 found that, of those who had left home, only 29 per cent had received financial help for any purpose since leaving, and only 12 per cent had received help explicitly for housing purposes (Pickvance and Pickvance, 1995). This was correlated with parental social class, and the average amount received was £1,900. When asked the purpose of the help, 7 per cent (of those who had left home) said it was to help with purchase of a flat or house. As many as 49 per cent of all respondents thought their parents could provide some help—£2,000 being the median figure—but only 20 per cent agreed that parents should provide financial help with housing. This suggests that even in a region where parental incomes are high and house prices are high, so that the capacity to provide and need for financial help are great, the extent of actual financial help was very limited.

---

unwilling to lend (Williams, 1976). At this time it contained a large majority of private rented housing. During the 1960s the landlords who owned this housing realized that they could make more money by converting the house for single-family occupation. Moreover, the government made available improvement grants to cover part of the cost of modernization. Ironically, these partial grants were only of use to owners who had savings to add to them or who planned to sell the house when it was renovated. Existing tenants, who were obstacles to renovation and resale, were evicted and the conversion of the area started. The result was that eventually Islington became a very safe area for investment and one in which today all lenders operate.

Unmortgageable Dwellings Just as certain neighbourhoods may be judged too risky by lenders, so individual houses may be avoided. Houses liable to subsidence or flooding, or newly built houses built on polluted land or on former waste sites giving off gases, may prove unsaleable by existing owners. Houses or flats containing asbestos or decaying concrete, or simply with basements, may also fall foul of risk-avoiding lenders.

Risky Occupations Finally, lenders pay attention to the borrower's occupation and are likely to discriminate against borrowers with 'risky' occupations. These include many self-employed occupations. (In 1997 13 per cent of the labour force in employment was self-employed.) Cyclical industries such as building are also considered risky.

One important conclusion which may be drawn from this is that mortgage lenders are selective in their lending policy since their aim is to meet their own financial objectives. They only meet the housing need of those who fit these criteria.

However, not all loans for house purchase come from major banks and building societies. There are other sources of loans, such as secondary banks and finance houses, used by some borrowers who have been rejected by the main lenders. How is this possible? The answer is that the mortgage market is segmented. Secondary banks offer loans at a higher rate of interest and for a shorter term; in turn they can offer higher rates of interest to savers—who take higher risks in the hope of greater rewards. The result is that loans are available at higher rates of interest and for shorter terms from these lenders. Each segment of the mortgage market involves different types of lender, dealing with different types of borrower and different types of house, and offering different terms.

In a sense the market works because even those with risky occupations or wanting to buy risky houses can obtain a loan on some conditions. However, the conditions may be prohibitive. Moreover, they mean that those who are least creditworthy (including the poor) pay most for mortgages or do not get one at all, while the most secure borrower pays least. This result may seem bizarre, but it is a completely normal effect of market operation. Gatekeepers in market institutions like mortgage lenders create rules of access which have nothing to do with housing need and everything to do with their internal needs; hence, for practical purposes, one cannot say that the housing market works.

Lending institutions generally defend their access rules and deny that red-lining takes place. But however it is described, a refusal to lend in an area by major lenders has inevitable consequences: that the area will go 'downhill'. This happens because any mortgages available are at a high cost and, to meet these costs, the owner has to crowd the house with more households in order to afford the repayments. The result is to worsen the reputation of the district and bring about the decline feared by the initial risk-averse lender.

Marginal Owner-Occupiers We can now examine the impact of owner-occupation on lower-income households. In the 1980s the rising share of households in owner-occupation came about because many households who would previously not have considered owner-occupation began to do so. They included those who privatized their council house or flat as well as many others too. The popularity of owner-occupation in the 1980s was due to the following factors:

- the decline in supply of private rented housing;
- the increasing cost and decreasing attractiveness of council housing as privatization proceeded;
- the desire for capital gains: in the 1970s and 1980s house prices rose much faster than inflation and produced 'capital gains' (at least on paper) to owner-occupiers;
- the increasing ability to pay for loans as more women entered the labour force;
- the large supply of funds available to mortgage lenders;
- a relaxation of lending criteria such that households were allowed to borrow a larger multiple of their income, e.g. 3 or more instead of 2.5. This allowed mortgage lenders to lend all the funds they had available. It also enabled households to borrow more, but increased the level of their repayments and made them more vulnerable to any fall in their income;
- tax policy which allowed unmarried couples or groups to borrow more.

As was shown in Tables 16.5 and 16.7, this mixture of constrained alternatives, changed access criteria by lenders, and individual desire to translate increasing incomes into capital gains led to the entry of a new swathe of households into the owner-occupied sector.

Unfortunately house prices rose to a peak in 1989 and then fell by 15 per cent to 1993, only reaching the 1989 level again in 1998. (If inflation is allowed for, the fall is much greater, and the 1989 level had not been reached by 1998.) As a result there was a 'shake-out' in which mortgage arrears and repossessions increased. The fall in house prices meant that some households wishing to sell could only do so at a price which was less than the value of their mortgage. In other words, the value of their house, after deducting the mortgage, was negative: hence the phrase **negative equity** (or negative net capital gain, in Saunders's terms). Research showed that in 1993 households affected by negative equity were most likely to:

- have purchased between 1988 and 1991;
- have been under 25 at the time of purchase;
- have purchased a house for under £40,000;
- have had manual or clerical occupations; and
- have had an annual joint income of between £20,000 and £30,000. (Dorling and Cornford 1995)

In brief, they were precisely the marginal owner-occupiers who had been attracted into the sector in the 1980s.

Other symptoms of the late 1980s and early 1990s were mortgage arrears and repossessions. Any threat to a household's income has an immediate impact on its ability to keep up mortgage payments. The easing of lending criteria in the 1980s, the rise in interest rates in the late 1980s, and the increase in unemployment in 1990 had a direct impact on owner-occupiers' ability to maintain mortgage payments. This was particularly so for those who had bought a house in the late 1980s and whose housing costs were a high proportion of their incomes.

This led first to the increase in households experiencing **mortgage arrears,** payments which have not been made and which are owed to the lender. Between 1988 and 1991 the proportion of households with mortgages who had arrears rose from 0.6 per cent to 2.3 per cent. For a mortgage lender this poses a problem: it can either allow a grace period, during which arrears build up, in the hope that the mortgagee will be able to pay later, or it can repossess the house. This means that the household has to give up the house and the lender then sells it, hoping to recoup the value of its loan. In a significant minority of cases repossession did take place, and from 1989 to 1992 the level of repossessions rose from 0.2 per cent to 0.8 per cent of households with mortgages, or 76,000 houses (Bramley 1994).

The fall in interest rates in the mid-1990s and the recovery of the economy had the effect of reducing mortgage arrears and repossessions. Taken together with the decline in house prices, a new mood emerged. The government became cautious about the desirability of expanding occupation any further. It feared that the dream of a property-owning democracy was turning into a nightmare, and that voters would remember this at election time. Between 1991 and 1996 the proportion of owner-occupied housing rose only from 66 to 66.9 per cent (Table 16.2). The lending institutions also showed a new caution: the experience of negative equity, mortgage arrears, and repossessions led them to adopt less generous lending policies. On the demand side, labour market uncertainty made households rethink their attitudes to house purchase. The idea that owner-occupation was a source of security or a way of making large capital gains seemed to belong to an age long past. But by the late 1990s confidence in slowly rising house prices had returned.

Council Housing in Practice

To understand how households get access to housing in the council sector it is necessary to be aware of supply as well as demand. Councils own large and diverse stocks of housing. Council housing differs in age from inter-war to modern, in type from flats in low- and high-rise blocks to semi-detached houses, in size (such as the number of bedrooms), in the attractiveness and location of the neighbourhood (from inner-city to urban periphery), and in condition from unmodernized to renovated. Councils can also make use of bed-and-breakfast accommodation.

The character of this stock reflects past building policy, modernization policy, and council housing sales. The effect of the latter in removing the more attractive housing from the sector has already been discussed. Councils are selective in their modernization efforts, with the effect that differences in quality are preserved; and the heterogeneous stock means that councils are gatekeepers to a variety of housing types.

Turning to how councils allocate their housing, they are subject to some national legislation about which groups are eligible. Councils are obliged to rehouse families whose houses were demolished, which was very important in the period of slum clearance in the 1950s and 1960s. Since 1977 they have been obliged to provide housing for the unintentionally homeless in priority categories. Finally, the 'waiting list' has been the access channel for those in need who did not fit any specific category. For completeness, one should add that tenancies can also be passed on to children, and transferred to or exchanged with other tenants. Normally moves by existing tenants are made before tenancies are offered to new tenants.

Councils have considerable discretion about what criteria they use dealing with households applying through the waiting list. The most common type of allocation system is a **points system,** in which points are given for various measures of need such as having children, living in damp or overcrowded conditions, or suffering illness. More debatable criteria may also be included, such as years of residence in the area; but having a low income is not a criterion. Those with the highest number of points are offered housing. Other, less common schemes rely on the date of application ('first come first served') or discretion. There is no obligation to house households on the waiting list within a specific time. The length of time a household waits is dependent on the number of tenancies becoming available, whether they match the household's characteristics, and the number of households with higher positions on the waiting list. Some households fail to apply for council housing because they think the chance of a tenancy is remote. Likewise, some households give up hope but leave their names on the list—it is estimated that 40 per cent of names on waiting lists are 'dead wood'.

In 1995/6, 502,000 new lettings were made in Great Britain. Of these 197,000 (39 per cent) were to existing tenants wishing to move within the sector and 305,000 (61 per cent) to new tenants. Of the latter, 63 per cent were drawn from the waiting list and 25 per cent from among homeless households. (Department of Environment 1998: Table

9.8.) Of households on the waiting list, about 65 per cent are existing households and 35 per cent are concealed households. Despite the sale of council housing, the number of lettings to new tenants remained remarkably constant from 1983 to 1995.

The allocation of tenancies by councils has been extensively studied, and reveals the importance of the diversity of the housing stock. First, councils see themselves as public landlords with a duty to preserve the value of the stock. To do this they match households to 'appropriate' housing. This is partly a matter of matching household size with dwelling size. But, more controversially, councils make judgements about both the quality of the dwellings and the 'quality' of the households. Again, a deserving/undeserving distinction is implicit. Households are classified by their reputation as regular payers, consisting of 'problem' families, and so on. 'Good' tenants are then offered housing in estates or parts of estates with other 'good' tenants, while 'problem' families are placed together in the least attractive housing. Homeless households are allocated unattractive council housing or placed in temporary housing, such as low-quality private rented or bed-and-breakfast accommodation. In practice, although being homeless and on the waiting list are distinct access channels, some homeless households are on the waiting list. By making the housing offered to homeless households unattractive, councils seek to encourage people to use the waiting list rather than take a 'short cut' via the homelessness channel. This practice was later reinforced by legislation, and since 1997 councils have had to place homeless households in temporary accommodation and only allow them to obtain permanent council housing through the waiting list.

Second, contrary to what is often believed, the allocation of tenancies allows applicants some choice. Applicants can state a preference for an area and will receive several offers. They are not obliged to accept the first offer, but the snag is that if they do not they cannot be sure that a second or third offer will be better, and after three offers they may lose their place on the waiting list. Applicants are more likely to express preferences for the most attractive estates and dwellings, but councils need to let all their dwellings. To deal with the problem of how to find tenants for the least attractive dwellings, they offer the least attractive dwellings as 'first offers' to 'problem households' in the hope that they will be accepted. 'Good' households are more likely to be offered attractive dwellings initially. It has been found that households in most desperate need are likely to accept the poor-quality dwellings first offered to them, while those in less need wait and hope for something better. The effect of this is to create and preserve a hierarchy of council estates, and to make it likely that those households in greatest need find themselves in the worst council housing (Clapham and Kintrea 1986).

The way households get access to council housing therefore depends on the nature of the stock and on council allocation policies. These allocation policies are determined by national legislation and locally decided priorities. However, they are concerned with the management of the stock as well as with meeting housing need.

In conclusion, we have seen that both owner-occupation and council housing operate with rules of access which exclude some households and include but differentially treat others. Two categories of household are excluded from owner-occupation: those whose incomes are too low or too uncertain, and those who want to buy 'risky' houses, or houses in 'risky' areas. Although the segmentation of the mortgage market means that some households will remain 'included' but will have to cope with tough loan terms, others will be totally excluded. The rules of access here are probably resistant to change because they are part of the conventional wisdom of the wider financial system. In council housing the effect of the professional ideologies of council housing managers is to channel households to better or worse housing within the sector: differential treatment of the sort normal in a housing market. Exclusion also exists in the council sector, applying to homeless households who do not meet the legal criteria of being unintentionally homeless and in a priority group. But it also occurs because being on the waiting list does not guarantee inclusion, that is, eventually being offered council housing. This is why some households in housing need do not join the waiting list, while others do so but find their own housing, or remain as concealed households.

Thus whereas the normal functioning of owner-occupation means it cannot meet all housing need because access depends on ability to pay, even council housing, which is specifically aimed at those unable to pay, is unable to do so completely in practice. It would be reassuring to think that the private rented sector and housing associations cope with those excluded from these two sectors. Undoubtedly they do so to some extent, but the other options for those who are excluded from the two large sectors are to be homeless and/or to be a concealed household.

Conclusion

In this chapter we have answered the question of whether housing policy is social policy by rejecting the idea that it is simply a response to housing need. Rather, we have seen that throughout the history of housing policy it is political forces which determine whether state action in response to need takes place, and if so, what form it takes and which groups benefit from it.

The immense level of housing need in the nineteenth century met with minimal response until its last decades. What changed then was the rise of the working class as a political force. This led to housing policy with a 'social' character and, together with the wartime experience of solidarity, to the post-1918 government's major innovation of council housing. After 1945 there was quite a long period when both major political parties supported the building of both council housing and owner-occupied housing. Only in the 1970s did the inter-party differences become striking. After that the Conservative government defined council housing as an obstacle to increased owner-occupation, and took measures against it. The Labour government passed the 1977 Homelessness Act and briefly reversed the Conservative attack on council housing. But in the 1980s it abandoned its traditional identification with council housing, and accepted that there was widespread support among council tenants for the right-to-buy scheme. By the 1990s, therefore, housing policy was partly 'social' (such as council housing, housing associations, and housing allowances) and partly support for market provision (assistance to owner-occupiers and private landlords). The explanation of this policy shift is that housing policy became a means of winning votes from the middle-income groups. Their interests were therefore advanced at the expense of the low-income groups.

Paradoxically, this shift in the direction of housing policy has not corresponded to a reduction of state intervention. State regulation of housing has continued at a high level, and Table 16.3 shows that while there has been a reduction in the scale of state spending on council housing, and that subsidies in the form of mortgage tax relief have fallen since 1986, these have been compensated for by the fourfold expansion in housing benefit in twenty years. The latter trend is due to the difficulty of introducing market-level rents in the three rented sectors used by poorer households, and ultimately to the dual (pro-poor and pro-market) character of housing policy in the UK. Thus in the housing sphere it is not the question of whether state intervention is present or absent which is important, but rather what forms it takes and who benefits from it. It is likely that the income groups which benefit from housing policy in the future will depend on the same mix of economic, political, and social need considerations which have been evident in housing policy in the past.

Key Legislation

1972 Housing Finance Act Introduced 'fair rents' for council tenants and allowed councils to make a surplus on council housing. This initiated the rise in council rents.

1977 Homelessness Act Imposed a duty on councils to rehouse unintentionally homeless families and individuals permanently.

1980 Housing Act The 'Right to Buy' act, which gave council tenants the right to buy their dwelling at a discount. Previously councils had a right to sell but council tenants had no right to buy.

1988 Housing Act Reduced regulation of private rented sector, and forced housing associations to rely more on private finance. Increased rent levels followed, and helped lead to the increase in housing benefit payments.

1996 Housing Act Required councils to place unintentionally homeless people in temporary accommodation (either in social housing or private rented housing). Their access to permanent council accommodation to be only through the waiting list.

Glossary

building society Financial institution which attracts money from savers and lends it to house purchasers.

concealed household A single person or group of people who share a meal a day together or a living room with another single person or group of people. Typically it refers to single persons or couples who are living with their parents but who would like to live independently, that is, form separate households.

gatekeeper In the housing context, the owner or financier whose rules of access control who is able to gain access to a particular type of housing. It applies to mortgage lenders, councils, housing associations, private landlords, and so on.

household A single person or group of people who have a particular address as their only or main residence, and who either share one meal a day together or share a living room (definition used in the UK census from 1981).

housing stock The total stock of housing in a given area irrespective of its tenure, whether it is currently occupied or empty, or whether it is a second home.

housing tenure The legal relationship between household and dwelling. The main types of tenure, owning and renting, involve sets of rights and obligations which depend partly on national legislation and partly on rules applied by mortgage lenders, councils, and so on. Hence, for example, the rights of private tenants vary between countries and over time.

mandatory legislation Legislation which imposes a duty, for example, on a council to undertake certain actions.

mortgage arrears Households buying dwellings normally take out loans, or mortgages. The mortgage allows the purchaser to pay the whole cost of the dwelling to the seller, and in exchange the household undertakes to make monthly repayments of the loan to the mortgage lender. When the household fails to maintain these payments the mortgage is said to be in arrears.

negative equity Equity refers to the value of a household's investment in a dwelling. This value is calculated by estimating the value of the dwelling and then deducting the value of outstanding loans from it. If the result is positive, the household has positive equity; if it is negative, the household has negative equity.

permissive legislation Legislation which allows but does not require, for example, a council to undertake certain actions

points system System of allocating council housing in which applicants are given points based on criteria of housing need.

rent control Controls imposed by legislation on the level of rents which landlords can charge tenants.

residualization Process of social change in council housing, in which the composition of households changes to include more households in great housing need. This happens because households leaving council housing are less deprived than those entering, for example because of the right to buy and homelessness legislation.

rules of access Criteria applied by owners and financiers of housing governing who gains access to housing and under what conditions.

unintentionally homeless Not homeless by their own choice. A concept introduced in the 1977 Homelessness Act, which obliged local councils to provide housing only for those who were 'unintentionally' homeless (and who had a local connection), as opposed to those who were considered to have made themselves homeless by their own choice.

Guide to Further Reading

The References list contains some of the main texts and research monographs in the field. A new edition of Malpass and Murie's textbook will appear in 1999. Others useful books include: J. Dorling, *Comparative Housing Policy* (London: Macmillan, 1997), M. L. Harrison,

Housing: Race, Social Policy and Empowerment (Aldershot: Avebury, 1995), A. E. Holmans, *Housing Policy in Britain: A History* (London: Croom Helm, 1987), M. Kleinman, *Housing, Welfare and the State in Europe* (Aldershot: Edward Elgar, 1996), and P. Lee and A. Murie, *Poverty, Housing Tenure and Social Exclusion* (Bristol: Policy Press, 1997). The main sources of up-to-date government data are: *English House Condition Survey* and *Housing and Construction Statistics*, published by the Department of Environment; and *Family Spending*, *Living in Britain*, *Social Trends*, and *Survey of English Housing*, published by the Office of National Statistics. From 1997 the CSO and OPCS were combined into the Office for National Statistics.

References

Bailey, R. (1973), *The Squatters* (Harmondsworth: Penguin).

Bramley, G. (1994), 'An Affordability Crisis in British Housing: Dimensions, Causes and Policy Impact', *Housing Studies*, 9, 103–24.

Central Statistical Office (1993), *Family Spending: A Report on the 1992 Family Expenditure Survey* (London: HMSO).

Clapham, D. and Kintrea, K. (1986), 'Rationing, Choice and Constraint: The Allocation of Public Housing in Glasgow', *Journal of Social Policy*, 15, 51–67.

Department of Employment (1982), *Family Expenditure Survey 1980* (London: HMSO).

Department of Environment (1998), *Housing and Construction Statistics 1997–8* (London: HMSO).

Dorling, D. and Cornford, J. (1995), 'Who Has Negative Equity? How House Price Falls in Britain have hit Different Groups of Home Buyers', *Housing Studies*, 10, 151–78.

Engels, F. (1969), *The Condition of the Working Class in England* (1845, London: Panther).

Forrest, R. and Murie, A. (1988), *Selling the Welfare State* (London: Routledge).

Forrest, R., Murie, A., and Williams, P. (1990), *Home Ownership: Differentiation and Fragmentation* (London: Unwin Hyman).

Gauldie, E. (1974), *Cruel Habitations* (London: George Allen and Unwin).

Gilbert, B. B. (1970), *British Social Policy 1914–1939* (London: Batsford).

Hamnett, C., Harmer, M., and Williams, P. (1991), *Safe as Houses: Housing Inheritance in Britain* (London: Paul Chapman).

Hills, J. (1998), 'Housing', in H. Glennerster and J. Hills (eds.), *The State of Welfare* (2nd edn., Oxford: Oxford University Press).

Malpass, P. and Murie, A. (1994), *Housing Policy and Practice* (4th edn., London: Macmillan).

McCrone, G. and Stephens, M. (1995), *Housing Policy in Britain and Europe* (London: UCL Press).

Office of Population Censuses and Surveys (1996), *Living in Britain: Results from the 1994 General Household Survey* (London: HMSO).

Pickvance, C. G. and Pickvance, K. (1995), 'The Role of Family Help in the Housing Decisions of Young People', *Sociological Review*, 43, 123–49.

Pleace, N., Burrows, R., and Quilgars, D. (1997), 'Homelessness in Contemporary Britain: Conceptualization and Measurement', in Burrows, R., Pleace, N., and Quilgars, D. (eds.), *Homelessness and Social Policy* (London: Routledge).

Saunders, P. (1990), *A Nation of Home Owners* (London: Unwin Hyman).

Williams, P. (1976), 'The Role of Institutions in the Inner London Housing Market: The Case of Islington', *Transactions of the Institute of British Geographers*, 1, 72–82.

7 Crime, Justice, and Punishment

Tina Eadie and Rebecca Morley

Contents

Introduction: Crime—A Pervasive Social Policy Concern

We are surrounded by crime—as a problem and as entertainment—in the media, in novels, in everyday discussion. We have television programmes which implore us, the public, to help the police solve crimes in our communities and to help put right miscarriages of justice. The annual crime statistics for England and Wales make headline news. They are offered as key indicators of the moral condition of society. Periodic rises and falls in crime rates provide ammunition for political debate concerning the successes and failures of social policies in the 'fight against crime', as the main political parties battle for the high ground on 'law and order'. Dramatic incidents of crime—a senseless killing, a spate of stalking cases, a shocking rape, for example—reverberate in the daily conversations of ordinary citizens filling us with outrage, horror, fear, grief. We are aware that crime has risen dramatically during the latter half of this century. Opinion polls show crime to be a major public concern. Clearly crime is a central social policy theme.

In this chapter we touch on the following questions as they bear on social policy concerns: What is crime? How much crime is there? How is it changing? Who suffers from it? Who commits it? How is it dealt with? How much does it cost? Why does it occur? How can it be prevented? There are no simple answers to these questions, and debates concerning them are complex and often contradictory. Recognizing that this chapter can only offer a brief overview of some of these questions, we hope that readers will follow up the references and further reading.

What is Crime? Measurement, Statistics, and Trends

The impression often given by politicians and the media is that crime is a physical fact, like the air temperature or rainfall, which, with proper techniques, can be accurately measured and assessed. However, closer examination shows that crime is thoroughly socially produced—that it is a **social construction.**

The most common and apparently straightforward and unproblematic definition of crime is violation of the criminal law—'law-breaking'. But laws are 'man-made', both in the generic and specific sense of the word 'man'. Laws change over time and place. We need therefore to ask how and why certain acts are defined and legislated as criminal in certain places and times (and why others are not). Perspectives on this question vary and are underpinned by differing views concerning the nature of social order: simplistically, whether crime arises from a social consensus about morality and norms of conduct or is the outcome of social conflict and coercion. The first suggests that crime is politically neutral; the second, that we need to examine issues of power and politics—who has the power to define what is criminal, and whose interests do these definitions serve?

Proponents of this second view ask, for example, why property crimes and personal violence are much more likely to be considered crimes than environmental pollution, unethical business practices, and health and safety hazards in the workplace. Marxist-oriented criminologists (such as Reiman 1995) argue that the criminal law and its operation are biased towards crimes of the poor and powerless, protecting the economic and political interests of the powerful while ignoring acts which are arguably more socially harmful in terms of financial loss and personal injury or death. Feminists (such as Radford and Stanko 1996) argue that the law and criminal justice system ignore the bulk of men's physical and sexual violence against women ('private' violence as opposed to street violence), supporting the interests of men or 'patriarchal' power. Domestic violence, for example, was legally sanctioned until the late nineteenth century and is only now—patchily and falteringly—treated as crime by the criminal justice system; rape in marriage was legal in England and Wales until 1991.

The obvious limitations of **legal definitions** have led some to argue that crime should be defined as actions which are socially harmful or which violate human rights, whether or not they are legally sanctioned. Such **social definitions** would include racism, sexism, poverty, and imperialism as crimes. However, in terms of public and policy debate the most influential definition of crime is clearly law-breaking, and within this, law-breaking that comes to the attention of the police and media.

Measurement

Crime is not just socially constructed in definition, it is socially constructed in measurement. Official crime rates for England and Wales are culled from police records published each year in *Criminal Statistics*. Comparable statistics are produced for Scotland and Northern Ireland; however, those from England and Wales figure most prominently in policy debates and the media. Recorded crime is the end point of a complex series of decisions: crime must be recognized, reported, classified by the police as an offence, and actually recorded. Some crimes (such as car theft) are far more likely to survive this process than others (such as marital rape).

Further, police only record certain categories of crime—'notifiable offences'. Prior to April 1998, these broadly corresponded to 'indictable offences'—supposedly more serious crimes which are triable only in Crown courts, or are 'triable either way' in Crown or magistrates' courts—as opposed to 'summary offences', which can be tried only in magistrates' courts. Thus, for example, violence which the police classified as 'common assault' rather than 'actual bodily harm' (ABH) was not recorded even though incidents can be as injurious as ABH: Edwards (1989: ch. 4), for example, found that police routinely 'downcrimed' domestic violence in order to avoid paperwork and further investigation, which they regarded as wasted effort.

In 1998 the Home Office acknowledged the need for revising the way crime is recorded, by expanding notifiable offences to include:

some closely linked summary offences. This expanded coverage will result in offences such as common assault, assault on a constable, drugs possession, cruelty to or neglect of children, vehicle interference, and dangerous driving being included in the crime statistics. As a result, the overall number of offences which are reported to and recorded by the police will rise. (Home Office Press Release 135/98, April 1998)

Clearly, official views concerning the seriousness of various kinds of offence change over time, and these changes result in rises or falls in the recorded crime rate.

Even within the categories of notifiable offences, different police forces may concentrate their efforts on detecting different sorts of crime at different points in time for a wide variety of reasons. These decisions, too, will affect the volume of recorded crime. Undeniably, then, official crime rates are fragile creatures which require great care in interpretation.

Statistics and Trends

At face value, the overall picture of crime from official statistics is startlingly clear. Apart from a small sustained decline in the early 1950s and since 1992, the total volume of crime has risen steadily since the 1930s and particularly steeply since the mid-1950s (see Fig. 17.1): in 1950 recorded crime stood at 500,000, or 1 per 100 of population; in 1992 nearly 5.6 million, or 11 per 100 of population, an elevenfold increase (Home Office 1997).

The vast majority of recorded crimes are property offences: in 1997 property offences accounted for 91 per cent, while violent crime including robbery comprised only 8 per cent (see Fig. 17.2). Furthermore, less than 7 per cent of violent crime (only 0.5 per cent of total recorded crime) was homicide and other more serious violence (Povey *et al.* 1998: Fig. 6). However, crimes of violence have increased more rapidly than property offences, at least since 1987; indeed, property crimes have actually decreased since 1992 (accounting for the small overall decline in the crime rate) while violent crimes have continued to rise (Home Office 1997; Povey *et al.* 1998).

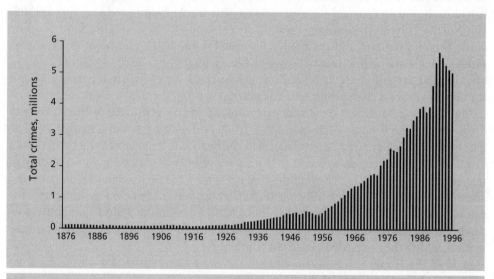

Figure 17.1 Crime recorded by the police, 1876–1996

Source: Maguire (1997: 158).

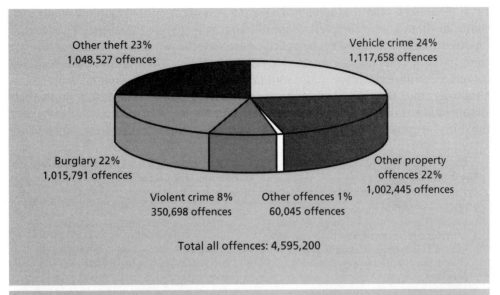

Other theft 23%
1,048,527 offences

Vehicle crime 24%
1,117,658 offences

Burglary 22%
1,015,791 offences

Other property
offences 22%
1,002,445 offences

Violent crime 8%
350,698 offences

Other offences 1%
60,045 offences

Total all offences: 4,595,200

Figure 17.2 Crime recorded by police by type of crime, England and Wales, 1997

Source: Povey *et al.* (1998): Fig. 1.

These trends can be and have been used to argue that crime is spiralling out of control. But they are capable of being selectively presented to support opposing ideological positions. Thus, for example, the Conservatives were able to celebrate winning the war against crime on the basis of the 1996 figures which revealed the fourth consecutive fall in crime, while the Labour Party's 1997 manifesto declared, 'Under the Conservatives, crime has doubled . . . the worst record on crime of any government since the Second World War. . . . Last year alone, violent crime rose 11 per cent' (Labour Party 1997: 22). More generally, there are important debates about the extent to which statistics represent real changes in criminal behaviour (the **realist approach**) as opposed to changes in reporting and recording (the **institutionalist approach**).

Crime Surveys and Victimology

Government-sponsored national crime surveys, comprising interviews with random samples of the population who are asked about their experiences of criminal victimization during a specified period, emerged in the USA in the early 1970s with the express aim of addressing the problem of interpreting official crime data. By 1980 researchers in the Home Office were arguing for a national crime survey on the grounds that policy-makers needed a better idea of the extent and shape of crime than that provided by official statistics, and that public misconceptions concerning crime levels and risk needed to be challenged (Mayhew and Hough 1988: 157).

The resulting **British Crime Survey (BCS)**, to date conducted seven times (1982, 1984,

1988, 1992, 1994, 1996, and 1998) and covering crimes committed in the previous year, claims to allow a more complete count of crime by including incidents which are not reported to and/or recorded by the police. In practice, the two sources cannot be directly compared since they do not count exactly the same things. For instance, the BCS counts common assault—which was not a notifiable offence until 1998—but does not count homicide, since the victims of homicide cannot talk to the interviewer about their victimization. (Table 17.1 compares the main features of the two sources.) However, for the subset of crimes which are comparable, estimates of the so-called 'dark figure' of un-

The British Crime Survey	Police recorded crime
• Starting in 1982, it measures both reported and unreported crime. As such it provides a measure of trends in crime not affected by changes in reporting, or changes in police recording rules or practices.	• Collected since 1857. Provides a measure of offences which are both reported to and recorded by the police. As such they are influenced by changes in reporting behaviour and recording rules and practices.
• Measures crime every two years.	• The police provide monthly crime returns, and figures are published every six months.
• Includes some offences the police are not required to notify to the Home Office.	• Only includes 'notifiable' offences which the police are required to notify to the Home Office for statistical purposes.
• The measure is based on estimates from a sample of the population. The estimates are therefore subject to sampling error and other methodological limitations.	• Provides an indicator of the workload of the police.
• Does not measure crime at the small area level well.	• Provides data at the level of 43 police force areas.
• Does not include crime against: – those under 16 – commercial and public sector establishments – those in institutions.	• Includes crime against: – those under 16 – commercial and public sector establishments – those living in institutions.
• Does not provide a measure of: – victimless crimes (e.g., drug, alcohol misuse) – crimes where a victim is no longer available for interview – fraud.	• Measures: – victimless crimes – murder and manslaughter – fraud.
• Collects information on what happens in crime (e.g., when crimes occur, and effects in terms of injury and property loss).	• Collects information about the number of arrests, who is arrested, the number of crimes detected, and by what method.
• Provides information about how the risks of crime vary for different groups.	• Does not show which groups of the population are most at risk of victimisation.

Table 17.1 Comparison of the BCS with crime recorded by the police
Source: Mirrlees-Black *et al.* (1998): 2 .

reported and unrecorded crime can be made. Further, the BCS collects other information such as the distribution of risk across different population groups, the impacts of victimization, and the public's fear of crime.

The BCS is now a source of major importance to policy-makers, rivalling official sources. Indeed, it has played a crucial role in the general shift in government policy since the 1980s from crime prevention towards 'victimization prevention' (Walklate 1998: 9). More generally, crime surveys have transformed the field of **victimology**—the study of victims—which originated in the 1940s as a concern with the relationship between the victim and offender, and which was much criticized for its preoccupation with victim typologies and notions of victim precipitation of crime (see Zedner 1997: 578–9).

The Picture of Crime from the British Crime Survey

As expected, the BCS uncovers many more crimes than official statistics—between three and four times more. However, the trends are broadly similar, though BCS rates have increased less steeply and continued to rise after 1992 until 1995, albeit at a much slower rate than before 1992. Under half (44 per cent) of all comparable BCS crimes uncovered in 1997 were reported to the police, and fewer than one-quarter (24 per cent) were estimated to have been recorded by the police (Mirrlees-Black *et al.* 1998). The 'dark figure' of unreported/unrecorded crime is thus considerable, though it varies substantially by type of offence (see Fig. 17.3).

Moreover, rates of reporting and recording have fluctuated since the BCS began in 1981. As Table 17.2 shows, these rose steadily to a peak in 1991, then fell—the fall in

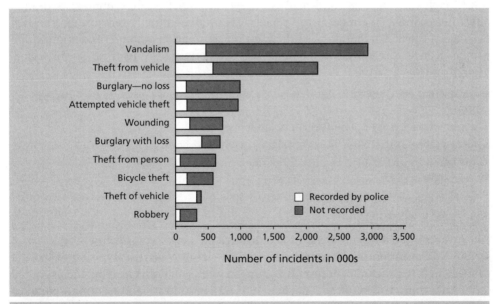

Figure 17.3 BCS estimates of recorded and unrecorded crime in 1997, by type of crime

Source: Mirrlees-Black *et al.* (1998): Fig. 4.1, 19.

Year	Reported crime[a] %	Reported crime recorded[b] %
1981	36	62
1983	39	59
1987	41	59
1991	49	60
1993	47	55
1995	46	50
1997	44	54

Table 17.2 BCS estimates of reported and recorded crime

[a] *The 1998 British Crime Survey*, Mirrlees-Black *et al.* (1998), from Table A4.1, 51.
[b] Ibid. from Table A4.4, 53.

police recording of reported crime between 1991 and 1995 being particularly dramatic. Maguire (1997: 167) argues that an analysis of these fluctuations

leads one to question very seriously whether *either* the dramatic increases in recorded crime between 1990 and 1992 (which helped to justify the equally dramatic switch in criminal justice policy and sentencing practices which has been evident since 1993) *or* the apparent fall in crime between 1993 and 1996 (which was trumpeted by the government as proof of the success of its tough new anti-crime strategies) ever 'really' happened (original emphases).

Although the first BCS confirmed the view that much more crime exists than is officially recorded, the tone of the report was overwhelmingly reassuring: 'the real message of the BCS is that it calls into question assumptions about crime upon which people's concern is founded. It emphasises the petty nature of most law-breaking' (Hough and Mayhew 1983: 33). Indeed, the authors calculated that:

assuming that rates remain at 1981 levels . . . a 'statistically average' person aged 16 or over can expect:

- a robbery once every five centuries (not attempts)
- an assault resulting in injury (even if slight) once every century
- the family car to be stolen or taken by joyriders once every 60 years
- a burglary in the home once every 40 years

. . . and a very low rate for rape and other sexual offences.

(Hough and Mayhew 1983: 15)

The authors offered further reassurance through an analysis of the differential risk of serious victimization. For example, the typical victim of assault was found to be a young, single male who spent several evenings a week out, drank heavily, and assaulted others (like himself) (Hough and Mayhew 1983: 21). In contrast, and seemingly paradoxically, fear of crime—measured by questions such as feelings of safety on the street at night—was found to be highest amongst those least at risk of victimization: women and the elderly. In addressing the paradox, the authors hinted at the possibility that fear is in part 'irrational or excessive', and concluded that 'in some areas, fear of crime appears to be a serious problem which needs to be tackled separately from the incidence of crime itself' (Hough and Mayhew 1983: 27). Fear reduction policies, aimed particularly at women and the elderly in the inner cities, were advocated (Maxfield 1984), and a number of policies emerged in the 1980s aimed at educating and reassuring the public concerning the 'reality' of crime.

Critical Responses to the BCS

This optimistic picture of the reality of crime has been contested, in particular by left realists (such as Young 1988) and feminists (such as Stanko 1988), who argue that the BCS provides a distorted picture of the distribution of risk, failing to uncover the disproportionate victimization of those most disadvantaged in society—the poor, ethnic minorities, and women—and thus misinterpreting the meaning of fear of crime. Since the mid-1980s a number of local crime surveys have been conducted in order to elucidate the victimization experiences of these groups.

For example, a survey of an inner city area of London—the first Islington Crime Survey (Jones *et al.* 1986)—found that a total of one-third of all households had experienced a burglary, robbery, or sexual violence within the previous year; that women were more likely than men to be victims of assault; and that while older people suffered less crime than younger, assaults against them were more likely to be serious in terms of level of violence, injury, and impact.

Feminist surveys have not only uncovered much higher levels of serious violence to women than the BCS, but have also documented the pervasiveness of women's experiences of acts which are not classified as crimes—for example sexual harassment, being touched up, leered at, followed, and so on—which constitute an ever-present climate of threat in women's lives. Radford's (1987) survey of women in Wandsworth, London, for

Type of violence	%[a]
Violent attack	44
Threatened in public place	13
Threatened/attacked by stranger in their home	10
Obscene telephone call	11
Sexual harassment at work	38
Threatened/attacked by men they were living with	12
Total assaulted or harassed	**89**

Table 17.3 The Wandsworth Violence Against Women Survey: proportion of 314 women experiencing various forms of men's violence during previous 12 months

[a] Percentages are not additive. Many women experienced more than one type of violence.

Source: Radford, J. (1987), 'Policing Male Violence—Policing Men', in M. Maynard and J. Hanmer (eds.), *Women, Violence and Social Control* (London: Macmillan), 35.

example, found that 89 per cent had suffered some form of assault or harassment during the previous 12 months, covering a wide range of type of incident (see Table 17.3). Most women had experienced more than one incident; some as many as thirteen (personal communication, Jill Radford 1998).

Findings such as these have impacted on the conduct of the BCS, and have undoubtedly been crucial to the recent reassessment by BCS researchers of the relationship of risk to fear of crime (such as Hough 1995: 42–6).

Theories about Crime and their Policy Implications

Theories about the nature and causes of crime are not just academic exercises. They serve both as stimuli to, and as rationalizations of, policy. Theories are thus crucial to understanding policy positions concerning crime control and prevention, although in practice political declarations and policy outcomes often represent a—sometimes muddled—coalescence of varying and potentially contradictory theoretical presumptions.

Traditional Paradigms of Crime

The two competing traditional paradigms of crime are classicism and positivism. **Classicism** emerged from eighteenth-century enlightenment thought which viewed humans as rational, self-interested, and exercising free will. It follows that crime is rationally motivated (freely chosen) by self-interest, and that offenders are fully responsible for their actions. What is required is punishment aimed at deterring (rational) individuals from committing crime. Punishment should be systematically applied, based on the nature and seriousness of the criminal act rather than the characteristics of the offender. In short, criminals should get their **just deserts**—proportional punishment with determinate (or fixed) sentences.

Positivism is rooted in nineteenth-century empiricist science, searching for the causes of phenomena through objective observation and measurement. In contrast to classicism, positivist theories of crime focus on the offender as determined. Crime is thus non-rational, caused by forces beyond the criminal's control. The earliest versions of positivism (still in evidence) focused on individual determinants—defects in the person's biological or psychological make-up which predispose him/her to crime. Because the problem is essentially a pathology or sickness, the appropriate response is treatment (not punishment) aimed at rehabilitation. Since appropriate treatment requires responding to individual needs, sentences should be indeterminate, taking into account not only the seriousness of the crime but the individual's diagnosis and prognosis.

The Rise of Social Positivism

Individual positivism dominated thinking about crime during the first half of the twentieth century. However, by the late 1950s a group of theories—originating in American sociology from the 1920s onwards—were coming to prominence which stressed the social causes of crime. Although these theories can be described as varieties of **social positivism** (see Table 17.4), most are more accurately viewed as theories which credit humans with freedoms within a determined social framework.

One strand focuses on the relationship between the propensity towards criminal behaviour and social norms and values. 'Social disorganization' theory suggests that crime is most likely to occur in specific urban areas where traditional norms and values have broken down due to immigration and migration. Alternatively, in 'strain theory', people at the bottom of the social structure—the working class and poor—are viewed as particularly susceptible to criminal behaviour precisely because they accept dominant norms and values but are denied legitimate means to achieve socially valued goals: crime is a meaningful solution to the disjunction between socially induced goals and the opportunity structures of society. 'Subcultural theory' maintains that these disjunctions are not solved by individuals in isolation, but by groups of people in similar structural positions who form deviant subcultures which may, over time, develop alternative, deviant norms and values. 'Differential association' examines the processes through which criminal behaviour is learned through acquiring skills, meanings, motives, and traditions in association with peer groups involved in criminal activity. All of the above imply that the solution to the problem of crime lies in social programmes designed

Theory	Argument	Policy implications
Social disorganization	breakdown of moral order of a community	community development; urban renewal; stamp out extreme criminal elements e.g. drug pushers
Strain theory	poverty, deprivation, blocked goals	anti-poverty programmes; equal opportunity
Subcultural theory	criminal behaviour socially valued	social mobility through economic growth; equal opportunity; education policies
Differential association	local peer/gang cultures	removal of gang leaders; breakup of peer groups
Labelling	people defined as criminal become criminal	decriminalization; diversion of first-time offenders to non-penal treatments
Marxist	inequalities of power and class conflict	collective ownership of means of production and control; redistribution of resources according to need
Feminist	patriarchy, women's economic and social subordination	social empowerment of women through economic, social, and political equality

Table 17.4 Varieties of 'social positivism' and their policy implications

to alleviate the precipitating social conditions of poverty, deprivation, unemployment, urban decay, and disorganization; in promoting equality of opportunity in education and employment; and through interventions to break up organized criminal groupings.

For labelling theorists, it is not that the poor are more deviant than other people, but that they are more likely to be labelled deviant by those who have the power to label. Once labelled, the person may take on a role or identity commensurate with the label, thus engaging in further deviant activity and seeking out the company of others with similar labels. The impact of labelling is potentially the creation of a criminal career, fuelled by a **deviancy amplification spiral**. Hence, it is argued, criminal justice policy should be geared towards decriminalization and keeping offenders out of formal justice systems as far as possible—radical non-intervention.

While labelling theory begins to question the assumption that there exists a social consensus of norms and values, it does not really challenge fundamental social structures. In contrast, Marxist theories focus centrally on issues of power and conflicts of interest in society: crime arises out of class divisions. The state, including the law and criminal justice system, is viewed as a tool used by those who own and control the means of production—those with power—to protect their interests; hence the criminal justice system targets crimes of the less powerful which threaten the powerful—property crime and public order offences. Unlike the other perspectives discussed so far, Marxist perspectives are interested not only in crimes of the less powerful but also in crimes of the powerful. It is argued that the latter (such as fraud, environmental destruction, and corruption) are caused by a desire to increase wealth or to gain competitive advantage, while the former are a result of economic necessity—ensuring subsistence—or are acts of alienation. Ultimately the solution of crime requires annihilating inequalities through overthrowing capitalism, collective ownership and control of the means of production, and redistribution of resources according to need. However, lesser demands—for public accountability, for democratization of institutions, and for social programmes to eliminate poverty and deprivation—have all been made in the name of Marxist thinking.

Feminist perspectives are also concerned with power and structural inequalities, but focus primarily on their relation to gender. Feminists argue that women are structurally disadvantaged; society is patriarchal, based on male domination and female subordination. Women's unequal position in society is key to understanding both female offending and victimization. Women who kill men, for example, have often been subject to violence from their victims; female property crime tends to be petty thieving and fraud done to support children. Women are vulnerable to sexual violence because of men's power over women constructed through double standards of masculinity and femininity. The solution to both lies in eradicating patriarchy—empowering women economically, socially, and politically. Feminist perspectives have also raised questions concerning male offending—what is it about men and masculinity that result in their greater involvement in crime?

The Theoretical Climate from the Late 1970s

Many commentators have pointed to a post-war consensus on crime, strongly based on the social positivist notion that improving social conditions and reducing inequalities through social policies would alleviate the crime problem. This consensus had fractured by the end of the 1970s for two interrelated reasons: first, the impact of the recession which resulted in calls for cuts in public expenditure, and second, the apparent failure of rising living standards to halt the rise in crime. Both were accompanied by a questioning of the ability of the welfare state generally, and social programmes specifically, to alleviate social problems.

'New right' approaches have gained prominence in this climate. They stress individual responsibility, law and order, and punishment and control of offenders; and include both revitalized classicism and positivism. They also have historical links with 'control theory', which holds that human nature is not naturally conforming but inherently anti-social, and that all people would commit crime if they were not subject to internalized and/or externalized controls.

'Rational choice theories' suggest that people make decisions to engage in criminal activity, and choose specific times and places, when economic benefits outweigh costs. The solution is deterrence which requires increasing the cost of criminal behaviour by making it riskier or more difficult to carry out, the policy emphasis being on victimization prevention. At the other extreme are theories which either find biological defects in criminals or imply that human nature is inherently anti-social, and blame crime on the 'permissive society', especially lack of discipline in the family (read 'single parents') and schools.

Particularly influential on the right has been the 'bio-social' thinking of James Q. Wilson (Wilson and Herrnstein 1985), for whom crime is caused by a combination of constitutional factors which determine the ease with which an individual's conscience can be conditioned, the quality of conditioning of conscience and self-control provided by the family and community, and the costs and benefits of crime. Though the larger constitutional and socialization causes of crime may be difficult to tackle, Wilson suggests that marginal gains can be made. As Young (1994) points out, these prioritize order over justice:

1. Police intervention should occur in terms of order on the streets rather than crime itself. For it is here that intervention would be seen to be effective, despite the fact that the individuals concerned have committed the least serious crimes—if any crimes at all.

2. Public intervention should occur in those areas that have not yet 'tipped' into 'irrevocable' decay: that is, *not* towards the most deserving areas but towards those which are deemed rescuable.

3. Intervention to control drug use should be directed not at the addicts (who are past reclaiming) or at the dealers, but at the first-time users, who may be deterred: that is, against those who have the least culpability.

4. Repeat offenders, whom Wilson sees as making a particularly high contribution to the crime problem, should be 'incapacitated' by imprisonment on a dual-track basis: that is, they should be punished both in terms of the seriousness of their crime and in terms of the public interest.

(Young 1994: 102, original emphasis)

This thinking has fed into calls to get 'tough on criminals' through lengthy prison sentences at one extreme, and 'zero tolerance' policies advocating heavy-handed policing of sub-criminal behaviour at the other, although these initiatives have now been questioned by Home Office researchers (Goldblatt and Lewis, eds., 1998).

A recent challenge to new-right thinking has come from 'left realist' approaches to crime. These emerged in the mid-1980s as an attempt to reclaim the law and order terrain for the left by acknowledging public anxieties about the rise of crime and disorder in society. A key cause of crime is seen to be relative deprivation—the belief that one's allocation of society's resources is unfair. Thus crime is not confined to those in absolute deprivation, the poor. However, 'it is among the poor, particularly the lower working class and certain ethnic minorities, who are marginalized from the "glittering prizes" of the wider society, that the push towards crime is greatest' (Young 1997: 488). While longer-term social change in the direction of social justice is clearly important in solving the crime problem, left realists emphasize the importance of more immediate interventions to control crime—for example, more responsive policing, community involvement, and support of victims.

Looking overall at the range of theoretical perspectives on crime, we can see that they are underpinned by a variety of contrasting views about human nature, the nature of social order, and resulting policy requirements for dealing with crime. It is also clear that the influence of certain theories and their underlying presumptions at certain historical periods is very much bound up with the larger economic and political climate of the time.

Welfare *vs.* Punishment

How those caught and convicted of a criminal offence are dealt with by the **criminal justice system** will be influenced by views on crime causation. Two models for dealing with offenders are outlined here—the **Welfare Model** and the **Justice Model.** Policies based on the former reflect positivist approaches to the treatment and rehabilitation of offenders—with welfare needs paramount. Policies based on the latter reflect a classicist and neoclassicist focus on the offence and its punishment rather than the personal characteristics or circumstances of the offender. A key dilemma for policy-makers is whether to provide help with problems associated with a person's offending in the hope of reducing or preventing future offending (an example of **reductive punishment**), or to punish solely in accordance with the seriousness of the offence (an example of **retributive punishment**), or indeed to attempt both.

The Rise and Demise of the Welfare Approach

Penal policy during the first half of the twentieth century became focused on the offender rather than the offence. The welfarist policy of rehabilitation through treatment created a 'soft machine' (Hudson 1987: p. x) of probation officers, social workers, therapists, and counsellors whose task was to provide diagnostic and curative services for offenders. This approach was probably at its height in the early 1960s. The White Paper, *The Child, the Family and the Young Offender* (Home Office 1965), is a good example of the welfare focus: 'what is needed is firm discipline and constructive treatment directed to the welfare or rehabilitation of the individual child or young person' (ibid.: 12). The White

Paper that followed, *Children in Trouble* (Home Office 1968), while less overtly welfare-oriented, continued to argue for the removal of young offenders from court and criminal procedures and for social workers to decide any treatment they should receive.

In the early 1970s the welfare approach began to be challenged from all sides. Not only were academics calling it a 'conceptual shambles' (Bean 1976: 143), the legal profession claimed that focusing on offenders' problems rather than on the crime resulted in disparities in sentencing which were discriminatory. Magistrates perceived the approach as a direct attack on their sentencing powers. Left-wing critics maintained it resulted in longer sentences, both prison and community, than would be imposed by a desert-based sentence. Finally, the fact that the previous twenty years had witnessed steadily increasing crime rates bolstered the growing right-wing charge that focusing on the welfare needs of offenders had failed to cure them of crime, and it was time to bring back punishment. The backlash against welfare is reflected in a statement by Ivan Lawrence QC, MP welcoming the new Conservative government's proposals which formed the basis of the Criminal Justice Act 1982:

One of the most important steps in the bill which I strongly welcome is the reflection of public opinion which says that we are fed up with letting sentences be decided by social workers rather than the courts . . . encouraged by wet socialist intellectuals from all over the place. (Quoted in Rutherford 1992: 63–4)

Social welfare professionals themselves were unable to demonstrate the effectiveness of their methods. Throughout the 1970s they were left reeling by research claiming that no sentence was more successful than any other in reducing recidivism (Martinson 1974). Welfare-based initiatives lost credibility with voters and politicians and the rehabilitative ideal, which had underpinned both institutional and community responses to crime, was rejected. In its place came a more desert-based approach, along with an increasingly punitive right-wing lobby.

Justice Through Punishment

The Justice Model, most strongly associated with Von Hirsch (1976), sought a return to classicist principles 'that the severity of the punishment should be commensurate with the seriousness of the wrong' (ibid.: 66), with the focus on the act committed rather than the person committing it. It was proposed that the principle of just deserts should guide punishment, that sentences should be **determinate** not **indeterminate,** and that sentencing guidelines should be introduced to reduce disparities in sentence length and time served.

The White Paper *Crime, Justice and Protecting the Public* (Home Office 1990) which preceded the Criminal Justice Act 1991, was an attempt to introduce a desert-based sentencing framework. The 1991 Act, however, was implemented in a political climate espousing a tough law-and-order rhetoric. It extended the White Paper's strict interpretation of desert by highlighting violent and sexual offences as giving grounds for going beyond desert in cases where the sentencer considered that the public needed protecting from a particular offender (Wasik and Taylor 1994: 23–4). During Michael Howard's period in office as Home Secretary from June 1993 to April 1997, an increasing emphasis on public protection moved sentencing away from both welfare and justice approaches and focused it on incapacitation as the only sure means of punishing the offender and preventing further offending. Charles Murray reflected this emphasis on punishment, stating provocatively, 'The broad proposition that "prison works" is not in question. Of course prison can work, if it is used with sufficient ruthlessness' (Murray 1997: 14). The Home Office Research Study, *Reducing Offending* (Goldblatt and Lewis, eds., 1998), challenged the use of imprisonment, and the headline in the *Guardian* newspaper (22 July 1998)—'Prison Doesn't Work: Official'—indicated the beginning of a possible change in direction.

Welfare *vs.* Punishment: A False Choice?

'Welfare *vs.* punishment' implies one or the other, and strict advocates of each approach argue that this is appropriate—that it is the mixing of welfare and punishment that leads to confusion of purpose. There has, however, been a long history of social work intervention with offenders; and disentangling help or treatment from punishment has in practice never been straightforward. Even in today's punitive climate there is growing interest in research claiming that treatment-oriented, **cognitive-behavioural programmes** are effective in reducing recidivism (McGuire 1995: 16; McIvor 1996: 107–19).

It can be argued that penal policy directed towards young offenders in the 1960s attempted to focus on welfare and not punishment, and that penal policy in the early 1990s attempted to focus on punishment and not welfare. The following two sections explore these opposing trends further.

Delinquency and Social Policy

We are told that a disproportionate number of offences against individuals are committed by young persons aged 10 to 17 years, especially by a small number of persistent offenders (Audit Commission 1996: 5). The vast majority of these are young men (Home Office 1995a: 19). There are opposing viewpoints regarding ways of transforming the delinquent youth into an upright citizen, and these have been reflected in official terminology—the 1968 White Paper referred to *Children in Trouble*, whereas the 1980 White Paper, *Young Offenders*, leaves us in no doubt that it is their criminality on which attention must focus, not their problems, that is, punishment, not welfare.

The Treatment of Juveniles: A Tendency to Moral Panic

The deviancy amplification spiral referred to earlier is particularly pertinent to juvenile offenders. Anti-social and criminal behaviour by young persons, described by Pitts (1996: 250) as 'a political "hot potato"', tends to be used as a barometer for the moral climate of the nation. Geoffrey Pearson demonstrates how successive generations have linked fears of social breakdown and moral degeneration with street crime and hooliganism by young persons—behaviour unheard of 'twenty years ago' (Pearson 1983: 9–11). The resulting **moral panic** (Cohen 1972) often leads to a government responding with tougher measures than are warranted by the original incident.

When the high wartime rates of juvenile offending failed to decline, the problem of juvenile delinquency attracted extensive political and press attention (Garland 1997: 58). Throughout the 1950s and 1960s both Labour and Conservative governments supported welfarist policies aimed at responding to social and psychological problems of which youth crime was believed to be a symptom. Had the Children and Young Persons Act 1969 been implemented as the Labour government intended, no young person under the age of 14 would have been prosecuted for any offence other than homicide. However, the election of a Conservative government back into power in 1970—combined with growing right-wing antagonism, legal criticism towards welfarist policies, and what Newburn (1997: 621) calls 'recurrent forms of moral panics . . . surrounding youthful forms of deviance'—set the stage for a more punitive, justice-based approach towards young offenders.

The Diversion of Juveniles: Systems Management

It is one of the ironies of penal policy this century that at times when welfarist policies have been strongest, numbers of young persons appearing in court and being incarcerated have been high. Conversely, in the mid-1980s when the Conservatives were pursuing a punitive criminal justice agenda, the number of young offenders aged 14 to 16 being processed through the system and receiving custodial sentences fell (Cavadino and Dignan 1997). This is illustrated in Table 17.5.

It will also be noticed that since 1990, numbers sentenced to immediate custody have risen again. How is the decrease and subsequent increase to be explained?

The 1970s and 1980s witnessed innovative attempts by social work practitioners to influence police and court responses towards young offenders. The development of methods known collectively as **Systems Management** included inter-agency diversion panels at one end of the system and the targeting of young persons at serious risk of receiving a custodial sentence at the other. Diversion panels were set up to decide whether young persons arrested by the police could be cautioned rather than prosecuted. By the end of the 1970s, half of all known juvenile offenders were being cautioned (Gelsthorpe and Morris 1994: 968). For those in danger of custody, credible alternative sentences were proposed by pre-sentence report writers, **Intermediate Treatment** (I.T.) schemes attached to a **Supervision Order** being particularly successful (Cavadino and Dignan 1997: 257–8).

Diversionary tactics are based on the belief that it is a young person's youth not his

Year	Males 14–16 (females in brackets)		Males 17–21 (females in brackets)	
1970	3,100	(N/K)	(N/K)	(N/K)
1975	5,900	(N/K)	(N/K)	(N/K)
1980	7,600	(100)	20,500	(700)
1985	6,100	(100)	25,700	(800)
1990	1,700	(<50)	1,700	(400)
1995	2,400	(N/K)	15,800	(N/K)

Table 17.5 Young persons sentenced to immediate custody 1970–95 (Crown and magistrates' courts)

Source: Home Office Research and Statistics Department Crime and Criminal Justice Unit, personal communication.

or her criminality that is a problem and that, with support and encouragement, he or she will 'grow out of' crime (Rutherford 1992: 29). Crucial to this policy is a means of identifying those young persons who demonstrate more serious delinquent tendencies —for which more formal intervention is required. While pursuing policies based on labelling theory and radical non-intervention succeeded in keeping many young persons both out of the system and out of custody, it also opened the door to criticisms that young people were being 'let off'.

The Punishment of Juveniles: Moral Panics Return

The deepening of the recession from the late 1980s coincided with official crime statistics published at the beginning of 1993 which showed figures for the previous year as being the second highest on record. An already disillusioned electorate sought a scapegoat. Crime, particularly that of young people, was back on the agenda. Tabloid newspapers ran stories on 'bail bandits', 'ram raiders', and 'twockers', and delighted in the following sorts of headlines:

> **Villains are getting younger but sentences are getting softer**
> **THE UNTOUCHABLES Jimmy is only 13. He has been a crook for 8 years**
> (Special report on Britain's tiny terrors)
> (*The Star*, Monday 30 November 1992)
>
> **One-boy crime wave**
> • **He started stealing from sweet shops at 11**
> • **Within two years he was a seasoned criminal**
> • **At 15, he has 220 offences on his record**
> (*Daily Mail*, Thursday 10 September 1992)

The tragic death of a 2-year-old at the hands of two truanting 10-year-old boys convinced the public that children and young persons were out of control and 'something had to be done'. The then Home Secretary, Kenneth Clarke, swiftly announced a package of measures, including the introduction of a secure training order for 12- to 14-year-old persistent offenders and a restriction on cautioning young offenders. Sentencers responded to the increasingly punitive climate and government focus on public protection by imprisoning more young people. The Crime and Disorder Act 1998 introduced a range of new measures specifically aimed at curbing the offending of young persons. The 1980s campaign for the abolition of custody for juveniles (Rutherford 1989: 29) belonged firmly to the previous decade.

Just as the response to young people's offending in the 1960s had been to impose more treatment, the response in the 1990s was to impose more punishment. The political climate will now be considered in more depth.

The Politics of Law and Order

As will have been clear from the discussion so far, crime, justice, and punishment do not exist in a political vacuum: political values determine definitions of crime, political beliefs about crime causation are reflected in the criminal justice response to crime and public disorder, and political decisions determine the social conditions which impact on crime. Law and order policy was largely uncontested during the first half of the twentieth century, with the exception of the debate on capital punishment, which was not party political. The second half witnessed an increasing divide between extreme right- and left-wing views, the right focusing on individuals' responsibility for offending and the need for punishment, the left on societal and economic factors which might influence offending behaviour as much as or more than personality factors. The 1990s has witnessed a return to consensus, but one which has moved both sides further to the right. As we consider the politics of law and order, it is important to bear in mind that the party political context, while influential, is not easy to disentangle from the influence of other players—senior civil servants, pressure groups, and the mass media.

The Political Divide

Downes and Morgan (1997: 90) argue that the 1970 General Election marked the real watershed in the policies of law and order; while all three main political parties devoted more space than ever before in their manifestos to these issues, it was the Conservatives who argued that the continued rise in the crime rate was related to policy, specifically Labour policy. They also began the process of criminalizing public demonstrations, a process that was to culminate in the Criminal Justice and Public Order Act 1994. Throughout the 1970s Labour's affiliation with the Trade Union Movement and the increasingly hostile and confrontational clashes between the unions and the government fed the Conservative line that Labour was not only incapable of controlling crime, but also encouraged civil disobedience. The different strategies taken by the Labour and Conservative parties in the General Elections of 1970, 1974, and 1979 reflected their different theoretical convictions: Downes and Morgan state (1997: 93), 'Labour devoted space to law and order issues but dealt with them *within* the context of creating 'one nation' by eliminating the evils of inequality, poverty and racial bigotry.' By contrast, the 1979 Conservative manifesto brought 'law and order' to the fore as a major election issue, and undertook to implement specific 'law and order' policies.

Elected on a 'law and order' ticket in 1979, the Conservatives set about restoring the 'rule of law' by focusing on police and sentencing reform. The numbers of offenders sentenced to imprisonment throughout the 1980s escalated and, despite a major prison-building programme, resulted in severe overcrowding and prison unrest. The Criminal Justice Act 1991 represented an attempt to manage both prison populations and risk to the public through a policy of bifurcation—reserving custody for offenders whose offences were so serious as to justify such a sentence, and punishing those whose offences were less serious in the community. The Act was immediately unpopular with sentencers and the police, and media ridiculing of radical reforms such as the **Unit Fines System** resulted in key sections of the Act being altered by means of the Criminal Justice Act 1993.

The Politics of Punishment

Cavadino and Dignan assert that, while approaches to punishment in this period did combine certain aspects of the justice model, they also included 'a generous dash of the populist, punitive ideology of "law and order"' (1997: 51). It is the latter that became the strongest force while the Conservatives remained in power. As the crime rate continued to rise, the Conservative response was to punish more and to punish harder; custodial sentences, which had shown a decline in 1992, began to increase once more. Tougher 'National Standards for the Supervision of Offenders in the Community' (Home Office 1995b) were imposed on the probation service for all aspects of their work, the aim of which was 'to strengthen the supervision of offenders in the community, providing punishment and a disciplined programme for offenders' (ibid.: 2).

Throughout this period, the Conservative administration was heavily influenced by New Right thinking in the USA that regarded crime as an inevitable part of modern life, and its management more important than discovering its cause (Wilson 1975: 53). Management of crime focused on incarcerating serious and repeat offenders on the basis that, 'Wicked people exist. Nothing avails except to set them apart from innocent people' (Wilson 1975: 209). In Britain, these sentiments were reflected in Michael Howard's statement to the Conservative Party Conference in October 1993 that 'Prison Works' (Howard 1993) and John Major's statement that 'we should condemn more and understand less' (Major 1994). The climate of moral panic was quick to criminalize specific groups—lone parents, child sexual abusers, drug misusers, persistent young offenders, and the mentally disturbed. Even certain breeds of dog were identified and legislated against in the ill-thought-through Dangerous Dogs Act 1991. Labour, desperate to rid itself of its 'soft on crime' label, joined the debate with the soundbite 'Tough on crime and tough on the causes of crime', an imaginative compromise of matching the Tory rhetoric of toughness while holding on to its own beliefs in crime being linked to societal and structural inequalities. Since Labour's victory in May 1997, the Home Secretary, Jack Straw, has stated that securing the safety of the public is his overriding priority (Parliamentary Debates 1997: 341). 'Tough on crime' is reflected in the implementation of mandatory sentences for certain offences, set out in the Crime (Sentences) Act 1997, and the Crime and Disorder Act 1998, to address youth crime. 'Tough on the causes of crime' is reflected in the government's 'Welfare-to-Work' programme for the young and long-term unemployed which the Home Secretary hopes will reduce 'both the temptation and opportunity for crime' (Parliamentary Debates 1997: 344).

Penal Policy: Costs, Numbers, and Outcomes

Costs

Crime imposes costs on victims, offenders, their families, and society as a whole. While attempts have been made to quantify the physical and emotional costs of crime for compensation purposes, the clearest financial cost is expenditure on the criminal justice system itself. This is shown in Table 17.6.

In addition, the Government spends a considerable amount of money on crime prevention, about three-quarters of which is spent by the Department of the Environment on urban and estate regeneration programmes.

Regarding sentencing, comparisons of the average net operating costs of custodial

Agency	Expenditure (£ million)	% of total expenditure
Police	6,498	65
Prisons	1,679	16
Lord Chancellor's department	744	7
Probation service	491	5
Magistrates' court	416	4
Crown prosecution service	297	3
Total	10,125	100

Table 17.6 Expenditure on the criminal justice system 1995/6

Source: *Criminal Justice Key Statistics, England and Wales* (London: Government Statistical Service, Jan. 1996).

sentences per inmate per month with community sentences always show custody to be more expensive; figures for 1995/6 were £1,776 per month in adult male prisons (NACRO 1997a: 9) compared with £180 for a supervision order, £190 for a probation order, and £140 for a community service order (NACRO 1997a: 14). It is important to remember that these figures are based on actual costs—the marginal cost of sending one more person into a prison at or near capacity is actually much smaller than the above figures suggest.

What is not included in official Home Office figures is any attempt to put a price on the human costs of imprisonment. Sir Alexander Paterson, an extremely influential member of the Prison Commission, wrote, 'Men (*sic*) come to prison *as* a punishment, not *for* punishment' (Ruck 1951: 13), but the prison environment continues to be a punishing one; in addition to cramped and unhygienic physical conditions, prisoners face bullying, drug misuse, and physical attack, including racist and sexual assaults (NACRO 1997b: 10). In 1997–8, there were 72 self-inflicted deaths in prison, including nine among young people aged under 21 and three women (NACRO 1998b: 9). When imprisoned, even for a short time, people may lose their homes, their employment, their family, and social ties. Additional, unquantifiable costs are suffered by prisoners' families.

Numbers

Prison is the most severe penalty available to the courts. Life imprisonment is reserved for the most serious offences, and is mandatory for murder and certain other grave offences (Crime [Sentences] Act 1997). Magistrates' courts can impose no more than six months imprisonment for any one offence, up to a maximum of twelve months, and the majority of custodial sentences are made at the Crown Court. The number of persons sentenced to custody rose until 1985 when it fell steadily until 1992. From 1993 onwards it began to rise rapidly, with the rate of increase for women being twice that of men (Penal Affairs Consortium 1996: 2).

In 1997, the average prison population in England and Wales reached a record 61,000 —greater than any previous year (Home Office 1998). The average female and sentenced young offender populations increased by 19 per cent and 17 per cent respectively (Home Office 1998). A disproportionate number of prisoners came from minority ethnic groups: on 30 June 1997 the figure was 19 per cent, comprising 18 per cent of the male and 24 per cent of the female populations (Home Office 1998). The large numbers of female foreign nationals imprisoned for drug trafficking contributes to the particularly high figure for women.

The prison population is made up of **remand** and **sentenced** prisoners. In 1994 the remand population accounted for approximately one-quarter of the total prison population (Home Office 1995a: 48). Twenty-nine per cent of women and 44 per cent of men remanded in custody in 1994 subsequently received a custodial sentence (Penal Affairs Consortium 1996: 2), raising the question of whether their detention was necessary in the first place. Fine defaulters add to the prison population and are held in custody for an average of about one week. There were an average of 141 fine defaulters in prison in 1997, compared to 180 in 1996 and 516 in June 1995. The main reason for the reduction in numbers is a 1995 Appeal Court judgment which clarified the requirements for courts to consider all methods of enforcement before committing a fine defaulter to prison (NACRO 1998a: 8).

Custody represented 17 per cent of sentences in 1994, with the fine and discharge making up 51 per cent of sentences between them. A further 28 per cent were **community orders** enforced predominantly by the Probation Service, but also by Social Services in the Youth Court. There was a 24 per cent increase in the use of **community sentences** as a whole between 1985 and 1994 (Home Office 1995a: 40). The use of the curfew order with electronic monitoring is set to increase with pilots in Manchester, Norfolk, and Berkshire showing that more than 80 per cent of offenders had successfully completed their curfew order, and sentencers liking the immediate detection of breach (NACRO 1997c: 15).

Outcomes

Two of the factors most closely associated with reconviction are age and gender; about two-thirds of offenders aged under 21 are reconvicted within two years of the date of conviction, compared with about half for those aged over 21. About 56 per cent of males are reconvicted within two years, as compared with 40 per cent of females. Previous criminal history is also found to be a good predictor of reconviction (Home Office 1995a: 60).

In considering the extent to which different punishments may affect future offending, 53 per cent of prisoners discharged from prison in 1993 were reconvicted within two years and 57 per cent of persons receiving a community sentence were reconvicted within two years. Statistical data therefore appear to demonstrate no significant difference between reconviction rates for custody and community penalties and were used by David Maclean MP, then Minister of State at the Home Office, to demonstrate 'positive proof that prison works'.

Statistics, as previously discussed, have to be handled with care; some of the reconvictions were for offences committed prior to the start of community orders, and therefore are unconnected with the effectiveness or otherwise of the order to influence further offending. Younger offenders, with a higher likelihood of reconviction, are more likely to be given community sentences early on, thus increasing rates of reconviction for community penalties.

Varieties of European Experience

There has been increasing interest in European experiences of crime and crime control. Some of the experiences reflect a more liberal approach to crime, justice, and punishment, especially in relation to the use of imprisonment. With opportunities for cross-border crime increasing in recent years, the need for co-operation between European nation states, including Britain, will increase. Particular crimes targeted as being of common concern include political violence and terrorist attacks, drug dealing, and organized business crime.

Countries throughout Europe have very different historical and cultural experiences. In France, transportation to the French colonies only ended in 1938. Spain did not begin its transition into democracy until after the death of Franco in 1975. Sweden's long-standing welfare-based social system is reflected in its humane penal policy. The Netherlands is beginning to question its reputation as having the most liberal and humanitarian criminal justice system in Europe. The opening up of Eastern European countries to the west, and the ending of strict state control, is having an impact on crime and crime control in those countries.

Varieties of Crime Control

While comparing statistics across national boundaries, each with different legal definitions and measurement of crime rates, is difficult, evidence suggests that crime rates have increased throughout most European countries since the Second World War. Without access to Eastern European data, this has been most noticeable in the West but, with capitalist economies replacing socialism, these countries are now beginning to experience rising crime rates. Increased crime has resulted in an increase in sentences of imprisonment and countries have demonstrated some imaginative policies. In the mid-1970s Norway introduced a 'waiting system' for less serious offenders sentenced to imprisonment. In 1982 Denmark reduced maximum sentences for property crimes and liberalized the rules concerning drunken driving. In 1983, Sweden introduced a system of parole halfway through a prison sentence for all but the most serious cases. Shorter sentences of imprisonment are the norm for many European countries, resulting in the paradox that Britain can sentence proportionately fewer people to imprisonment but still have a larger prison population.

Varieties of Prison Populations

Prison populations reflect criminalization processes. While large numbers of unemployed, poor, and homeless persons are routinely incarcerated throughout Europe, two specific groups are worth particular mention—women and minority ethnic groups, both indigenous and from different countries of origin. While the conviction and prosecution of women is still far below that of men there are indications throughout

Europe that increasing numbers are being sentenced to imprisonment and for longer (Ruggiero, Ryan, and Sim 1995: 13–15). As Maureen Cain (1989) demonstrates, a process of attempting to regulate, discipline, and normalize women and girls through criminal justice processes can be recognized across Western Europe. There is evidence of similar controls being applied to minority ethnic groups. 'Fortress Europe' (Christie 1993: 68–71) works to keep out the impoverished and marginalized, while policing heavily and imprisoning those groups inside whose lifestyles are believed to threaten order and stability—most notably immigrants (legal and illegal), asylum seekers, refugees, guest workers, and foreigners (Ruggiero, Ryan and Sim 1995: 10–13).

Varieties of Alternative Responses to Imprisonment

Three particular experiences show the range and variety of practice in Europe. The Netherlands maintained a steadily decreasing prison population between 1950 and 1975, despite rising crime rates, through achieving a culture of 'tolerance' (Downes 1988: 69–74) in which the ineffectiveness of long sentences of imprisonment was generally accepted. In France in the 1980s a social crime prevention initiative made a significant impact on the crime rate; introduced in 1981, older teenagers in ghetto suburbs were recruited to act as paid youth workers with younger teenagers and children. Linked into local and national structures, the initiative forged a link between the situational, social, and political dimensions of crime prevention (Pitts 1996). The West German prison population showed a 10 per cent decrease in the 1980s when many other European countries were experiencing a massive increase. Feest (1991) rules out economic, demographic, and legislative explanations and suggests that the reduction is attributable to changes in the behaviour of prosecutors and judges (1991: 135). He argues that this decrease, while not sustained, demonstrated that a substantial reduction of the prison population is possible without an increase in major crime and, therefore, without jeopardizing public safety.

Trends in European Experience

A shift to the right was experienced in most Western European countries in the 1980s and 1990s which resulted in deterrence-based crime control policies. Increased numbers of people received sentences of imprisonment, sentence length increased, and prison capacity was expanded. While the use of community sentences also increased, as in the UK, this had little or no impact on the prison population, suggesting that these were being used in addition rather than instead of imprisonment (Ruggiero, Ryan and Sim 1995: 3).

Throughout Europe there is evidence that the penal system has been used excessively to resolve all manner of conflicts and social problems which have not found resolution in civil or administrative spheres through effective social policies. Morgan (1997: 1144) states that the rate of imprisonment is not determined by factors beyond government control—it is ultimately a matter of political choice. Despite the fact that prison populations are increasing throughout Europe, the rate of incarceration is still nowhere near that of the United States. Governments are currently having to decide whether the huge costs of an incarcerative penal policy can be sustained, and how, if they decide they cannot, decarcerative strategies can be introduced which will be acceptable to those who voted them into power.

Key Legislation and White Papers

Children and Young Persons Act 1933 An Act of Parliament which clarified the legal distinction between an 'adult' and a 'child' and raised the age of criminal responsibility from 7 to 8 years old. (This was further raised to 10 in 1963, where it has remained). The six parts of the Act addressed a comprehensive range of issues relating to the treatment of children and young persons. These included the prevention of cruelty and exposure to moral and physical danger, the employment of children, and the protection of children and young persons in relation to criminal and summary proceedings. It introduced the provision of remand homes, approved schools, and fit persons for different classifications of children and young persons. Courts dealing with a child or young person, either as an offender or otherwise, were to have regard for his or her welfare and given powers to remove a child or young person from 'undesirable surroundings'.

***The Child, the Family and the Young Offender* (Cmnd. 2742, 1965)** A Home Office White Paper outlining the 'welfarist' approach. This included the radical suggestion that juvenile courts be replaced with local authority 'family councils' and 'family courts' which would deal with cases as far as possible in consultation and agreement with the parents.

***Children in Trouble* (Cmnd. 3601, 1968)** A Home Office White Paper which replaced the 1965 White Paper, *The Child, the Family and the Young Offender*, following widespread criticism of its proposals. It preserved the juvenile court system. The White Paper introduced Intermediate Treatment (I.T.), which developed around a number of community-based programmes including remedial education, work training, community service, group activities, and the development of skills and interests. The White Paper formed the basis of the Children and Young Persons Act 1969.

Children and Young Persons Act 1969 An Act of Parliament designed to implement the welfare-orientated strategy favoured by left-wing policy-makers for juveniles throughout the 1960s. The Act introduced the supervision order and the care order. The latter, effectively an indeterminate sentence to reside in the care of the local authority, was removed as a response to offending by the Children Act 1989. The partial implementation of the 1969 Act was due to the election of a Conservative Government in 1970 and a changing criminal justice climate throughout the 1970s and beyond.

***Young Offenders* (Cm. 8045, 1980)** A Home Office White Paper outlining a series of proposals which demonstrated an apparent commitment to move away from the use of custody and towards community-based measures for young offenders.

The Criminal Justice Act 1982 An Act of Parliament containing certain restrictions on the custodial sentencing of persons under the age of 21 and introducing a new 'supervised activities requirement' to be attached to supervision orders. The Act replaced the semi-determinate sentence of Borstal training with the determinate sentence of youth custody, and reduced the existing detention centre sentence to a minimum of three weeks and a maximum of four months (the 'short, sharp shock'). The Act made provision for community service orders to be made in respect of 16-year-olds.

***Crime, Justice and Protecting the Public* (Cm. 965, 1990)** A Home Office White Paper aiming to obtain better justice through greater consistency in sentencing. Prior to this, courts had been given little advice on sentencing other than the setting of maximum penalties for offences and Court of Appeal decisions. The proposed sentencing framework was based on achieving proportionality between the seriousness of the offence and the subsequent restriction of the offender's liberty. The concept of public protection was central to the White Paper, with the introduction of an explicit twin-track approach whereby sexual and violent offenders were to be sentenced 'beyond desert', and less serious and property offenders were to receive 'punishment in the community'. The White Paper formed the basis of the Criminal Justice Act 1991.

Criminal Justice Act 1991 An Act of Parliament which represented a major development in sentencing law and practice. As set out in the White Paper which preceded it, it attempted to establish proportionality, or just deserts, as the guiding principle for sentencers and introduced a coherent sentencing framework for the use of financial, community, and custodial punishments. It set out new provisions for the release of prisoners and for the supervision of offenders in the community, whether as a sentence or on release from custody. It introduced two new community orders: the combination order (combining a probation order with a community service order) and the curfew order (to which a requirement for electronic monitoring was to be attached). It also renamed the juvenile court the youth court, and raised the age limit to include 17-year-olds.

Criminal Justice Act 1993 An Act of Parliament used to make statutory amendments to the Criminal Justice Act 1991 within a year of the 1991 Act's implementation. The announcement to abolish the system of income-related unit fines was made by the then Home Secretary Kenneth Clarke in May 1993. This was followed by a new Section 29 which stated that, in assessing the seriousness of any offence, previous convictions and any failure to respond to previous sentences could now be taken into account. Section 66 of the 1993 Act effectively deleted the 1991 Act's restriction on sentencers to focus on a maximum of two offences per offender when assessing offence seriousness. In addition, offences on bail were to be treated as an aggravating factor (making more serious) in considering the seriousness of any offence. The consequences of the 1993 Act were to move away from the notion of desert-based sentencing.

Criminal Justice and Public Order Act 1994 An Act of Parliament which addressed a diverse selection of criminal justice issues, including some which had arisen from moral panics throughout 1983. Provisions included the introduction of a new custodial sentence, the secure training order, for 12- to 14-year-olds, the ending of the 'right to silence', the lowering of the age of homosexual consent from 21 to 18, and the extension of the privatization of the prison service. A central feature leading to considerable public protest was the increase in police powers to remove trespassers on land—'squatters', 'new age travellers', 'unauthorized campers', those organizing or attending 'raves', 'hunt saboteurs' and other protesters.

Crime (Sentences) Act 1997 An Act of Parliament which introduced mandatory and minimum custodial sentences for specific serious offences, court powers to make a community service order or curfew order for fine default, and the abolition of the need for the court to seek an offender's consent to a community sentence. Some parts not implemented by the Labour Government.

Crime and Disorder Act 1998 The overall purpose of the Act was to tackle youth crime and, in particular, disorder; to involve victims more in the youth justice system; and to help create safer communities. Multi-agency offending teams, created to provide a more co-ordinated approach, include social workers, probation officers, police officers, and education and health authority staff.

Glossary

British Crime Survey (BCS) A series of large household surveys of people's experiences and perceptions of crime in England and Wales. The first one was undertaken in 1982.

classicism A traditional, punishment-oriented approach to crime most commonly associated with the eighteenth-century Italian philosopher Cesare Beccaria. It emphasizes clarity in the law and due process in criminal procedure, combined with certainty and regularity of punishment. Classicists regard human beings, including offenders, as having free choice and therefore as being deterred from certain acts prohibited by the law by the anticipation of swift and certain punishment.

cognitive-behavioural programmes Individual or groupwork intervention based on a synthesis of methods drawn from behavioural and cognitive psychology which aim to change the way people think about themselves and their environment. Applied to offenders, the programmes attempt to change offenders' attitudes towards their offending behaviour and hence change the behaviour itself.

community orders Court orders making up Community Sentences and encompassing each of the following: a probation order (16 years and over), a community service order, a combination order (combining both a probation order and community service order), a curfew order (with electronic monitoring attached), a supervision order (17 years and under), and an attendance centre order.

community sentences A collective term introduced by the Criminal Justice Act 1991 to describe the tier of sentences between financial penalties and custodial sentences. In addition to community orders, community sentences include attendance centre orders (supervised by the police) and curfew orders (not yet fully implemented in all areas).

criminal justice system The term most commonly used to refer to the group of agencies concerned with different stages in the delivery of criminal justice. These are the Police, the Crown Prosecution Service, the Courts, the Prisons, and the Probation Service. Also referred to as the criminal justice process.

determinate sentence One in which the period is fixed, and made known, in advance.

deviancy amplification spiral A process whereby certain types of youthful deviance arouse public attention, and are focused on by, for example, the media and the police. The activity then appears to increase (and may in fact increase) through heightened awareness, reporting, recording, and research.

indeterminate sentence One which will expire only when a decision to that effect is made, as with life imprisonment.

institutionalist approach An approach to interpreting crime statistics which suggests that they are more a product of the institutions that define and measure crime than 'real' phenomena.

Intermediate Treatment (I.T.) schemes A form of treatment for children and young persons introduced by the Children and Young Persons Act 1969. I.T. provides an intermediate possibility of allowing young persons to remain at home while attending supervised activities designed to have a positive impact on their behaviour rather than their having to enter a residential establishment.

just deserts The classical notion that wrongdoers should be punished in proportion to the harm done—literally that they receive their 'just deserts'. Desert-based sentencing is based on this principle.

justice model An approach which seeks to reduce official discretion in the justice system, and to ensure that like cases are treated alike—punishment to fit the crime, not the criminal.

legal definitions (of crime) The definition of a crime simply as an act defined as criminal by the law, irrespective of how current social values define the act.

moral panic The term used by Stanley Cohen (1972) in *Folk Devils and Moral Panics* to indicate a process of collective over-reaction to a form of apparently widespread deviance. The media initially 'identify' the 'crisis' and the inevitable societal reaction is to demand greater control through increased policing and more retributive law.

positivism Most commonly associated with another Italian, Cesare Lombroso, but in most respects diametrically opposed to the classical school of thought. The positivist school of criminology views crime as caused by factors and processes which can be discovered by observation and scientific investigation. Positivists often subscribe to the doctrine of determinism: that human beings, including criminals, do not act from their own free will but are impelled to act by forces beyond their control.

realist approach An approach to interpreting crime data which suggests that they reflect 'real' trends in criminal behaviour, as opposed to the practices of the institutions that produce this data.

reductive punishment Punishment which seeks to reduce the incidence of the types of behaviour prohibited by the criminal law, whether committed by the person punished (individual deterrence) or by others (general deterrence).

remand prisoners Unconvicted or unsentenced persons committed to custody rather than released on bail pending a further stage of criminal proceedings. The defendant is said to be 'on remand' during the adjournment.

retributive punishment Punishment which sets out to impose an amount of pain proportionate to that caused by the criminal act. The criminal receives his or her 'just deserts'—literally, what is deserved.

sentenced prisoners Persons committed to custody following conviction of a criminal offence in a court of law.

social construction The notion that a phenomenon—in this case crime—is not an objective, observable entity in the world waiting to be discovered, but rather is created (constructed) by social values and preconceptions.

social definitions (of crime) Definitions which are based, not on whether or not an act is against the law (legal definitions) but on the basis of broader social criteria; for example, social values and norms or social justice.

social positivism The positivist belief that the main cause of crime is to be found in social conditions rather than in the biological or psychological make-up of the individual.

supervision order Young persons found guilty of any offence may be ordered by the court to be supervised by the local authority for a maximum of three years. Requirements may be imposed, as to residence or for intermediate treatment, for example.

systems management The collective term for methods developed throughout the 1970s and 1980s to impact positively on rates of juvenile custody, juvenile prosecution, and juvenile crime itself by attending to the mechanics of the criminal justice process. Methods included cautioning panels, discontinuance from prosecution, and Intermediate Treatment.

unit fines system Introduced by the Criminal Justice Act 1991 as a means of reflecting 'equal impact' in financial penalties.

victimology The study of the relationship between victims and offenders. The academic 'discipline' of victimology was founded in the late 1940s.

welfare model Most commonly referred to in the context of juvenile justice to describe a 'positivistic' approach, which holds that young offenders should be helped rather than punished. Transferable to the young adult offender and adult context.

Guide to Further Reading

Mike Maguire, Rod Morgan, and Robert Reiner (eds.) (1997), *The Oxford Handbook of Criminology* (2nd edn., Oxford: Clarendon Press; 1st edn. 1994). Both editions of this handbook contain a number of stimulating articles relating to crime, justice, and punishment. Part II of the 1997 edition addresses the social dimensions of crime, and includes Tim Newburn's 'Youth, Crime, and Justice' and Frances Heidensohn's 'Gender and Crime', which offer excellent overviews of these areas of study. Charles Murray (ed.) (1997), *Does Prison Work?* (London: IEA Health and Welfare Unit) includes Charles Murray's own provocative essay on the subject, alongside three critical responses. Jeffrey Reiman (1995), *The Rich Get Richer and the Poor Get Prison* (4th edn., Needham Heights, Mass.: Allyn & Bacon), is a classic Marxist-oriented account of the American penal system. Sandra Walklate (1998), *Understanding Criminology: Current Theoretical Debates* (Buckingham: Open University Press), is a clear and readable textbook which introduces current debates in criminological theory. Catriona Mirrlees-Black, Tracey Budd, Sarah Partridge, and Pat Mayhew (1998), *The 1998 British Crime Survey, England and Wales* (Home Office Statistical Bulletin, Issue 21/98, London: Home Office) reports on the seventh British Crime Survey, a sample survey of crimes against people in private households in England and Wales which was first conducted in 1982.

References

Audit Commission (1996), *Misspent Youth*, Audit Commission for Local Authorities and National Health Service in England and Wales (London: The Commission).

Bean, P. (1976), *Rehabilitation and Deviance* (London: Routledge and Kegan Paul).

Cain, M. (ed.) (1989), *Growing up Good: Policing the Behaviour of Girls in Europe* (London: Sage Publications).

Cavadino, M. and Dignan, J. (1997), *The Penal System: An Introduction* (2nd edn., London: Sage Publications).

Christie, N. (1993), *Crime Control as Industry* (London: Routledge).

Cohen, S. (1972), *Folk Devils and Moral Panics: The Creation of the Mods and Rockers* (London: MacGibbon and Kee).

——(1985), *Visions of Social Control* (Cambridge: Polity).

Downes, D. (1988), *Contrasts in Tolerance: Post War Penal Policy in the Netherlands* (Oxford: Oxford University Press).

Downes, D. and Morgan, R. (1997), 'Dumping the "Hostages to Fortune"? The Politics of Law and Order in Post-War Britain', in M. Maguire, R. Morgan, and R. Reiner (eds.), *The Oxford Handbook of Criminology* (2nd edn., Oxford: Oxford University Press).

Edwards, S. S. M. (1989), *Policing 'Domestic' Violence: Women, the Law and the State* (London: Sage Publications).

Feest, J. (1991), 'Reducing the Prison Population: Lessons from the West German Experience?', in J. Muncie and R. Sparks, *Imprisonment: European Perspectives* (Hemel Hempstead: Harvester Wheatsheaf).

Garland, D. (1997), 'Of Crimes and Criminals: The Development of Criminology in Britain', in M. Maguire, R. Morgan, and R. Reiner (eds.), *The Oxford Handbook of Criminology* (2nd edn., Oxford: Oxford University Press).

Gelsthorpe, L. and Morris, A. (1994), 'Juvenile Justice 1945–1992', in M. Maguire, R. Morgan, and R. Reiner (eds.), *The Oxford Handbook of Criminology* (Oxford: Oxford University Press).

Goldblatt, P. and Lewis, C. (eds.) (1998), *Reducing Offending: An Assessment of Research Evidence on Ways of Dealing with Offending Behaviour*, Home Office Research Study 187 (London: Home Office).

Home Office (1965), *The Child, the Family and the Young Offender*, Cmnd. 2742 (London: Home Office).

——(1968), *Children in Trouble*, Cmnd. 3601 (London: Home Office).

——(1990), *Crime, Justice and Protecting the Public*. The Government's Proposals for Legislation, Cmnd. 965 (London: HMSO).

——(1995a), *Information on the Criminal Justice System in England and Wales*, Digest 3 (London, HMSO).

——(1995b), *National Standards for the Supervision of Offenders in the Community* (London: HMSO).

——(1997), *Criminal Statistics, England and Wales 1996*, Cmnd. 3764 (London: HMSO).

——(1998), *The Prison Population, 1997*, Home Office Statistical Bulletin Issue 5/98 (London: Home Office).

Hough, M. (1995), *Anxiety About Crime: Findings From the 1994 British Crime Survey*, Home Office Research Study, 147 (London: Home Office).

——and Mayhew, P. (1983), *The British Crime Survey: first report*, Home Office Research Study No. 76 (London: HMSO).

Howard, M. (1993), *Speech by the Rt. Hon. Michael Howard QC MP, the Home Secretary, to the 110th Conservative Party Conference, 6 October* (London: Conservative Party Central Office).

Hudson, B. (1987), *Justice Through Punishment: A Critique of the 'Justice' Model of Corrections* (Basingstoke: Macmillan).

Jones, T., MacLean, B., and Young, J. (1986), *The Islington Crime Survey: Crime, Victimization and Policing in Inner-City London* (Aldershot: Gower).

Labour Party (1997), *New Labour: Because Britain Deserves Better* (London: The Labour Party).

Maguire, M. (1997), 'Crime Statistics, Patterns, and Trends: Changing Perceptions and their Implications', in M. Maguire, R. Morgan, and R. Reiner (eds.), *The Oxford Handbook of Criminology* (2nd edn., Oxford: Oxford University Press).

Major, J. (1994), *Speech by the Prime Minister, Rt. Hon. John Major, MP, at Church House, London, 9 September* (Press Notice: PM's Office).

McGuire, J. (ed.) (1995), *What Works: Reducing Reoffending* (Chichester: Wiley).

McIvor, G. (ed.) (1996), *Working with Offenders*, Research Highlights in Social Work 26 (London: Jessica Kingsley Publishers).

Martinson, R. (1974), 'What Works?—Questions and Answers about Prison Reform', *Public Interest*, 35, Spring.

Maxfield, M. G. (1984), *Fear of Crime in England and Wales*, Home Office Research Study No. 78 (London: HMSO).

Mayhew, P., and Hough, M. (1988), 'The British Crime Survey: Origins and Impact', in M. Maguire and J. Pointing (eds.), *Victims of Crime: a New Deal?* (Milton Keynes: Open University Press).

Mirrlees-Black, C., Budd, T., Partridge, S., and Mayhew, P. (1998), *The 1998 British Crime Survey, England and Wales*, Home Office Statistical Bulletin, Issue 21/98 (London: Home Office).

Morgan, R. (1997), 'Imprisonment, Current Concerns and a Brief History Since 1945', in M. Maguire, R. Morgan, and R. Reiner (eds.), *The Oxford Handbook of Criminology* (2nd edn., Oxford: Oxford University Press).

Murray, C. (1997), *Does Prison Work?* (London: the IEA Health and Welfare Unit).

NACRO (National Association for the Care and Resettlement of Offenders) (1997a), *Criminal Justice Digest*, February (London: NACRO Communications Department).

——(1997b), *Criminal Justice Digest*, April (London: NACRO Communications Department).

——(1997c), *Criminal Justice Digest*, October (London: NACRO Communications Department).

——(1998a), *Criminal Justice Digest*, April (London: NACRO Communications Department).

——(1998b), *Criminal Justice Digest*, July (London: NACRO Communications Department).

Newburn, T. (1997), 'Youth, Crime and Justice', in M. Maguire, R. Morgan, and R. Reiner (eds.), *The Oxford Handbook of Criminology* (2nd edn., Oxford: Oxford University Press).

Parliamentary Debates (1997), *House of Commons 30 July 1997—Criminal Justice* (Hansard), 341–4 (London: HMSO).

Pearson, G. (1983), *Hooligan: A History of Respectable Fears* (London: Macmillan).

Penal Affairs Consortium (1996), *The Imprisonment of Women: Some Facts and Figures*, March (London).

Pitts, J. (1996), 'The Politics and Practice of Youth Justice', in E. McLaughlin and J. Muncie (eds.), *Controlling Crime* (London: Sage Publications/The Open University).

Povey, D., Prime, J., and Taylor, P. (1998), *Notifiable Offences England and Wales, 1997*, Home Office Statistical Bulletin, 7/98 (London: Home Office).

Radford, J. (1987), 'Policing Male Violence—Policing Men', in M. Maynard and J. Hanmer (eds.), *Women, Violence and Social Control* (London: Macmillan).

——and Stanko, E. A. (1996), 'Violence against Women and Children: The Contradictions of Crime Control Under Patriarchy', in M. Hester, L. Kelly, and J. Radford (eds.), *Women, Violence and Male Power* (Buckingham: Open University Press).

Reiman, J. (1995), *The Rich Get Richer and the Poor Get Prison: Ideology, Crime, and Criminal Justice* (5th edn., Boston: Allyn & Bacon).

Ruck, S. K. (ed.) (1951), *Paterson on Prisons* (London: Frederick Muller).

Ruggiero, V., Ryan, M., and Sim, J. (eds.) (1995), *Western European Penal Systems: A Critical Anatomy* (London: Sage Publications).

Rutherford, A. (1989), 'The Mood and Temper of Penal Policy. Curious Happenings in England during the 1980s', *Youth and Policy*, 27.

——(1992), *Growing Out of Crime* (2nd edn., Winchester: Waterside Press).

Stanko, E. A. (1988), 'Hidden Violence Against Women', in M. Maguire and J. Ponting (eds.), *Victims of Crime: A New Deal?* (Milton Keynes: Open University Press).

Von Hirsch, A. (1976), *Doing Justice: The Choice of Punishments* (New York: Hill and Wang).

Walklate, S. (1998), *Understanding Criminology: Current Theoretical Debates* (Buckingham: Open University Press).

Wasik, M. and Taylor, R. D. (1994), *Blackstone's Guide to the Criminal Justice Act 1991* (2nd edn., London: Blackstone).

——(1995), *Blackstone's Guide to the Criminal Justice & Public Order Act 1994* (London: Blackstone Press).

Wilson, J. Q. (1975), *Thinking About Crime* (New York: Basic Books).

Wilson, J. Q. and Herrnstein, R. (1985), *Crime and Human Nature* (New York: Simon and Schuster).

Young, J. (1988), 'Risk of Crime and Fear of Crime: a Realist Critique of Survey-Based Assumptions', in M. Maguire and J. Ponting (eds.), *Victims of Crime: A New Deal?* (Milton Keynes: Open University Press).

Young, J. (1994), 'Incessant Chatter: Recent Paradigms in Criminology', in M. Maguire, R. Morgan, and R. Reiner (eds.), *The Oxford Handbook of Criminology* (Oxford: Oxford University Press).

Young, J. (1997), 'Left Realist Criminology: Radical in its Analysis, Realist in its Policy', in M. Maguire, R. Morgan, and R. Reiner (eds.), *The Oxford Handbook of Criminology* (2nd edn., Oxford: Oxford University Press).

Zedner, L. (1997), 'Victims', in M. Maguire, R. Morgan, and R. Reiner (eds.), *The Oxford Handbook of Criminology* (2nd edn., Oxford: Oxford University Press).

18 The Environment and Green Social Policy

Michael Cahill

Contents

Introduction: The Legacy of Industrialization

It is widely acknowledged today that environmental considerations need to be built into all government policies, into the work of business, the management of the economy, and even into social policy textbooks. The environment has ceased to be the sole concern of the political and academic fringe and become an important policy area. This chapter surveys the rise of environmental and green thinking, shows the ways in which the concept of **sustainability** has been utilized and its connections with social policy, and reviews those policy proposals which could be said to have been informed by green thinking.

Social policies first emerged as responses to the social problems produced by industrialization, a process which simultaneously was making a profound impact upon the natural environment. Industrialization had promised to take humankind out of a period of scarcity, where life was precarious and short, and into an age of plenty. Judged against a historical perspective of centuries, in general this was achieved in the advanced industrial societies of the North, where even the poor live in relative and not subsistence poverty. But it is also the case that the activities of the past 250 years have led to insupportable burdens for the planet. The advances in science, medicine, and telecommunications have been beneficial, but they have been gained at the expense of the natural world. In order to achieve the levels of economic growth witnessed over the last 250 years, the environment has been pillaged: millions of hectares of forests have been removed, the seas and rivers have been used as dumps for chemicals, waste, and other pollutants, and this in turn has meant that the habitats of marine life, birds, and most mammals other than man have been seriously damaged. The continuing world population growth, consequent upon the vast expansion in material wealth, has in turn produced yet greater pressures on the natural environment, leading to increasing demands for food and living space.

During the last half-century the damage to the natural environment wrought by humankind has accelerated. Advances in science and technology have meant that manufactured consumer products are now universally used by people in the industrialized West. Some of these have quite catastrophic impacts upon the natural world: the motor car, for example, symbolizes the consumer society, in that it is privatized and endows its driver with the freedom to travel; but in its manufacture, use, and disposal it consumes vast quantities of water, minerals, and petroleum, and is a major source of environmental pollution (Whitelegg 1997). The first major realization of the impact of humankind's unsustainable activity was the fear in the early 1970s that minerals and natural resources were being depleted at such a rate that the Western way of life would become insupportable. Although the more dire predictions have not yet been borne out, it remains a real probability that resource depletion will just take longer to occur; it is expected that reserves—oil, for example—will be depleted by the middle of the next century rather than, as was earlier forecast, by the end of the 1990s. As the twentieth century draws to a close the risk from environmental hazards—from nuclear waste, from genetic engineering, from contaminated food—has led some social scientists to define ours as a **risk society** (Beck 1992; Giddens 1991). Uncertainty, insecurity, and hazard abound for individuals in a society where traditional ways of acting have come to an end, while the advance of science and technology has meant that nuclear power and genetic engineering, to take two examples, pose risks on a global scale.

Green Parties, Green Pressure Groups, and Social Welfare

The Green Parties which emerged in Western Europe in the 1980s claimed that they were 'neither left nor right but in front'. They offered a political programme which embraced far more than the environmental agenda, having policies on health services, income maintenance, and the other traditional areas of political controversy. Although Greens achieved some limited success in countries which have a proportional representation system, in the UK the Green Party has never polled more than 1 per cent of the vote at general elections (Carter 1997). In retrospect, its vote of 14.9 per cent in the 1989 European elections in England and Wales was an aberration. In this country the running on environmental policy has been made by green pressure groups which boast large memberships. Greenpeace has a membership of over 300,000 and Friends of the Earth of over 200,000, while the membership of the Green Party is now around 5,000, having fallen from a peak of 20,000 in 1990 (Green Party Press Office 1998; Garner 1996). Friends of the Earth and Greenpeace, both radical environmental groups, have moved over the last five years from a position of being outsiders to insiders in the policy networks. Friends of the Earth has shifted its stance to include discussion of broader social as well as environmental policies (Lamb 1996). At the 1997 General Election, the Real World Coalition brought together more than thirty voluntary and campaigning bodies, including third-world charities such as The Save the Children Fund, Christian Aid, and Oxfam, together with voluntary organizations such as the Town and Country Planning Association, as well as Friends of the Earth, on a platform of action against poverty in the UK and in support of sustainable policies worldwide. Although it did not have an impact on the General Election of 1997 it augurs a new campaigning coalition and a merger of environmental and social concerns (Jacobs 1996).

There has been a corresponding shift in the stance of the major political parties and the political culture in the UK. As the environment has now become part of mainstream politics, it was noticeable that there was no great difference between the positions of the Labour Party and the Conservative Party in their 1997 General Election manifestos, although the Liberal Democrats have, it is true, a much harder-edged approach. In 1988 the Conservative Prime Minister, Mrs Thatcher, transformed the Conservative government's approach to the environment with a speech to the Royal Society in which she identified global warming as a serious international problem. Another decisive change occurred in 1992 when, following the Rio Summit, the UK Government headed by John Major committed itself to **sustainable development** across all policy areas. Since then the government has published an annual statement on progress towards sustainable development (see, for example, Department of the Environment 1996). The Department of the Environment, Transport and the Regions formed by the new Labour government in 1997 was designed to give environmental considerations a much greater prominence in the work of the merged department.

Much environmental policy in the UK is concerned with regulation and standard setting in the areas of water, energy, wildlife, and nature conservation. This is implemented through the work of the Environment Agency, a government quango, whose role is 'to protect or enhance the environment, taken as a whole, as to make the contribution towards attaining the objective of achieving sustainable development that Ministers consider appropriate' (Environment Agency 1997: 5). It started work in 1996, and has taken over the responsibilities previously carried out by the National Rivers Authority and Her Majesty's Inspectorate of Pollution.

Any picture of consensus across the political spectrum on sustainability would be misleading. There is much debate as to the meaning and consequent priorities of sustainability: should primacy be given to state or market in achieving sustainability; can sustainability coexist with the present national degree of commitment to the consumer society and the existing distribution of income and wealth? 'Sustainable development', defined by the Brundtland Commission as 'development which meets the needs of the present without compromising the ability of future generations to meet their own needs' (World Commission on the Environment 1987) became a popular term in the 1990s because it embraced aspirations for conservation with an apparent acceptance of the importance of economic growth. Within the concept lies the important commitment to 'inter-generational equity'. Given this expansive, all-embracing definition it could not fail to win favour. Since then employers, government agencies, and pressure groups have all sprayed 'sustainable' on to policies and titles. But what are today's environmental needs and who should define them? Similar questions lie at the heart of social policy debates where there is, in particular, a developed body of literature on the difference between wants and needs (see Chapter 6).

Ecological modernization is an increasingly influential theme in the politics of environmental problems. This is the argument that the environmental restructuring necessary for sustainability can occur within capitalist economies, but will require widespread industrial change. The tools of industrial management can be utilized to achieve more environmentally benign economic behaviour. These would involve recycling, much greater use of renewable energy sources, and shifts from industrial activity which has a major impact on the environment to that which has a much smaller impact, like the service sector (see Weale 1992). Pollution abatement, renewable energy, and environmental management are all areas where new jobs can be created. Stricter environmental regulations in the UK will mean that there is the domestic incentive for UK firms to develop the requisite technology which can then be sold abroad (Tindale 1996).

Although there is a growing international consensus that global warming, species extinction, and holes in the ozone layer (to name but three major environmental problems) are serious threats to the future of the human race, the scientific evidence does not all point in the same way, and there is a body of opinion within social science which treats environmental claims with considerable scepticism. The rationale of capitalist society is to provide for the needs of the population, and many would claim that this it has done spectacularly well in raising the standard of living of countries around the globe (see, for example, Saunders 1995). Many Greens, however, would argue that consumer capitalism manufactures needs in order to stimulate production, and this is being done at the expense of the world's poorest people. Moreover, despite the undoubted success of capitalism, the fact remains that it is the richest 20 per cent of the world's population, mostly in the industrialized countries, who consume over 80 per cent of the world's resources. Because the population of the industrialized world has had a hugely disproportionate impact upon the natural environment it may have put the very survival of the industrial way of life at risk.

Green Ideologies

There are many varieties of environmentalism with a continuum in green thinking from the **ecocentric** to the **technocentric** (Pepper 1996), from **dark green** to **light green** (Porritt 1984; Dobson 1995), from **deep ecology** to shallow ecology (Naess 1988), or, as the German Greens say, from fundamentalist to realist positions (Hulsberg 1987). The terms may vary, but the continuum is essentially from revolutionary through radical to reformist. Contemporary ecological thought also contains elements of anarchism and decentralization, and this is hardly surprising, because as long as there has been industrialization there have been forms of opposition to it to be found in all the UK political parties (see Bramwell 1989).

Indeed, there is much debate as to whether the Greens do represent a new ideology at all. Granted, their concerns are new: previous generations did not know the environmental impact that their car journeys were making, or were not able to take their holidays in their millions on the other side of the planet. Although there was concern among a small number of natural scientists and ecologists, there was not the popular interest that has emerged in the last two decades. Today one of the defining characteristics of the ecocentric Greens is their commitment to the earth and the planet, and the insistence that humans are but one species. This means that many believe that change can only come about if there is a change of heart and change of way of life among the population. As a result some in the Green parties are not wholehearted about their political engagement, believing that being a Green is more a way of life than merely being a member of a political party.

Population size is a major concern for many environmentalists, and one of the best-known arguments was developed by Garrett Hardin: 'the tragedy of the commons'. The simple but effective analogy is with the practice before the enclosure movement, when common land was used for grazing. The common land was intended to be shared by a small number of cattle. It was in the interests of each individual to bring as many cattle as possible onto the land; but the net result of this was overgrazing and the decline in quality of the land. Hardin argues we have the same problem today, but on a world scale. There are too many people in the world, and, by extension, we are overburdening not just the land but also the sea and the air. His arguments are neo-**malthusian,** in that he believes that we have to stop giving a 'lifeline' to people in the poorer world, and allow them to starve to death. The 'tragedy of the commons' highlights the immense strains that we are putting on our planet; but an obvious rejoinder is that the industrialized countries, particularly in their consumer capitalist phase, are putting much more strain on the resources of the planet than the people of the south (Hardin 1968).

'Ecofeminism' is another strand in recent green thinking. It makes a strong connection between the exploitation of the natural world and the exploitation and undervaluing of women. Ecofeminists share the belief that the natural world is but one, and that human beings are a part of nature. Arguing that women have always been closer to nature than men, ecofeminists believe that women's subordination is linked with the treatment of nature (Mellor 1997).

'Ecosocialism' is to be found in many different varieties, ranging from those in the Labour Party who are green, to those in the Green Party who are socialists. However, most ecosocialists in the UK are members of neither party, and are more likely to be in pressure groups. Ecosocialism attributes the parlous state of the world's environment to the depredations of the market system and suggests that it is capitalism which needs to be overthrown if the planet is to be saved from destruction. In many ways it is the successor to the revolutionary movements that were so popular among students in the 1960s; it offers a goal for the future rooted in an implacable opposition to contemporary capitalism. Its best-known exponents were to be found among the West German Greens, principally within its fundamentalist tendency, and in the writings of the late

Rudolph Bahro (Bahro 1982, 1986). The German Greens since their inception in 1980 have been an alliance between the non-aligned left, peaceniks, and feminists. 'Ecology is only a factor in their identity' (Jahn in Jacobs 1997: 175). Many ecosocialists draw upon Marxism for their understanding of environmental problems, believing that it is within the social relationships of capitalist society that change must be effected, rather than focusing on lifestyle change among the mass of the population. They argue that industrial progress can go further without damage to the environment, but only if it is within the context of a society organized around the common ownership of the means of production (Ryle 1988; Pepper 1993).

Green conservatism is not an especially prominent aspect of contemporary thinking on the environment. Conservative ideas, however, pervade much thinking about the environment, although this is in the sense of conservation rather than political conservatism with a large C. The political philosopher John Gray has elaborated a basis for green conservatism in his book *Beyond the New Right: Markets, Governments and the Natural Environment* (Gray 1993) in which he explores the limitations of the market in dealing with environmental issues.

Local Agenda 21

Local Agenda 21, a resolution which emerged from the Rio Earth Summit in 1992, aims to make sustainable development a reality in localities. It is about people and their interaction with the environment, taking as its focus the work of the local authority and the range of responsibilities that it has: for example, environmental health, transport, recycling, and energy are core areas of LA 21 activity. In this way environmental issues are now being integrated with other policy areas, with a stress on how people and their actions can improve or damage the environment. In the UK local authorities have reviewed their activities in the light of the principles of sustainability; many have implemented environmental audits, while others have integrated the Local Agenda 21 process into their system of corporate management. Some councils have drawn up indicators which will measure progress towards local sustainability. These generally cover two areas: those that measure the quality of the environment and the way in which the local authority can respond to the stresses on it; and those which measure environmental efficiency in areas such as transport, industry, and energy (Selman 1996; Buckingham-Hatfield 1998). Local authorities have on the whole been sensitive to the ways in which these indicators can be constructed. There has been an awareness that it is easy to ignore the views of those who do not naturally participate in environmental policy-making, but who are concerned about the environment: that is to say, the great majority of the population! Recent research has revealed that most people have not even heard of the concept of sustainability (Macnaghten *et al.* 1995).

The thrust of Local Agenda 21 enables issues of access and inequality to be encompassed in the drive for sustainability. Lancashire County Council has incorporated social objectives in its green audit. One of the indicators that it has used in its review of the population of Lancashire is the percentage who live more than one kilometre from five basic services: post office, primary school, food shop, GP surgery, and bus stop. In this way the concept of accessibility is operationalized. A key link between sustainable development and social policy issues is the concept of 'quality of life'.

Box 18.1 Key areas of action in the Local Agenda 21 process

Three areas for action within the local authority

Managing and improving the local authority's own environmental performance

- corporate commitment
- staff training and awareness raising
- environmental management systems and budgeting
- cross-sectoral policy integration

Integrating sustainable development aims into the local authority's policies and activities

- green housekeeping
- land use planning, transport, housing, and economic development
- tendering and purchasing
- tourism and visitor strategies
- health, welfare, equal opportunities, and poverty strategies
- explicitly 'environmental' services

Awareness-raising and education

- support for environmental education and voluntary groups
- visits, talks, and awareness-raising events
- publication of local information and press releases
- initiatives to encourage behaviour change and practical action

Three areas for action within the wider community

Consulting and involving the general public

- public consultation processes
- forums, focus groups, and feedback mechanisms
- 'planning for real' and parish maps

Partnerships

- meetings, workshops, conferences, roundtables, working/advisory groups
- Environment City model
- partnership initiatives
- developing-world partnerships and support

Measuring, monitoring, and reporting on progress towards sustainability

- environmental monitoring and state of environment reporting
- sustainability indicators and targets
- environmental impact assessment and strategic environmental assessment

Source: Based on Table 5.4 in Selman (1996).

Quality of life is a slippery concept, but is used in discussions of sustainability to refer to the environmental and social goods which lie outside market regulation (see Jackson 1996; Offer 1996; Seed and Lloyd 1997). It can embrace the proximity of public libraries as well as bus stops, or even the very existence of public libraries. 'Quality of life' is subjective: it will be interpreted differently from one individual to the next. People in Lancashire were asked to define what they meant by 'quality of life', and they responded by choosing the following: having a more local job, not having to worry about money, better relationships with friends and family, more community spirit, and better amenities, especially for children (Lancashire County Council 1997). Similarly, in Leicester 'quality of life' has been central to Agenda 21 policy being interpreted as a sense of community which 'supports individuals, supports a diverse and vibrant local economy, meets the needs of food and shelter and gives access to fulfilling work that is of benefit to the community' (Selman 1996: 106). For many people their quality of life is better measured by the number and range of consumer durables which they possess, and this is perhaps the dominant view in our society. When questioned, however, people agree that for them public amenities such as parks, libraries, and public conveniences are also part of their quality of life. These are what economists call 'social goods', for they are enjoyed in common and have to be provided collectively, unless one is very rich indeed (Jacobs 1997). The extent to which the mass of the population can be mobilized in support of these social goods, such as when they are threatened by developers or roadbuilders, is unpredictable because the values of individual self-advancement and private consumption are often stronger. There is none the less a widespread perception that there has been an erosion of the 'quality of life' in our society despite the increases in personal consumption.

The New Economics Foundation argue that there has been a decline in the quality of life in the UK over the last 25 years, and has attempted to measure this. Their **Index of Sustainable Economic Welfare** (ISEW) uses the volume of consumer expenditure as the main constituent of the Gross Domestic Product (GDP) and then makes additions and subtractions based on such factors as increased traffic congestion, resource depletion, and positive additions such as unpaid household labour. The ISEW measure, unlike GDP, also takes account of environmental factors, for example, by building in a measure for the depletion of North Sea oil and the impact of climate change. The ISEW has fallen by around 22 per cent since 1980 in the UK. The UK's per capita GDP is 2.5 times greater in real terms in 1996 than it was in 1950, an average year-on-year growth of 2 per cent. But the level of the ISEW is only up by 31 per cent on the 1950 figure (Friends of the Earth/New Economics Foundation 1997; Jackson *et al.* 1998). Clearly the environmental measures used by the New Economics Foundation can be contested, but their arguments also demonstrate weaknesses in conventional measures of the standard of living and social welfare.

These arguments are an example of a growing body of work which attempts to construct a 'new economics' where basic human needs are not measured only by indices of material consumption. In conventional economics consumption has been seen as a proxy for welfare. Green economists define welfare in terms of the satisfaction of basic human needs and wants, building on the work of Maslow (1954), who argued that material needs have first to be satisfied before the human wants of love, truth, and

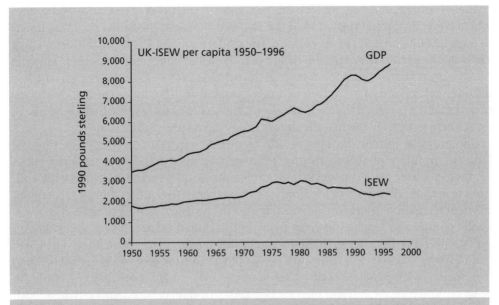

Figure 18.1 The Index of Sustainable Economic Welfare in the UK

Source: Friends of the Earth/New Economics Foundation (1997), *Quality of Life Briefing Paper No. 3* (London).

justice can be met. The Chilean economist Max Neef has expanded on this list to include affection, understanding, participation, identity, idleness, creativity, and freedom (Max Neef 1992; Jackson 1995).

Work, Paid Employment, and the Green Policy Agenda

In pursuing their arguments, Greens and the 'new economists' have also contributed to a reassessment of the value of work and production in the creation of welfare (Robertson 1989). In European Union countries there are over 20 million unemployed people who are not in the formal labour market. The way in which advanced industrial countries have moved from being primarily manufacturing economies to becoming primarily service-sector economies has meant that many unskilled jobs have disappeared. In our post-industrial society employment has been transformed by the massive restructuring generated by globalization and the technological revolution of the last two decades. In the process millions of jobs have been lost in labour-intensive industries as machines have replaced people or as jobs have moved to cheaper countries. The decline in manufacturing industry has reduced the number of jobs for unskilled, particularly male, workers: the male family breadwinner has been consigned to the dustbin of history. At the same time consumerism has ensured that the attachment to paid work as a source of cash and hence identity has permeated all sections of society.

The crisis of growing unemployment goes right to the heart of the industrial system which has transformed the world in the past two centuries, revealing the attachment to wage labour which lies at the centre of the modern economic system. Job losses affect not only the person who loses his or her job: the wider community loses not only the purchasing power in that area, but often the benefits of the job that was axed. The loss of the park-keeper means that there is more vandalism. The loss of the bus conductor means that some older and infirm people cannot use the bus because there is no one to assist them in the (for them) difficult task of getting on and off the vehicle.

One proposal to remedy this position is to better distribute work by limiting the hours of the full-time workers in order to create more jobs in the economy. However, as yet there has been little support for this among the workforce. The obsession with work can mean that other parts of life time spent together with families, hobbies, pastimes, physical recreation, sport—are all downgraded in the individual's priorities. The work-aholic culture has reached its high point in the United States of America, where on average workers have fewer holidays and work longer hours than their European counterparts. The fixation with work is part of the consumerism that pervades American society, with people working long hours in order to get more money in order to buy consumer goods and durables (Schor 1992). In dual-earner families where both parents are working full-time there is much less time for the children, with the result that caring services have to be bought by the parents in the form of nannies, au pairs, and others. In the USA the amount of time spent in parent–child interaction has decreased (Etzioni 1995). It is argued that similar trends are becoming apparent in the UK (Leach 1994). In 1997 the number of women in the UK workforce overtook the number of men for the first time. Now some contemporary feminist writers have begun to question seriously the feminist strategy of putting emphasis on waged work as a means of achieving sex equality, when it has led to a devaluing of motherhood for women and increasingly frantic lives for both sexes (Benn 1998).

The indices used to track our economy do not measure the amount of unpaid work. Therefore it is not included in the value of the Gross Domestic Product, yet calculations show that it is a considerable amount of labour. The increased role of women in formal employment has meant that their unpaid family labour is more apparent, especially in those households which pay for this work to be performed by purchasing childcare or cleaning services. The market now provides the goods and services which are needed by those with little time. For example, many working people think that cooking meals from fresh ingredients is too lengthy a process after the working day, and there has been a large increase in the amount of convenience food sold.

Given the fact that the labour market will not be able to fulfil the demand for employment either in the present or in the foreseeable future, the arguments of greens and others for a revaluation of work are coming to be seen as more relevant. Basic Income, often known as Citizen's Income, is one of the most powerful of the policy proposals popularized by the Greens in the 1980s, and has now been taken up by many others, both on the left and the right. Briefly, this is an income which will be paid to all citizens, irrespective of their age. For children it would replace child benefit, and for older people it would replace the retirement pension. The attractions of Basic Income are that it will get rid of many social security benefits, and most particularly means-tested benefits. The income would be paid to all, irrespective of whether they were in work or not. Their savings, other income, or marital status would not affect the payment.

Basic Income is intended to give everyone the opportunity to work in the economy in the way in which they want. It recognizes the value of unpaid work—domestic labour and caring work—by giving those who perform this work a wage. It acknowledges the value of low-paid work, often carried out for community purposes, by providing a supplement that will enable people to be able to afford to do it. Additionally, Basic Income is an increasingly useful tool in the employment market of the late twentieth century, where part-time work has multiplied at the expense of full-time jobs. The problems regarding its implementation lie in the area of cost, how it will be possible to afford the income, and the level at which the income should be set. Clearly it is an extremely contentious proposal, for it goes against the grain of the emerging bipartisan consensus on social security and employment summarized in the phrase 'welfare to work'. Among the main objections to a universal Basic Income without qualification is that it would offend notions of fairness, the very same principle which makes some kinds of social security fraud so unpopular. The Commission on Social Justice called for a 'Participation income', a variation on Basic Income which tackles the problem of 'getting something for nothing' by requiring some evidence of participation, either by having caring responsibilities or being 'available for work' (Commission on Social Justice 1994). Another fundamental objection is that the Basic Income is predicated upon a redistribution of resources from one citizen to another which will require a state with tax-raising and tax-spending powers, something that the anarchist wing of the Greens want to rule out. Basic Income has been around as an idea (under other names) since the 1920s, long before the current wave of green thinking.

Other proposals espoused by Greens are of much more recent provenance. Local Exchange Trading Schemes (LETS) have proliferated, particularly in the USA, Canada, and the UK. These are token economies which enable services and work to be performed for tokens or credits which can then be used to obtain other services. Members of the schemes themselves decide who they are going to exchange their tokens with and for which services. The coverage of these schemes is haphazard in the UK and they have not made major inroads into local economies. One study of five LETS in the UK found that about 40 per cent of the activities were domestic work and all could have been paid for in cash (Seyfang, cited in O'Riordan 1997: 18). LETS schemes do, however, constitute an acknowledgement of the amount of work which goes on outside the formal economy.

Community enterprise schemes aim to provide work in areas which are run down and have suffered greatly from the restructuring of the British economy over the past two decades. These areas are characterized by high unemployment, poor housing, underperforming schools, and poor public transport. They are often in inner-city areas or outer 'sink' estates. Credit Unions are a key form of community enterprise. Financial exclusion is linked to social exclusion: it is estimated that 26 per cent of people have no current account with a bank or a building society. 'The groups without bank accounts tend to be women, the young, the old, the unemployed, those both in low-paid jobs and more likely to live in rented accommodation' (Conaty and Mayo 1997). Credit Unions offer saving facilities for those who are outside the traditional banking system, providing loans at low interest to their members. The rules of Credit Unions generally require members to live and work locally (Pearce 1993).

Ecological Tax Reform

Taxation is at the heart of social policy. It allows the state resources to redistribute between citizens if it so chooses and permits it sufficient income to provide services for those citizens. Taxes are raised in a variety of ways: on incomes, in the form of social insurance contributions, on sales of goods in shops, and on imports of goods into the country. Fifty per cent of taxes in the European Union are taxes on employment (Tindale 1997). Greens argue that if governments want to move towards more sustainable policies then they have to consider changing the nature of taxation. Given the fact that all governments wish to encourage the level of employment, then taxes on a 'good' such as a job should be reduced, while taxes on 'bads' such as pollution should be increased. There is an additional benefit claimed for pollution and environmental taxes, namely that they could enable the reduction of taxes on employment, such as National Insurance in the UK. Thus there would be a 'double dividend' of more employment, and the cost to employers of an extra worker would fall.

Clearly poor people might need protection from such changes. Pollution taxes can be socially regressive, that is to say, they may fall most heavily on those who are least able to bear the cost. This can be illustrated by one of the most debated examples of an ecological tax proposal—a continuing and substantial increase in the tax on petrol. Such a tax would penalize those who live in rural and semi-rural areas where there is no alternative for many people to using the car if they wish to reach their work and other amenities. Proponents of ecological taxation admit the force of this argument, and propose that payments should be made to such motorists to compensate them for the extra costs which they would have to bear. However, this is not the only tax that could be levied in support of an environmentally friendly transport policy. It is widely acknowledged that the existence of free parking at work has been one of the major reasons why the use of the car has greatly increased for commuter journeys over the last twenty years. Taxing employers for this parking space would, if it was passed onto the employee, discourage the use of the car for these journeys. Those on low incomes are clearly hit the hardest when domestic fuel taxation is increased, and the state would need to protect them with rebates and by subsidizing better standards of insulation in the home.

The green perspective on health policy is a preventive one, with an emphasis on clean environments, alternative medicine, and reducing pollution levels (Draper 1991). The new emphasis on public health by the Labour government reinforces the links between health and other policy areas, particularly housing. Housing represents a major area where the impact of environmental 'goods' and 'bads' can be seen. Houses and the households that live in them use a great deal of energy and generate considerable waste: energy and materials are used to construct the houses in the first place; they use a range of fuels for lighting, heating, cooking, and the running of the household appliances; and the occupants produce waste that has to be disposed of. These are all areas where environmental gains and losses are considerable, and where social policies can seek a better balance (Bhatti, Brooke, and Gibson 1994). The growth in household formation has highlighted the conflict between protection of the green belt and the desire of many house buyers to live in country locations. The Department of the Environment has estimated that housing for another 4.4 million extra households will be required by 2016 but, as McLaren *et al.* note, 'While car travel is cheap, demand for detached and semi-detached country homes remains high' (McLaren *et al.* 1998: 129).

A major area for environmental taxation is water consumption. Water is a precious asset, vital for human beings and all life forms on the planet, yet in the Western industrialized countries it is used profligately. There are now well-worked-out policies to cut back on water use: a combination of water metering and different tariffs for different household sizes. Here again low-income consumers need protection. Water tariffs need to be designed so that where there is extra demand in a household, it can be compensated for; for example, those receiving child benefit could claim an additional allowance (Herrington in O'Riordan 1997). In 1994 almost 2 million households defaulted on their water bills, 9 per cent of all households in Britain (Herbert and Kempson 1995). A great many of these were either on low incomes or on social assistance.

Conclusion: How New is Green Social Policy?

Green perspectives are usually concerned with welfare in the widest sense: green writing has been hostile to the notion of the welfare state, drawing on a tradition of anarchism with its critiques of large-scale, bureaucratic state structures. From this perspective the idea of the welfare state is a contradiction in terms. Welfare and community care should come from the activities of families, friends, and the local community. Professionals can all too easily become disempowering, removing the capacity of men and women to help themselves. Greens believe that individuals and communities need to define their needs for themselves. Much of this thinking is not new or different from mainstream social policy ideas on community development, although some versions of community enterprise are 'greener' than others. Recently it has been suggested that Paul Hirst's vision of an 'associative democracy', where self-governing community organizations become the primary forms for political life and public services and the state becomes secondary, are a possible 'greenprint' for community development (Achterburg, in Doherty and de Geus 1996; Hirst 1994).

In most areas of social policy the green perspective offers nothing new in the sense of policy ideas. Any novelty comes from the priority which it accords an environmental perspective. To some extent this is because the practice of those who work in and those who direct the welfare state is still conducted within a framework of everyday institutions—hospitals, social services departments, and social security offices—which are predicated upon profligate use of energy. This is especially the case with the car, a technology which has transformed the practice of welfare state professionals but on the other hand made some vital facilities expensive and time-consuming to visit for the carless. Among these we can number not only the poorest and many disabled people but also all children and many adults. Hillman *et al.* have shown how the right of children to walk the streets safely to school has been largely removed in this country (Hillman, Adams, and Whitelegg 1990) but the rights and welfare of the carless in general have been severely curtailed by the hegemony of the motor vehicle, thus contributing to a decline in their welfare.

The green perspective will not change whole areas of policy. However, the commitment to sustainable development at both local and central government level means that the debate is now beginning to concern itself with the 'how' rather than the 'why' of sustainability. The discourse around 'quality of life' does have the potential to link environmental issues and social policy. For example, community care services are going to be needed in a society informed by environmental considerations just as much as the present capitalist society, though their nature and form will change. Sustainability implies a commitment to local services on grounds of energy-saving and access. As we have seen, in the example quoted earlier of Lancashire County Council, how far people have to travel to services, the mobility cost of access, is important. For social service departments to take this seriously would mean returning to the ideas of local patch organization recommended by Roger Hadley twenty years ago (Brown, Hadley, and White 1982).

Ecological citizenship is promoted by some Greens as a way for populations in the advanced industrial societies to remember their obligations to the poor world and hence to restrain their consumption: 'to live more simply so that others may simply live'. The twenty-first century could mean that 'First world communities . . . will need to accept declining material living standards, the elimination of employment in certain industry sectors and geographic regions . . . and significant transfers of resources back to the Third World' (Christoff, in Doherty and de Geus 1996). In any version of sustainable development, even in its weakest interpretation, behavioural change is required. But this is politically unpopular, and governments in Western democracies are dependent upon responding to the mood of electorates. These are not necessarily selfish in their attitudes—the public opinion polls show that there is a widespread support for environmental and green views—but change can be much harder to achieve. A good test of this will come in the next few years as the Labour government grapples with weaning the British public away from its over-reliance on the car. Car dependency is now firmly entrenched in the UK and other advanced industrial societies, yet the use of the car has to be cut back drastically if the carbon emissions which lead to global warming are to be reduced.

The social policies discussed will improve the 'quality of life' for some people. But far too many people, it must be said, are also registering their dissatisfaction with the way that some other people behave which affects their local environment—allowing their dogs to foul the pavement, vomiting in their doorway after a heavy session at the pub, thieving from cars, playing loud music at all hours of the day and night, and drug dealers plying their trade on the street. This behaviour degrades not only the local environment but also the 'quality of life' for their neighbours. Some of the worst of this behaviour is to be found in the poorest areas of our cities and on 'sink' estates: the unacceptable face of a society which is committed to freedom, choice, and privatized lifestyles. Communitarianism offers one response which stresses that communities need to be supported in enforcing their collective majority view about what passes for acceptable behaviour (Etzioni 1995; 1997). Green citizenship is related to this in the sense that, like communitarians, its exponents believe that individuals gain much of their identity from the local community and presumably communitarians would not want to damage the local environment as well. Indeed, they are active in fostering a social ecology of sound local relationships.

A sustainable social policy will have to be one which protects the poorest and vulnerable while at the same time delivering environmental benefits. The environmental agenda of the twenty-first century will need to address the traditional concerns of Social Policy —need, welfare, social justice, equity—but in the context of sustainable development.

Glossary

dark green Broad term describing the ideology of those who take a tough view of the changes needed to preserve the natural environment and to return it to ecological balance. Generally dark greens believe very substantial, possibly revolutionary, changes to the economy and other social institutions are necessary. Contrasted with **light green.**

deep ecology The welfare of human and non-human forms of life on the planet have value in themselves. Change will come about for humans at the individual level, and there is value in all viewpoints, so that change has to come through non-violent persuasion.

ecocentric view Sees humans as one part of the natural ecosystem and argues for a sense of respect for nature. Usually allied to a deep suspicion of bureaucracy and technology.

ecological modernization The view that economic growth need not lead to greater environmental damage. Its proponents argue for environmental policy controls because they believe that these will lead the economy towards innovation, which will not only reduce the environmental impact, but promote resource-intensive industries.

Index of Sustainable Economic Welfare Conventional economic indicators such as GDP—Gross Domestic Product—do not necessarily measure welfare. The Index of Sustainable Economic Welfare takes into account personal consumer expenditure, but then adjusts this to take account of such factors as income inequality, unpaid domestic labour, environmental degradation, depletion of natural resources, long-term environmental damage, and so on. It was pioneered by Cobb and Daly (1990) in the USA, and has been adapted for the UK (Jackson et al. 1998).

light green Broad term describing the ideology of those who believe in the possibility of policies that will sustain and improve the quality of the natural environment and which are at the same time largely compatible with existing economic and social arrangements. Contrasted with dark green.

malthusian Pertaining to the views of Thomas Malthus (1766–1834), who in his book *Essay on the Principle of Population* argued that there were natural limits to growth in human population and in the capacity of the economy to provide for them.

quality of life Used in Green debates to refer to a view that individual and collective welfare is not solely provided by consumption, but must also include such environmental 'goods' as clean air, clean water, and lack of noise pollution, as well as social goods such as low crime rates, public parks, and health and social services.

risk society A society with uncertainties and hazards created by the limited ability of humankind to dominate nature and the environment. Also used to describe the uncertainties faced by individuals in their personal lives as the result of the demise of tradition.

sustainability/sustainable development Classically defined by the Brundtland commission as 'development that meets the needs of the present without compromising the ability of future generations to meet their own needs'. Embodies the notion of inter-generational equity, meaning that the stock of resources bequeathed to our children, both natural and man-made, should be the same as that inherited by us. Similarly includes the concept of intra-generational equity or social justice between the rich and poor worlds. Equally, there is a commitment to participation for all people who will be affected by decisions which will impinge upon their quality of lives.

technocentric The belief that the application of science and technology can deal with environmental problems without any fundamental alteration to the economic system.

Guide to Further Reading

Meg Huby's *Social Policy and the Environment* (Buckingham: Open University Press, 1998) is the most recent challenge to the discipline of social policy to address environmental issues more directly. Dobson, A. (1995), *Green Political Thought* (2nd edn., London: Unwin Hyman) is a lucid guide to green thought, with an emphasis on the challenges for contemporary society from dark greens. *Wealth Beyond Measure: An Atlas of New Economics* by Paul Ekins, Mayer Hillman, and Robert Hutchison (London: Routledge, 1992) is an attractively presented guide to the 'new economics'. Robert Garner's *Environmental Politics* (1996: Prentice Hall/Harvester Wheatsheaf) covers green ideology, the environmental movement, environmental policy-making in the UK, and the role of pressure groups. Michael Jacobs' edited collection (1997), *Greening the Millennium: The New Politics of the Environment* (Oxford: Blackwell) is a very useful set of essays from *Political Quarterly* on ideologies, political economy, political parties, and European perspectives, while his earlier book, *The Green Economy* (1991: Pluto), is essential for its exposition of environmental economics. Luke Martell's *Ecology and Society* (Cambridge: Polity Press, 1994) is a clear and readable sociological account. Duncan McLaren, Simon Bullock, and Nusrat Yousuf, *Tomorrow's World: Britain's Share in a Sustainable Future* (London: Earthscan, 1998), makes the case for reducing consumption and improving our quality of life using the concept of 'environmental space'. David Pearce *et al.* (1989), *Blueprint for a Green Economy* (London: Earthscan), showed the kind of changes that were required in order to move towards sustainability. The analysis continues with *Blueprint 3; Measuring Sustainable Development* (London: Earthscan, 1993), on the UK, and *Blueprint 4: Capturing Global Environmental Value* (London: Earthscan, 1995). David Pepper's *Modern Environmentalism: An Introduction* (London: Routledge, 1996) is an extremely thorough and authoritative guide to the varieties of green thought and environmental movements situating them in the context of the history of ideas. Paul Selman, *Local Sustainability* (London: Paul Chapman, 1996) examines the progress towards sustainable development in the locality. John Whitelegg, *Critical Mass: Transport, Environment and Society in the Twenty-First Century* (London: Pluto Press, 1997) demonstrates how our car dependency has produced enormous problems of congestion, ill health, and inequality.

References

Achterburg, W. (1996) (eds.), 'Sustainability, Community and Democracy', in Doherty, B. and de Geuss, M.

Bahro, R. (1982), *Socialism and Survival* (London: Heretic Books).

——(1986), *Building the Green Movement* (London: Green Mantel Press).

Barclay, P. (1982), *Social Workers: Their Roles and Tasks* (London: National Institute for Social Work, Bedford Square Press).

Beck, U. (1992), *Risk Society: Towards a New Modernity* (London: Sage).

Benn, M. (1998), *Madonna and Child: The Politics of Modern Motherhood* (London: Cape).

Bhatti, M., Brooke, J. and Gibson, M. (1994) (eds.), *Housing and the Environment: A New Agenda* (London: Chartered Institute of Housing).

Bramwell, A. (1989), *Ecology in the 20th Century: A History* (London: Yale University Press).

Brown, P., Hadley, R., and White, K. J. (1982), 'A Case for Neighbourhood-Based Social Work and Social Services', in Barclay, P. (1992), *Social Workers: Their Roles and Tasks*.

Buckingham-Hatfield, S. P. (1998), *Constructing Local Environmental Agendas* (London: Routledge).

Carter, N. (1997), 'Prospects: The Parties and the Environment in the UK', in Jacobs, M. (ed.) (1997).

Commission on Social Justice (1994), *Social Justice: Strategies for National Renewal* (London: Vintage).

Conaty, P. and Mayo, E. (1997), *A Commitment to People and Place: The Case for Community Development Credit Unions* (York: Joseph Rowntree Foundation).

Daly, H. E. and Cobb, J. B. (1990), *For the Common Good: Redirecting the Economy towards Community, the Environment and a Sustainable Future* (London: Green Print).

Department of the Environment (1996), *This Common Inheritance: UK Annual Report 1996* (London: HMSO).

Dobson, A. (1995), *Green Political Thought* (2nd edn., London: Unwin Hyman).

Doherty, B. and de Geus, M. (1996) (eds.), *Democracy and Green Political Thought: Sustainability, Rights and Citizenship* (London: Routledge).

Draper, P. (1991), *Health through Public Policy: The Greening of Public Health* (London: Green Print).

Ekins, P. and Max-Neef, M. (eds.) (1992), *Real-Life Economics: Understanding Wealth Creation* (London: Routledge).

Environment Agency (1997), *Environment Agency Annual Report and Accounts 1996–7* (Bristol: HMSO).

Etzioni, A. (1995), *The Spirit of Community: Rights, Responsibilities and the Communitarian Agenda* (London: Fontana Press).

Etzioni, A. (1997), *The New Golden Rule: Community and Morality in a Democratic Society* (London: Profile).

Friends of the Earth/New Economics Foundation (1997), *Quality of Life Briefing Paper No. 3* (London: New Economics Foundation).

Garner, R. (1996), *Environmental Politics* (Hemel Hempstead: Prentice Hall/Harvester Wheatsheaf).

Giddens, A. (1991), *Modernity and Self Identity: Self and Society in the Late Modern Age* (Cambridge: Polity).

Gray, J. (1993), *Beyond the New Right: Markets, Governments and the Natural Environment* (London: Routledge).

Hardin, G. (1968), 'The Tragedy of the Commons', *Science*, 162, 1243–8.

Herbert, A. and Kempson, E. (1995), *Water Debt and Disconnection* (London: Policy Studies Institute).

Hillman, M., Adams, J., and Whitelegg, J. (1990), *One False Move . . . A Study of Children's Independent Mobility* (London: Policy Studies Institute).

Hirst, P. (1994), *Associative Democracy: New Forms of Economic and Social Governance* (Cambridge: Polity).

Hulsberg, W. (1987), *The West German Greens, A Social and Political Profile* (London: Verso).

Jackson, T. (1995), *Material Concerns: Pollution, Profit and Quality of Life* (London: Routledge).

——Marks, N., Ralls, J. and Stymme, S. (1998), *Sustainable Economic Welfare in the UK 1950–1996* (London: New Economics Foundation).

Jacobs, M. (1996), *The Politics of the Real World: Meeting the New Century* (London: Pluto).

——(ed.) (1997), *Greening the Millennium: The New Politics of the Environment* (Oxford: Blackwell).

Lamb, R. (1996), *Promising the Earth* (London: Routledge).

Lancashire County Council (1997), *Lancashire's Green Audit 2: A Sustainability Report* (Preston).

Leach, P. (1994), *Children First: What our Society Must Do—And Is Not Doing—for Children Today* (London: Penguin).

McLaren, D., Bullock, S., and Yousuf, N. (1998), *Tomorrow's World: Britain's Share in a Sustainable Future* (London: Earthscan).

Macnaghten, P. (1995), *Public Perceptions and Sustainability in Lancashire* (Lancaster: Lancaster University).

Maslow, A. H. (1954), *Motivation and Personality* (New York: Harper).

Max Neef, M. (1992), 'Development and Human Needs', in Ekins, P. and Max-Neef, M. (eds.), *Real-Life Economics: Understanding Wealth Creation* (London: Routledge).

Mellor, M. (1997), *Feminism and Ecology* (Cambridge: Polity).

Naess, A. (1988), 'The Basics of Deep Ecology', *Resurgence*, 126, 4–7.

Offer, A (ed.) (1996), *In Pursuit of the Quality of Life* (Oxford: Oxford University Press).

O'Riordan, T. (ed.) (1997), *Ecotaxation* (London: Earthscan).

Pearce, J. (1993), *At the Heart of the Community Economy: Community Enterprise in a Changing World* (London: Calouste Gulbenkian Foundation).

Pepper, D. (1993), *Eco-Socialism: From Deep Ecology to Social Justice* (London: Routledge).

——(1996), *Modern Environmentalism: An Introduction* (London: Routledge).

Porritt, J. (1984), *Seeing Green: The Politics of Ecology Explained* (Oxford: Blackwell).

Report of the Commission on Social Justice (1994), *Social Justice: Strategies for National Renewal* (London: Vintage).

Robertson, J. (1989), *Future Wealth: A New Economics for the 21st Century* (London: Cassell).

Ryle, M. (1988), *Ecology and Socialism* (London: Radius).

Saunders, P. (1995), *Capitalism: A Social Audit* (Buckingham: Open University Press).

Schor, J. (1992), *The Overworked American: The Unexpected Decline of Leisure* (New York: Basic Books).

Seed, P. and Lloyd, G. (1997), *Quality of Life* (London: Jessica Kingsley Publishers).

Selman, P. (1996), *Local Sustainability: Managing and Planning Ecologically Sound Places* (London: Paul Chapman).

Tindale, S. (1996), *Jobs and the Environment* (London: Institute for Public Policy Research).

——(1997), 'The Political Economy of Environmental Tax Reform', in Jacobs, M. (ed.) (1997).

Weale, A. (1992), *The New Politics of Pollution* (Manchester: Manchester University Press).

Whitelegg, J. (1997), *Critical Mass: Transport, Environment and Society in the Twenty-First Century* (London: Pluto Press).

World Commission on Environment and Development (chairman: Gro Brundtland) (1987), *Our Common Future* (Oxford: Oxford University Press).

19 Arts and Cultural Policy

Mark Liddiard

Contents

Introduction

The **arts** and **culture** permeate almost every aspect of social life. Whatever our appreciation of the arts, all of us are enveloped by the ubiquitous culture—popular and otherwise—that surrounds us. Most of us enjoy music, visit the cinema, watch television, listen to the radio, or read newspapers. In simple terms, the arts and culture are a fundamental and highly pervasive feature of society. Yet this is an area which has been woefully neglected by social policy, with just a few notable exceptions (such as Cahill 1994). This is all the more surprising when one considers that there are a number of ways in which issues surrounding the arts and culture closely reflect wider social policy debates and present policy-makers with a variety of conundrums. The very real inequity in people's participation and enjoyment of the arts and culture has many implications for society, and closely reflects some of the wider debates about inequality. Just as questions of inequality in other areas of social provision lead to questions of social need, so the clear inequity in participation in the arts and culture raises important questions about **cultural need**. Namely, how important are the arts and culture, and participation in them, for creating a balanced and healthy society? Might they conceivably be a part of citizenship? In which case, what should be the role of the state in providing for cultural enrichment? Should they subsidize the arts? Yet how does one decide how much the arts and culture should get in relation to other areas of social need? Moreover, what are the most appropriate ways to raise and distribute money and financial support for the arts? These are important policy questions which have long challenged policy-makers and have recently been closely examined in the UK as the **National Lottery** has been established.

Yet debate about the arts and culture is not simply a reflection of other social policy discussions. They present many new issues for policy-makers, not least the very real potential of the media for informing important debates among both the public and policy-makers. We are surrounded by **mass media** of many types—television, radio, newspapers, and even the Internet—all of which are increasingly important and influential sources of information and have enormous potential for framing the ways in which we understand current news and issues. The media are crucial for understanding the nature of social policy controversies. The mass media can play very significant roles in the policy process, by placing topics and issues on the agendas of government, politicians, and, of course, the public. They may also be very important for influencing and informing the very nature of these debates, although the impact of the media is both inconsistent and complex. None the less, their influential role in modern society raises a multitude of questions and debates. What control, if any, should there be over the content and form of the mass media? What are the implications for media freedom? In the global environment in which we live, should there be more restrictions and regulations upon the carriers of global information, such as satellite and cable television or even the Internet? At what point does regulation of the media lead to **censorship**?

In short, the arts and culture raise a number of important issues for social policy which to date have been largely ignored, much to the detriment of the discipline. This chapter will seek to explore and consider some of these issues. Let us begin by looking at participation in the arts and culture, and the vexed question of cultural need.

Cultural Need

Participation in the arts and culture is often profoundly inequitable. Divisions of class, age, gender, and ethnicity can all have a dramatic impact upon participation in various cultural endeavours. Even a cursory examination of Table 19.1 reveals profound differences in the level of participation in selected leisure activities.

It is evident from this table that there are considerable class disparities in the level of participation for a range of cultural and leisure pursuits. The question is, why? Of course, these disparities may simply be a consequence of choice. However, in recent years access to the arts and culture has increasingly been left to the vagaries of the market. Consequently, many in the arts world have argued that those in financial poverty

	Percentages aged 16 and over participating in each activity in the three months prior to interview					
	AB	C1	C2	D	E	All adults
Library	59	43	31	30	31	39
Cinema	47	42	35	30	21	36
Historic building	41	31	17	15	10	24
Spectator sports event	30	25	23	18	7	22
Theatre	35	26	17	11	7	20
Museum or gallery	36	24	14	11	12	20
Exhibition (other than museum/gallery)	24	18	13	7	4	14

Table 19.1 Participation in selected leisure activities away from home: by social grade, Great Britain, 1996
Source: Office for National Statistics (1998).

have effectively been condemned to a cultural poverty—unable to afford even to enjoy their own heritage, for instance, excluded from museums by the gradual introduction of entry charges. The question arises, therefore, as to whether or not the arts and culture should be included in the wider debates about social need. In short, what should be the role of the state in the context of the arts, culture, and leisure? Should the state invest resources to ensure that no-one is financially excluded from the benefits of cultural participation? These are complex debates which raise a number of different issues. Let us consider some of the questions.

Arguments Against State Support

The arts account for just one and a half per cent of state expenditure (Social Trends 1998). Yet state support for the arts is a highly contentious issue, which has attracted vociferous and highly vocal comment from a variety of sources. The launch of the National Lottery in 1994 and the expressed commitment to using the proceeds to subsidize and support areas like the arts otherwise receiving scant state assistance has ensured that the issue of state support for the arts remains firmly on the popular agenda. But concern about state involvement in the arts has been a recurring issue for some time. The widespread closure of many provincial theatres and cinemas, and restricted opening hours imposed on many libraries, have all precipitated a wide-ranging debate about whether or not local authorities have an obligation to provide cultural amenities, such as cinemas or libraries, or whether their provision must rest wholly in the hands of the free market.

In principle, and with largely unlimited funds, the arts may indeed have a strong claim upon government resources. However, government funds are limited, restrictively so in many areas of social policy, and so it may be difficult to justify government financial support for the arts when other areas of need present themselves. Nevertheless, the fact that more money should be spent by the state on concrete social need, such as education or housing, does not—or at least should not—consequently imply that less should be spent on the arts and meeting cultural need.

A somewhat different argument is that state subsidies simply displace private funds and contributions to the arts. This is an interesting claim, not least because one could argue that the relatively low levels of private support in the UK and elsewhere are indicative of the impact of state subsidies in discouraging private funds from the arts. However, it is equally possible to argue that the general paucity of private finance is the very reason for state subsidies. Historically, it is certainly true that **philanthropy** has tended to focus upon areas of unmet social need, and when these areas of need are actually recognized and addressed by society so it has tended to move to other areas. Yet it is difficult to see how these arguments could be credible in the context of the arts— the arts present a huge pool of unmet need and the scale of state support is still tiny, such that the need for private donors is as pronounced as ever. In fact, the evidence suggests that private support is more likely to be forthcoming when an element of state support has already been committed. Indeed, a recognition of the potential for partner- ships between the state and private finance and for **plural funding,** by way of local and central government, turnstiles and box offices, business sponsors, and patrons seems to be central to current arts policy in the UK and elsewhere.

Related to the above theme, some commentators such as Sawers (1993) argue that state support is simply not necessary for the artistic and cultural enrichment of society. Namely, good art and culture will prosper regardless of whether or not the state is offering support. This is a very interesting point, not least because it introduces some of the many difficulties with measuring and quantifying the impact and effectiveness of the money which is spent on the arts and culture. In short, how does one quantify or measure the impact of state—and in turn, public—money spent on the arts? While he was Secretary of State for National Heritage, Peter Brooke declared that a good test of the state's financial involvement in the arts was the extent to which the arts 'flourish'. Yet just what does this mean? Does it refer to the attainment of critical acclaim? Does it mean commercial recognition and success? Does it concern an expansion in the number of artistic and cultural endeavours or a broadening of the types of artistic and cultural endeavours? In the context of museums, for example, the efficient use of funds is fre- quently assessed simply in terms of the number of visitors that a particular museum attracts. Yet such a measure can be highly unsatisfactory in terms of assessing the effectiveness of subsidies and the quality of the experience that they provide.

Some authors have actually gone so far as to suggest that state support may actually be to the detriment of the arts and culture. On the one hand, government funding may mean that cultural organizations and institutions become complacent, immune to market and commercial pressure, and may subsequently err towards financial irre- sponsibility. Whilst this has often been a dominant theme in the government's attitude towards the arts, and has been reflected in the state funding of museums, for instance, the fiscal prudence which has now come to thoroughly permeate the arts world means that notions of financial complacency and irresponsibility are somewhat misguided.

A more potent suggestion is that art subsidies can be detrimental by effectively stifling innovation. The way in which financial support is often directed at the well-established bodies and organizations is such that conceivably artistic projects may come to lack originality and become somewhat staid, because established projects are seen to be a 'safe bet' for support. The result is that the dynamism and innovation on which art so clearly rests can become somewhat stifled—a point which has often been raised about the **Arts Council of England** and similar bodies abroad. This is a difficult point, namely because the finance available for the arts is so restricted that decisions—very difficult and vexed decisions—have to be made about what art is worthy of support and which art is not, such that good art is financed and encouraged while poor art is not. Yet these issues rest heavily upon questions of artistic quality and how one assesses it, which are notoriously subjective and to which there are no agreed answers. However, these concerns are not necessarily questioning the appropriateness of art subsidy, simply questioning the way in which the financial cake is divided and the criteria by which this is done.

Perhaps the most vociferous attack on art subsidies of late—and one which has especially been highlighted by the advent of the National Lottery—is their inequity. Why should the many fund and subsidize the entertainment of the few? As Anthony Everitt said about the Royal Opera House's annual grant of some £20 million, 'Never in the history of British culture has so much been given by so many for so few' (Everitt 1994). By the logic of supply and demand, if audience demand for the arts is insufficient to cover the costs of supplying opera or ballet through admission charges, why should society and taxpayers as a whole subsidize them? After all, art subsidies involve the application of resources which are supplied involuntarily by all the public in the form of taxes, and yet these resources are inevitably distributed inequitably. As we shall see, the National Lottery had initially been envisaged as the answer to this problem of inequity, but in fact the distribution of Lottery grants has become an issue in itself.

Of course, this inequity may be more perceived than real—and the media have undoubtedly played an important role, particularly in the context of the National Lottery, in shaping public perception of injustice. None the less, there is still good evidence to suggest that this concern with the inequity of state support for the arts may be real. The influential work of Julian Le Grand, for instance, focused on the iniquitous workings of the welfare state and claimed that, in the UK, the top 20 per cent of households receive some 40 per cent of public expenditure on the arts, while in contrast the bottom 25 per cent receive just 4 per cent (1982: 157–8). These calculations are unsurprising—opera and ballet, for instance, are regular recipients of very considerable support from the Arts Council, and yet, as we saw at the beginning of the chapter, the audiences for these activities are disproportionately distributed between different social classes.

These are potent arguments, although it is important to ensure that meeting cultural need is not viewed any differently to meeting other social need. After all, it is now widely acknowledged and accepted that the welfare state itself is thoroughly permeated by inequity. Indeed, one can also argue that precisely because access to the arts and culture is so unequally spread, this is even more justification for state intervention. None the less, the perceived inequity in state support for the arts—whether real or not— is important because of the impact that it has upon public perception and attitudes to which, in theory at least, politicians and policy-makers are ultimately subservient.

It is very interesting that survey evidence, such as the data in Table 19.2 from the British Social Attitudes Survey, appears to suggest that state support for the arts is gen-

Item of spending	% wanting government to spend		
	More	Same as now	Less
Health	87	9	1
Education	79	16	1
Unemployment benefits	48	39	8
Culture and the arts	10	38	44

Table 19.2 Attitudes to government spending
Source: Jowell *et al.* 1994.

erally not perceived as a legitimate use of public money by the public. In short, for every person who wants more money spent on the arts, more than four people want less spent. Additionally, there is a very interesting class influence upon this figure: amongst the **salariat**, one in seven want more public money spent on the arts and culture, which compares to just one in twenty among the working class. Clearly, there may be a variety of reasons for this pattern of support. One explanation rests with the pattern of participation in the arts and culture which we outlined at the beginning. In short, the higher social classes are generally more likely to participate in the arts and high culture, and are therefore both more likely to appreciate the virtue of investing more money in the arts and, of course, are more likely to benefit directly from any increase in spending. We have already seen that public attitudes to welfare closely reflect self-interest. Other factors may also play a role here, not least the media for presenting state support for the arts and culture as necessarily benefiting the few when this may not necessarily be the case. We will see shortly that the media can certainly be important in framing and influencing debates such as this in the public arena.

To reiterate, in recent years there has been a marked shift in policy towards the arts on the part of government in the UK, a move away from state subsidies and towards market provision. In other words, people are expected to pay the market price for their enjoyment of the arts. The arts have therefore become increasingly dependent upon a simplistic 'market test'—in a crude supply-and-demand scenario, if the public are not prepared to pay the market price to see or enjoy something, then the state cannot be expected to support it. This is a policy approach which has applied the free-market ideology of the New Right to the arts, an arena in which crude notions of financial supply and demand are simply inappropriate. In response, a number of pertinent arguments have been presented to justify state expenditure on the arts.

Arguments For State Support

The widening of opportunity and allowing all to appreciate the arts and culture, irrespective of their financial power, lies at the heart of arguments in favour of state subsidy. Indeed, this is why the Victorians were such avid supporters of cultural endeavours like museums, and it is why the widespread introduction of museum charges was met with such disdain throughout the profession. One of the core functions of the Arts Council of England, for example, is to increase the accessibility of the arts to the public; and yet it is difficult to see how this role can be compatible with a crude market test. It may be true that opera or ballet only have a limited audience, but with average ticket prices of £30 or more this may be more indicative of the public's economic weakness than a lack of interest. Indeed, even if there is less apparent demand for opera or ballet among some of the public, this may simply reflect the fact that much of the population have never had the opportunity to appreciate opera or ballet. In this sense, subsidies are necessary in order to nurture the audiences of tomorrow.

This relates to the next point, namely, that the opportunity to enjoy and appreciate the arts and culture are crucial for the development of a healthy and balanced society and cannot be reduced to a simple market test of demand and supply. This is even more pronounced if one is considering the nebulous and ultimately very broad notion of 'cultural enrichment'. However, there is no doubt that Britain has considerable international prestige courtesy of its performing arts—indeed, this is a point that respective Governments are often very fond of reiterating—and yet it is difficult to see how this can possibly be compatible with a crude market test.

There are a wide range of potent arguments to be made in favour of public arts subsidy, and there are also powerful arguments by precedent—the Victorians were avid funders of leisure and cultural facilities, believing as they did in the central notion of self-education and the role of cultural fulfilment in pulling together a highly polarized society. Similarly, it is important to recognize that cultural need is not necessarily unrelated to other forms of need which are often unquestionably the role of the state. The arts and culture have a real role to play in the provision of employment opportunities. Similarly, the advent of the National Curriculum has seen an enhanced acknowledgement of the important educative role of museums. In a variety of respects, therefore, state support for the arts closely impinges upon areas of social need which are more widely acknowledged as appropriate recipients of state intervention, such as employment and education.

It is true that there are a number of real problems and difficulties with the notion of cultural need, not least the fact that it is such an intangible notion that assessing or quantifying the impact of state expenditure upon the arts can be difficult. Nevertheless, the meeting of other areas of need are also beset with problems in terms of quantifying the impact of the state. Indeed, in the same way as other forms of social need form an important component of citizenship, so one can argue that cultural need—which can take many different forms—should also be a component of citizenship. Certainly, T. H. Marshall himself, in his exposition of citizenship, implied that full citizenship should include the right to culture: 'By the social element I mean the whole range from the right to a modicum of economic welfare and security to the right to share to the full in the social heritage and to live the life of a civilized being according to the standards prevailing in society' (Marshall 1963: 74).

The problem, however, is that since the 1970s access to the arts and culture, and indeed to many areas of social life, has been generally determined not by citizenship, but by consumerism and the ability to pay. The result has been a predictable one, as economically weak individuals have experienced varying degrees of exclusion from many areas of social life, especially the arts and culture, where access has been left largely to the vagaries of the market. The result has been to effectively compound the existing inequalities in participation in the arts. One can claim, therefore, that access to culture is an important, even fundamental, component of a citizen's rights. The exclusion and inequalities in access which result from this move towards the operation of the market, and the emphasis on individual consumption, arguably necessitates state support and intervention.

The new Labour government have certainly shown themselves to be more willing to engage with enhanced state involvement in the arts and culture in many ways. From their encouragement of the British film industry through favourable tax regimes, to their announcement of £100 million to enable national museums and galleries to introduce universal free entry by the year 2001, the arts world have broadly welcomed the arrival of a new government, albeit with some reservations. However, the area in which the Labour opposition most successfully courted public opinion in relation to the arts before the General Election was in the context of the National Lottery.

The National Lottery

To some extent, the advent of the National Lottery was widely seen as the answer to some of these dilemmas concerning state funding of the arts. Run by Camelot, the National Lottery was established in the UK in November 1994. Since then it has become firmly established in the nation's psyche. Indeed, the initial scale of uptake was quite phenomenal, as Table 19.3 illustrates.

In the first 13 months of its operation until the end of 1995, for instance, lottery sales totalled some £5.1 billion—approximately 3 per cent of all retail spending! Clearly, this is a very significant economic development, diverting discretionary consumer spending away from other retail sectors. In short, the National Lottery has been a huge success, beyond the expectations of both its promoters and detractors. It has also generated huge revenue for the Government in terms of lottery duty—a projected £3.84 billion over the seven-year licence period—along with very substantial amounts of money for the five good causes of the arts, charity, heritage, sport, and the celebration of the Millennium: a projected £9 billion over the seven-year licence period. In many respects, therefore, the Lottery has been a profound success. Many in the arts world were initially hopeful that Lottery funds would help to revitalize the arts and culture in this country, and begin to resolve the notable inequity in cultural participation. Some four years on from the establishment of the Lottery, however, many are not so optimistic. In short, the National Lottery ran into a variety of difficulties.

The Distribution of Grants

The number of grants made by bodies distributing cash to the 'good causes' was far lower than originally expected, although the average size of the grants given was considerably larger than anticipated. The original promise was that literally thousands of grants would be made reaching every corner of the country. Yet this was simply not the case. The net result was that smaller organizations seeking Lottery money were largely

	Total to 31.12.95	of which	Projection over 7-year licence	of which
Sales	£5.1 billion	Weekly draw £3.8 billion (75% of sales)	£32.06 billion	
		Scratch cards £1.3 billion (25% of sales)		
Lottery duty (12%)	£600 million		£3.84 billion	
Retailer commission (5%)	£225 million		£1.66 billion	
Camelot costs and profit	£312 million[a]		£1.6 billion[b]	
operating costs (4%)				£1.28 billion
after tax and profits (1%)				£320 million
Prizes (50%)	£2.4 billion	Weekly draw £1.7 billion (45% payout)	£16 billion	
		Scratch cards £720 million (55% payout)		
Good causes (28%) awarded in grants	£1.4 billion		£8.96 billion	
		£991 million		
		Art £225 million		£1.79 billion
		Charity £159 million		£1.79 billion
		Heritage £96 million		£1.79 billion
		Millennium £328 million		£1.79 billion
		Sport £153 million		£1.79 billion

Table 19.3 Lottery sales and payout, 13 months to 31 December 1995

There is a 'missing' 2.5% or £133 million. This seems to consist mainly of money held for rolled-over or unclaimed or unallocated prizes.

[a] 6 per cent.

[b] 5 per cent.

Source: Fitzherbert, Giussani, and Hunt 1996.

excluded. In terms of grants given to the arts in England, projects requesting more than a million pounds received more than 80 per cent of the total cash distributed. Just 1 per cent went in grants of less than £30,000 (Fitzherbert, Giussani, and Hunt 1996).

There has also been a very real concern about the geographical distribution of grants. At the inception of the Lottery there were fears that arts and heritage grants would be heavily concentrated in London and the South-East. This concern appears to have been justified. London, for instance, certainly received a considerably higher share of arts, heritage, and sport money. Per head of population, London got an average of £26.07 from these sources, compared to the East Midlands—which is already experiencing fewer resources, remember—of £3.21 (Fitzherbert, Giussani, and Hunt 1996). There has therefore been a considerable geographical problem here.

In short, the National Lottery was welcomed initially as a development which had the power and potential to redress the real inequity in people's enjoyment and participation in the arts, culture, and their own heritage. Yet this potential has not been realized.

This inequity is even more difficult to accept when one considers that, in many respects, it is the lowest income groups who invest most in the Lottery and yet receive the fewest benefits. The Family Expenditure Survey has shown, for instance, that in the first three months of 1995, amongst purchasers of lottery tickets the families from the very poorest 10 per cent of the population spent just under £2 per week, although this represented some 30 per cent of their leisure spending. In contrast, whilst the families from the richest 10 per cent spent about £4 per week, this represented just 4 per cent of this group's leisure spending (Social Trends 1998). Moreover, the lower socio-economic groups, through volume of numbers, purchase more lottery tickets and so in turn contribute most to the money available for good causes. Yet it is felt that the National Lottery money is being largely distributed to artistic endeavours more commonly frequented by higher social groups.

The Impact on Charities

Since the inception of the National Lottery concern has been voiced about its impact

Box 19.1 How has the National Lottery contributed to social problems?

Source: Guardian 1996. Reprinted with permission.

upon charitable giving, so important in many areas of social need. To some extent these concerns have been borne out by the evidence. The National Council of Voluntary Organizations, for instance, found that individual donations to charities dropped by £344 million in 1995. Whilst the National Lottery Charities Board made grants of £240 million, the net loss to charities has none the less been some £104 million (Fitzherbert, Giussani, and Hunt, 1996). However, the evidence on the impact of the Lottery upon charities remains unclear, and more research is currently taking place.

Creation of Social Problems

It is still very difficult to know whether or not the National Lottery has created or exacerbated social problems such as gambling. Certainly the experience of National Lotteries elsewhere, such as the US and Canada, suggest that problem gambling will increase as a result of the National Lottery. Despite government assurances to the contrary, the National Lottery has signalled a widespread dismantling of restrictions on other forms of gambling (Sambrook 1997).

To summarize, the National Lottery has had a profound impact upon many areas of social and economic life. Yet whilst it was initially hailed as the shot in the arm that the arts needed, to date it has simply failed to deliver on its potential. If anything, the workings of the Lottery appear to have made existing inequity in participation in the arts—both social and geographic—more pronounced. The perceived inequity in benefits from the Lottery has certainly attracted much debate, and has raised wider questions about the role of public finance in terms of cultural life. It is certainly interesting that in 1994, at the inception of the National Lottery, some 12 per cent of the population thought that there should be more spending on culture and the arts. Yet within just two years, this figure had halved to only 6 per cent (Social Trends 1998). In the sense that the Lottery has provoked debate about the role of public support for the arts and culture, it has been very important indeed. Yet these debates, as with many other policy debates, have only really entered the public arena by virtue of the mass media. The fact that we live in an increasingly media-conscious political and social environment means that the mass media are simply too important for social policy to ignore.

The Mass Media

The mass media are crucial to social policy for a variety of reasons, not least because they often perform an influential role in framing many social policy debates. With the advent of television we are exposed to the mass media more than ever before. In this way, the mass media have become crucial to how we understand the world, and it is perhaps not surprising that some mass media content has attracted concern and condemnation for being offensive and inflammatory (see Box 19.2). What is considerably less clear, however, is the precise way in which audiences interpret and receive the myriad of messages and images that they receive. There are important questions here about the role of the mass media in terms of influencing public opinion in relation to welfare issues and even the welfare state itself: questions which, with just a few notable exceptions (e.g. Golding and Middleton 1982), are largely neglected by social policy. Yet

Box 19.2 What impact does mass media content have upon public opinion and policy-makers?

"I SAID WE'D HAVE NO TROUBLE GETTING THROUGH!"

Source: Sun, 16 October 1986. Reprinted with permission.

given the very real importance that some interest groups and agencies attach to securing favourable media coverage and exposure in their efforts to secure policy changes, just what influence does the mass media have upon policy-makers? Given the potential power held by the mass media in influencing and even manipulating policy debates, what should be the appropriate role of the state in terms of the control and regulation of the mass media?

The Impact of the Mass Media upon Public Attitudes

Many areas of welfare provision attach considerable importance to achieving favourable media coverage. There is often something of an implicit assumption on the part of involved agencies and commentators that media coverage is important for changing public perceptions and helping to change and modify policy. But is this really the case? What kind of impact does the mass media have upon public attitudes towards different social problems?

The first point, of course, is to recognize that the media are far from homogeneous. The content and style of presentation, for example, may vary widely and dramatically between the press and television. Moreover, even if one is only considering the press, they too are far from homogeneous. On the simplest level there is an obvious distinction between the tabloids and the broadsheets. The heterogeneity of the mass media, however, may be important because their impact upon public attitudes may differ widely. A recent survey, for instance, showed that in the UK the public view the credibility of news coverage very differently depending upon the medium concerned. Whilst some 85 per cent of respondents believed that television news reporting was exactly in line or approximately in line with what really happened, the corresponding figure for newspaper coverage was just 48 per cent (Smith 1998).

The styles of media presentation can also be important because of the influence that they may or may not have upon the public. Often, political and social issues may be treated as if they were a form of public entertainment. Whilst this may be useful for encouraging public interest in a topic such as homelessness, it can none the less leave misconceptions and stereotypes, trivialize serious social issues, and may ultimately do little to rectify misapprehensions or modify attitudes (Hutson and Liddiard 1994).

It is important too to recognize that the media operate with their own agendas, which can take many different forms. The implication is an important one because of the way in which only the issues, notions, and concepts which are consistent with pre-existing media agendas will be accepted and promoted. In this sense, whilst agencies may rightly or wrongly view the media as being in a position of enviable power to influence public opinion and policy-making, in order to actually attract media interest, agencies must first subscribe to media agendas and modify their messages and concerns. For instance, in the context of homelessness, journalists and politicians regularly employ crude and stereotypical images of the homeless because they make good copy (Kemp 1997). Importantly, homeless agencies will often collude with such images in their enthusiasm to attain coverage (Beresford 1979; Liddiard and Hutson 1998).

There is no doubt that the media can provide a very important and powerful source of communication, enabling issues to be conveyed to millions of people who may not otherwise have been involved or particularly interested. The ability to reach and sensitize so many people to social policy concerns is not to be minimized. Yet the assumption that media coverage of a social issue will have a direct impact upon both public opinion and policy-makers is a questionable one.

Public attitudes towards many different areas of social welfare are notoriously difficult to delimit. Public opinion is profoundly heterogeneous, and levels of knowledge and interest in social issues vary widely. As studies such as the British Social Attitudes Survey have shown, eliciting accurate information about public attitudes towards different areas of welfare is difficult and laden with methodological problems. None the less, a number of points can be made about the role of the media in terms of public attitudes.

The question of how the media impacts upon public attitudes has long concerned academics, and there have been a number of important shifts in how they have approached the issue. One view is known as the 'hypodermic syringe' model, and perceives the media as somehow having a direct and inherently straightforward impact upon the viewing audience. However, this approach has now been largely discredited because of the way in which it implies a passive audience unquestioningly absorbing whatever they are presented with by the media. Instead, the impact of the media upon the public is more complex, not least because there is now much agreement about the fact that the public select and interpret media messages according to their existing viewpoints. In other words, far from being passive recipients of media messages, the public are actually highly active in their interpretation of the images and messages with which they are presented. Only those media messages which reinforce what individuals already believe are selected by the audience. In this way the same media item can be interpreted differently by different categories of people. Arguably the result is a mass public largely ill-informed of key social issues, whose knowledge is only modified or mediated on the basis of their own pre-existing agendas and misapprehensions. In short, the role of media coverage upon public attitudes towards social issues is far from clear. Yet just what impact does the media coverage have upon policy-making?

The Impact of the Media on Policy-Making

Does media coverage of homelessness and other social problems have a significant influence upon policy-makers, promoting the importance of some issues over others? This is a difficult issue to address, because we know surprisingly little about the impact of the mass media upon the decision-making process. None the less, a number of points can be made. In the initial stages of policy-germination, for instance, pressure groups will seek to place certain issues onto the political agenda. The media certainly perform an important role at this early stage of the policy and decision-making process, with pressure groups depending heavily upon their ability to excite the interest of the media. Without such assistance, many campaigns would never get off the ground.

However, it remains very difficult to actually identify concrete effects that media coverage—and, in turn, public concern—may have had upon subsequent policy, although it does seem that the influence of media coverage depends upon the wider social context in which this coverage is taking place. If media coverage is compatible with the surrounding socio-economic and, of course, political environment then it is likely to have more impact. It is important, too, to remember that the link between the media and policy-making operates in both directions, with policy-makers and politicians often playing a crucial role in terms of informing, even manipulating, the media. The work of the Glasgow University Media Group and others have shown how government accounts and interpretations can permeate into mass media accounts, often through subtle manipulation of journalistic processes and information collection (see Broadbent 1993, Miller 1994). Policy responses to social problems such as homelessness may have much less to do with media coverage and public opinion than with wider political ideologies and agendas (Liddiard 1998).

For these reasons, it is probably fair to suggest that the media have only a limited impact upon policy-making. After all, policies are made in response to a variety of diverse pressures, of which agenda-setting by the media is only one. None the less, it does seem that the media may have a role to play in terms of actually setting the parameters for policy debates, and at least play a small part in framing policy discussions. Golding and Middleton, for instance, claim that the mass media are important for shaping the political climate:

so that ultimately legislation and the overall allocation of resources are influenced by mass mediated versions of priorities and necessities (and) they influence the cultural context . . . by setting the tone for public discussion and providing the imagery and rhetoric . . . (for) administrators. (1979: 19)

In light of the real potential of the mass media for influencing social policy debates on the part of both the public and policy-makers, some concern has been raised about their role and content in the UK and elsewhere. How can we ensure that the mass media are free to deal with whatever issues they wish, while at the same time ensuring that they behave responsibly? These issues have come to the fore in recent debates concerning the freedom and regulation of the mass media, particularly the press.

Regulation of the Press?

The freedom of the press is often presented as a central feature of democracy. In other words, the public are seen to have the right to full and complete knowledge of the world in which they live without government interference, selection, or suppression. Indeed, it is often argued that censorship and other restrictions on the press are the hallmark of totalitarian and suppressive regimes. In fact, this is a somewhat misguided notion—censorship can be both subtle and insidious. In the UK, for instance, government interference with the media may be less explicit than that experienced in totalitarian regimes, but it can be just as problematic. Indeed, there are a number of notable cases when the UK Government has been far from subtle in attempting to prevent information from entering the public domain:

- Reporters' rights to privacy of notes and anonymity of sources has regularly been attacked by the Government, most infamously in 1986, when a film about the secret spy satellite, Zircon, was seized from the BBC under a court order.

- The Government may attempt to censor books and newspapers before publication. In the late 1980s, for instance, the press were taken to court by the Government to prevent them from publishing extracts from 'Spycatcher', the book by ex-MI5 officer Peter Wright.

- The Government can also restrict access to news and even the scene of events in a way which makes accurate reporting more difficult. This was seen to be particularly pronounced in the context of the 1982 Falklands War.

These few examples are all clear instances of explicit government interference and attempted control of media content. Yet they also highlight the stark dilemmas faced by policy-makers and academics when they discuss regulation and control of the mass media. Each case was justified on the grounds of protecting 'national security'. Even if this argument has often been abused in the UK, simply to prevent politically damaging revelations—as it was in the 'Arms to Iraq' scandal—it can still be difficult to know when media restrictions are appropriate and when they are not.

The debate about media regulation, however, also rests heavily upon the media themselves. Those who gather, report, edit, and disseminate the news and views have a very large responsibility to report events and views in an accurate and objective manner. However, this responsibility for accuracy and truth, for interpretation which corresponds to the facts, for reporting that is balanced and not selective or biased, as well as the need to provide a proper background and context to issues being discussed, are all becoming more problematic in the context of the contemporary media. The growing competition and dramatic requirements of the modern mass media are often seen to be encouraging irresponsible practice—a debate which came most poignantly to the fore with the death of the Princess of Wales and the question of privacy and press intrusion. Similarly, Lasch (1995) has argued that the mass media's increasing emphasis upon sensationalist entertainment has actually led to a decline of informed political debate in the US and elsewhere, implying a real need for more control of the media in the interests of the public and democracy.

None the less, a number of pertinent arguments have been presented arguing against any further moves towards state regulation and control of the mass media. Most obviously, the law of the marketplace prevails, and no amount of public control can change that. In other words, the public buy what the public wants—and if they do not want to read or watch something, then they will not buy the papers or watch the television channels. There is certainly an element of truth to this claim, although it fails to acknowledge that the media can also help to determine public tastes. None the less, there are some interesting examples of this—the mass boycott of the *Sun* newspaper in Liverpool, following its coverage of the 1989 Hillsborough disaster, is one such example. Similarly, advertisers can and do withhold their advertising for various reasons, hitting at the financial heart of the media.

Indeed, it can be argued that the true function of the mass media—the dissemination of information—has been distorted by the pressures of financial interests. The tabloid press, for instance, may often resort to sensationalist and superficial entertainment in a bid to boost their circulation figures. There is no doubt that the popular press in particular is often guilty of gross errors of taste, in terms of both the kind of news that it provides and in the methods used to obtain it. Soothill and Walby (1991), for example, show how sex crimes have increasingly been exploited as a form of titillation by the press, in their efforts to increase circulation. The question here, however, is whether or not the press are simply reflecting what the public want, or whether public preferences are being influenced and determined by the press. This raises the important question of media ownership. There is no doubt that the presentation and interpretation of news may be subject to the personal predilections of the proprietors and the interests that, openly or otherwise, they represent.

The power and influence of Rupert Murdoch and his News International empire has long been the focus of scrutiny given his ownership of a number of national newspapers, including the *Sun* and *The Times*. Indeed, it is important not to underestimate the sheer size of the potential audience for this medium. Even in the age of electronic and televisual news dissemination, the scale of newspaper circulation in the UK remains very high, as Table 19.4 illustrates.

In short, Britons purchase more than 10 million newspapers every day—more than any other Europeans (Smith 1998). Yet the figures for the readership of these newspapers is even higher than their circulation. The *Sun*, for instance, is the nation's most popular weekday newspaper and has a daily readership of over 10 million people (Social Trends 1998). With such a huge potential audience, the crude political bias of such newspapers and their proprietors (see Box 19.3) certainly strengthens the case for greater regulation of press content and ownership.

These issues have been given added urgency by a number of technological developments, particularly the expansion of satellite television and the **Internet.**

	August 1998
Daily Papers	
Sun	3,707,471
The Mirror	2,377,782
Daily Record	698,074
Daily Star	664,233
Daily Mail	2,312,285
The Express	1,151,583
Daily Telegraph	1,064,813
Guardian	380,857
The Times	739,285
Independent	221,915
Financial Times	358,019
Sunday Papers	
News of the World	4,294,318
Sunday Mirror	2,019,928
People	1,775,252
Mail on Sunday	2,224,776
Express on Sunday	1,072,858
The Sunday Times	1,322,537
Sunday Telegraph	842,055
Observer	387,342
Independent on Sunday	256,826

Table 19.4 National newspaper circulation
Source: Audit Bureau of Circulations.

Satellite, Cable, and Digital Television

Many of the questions of media regulation that we have already touched upon are illustrated in heightened form in the debates about television. The medium of television has experienced very dramatic change and development in recent years, and the launch of digital television seems set to revolutionize viewing opportunities.

The main debates have largely reflected the development of television into a global system of news, information, and entertainment. In particular there has been some real concern that the production of this news, information, and entertainment is increasingly concentrated in the hands of huge corporations which are simply dedicated to the pursuit of profit by selling a standardized product around the world. Marshall McLuhan (1989) first suggested that television was making a 'global village' and was shrinking the world and homogenizing its culture and differences. Of course, this process of globalization is not necessarily a bad thing. Global images and messages certainly have the potential to lead to greater tolerance and understanding of different cultures and interpretations. None the less, the manner in which this process has taken

Box 19.3 Is there a case for more regulation and control of the press?

FRANKLIN

BRITAIN VOTES TODAY

"THEY MUST BE HOPING LABOUR WIN!"

Source: Sun, 11 June 1987. Reprinted with permission.

place is often seen to be highly problematic, and a real concern has been the dominance of the US television industry. The implication has been that the images and interpretation carried on the global network are increasingly homogenized, increasingly excluding the local and the politically oppositional.

Closely linked to this concern is the question of deregulation of television. In Western Europe there has been a discernible process of 'deregulation'. In the UK, the 1988 White Paper on broadcasting endorsed principles first established in the 1962 Pilkington Committee's report on broadcasting, which was worried about the dangers of a 'one-sided presentation of affairs of public concern' if two or more mass communications media were ostensibly owned by the same people. Yet such principles were notable by their absence from the 1990 Broadcasting Act, which applied limits on concentrated and cross-media ownership only to commercial channels using UK broadcasting frequencies, and not to channels transmitted from private or non-UK satellite operations. The Murdoch-led News International was therefore excluded from regulation. The unregulated role of Murdoch's media empire was very interesting, given its long-standing support for the Conservative Party. Similarly, the 1990 Act also reversed previous restrictions on ownership of terrestrial television franchises whereby one company could hold only one franchise, and overseas ownership was forbidden. The spate of takeovers (Meridian/ Anglia; Granada/London Weekend Television) has led to a regrouping of the larger companies with the smaller ones isolated and under threat on the margins.

European television systems have been predominantly state-run or state-regulated, operating a variety of 'public service' models. However, deregulation seems to have increasingly resulted in what is known as the 'Canadianization' of television. Canada was one of the earliest examples of the subordination of domestic television by the US, pre-empting a phenomena that is now worldwide. Arguably, however, what we have seen is not 'deregulation', but actually 'reregulation' according to the less visible but equally powerful laws of the global marketplace, in which the US industry dominates, as do US agendas. These developments undoubtedly have very important implications for public service broadcasting, in that 'public service' stations are changing their priorities to compete. This is a phenomenon described in the context of US news coverage as 'dumbing down'—the erosion of quality television news and programming under pressure to sensationalize the news and attract the maximum audience and, in turn, the maximum revenue.

The main argument by proponents of 'deregulation' is that the few should not be able to determine what the many should and should not watch. In other words, the boards of the BBC deciding what we should watch is simply unacceptable. Instead, the market will reflect the popular will, giving people what they want. By the laws of the marketplace, if you do not give people what they want, they will not buy it! However, this is a somewhat crude understanding of the workings of the market, which is determined instead by a quest for profit which can be incompatible with public preferences.

In the UK, for instance, surveys have shown that many people want entertainment together with informing or educational programmes, and that an exclusive diet of entertainment is not what the public want (Williams 1996). Yet satellite television is remarkably devoid of their own educational programmes, for the simple reason that producing such quality programmes is expensive and does not make as much money as cheap gameshows and other forms of entertainment. The result is a growing world dominance of exclusively entertainment-led television, which may not reflect public preferences for a more mixed diet of programmes.

As we saw at the beginning of this chapter, when talking about the marketization of many forms of culture and the growing importance of consumption, so the marketization of television has dramatically affected the socially and economically marginalized in society. Without the finance to subscribe to particular channels, large groups of people have been excluded from viewing a variety of events, most obviously national sporting events. Moreover, deregulation, far from allowing lots of competition, as its protractors have argued, has instead resulted in a virtual monopoly of television within a deregulated system, which may then consciously promote certain ideas and interpretations. In Italy, for instance, there was very real concern at the way in which Prime Minister Silvio Berlusconi owned a number of television stations and newspapers, which in turn were strongly supportive of his political ideals. Certainly, free-marketeers have argued forcefully that the absence of state intervention in a deregulated television system is a guarantee of political freedom. In fact, in many South American countries those interested in democratic expression are fighting for more regulation of television. Campaigners are seeking many of the rules and ideals now being abandoned in Europe (Negrine 1988).

These concerns have been especially pronounced in the UK, where concern over the role of Rupert Murdoch as a media mogul has been very vocal. Murdoch used the huge profits from his newspaper empire to finance News International's expansion in Australia, the US, and the Far East. He paid some $325 million for his Asian satellite operation, Star TV, covering some two-thirds of the world's population, from Turkey to Japan. Linked to his European and American operations, this means that Murdoch has virtually a global reach for his satellite transmissions. Yet questions of quality or ethics seem secondary to the pursuit of money. For instance, in 1993 he dropped the BBC World Service from Star TV and replaced it with an internal version of Sky News, because of an alleged bias against China. In fact, this decision arose because China objected to the BBC's coverage of dissidents, labour camps, and the sale of body parts from executed prisoners, and threatened to restrict satellite access to the world's most populous country (Williams 1996).

In short, some commentators have argued that Rupert Murdoch actually poses a democratic threat, whereby he is so powerful that no political group dare confront his interests and try to reduce his power and influence for fear that his media power will be directed against them. The courtship of Rupert Murdoch by Tony Blair and the Labour Party before the 1997 General Election was seen by some as indicative of this point, and a compelling case for greater state regulation of media content and ownership. If regulation in the context of television is becoming an issue of growing concern and debate, nowhere is the entire question of cultural regulation more evident than in the context of the Internet.

The Internet

The next Millennium will undoubtedly be the age of the 'information superhighway', to quote US vice-president Al Gore. Information, and our access to it, is experiencing a profound revolution which seems set to alter many aspects of our lives in fundamental ways. Yet these developments also seem set to present difficult conundrums for policy-makers and social policy, if they are not already doing so. It is perhaps ironic that the contents of this chapter are destined for a printed book, when increasingly information and data, and in turn political and academic debate, is taking place not through the medium of the printed word, but electronically, through the medium of the Internet and the World Wide Web.

The development of the Internet evidently has many implications. It is certainly an excellent illustration of globalization, and some of the dilemmas that this may imply. A global village of information already exists and is growing in size and importance at a staggering rate. The opportunities to transmit and access huge quantities of data globally could have many consequences, some of which are of real importance for social policy. The educational implications of the Internet, for instance, remain to fully manifest themselves. But there is already growing concern that access to information is likely to be highly iniquitous, in turn reflecting and compounding existing inequality in educational performance, already driven as it is by stark divisions of class and income.

Box 19.4 Internet use in Great Britain

The consumer magazine *Which? Online* surveyed 2,124 people throughout Britain about the Internet in 1998. The results were very interesting.

- Approximately 14 per cent of Britons—some 7 million people—use the Internet.
- Of these, half of all users signed on in the past year.
- More than half of users were under 35, while just 7 per cent were over 55.
- Three out of four users were online for five or fewer hours a week, while 5 per cent used it for 20 or more hours a week.
- One in three users claimed that the Internet had improved their overall quality of life.
- One in ten admitted spending too much time on the Internet.
- 22 per cent of all respondents suggested that the Internet spawned unsociable computer 'anoraks' in danger of losing their grip on reality.
- 72 per cent of all respondents believed that the Internet should be regulated.
- 58 per cent of all respondents believed that the Internet undermined public morality.
- Only 13 per cent of all respondents said that they would feel comfortable allowing their children to use it unsupervised.

Yet the Internet also presents vexed questions of national regulation and control, which in turn may have important social implications. The pervasiveness of offensive material on the Internet, and the ease of its cross-national transmission and reception, has already provoked widespread anxiety (Miller 1998). Whilst this potential has most evidently come to the fore in recent child pornography, the sex industry more generally has been attracted by the ease and low cost of conveying pornographic imagery that the Internet offers. A recent estimate suggested that there are already more than 70,000 pornographic sites on the Internet, and the number is growing fast. On an immediate level, there is no doubt that the Internet is fuelling an expansion in the sex industry, which is already worth a staggering $10 billion dollars in the US (Lillington 1998). Whilst the links between pornography, sexual offences, and violence against women has long been a source of inconclusive debate (see Itzen 1992), the pervasiveness of disturbing material freely available on the Internet—from sexually explicit imagery to racist literature and almost every conceivable range of offensive content—is of growing concern to the public and policy-makers alike.

The manner in which Internet content is able to transcend national barriers with ease has raised similar questions of regulation and control to the pervasiveness of satellite and cable television. Restricting access to some Internet content raises not simply technological difficulties, but also profound questions of censorship which go to the heart of democratic society. This area is further clouded by the fact that no-one really owns the Internet, so it is not always clear who in turn is responsible for its contents.

The recent conviction of the former head of the CompuServe online service in Germany for aiding and abetting the spread of child pornography raised more questions than it answered (Traynor 1998). It was the very first occasion anywhere in the world that a representative of a firm providing access to the Internet had been criminalized because of the content of material available in cyberspace. Yet these conundrums are not going to go away for policy-makers and social policy. On the contrary, it seems certain that they will continue to grow in importance and significance. The fact that social policy has been so slow to react to these developments is clearly to the detriment of the discipline.

Conclusion

This chapter has sought to achieve a number of things. Most importantly, it has attempted to illustrate the importance of the arts and culture for social policy. It is a field which lies at the very heart of society, its cohesiveness, and its problems. Some of the themes raised in this field mirror fundamental debates in social policy. The whole question of cultural need and the inequity in cultural participation raises similar dilemmas to those surrounding social need. The long-standing debate about the importance of cultural need and the appropriateness of state intervention for meeting such need—a debate which has come to some prominence with the National Lottery—is finally being acknowledged by the Labour Government. Yet social policy continues to see the arts and culture as largely irrelevant. This is even more surprising when one considers that many social policy debates, and their political manifestations, take place in an increasingly media-conscious and media-dominated environment. The impact of the media upon social policy debates should be viewed with much more urgency and importance by the social policy community than it currently is. Many of these issues, and their social implications, are set to become increasingly pronounced as we enter the new millennium. It is time for social policy to broaden its traditional focus, and to view these concerns with the seriousness that they deserve.

Glossary

Arts The diverse body of creative endeavours concerned not simply with the visual arts, but also with music, theatre, cinema, and literature.

Arts Council of England The funding body through which the state funds the arts in England, supporting music, drama, and the visual arts with Government funds, and which is responsible to the Secretary of State for Culture, Media, and Sport. In 1994, the Scottish and Welsh Arts Councils became autonomous, directly accountable to their respective Secretaries of State.

censorship The suppression by authority of material deemed to be immoral, heretical, subversive, libellous, damaging to state security, or otherwise offensive. Censorship is not always the prerogative of Government—the media can and do exercise self-censorship.

cultural need Need defined in terms of being unable to fully participate in the cultural life of society. The growing commercialization of culture and leisure has exacerbated the exclusion of economically weak individuals from even the most basic cultural and leisure opportunities.

culture A very broad term, which literally means the way of life of a particular society or group of people. The term is often used more specifically to refer to art, music, and literature.

Internet A global system of electronic networks or a World Wide Web, through which global computer sites and addresses—and in turn the information they contain—can be easily accessed via a computer and a modem. The Internet is not owned or controlled by anyone.

mass media The techniques and institutions through which information and communication is broadcast to a large, heterogeneous, and geographically dispersed audience. In the twentieth century, the mass media include books, newspapers, radio, cinema, television, and the Internet.

National Lottery A national game of chance in which tickets sold may win a substantial prize. Established in 1994, the main National Lottery game in the UK involves trying to correctly guess the numbers of 6 balls randomly drawn from a choice of 49—at odds of 14 million to one!

philanthropy Practical charity, often in the form of funding.

plural funding The funding of arts projects through partnerships between the state (in the form of local or central government) and private finance of different kinds (such as business sponsors and individual patrons). This approach has become increasingly important in the arts world and is a condition of securing Lottery funding.

salariat The salaried class. These employees often have greater job security and face a more definite career structure than employees paid weekly. They may therefore have a greater vested interest in the organizations they work for.

Guide to Further Reading

Cahill, M., *The New Social Policy* (Oxford: Blackwell, 1994). A very influential book, and one of the few attempts to broaden the traditional focus of social policy towards new areas such as communicating, viewing, travelling, shopping, and recreation. Cahill argues that the development of an increasingly consumerist society has led to the emergence of profound inequalities in these areas, which warrant much more attention from the social policy community than they generally receive.

Curran, J. and Seaton, J., *Power Without Responsibility: The Press and Broadcasting In Britain* (4th edn., London: Routledge, 1991). An excellent overview of the debates surrounding media freedom and regulation in the UK. Whether interested in the freedom of the press, media ownership, or the development of satellite television, this is a good starting-point.

Eldridge, J. (ed.), *Getting the Message: News, Truth and Power* (London: Routledge, 1993). A collection of some of the more recent research by the Glasgow University Media Group. A variety of rich empirical articles on a diverse array of topics illustrate the complexities of the transmission and reception of ideological messages through the mass media.

Fitzherbert, L., Giussani, C., and Hunt, H. (eds.), *The National Lottery Yearbook* (London: Directory of Social Change, 1996). The consummate guide to the National Lottery and the vexed questions it raises. Drawing together Camelot's statistical data, it also offers a critical and comprehensive overview of issues such as the distribution of grants, and the impact of the National Lottery upon charitable giving and problem gambling.

Golding, P. and Middleton, S., *Images of Welfare: Press and Public Attitudes to Poverty* (Oxford: Robertson, 1982). One of the few attempts in social policy to unpack the influence of media accounts upon welfare debates and public perception of social problems like poverty. Somewhat dated in places, but the authors still make some astute points of considerable contemporary relevance.

Negrine, R., *Politics and the Mass Media in Britain* (2nd edn., London: Routledge, 1994). A comprehensive overview of the many arguments and debates surrounding the mass media in Britain. Negrine's examination of the relationship between media coverage, public opinion, and policy-making is an excellent introduction to the topic, presenting a wealth of ideas and evidence.

Social Trends, *Social Trends: The 28th Report* (London: Office for National Statistics, 1998). An invaluable sourcebook of statistical data for social policy students and academics alike. It draws together a wealth of information on the arts, culture, and leisure from a number of sources, such as the Family Expenditure Survey, the General Household Survey, and the British Social Attitudes Survey, which it then presents in a highly accessible manner.

References

Beresford, P. (1979), 'The Public Presentation of Vagrancy', in T. Cook (ed.), *Vagrancy: Some New Perspectives* (London: Academic Press).

Broadbent, L. (1993), 'Backyard on the Front Page: The Case of Nicaragua', in J. Eldridge (ed.), *Getting the Message: News, Truth and Power* (London: Routledge).

Cahill, M. (1994), *The New Social Policy* (Oxford: Blackwell).

Curran, J. and Seaton, J. (1991), *Power Without Responsibility: The Press and Broadcasting In Britain* (4th edn., London: Routledge).

Everitt, A. (1994), 'Lose the Life Support?', *Guardian* (23 May).

Fitzherbert, L., Giussani, C., and Hunt, H. (eds.) (1996), *The National Lottery Yearbook* (London: Directory of Social Change).

Golding, P. and Middleton, S. (1979), 'Making Claims: News Media and the Welfare State', *Media, Culture and Society*, 1, 5–21.

——(1982), *Images of Welfare: Press and Public Attitudes to Poverty* (Oxford: Robertson).

Hutson, S. and Liddiard, M. (1994), *Youth Homelessness: The Construction of a Social Issue* (London: Macmillan).

Itzen, C. (ed.) (1992), *Pornography: Women, Violence and Civil Liberties* (Oxford: Oxford University Press).

Jowell, R., Curtice, J., Brook, L., and Ahrendt, D. (eds.) (1994), *British Social Attitudes: The 11th Report* (Aldershot: Dartmouth).

Kemp, P. (1997), 'The Characteristics of Single Homeless People in England', in R. Burrows, N. Pleace, and D. Quilgars (eds.), *Homelessness and Social Policy* (London: Routledge).

Lasch, C. (1995), *The Revolt of the Elites and the Betrayal of Democracy* (London: Norton).

Le Grand, J. (1982), *The Strategy of Equality: Redistribution and the Social Services* (London: Allen and Unwin).

Liddiard, M. (1998), 'Homelessness—The Media, Public Attitudes and Policy-Making', in S. Hutson and D. Clapham (eds.), *Homelessness: Public Policies and Private Troubles* (London: Cassells).

——and Hutson, S. (1998), 'Youth Homelessness, the Press and Public Attitudes', *Youth and Policy*, 59, 57–69.

Lillington, K. (1998), 'Surfing for Sex', *Guardian* (14 May).

Marshall, T. H. (1963), 'Citizenship and Social Class', in *Sociology at the Crossroads* (London: Heinemann).

McLuhan, M. (1989), *The Global Village* (Oxford: Oxford University Press).

Miller, D. (1994), *Don't Mention the War: Northern Ireland, Propaganda and the Media* (London: Pluto Press).

Miller, J. (1998), 'Tangled Web', *Guardian* (28 July).

Negrine, R. (ed.) (1988), *Satellite Broadcasting: The Politics and Implications of the New Media* (London: Routledge).

——(1994), *Politics and the Mass Media in Britain* (2nd edn., London: Routledge).

Office for National Statistics (1998), *Social Trends* (London: HMSO).

Sambrook, C. (1997), 'A Gamble we Can't Afford', *Guardian* (23 April).

Sawers, D. (1993), *Should the Taxpayer Support the Arts?* (London: Institute of Economic Affairs).

Smith, A. (1998), 'Britons Buy More Papers than Other Europeans but Doubt Contents', *Guardian* (29 January).

Social Trends (1998), *Social Trends: The 28th Report* (London: Office for National Statistics).

Soothill, K. and Walby, S. (1991), *Sex Crime in the News* (London: Routledge).

Traynor, I. (1998), 'Child Porn Verdict Stuns Net Lawyer', *Guardian* (29 May).

Which? Online (1998), *Conspiracy, Controversy or Control: Are We Ready for the E-Nation?* (London: Consumers' Association).

Williams, G. (1996), *Britain's Media: How They are Related—Media Ownership and Democracy* (2nd edn., London: Campaign for Press and Broadcasting Freedom).

Part Five

Consequences and Outcomes of Social Policy

20 The Impact of Social Policy

Chris Pickvance

Contents

Introduction: Assessing the Impact of Social Policy

Social policy is inextricably linked with the idea of need. In the earlier chapters in the book, and particularly in Section Four, the way in which government action has addressed need in the different fields of social policy has been detailed. In this chapter we examine systematically what the effects of these policies have been, and in particular whether need has been met and how this varies between social groups and by social policy.

The Definition and Scope of Social Policy

In this section we discuss what is meant by social policy, and how to measure its impact, and in subsequent sections we go on to examine the impact of social policy on individuals and on society as a whole.

In this book the variety of sources of welfare has been emphasized: state, occupational, charitable, family/household, and commercial or private. However, for practical reasons, in this chapter we are concerned only with social policy, which we interpret as a category of government policy. This still leaves for discussion the question of which policies belong to this category.

Social policy has widened in scope over the last 150 years. This has reflected changing beliefs about the proper role of public action. The belief in the duty and capacity of government to take action in the face of social problems grew only gradually as a result of political pressure and the demonstrated success of government action. This process of rising expectations driving an expansion in the scope of social policy met with a counter-force from the 1970s on, when the belief that government action created more problems than it solved started to take root. Although this view never became dominant, it meant that the assumption that the scope of social policy would expand endlessly could no longer be taken for granted.

However, even if we ignore these changes over time there remains disagreement over what should be counted as social policy in the UK today.

The first issue is whether social policy should be defined narrowly as policy which seeks to ensure a minimum level of welfare for all, or to reduce inequalities in welfare, or whether broader definitions should be used, so as to include policy which aims at a high level of welfare, for example, or even to include all policy which seeks to achieve social as opposed to economic goals. It is widely agreed that social policy covers the efforts by government to ensure an adequate income for all, to prevent and treat illness, and to provide adequate housing, education, and social services for those in need. This leaves disagreements about what is meant by 'adequate', and about where the responsibilities of parents end and those of the state begin. (For example, the restriction of benefit entitlements of young people under 25 is intended to increase the role of family in looking after young people.) But beyond this, disagreement increases. Is higher education also social policy? It goes well beyond the minimum level of welfare, but contributes to the social goal of a more educated workforce. Here higher education will be included.

The second issue is whether we should restrict ourselves to what is conventionally labelled as social policy. There are two points:

- A number of policies are indirectly aimed at helping the poor though they are not labelled social policy. Examples include urban and regional policies which support activities in deprived areas and industrial policies which are guided by the need to reduce unemployment. In practice the amount of spending covered by such examples is low compared with that on social policy as conventionally defined.

- Labels are not an accurate guide to the purposes of a policy. Housing policy is not primarily about providing minimum or even good housing for all: in recent decades it has been mainly about increasing the scope of home-ownership as an end in itself irrespective of condition, cost, or amenity levels. Likewise, the pegging of increases in the state pension to inflation rather than to average earnings means that by 2040 the state pension is expected to fall to 7.5 per cent of average earnings. Hence pensions policy makes a difference to people's welfare, but is far from meeting their basic needs. Other objectives, such as controlling government spending, play a major role. This suggests that social policies reflect a mix of objectives and that their 'social' content is less than figures of spending on social policy would suggest.

Measuring Social Policy

Whatever choice is made about the definition of social policy, in order to establish its impact it is necessary to know whether 'more' or 'less' of a social policy has been provided. In other words we must be able to measure the volume of social policy in existence at any time. This appears to be a simple question, but turns out to be more complex. To explore it we examine in turn what is meant by meeting need, since this is the usual description of the purpose of social policy, and how to measure the volume of social policy.

Social policy comes in three forms:

- Regulation, that is, the establishment of constraints on the actions of individuals and firms so as to increase social welfare. This includes building, energy, and planning standards in housing; regulations about the handling of food, the labelling of food, and food additives; and rules about the training needed by the different categories of workers in the health service.

- Taxation, that is, the differential levying of taxes so as to protect the poorest groups or groups with a particular need. Two examples are income tax, which exempts those with the lowest income, and is set at increasing rates at higher income levels, and the lower rate of VAT on electricity and gas, which recognizes that energy represents a larger proportion of household budgets for poor households.

- Provision, where government spending is used in pursuit of social welfare aims. This takes two main forms:
  1. Benefits in kind, or services, such as healthcare, education, public housing, and personal social services; and
  2. cash benefits, such as pensions, 'jobseekers' allowance', housing benefit, income support, and incapacity benefit.

For reasons of space this chapter will only be concerned with provision in the form of services and cash benefits. In some cases the arguments of the chapter apply to both forms of provision equally, but in other cases we shall consider services and cash benefits separately.

Let us first consider what is meant by 'meeting welfare needs'. This concept has two aspects: what is meant by need, and what is meant by meeting it. We shall also consider here a third issue: the match between the volume of benefits provided by a social policy relative to the scale of need.

The most debated issue concerns how to measure need quantitatively. (See Chapter 6 for a fuller discussion.)

There are three approaches to measuring need. One can

- rely on subjective judgements (by asking service users, say). This is often referred to as 'felt' or 'expressed' need.
- rely on expert judgements (such as by asking professionals or managers involved in providing a service). This is usually referred to as 'normative need'.
- assume that existing provision meets needs (by taking the current cost per capita of meeting a particular need for each person in a need category as a measure of need).

Each approach has certain drawbacks. The first is open to the possibility that people will express 'unrealistic' needs, and the second is open to the objection that professionals and managers will define needs 'generously' so as to expand employment opportunities in their organizations, though they may also defend the status quo. The third approach is optimistic, since it does not allow for any shortfall in meeting need, and is also crude, since it is based on numbers of people in categories rather than individuals and their needs. In practice the second and third approaches overlap, since existing provision is partly based on expert opinion: but it is also based on cost constraints. Most often, calculations of need for a category are based on the third method, by multiplying the cost of existing provision per person and demographic estimates of the number of people in the need category. For example, the healthcare needs of the over-85s in an area are calculated by estimating their size in the population and the average healthcare spending per capita in this group, or the need for primary education is based on the number of children of primary school age in an area and the average education spending per child. The fact that need is often calculated in respect of those living in an area, and that there are inter-area variations in need, is central to the idea of territorial justice discussed below.

A further useful distinction is between the **horizontal** and **vertical dimensions of need.** These are closely related to the concepts of 'breadth' and 'depth' (or 'intensity') of need. The proportion of the population in need is referred to as the 'horizontal' dimension, while the average level of need per person (and hence the level of service, or benefit, provided to each) is referred to as the 'vertical' dimension. A given sum of money could be used to provide a limited service to many or a more adequate service to a minority. The horizontal dimension thus reflects the level of **take-up,** the proportion of those eligible who actually receive the service or benefit. This is a misleading term, since it implies that the cause is ignorance, lack of effort or interest, or pride among the potential recipients, rather than any poor management or lack of effort by the providers.

The debate about measuring need tends to leave aside the more fundamental question of whether the forms in which education, healthcare, housing, or personal social services are provided do meet people's needs. Policy debates often take for granted that existing forms of provision are largely on the right lines, and that if the right groups are gaining access to a service their needs are being met. But radicals, who question existing forms of provision, would argue that they often represent the interests of the providers rather than those of the consumers, and that people's expressed needs are highly conditioned by what is available in society. Hence it is less likely that people will say they have a need for alternative forms, such as complementary medicine, or radical methods of education and housing provision (self-build, co-operatives, and so on). The debate about whether services meet needs is therefore often about who is receiving the service, which is a different question. It starts from the expert's view rather than the recipient's, and does not ask what benefit recipients derive from the service or benefit. However, innovation in service provision does take place, both instigated by professionals ('community care' for elderly people) and by users, for example some forms of 'community care' demanded by disabled people.

What is meant by meeting need? This is a simple question with a complex answer.

A primary-school-age child has a need for education. This is a societal value embodied in the state requirement, in the UK, that compulsory education extends from 5 to 16. If state schools were the only way of meeting this need, then we could say that the need for primary-level state education in an area depended on the number of primary-age children. This leads to the **principle of uniform service provision,** which implies that uniform provision enables uniform meeting of needs. It could, for example, lead to an identical per pupil allocation of funds for primary education in all areas. But this is only one possibility.

An alternative is that in some areas, such as in inner cities or deprived outer council estates, a greater input of resources is needed in primary schools to compensate for the disadvantaged situation from which the children come. In other words, to provide equality of opportunity, unequal provision is required to meet needs equally. This is the **principle of proportional service provision,** and implies that where needs among a population group are unequal, provision should be proportional to need. (The parallel principles in the case of cash benefits are universalism and selectivity: see Chapter 11.)

The two principles may be used together. For example, in education resources are allocated partly on a per-pupil basis and partly in recognition of special situations. Schools in deprived areas do receive additional resources, as do schools with many 'special needs' pupils.

Finally it is worth mentioning a closely related idea: the principle of **territorial justice.** This concept was introduced by Davies (1968) (see also Boyne and Powell, 1991) in recognition of the fact that most services are provided on an area basis and need varies from one area to another. Territorial justice refers to a situation where the provision of services (health, personal social services, and so on) in different areas varies in proportion to inter-area differences in need. It should be noted that territorial justice is a relative concept, since it does not concern the absolute level of provision. It could mean that need is met equally badly in different areas or that it is met equally well.

The final issue in measuring social policy is whether a growth in spending on a service, or in the number of direct service providers (teachers, GPs, or social workers), means that more welfare is being produced and need is being better met than before.

Two types of measure of social policy will be considered here: input measures and output measures. A third type of measure, an outcome measure, is discussed in the next section, since it refers to the impact of social policy. We will use the example of a service here; cash benefits will be discussed later.

An **input measure** of a social policy is a measure of the various inputs used to provide a service. The simplest input measure is spending. This covers the wages and salaries of the staff employed (administrative and manual as well as professional staff in health or education), the goods and services used (drugs, books, and so on), and capital spending (on new buildings and equipment, for example). But what improves the overall state of welfare in a service area is how much of the service is produced and how appropriately it is allocated. This depends partly on the amount of spending on the budgetary items listed above, and partly on how they are combined together and managed. Input measures bear some relation to the service provided, but cannot tell us how efficiently or wastefully services are being provided and how well they are being directed to those in need.

There are other input measures besides spending, such as the number of GPs or teachers employed, or, more commonly, the number of GPs per 100,000 population (the average GP list size) or the average class size. These are more direct measures of input, since they refer to the direct providers of social services. Their weakness is that social policy outcomes depend on all inputs (and not only the number of direct providers) and how they are combined. For example, however appealing the idea, it does not follow that if all administrative staff were replaced by teachers or GPs a more efficient service would result. A certain level of administrative staffing is necessary to ensure that the efforts of direct providers are effectively channelled.

A second type of measure is known as an **output measure**, because it measures not the service inputs but the volume of the service itself, such as healthcare or personal social services, and hence gets closer to the idea of a measure of the welfare produced by the service. There are two types of measure: service-based and access-based. The former include the number of 'patient treatment episodes' in hospitals (since one patient may need a series of treatments) or the number of children living in local-authority-run children's homes, and the latter include the proportion of people waiting more than one year for hospital treatment. Obviously there is some connection between input measures and output measures, since without resources no services could be provided, but output measures take account of how spending feeds through into the provision of services. The problem with service-based output measures is that they do not distinguish between more and less appropriate or successful service provision. For example, repeated attempts to treat the same illness would show up as increased healthcare provision even if it was misdirected. The problem with access-based measures such as waiting-list length, which is popular with politicians, is that they assume that people's need for the service is equal. In fact, the need for hospital treatment varies in urgency, and overall welfare may be better served by the proportional than by the uniform principle of provision: by giving priority in treatment to those with the most urgent need, even if they have not waited very long.

Since it would make little sense to spend more on or provide more of a service irrespective of the need for it, both input and output measures are usually calculated *for a region or district*, and are considered in conjunction with the need for treatment *in that area*. In other words, territorial justice is sought.

Thus the assumption that more spending on a social policy means more welfare turns out to be questionable. Everything depends on how the spending is used, how it is allocated between areas, and how it is targeted on groups in need.

Finally, we turn briefly to the question of measuring social policy provided through cash benefits. In the case of social policies which take the form of cash benefits, input measures (spending) are usually used. The main limitation of *total* spending measures of cash benefits is that they are a product of the numbers receiving the benefit (which itself depends on the number eligible and the level of take-up) and the level of the benefit. A rising trend in spending on a cash benefit may be because of an increase in claimants rather than because of an increase in generosity of benefit levels. Ideally, therefore, both take-up and benefit level need to be known.

In contrast, output measures are not generally used. One reason for this is that cash benefits are used directly by those receiving them to obtain increased welfare. No professionals are involved, as in the case of service-based social policies like health or education. In theory one could examine whether inputs in the form of cash benefits are converted into a welfare 'output' by the recipient, or whether they are 'diverted' to some other purpose. The possibility that cash benefits are not translated by their recipients into welfare outputs leads to the provision of benefits in a non-transferable form (as in the US system of food stamps, for example) or the payment of cash directly to the provider of welfare (such as in the UK when housing benefit is paid direct to landlords).

In sum, both input and output measures of social policies are all either conceptually debatable or difficult to apply in practice, and hence need to be treated with caution.

Measuring the Impact of Social Policy

The question of how to establish the impact of social policy is a particular case of the general issue of how to identify cause–effect relations. This is a thorny problem in all social scientific work. There are two main reasons for this.

First, society is complex and many possible causes operate simultaneously, which makes it difficult to identify the effect of a single cause (or rather, collection of causes) such as a social policy. For example, the number of people experiencing poverty depends on the effectiveness of social policy, but also on demographic and labour market processes (such as birth rates, household formation and dissolution rates, migration rates, the availability of jobs in different sectors of the labour market, and wage levels) which increase or decrease the number of individuals potentially in poverty.

Second, because the success of policies is economically significant and politically important, politicians, officials, and others involved will make claims about the effect of social policy which may be more intended to take credit and avoid blame than to make a careful assessment. Social science thus has to find a path through the thicket of claims by actors for whom social policy is important.

To claim that social policy has had an impact of some type, three conditions must be met:

- the social policy must occur before the effect claimed for it. This is perhaps too obvious to need stating. But it is not uncommon for writers to claim that trends which had been in existence for some time are evidence of the success of a new policy;
- variations in the policy must be associated with variations in the claimed effect. This is the

familiar point that if two things are causally related they will vary together. However, the reverse is not true. Events or processes which occur together or rise and fall over time together are not necessarily linked by cause–effect relations: causation is more than correlation. This is not an easy condition to meet, since the presence of multiple causes means that cause–effect relations may be concealed. Multivariate statistical analysis allows a disentangling of such complexities if certain simplifying assumptions are accepted;

- the nature of the causal process(es) linking the policy with its claimed effect must be identified or hypothesized. This requirement is also difficult to meet. First, causal connections are not directly observable, but are matters of inference. Writers belonging to different theoretical schools disagree both about what causal connections are likely to exist and about what evidence would establish that they do. Debates about causal connections cannot be settled by an 'appeal to the facts' because of the disagreement about which 'facts' are relevant. Second, as mentioned above, many causes are in operation, and they may be hard to identify and disentangle. Comparison with other countries, or with the same country in the past, may be helpful, but only if it is assumed that there are common processes operating and no significant differences—a matter which, again, may be debated between theoretical schools. Third, we are only aware of some of the causes which operate. Scientific progress involves identifying new causal links and improving our understanding of policy impact.

For all these reasons the general problems of identifying cause–effect relations apply to the question of the impact of social policy, and any claims about this impact are best regarded as provisional.

This can be demonstrated if we examine what are known as **outcome measures** of social policy because they are believed to measures the result of the policy. Examples are the level of morbidity (ill-health) in an area, school examination results, or the life expectation of elderly people receiving 'community care'. The attraction of this type of measure is that it comes closest to being an indicator of impact, in the sense of additional welfare due to social policy. The drawback of outcome measures is that that they measure the outcome of a large number of processes, of which the social policy of interest is only one. (The term 'outcome measure' is thus a misnomer.) For example, school exam results reflect the ability of children admitted to a school and the extent of parental support, as well as the efforts of the school; and morbidity reflects nutrition, living and working conditions, and environmental effects as well as healthcare. Unless the causal influence of these processes can be taken into account the impact of a social policy cannot be identified. A further issue concerns when outcomes should be measured. While in some cases an immediate measure is appropriate, in others, such as preventive healthcare, outcomes need to be measured over a longer period. Social policy can also have wider impacts on society generally. These are considered later in the chapter.

Finally, two more general points about assessing the impact of social policy must be made. First, it is important to distinguish between the aims and the effects of a social policy. The aims of a policy refer to the intentions of policy-makers or of those involved in implementing the policy, which may themselves conflict or change over time: in some cases they are even modified retrospectively in the light of changing government priorities. Hence, although every policy has aims, there is a degree of flexibility about them which makes them an unstable yardstick by which to judge the success of a policy. In our case this does not matter since we are concerned with the effects of social policy, and aims are distinct from effects.[1] However, in practice it is difficult to avoid some reference to aims. Second, there is no necessary connection between pressure groups who are influential in bringing a policy into existence and the effects of the policy. One cannot say that because a pressure group was influential that the population category the group is fighting on behalf of is the main beneficiary. The effects of a policy can only be assessed in the way indicated above.

In sum, there are very considerable problems in establishing the effects of social policy, and we need to pay attention to the methods used by those who claim to have identified their effects.

The Impact of Social Policy on Individual Households

We consider, first, the substantive question of the impact of social policy on individual households; in the next section we discuss its impact on society as a whole. Before considering the different fields of social policy, some general comments will be made.

First, it is useful to have a general picture of the pattern of spending on social policy. The shares of social policy spending going on services and on cash benefits are roughly equal. In 1995 public spending on health accounted for 5.7 per cent of GDP, on education 5.1 per cent, on personal social services 1.2 per cent, and on housing 0.6 per cent (excluding housing benefits, which account for 1.7 per cent). Spending on cash benefits including housing benefits amounted to 13.1 per cent of GDP.[2]

Second, it is helpful to list the different elements which may be present in an increase of spending. The increase may be:

- to meet increasing horizontal need, that is, to provide the service or benefit to more people;
- to meet increasing vertical need, that is, to provide a higher level of benefit or a more adequate service to each recipient;
- to allow for inflation; and
- to allow for decreased efficiency.

The main difficulty of assessing the impact of social policy from spending figures is to assess the roles of these four elements.

Horizontal need is easy to estimate in some cases (such as the number of school-age

---

[1] There are various reasons why policy aims may not be achieved: the level of funding may be inadequate, people may respond to the policy in unexpected ways (people may fail to take up a benefit because it is felt to be stigmatizing, say, or elderly people may divest themselves of assets in order to be eligible for state support for their housing), or countervailing processes are present (for example, low-income households who need home improvement grants most are less likely to take them up if they cover only part of the cost of the work needed). More generally, it is common for policies to have unintended consequences. For example, in order to succeed in terms of one outcome measure, effort is diverted from activities which are not being measured.

[2] Unless otherwise stated, all the figures in this section of the chapter are taken from Glennerster and Hills (1998). This is an indispensable work which provides a comprehensive and convenient source of data on social policy inputs, outputs, and outcomes. It also contains numerous data sets which are not available elsewhere.

children) but difficult in others (such as the number entitled to mobility allowance, which depends on a doctor's assessment). Vertical need is more difficult to estimate, because it implies that different people within a need category have different needs (for example, different children have different intensities of need).

Inflation can be taken into account in either of two ways. Actual spending each year is recorded in 'money terms' or 'current prices', and will therefore rise simply because of inflation. If allowance is made for the rise in the general price level (that is, for the increase in prices for *all* goods and services) the result is a figure referred to as **real spending**. Alternatively, if allowance is made for the rise in prices of those goods and services in the sector concerned (such as health or education), the result is referred to as 'volume terms spending' or **volume spending**. If the prices of the goods and services bought with social policy spending rose at the same rate as prices generally, real spending and volume spending would be identical. In practice, the price of goods and services purchased with most types of social policy spending goes up relatively faster than the general rate of inflation.[3] Spending in 'real terms' or 'real spending' thus underestimates the rate of inflation in the field of social policy and overestimates the value of social policy inputs. 'Volume spending' allows for inflation experienced in the social services, but understates the value of social policy inputs, since it assumes that if the volume of, say, teachers remains the same their productivity remains the same. In practice, through the use of computers or improved management these teachers may become more productive. Neither real nor volume spending is therefore a perfect measure of inputs, and Sefton (1997) suggests that the truth lies somewhere between them.

Lastly, efficiency is the most difficult element to measure, as it relates to the conversion of inputs into outputs and is therefore affected by the uncertainties surrounding both of these measures. (Chapter 5 includes a discussion of different types of efficiency.)

We now examine in turn the impact of healthcare, education, housing, personal social services, and cash benefits.

Healthcare

Health is the largest service in terms of public spending. Although 10 per cent of the population is covered by private health insurance, this is used mainly for elective surgery, and private expenditure on healthcare accounts for less than 3 per cent of public healthcare costs (Le Grand and Vizard 1998: 98). Public spending on healthcare is therefore the dominant form of healthcare. The overall aim of health policy is to improve the nation's health. Secondary aims are to achieve greater equity between groups and places, to use resources efficiently, and to be responsive to changes in need and in medical knowledge. The majority of spending is on hospital care.

---

[3] This is known as the 'relative price effect' and occurs because employees are a crucial part of the service being provided in the social policy sphere and hence the chance of saving money by substituting employees by machines is very limited. In contrast in manufacturing industry this option is normal; the consumer does not mind if higher wages lead employers to replace workers by machines. Indeed, the involvement of robots becomes a selling-point in the marketing of cars. There is no sign of this happening in the social policy field: the caring quality of nurses or the ability of teachers to inspire cannot be replaced by machines. It is true that computers are heavily used in education and in administration in all areas of social policy, but they only partly save money, since they require new staff to be employed and may raise the quality of the service.

How much health service provision is taking place and what is its impact?

The simplest input measure of healthcare is health spending. In general increased spending can only be taken to mean that need is being better met (either horizontally or vertically) if we can be sure

- that the need for the service has not increased;
- that costs have not gone up so that the same spending buys less of the service. Hence the need to look at real and volume spending; and
- that efficiency, that is, the conversion of inputs into outputs, has not fallen.

If need has increased, costs have risen, or efficiency has fallen, higher spending will be needed to meet need at the same level.

Between 1981 and 1995 real spending on the National Health Service rose by 55 per cent, but volume spending rose by only 28 per cent (Le Grand and Vizard, 1998: Table 4.1).[4] But how did this increase in inputs match the change in needs? A demographically based estimate of needs suggests that between 1981 and 1995 a 10 per cent increase was needed simply to meet the greater demands on healthcare due to people living longer (Le Grand and Vizard 1998: Table 4.4). This estimate is likely to be an underestimate, since it assumes that people's health needs were being adequately met in the base year, which can only be an assumption. Hence volume spending on health inputs increased by about 1.8 per cent per year faster than needs in this period, or less if health needs were not being met adequately in the base year.

How did these inputs vary by region and by social group? The regional distribution of real health spending per capita on all items (including both hospitals and primary care provided by GPs) between 1985 and 1994 shows an increase in the spread between regions: the 'coefficient of variation', a statistical measure of spread between regions, increased from 0.103 to 0.143 (Le Grand and Vizard 1998: Table 4.8). No data is available to compare this with the changing regional distribution of need for healthcare. But 'unless there was also a growing and matching inequality in need, this suggests that regional inequalities may be increasing' (Le Grand and Vizard 1998: 104.) In other words, territorial injustice in this respect is increasing. This trend is despite an explicit policy introduced in 1976 aimed at reducing regional inequalities.

Another measure of variation of inputs by region, the number of GPs per 100,000 population, shows that here, too, regional variation increased between 1975 and 1995. Thus while the average number of GPs per 100,000 in the UK rose from 48 to 61, it ranged from 43 (Trent) to 58 (Scotland) in 1975, and from 53 (North Western) to 76 (in Scotland) in 1995 (Le Grand and Vizard 1998: Table 4.9).

The variation in inputs used by different social groups has been studied, but while research in the 1970s showed that professionals and managers received 40 per cent higher spending per ill person than the semi- and unskilled, later studies found no such bias (quoted in Le Grand and Vizard 1998: 107).

Thus, while overall, inputs may have increased faster than needs, the distribution of these inputs between regions implies considerable and possibly widening territorial

---

4 In places my classification of services as inputs or outputs or my interpretation of the data diverges from that in Glennerster and Hills (1998).

injustice. As a result the impact of health service provision on health is likely to have been less than otherwise.

Turning to output measures of healthcare, two types are available: measures of the services received by different social groups, and access-based measures. In the case of the former, studies of the use of services suggest that poorer groups visit GP surgeries more than better-off groups (assuming their need is reflected in their age-distribution) and are more often hospital in-patients, whereas better-off groups phone their GPs more and make more use of outpatient treatment (Evandrou, referred to in Le Grand and Vizard 1998: 107). On the other hand, South Asians and Caribbean make less use of both in-patient and out-patient services than their needs would suggest.

As far as access-based measures are concerned, waiting lists for in-patient treatment grew from 628,000 in 1981 to 729,000 in 1991, and for all treatment from 948,000 in 1991 to 1,164,000 in 1997 (Le Grand and Vizard 1998: 99). However, the proportion waiting over one year fell from 24 per cent in 1988 to 1 per cent in 1996 (Le Grand and Vizard 1998: Table 4.6). The latter reflects the targeting of policy to reduce waiting times.

What was the impact of these healthcare inputs and outputs on health?

The most commonly used outcome measures are mortality and morbidity rates. There is conflicting evidence about mortality rates. The life expectation for men and women, allowing for differences in the size of each age cohort, increased from 70.4 to 71.5 between 1974 and 1994, and the male–female gap narrowed slightly. On the other hand, class differences for males dying between 20 and 64 have increased: unskilled workers in this age range were 1.8 times more likely to die than professionals in 1970/2, but 2.9 times more likely to do so by 1991/3 (Le Grand and Vizard 1998: Table 4.10).

Evidence on morbidity shows an increase in self-reported chronic and acute illness between 1974 and 1994, even when the effect of the ageing population is taken into account. This may be linked with the increase in waiting lists mentioned earlier. But class differences in chronic and acute illness have not increased over time (Le Grand and Vizard 1998: Fig. 4.2 and Table 4.12).

As mentioned earlier, these outcomes reflect many other processes besides the public spending on health. However, if inputs have indeed risen faster than needs in total, then it is likely that it is the maldistribution of inputs and outputs (such as access to hospital and GP care) between need categories (social or spatial), which explains why the effect on morbidity has not been greater. On the other hand, non-health-service factors such as lifestyles, and domestic, work, and environmental situations may have counteracted the positive effects of health services.

Education

The aims of education policy are a mix of social and individual goals. Education provides benefits to society and employers, but also facilitates individual advancement. In recent years central government has challenged the power of local authorities and teacher unions, and has imposed a core curriculum and set standards of attainment to be reached at specific ages.

Education is the second largest service after health in terms of public spending: it covers primary, secondary, special, further, and higher education. As in the case of health, private spending on education is dwarfed by public spending, though its share is larger than that of private health spending: private education spending accounted for 15.1 per cent of total education spending in 1995. Public expenditure on education went up by 32 per cent between 1973 and 1995 in real terms, but by only 6 per cent in volume terms (Glennerster 1998: Tables 3A1 and 3A2).

However, these figures are not very meaningful, since demographic processes can produce large fluctuations in the number of children. Hence it is worth examining the figures for spending per pupil.

Real education spending per pupil between 1973 and 1995 rose 101 per cent for primary pupils, 62 per cent for secondary pupils, and 62 per cent for post-school age students. The corresponding figures for volume spending were 57 per cent, 27 per cent, and −48 per cent, or roughly 2.6 per cent, 1.2 per cent, and −2.2 per cent per year. The effect of taking into account demographic change is thus to show high rates of increase of spending for primary and secondary education, but a decline in spending levels for post-school education. This is because the size of the primary and secondary school cohorts fell over the period, while the number of post-school students increased sharply as the level of participation in higher education was increased as a matter of policy from 1988. Interestingly, the figures for primary and secondary education show increases only slightly less than those for health spending.

There is some evidence on the distribution of education spending by area and social group. The level of variation between local education authorities in spending per pupil rose in both primary and secondary education between 1974 and 1993: the coefficient of variation rose from 9.2 to 19.1 for primary schools, and from 8.8 to 14.6 for secondary schools (Glennerster 1998: Table 3.9). This is hard to interpret in the absence of measures of need but, as argued above in relation to similar divergent trends in the health field, unless the variation is due to corresponding variations in need it must be concluded that the distribution of educational spending is becoming less equitable, that is, that there has been a decline in territorial justice.

We now examine educational output measures. Class sizes in primary schools in England fell from 27 in 1977 to 25 in 1980 and rose to 27 in 1995, while in secondary schools class sizes fell from 21 in 1977 to 20 in 1985 and rose to 22 in 1995 (Glennerster 1998: Table 3.4). From 1986 the proportions of 17-year-olds staying on at school started to increase, rising to 60 per cent in 1994. In higher education the participation rate doubled in the five-year period between 1989 and 1994, reaching 30 per cent, but spending rose only slightly, creating the fall in spending per student mentioned above.

What was the impact of these educational inputs and outputs? Indicators of educational outcomes such as examination results and performance-based league tables of schools have become increasingly central to policy debates in the last two decades. The proportion of 17-year-olds gaining one or more 'A' level rose from 16 per cent in 1970 to 22 per cent in 1993, and the proportion of 15-year-olds gaining an A to C grade at GCSE or 'O' level rose from 42 to 70 per cent in the same period (Glennerster 1998: Table 3.5). There is an unresolved debate about how far this is due to an alleged easing of examination standards, to the efforts of schools and pupils, and to external factors. It has been speculated that schools are becoming more selective about entering pupils for exams in order to obtain a higher school-based pass rate, but this would reduce the proportion of an age group passing exams. There is also evidence of non-white pupils (especially Asians) being particularly successful in exams.

As in the case of health outcomes, educational outcomes are the result of processes outside as well as inside the school. Social class and home background are particularly influential. Since the class structure of the population is shifting upwards, that in itself should lead to an improvement of exam results. However, from 1974 to 1990, while there remained a correlation between parental class and a person's highest qualifications, this was becoming less strong (Glennerster 1998: Table 3.11). This implies that higher qualifications ('A' levels and degrees) are spreading beyond the professional, managerial, and other non-manual groups, and that this is an effect not due to social class-related social processes. It reinforces the idea that the educational system can take responsibility for some of the improved educational outcomes.

Increasingly, league tables are being drawn up containing a wider range of measures of school performance, including truancy and expulsions as well as exam results. These tables do not generally take into account the social characteristics of the children admitted, their home background, and so on. In the near future it is likely that this will be done, and that the 'value added' by the school will become apparent.

Housing

In health and education we noted that private expenditure played a marginal role and social policy operated through public provision. Housing is a contrast in both respects. Private expenditure is dominant, and social policy is as much directed towards what happens in the private sector of housing as it is to public housing provision. This has three consequences: public spending on housing provision is minute compared with health and education, public subsidies to private housing are significant, and the public regulation of private housing is substantial. As shown in Chapter 16, public spending on housing now takes the form mainly of housing benefits,[5] though tax relief on mortgage interest, which is a tax expenditure rather than public spending, is similar in value to public spending on housing excluding housing benefits.

This leads to a further distinctive feature. In the 1950s and 1960s the aim of housing policy was to provide adequate housing for all at an affordable cost, a clearly social goal, and this involved a large council house building programme. In the last two decades, however, the prime aim of housing policy has been the promotion of owner-occupation, a political rather than a social goal. As will be seen, this leads to some problems in measuring policy inputs, outputs, and impacts.

The main elements of public spending on housing are subsidies to council housing, housing benefit, loans to local councils, and grants to private owners (for improvement) and to housing associations for building. These five elements of spending fell by 3 per cent in total in real terms in the 1973 to 1996 period. Housing benefits rose from 25 to 81 per cent of the total, while the other items shrunk from 75 to 19 per cent as council housebuilding has all but stopped and subsidies to councils have shrunk. Mortgage interest tax relief has fallen by 27 per cent in real terms over a period when the number

---

[5] Housing benefits are a cash benefit but are considered here because they are so clearly linked to a specific sector of social policy.

of owner-occupiers was expanding. The concept of outputs is clear in the case of government provision (of public housing, for example). It is less so where government provides incentives or partial finance, as in the case of housing-association housing or improvement grants. In these cases the output is the joint responsibility of government and other actors, and is best seen as an indirect output. Between 1973 and 1995 council housebuilding fell from 97,000 to 2,000 dwellings per year, while housing association building rose from 9,000 to 39,000. Both efforts were dwarfed by private building of between 140,000 and 190,000 dwellings throughout the period (Hills 1998: Table 5.5).

Turning to the impact of these inputs and outputs, the concept of housing 'outcome' is ambiguous for two reasons. First, since housing policy has been so tied to promoting owner-occupation in recent years it can be argued that the level of owner-occupation should be the only or at least the primary measure of policy success. Second, as the council-housing sector shrinks, most housing outcomes are due to market processes (in which government has some regulatory involvement, but which have their own dynamic), and can thus only partly be regarded as outcomes of policy.

In terms of traditional social measures of housing conditions, we can measure the adequacy of housing in physical terms and in terms of affordability. It was shown in Chapter 16 that, despite increases in the number of dwellings, the housing stock is less than the number of households, and that over 100,000 households each year have been accepted as statutorily homeless by local authorities since 1985. Measures of the quality of the housing stock show that the proportion of dwellings in England which were unfit, lacked one or more amenity, or were in serious disrepair fell from 19.7 per cent in 1971 to 9.5 per cent in 1986 (Hills 1998: Table 5.15), and that the worst conditions were in the private rented sector. Poorer households, and Asian and black households, were disproportionately living in the worst housing conditions. There was a fall in the proportion of households living in overcrowded conditions (one or more persons per room) from 1974 to 1990 and a slight rise in 1994. The 1994 proportion is 8.8 per cent of adults, which rises to 21.4 per cent for adults born outside Europe and North America. Thus there have been improvements in the overall housing situation, but particular groups, including the poor and ethnic minorities, are disproportionately in the worst housing.

Affordability is best measured by the proportion of income devoted to housing costs after receipt of mortgage interest tax relief or housing benefit. From 1987 to 1994 this proportion fell for mortgagors from 14 to 13 per cent and for housing association tenants from 12 to 11 per cent, but rose for council tenants (from 8 to 10 per cent), private furnished tenants (10 to 16 per cent), and private unfurnished tenants (18 to 25 per cent) (Hills 1998: Table 5.22). In other words, excluding housing association tenants, affordability problems increased for the poorer and decreased for the better-off. If we focus on the proportions who were paying over 25 per cent of their income on housing this figure increased by one-third or more for the latter three tenure groups, while it fell by one-quarter or more for the former two tenures. This reinforces the picture of a polarization process in which the poorest households have not shared proportionately in improvements in housing conditions and are, on average, living in less affordable housing than before.

So far we have considered traditional social measures of housing conditions. But since the main aim of housing policy in the last twenty years has been the expansion of owner-occupation, success in this respect needs to be examined. It was shown in Table 16.2 that the proportion of owner-occupiers in Great Britain had risen from 50.5 per cent in 1971 to 66 per cent in 1991 and 66.9 per cent in 1996. This was a product of the promotion of the sale of council houses, the raising of council rents, and the subsidizing of owner-occupation. It is difficult to see it as entirely a process of 'choice', since the declining size of the private rented and council rented sectors introduced severe constraints on the housing available. The mortgage arrears and negative equity problems experienced by owner-occupiers when house prices started to fall have led to a more measured attitude to owner-occupation by the government. The idea that different housing tenures should receive equal amounts of subsidy, 'tenure neutrality', is far from being accepted by government, but the excesses of the promotion of owner-occupation are now acknowledged.

Personal Social Services

As a field of social policy the personal social services are smaller than health and education in spending terms, but they have grown considerably since the 1960s. They are the services provided to a diverse range of groups, including physically disabled people, people with learning disabilities, people with mental illness, children in need of protection, delinquents, and elderly people who cannot live independently or who cannot afford to pay for their residential care. The services provided seek to integrate these groups into society. This is done by a variety of means, including residential provision on the one hand, and day care and domiciliary care by social workers and others for those living in the 'community'. The main policy developments over the last decade have been to close hospital and residential provision for mentally ill and elderly people, and to encourage 'community care', which involves an extended range of services tailored to the needs of the individual under the management of a professional social worker. A further change has been to shift the role of the local authority from provider towards that of enabler, where the local authority has the responsibility for paying for a service, but does not have to provide the service itself. Private and charitable organizations may provide the service instead, and social security benefits may be drawn on. The fact that cash benefits are increasingly involved in maintaining people in the 'community' means that comparing spending on personal social services from year to year is not comparing like with like.

Between 1973 and 1993 real spending on personal social services rose at 3.8 per cent per annum, and volume spending at about 3.5 per cent per annum. This is in excess of the amount thought necessary to meet demographic and 'inescapable' increases in need (a rather imprecise concept). Between 1986 and 1994 real spending (net of charges) rose by 6.4 per cent per annum for elderly people as a group, 9.3 per cent for younger physically disabled people, and 15.8 per cent for mentally ill people (Evandrou and Falkingham 1998: Table 6.5a).

The meaning of these spending statistics are particularly difficult to analyse. In addition to the question of the size of the need group we discussed earlier, there is the effect of the change in form of provision from hospital and residential care to daycare. In practice, while there has been a decline in the number of sponsored residential places and an increase in the number of day places for elderly people, for people with mental illness there was an increase in both residential places and daycare places, while for people with physical disabilities there was a decline in both (Evandrou and Falkingham 1998: Table 6.6).

Considering the three groups in turn, Evandrou and Falkingham (1998) show that, for elderly people, the group with the lowest rate of annual real spending increase, neither residential care nor home help provision has kept pace with demographically estimated demand; meals provided in the home also fell behind need until 1994. There is some evidence that those who do receive home helps and meals are in the greatest need (that is, they need help with mobility or looking after themselves), but only two-thirds of this group had received help in the previous month, suggesting incomplete coverage.

Moreover, the proportion of elderly people receiving local-authority-organized home help has fallen from 62 per cent in 1980 to 45 per cent in 1994—though this figure rose with increasing age and lower income. Evandrou and Falkingham point out that local authorities are not subject to sanctions if they fail to meet targets for providing (or paying for) adequate care for elderly people. Another author points out that it is the second **income quintile** of elderly people, rather than the first (lowest) quintile who received most spending on residential care (Sefton 1997: Table 5.2).

Mentally ill people, the group with the highest rate of annual real spending increase between 1986 and 1994 and who experienced a rise in both residential and day care places, have also benefited from an increase in those who live at home financed by social security payments and by an increase in community mental-health nurses. This suggests that a real increase in their level of welfare has taken place.

For younger people with physical disabilities who as a group have seen an intermediate increase in spending, there has been a decline in residential places without any increase in daycare places. This group seems to have experienced a decline in welfare, on average.

Finally, it should be noted that the above spending figures are in real rather than volume terms (which tend to exaggerate the value of services provided), and are also affected by the change from hospital and residential provision to daycare and domiciliary services (which are cheaper to provide per head, other things being equal). This makes them particularly hard to interpret. It has also been suggested that there has been a fall in efficiency of service provision in this field (Evandrou and Falkingham 1998: 227–9).

The impact of the personal social services requires a variety of measures to assess it. Provision for delinquents should reduce the level of youth crime. Children who are in care should have better living conditions—though there have been a number of scandals involving the abuse of children in residential homes by staff. Disabled people should be able to participate more fully in every aspect of life. People with learning difficulties should be able to have appropriate education and facilities; and for each group the criteria for evaluating the impact of policy are slightly different.

We consider only services for the largest group, that of elderly people, which has been the subject of numerous studies to evaluate the impact of community care. A study by Challis *et al.* (1990) made a comparison of two groups of elderly people with high needs for care. One group was given the standard domiciliary services, while the other received a higher level of services and more intensive case management. A careful attempt was made to match the individuals in the two groups in terms of their need and social characteristics. At the end of a one-year period it was found that 63 per cent of those receiving enhanced community care were still living at home, compared with only 36 per cent of the comparison group, which was taken as a measure of the success of the scheme. In addition, those receiving community care were less likely to feel lonely or depressed than the comparison group, and more likely to feel able to cope. The authors do point out, however, that those who had been admitted into residential homes during the year were also relatively satisfied. The strong contrast was with those who received standard domiciliary services.

The Impact of All Services by Income Quintile

Table 20.1 summarizes the effects of the four services considered above across the different income quintiles. The assumption is that the cost of providing a service can be treated as the value of this service as a 'benefit in kind'. The figures are given at constant prices which means that increases between 1979 and 1993 are not due to inflation. However they probably overstate the value of the benefits since, as explained, real spending underestimates the effect of inflation in social services, while volume spending overestimates it. It should be noted that the coverage of housing is partial: spending on council housing and subsidies to council tenants buying their houses are included, while other items are excluded. The table refers to individuals rather than households.

What distribution should we expect this table to show? It should reflect the pattern

	Income quintile				
	Bottom	2	3	4	Top
1979					
Health	530	420	350	340	340
Education	360	480	490	420	330
Housing	170	140	130	100	70
Personal social services	50	20	10	10	0
Total	1110	1060	980	870	740
1993					
Health	580	660	560	470	430
Education	620	510	550	470	410
Housing	200	200	110	70	20
Personal social services	80	120	50	30	10
Total	1480	1490	1270	1040	870

Table 20.1 Distribution of benefits in kind, 1979–93, £, in 1993 prices, all persons

Source: Sefton (1997, Table 2.2).

of need and use of the four services, which overlap to a large extent, but not entirely. For example, in the case of health, if lower income groups have more illness they should use health services more and receive a larger share of benefits. In education, on the other hand, the distribution will reflect the fact that staying on after 16 and going on to higher education are biased towards the middle class.

Looking along the rows, we can see how the value of benefits of each service varies by income quintile. Housing and personal social services benefit the lowest quintiles most, while education and health also benefit the lowest quintiles most, but to a lesser degree. This is because health and education are services used by all, whereas council housing and personal social services are used disproportionately by lower-income groups: higher-income groups will use private provision in both cases.

Comparing 1979 and 1993, we can see that the values of healthcare and personal social services provided have increased most, education has increased less, and housing has remained constant. This is in line with the overall spending figures given above. Looking at the distributions in each year we can see that:

- in 1979 the value of benefits of each service fell as one went from the lowest quintile to the highest quintile, except in education, where the third quintile received more and the first quintile less than would be expected if education benefits were proportional to income, and

- in 1993 health shows the lowest quintile, receiving less in benefit than the second quintile, which is peculiar. In education there is a reversal of the 1979 position for the lowest two quintiles, and a perhaps surprising degree of progressiveness in the distribution of benefits. For housing there is a focusing of benefits on the lowest quintiles as council housing becomes more synonymous with low incomes. In personal social services the second quintile has gained unexpectedly.

Sefton (1997) has suggested that one reason for the 1993 pattern is that there was a change in the age-and-income distribution between 1979 and 1993. There was a decrease of elderly people in the bottom quintile and an increase in the second quintile, and a decrease of children in the third quintile and an increase in the first quintile. This partly explains why personal social services consumption by the second quintile has risen so much in 1993: that elderly people are the main users of personal social services.

	Income quintile				
	Bottom	2	3	4	Top
Health	21.5	24.4	20.7	17.4	15.9
Education	24.2	19.9	21.4	18.4	16.0
Housing	33.3	33.3	18.3	11.7	3.3
Personal social services	27.6	41.4	17.2	10.3	3.4

Table 20.2 Distribution of percentage share of benefits in kind, 1993, all persons

Source: calculated from Table 20.1 above.

It also helps explain why the lowest quintiles are receiving a higher share of education spending.

Finally to express the benefits received by each quintile as a share of the total we can calculate a new table. If each quintile received an equal share of benefits of a particular service, every figure in Table 20.2 would be 20. Figures above 20 indicate that an income quintile is receiving a more than equal share of cash benefits, while a figure under 20 would show that it is receiving a less than equal share. This table may be compared with Table 20.3 showing the distribution of social security benefits below.

Social Security

Finally we turn to spending on cash benefits, which account for about half of all spending on social policy. The main categories of cash benefit included under the heading of social security are (in order of magnitude): retirement pensions, supplementary allowance/non-pensioner income support, invalidity benefit/incapacity benefit, child benefit, disability allowances, supplementary pension/pensioner income support, attendance allowance, family credit, war pensions, unemployment benefit/jobseekers allowance, and widows benefit, all of which cost £1 bn or more in 1995 (Evans 1998: Table 7A.1).

There is no single aim underlying all of these types of benefit, and entitlement to them follows different patterns. (For more information see Chapter 11.)

- **means tested,** where eligibility is based on income. (This can be seen both as a way of targeting benefits on those most in need, and as a way of restricting the availability of a benefit.)
- non-means-tested **contributory.** Contributory benefits are those for which National Insurance contributions are made, and where entitlement depends on a person's record of contributions.
- non-means-tested non-contributory.

The aim of preventing poverty is most clear in the case of means-tested benefits such as income support and family credit. However, it is also present in some of the non-means-tested benefits such as (non-contributory) child benefit and (contributory) retirement pensions. Other benefits are intended to cushion people against adverse circumstances such as sickness or unemployment.

As indicated earlier, one can analyse the impact of cash benefits in terms of inputs, since the category of 'output' only applies in the case of services. The input measure is obviously spending, but aggregate spending levels are not a measure of the input of social policy to the individual, since they are a product of numbers of recipients and levels of benefit. We shall therefore pay attention to both these elements, as well as to data which summarize the impact of all benefits on the distribution of income.

A general point about expenditure on social security benefits is that it is highly responsive to labour market conditions, demographic change, and changes in the role of the family. For example, the rise in unemployment from the late 1970s to the mid-1980s led to a sharp increase in claims for unemployment benefit, sickness benefit, and supplementary benefit. Spending on these measures is therefore more unpredictable. By comparison, the number of pupils in different age groups is highly predictable.

Social security spending grew in total at 3.4 per cent per annum in real terms between 1973 and 1995. Spending on means-tested benefits grew much faster (9.3 per cent per annum) than spending on contributory (2.2 per cent) and non-contributory benefits (3.3 per cent). Means-tested benefits account for 23 per cent of social security spending (or 30 per cent if housing benefit is included).

Benefit Levels The changing level of benefits over time can be measured either in relation to inflation or to average personal incomes. Between 1974 and 1996 invalidity benefit rose from around £47.19 to £61.15 in real terms (30 per cent), basic pensions from £54.88 to £61.15 (11 per cent), and unemployment benefit from £47.19 to £48.25 (2 per cent). Child benefit rose from £7.12 in 1978 to £10.80 in 1996 (52 per cent). The proportionate increases show a hierarchy, in descending order: child benefits, invalidity benefit, pensions, and unemployment benefit. In other words, child benefit, the non-means-tested benefit, has gone up more than the others—which suggests that helping the poorest is not the only aim of social security policy. But in relation to personal incomes these benefits have all fallen; the growth rates have been less than that of personal incomes generally. This means that those dependent on them are not sharing in national economic growth, and are falling behind the rest of the population. For example, pensions and invalidity benefit fell from around 49 per cent of average personal net disposable income in 1974 to around 37 per cent in 1995 (Evans 1998: Table 7.7). This is a means of keeping down total spending on benefits.

Take-Up The impact of benefit levels on welfare depends on take-up levels. In the case of contributory benefits, such as pensions, take-up is near 100 per cent, since there is a central record of entitlement. In the case of means-tested benefits, Evans (1998) shows there has been a gradual rise from 1976 to 1994 in take-up of supplementary benefit/income support, and family income supplement/family credit. But even in 1994 take-up levels are only in the 70 to 80 per cent range measured by numbers of recipients, and 85 to 90 per cent if measured by amount of money claimed (Evans 1998: Table 7.19). He suggests that 1.5 million people may not be claiming income support. Clearly then there are major gaps in access to benefits.

Pensions The growth of pensions spending between 1973 and 1994 was made up of a 29.6 per cent increase in number of pensioners and an 18.2 per cent increase in average payments in real terms (Evans 1998: 273). This was partly due to an increase in the number of pensioners who had paid extra contributions and who therefore received higher pension payments.

Invalidity Benefit (Paid for Long-Term Sickness) Spending on this has grown by 408 per cent in real terms between 1973 and 1994, or 19 per cent per annum. Since the level of invalidity benefit rose 30 per cent in real terms between 1974 and 1996, which is 1.4 per cent per annum, the growth in spending can be seen as almost entirely due to a growth in the number of people with long-term incapacity. There has been much debate about the reasons for this growth in long-term sickness. One hypothesis is that as the benefit is higher than provision for the unemployed, gives entitlements to additional means-tested help, and cannot be revoked, there is an incentive for those with any health problem to claim it. This assumes collusion by GPs who have to certify long-term sickness. The largest group of recipients is within ten years of retirement age.

Disability Benefits These are non-contributory, non-means-tested benefits, and spending on them has grown faster than social security spending generally. This is partly due to rising numbers of recipients—though previously they would have been entitled to some means-tested benefits. Some recipients are elderly people living at home rather than in residential homes or hospital. This shows how, as discussed earlier, an increase in social security benefits helps to finance the change in personal social services away from residential care. It is also due to a lowering of the need threshold (which means an increase in the intensity of need recognized). Because of these changes in forms of provision and entitlement it is difficult to divide the increase on spending into an increase in claimants and an increase in the value of the benefits.

The Impact of Cash Benefits

Social security benefits are not simply aimed at reducing poverty. They are a diverse group, among which contributory and non-means-tested non-contributory benefits account for the large majority of spending (77 per cent in 1995) and means-tested benefits a minority (23 per cent), though this was the fastest-growing category.

Hence it would be an unreasonable test of the impact of social security spending to expect it solely to increase the income share received by the lowest quintile. Nevertheless, given the presence of some means-tested benefits which are restricted to low-income groups, and of non-means tested benefits such as invalidity benefit and unemployment benefit which in practice are likely to go more often to low-income groups, we can hypothesize that the effect of social security benefits will be to increase the share received by low-income groups relatively more than that received by higher-income groups.

Table 20.3 shows the distribution of social security spending by household income quintile. Two conclusions can be drawn. First, for each year except 1995 the lowest income quintile receives the largest share of benefits and the highest quintile receives the lowest share. This gradation is what we would expect due to the combination of means-tested and non-means-tested benefits involved. The 1995 figures, however, are unexpected, since the second quintile receives more than the lowest quintile. Second, while the trend over time shown between 1980 and 1987 was for the lower quintiles to receive a larger share of benefits and the upper quintiles to receive a lower share, that is, an egalitarian trend, from 1987 to 1995 the trend is the reverse. In 1995 the two lower quintiles received less than in 1987, while the two higher ones received more. To explain this one would need to examine the effects of the labour market, demography, and wider social change, such as the increase in elderly people in the second quintile. It should be borne in mind that the effects of any differential take-up of cash benefits between income quintiles are also reflected in this table.

A second measure of the impact of social security spending is to ask what proportions of households are kept out of poverty due to cash benefits. The debate about definitions of poverty has been outlined in Chapter 6. Here we use a relative definition: those whose income is less than 50 per cent of the mean income. It has been estimated that the proportion of households in poverty would rise from 18 to 35 per cent in 1995 in the absence of social security benefits (Piachaud, quoted by Evans, 1998). One can read this in two ways. On the one hand, benefits have cut the figure by about half; on the other hand, they have left 18 per cent in the 'below 50 per cent of mean income' category.

	Income quintile				
	Bottom	2	3	4	Top
Old series					
1980	41.6	27.9	12.7	9.5	8.3
1985	38.4	30.3	14.1	9.3	7.9
1987 old	39.0	30.0	14.1	9.6	7.2
New series					
1987 new	33.2	29.1	19.6	11.2	7.0
1990	33.6	29.7	19.2	11.2	6.3
1995	25.8	30.9	21.0	12.9	9.4

Table 20.3 The distribution of social security spending among households by income quintile, 1980–95

Note: The two series are drawn up on slightly different bases and cannot be compared.

Source: Evans 1998: Table 7.20a.

Since reducing poverty is only one aim of cash benefits, it would be very surprising if the result of these benefits was to reduce the proportion in poverty from 35 per cent to nil. However, given that the trend has been for an increase in the role of means-tested benefits, the fact that 18 per cent of all households, around 4 million, are left with such a low income suggests that benefit levels are either too low or that they are not sufficiently concentrated on the lowest-income households. The former possibility is confirmed by the earlier evidence that benefit levels were falling behind average incomes: the latter is suggested by Table 20.3. This suggests that the effect of greater targeting of benefits through means tests is swamped by the decline in value of benefits relative to average income.

The Combined Impact of Spending on Services and Spending on Cash Benefits

Debates about the impact of social policy have centred around two propositions. The first is that social policy helps the poor, and this is because it was set up to do so and because it achieves its aims. The second is that social policy benefits the middle class disproportionately. This claim was advanced by Le Grand (1982) in *The Strategy of Equality*, who argued that there had been a middle-class 'capture' of the welfare state preventing it from realizing its aims.

The analyses presented in this chapter can be combined to give a rough answer to the question of who benefits from social policy.[6] The 'who benefits' question is a straightforward one, but conceals some difficult issues.

---

[6] We cannot consider here the other traditional question, namely whether social policy is redistributive, in the sense that the poor receive more in services and benefits than they contribute in taxes, since taxation is not discussed here.

First we shall discuss this question in terms of which social groups receive what shares of services and cash benefit. There is another side to the 'who benefits' question, which goes beyond the effects on the recipients to consider indirect effects such as those on the economy, polity, and society generally. These will be discussed in the next section.

Second, since, as has been shown, different households have different levels of need, a calculation of who benefits is only an approximate answer to the more interesting question of who benefits and whether it was in proportion to need. To answer this we need to take into account different levels of need related to age, gender, ethnicity, and so on.

Third, there are some questions of method. In the case of cash benefits the value of the benefits received by the individual is clear. In the case of services in kind, their value has to be inferred. This is usually done by

- establishing the total cost of a particular service;
- establishing what use is made of this service by different social groups or categories (income group, gender, ethnic group, family type);
- breaking down the total cost of the service among groups in proportion to their usage of it; and
- assuming that this share of the cost is equal to the service's value to the group.

To say that the cost of providing the service is the same as its value to the recipient is a good example of the third approach distinguished earlier in discussing how to measure need. This is a crude assumption since it uses an input measure (spending) and an output measure (service produced) to arrive at the value of the benefit (outcome in increased welfare) produced. This approach ignores questions of inefficiency and poor targeting (by need group and spatially), inappropriate service provision, needs which are unmet, and so on, as discussed earlier.

A further question of method concerns the unit of measurement. If the household is chosen it means that large and small households are equated, and the fact that the value of benefits and services is split between all the members of the household is not allowed for. In 1993 the average household size was highest in the lowest income quintile and lowest in the highest income quintile, and the second income quintile had the largest share of elderly people. Hence if the household is the unit the two lowest income quintiles need more than 20 per cent each of the value of services and benefits. If the individual is chosen as the unit of measurement this problem is avoided, but the lower cost of living with others is also ignored.

Tables 20.2 and 20.3 show the distribution between income quintiles of the value of services for individuals in 1993, and of the value of cash benefits for households in 1995. The crude comparison shows that services and cash benefits are both distributed in a pro-poor direction, and that services are more pro-poor than cash benefits. However, as just explained, the tables are not comparable because of their different units of measurement: Table 20.3 would show a greater pro-poor distribution if it was based on individuals. Moreover, Table 20.2 excludes housing benefits, so that the main spending item on housing is omitted from both tables. Since it is a highly pro-poor item of spending, it would lead a more pro-poor picture in whichever of the tables it was included.

In sum, the pro-poor distribution of social policy spending is greater than indicated in either table. Frustratingly, only Table 20.2 takes account of differences in need by age and gender. Hence we cannot answer the question of whether the distribution of cash benefits as well as services is sufficiently pro-poor to meet the greater needs of poorer individuals.

At the end of this discussion of the impact of social policy on individuals, we can see that the easier data to present are on real and volume spending. Information on efficiency has rarely been referred to, and is a source of potential error. However, the major difficulty in estimating the impact of social policy lies in measuring the scope and intensity of need. The eagle-eyed reader will have noticed that statements about need have usually been either statements attributed to unidentified experts or assumptions based on demographic trends which assume that provision at some time in the past was meeting need adequately. This source of uncertainty is frustrating given the scale of spending on social policy and the importance of need in measuring the outcome of this spending.

The Impact of Social Policy on Society

We now consider the wider social impacts of social policy. This is a very large field, and we shall be selective.[7] We examine the following arguments:

- that social policy increases social stability; and
- that social policy undermines the market mechanism for allocating resources.

One preliminary point needs to be made. This is that the discussion of wider effects encounters even more problems of identifying cause–effect relations than our discussion of the impact of social policy on different social groups. One reason for this is because the causal links in question relate to broader and more nebulous concepts like 'social stability'. The other reason is that in saying that social policy has a wider impact of a particular type, a comparison has to be made with a hypothetical situation in which that social policy was absent, or took a different form, that is, what is known as the 'counterfactual' because it is something that did not happen! This can be done by comparing the UK today either with the UK previously, when the social policy was absent or different in form, or with other advanced capitalist societies. The problem in the first case is to allow for the other changes which will have occurred since the policy was introduced or changed, and in the second to allow for the other relevant differences between the UK and the other societies chosen. These two difficulties mean that there is inevitably greater reliance on the plausibility of the causal inference, and this means that writers of different theoretical persuasions will tend to advance their own interpretations of the wider impact of social policy. Thus the reader needs to be particularly cautious about accepting claims made about the wider impacts of social policy.

---

[7] For a more extensive discussion of the societal impacts of social policy see George and Wilding (1984: chs. 4–7). The effects of social policy on the labour force and particularly on women's employment are also very significant.

Social Policy and Social Stability

One of the most widely held views about social policy is that it contributes to the stability of society. This belief has often been used by politicians and reformers in advocating social policy measures. They have asserted that by introducing reforms, social disorder or even revolution would be avoided. The clear message is that social policy has a stabilizing effect. But advocates of reform have a vested interest, and are likely to adopt whatever arguments they think will help win support for their case. The fact that claims are made that social policy has a stabilizing effect does not mean that such effects actually exist. To establish whether they do or not we need to look beyond the statements of interested parties. We examine the three elements of the claim that social policy has a stabilizing effect: that it reduces the number of deprivations, that it individualizes social problems, and that it reduces conflict.

Social Policy Reduces the Number of Deprivations Social policy undoubtedly averts or ameliorates some of the situations which arose before it existed. As we have seen, cash benefits and services are available to a wide variety of groups in need. Even allowing for a certain degree of mistargeting, incomplete take-up, stigmatization, inappropriate services, and cash benefits which are too low in value, it is undeniable that social policy has the effect of reducing the level of deprivation. However, social policy also has a second effect: to increase the number of deprivations and increase the demands made for policy measures. This is because the number of deprivations is not fixed, but is subject to a 'demonstration effect' by which the success of social policy measures in one sphere creates a pressure for further intervention in the same or other spheres. For example, the precedent of state intervention in the form of council housing led to subsequent pressure on government to widen the responsibilities of councils to include provision for homeless people. Paradoxically, therefore, social policy can *increase* the number of deprivations which are labelled as social problems, as well as averting or lessening the impact of such problems through remedial action.

Social Policy Individualizes Social Problems Typically the individualized mode of dealing with problems in the social policy sphere leads people to experience deprivations as individuals. For example, if a particular job or workplace is hazardous, the individual workers may be treated by health services as individuals and no attempt may be made to discover the common cause of their symptoms. Likewise, if there is a recession the consequent job losses lead individuals into unemployment and poverty, and they are treated as individuals by the agencies they contact in order to obtain social security benefits and services. The common source of their situation is eclipsed from view. In the case of contributory and means-tested benefits there is a stronger sense of fragmentation, with some individuals being entitled to them and others not. Clearly the various social services are set up in a way which emphasizes individual need and the provision of services and benefits to meet it, rather than the common sources which give rise to these needs. This has an isolating or fragmenting effect and reduces the probability of group action among those involved. However, it does not rule it out altogether. The effectiveness of the movement of disabled people is a case in point (Campbell and Oliver, 1996).

Less Deprivation Means Less Conflict and Greater Social Stability The third argument is that by reducing the number of deprivations and individualizing social problems social policy makes it less likely that groups will demand change, and this strengthens social stability.

The connection between deprivation and social instability is a complex one. Every society generates a wide variety of situations, ranging from ill health to unemployment and poverty. There are three factors which determine whether they lead to conflict. First, people's expectations must be high enough to regard them as deprivations. Second, people must feel they are deprivations that can be changed, rather than that they are unalterable. Third, people must believe that the government or other agency is capable of responding to group action.

But is it correct to assume that, in the absence of social policy, deprived groups would engage in social conflict? In fact this is debatable. Research on social movements suggests that the most deprived groups typically lack confidence in themselves and are much less likely to engage in collective action than groups which are not deprived but have high expectations and are effective in mobilizing themselves (Neidhardt and Rucht 1991).

The further question of whether, if conflict occurs, it is a source of instability is a large one. There are various views about how stable advanced capitalist societies are and what the main sources of division within them might be. Marxist writers argue that capitalist–worker conflicts have the greatest potential to destabilize society, and that conflicts around consumption issues such as social services are of secondary importance. Others would argue that the consumption sphere is at least as important, if not more so, as a source of conflict, and that consumption-based conflicts can be just as destabilizing for society. For example, for owner-occupiers housing is a large investment and the largest monthly expenditure, and hence could generate strong conflicts. Taking the two views together, one might suggest that if the lines of division in consumption conflicts co-incide with those in work-based conflicts there is a greater potential for instability, but where consumption divisions cross-cut production divisions the effect is to mitigate the strength of conflict.

To explore these ideas Dunleavy and Husbands interviewed a sample of people about their voting in the 1983 general election. This revealed that within each social class, council tenants were more likely to vote Labour and home-owners to vote Conservative, with those in other tenures having an intermediate position (Dunleavy and Husbands 1985: Table 6.13). This made clear that housing tenure had an association with voting over and above the relation between class and voting. They went on to reason that dependence on public transport or access to a private car might also affect voting. They found that those without a car were least likely to vote Conservative, those with one car more likely, and those with two or more cars most likely, and that this was true within each class category (Dunleavy and Husbands 1985: Table 6.14). These two findings are consistent with the idea that housing and transport consumption do generate different interests (as measured by voting), though this may not lead to conflict. Other writers argue that prior values condition both voting and consumption choices (Heath *et al.* 1985: 44–57).

Another example of consumption-based interests concerns people receiving cash benefits. On the one hand it can be argued that this creates a common interest (in higher benefit levels, for example) among recipients. On the other hand there are divisions between those receiving different benefits which makes common action more difficult. As was shown, government policy has been to increase benefit levels at different rates for different benefits. This reinforces divisions among claimants and places them in a competitive relationship. Lastly, whether claimants act together depends also on how they think of themselves, and this is likely to emphasize the differences between those receiving different benefits; for example, those receiving state pensions to which they have contributed are likely to feel little in common with people receiving means-tested benefits to which a stigma may be attached.

Hence the consumption sphere is a source of different interests as well as common interests. As suggested above, whether consumption-based interests give rise to conflict depends on how far consumption divisions coincide with work-based divisions. It also depends on two other considerations: the types of demand made by those with common interests, and the institutions available for handling conflict. On the former point there are two arguments. The first is that demands which challenge the way society is organized have a greater destabilizing potential than those which do not. However, in practice this potential is not realized, since only small minorities make radical demands. This leads to a second view: that it is demands which do not challenge society but which have considerable support which give rise to the most conflict, and that these can be destabilizing although they are not demands for radical change. This could be seen in trade union demands in the late 1970s.

On the latter point, whether conflict is destabilizing depends on the institutions available for reaching compromise. Compared to France, where direct and often violent action is quite usual, in the UK government is relatively open, and this encourages negotiation and the channelling of protest into peaceful and less destabilizing forms.

In sum, it has been argued that the likelihood that deprived individuals will engage in collective action and conflict, and that any action will be destabilizing, is much smaller than often suggested. In the absence of social policy most deprivations would lead to resignation rather than collective action, and any conflict would not necessarily be destabilizing. It follows that in so far as it reduces deprivation social policy increases social stability only to a limited extent, contrary to what is often claimed.

We have thus suggested that social policy both expands and reduces deprivations, that it encourages a view of social problems as something experienced individually, and that to a limited extent it reduces the amount of collective action that would be taken by deprived groups. It can thus be concluded that social policy on balance helps social stability, but that it encourages forces in both directions.

Social Policy and the Market Mechanism

A second argument about the wider impact of social policy is that it introduces a system of allocating resources which is in contradiction with the market mechanism, and that that is incompatible with a capitalist type of society.

The starting-point is the idea that markets are the central means of allocating resources in capitalist societies. They allow people to obtain resources according to their ability to pay the current price. This is held to be an efficient mechanism, because the price people are willing to pay is taken to be a measure of the value they give to that resource, so that if they value it more highly they will be willing to pay more for it. Hence the market is an efficient way for society to allocate resources between individuals, and an efficient way to enable individuals to choose between different items of spending. This leads to the idea that the market mechanism provides people with an incentive to earn more so that they can obtain more resources. In all these respects, therefore, the market mechanism is held to be socially beneficial.

By contrast, the allocation of services and cash benefits according to need has no place for ability to pay as a principle. It is held to be more socially efficient because need is not necessarily indicated by ability to pay, and groups with low incomes would consume less than they need if the market mechanism was the only one operating. Instead, need-based allocation relies on expert judgements about what levels of need people have, and this is claimed to lead to a more efficient allocation of resources. Critics, however, would say that allocation according to need is unsatisfactory because

- expert opinion is not reliable, due to experts' self-interest arising from their role in the process of provision;
- it leads to both overconsumption and overproduction, because price does not act as a rationing device to indicate people's preferences; and
- it weakens the motivation to work, since services and cash benefits are not allocated according to effort.

In appearance, therefore, social policy introduces a principle of allocation which threatens the market principle central to the operation of capitalism. Let us examine the arguments for and against.

The arguments for the idea that social policy is incompatible with the market principle are as follows:

- services and cash benefits in social policy are allocated according to need, not ability to pay. We have seen that this is the case in principle in health, education, and personal social services and cash benefits. In practice these services and benefits do not meet need adequately, but that does not alter the fact that the principle is one of needs-based allocation. In the case of housing, on the other hand, policy is concerned with political goals as much as with meeting need (see Chapter 16). The implication is that people whose need is less than their ability to pay receive more than they would receive if social policy did not exist, and they had to rely on their wages and purchase education and healthcare through the market. The market principle would lead to the callous view that these groups deserve less and are overconsuming. But such a view is so extreme that it would be difficult to find a serious advocate for it. This suggests that in capitalism the market principle of allocation is combined with values which limit its application.
- A second argument is that social policy weakens the incentive to work, and is thus threatening to market allocation. This argument is applied particularly to cash benefits paid to those without work and those looking for it. This argument would be most convincing if all allocation was according to need, rather than only social policy measures. In fact, as long as most people are reliant on wages for their income, the incentive to work is considerable. In the case of benefits paid to unemployed people, it is claimed that if benefits are a high percentage of the wages people receive when in work they will be discouraged from finding employment. But, as was indicated earlier, the failure of benefit levels to keep pace with wages means that the proportion of unemployed people who would be discouraged from taking

employment by the level of benefits is declining continuously (see Chapter 11 and Evans, 1998).

The arguments that need-based allocation does not undermine market allocation are as follows:

- The most challenging argument is that market allocation is not as efficient in resource allocation or as crucial to motivation as it claims. (Chapter 5 explains why markets are likely to be inefficient.) One example would be to ask whether in the USA, where total spending on healthcare is much higher as a share of GNP than in the UK, and mostly takes place through market allocation (e.g. private health insurance), this is a more efficient allocation of resources. Critics would argue that the 'market' in healthcare leads to over-treatment, as hospitals and doctors are paid by insurance companies rather than directly by patients. In contrast, advocates of need-based allocation would say that it discourages over-consumption of health services because of the public spending constraints applying to it.

- The second argument complements the last one: that need-based allocation is actually indispensable in advanced capitalist societies. Social policy spending helps create a productive (healthy, educated, and disciplined) labour force, and shields the private sector from direct responsibility for workers who are made redundant. It also embodies values about minimum welfare levels and preferences for greater equality which are social values which exist within advanced capitalist societies but which cannot be achieved by the market principle.

  This is part of a broader view about the role of the public sector in capitalist societies. The dominant idea is that public spending is unproductive and parasitic on the private sector, because it is a burden on taxes which could either be cut or used to benefit the private sector directly. But this is a very one-sided view. Public sector employment is 23 per cent of the total and generates income tax itself, and the private sector is highly dependent on public spending on infrastructure, industrial support, public sector orders, and on loan guarantees for exports. (For example, almost all health service spending on equipment and drugs goes to private suppliers.) This suggests that the private and public sectors are interdependent, the productivity of one depending on the other. Hence the indispensability of need-based allocation in capitalist societies.

We would therefore suggest that social policy introduces a principle of allocation which is complementary rather than contradictory with market allocation, as long as values favouring the achievement of minimum levels of welfare for all and some steps towards equality are prevalent in society. If need-based allocation were to become dominant rather than subordinate as a principle, that would undermine the functioning of capitalism. But this is not the case.

Conclusion

In conclusion, the two wider impacts of social policy we have discussed show that it contributes to social stability, and that it is not threatening to capitalism despite being based on a principle which contradicts the market principle. Earlier, when looking at the impact on individuals and households, we concluded that on balance social policy distribution is pro-poor, but we found it difficult to be clear about the amounts by which social policy raises social welfare, for some people absolutely, or in terms of reducing inequality, because initial definitions of needs are so varied and so open to question and judgement.

Glossary

contributory benefit Benefit to which contributions have been made, through National Insurance payments, for example. Eligibility for contributory benefits is restricted to contributors.

horizontal dimension of need Number of people with a given level of need.

input measure Measure of resources used in providing a service or benefit: spending, number of staff employed, and so forth.

income quintiles The division of a population, such as individuals or households, into a hierarchy of five parts, each containing equal numbers. The bottom quintile would contain the fifth with the lowest incomes and so on, to the top fifth, containing those with the highest incomes. The income of each quintile is usually given in the form the average income of all the units in it. The income distribution is also sometimes divided into deciles (tenths) in a similar way.

means-tested benefit Benefit where eligibility is subject to test based on income.

outcome measure Type of measure (of social policy) which looks at final impact, such as level of illness, examination results, and so on.

output measure Measure of volume of service produced using resource inputs, such as number of patients treated, number of council houses built, number of people receiving home help.

principle of proportional service provision Principle according to which provision varies in proportion to need.

principle of uniform service provision Principle according to which provision is equal per member of group in need.

real spending Spending which has been adjusted for the effect of the general level of inflation in the economy.

take-up Extent to which all those entitled to a service or benefit receive it.

territorial justice A situation where the provision of services in different areas varies in proportion to inter-area differences in need.

vertical dimension of need Need defined in terms of its hierarchical distribution amongst similar units, such as individuals or households, such that some are said to have higher needs than others.

volume spending Spending which has been adjusted for the effect of the level of inflation experienced in a particular sector, such as education.

Guide to Further Reading

The Glennerster and Hills (1998) collection (*The State of Welfare*, 2nd edn., Oxford: Oxford University Press) is an indispensable and up-to-date source of data and interpretation on the impact of social policy. The earlier book by George and Wilding (*The Impact of Social Policy*, London: Routledge 1984) is particularly useful for its discussion of societal impacts of social policy. Books which explore the role of taxation as a social policy measure are

J. Hills, *New Inequalities: The Changing Distribution of Income and Wealth in the U.K.* (Cambridge UP 1996), and J. Hills, *The Future of Welfare* (2nd edn., Joseph Rowntree Foundation, 1997). A stimulating account of the degree to which industrial societies, and particularly the UK, remain affected by differences in most measures of welfare is provided by Richard Wilkinson's highly readable *Unhealthy Societies: The Afflictions of Inequality* (Routledge 1997).

References

G. Boyne and M. Powell (1991), 'Territorial Justice—A Review of Theory and Evidence', *Political Geography*, 10, 263–81.

J. Campbell and M. Oliver (1996), *Disability Politics* (London: Routledge).

D. Challis, R. Chessum, J. Chesterman, R. Luckett, and K. Traske (1990), *Case Management in Social and Health Care: The Gateshead Community Care Scheme* (Canterbury, Personal Social Services Research Unit: University of Kent).

B. P. Davies (1968), *Social Needs and Resources in Social Services* (London: Michael Joseph).

P. Dunleavy and C. T. Husbands (1985), *British Democracy at the Crossroads* (London: George Allen and Unwin).

M. Evandrou and J. Falkingham (1998), 'The Personal Social Services', in H. Glennerster and J. Hills (eds.), *The State of Welfare* (2nd edn., Oxford: Oxford University Press).

M. Evans (1998), 'Social Security: Dismantling the Pyramids?', in H. Glennerster and J. Hills (eds.), *The State of Welfare* (2nd edn., Oxford: Oxford University Press).

V. George and P. Wilding (1984), *The Impact of Social Policy* (London: Routledge).

H. Glennerster (1998), 'Education: Reaping the Harvest?', in H. Glennerster and J. Hills (eds.), *The State of Welfare* (2nd edn., Oxford: Oxford University Press).

H. Glennerster and J. Hills (eds.) (1998), *The State of Welfare* (2nd edn., Oxford: Oxford University Press).

A. Heath, R. Jowell, and J. Curtice (1985), *How Britain Votes* (Oxford: Pergamon).

J. Hills (1998), 'Housing: A Decent Home Within the Reach of Every Family?', in H. Glennerster and J. Hills (eds.), *The State of Welfare* (2nd edn., Oxford: Oxford University Press).

J. Le Grand (1982), *The Strategy of Equality* (London: George Allen and Unwin).

J. Le Grand and P. Vizard (1998), 'The National Health Service: Crisis, Change or Continuity?', in H. Glennerster and J. Hills (eds.), *The State of Welfare* (2nd edn., Oxford: Oxford University Press).

F. Neidhardt and D. Rucht (1991), 'The Analysis of Social Movements: The State of the Art and Some Perspectives for Further Research', in D. Rucht (ed.), *Research on Social Movements* (Frankfurt: Campus and Boulder: Westview).

T. Sefton (1997), *The Changing Distribution of the Social Wage* (STICERD Occasional Paper No 21, London: London School of Economics).

21 The Future of Social Policy

Peter Taylor-Gooby

Contents

Introduction: A Crisis of Confidence in Welfare

The welfare state is in crisis. There are three aspects to the current dilemmas. First, the demand for welfare provision is rising at a rate not seen in Western countries since the period of secure post-war economic growth of the 1950s and 1960s. Amongst the industrial nations the proportion of the population made up of the most important group of consumers of welfare services—retired people—is increasing rapidly. Other social groups that run a high risk of welfare dependency are also growing, as a result of demographic and labour market change. The number of unemployed or sub-employed people has risen sharply since the early 1980s. These changes feed on each other, since access to good-quality pensions and healthcare in most countries is effectively linked to work and to social security contribution records. Those with unstable working lives run a greater risk of becoming dependent on state welfare later in their lives.

The second aspect to the current crisis concerns the willingness of populations to pay for increased welfare spending. Throughout Europe governments are cutting back on welfare provision. The requirements for budgetary stability in the Maastricht Treaty's rules for progress towards European monetary union reinforce the determination to contain spending just at the time when demand for welfare is rising. The view of citizens on the desirability of these cutbacks is unclear. Opinion polls indicate that cuts are opposed by considerable majorities, yet political parties of both the right and left committed to retrenchment are returned to government. The determination of governments to reverse the trend to expansion in welfare spending is clear.

Welfare states have experienced crises before in their relatively brief history. The oil price shocks in the mid-1970s brought the period of confident post-war expansion to an end. In the early 1950s, the strong opposition of Conservative parties to the development of welfare states had to be contained before the era of welfare expansion could get under way. The third and qualitatively new feature of the current crisis arises from the nature of the political debate about welfare. Put simply, the advocates of state welfare have lost confidence. This is particularly clear in the UK where the policies of the current Labour government on issues like the retrenchment of public spending, the expansion of the private sector, and the development of ever more stringent controls in welfare closely resemble those of the Conservatives. In most European countries there are few mainstream politicians who will advocate the kind of expansionism associated with the experiment in **Keynesian economic management** in France in the early 1980s or the building of a comprehensive social insurance system in Spain between the late 1970s and 1989. The accent of much academic discussion of welfare is on the containment of spending, the expansion of non-state provision, and the development of family-based care systems. In previous crises the desirability of strengthening state provision was presented as a long-term objective, to be pursued when economic circumstances permitted. Now the welfare state seems to have lost its way. The decline of welfare advocacy is the key feature of the current crisis, and one that raises the question of whether these developments may be terminal.

The gift of the West to the world in the eighteenth century was **mercantile capitalism,** expanded to a world system under imperialism in the nineteenth. One of the successes of the twentieth, at least from the point of view of the life chances of millions of ordinary people in Western countries, was state welfare. Indeed many writers, drawing on Marshall's historical account of the progression from legal to political and finally to social rights in the UK, saw universal redistributive government services as the logical outcome of mass democracy. The **globalization** of commodity, capital, and labour markets in a large number of fields have diminished the power of nation states. Technological developments affect patterns of work and employment, reducing opportunities for less skilled workers and subjecting substantial parts of the labour force to the uncertainties associated with the possibilities of cybernetic substitution or the export of their jobs. International competitive pressures shift jobs between countries according to the logic of markets. The capacity of governments to control the impact of these changes is increasingly limited. Politicians in most countries are convinced that state spending must be rigorously constrained, since higher taxes will increase production costs and render national industries less competitive. Towards the end of the twentieth century it seems that the Western invention of globalized capitalism will undermine the Western system of state welfare as a citizen right (Fukuyama 1989).

In this chapter we will review some of the available evidence in relation to the various pressures on modern welfare states and consider the possibilities for the future.

To review the pressures and possibilities effectively, we will have to set some of the changes affecting national welfare states in their international context. We will also need to examine the intellectual underpinning to debates about welfare, since it is this that establishes the scope and direction of discussion and determines what is included on the agenda and what gets left off. The welfare state is not only undermined by practical difficulties such as changes in the level of need for its services and in the economic and political environment of its practice, but also by a shift in the intellectual climate, which is perhaps the most important factor in explaining why the future is unlikely to resemble the past. First, the practical issues.

The Growing Demand for Welfare

The most important factors here are the ageing of the population and the increased numbers of un- and sub-employed people (see Chapter 7). These changes imply larger spending commitments in future years, although the impact of population ageing is not so great in the UK as in most other countries, due to its relatively low level of health spending and of state benefits, and its comparatively favourable age-structure (OECD 1998: see ch. 6).

The demographic problem is the result of three factors. First the ratio of elderly people compared to those of working age has risen sharply in recent years, and stands to increase dramatically in the first half of the next century. Secondly, participation in the labour force by those of working age has fallen and appears likely to continue to fall. This is particularly true of two age-groups—those aged under 25 are more likely to be in education and training than in the past, and those over 50 are more likely to retire early. Thirdly, unemployment has risen and seems unlikely to fall in the immediate future. At the same time the proportion of women who enter the labour force has increased, and this trend seems set to continue. Migration into European Union (EU) member countries may tend in the short term to increase the proportion of people of working age, but is unlikely to be sufficiently large to have a substantial effect.

The combined effect of these factors is hard to gauge. A positive outcome is technically possible. The European Statistics Office estimates indicate that, if unemployment in EU countries were to return to the level of the early 1970s, before the oil crisis (2 to 3 per cent of the labour force), and the upward trend in labour force participation on the part of women were to continue, the problem of financing pensions and other services for those aged 65 or over would be resolved in most European countries. However, if unemployment remains at current levels of over 10 per cent then 'the difficulties of achieving the necessary transfer from those below 65 to those above will be acute and the pressure radically to reform pension systems could prove irresistible' (EU 1996: 43).

There has been considerable debate about the sustainability of current levels of state provision. European governments have tended to argue consistently for retrenchment and for the substitution of individual responsibility and private services for state provision. For example the UK's Green Paper on social security reform states bluntly that

> ### Box 21.1 The pressure of population ageing
>
> In 1995 around 15 per cent of the population of the EU was aged 65 or over, equivalent to about 23 per cent of the population of working age. By 2005 the number of those aged 65 and over will be equivalent to 26 per cent of the working-age population, by 2015 30 per cent, and by 2025 36 per cent (EU 1996: 43–4). The situation varies between countries. By 2025 the number of pensioners will be equivalent to 40 per cent of the working-age population in Italy, and over 36 per cent in Belgium, Germany, France, and Sweden. Only in Portugal will it be less than 30 per cent, and in Ireland and Luxembourg less than 32 per cent
>
> *Source*: EU (1996), graph 6.

'pension provision needs to increase, but the proportion financed by taxpayers will not', and discusses a variety of methods for expanding the role of private pensions (DSS 1998: 3; see also DHSS 1985: para. 1.4 on using private services to contain the escalating costs of health and social care).

Pressures on Provision

These shifts in demand combine with a number of factors in the international context to call into question the viability of the traditional model of the welfare state. Two are of most significance—shifts in the international political economy, and those in styles of economic organization.

The Changing International Political Economy

First, the control of government over key features of national economies that was central to the Keynesian apparatus of economic management has been significantly curtailed. Several developments are important in this area. The growing importance of international currencies other than the dollar (particularly the yen and the mark) since the late 1960s, the availability of the liquid funds for speculation resulting from the 1970s oil-price rise, and the decline of exchange controls have created an international market in which speculators can shift money in ways which can undermine the stability of a country's economy. The confidence of the international currency market in a country's economic management is critical to the stability of its currency and hence its trading position. The examples of the decline of the franc following a slide in confidence at the time of the French experiment in strong Keynesian economic management in the 1980s, the departure of Italy and the UK from the European Monetary System when they were effectively forced to devalue in 1992, and the fact that the Swedish government could not avoid an unprecedented programme of spending cuts in 1995 to maintain the value of its currency, all demonstrated that governments are no longer in exclusive control of their own domestic policies. Retrenchment in developed Western economies following the world financial crisis of 1998/9 drives home the point.

Second, the expansion of international trade following the growth of new industrial economies, especially in South-East Asia, and the collapse of communism in Europe imposes additional pressures on governments in relatively high-waged European economies. Although Asian exports make up a relatively small proportion of European imports, these countries have succeeded in capturing from Europe much of the growth in developing markets elsewhere in Asia and in Africa. This has powerful implications for the future position of economies which traditionally responded to the imperative: 'Export or die!' (United Nations 1994: Tables A.15, A.16). In addition, the proportion of European and US trade made up of low-cost Southern imports is estimated to have doubled over the 15 years to 1990 (Wood 1994).

The third factor undermining national economic authority is the growth in multinational companies and political institutions within the freer international markets. Marginson estimates that about two-fifths of the jobs created by British-origin multinationals are abroad (1994: 64). This has highlighted the importance of international political responses in creating organizations such as the EU, with its Single European Market, and the recently established North American Free Trade Association. The EU already exerts a strong influence on UK policy-making in respect of equal opportunities, health and safety, agricultural and fisheries policy, and employment law. This influence will grow following government acceptance of the Maastricht Treaty social provisions and commitment to join the European Monetary Union, effectively conceding fiscal policy to a central bank which includes the control of inflation but not of unemployment among its targets.

New Styles of Economic Organization

The most significant development in the structure and organization of the economy is the shift from manufacturing to service-sector employment detailed in Chapter 7, compounded for the UK in recent years by an actual decline in the size of the manufacturing sector. The industrial system provided an obvious basis for the traditional division of the population into social classes, providing both the motor (class politics) and the goal (redistributive welfare) for the distinctively European contribution to social cohesion—the **Keynesian welfare state.** Greater flexibility in patterns of work may lead to more complex patterns of social identity and of political interests, centred around **life-politics** (Giddens 1998) or **consumption sectors** (Dunleavy and Husbands 1985: 18–25). At the same time, the new information technology opens up the possibility of co-ordinating the activities of enterprises without the need for direct chains of command, so that industrial firms no longer find it desirable to establish control over all aspects of their operation from raw materials to after-sales service by bureaucratic management. Public-sector organizations have also followed the trend to more decentralization and flexibility in management. The new welfare state managerialism emphasizes the use of markets to co-ordinate the activities of a multiplicity of public and sometimes private or voluntary service providers (Flynn 1993: 126–39; Taylor-Gooby and Lawson 1993: 133–6).

These changes in employment, work, and social organization are supposed by some to lead to a radically new social structure which will both require and nourish new forms of welfare operating according to different principles from those of the **Keynes/ Beveridge welfare state.** The previous welfare settlement was part and parcel of the social arrangements summed up as **Fordism.** This notion referred to a society regimented by its factory-based industrial and nuclear-family-based consumption systems, so that welfare could be provided conveniently on mass lines through a centralized government system of taxation of those in work and redistribution to households in defined categories of need, typically via a male 'head of household'. Burrows and Loader argue that if the politico-economic settlement of Fordism was characterized by a correspondence between 'mass production, mass consumption, modernist cultural forms and mass public provision of welfare, then post-Fordism is characterized by an emerging coalition between flexible production, differentiated and segmented consumption patterns, post-modernist cultural forms and a restructured welfare state' (1994: 1—see Box 21.2).

It is the **post-Fordist** system that is seen as appropriate to the internationalized world with its less significant role for the welfare state. Governments are now concerned to secure success in international markets, to promote flexibility in labour markets to attract overseas and retain domestic investment, and to foster a business environment that makes innovation possible. Policies are driven by the forces of economic competition. Jessop terms the new settlement the **Schumpeterian workfare state:** 'It marks a clear break with the Keynesian Welfare State as domestic full employment is deprioritized in favour of international competitiveness, and redistributive welfare rights take second place to a productivist re-ordering of social policy' (1994: 24). The nation state

---

Box 21.2 From Fordism to post-Fordism

	Fordism	Change Agent	Post-Fordism
Economic system	National: mass production/mass consumption	Economic globalization plus new technology plus flexible demand	Production for highly competitive global market plus flexible consumption
State system	Keynes/Beveridge: Full employment plus redistributive social policies	Shift towards liberalism, privatization, and markets	Imperative to ensure that the workforce remains internationally competitive and flexible
Cultural system	Urban/industrial: nuclear family with male 'breadwinner'/ class division between non-manual middle and manual working classes	'High modern': diversity in life-styles, life-interests, and life-politics	Fragmented

loses its effective capacity to exert authority and is 'hollowed out' by a combination of technological change, growing internationalization, and the regionalization of economies. As capital markets and (in some fields) markets in goods and services become more international, economies must respond to pressures which are not under the control of the nation state. New technologies assist this process, allowing for the integration of geographically dispersed (and competing) suppliers of components into the production process and for the swifter exchange of managerial and marketing information.

It is argued that the previous pattern of national regulation of mass production and consumption cannot be sustained. Welfare is increasingly about regulation rather than redistribution; centralized, universal services are increasingly difficult to sustain; and the diversity and uncertainty of social circumstances calls for decentralized provision and greater individual responsibility for meeting need and the growth of the private sector. The capacity of government to plan and manage the economy has been undermined, and government must also limit its responsibility for the dis-welfares that result from economic and social change.

This approach contains some truth, but like all holistic models of social change, there are substantial uncertainties about its applicability to current developments. First, governments do have considerable room to manœuvre, as evidenced by the success in international markets of states which have rather different internal arrangements and differ in their welfare settlements. A considerable number of cross-national comparative studies have examined the relationship between measures of welfare state provision (social security spending, spending on services in kind, redistributive impact of state welfare, and so on) and measures of economic success (growth rates, strength of the currency, and economic competitiveness, understood in different ways). The conclusions are entirely equivocal—some studies indicate that welfare does inhibit economic expansion while others show the reverse. The implication is that much depends on the detail of the exact nature of welfare provision and the international trading and competitive position of the nation involved (for careful reviews of this literature see Atkinson 1995; Esping-Andersen 1994: 720–6; Gough 1996: 219). Secondly, nation states have the capacity to negotiate with each other and create institutions which may resist, or at least moderate, the play of international forces such as the EU. The introduction of a 'fair trade' clause into commercial treaties, insisting that competitors maintain minimum standards of conditions for workers, and of controls on speculation to prevent a repetition of the 1998/9 financial crisis, are currently under debate. Finally, the extent to which current trends in the internationalization of capital will continue into the future are simply unclear. However, it is the case that welfare states at the least must adapt to external pressures from globalization and to internal pressures from changes in patterns of work.

Support for the Welfare State

Virtually all research that examines popular support for government spending on welfare points to three conclusions. First, state welfare services are highly popular. Second, the welfare state is not a seamless web—some aspects are far more popular than others. Third, there is considerable support for the coexistence of the private sector in some areas of provision, alongside the state. The best source of information for the UK is the British Social Attitudes survey, an annual series of detailed attitude surveys starting in 1983, which repeat and occasionally add to a battery of questions on various aspects of welfare provision.

Since 1983 respondents have consistently named health and education as spending priorities, effectively jostling out all other contenders. Support for both has increased steadily during the 1980s and 1990s. Moreover, when tax and spending are explicitly linked a substantial majority opts for higher taxes and higher social spending. Even when the question specifically states that spending increase 'might require a tax increase to pay for it', there are large majorities expressing a preference for higher spending on education, health, pensions, the environment, and, increasingly, law enforcement. The discrepancy between these findings and the fact that the British public voted for parties committed to no increase in personal taxation at the five general elections between 1979 and 1997 has led many commentators to question the accuracy of polls. In 1995 and 1996 the survey asked highly detailed questions and presented scenarios that allowed individuals to choose between realistic mixes of tax increases and reductions and changes in the level of service (see Brook 1996 for details of the survey).

The level of support for state spending, especially on the mass services of education, health, and pensions, revealed by surveys in the UK is only matched by the enthusiasm of politicians of both the main parties to reduce their spending commitments. One approach is to see this as indicating the shortcomings of the electoral system: policy platforms imperfectly represent what the population actually wants. Another is to suggest that the opinions expressed in surveys do not necessarily correspond to behaviour at the ballot box. However, the attitude data is remarkably consistent across a large number of studies (for example, Jowell *et al.* 1983 onwards; see also Judge and Solomon 1993: 304–5; Dunleavy and Husbands 1985; and Edgell and Duke 1991). In addition there is a clear linkage between self-interest in the use of particular services and the strength of public opinion in relation to them—the services that meet mass needs or cope with mass risks, such as education and the NHS, are more strongly supported than provision for one parent families or homeless people, which cater only for minorities in the population. It seems likely that there is a strong current of citizen support for the main welfare state services and for increased public spending on them, but perhaps also a willingness to see welfare provision for more marginal and stigmatized groups curtailed.

The same pattern is evident in analyses of the data from European attitude studies, of which the most substantial is Ferrerra's summary of EU surveys (1993). It is also borne out in the popular response to attempts by European governments to institute substantial public spending cutbacks, such as the Juppé Plan of 1995/6 in France, the German 1995–6 *Sparpaket*, which sought to cut spending on pensions and healthcare, and the Spanish pension and benefit cuts of 1989. In each case widespread protests and demonstrations forced the governments to moderate the cuts, particularly where these have involved job losses or changes to conditions of service in the public sector.

Remodelling Welfare: Responding to Consumer Interests

Welfare systems face considerable external pressures that demand change. Things simply cannot go on as they have in the past, because the books won't balance. It is not clear, however, that this situation requires the abandonment of the welfare state approach to meeting social needs and maintaining the casualties of the market. One solution to the problem of a changing demographic balance is to move to a different system of finance for pensions and for health and social care for elderly people, or simply to increase taxation and social contributions. Changes in finance have already taken place in a number of countries with the expansion of private or state-regulated private systems and the extension of **funded pension financing** whereby individuals are responsible for building up the resources necessary to pay for their pension over their working life. The argument that citizens are no longer willing to pay for state services does not seem in tune with the facts. The heartland of state welfare services—healthcare, education, and pensions—seem to be highly popular. The crisis of welfare is a crisis of political will. However, shifts in political perspectives correspond to assumptions that can be traced to roots in social science theory. To these we now turn.

Public policy is built on assumptions about the factors that influence human behaviour. Policy-makers often wish to reinforce particular behaviour patterns—for example, those involved in the family or the work ethic, or in entrepreneurship, or in taking responsibility for one's own welfare and those of one's family, or in altruism towards those in need—and to weaken others, such as fraudulent claiming, dropping out from schooling, or welfare dependency. Recent uncertainties about welfare, and particularly the restructuring of the public sector towards greater use of market competition, have been driven in part by a new understanding of why people behave as they do that has come to inform policy-making. The traditional model of the welfare state corresponded to an influential strand in the political science of the expansionist years of the post-war public sector. Almond and Verba's account of the civic virtues appropriate to a modern democratic society argued for a 'mixed political culture' (1965: 29). 'The model . . . that required that all citizens be involved and active . . . by itself . . . could not sustain a stable democratic government. Only when combined . . . with its opposites of passivity, trust and deference to authority and competence was a viable, stable democracy possible' (Almond and Verba 1989: 16). The civic culture of the welfare state assumed that activism, involvement, and altruism were the province of providers, while service users were required to trust and defer, confining their political involvement to voting when elections were called. These assumptions have been challenged in relation to each of the three groups discussed below.

The post-war welfare system was based on tax-financed, state-administered provision. Three distinct groups of actors were involved in the traditional model of state welfare—the makers and suppliers of policy (politicians, civil servants, and the professionals and officials who actually ran the services), the taxpayers who financed most social provision, and the service users. Planners and providers were seen as motivated primarily by considerations of public service and pursuit of the common good, regulated by their professional ethics. Altruism, or at least the desire for a secure safety-net, motivated citizens to accept the increasing levels of progressive taxation necessary to finance the services. The service users were seen as essentially passive, content to accept bureaucratically administered state provision designed by those who knew best and acted for the best. In an important analysis of the assumptions about behaviour built into social policy, Le Grand points to the disjunction between the roles of policy-maker, service provider, and taxpayer, where the primary motivation is active and altruistic, and that of recipient, where behaviour is seen as passive and accepting. He dubs the former the 'knights' and the latter the 'pawns' of the traditional welfare state (1997: 154—see Box 21.3).

The assumptions underlying this altruistic/deference model of public policy in the UK have been called into question. New approaches to public policy imply a different approach to motivation. The welfare reforms of the past two decades have been increasingly based on the assumption that people are essentially individualistic and self-interested in their motivation, and, as a consequence, active in their response to the circumstances they encounter. Citizens are unwilling to pay higher taxes for improvements in collective provision, unless they think they will themselves benefit. Service providers may act to improve their own circumstances rather than serve the public interest if the structure in which they work permits them to do so. Service users are active, on the one hand as beneficiaries who will modify their behaviour in response to incentives implicit in entitlement rules, and on the other as consumers seeking the best bundle of provision to meet their own needs and willing to exit from the state to the private sector if that serves their interest best. Thus, the availability of unemployment benefits may undermine work incentives or means-testing for social care may lead people to reduce or disguise their assets.

Box 21.3 From altruism plus deference to self-interest plus proactivity

Social Actors	Traditional Model	Rational Choice Model
Politicians and Planners	Altruistic/Active (act in public interest)	Self-interested/Proactive (seek favour of voters)
Managers and Professionals	Altruistic/Active (pursue service user interest)	Self-interested/Proactive (seek to enlarge bureau/ budget)
Citizens as Taxpayers	Deferential/Passive (happy to pay set taxes)	Self-interested/Proactive (tax revolt)
Citizens as Service Users	Deferential/Passive (accept given standards and priorities)	Self-interested/Proactive (challenge standards of provision, jump queues, cheat on benefits)

This shift in assumptions about motivation led to an emphasis on decentralized market structures in provision rather than monolithic provider organizations driven by the allocation decisions of officials, and to new measures to regulate the possible perverse incentive effects of benefits and services. These concerns are evident in the programmes of both the main political parties and in broader policy discussion. They are reinforced by assumptions about expectations.

One authoritative review of recent developments points to the paradox that, while the welfare state performed well during the 1980s and 1990s—despite tightly constrained resources, rapid increases in the numbers of unemployed and older people, and a hostile political environment—most policy-makers seek to cut state provision further, rather than support a successful system (Glennerster and Hills 1998: ch. 8). The answer suggested is that improvements in the quality and variety of goods delivered by private consumer markets simply outpaced the necessarily more modest improvements in state welfare. The proportion of the population who enjoy home videos, foreign holidays, central heating, regular meals out, microwaves, dishwashers, mobile phones, and the other amenities of life has risen rapidly (ONS 1998, Table 15.4). The welfare state cannot keep up, and it is hardly surprising that it falls from favour with politicians and policy-makers. In fact the attitude survey evidence shows that state welfare solutions remain highly popular in relation to many needs outside the field of commodity consumption discussed above. None the less, assumptions about expectations drawn from comparisons with consumer goods colour the debate.

Arguments for New Forms of Welfare

Real pressures for radical changes in welfare policy exist. First, many studies show that middle-class voters exit from state provision where they can to private pensions, owner-occupied housing, and to a lesser extent private medical care and schooling. Within the state sector, more influential groups (middle-class people and men) are able to gain access to preferential treatment within the NHS, better access to social care and to the most costly parts of the state education system, and to enjoy the lion's share of the fiscal and other subsidies to private pensions, housing, and transport. Social policy writers from Titmuss (1962) to Le Grand (1982) have drawn attention to the significance of the 'social division of welfare', and political scientists have refined this to argue that consumption sectors can form a basic axis of **social cleavage** (Dunleavy 1980).

Second, a number of writers influenced by the work of Murray (1984) and Mead (1986) in the US argue that lower- as well as higher-income groups respond to the incentives built into social policy. Benefits for unemployed people and the provision of both benefits and services such as housing for one-parent families, it is argued, provide perverse incentives which undermine the work and family ethics seen as core elements in social cohesion. While the evidence for the construction of a 'dependency culture' as a result of welfare policy is weak (Dean and Taylor-Gooby 1992: ch. 1; Walker 1990), concerns about welfare dependency colour current policy debates.

Third, commentators on welfare citizenship stress an active approach. One perspective advocates active citizenship, understood as enhanced 'neighbourliness' (Hurd 1988).

Another argues that 'we need to build from the bottom up, by creating structures of power that release the talents and potential of ordinary people . . . there is no limit to what people and communities can be enabled to do for themselves' (Commission on Social Justice 1994: 22). Such an approach implies that the focus of citizenship widens to include the empowerment of minorities and groups who are disadvantaged in relation to employment or the domestic sphere (Lister 1990: 464). At a more theoretical level, this leads to a concern with 'positive welfare', understood as 'the mobilizing of life-political measures, aimed once more at connecting autonomy with personal and collective responsibilities' (Giddens 1994: 34; 1998: 44).

All these arguments are hotly contested. None the less, they are highly influential in policy-making. As Chapters 11 to 16 have shown, reforms in the UK across the range of welfare services are concerned to reduce direct state provision (for example, in the encouragement of private medical insurance, schooling, pensions, nursery education, owner-occupied housing, the transfer of social housing from local government to private landlords and housing associations, and the cutbacks in benefit budgets and abolition of national insurance unemployment and sickness benefits) and expand markets and quasi-markets (in the decentralization of provision and the encouragement of competition between state, private, and voluntary provider agencies in hospital care, pre-schooling, schooling and further education, and community care). Regulatory measures defend the family and work ethics (such as the Child Support Agency or the linking of the Jobseekers Allowance to approved work-seeking behaviour). Individual welfare consumers (or, in the case of medical and some aspects of social care, professionals acting as their proxies) are encouraged to make active choices between different providing agencies. School and hospital league tables are designed to improve the availability of information on quality of service. Restrictions on access to different providers have been cut back through such measures as the abolition of formal school catchment areas. Decentralization of budgets linked to the number of users of the agency has strengthened the incentives for providers to respond to consumer demand.

The new direction in welfare is sometimes seen as a shift from a provider to a regulatory welfare state (see Box 21.4). The traditional welfare state provided a wide range of services to all or most of its citizens, with the private sector playing a comparatively minor role. Increasingly government does not attempt to maintain mass provision directly, but instead seeks to influence the pattern and structure of non-state provision through the regulation of non-state services. Politicians think such an approach will meet the aspirations they believe to exist for greater individual choice and diversity in provision and also allow government to reduce the tax bill.

The picture that emerges from this review is that the original intellectual underpinning of the welfare state model has been largely abandoned by policy-makers, despite the fact that the evidence against it is entirely controversial. It is simply unclear whether welfare state services are likely to be dominated by the kind of inefficiencies and lack of responsiveness outlined above, and whether market and private-sector alternatives can do much better. None the less, the approach that argues vigorously for the supremacy of liberal ideals in the development of capitalist market systems seems likely to dominate discussion of welfare for the foreseeable future.

Box 21.4 Regulatory and provider welfare states

Provider Welfare State	Regulatory Welfare State
High levels of taxation	Low taxation
Universal state services	Residual targeted state services
Small private sector	Extensive private sector
State responsibility for meeting citizen needs	Private responsibility for arranging to meet one's own needs
Little regulation of private services	Extensive regulation of standards and services in private sector
Little concern with 'perverse incentive effects of state provision'	Measure to regulate the behaviour of those using state services
No compulsion on individuals to insure privately	Possible compulsion
No compulsion on employers to provide occupational welfare (e.g. sick pay, pensions, health insurance)	Possible mandatory provision in such areas

---

Conclusion

The traditional welfare state faces very considerable pressures from changes in population structure and in the labour market, at a time when it is widely believed that the political resources to generate the levels of spending to meet these pressures are not available. The evidence from surveys indicates that this belief is erroneous. New approaches to welfare, influenced in part by the pressures to achieve efficiency savings and greater public acceptability for welfare and in part by liberal market ideology, point to more market-based solutions within a slimmed-down welfare state. These conclusions are themselves open to challenge. The future of welfare is open, and welfare studies can no longer rest content to fill in the policy details on a canvas dominated by economists' views on human behaviour. The extent to which the welfare policies of the twenty-first century succeed in meeting citizen needs will, in part, be determined by the influence which those whose interests extend beyond competitiveness, labour market flexibility and economic growth exert on the policy agenda.

Glossary

consumption sectors The classification of groups in society according to significant consumption differences, in contrast to a classification in terms of occupational class. Access to private-sector consumption in areas like housing (owned, as against council-rented), transport (car against bus), or health care (private insurance against the NHS) is seen as particularly significant.

family-based care Welfare systems in which kin are the primary source of support for family members.

Fordism A social structure organized around mass production employment, consumerist mass consumption, and the nuclear family as the unit that services the worker in the first sector and manages consumption in the second. Seen to presuppose class politics, a bureaucratically organized nation state, and large industrial firms.

funded pension financing A system of paying for pensions whereby individual contributions are invested over a person's working life to produce their pension, rather than the pay-as-you-go system, which simply uses the contributions of current workers to pay for the pensions of current pensioners.

Keynesian economic management A system whereby national government manipulates interest rates, credit, and investment (and in some versions direct state investment in nationalized industries and capital projects) in order to ensure high rates of employment and a smooth rate of growth. Assumes that the nation state has a high degree of control over the national economy.

Keynes/Beveridge welfare state A welfare system presupposing Keynesian economic management, together with government policies which redistribute income over a typical working-class life-cycle, and from better-off to poorer groups in the population, to meet a defined range of needs.

globalization The fact that in the modern world activities in different parts of the planet are swiftly affected by distant events and developments, through widespread international trade, cheap communications, and international media.

life-politics Theory associated with the prominent British sociologist, Giddens, that in an increasingly diverse and uncertain society political interests become more diffuse and concerned with a wide range of personal, ecological, gender, and identity-related issues, rather than being dominated by a rigid class structure.

Marshall Prominent post-war British sociologist, who argued that social rights developed in historical progression from political rights, which developed in turn from legal rights.

Mercantile capitalism Variant of capitalism wherein the state plays an active role in creating and defending markets for a nation's goods.

post-Fordism The breakdown of Fordism, as short-run production replaces mass production, individuals demand personally tailored consumption goods, and a greater diversity of family forms emerges. Associated with the weakness of the nation state in managing production and successful trading in the face of globalization.

Schumpeterian workfare state Term used by the British sociologist Jessop to describe development of a system to replace the Keynes/Beveridge welfare state, in which the political emphasis is on the creation of a highly competitive, low-waged, flexible labour force rather than redistribution to guarantee reasonable working-class living standards. The system is seen as better adapted to cope with the demands of a globalized economic system.

social cleavage A division within society usually based on occupation or forms of consumption, but sometimes also on such factors as ethnicity, regional identity, culture, and religion, which lies behind significant behaviour such as voting and political allegiance.

Guide to Further Reading

Esping-Andersen, G. (1996), *Welfare States in Transition* (London: Sage). A clear account of different approaches to the pressures of social and economic change on the different welfare systems that exist in industrialized countries.

Giddens, G. (1994), *Beyond Left and Right* (Cambridge: Polity), and (1998) *The Third Way* (Cambridge: Polity). These books argue that economic and cultural globalization and the growing importance of risk and uncertainty render the traditional patterns of political debate redundant. Highly controversial, extremely well-written, and influential with key political figures.

Hutton, W. (1996), *The State We're In* (London: Vintage). A seminal work of radical political economy of the early 1990s, this book argues that major changes to economic and social policy are needed to make the British economy competitive on the world market.

Pierson, C. (1998), *Beyond the Welfare State?* (2nd edn., Cambridge: Polity). This book gives a highly accessible review of the challenges to traditional approaches to social welfare provision in the UK.

Pierson, P. (1994), *Dismantling the Welfare State?* (Cambridge: Cambridge University Press). A study of recent developments in the UK and the US which shows that it is difficult for politicians to alter welfare policy by head-on confrontation, and that policies that change the context in which welfare is made and that undermine the interests supporting state welfare are much more successful in achieving long-term change.

Taylor-Gooby, P. (1991), *Social Change, Social Welfare and Social Science* (Hemel Hempstead: Harvester Wheatsheaf). This book reviews the main pressures on the UK welfare state and argues that the demands for change are not as ineluctable as is often suggested.

Taylor-Gooby, P. (1997) (ed.), *Choice and Public Policy* (London: Macmillan). A research-based analysis of the new welfare consumerism which shows that the behavioural assumptions on which much policy-making is based are mistaken and the resultant policies likely to suffer shortcomings.

Williams, F. (1989), *Social Policy* (Cambridge: Polity). The most readable account of the main theoretical positions in social policy writing.

References

Almond, G. and Verba, S. (1965), *The Civic Culture* (Boston: Little, Brown).

——(1989) (eds.), *The Civic Culture Revisited* (Boston: Sage).

Atkinson, A. (1995), *The Welfare State and Economic Performance* (Welfare State Programme Discussion Paper 109, STICERD, LSE, May).

L. Brook (1996), 'Public Spending and Taxation', in R. Jowell (ed.) (1996), *British Social Attitudes* (SCPR/Dartmouth: London).

R. Burrows and B. Loader (1994) (eds.), *Towards a Post-Fordist Welfare State?* (London: Routledge).

Commission on Social Justice (1994), *Social Justice: Strategies for National Renewal* (London: Vintage).

Dean, H. and Taylor-Gooby, P. (1992), *Dependency Culture* (Hemel Hempstead: Wheatsheaf).

Deakin, N. (1987), *The Politics of Welfare* (London: Methuen).

Dennis, N. and Erdos, G. (1992), *Families without Fatherhood* (London: IEA).

Department of Health and Social Security (1985), 'The Reform of Social Security' (Green Paper), Cmnd. 9517 (London: HMSO).

Department of Health and Social Security (1989), *Working for Patients*, Cmd. 555 (London: HMSO).

Department of Social Security (1998), *A New Contract for Welfare*, Cm. 3805 (London: HMSO).

Dunleavy, P. (1980), 'The Political Implications of Sectoral Cleavages and the Growth of State Employment, Parts I and II', *Political Studies*, 28/3, 364–83 and 527–49.

Dunleavy, P. and Husbands, C. (1985), *British Democracy at the Crossroads* (London: Allen & Unwin).

Edgell, S. and Duke, V. (1991), *A Measure of Thatcherism* (Hammersmith: HarperCollins).

Esping-Andersen, G. (1996), *Welfare States in Transition* (London: Polity).

——(1994), 'Welfare States and the Economy', in N. Smelser and R. Swedborg (eds.) *The Handbook of Economic Sociology* (Princeton: Princeton University Press).

EU (1996), *Social Protection in Europe: 1995* (Luxembourg: European Commission).

Ferrerra, M. (1993), *European Community Citizens and Social Protection* (Commission of the EU, Luxembourg).

Flynn, N. (1993), *Public Sector Management* (Harlow: Wheatsheaf).

Fukuyama, F. (1989), 'The End of History', *The National Interest*, 16 (summer), 3–18.

Giddens, A. (1998), *The Third Way* (Cambridge: Polity).

——(1994), *Beyond Left and Right* (Cambridge: Polity).

Glennerster, H. (1992), *Paying for Welfare: The 1990s* (Hemel Hempstead: Wheatsheaf).

——and Hills, J. (1998), *The State of Welfare: The Economics of Social Policy* (2nd edn., Oxford: Oxford University Press).

Gough, I. (1996), 'Social Welfare and Competitiveness', *New Political Economy*, 1/2, 209–24.

Gray, J. (1996), *After Social Democracy: Politics, Capitalism and the Common Life* (London: Demos).

Hurd, D. (1988), 'Active Citizens', *Guardian* (19 September).

Hutton, W. (1996), *The State We're In* (rev. edn., London: Vintage).

Jessop, B. (1994), 'The Transition to Post-Fordism and the Schumpeterian Welfare State', in R. Burrows and B. Loader (eds.), *Towards a Post-Fordist Welfare State?* (London: Routledge).

Jowell, R. *et al.* (1983–97 annual), *British Social Attitudes* (SCPR/Dartmouth, London).

Judge, K. and Solomon, M. (1993), 'Public Opinion and the NHS', *Journal of Social Policy*, 22/3, 299–328.

Le Grand, J. (1997), 'Knights, Knaves or Pawns? Human Behaviour and Social Policy', *Journal of Social Policy*, 26/2, 149–70.

Le Grand, J. (1982), *The Strategy of Equality* (London: Allen and Unwin).

Le Grand, J. and Bartlett, W. (1993) (eds.), *Quasi-Markets and Social Policy* (Basingstoke: Macmillan).

Lister, R. (1990), 'Women, Economic Dependency and Citizenship', *Journal of Social Policy*, 19/4, 445–67.

Lowe, R. (1993), *The Welfare State in Britain since 1945* (London: Macmillan).

Marginson, P. (1994), 'Multinational Britain: Employment and Work in an Internationalized Economy', *Human Resource Management Journal*, 4/4, 63–80.

Mead, L. (1986), *Beyond Entitlement: The Social Obligations of Citizenship* (New York: Free Press).

Murray, C. (1984), *Losing Ground: American Social Policy 1950–1980* (New York: Basic Books).

Niskanen, W. (1973), *Bureaucracy—Servant or Master?* (London: IEA).

OECD (Organization for Economic Co-operation and Development) (1998), *Maintaining Prosperity in an Ageing Society* (OECD: Paris).

ONS, Office of National Statistics (1998), *Annual Abstract of Statistics* (HMSO: London).

Pierson, C. (1998), *Beyond the Welfare State?* (2nd edn., Cambridge: Cambridge University Press).

Pierson, P. (1994), *Dismantling the Welfare State?* (Cambridge: Cambridge University Press).

Taylor-Gooby, P. (1991), *Social Change, Social Welfare and Social Science* (Hemel Hempstead: Wheatsheaf).

Taylor-Gooby, P. and Lawson, R. (1993) (eds.), *Markets and Managers* (Milton Keynes: Open University Press).

Taylor-Gooby, P. (1997) (ed.), *Choice and Public Policy* (London: Macmillan).

Titmuss, R. (1962), *Income Distribution and Social Change* (London: Allen & Unwin).

UN (1994): United Nations, *World Economic and Social Survey* (New York: United Nations).

Walker, A. (1990), 'Blaming Victims', in C. Murray (ed.), *The Emerging British Underclass* (London: IEA).

Williams, F. (1989), *Social Policy* (Cambridge: Polity)

Wood, A. (1994), *North–South Trade, Employment and Inequality* (Oxford: Oxford University Press).

Index

List of Boxes

List of Figures

List of Tables